Consulting Editor

Russell C. Brinker

Professor of Civil Engineering
New Mexico State University

1777
REVIEW PROBLEMS

from EIT and ENGINEERING
REGISTRATION EXAMINATIONS
with answers and typical solutions

1777
REVIEW PROBLEMS

from EIT and ENGINEERING
REGISTRATION EXAMINATIONS
with answers and typical solutions

by

RUSSELL C. BRINKER
New Mexico State University

and

JACK J. BOURQUIN **PAUL C. HASSLER**
JOHN A. WHITACRE, JR. **PHILIP W. YOUNG**
University of Texas at El Paso

INTERNATIONAL TEXTBOOK COMPANY

B-W-RK

FIRST EDITION TITLED 1301 REVIEW PROBLEMS

 Printed in the United States of America by The Haddon Craftsmen, Inc., at Scranton, Pennsylvania. Library of Congress Catalog Card Number: 67-16241. ISBN: 0-7002-2123-9

INTEXT EDUCATIONAL PUBLISHERS
666 FIFTH AVENUE
NEW YORK, N.Y. 10019

Contributors

TO SECOND EDITION

Dr. Harold E. Alexander	*University of Texas at El Paso*
Dr. Harold Belken	*New Mexico State University*
Dr. Elton Endebrock	*New Mexico State University*
Dr. Kermit L. Holman	*New Mexico State University*
Dr. Ray Lutz	*New Mexico State University*
Carlos McDonald	*University of Texas at El Paso*
Dr. Bruce Wilson	*New Mexico State University*
Dr. Roger Zimmerman	*New Mexico State University*

TO FIRST EDITION

Dr. Harold E. Alexander	*University of Texas at El Paso*
Harold N. Ballard	*University of Texas at El Paso*
John R. Ballentine	*Convair Division, General Dynamics Corp.*
Howard P. Emerson	*University of Tennessee*
Robert L. James	*U. S. Army Corps of Engineers*
Robert M. LaForge	*University of Tennessee*
Jose McDonald, Jr.	*University of Texas at El Paso*
Henry DeForest Ralph, Jr.	*Standard Oil Company of Texas*
Robert E. Rimkus	*Pennsalt Chemicals Corp.*
Dr. Robert W. Truitt	*North Carolina State University*

Preface to Second Edition

This Second Edition of the Review Problems book, "1777," retains the format and objectives of "1301." Additional problems and more complete actual examinations have been included with some rearrangement of material made to accommodate them. Answers for all problems except the single general examination have been tabulated in Appendix A. Over 200 mathematical solutions are shown in "1777," and a solutions manual is in preparation.

Progress toward a National EIT test has been attained and more than 30 states now use a common one-day, eight-hour examination on 10 fundamental subjects given on the fourth Saturday in April and the first Saturday in December. Examinations 20-A, 20-B, and 20-C are the most recent ones. Each state pays for the test papers and (optionally) for having its candidates graded collectively with others. A number of states continue using the Southern Zone examination, which is similar to the National test. A few states still prepare their own EIT examinations and California, showing a preference for some multiple-choice questions, is a good example.

Professional registration examinations are individual, varied, and now held confidential by most states, California again being an exception. Professors and men in practice are paid at a very nominal rate (as are registration board members) to submit problems in their specialties. Little progress has been made toward a national PE license examination.

In many states, 70 to 80 percent of applicants taking EIT tests succeed on the first try by intensive study and perhaps the help of a refresher course if available. Generally, a second attempt is permitted without an added cost. In certain states, however, the pass rates for men taking the PE examination in Civil, Electrical, and Mechanical Engineering, Land Surveying, etc. are as low as 10 percent. Two men recently passed the PE examination on their 16th try! Experience proves that taking the EIT or PE examinations without considerable advance special study exhibits poor engineering judgment. In fact, each semester, far-sighted undergraduate engineering students should check their ability to solve the problems given on EIT examinations as they progress through the fundamental areas of mathematics, chemistry, physics, etc.

Many people were helpful in compiling problems and answers for "1777," including Dr. Quentin Ford, New Mexico State University; Mr. Charles Grosvenor, Asphalt Institute; Gabriel Armijo, Schellenger Research Laboratory; Dr. W. Garth Henderson, University of Texas at El Paso; and Dr. Calvin Woods, University of Texas at El Paso.

R. C. Brinker
J. J. Bourquin
P. C. Hassler
J. A. Whitacre, Jr.
P. W. Young

University Park, New Mexico
May, 1967

Preface to First Edition

The purpose of this book is to provide an intensive practical review for persons planning to take the Engineer-in-Training (EIT) and Professional Registration examinations. It serves also as a review for men in practice and administration who are interested in keeping their technical knowledge from slipping away.

All problems in the book have come from actual state registration examinations given in one or more of the 35 states whose tests were available. Questions are not, and cannot be, identified by their state of origin. Many of the problems are ageless and have appeared in several examinations over a period of years. Registration examinations will doubtless continue to follow the evolution of college curricula and engineering practice, but the basic principles reviewed herein will change little, if at all. Individual problems form the basic review material, but nine complete typical actual examinations are given in Chapter 20 so that students can put the pieces together and take a final test in accordance with the official ground rules set up by the particular state.

In most states, registration as a professional engineer requires the following steps: (1) procurement of an engineering degree from a 4- or 5-year accredited engineering college or university, or 10 to 12 years of practical experience; (2) passing a 1- or 2-day EIT examination; (3) acquiring 2 to 4 (usually a minimum of 4) years of "satisfactory" practical experience; and (4) passing a 1-day Professional examination. The "grandfather" clause which is normally effective for one year following passage of a professional engineering registration law (to permit registration by experience without examination) has run out. Registration by reciprocity is possible in most states if the original registration was obtained by passing an examination comparable with that required in the reciprocating state. The Model Registration Law is generally followed in most states but the versions and applications differ. Registration Boards have rules which enable them to hold the line if desired in doubtful cases, but permit concessions to be made at their discretion.

Most EIT examinations consist of two parts: (1) General, and (2) Engineering. The General section covers some or all of the following subjects: Mathematics, Chemistry, Statics, Dynamics, Physics, Strength of Materials, Thermodynamics, Fluid Mechanics, Electricity, Engineering Economy, and Ethics, Contracts, Specifications, and Practice. Usually one day, broken into two four-hour examination periods, is allotted for this part.

The Engineering, or Applied Engineering, examination is given in two four-hour periods on the second day and covers the applicant's special branch of Engineering, such as Civil, Electrical, Mechanical, Chemical, and so forth. If the material is not broken into specialties, a large number of problems may be given from which the examinee selects the required number of most familiar types (or perhaps the least unfamiliar kind) to be answered. Examination I in Chapter 20 illustrates this kind of examination. Many states do not give examinations in Mining, Industrial, and Aeronautical Engineering, hence the selection of questions was more limited. In this book Part I, *Fundamentals*, covers the eleven General subjects; Part II, *Applied Engineering*; and Part III, *Typical Examinations*.

The same EIT examination is now given simultaneously for a large section of the country on the same day, but many states still do not participate in this joint arrangement. Perhaps at some future time, all states will agree upon a uniform examination to be given on a specified day or days, twice each year. Better examinations and automatic reciprocity between states would result. At present, some states permit *bound* references for all or parts of the examination, others do not. The same problem has been found on open-book and closed-book examinations.

The one-day Professional examination, if taken after a specified number of years of practical experience, consists of one or more broad problems requiring the exercise of judgment expected of persons at that stage of their careers. For example, a Civil Engineer might be asked to lay out a railroad station and design some typical structural members, being given the number of trains and passengers per day, the tonnage of freight to be handled, etc. Some of these "professional" questions are more closely held by the Boards and difficult to review because of their character.

As previously noted, variable regulations govern (1) the use or denial of the use of reference books in registration examinations; (2) the number of days of examination required; (3) the number of years of satisfactory experience to be acquired after the EIT test before the next step can be taken, and the definition of what constitutes satisfactory experience; (4) registration by endorsement, reciprocity, or reputation("eminence"). These points can be clarified only by contact with the pertinent state registration board. Addresses of the 50 State Boards are listed in the Appendix. Engineers who move from state to state or find it necessary to become registered in a number of states can clear their credentials through the National Bureau of Engineering registration (NBER). Submission of experience records and letters of reference is simplified and the process of registration by endorsement expedited if a Certificate of Qualification is secured from the NBER.

Registration examinations are not passed by memorizing any number of problem solutions. The important thing for an applicant to know is what kind of problems to expect, and thus what to prepare for. The large number of problems selected herein have come from many state examinations to provide a broad cross section in every field requiring review. Problems are placed in somewhat related groups in each chapter, and solutions given for what have been discovered to be common types among the various states. Some questions could readily have been included in any one of several classifications, for example: Physics, Mechanics, Fluids. Answers to most problems are given in the Appendix, but the authors consider these of lesser importance than the wide variety of problems presented. Some questions have been restated in cases where they were too ambiguous, although it is evident that examinees are expected to make assumptions as necessary. Such assumptions must be listed, of course, and their reasonableness is considered in grading.

The authors believe that registration of professional engineers will become more important in all branches of engineering (and the examinations and requirements more difficult) with each succeeding year. It is therefore imperative that all engineering students and practitioners take the necessary steps to secure registration as soon as possible. Without registration, the practitioner's horizon is seriously limited since he cannot use the designation "Engineer" and is prohibited from doing work above the technician level unless a licensed engineer checks and stamps the work, and assumes the responsibility. The standard registration law clearly defines the limitation of a nonregistered practitioner by stating that it shall be a misdemeanor to practice or to offer to practice engineering without registration. The penalty imposed may be a fine, imprisonment, or both.

The authors gratefully acknowledge the help provided by the many persons who aided in the preparation of this book. In addition to those persons who are listed as Contributors, they would like to specifically thank Manuel Gomez, Jr., David Rozendal, and Joseph F. Friedkin for their assistance.

Concerted efforts have been made to eliminate errors in the text and answer tabulation but if any remain, the authors will appreciate information of their presence.

R. C. BRINKER
J. J. BOURQUIN
P. C. HASSLER
J. A. WHITACRE, JR.
P. W. YOUNG

El Paso, Texas
September, 1960

Contents

1777
REVIEW PROBLEMS

from EIT and ENGINEERING
REGISTRATION EXAMINATIONS
with answers and typical solutions

part one

FUNDAMENTALS

Mathematics 1

Mathematics problems given in recent Engineer-in-Training examinations fall into categories which involve (1) algebra, (2) logarithms, (3) trigonometry, and (4) calculus.

The first twelve problems have been solved in outline form with some details omitted between the steps shown. These examples are representative of other problems selected for the chapter.

1–1. A rectangular room is 4 ft longer than it is wide. If the width were increased by 2 ft and the length by 5 ft, the floor area would be increased by 179 sq ft. Find the dimensions of the room.

Solution: $y=x+4 \qquad (x+2)(y+5)=A+179 \qquad x(x+4)=A$

$$(x+2)(x+9)=x(x+4)+179 \qquad x=23, \quad y=27$$

1–2. A parabola having the equation $x^2=2y-\frac{1}{4}$ is intersected by the straight line whose equation is $x+2y=1$. What are the coordinates of the points of intersection?

Solution:

$$x^2-2y+\tfrac{1}{4}=0 \qquad x+2y=1 \qquad 2y=1-x$$

$$x^2-(1-x)+\tfrac{1}{4}=0 \qquad x=-\tfrac{3}{2}, \quad y=\tfrac{5}{4}$$

$$-\tfrac{3}{2}+2y=1 \qquad x=\tfrac{1}{2}, \quad y=\tfrac{1}{4}$$

$$\tfrac{1}{2}+2y=1$$

1–3. The sides of a triangle are measured, and the area is calculated. If the sides are measured as 90 ft, 100 ft, and 110 ft with a possible error of 0.1 ft in each measurement, find the largest possible error in the area and the largest possible relative error. (The use of differentials is suggested.)

Solution:

$$A=[s(s-a)(s-b)(s-c)]^{\frac{1}{2}}, \text{where } s=(a+b+c)/2$$

$$\ln A=\tfrac{1}{2}[\ln s+\ln(s-a)+\ln(s-b)+\ln(s-c)]$$

$$\frac{dA}{A}=\frac{1}{2}\left[\frac{ds}{s}+\frac{ds-da}{s-a}+\frac{ds-db}{s-b}+\frac{ds-dc}{s-c}\right] \qquad ds=\tfrac{1}{2}(da+db+dc)$$

$$ds=\pm\frac{da}{2} \quad \text{or} \quad \pm\frac{3}{2}\,da$$

$$\frac{dA}{A}=\frac{1}{2}\left[\frac{3}{2}\frac{da}{s}+\frac{1}{2}\frac{da}{s-a}+\frac{1}{2}\frac{da}{s-b}+\frac{1}{2}\frac{da}{s-c}\right] \qquad s=150,\ s-a=60,\ s-b=50,\text{ and } s-c=40$$

$$\frac{dA}{A}=\frac{0.1}{4}\left[\frac{3}{150}+\frac{1}{60}+\frac{1}{50}+\frac{1}{40}\right]=2.05\times 10^{-3}$$

1–4. A spherical balloon is inflated with a gas having a constant specific weight of 0.05 lb/cu ft at a steady flow rate of 15.0 lb/min. At what rate, in inches per minute, is the radius changing when the balloon has a diameter of 20 ft?

Solution:

$$V=\tfrac{4}{3}\pi r^3 \qquad \frac{dV}{dt}=\tfrac{4}{3}(3)(\pi r^2)\frac{dr}{dt} \qquad \frac{dr}{dt}=\frac{dV/dt}{4\pi r^2}$$

$$V=\frac{\text{weight}}{\text{density}}=\frac{w}{d} \qquad \frac{dV}{dt}=d^{-1}\left(\frac{dw}{dt}\right)$$

Substituting for $\frac{dV}{dt}$

$$\frac{dw/dt}{d\,4\pi r^2}=\frac{dr}{dt} \qquad \frac{15}{0.05(4\pi\times 10^2)}=\frac{dr}{dt}=\frac{3}{4\pi}\text{ fpm}$$

1–5. Determine the area bounded by the parabola $y=x^2$, the x axis, and the two lines $x=2$ and $x=4$.

Solution:

$$dA=y\,dx \qquad y=x^2 \qquad dA=x^2\,dx$$

$$A=\int_2^4 x^2\,dx=\frac{56}{3}$$

1–6. Find the coordinates of the point of intersection of the two tangents to the curve $y=x^2+4$ at the points (1,5) and (2,8).

Solution:

$$y=x^2+4 \qquad \frac{dy}{dx}=2x \qquad \left.\frac{dy}{dx}\right|_1=2 \qquad \left.\frac{dy}{dx}\right|_2=4$$

$$y=m_1x+b_1=2x+b_1 \qquad 5=2(1)+b_1 \qquad b_1=3,\quad y=2x+3$$

$$y=m_2x+b_2 \qquad 8=4(2)+b_2 \qquad b_2=0,\quad y=4x$$

$$y=2x+3 \qquad y=4x$$

Equating and solving

$$x=\tfrac{3}{2},\quad y=6$$

1–7. Determine the largest positive value for y on the curve $y=-3x^2+6x+5$.

Solution:

$$y=-3x^2+6x+5 \qquad \frac{dy}{dx}=-6x+6=6(-x+1)=0$$

For $x=1$, $y=8$ maximum value

1–8. Find the mass of a right circular cone whose height is 10 ft and whose base is 16 ft in diameter if the density (pounds per cubic foot) at any point is known to be numerically equal to 25/16 of the distance to the base of the cone.

Solution: y = altitude, x = radius at any height.

$$dV = \pi x^2\,dy \qquad dm = p\,dV = p\pi x^2\,dy \qquad p = ny$$

$$dm = \pi n y x^2\,dy$$

$$\int dm = \pi n \int_0^h y x^2\,dy \qquad y = kx + b$$

$$x = \frac{y-b}{k} \qquad x^2 = \left(\frac{y-b}{k}\right)^2 \qquad dx = \frac{1}{k}\,dy$$

$$m = \int dm = \pi n \int_0^h y \left(\frac{y-b}{k}\right)^2 dy = \frac{\pi n}{k^2} \int_0^h y(y^2 - 2yb + b^2)\,dy$$

$$m = \frac{\pi n}{k^2}\left(\frac{h^4}{4} - \frac{2h^4}{3} + \frac{h^4}{2}\right)$$

Substituting

$$k = \frac{-h}{r} \qquad n = 25/16, \quad h = 10, \quad r = 8, \quad m = \frac{\pi}{12} \times 10^4 \text{ lb}$$

1–9. Given two point sources of light 100 ft apart and of intensity 512 and 64 foot-candles. If the intensity of illumination at any point due to a given point source is directly proportional to the intensity of the source and inversely proportional to the square of the distance from the source, find the point on the line joining the two sources at which the illumination will be the least. Give the distance from the 64-foot-candle source.

Solution:

$$E_1 = \frac{I_1}{x^2} \qquad E_2 = \frac{I_2}{(d-x)^2} \qquad d = 100 \text{ ft}$$

$$E = E_1 + E_2 = I_1 x^{-2} + I_2 (d-x)^{-2}$$

$$\frac{dE}{dx} = -2I_1 x^{-3} + 2I_2 (d-x)^{-3}$$

Set $\frac{dE}{dx} = 0$

$$I_1 x^{-3} = I_2 (d-x)^{-3}$$

$$I_1 (d-x)^3 = I_2 x^3$$

$$I_1 (d^3 - 3d^2 x + 3dx^2 - x^3) = I_2 x^3$$

$$\frac{I_2 + I_1}{I_1} x^3 - 3x^2 d + 3xd^2 - d^3 = 0 \qquad \frac{I_2 + I_1}{I_1} = 9$$

$$9x^3 - 3x^2 d + 3xd^2 - d^3 = 0$$

$$x = \frac{d}{3} = 33.3 \text{ ft}$$

1–10. Evaluate the following, slide-rule accuracy sufficient: (a) $\text{Log}_{3.2}\, 30 = x$. Find x. (b) $\text{Log}_e\, 0.0028 = x$. Find x.

Solution: (a)

$$\text{Log}_{3.2}\,30 = x \qquad 3.2^x = 30$$

$$x\ \text{Log}\ 3.2 = \text{Log}\ 30 \qquad x = \frac{1.477}{0.505} = 2.92$$

(b)

$$\text{Log}_e\ 0.0028 = x \qquad e^x = 0.0028$$

$$x\ \text{Log}\ e = \text{Log}\ 0.0028 \qquad x = \frac{7.448 - 10}{0.434} = -5.90$$

NOTE: These problems can be solved by using the LL slide-rule scales.

1–11. Points A and B are 800 ft apart horizontally, and B is 150 ft higher than A. Point C lies in a valley between them. A transit line from A to C dips 45°, from B to C it dips 60°. How far is C below A?

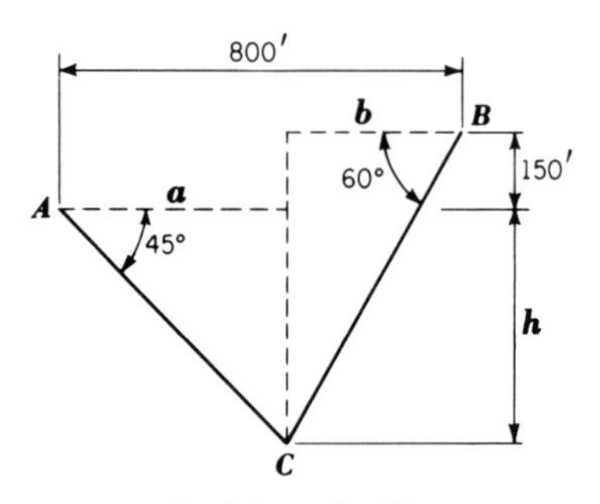

Problem 1–11.

Solution:

$$a + b = 800 \qquad a = h$$

$$\tan 60° = \frac{150 + h}{b} = \frac{150 + h}{800 - h} = 1.732$$

$$150 + h = 1385 - 1.732h \qquad h = 452\ \text{ft}$$

1–12. What is the probability of rolling either a 7 or an 11 with one roll of a pair of dice?

Solution: There are 36 possible combinations with one roll of a pair of dice, and 8 ways of rolling a 7 or an 11 as follows: 1-6, 2-5, 3-4, 5-6, 6-5, 4-3, 5-2, 6-1. Probability $= 8/36 = 0.222$.

1–13. Find to three significant figures the root of $x^4 + 2x^3 + x^2 - 6x - 12 = 0$ which lies between 1 and 2.

1–14. One end of a ladder 50 ft long is leaning against a perpendicular wall standing on a horizontal plane. Supposing the foot of the ladder to be pulled away from the wall at a rate of 3 fpm, how fast is the top of the ladder descending when the foot is 14 ft from the wall?

1–15. Given the equations $x-y=10$ and $x^2-y^2=300$. What are the values of x and y?

1–16. A man walks into the country at the rate of 4 mph and rides back to his starting place at the rate of 20 mph. If the whole trip takes $4\frac{1}{2}$ hr, how far did he walk?

1–17. Three times the sum of two numbers equals 63, and the difference of the squares of these two numbers also equals 63. What is the difference between these two numbers?

1–18. Solve for the value of x in the following equation; show all work.

$$4+\frac{x+3}{x-3}-\frac{4x^2}{x^2-9}=\frac{x-3}{x+3}$$

1–19. What is the equation of the line through the intersection of $2x+3y-4=0$ and $x+2y-5=0$ and the point $(2,3)$?

1–20. Find, correct to two decimal places, the values of t for which $5t^2-12t = -7$.

1–21. Given equations: $x^2\sin 2\phi+10\tan\phi=20$, and $x \cos\phi+20=23$. What are the values of x and ϕ?

1–22. In a rectangular coordinate system, find the equation of the straight line that goes through the point of intersection of $2x+y-7$ and $x-y=5$, and that is perpendicular to $2x+3y=4$.

1–23. What is the probability of obtaining at least one six in three throws of one die?

1–24. A factory has measured the diameter of a hundred random samples of its product. The results, arranged in ascending order, were (45 results between 0.859 and 0.900, inclusive) : 0.901, 0.902, 0.902, 0.902, 0.903, 0.903, 0.904, 0.904, 0.904, 0.904 . . . . (45 more different results from 0.905 to 0.958, inclusive).

The sum of all 100 observations is 91.170. No observed value among those not numerically shown occurred more than twice. The smallest observed value was 0.859; the largest was 0.958. From the data given, find the mean, the median, and the mode for these observations.

1–25. Given three points in space describing a plane, $x=1$, $y=2$, $z=3$, determine the intersection point in space, x, y, z, between this plane and a normal line which passes through the origin.

1–26. The cost per cubic yard of fill for a highway construction job is \$2.00 plus \$0.02 per station (100 ft) hauled. The cost of opening a borrow pit is \$4000.00. If a uniform fill of 500 cubic yards per station is required, what is the economical spacing of the borrow pits?

1–27. Calculate by logarithms

$$x=\sqrt[3]{\frac{1.4321\ (0.81406)}{42.621\ (0.04260)}}$$

Limit the number of digits in the answer by the accuracy of your tables or by the indicated accuracy of the data, whichever is more restrictive.

1–28. Solve each of the following for x: (a) $\log_2 65=x$; (b) $\log_e 753.6=x$; (c) $x^2-2x+2=x$; (d) $\cos^2 x-2\tan^2 x=\sec^2 x$. In (d) find the principal values of x.

1–29. What is the logarithm of 243 to the base 3? What is the number whose logarithm is 5 to the base 1?

1–30. Find the value of $(0.085)^{3/2}$.

1–31. Solve the following equation mathematically for x: $\text{Log}_{10}(x-1)+\text{Log}_{10}(x)=1$.

1–32. Find, to the nearest degree, the largest angle of a triangle whose sides are 7 in., 8 in., and 13 in. long, respectively.

1–33. One side of a triangle is 1 ft and the adjacent angles are B and C. Write expressions for the lengths b and c and the area of the triangle.

1–34. A certain observation tower B is 1 mile due east of tower A. A third tower is northeast 45° from B 1.41 miles. Clocks at B and C strike at the same instant. (a) What time interval will elapse between the two sounds, as heard by an observer at A? (b) If the distance BC is the diagonal of a square piece of land, how many acres would be included in the square area?

1–35. A tree, growing vertically upward, stands on a slope which is inclined 12°30′ with the horizontal and casts a shadow 105 ft long directly down the slope. The altitude of the sun above the true horizon is 42°30′. Determine the height of the tree.

1–36. Two angles of elevation of a balloon are observed simultaneously from two points in the same vertical plane as the balloon and on level ground beneath the balloon. The two points are ½ mile apart, and the two angles are 45° and 15°, respectively. Determine the height of the balloon (a) when the two points are on the same side of the balloon and (b) when the two points are on opposite sides of the balloon.

1–37. In the figure, *ABC* is a triangular tract of land. The 1-acre tract *DEFG* is to be cut off. Dimensions given are $AE=400$ ft, $EF=480$ ft, $DC=200$ ft. Calculate the length of *DG* and *CB*.

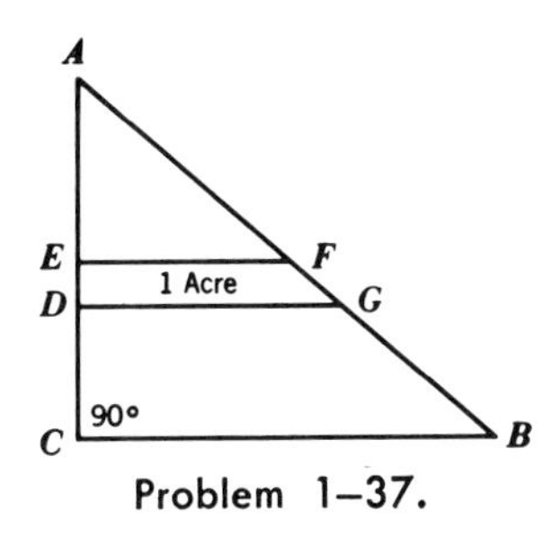

Problem 1–37.

1–38. Two observers 5 miles apart on a plane and facing each other find that the angles of elevation of a balloon in the same vertical plane with themselves are 55° and 58°, respectively. Determine the height of the balloon above the plane.

1–39. Prove the following trigonometric identity:

$$\frac{\cos^4\theta-\sin^4\theta+1}{2\cos^2\theta}=1$$

1–40. On an exploring expedition, the height of a newly discovered mountain is measured in the following manner: From a point "*A*" whose elevation was judged to be 8000 ft, a measurement of 10,000 ft was made toward the peak to point "*B*" whose elevation is 200 ft higher than "*A*'s". From *A*, the line of sight to the peak sloped 15.25°, and from *B* it was 21.40°. To slide rule accuracy, how high is the new peak above sea level?

1–41. Find the values of the angle x which lie between 0° and 360° which satisfy the condition that $3\sin x=2\cos^2 x$.

1–42. The area of a right triangle is 210 sq ft. If the hypotenuse is 29 ft, what are the lengths of the other two sides?

1–43. If $y=x(2-x)^2$, find dy/dx. Find the value of

$$\int_1^3 (3x^2-2)\,dx$$

1–44. Power (P) is defined as the time rate of doing work (work denoted by W). If the work being done by a force is $W=3t^2+4t+6$, where t is in seconds and W is in footpounds, find the power when $t=2$ sec.

1–45. The height s, in feet, reached in t seconds by a body projected vertically upward with a velocity of v_1 feet per second is given by the formula $s=v_1t-16.1t^2$. If $v_1=300$ fps, find the velocity and acceleration (a) at the end of 2 sec and (b) at the end of 15 sec. Resistance of air is neglected. Solve by calculus.

1–46. If $d^2y/dx^2=x$ and if when $x=60$, $y=1$ and $dy/dx=0$, find y in terms of x.

1–47. Evaluate the following integrals:

$$\int_0^1 \frac{dx}{\sqrt{x^2+2}} \qquad \int_0^\pi e^x \sin x \, dx \qquad \int \frac{\sqrt{x}\, dx}{1+x\sqrt{x}}$$

1–48. Evaluate the following integral:

$$\int_0^2 \frac{\cos\theta \, d\theta}{1+\sin^2\theta}$$

1–49. Determine the area of the triangle formed by the x axis and the tangent and normal to the curve $y^2=6x$ at the point $x=6$ and $y=6$. Determine the area enclosed by the curve and the line $y=x/2$.

1–50. Given the area bounded by the curve $y=x^4$, the line $x=2$, and the x axis; find the volume generated by revolving this area around (a) the x axis and (b) the y axis.

1–51. Find by integration the area under the curve $y=x^2 \sin x$, between $x=0$ and $x=\pi$.

1–52. Determine the equations of the tangent and the normal to the circle $(x-4)^2+(y+3)^2=25$ at point (7,1).

1–53. A rectangular box with a square base and top is to be made to contain 1250 cu ft. The material for the base costs $0.35 per square foot, for the top $0.15 per square foot, and for the sides $0.20 per square foot. Find the dimensions and the total cost such that the cost will be a minimum.

1–54. An open tray is to be made by cutting an equal square from each corner of a piece of sheet metal 6 in. × 10 in. What should be the size of the squares to give maximum volume?

1–55. The space within a ¼-mile running track consists of a rectangle with a semicircle at each end. To make the rectangular area as large as possible, how much of the ¼-mile track (440 yd) should be given to the straight sides and how much to the curved ends?

1–56. A manufacturer has 30 machines with an average daily output of 400 parts per machine. For each additional machine, the average daily output per machine is reduced by 10 parts. How many machines will give the largest total number of parts per day?

1–57. A transformer core is to be built up of sheet-steel laminations, using two different strip widths, x and y, so that the resultant symmetrical cross section will fit within a circle of diameter D. Compute the values of x and y in terms of D so that the cross section of the core will have maximum value.

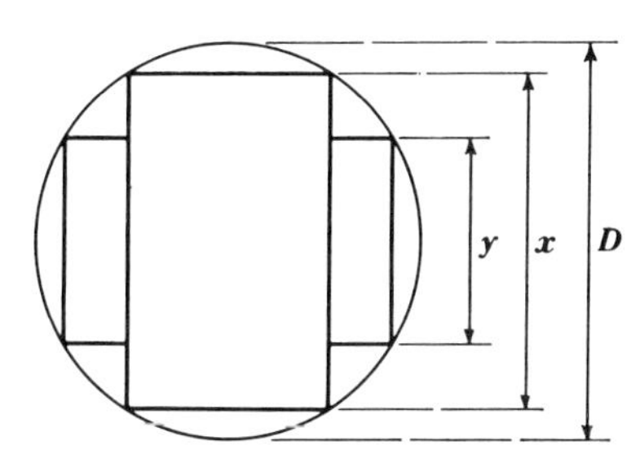

Problem 1–57.

1–58. A parabolic tunnel is 16 ft wide at the base and 16 ft high at the middle. What is the maximum height of a moving van (8 ft wide at its top) that could pass through the tunnel?

1–59. A cylindrical tank is to contain 1125 cu ft and is to have a flat bottom and a hemispherical screen for a roof. The bottom costs $0.40 per square foot, the curved wall $0.30 per square foot, and the roof $0.20 per square foot. Find (a) the proportions of the tank so that the cost of materials will be a minimum, (b) the cost.

1–60. Determine the optimum dimensions for the cheapest construction of a cylindrical tank with flat ends if the side is made of a material costing twice as much per unit area as the material for the ends. The volume is to be exactly 1 cu ft.

1–61. What is the greatest number of solid spheres 1 ft in diameter that can be packed in a covered box 10 ft × 10 ft × 10 ft, inside dimensions? What per cent of air space will be left?

1–62. When a plane surface of inclination θ moves through the air horizontally and at a fixed speed, the lifting power of the resisting air is given as $Q=K \sin^2 \theta \cos \theta$. Find the value θ which makes Q a maximum if K is made equal to 1.

1–63. A semielliptical culvert having dimensions as shown is found to need additional support at points A and B, 6 ft from the center line. These supports are to be placed normal to the curvature of the surface at these points. How many feet of material will be needed to make these supports?

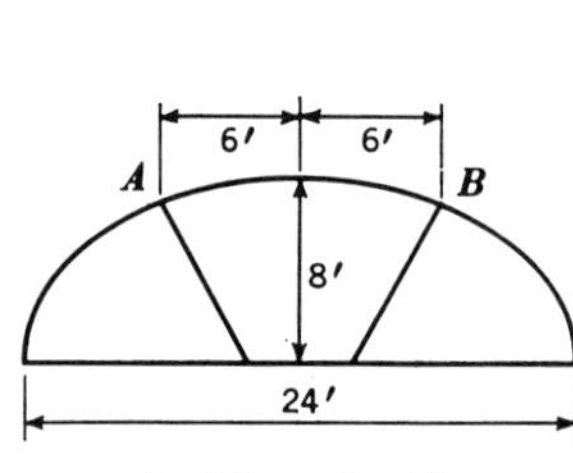

Problem 1–63.

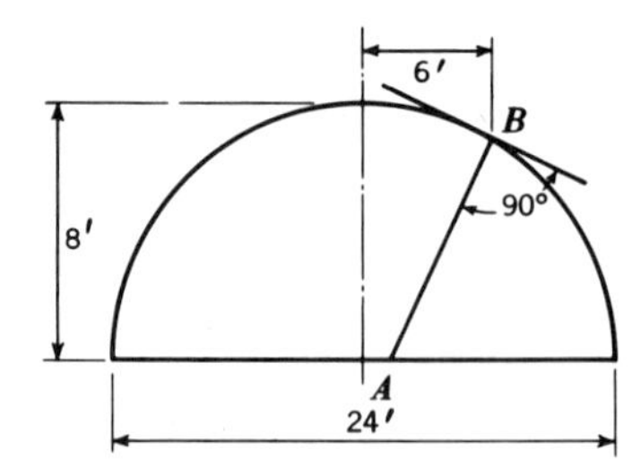

Problem 1–64.

1–64. A parabolic-arch bridge 8 ft high and 24 ft wide is to be formed as shown in the sketch. Determine the length of the inserted brace AB. (NOTE: The point A is not at mid-span.)

1–65. A cubical open-topped tank rests on one edge and is tilted 30° from the vertical. It is filled with water until the water runs over the lowest upper edge. Through what additional angle must the tank be tilted to pour off one-half of the water?

1–66. A load of 1000 lb is to be lifted 100 ft using a cable weighing 1 lb/ft. How long will it take a completely efficient 10-hp motor to lift the load the required distance?

1–67. An ornamental pillar 20 ft in height has a circular cross section at every point. The diameters measured at 0, 5, 10, 15, and 20 ft from the ground are found to be 5, 2, 1, 2, and 5 ft, respectively. Estimate the volume.

1–68. An elevator starts from rest and acquires an upward velocity of 900 fpm in a distance of 30 ft. The elevator weighs

3220 lb. If the acceleration is constant, what is the tension in the elevator cable?

1–69. An object is shot upward from the ground at an initial velocity of 100 fps. At the same instant another object is dropped from a place 100 ft above the ground. After what interval of time and at what distance above the ground will the two objects pass? Neglect air resistance.

1–70. The velocity of a body starting from rest is $5t^2$ feet per second after t seconds. How far will it be from the point of starting in 4 sec? In what time will it pass a distance of 570 ft measured from the starting point?

1–71. In counting traffic passing a certain point it is found that in general the rate at which vehicles pass the point per hour follows a sine curve for a 24-hr period with a minimum of 40 per hour at midnight and a maximum of 1600 per hour at noon. From these data write an equation which will give the rate per hour at any time of the day measured in hours from midnight and calculate the rate at 8 A.M. How many vehicles pass the point between 8 A.M. and noon?

1–72. A bombardier is sighting on a target on the ground directly ahead. If the bomber is flying 2 miles above the ground at 240 mph, how fast must the sighting instrument be turning when the angle between the path of the bomber and the line of sight is 30°?

1–73. Determine the length of the catenary from $x=0$ to $x=x_1$ by using the exponential equation $y=\frac{1}{2}a(e^{x/a}+e^{-x/a})$.

1–74. Sawdust is carried off by a blower and deposited in a conical pile whose radius is always three-fourths of its height. The blower discharges sawdust at the rate of 2 cfm. How fast is the altitude of the pile increasing when the base of the pile is 12 ft in diameter? (Volume of a cone $=\frac{1}{3}$ height $\times$ area of base.)

1–75. A swimming pool is 60 ft long, 30 ft wide, 1 ft deep at one end, and 10 ft deep at the other, the bottom of the pool being a plane surface. Water input is 600 $\text{ft}^3\text{-min}^{-1}$. At what rate is the water surface rising when the maximum depth is (a) 5 ft and (b) 9.5 ft?

1–76. What should be the dimensions of the largest possible rectangular box with square base and open top which is to be made from 300 sq ft of material?

1–77. Determine the centroid of a half-circle.

1–78. Given the equation of a curve $y=10x-x^2$. What is the area between this curve and the x-axis from $x=0$ to $x=7$ ft? What is the x coordinate of the center of gravity of this area?

1–79. Find the limit of $\dfrac{x^2-3x+2}{x^2+x-2}$ as x approaches the limit of 1.

1–80. An automobile is moving horizontally at the rate (dx/dt) of 30 miles per hour toward the base of a tower which is (z) 360 ft high. Compute the rate (dy/dt) at which the automobile is approaching the top of the tower when it is (x) 100 ft away from its base.

Chemistry 2

The problems and questions in this chapter require only a general knowledge of chemistry. The examples for which solutions are given encompass all of the chemical principles, laws, and theories involved in the problems of the chapter. Several applications of each principle, and related principles, may be combined in one problem. The following general sequence is used in the presentation: gas laws, Avogadro's number, molar volume, calculations based on chemical equations (weight and volume), percentage composition, normal concentrations of solutions and equivalent weights, molal freezing-point effect, ionic equilibria and pH, and electrolysis. The principles utilized most frequently on past examination questions are emphasized by the selection of typical problems included herein.

2–1. Compute the number of molecules of hydrogen in 1 ml at 20°C and 1 mm (mercury) pressure.

Solution:

$$pV = nRT \qquad \frac{1}{760}\left(\frac{1}{1000}\right) = n(0.082)(293) \qquad n = 5.47 \times 10^{-8} \text{ mole}$$

$$1 \text{ mole} = 6.02 \times 10^{23} \text{ molecules}$$

$$\text{Number of molecules} = (5.47 \times 10^{-8})(6.02 \times 10^{23}) = 3.29 \times 10^{16}$$

2–2. An empty steel cylinder has a capacity of 2 cu ft. Its weight empty, with valve, is 135 lb. The cylinder is filled with oxygen at 1900 psi and 77°F. Assume the validity of the gas laws. A pound mole of a gas at standard conditions occupies approximately 358 cu ft. (a) Calculate the number of cubic feet of atmospheric air at 77°F required to fill the tank under the given conditions. (b) Calculate what per cent of the total weight of the full tank is oxygen when the tank is filled with oxygen.

Solution:

(a) $p_1V_1 = p_2V_2 \qquad 14.7V_1 = 1900(2) \qquad V_1 = 258.5 \text{ cu ft}$

(b) $V_{STP} = V_1\left(\frac{P_1}{P_{STP}}\right)\left(\frac{T_{STP}}{T_1}\right) = 2\left(\frac{1900}{14.7}\right)\left(\frac{491°R}{536°R}\right) = 236.8 \text{ cu ft}$

$$\text{Moles of } O_2 = \frac{236.8}{358} = 0.661 \qquad \text{Weight of } O_2 = 32(0.661) = 21.2 \text{ lb}$$

$$\text{Per cent } O_2 = \frac{21.2(100)}{135+21.2} = 13.6$$

2–3. What is the composition, in volume per cent, of the gases obtained from burning FeS_2 with 50 per cent excess air, assuming all of the iron goes to Fe_2O_3 and the sulfur to SO_2?

Solution: $$11O_2 + 4FeS_2 \rightarrow 2Fe_2O_3 + 8SO_2$$

$$\text{Total } V_A = 55 + 27.5 = 82.5 \text{ volumes}$$

$$\text{Volume } N_2 \text{ left} = 82.5(0.8) = 66 \qquad \text{Volume } O_2 = 27.5(0.2) = 5.5 \text{ volumes}$$

$$\text{Volume } SO_2 = 8 \text{ volumes} \qquad V_T = 66 + 5.5 + 8 = 79.5$$

$$\text{Per cent } N_2 = 83 \qquad \text{Per cent } O_2 = 7 \qquad \text{Per cent } SO_2 = 10$$

2–4. Six grams of carbon are burned, 14 g of oxygen being used for the purpose. Some CO is formed, and the rest is CO_2. What fraction of the final volume of gas mixture is CO_2? Atomic weights: C=12, O=16.

Solution: $$2C + O_2 \rightarrow 2CO \qquad C + O_2 \rightarrow CO_2$$

$$\frac{6\text{g}}{12 \text{ g/g}-\text{atom}} = 0.5 \text{ g}-\text{atom of C} = 0.5 \text{ mole gas formed}$$

$$x = \text{moles of } O_2 \text{ used in forming CO} \qquad 2x = \text{moles of CO formed}$$

$$\frac{14\text{g}}{32 \text{ g/mole}} = \tfrac{7}{16} \text{ mole (total } O_2 \text{ used)}$$

$$\tfrac{7}{16} - x = \text{moles of } O_2 \text{ used in forming } CO_2 = \text{moles of } CO_2 \text{ formed}$$

$$2x + (\tfrac{7}{16} - x) = 0.5 \qquad x = \tfrac{1}{16} \qquad 2x = \tfrac{1}{8} \qquad \tfrac{7}{16} - x = \tfrac{3}{8} \text{ mole of } CO_2$$

$$\text{Mole fraction of } CO_2 = \tfrac{3}{8} \div \tfrac{1}{2} = \tfrac{3}{4}$$

2–5. Caustic soda, NaOH, is an important commercial chemical. It is often prepared by the reaction of soda ash, Na_2CO_3, with slaked lime, $Ca(OH)_2$. (a) How many pounds of caustic soda can be obtained by treating 11.023 lb of soda ash with slaked lime? (b) What weight, in pounds, of lime, CaO, would be required? Assume complete reaction. Use approximate atomic weights: Ca=40.1, Na=23, C=12, O=16, H=1.

Solution: (a) $$Na_2CO_3 + Ca(OH)_2 \rightarrow CaCO_3 + 2NaOH$$

Molecular weights are as follows: $Na_2CO_3 = 46 + 12 + 48 = 106$ and $NaOH = 23 + 16 + 1 = 40$, whence 106 lb Na_2CO_3 gives 80 lb of NaOH.

$$\frac{106}{80} = \frac{11.023}{x} \qquad x = 8.32 \text{ lb NaOH}$$

(b) $CaO + H_2O \rightarrow Ca(OH)_2$ Molecular weight of $CaO = 40.1 + 16 = 56.1$

$$\frac{56.1}{80} = \frac{x}{8.32} \qquad x = 5.83 \text{ lb CaO}$$

2-6. Borax is made from the mineral colemanite by the reaction $Ca_2B_6O_{11} + Na_2CO_3 + H_2O \rightarrow CaCO_3 + Na_2B_4O_7 + NaOH$ (not balanced). Determine the pounds of pure borax obtainable from the treatment of 1 ton of colemanite ore that analyzes 10 per cent boron by weight. Atomic weights are Ca = 40, Na = 23, B = 11, C = 12.

Solution:

$$2Ca_2B_6O_{11} + 4Na_2CO_3 + H_2O \rightarrow 4CaCO_3 + 3Na_2B_4O_7 + 2NaOH$$

Molecular weights are $Ca_2B_6O_{11} = 322$, $Na_2B_4O_7 = 202$.

$$\frac{66/322\ (w)}{2000} \times 100 = 10 \text{ per cent} \qquad w = \text{weight of } Ca_2B_6O_{11} = 976 \text{ lb}$$

From the equation,

$$\frac{2(322)}{3(202)} = \frac{976}{x} \qquad x = 918 = \text{weight of borax obtained}$$

2-7. A water having the following composition is to be softened by the lime-soda process: $Na^+ = 69$, $Ca^{++} = 70$, $Mg^{++} = 30$, $HCO_3^- = 213.5$, $SO_4^= = 120$, and $Cl^- = 106.5$, all in parts per million. What would be the theoretical number of pounds of slaked lime (90 per cent lime by weight) and soda ash required for the treatment of 1000 gal of water?

Solution:

$$W_W = 8340 \text{ lb} \qquad \text{Pound-mole } HCO_3^- = \frac{213.5}{10^6}\ \frac{(8340)}{(61)} = 0.0292$$

$$\text{Pound-mole } Mg^{++} = \frac{30(8340)}{10^6(24.3)} = 0.0103 \qquad \text{Pound-mole } Ca^{++} = \frac{70(8340)}{10^6(40)} = 0.0146$$

$$CaO + H_2O \rightarrow Ca^{++} + 2OH^- \qquad Mg^{++} + 2OH^- \rightarrow Mg(OH)_2$$

$$HCO_3^- + OH^- \rightarrow CO_3^= + H_2O \qquad Ca^{++} + CO_3^= \rightarrow CaCO_3$$

Moles CaO required to convert HCO_3^- to $CO_3^= = 0.0292/2 = 0.0146$

Total Ca^{++} present $= 0.0146 + 0.0146 = 0.0292$ moles = total $CO_3^=$ formed

Moles of CaO required to precipitate all of Mg^{++} as $Mg(OH)_2 = 0.0103$

Total CaO added $= 0.0146 + 0.0103 = 0.0249$ mole

Weight of CaO $= 0.0249(56) = 1.39$ lb

Weight of slaked lime required: $0.9(x) = 1.39$; $x = 1.54$ lb

Weight of Na_2CO_3 required $= 0.0103(106) = 1.09$ lb

2-8. If you were to make 110 lb of glass having the composition $Na_2O \cdot CaO \cdot 7SiO_2$, calculate the weight of the pure (a) $CaCO_3$, (b) Na_2CO_3, (c) SiO_2 to be used.

Solution: Molecular weights are $Na_2O \cdot CaO \cdot 7SiO_2 = 539$, $Na_2CO_3 = 106$, $CaCO_3 = 100$, and $SiO_2 = 60$.

$$\frac{539}{110} = \frac{100}{x} \qquad x = 20.4 \text{ lb } CaCO_3 \qquad \frac{539}{110} = \frac{7(60)}{x} \qquad x = 85.7 \text{ lb } SiO_2$$

$$\frac{539}{110} = \frac{106}{x} \qquad x = 21.6 \text{ lb } Na_2CO_3$$

2–9. The number of moles of sulfuric acid in 400 ml of 6 N sulfuric acid is ________?

Solution:

$$EW = \frac{MW}{\text{(number of replacable H atoms)}} \qquad \text{MW of } H_2SO_4 = 98 \qquad EW = \frac{98}{2} = 49$$

$$6\,N(0.40) = 2.4 \text{ equivalents (eq.)} \qquad \text{Number of moles} = 1.2$$

2–10. The number of grams of pure sulfuric acid (hydrogen sulfate) in 1 liter of 6 N sulfuric acid is ________?

Solution: $6\,N\ (1) = 6$ eq., $EW = MW/2 = 49$.

$$\text{Weight } H_2SO_4 = 6(49) = 294 \text{ g}$$

2–11. The volume, in milliliters, of a 0.5 N sulfuric acid solution needed to neutralize completely 500 ml of 0.2 M sodium hydroxide is ________?

Solution:

$$EW = \frac{MW}{\text{number of OH groups}}$$

For NaOH,

$$EW = MW \qquad \text{molarity} = \text{normality}$$

$$N_A V_A = N_B V_B \qquad 0.5 V_A = 0.2(500)$$

$$V_A = 200 \text{ ml} \qquad \text{volume } H_2SO_4$$

2–12. A gas stream containing hydrogen chloride and air at 1 atm and 20°C was analyzed by passing a sample of the gas through sodium hydroxide in a gas-scrubbing bottle. Sufficient gas was passed through 250 ml of 0.01 N sodium hydroxide to cause the normality to drop to 0.008. The volume of the air after the removal of the HCl was 1000 ml at 20°C and 1 atm. Determine (a) the partial pressure of the HCl in the original mixture and (b) the weight per cent and mole per cent of HCl in the original mixture.

Solution: (a)

Meq. NaOH reacted $= 0.01(250) - 0.008(250) = 0.5$

Meq. HCl reacted $= 0.5$, or 0.0005 mole

$pV = nRT \qquad V = 0.0005(0.082)(293°K) = 0.012 l = 12$ ml

V_T Gas $= 1000 + 12 = 1012$ ml

$$\text{Partial pressure of HCl} = \frac{12}{1012}(1) = 0.0119 \text{ atm} = 0.0119(760) = 9 \text{ mm}$$

(b)

$$\frac{\text{Moles HCl}}{\text{Total moles}} = \frac{\text{vol HCl}}{\text{total vol}} = \frac{12}{1012} = 0.0119$$

$$\text{Mole per cent HCl} = 0.0119(100) = 1.19 \text{ per cent}$$

$$\text{Mole per cent air} = 100 - 1.19 = 98.8 \text{ per cent}$$

$$\text{Average MW of air} = 28.8 \qquad \text{MW HCl} = 36.5$$

$$\text{Weight per cent of HCl} = \frac{36.5(1.2)(100)}{98.8(28.8)+36.5(1.2)} = 1.52 \text{ per cent}$$

2–13. How many milliliters of concentrated sulfuric acid must be mixed with sufficient water to make 1000 ml of a sulfuric acid solution, 15 ml of which are required to neutralize 27 ml of 0.1 *N* sodium hydroxide solution? Specific gravity of the concentrated sulfuric acid is 1.84 and is 95 per cent H_2SO_4 by weight.

Solution:

$$N_AV_A = N_BV_B \qquad \text{EW of } H_2SO_4 = \frac{\text{MW}}{2} = 49 \qquad \begin{array}{c} N_A(15) = 0.1(27) \\ N_A = 0.18 \end{array}$$

$$\frac{1.84(1000)(0.95)}{49} = 35.7\ N \qquad \text{concentrated } H_2SO_4$$

$$35.7V_1 = 0.18(1000) \qquad V_1 = 5.05 \text{ ml of concentrated } H_2SO_4$$

2–14. The freezing point of a solution containing 1.60 g of solute per 150 cc of water was $-0.110°C$. What was the approximate molecular weight of the solute, assuming that it is a non-electrolyte?

Solution: Molal freezing-point constant for water = 1.86°C

$$\text{Weight of solute /1000 g water} = \frac{1.6}{150}(1000) = 10.7 \text{ g}$$

Weight of solute to lower freezing point to $-1.86°C$

$$W = \frac{10.7(1.86)}{0.110} = 180 \text{ g} \qquad \text{MW} = 180$$

2–15. The (a) hydrogen ion concentration (gram-ions per liter) and (b) the pH of a 0.1 *M* acetic acid solution are (a) ________ and (b) ________ at 25°C. The ionization constant of acetic acid is 1.8×10^{-5} at 25°C.

Solution: (a)

$$HC_2H_3O_2 \leftrightarrows H^+ + C_2H_3O_2^-$$

$$K_i = \frac{[H^+][C_2H_3O_2^-]}{[HC_2H_3O_2]}$$

$$x = [H^+] \qquad x = [C_2H_3O_2^-] \qquad [HC_2H_3O_2] = 0.1 - x$$

Concentration of ions very small compared to concentration of non-ionized acid

$$1.8 \times 10^{-5} = \frac{(x)(x)}{0.1} \qquad x = 1.34 \times 10^{-3} = [H^+] \text{ gram-ion/liter}$$

(b)

$$\text{pH} = \log \frac{1}{[H^+]} = \log \frac{1}{1.34 \times 10^{-3}} = 2.87$$

2–16. In an electroplating process, how many grams of copper metal would be deposited from a copper sulfate, $CuSO_4$, solution in

1 hr when a current of 10 amp passes through the solution? (1 amp=1 coulomb/sec; 1 faraday=96,500 coulombs; atomic weight of copper is 63.5.)

Solution:

1 faraday will deposit 1 gram equivalent weight of metal.

Half-cell reaction for Cu^{++}: $Cu^{++}+2e^{-}\rightarrow Cu^{0}$

$EW=MW/2=31.75$

1 faraday will plate out 31.7 g Cu metal from $CuSO_4$

$10(60)(60)(1)=36{,}000$ coulombs

$31.7(36{,}000)/96{,}500=11.8$ g (weight of Cu deposited)

2–17. A transportation company specializes in the shipment of gaseous materials. If they had standard size tanks of 10 liters, 20 liters, and 30 liters and they received an order for 100 liters of a gas at standard temperature and pressure, which size container would be required if the gas were to be shipped at a temperature of 80°F and at a maximum pressure of 8 atm?

2–18. A tank tested to withstand a pressure of 15 atm is filled with gas at 20°F and 12 atm pressure. If the temperature goes up to 65°F, what percentage of the margin of safety has been lost?

2–19. An Orsat analysis of flue gas yields the following volumetric analysis, in per cent: $CO_2=12.5$, $CO=0.5$, $O_2=6.4$, and $N_2=80.6$. Convert this analysis to an analysis by weight.

2–20. An oxygen cylinder contains 4.0 cu ft of O_2 at 70°F and 2200 psig. What is the weight of the O_2? The gas constant for O_2 is 48.2 ft-lb/(lb) (°F abs).

2–21. A standard cylinder of O_2 contains 240 cu ft of gas measured at 60°F and 1 atm pressure. If the actual tank pressure when filled is 2400 psig at 70°F, what is the actual volume of the cylinder? What is the weight of the cylinder filled if the empty cylinder weighs 55 lb?

2–22. Gasoline may be designated approximately as C_8H_{18}. Write the correct chemical equation which shows the theoretical moles of oxygen, O_2, required to burn gasoline and the moles of products of combustion.

2–23. In the thermite process, ferric oxide reacts with aluminum metal to produce iron metal and aluminum oxide according to the following equation: $Fe_2O_3+2Al\rightarrow Al_2O_3+2Fe$. The reaction liberates so much heat that the iron is molten and flows easily. This process is used for on-the-spot welding of broken iron rails or large parts of machinery. Calculate how many kilograms of ferric oxide would be used to produce 15.0 kg of iron required for a welding job. (Assume that sufficient aluminum is available to react with all the ferric oxide needed.) Atomic weights: Fe=56, O=16, Al=27.

2–24. Write the chemical equation for, and calculate the weight of, water and copper formed by the reaction of hydrogen with 10 g of cupric oxide.

2–25. Gasoline may be represented approximately by the compound C_8H_{18}. Write the equation for the complete combustion of gasoline with oxygen and determine for 1 lb of fuel the weight of oxygen required and the weight of each of the products of complete combustion with 40 per cent excess air.

2–26. In the complete combustion of 15 lb of hydrogen sulfide, H_2S, to sulfur dioxide, SO_2, and water, how many pounds of each product are formed? How many pounds of oxygen are needed?

2–27. Phosphorus is prepared in an electric furnace according to the chemical equation

$$Ca_3(PO_4)_2 + 3SiO_2 + 5C \rightarrow 3CaSiO_3 + 5CO + 2P$$

Atomic weights: Ca=40, P=31, O=16, C=12, Si=28. (a) Calculate the number of pounds of phosphorus formed for each pound of $Ca_3(PO_4)_2$ used. (b) Calculate the number of grams of SiO_2 required for each grain of P produced.

2–28. Soda ash, Na_2CO_3, is produced commercially by the Solvay process, which may be represented by the following chemical equations:

$$CO_2 + NH_3 + NaCl + H_2O \rightarrow NaHCO_3 + NH_4Cl$$

$$2NaHCO_3 + \text{heat} \rightarrow Na_2CO_3 + H_2O + CO_2$$

In order to produce 2.2 kg of soda ash, how many grams of salt, NaCl, are required? Use atomic weights: Na=23, C=12, O=16, Cl=35.5.

2–29. A solution of silver nitrate, $AgNO_3$, is standardized by reacting it with pure NaCl as follows:

$$AgNO_3 + NaCl \rightarrow AgCl + NaNO_3$$

Atomic weights are O=16, Ag=107.9, Na=23, Cl=35.5, N=14. When 0.22 g of NaCl reacts with 34.1 g of the solution, determine (a) the weight of silver nitrate in the solution and (b) the per cent by weight in solution.

2–30. Calculate the weight of lime, CaO, that can be prepared by heating 200 lb of limestone containing 85 per cent by weight of $CaCO_3$ and 15 per cent by weight of inert material.

2–31. Phosphoric acid is made from phosphate rock by the reaction $Ca_3(PO_4)_2+H_2SO_4 \rightarrow CaSO_4+H_3PO_4$ (not balanced). How many pounds of phosphoric acid of 30 per cent P_2O_5 content by weight can be obtained per ton of 93 per cent strength sulfuric acid? The compound P_2O_5 is the anhydride of phosphoric acid.

2–32. What is the per cent of sulfur in aluminum sulfate, $Al_2(SO_4)_3$?

2–33. A flat piece of metal measuring 6 cm by 5 cm (of negligible thickness) is electroplated with copper using a solution made by dissolving $CuSO_4 \cdot 5H_2O$ in water. The copper plate is 0.002 cm in thickness. The density of copper is 8.9 g/cc. Calculate the grams of $CuSO_4 \cdot 5H_2O$ which were necessary to furnish the copper which was plated out.

2–34. Propane gas burns in air as indicated by the following equation: $C_3H_8+5O_2 \rightarrow 3CO_2+4H_2O$. Determine the cubic feet of O_2 necessary to burn 4.0 cu ft of C_3H_8.

2–35. (a) Write a balanced equation for the complete combustion of methane gas, CH_4. (b) From this equation, calculate the volume of air (21 per cent O_2 by volume) which is necessary to burn completely 100 cu ft of CH_4 gas measured at the same temperature and pressure as the air.

2–36. The complete combustion of propane gas is represented by the following skeleton equation: $C_3H_8+O_2 \rightarrow CO_2+H_2O$. (a) Balance the equation. (b) How many cubic feet of air (air is 21 per cent O_2 by volume and 79 per cent N_2 by volume) measured at 25°C and a pressure of 760 mm of Hg would be required to burn 20,000 cu ft of propane gas measured at the same conditions of temperature and pressure?

2–37. Potassium chlorate, $KClO_3$, will liberate all of its oxygen if heated to the proper temperature. Potassium nitrate, KNO_3, will liberate part of its oxygen if heated to the proper temperature, yielding KNO_2+O_2. What weight of KNO_3 is required to deliver the same amount of oxygen as 1 lb of $KClO_3$? Atomic weights: K=39.10, Cl=35.46, N=14.01, O=16.00.

2–38. Twenty grams of aluminum were treated with sulfuric acid. Calculate (a) the weight of H_2SO_4 necessary to react with

20 g of aluminum and (b) the volume of hydrogen liberated (measured at standard temperature and pressure). The equation representing this reaction is $2Al+3H_2(SO_4) \rightarrow Al_2(SO_4)_3+3H_2$. Atomic weights used are as follows: Al=27.0, H=1.0, S=32.0, O=16.0, Ca=40.0, N=14.0.

2-39. The mineral iron pyrites, FeS_2, may be converted to ferric oxide by reacting according to the following equation: $4FeS_2+11O_2 \rightarrow 2Fe_2O_3+8SO_2$. (a) Calculate the number of pounds of oxygen required for the complete conversion of 100 lb of pyrites to the oxide. (b) How many liters of SO_2 at standard temperature and pressure would be produced by each pound of iron pyrites converted? Use the following atomic weights: Fe=55.9, S=32.0, O=16.0.

2-40. Hydrogen sulfide gas, H_2S, is used to precipitate lead sulfide, PbS, in a solution of hydrochloric acid. Atomic weights: H=1.008, S=32.06, Pb=207.2, Cl=35.46.

$$\_\_\_\_ H_2S + \_\_\_\_ PbCl_2 \rightarrow \_\_\_\_ PbS + \_\_\_\_ HCl$$

(a) Balance the chemical equation and state how many moles of H_2S are required to produce 1 mole of PbS. (b) How many pounds of H_2S are required to produce 1 lb of PbS? (c) How many cubic feet of H_2S gas at 70°F and atmospheric pressure are required to produce 1 lb of PbS? The gas constant for H_2S is 23.7 ft-lb/(lb) (°R).

2-41. A limestone analysis is given below. Atomic weights are as follows: Ca=40.07, Mg=24.3, C=12, O=16. The limestone is $CaCO_3$=92 per cent, $MgCO_3$=5 per cent, insoluble=3 per cent. (a) How many pounds of calcium oxide can be obtained from 5 tons of this limestone? (b) How many pounds of CO_2 could be obtained from 1 ton of limestone? (c) How many cubic feet would the CO_2 gas occupy at standard conditions?

2-42. Limestone containing 60 per cent by weight of $CaCO_3$ and 40 per cent by weight of $MgCO_3$ upon heating in a kiln undergoes the following chemical reactions: $CaCO_3 \rightarrow CaO+CO_2$; $MgCO_3 \rightarrow MgO+CO_2$. Atomic weights are Ca=40.1, Mg=24.3, O=16.0, C=12.0. One molecular weight of a gas occupies 380 cu ft at conditions of production. Determine the production from 3 tons of limestone of (a) pounds of MgO and (b) cubic feet of CO_2.

2-43. A certain limestone contains 25 per cent $MgCO_3$ and 75 per cent $CaCO_3$ by weight. Atomic weights are Ca=40, Mg=24.3, C=12, O=16. One pound molecular weight of gas occupies 359 cu ft at 32°F and 1 atm pressure. Determine how many cubic feet of CO_2 are formed by burning 100 lb of limestone if the volume is measured at 170°F and 1 atm.

2–44. Methane gas burns according to the chemical equation $CH_4+2O_2 \rightarrow CO_2+2H_2O$. Atomic weights are C=12, H=1.0, O=16. (a) If air contains 23 per cent by weight of oxygen, how many pounds of air are required to burn 30 lb of methane? (b) If air is 21 per cent oxygen by volume, how many cubic feet of air would be required to burn 300 cu ft of methane measured at the same temperature and pressure?

2–45. When calcium fluoride is treated with sulfuric acid, the following reaction results: $CaF_2+H_2SO_4 \rightarrow 2HF+CaSO_4$. If 100 g of flourspar containing 20 per cent insoluble (inert) material is treated with the theoretical amount of sulfuric acid and 5 per cent of the hydrogen fluoride produced remains in the residue, how many grams of residue will there be and how many cubic centimeters of HF will be given off at 1 atm absolute and 100°F? Atomic weights: Ca=40, F=19, H=1, S=32, O=16.

2–46. Assuming no heat loss in the process, calculate the weight of water, in grams, which could be raised in temperature from 25°C to 100°C by the complete burning of 2.2 kg of carbon to carbon dioxide. The thermochemical equation for the combustion of carbon to carbon dioxide is $C+O_2 \rightarrow CO_2+95$ kilocalories. Use atomic weight C=12.

2–47. How many grams of $Ca(NO_3)_2$ are needed to make 1 liter of a molar solution?

2–48. Twenty-eight milliliters of a normal solution of sodium hydroxide, NaOH, just neutralize 20 ml of a solution of sulfuric acid, H_2SO_4. Calculate the strength of the acid solution in terms of the weight of sulfuric acid in 1 liter of solution.

2–49. How many grams of sodium hydroxide (98.5 per cent NaOH by weight) are required to prepare a liter of sodium hydroxide solution, 28.8 ml of which will neutralize 24 ml of a 0.12 *N* solution of hydrochloric acid?

2–50. A 20-qt radiator has a solution of 80 per cent water and 20 per cent antifreeze. It is desired to increase the antifreeze to 25 per cent. What is the minimum amount of solution to be withdrawn so as to satisfy the condition by adding antifreeze?

2–51. Determine the liters of NH_3 gas measured at 1 atm and

25°C to make enough ammonium hydroxide to neutralize 100 cc of 3 N H_2SO_4. Atomic weights: N=14, S=32, O=16.

2–52. How many liters of hydrochloric acid (specific gravity 1.18, HCl 38 per cent by weight) are required to liberate 4.17 liters of hydrogen (at standard conditions) when the hydrochloric acid reacts with zinc metal? How many grams of zinc are consumed?

2–53. A current of 1 amp flowing through a cell (containing 15 per cent NaOH) for 13.4 hr liberates 4.17 liters of hydrogen at standard conditions. What is the efficiency of the cell?

2–54. (a) Of what advantage is it to write equations in the ionic form? (b) What is a "half-cell" reaction? Give two examples. (c) Balance the equations:

(1) $\_\_\_\_ OH^- + \_\_\_\_ NO_2 \rightarrow$
$\_\_\_\_ NO_3^- + \_\_\_\_ NO_2^- + \_\_\_\_ H_2O$

(2) $\_\_\_\_ HBrO \rightarrow$
$\_\_\_\_ H^+ + \_\_\_\_ Br^- + \_\_\_\_ O_2$

2–55. (a) Carbon in living matter contains a definite proportion of radiocarbon, C^{14}. Upon death of this living matter, the radiocarbon decreases at the rate of 1 part in 8000 per year. Derive an equation where A is the original amount of C^{14} at the death of the living matter and y is the amount of C^{14} left at any time t, in years, measured from the death of the living matter. (b) Charcoal from a tree killed by the eruption of the volcano which formed Crater Lake is assayed at 44.5 per cent radiocarbon. How many years ago did the eruption occur?

2–56. A metal has a specific heat of 0.279 cal/g. If 6.08 g of the metal reacts with an excess of acid, 6.20 liters of hydrogen, H_2, are released at 23°C and 745 mm (dry hydrogen). (a) What is the approximate atomic weight of the metal? Name the method used in this step. (b) What is the equivalent weight of the metal? (c) What is the best value for the atomic weight you can furnish from the above data?

2–57. Balance the following chemical equation and name the elements and radicals represented by the chemical symbols:

$\_\_\_ Ag + \_\_\_ O_2 + \_\_\_ NaCN + \_\_\_ H_2O \rightarrow NaAg(CN)_2 + \_\_\_ NaOH.$

Ag: ________	C: ________	CN: ________
O: ________	N: ________	OH: ________
Na: ________	H: ________	

2–58. On what does the rate of a reaction depend?

2–59. How do changes in 1) temperature and 2) pressure affect the equilibrium expressed by the equation $N_2+3H_2 \rightleftharpoons 2NH_3+21{,}880$ calories?

2–60. What is meant by the pH of a solution?

2–61. Explain the purpose and the chemical bases of the use of the following materials or groups of materials in water treatment: (a) sodium phosphate, (b) sodium carbonate, (c) chlorine, (d) chlorinated lime, (e) ozone, (f) anionic resins, (g) cationic resins, (h) inorganic ion exchange reagents. In your discussion, point out the specific advantages and limitations of the particular agent.

2–62. Explain in some detail, through diagrams, discussion, etc., the electrolysis of sodium chloride under each of the following conditions: (a) dilute aqueous solutions at low potentials, (b) concentrated aqueous solutions at low potentials, (c) dilute aqueous solutions at high potentials, (d) concentrated aqueous solutions at high potentials, and (e) pure molten. State the applications, if any, of each of these electrolyses.

2–63. Distinguish by definitions and comparative statements the meaning of each of the following terms: (a) the electrovalent bond, (b) the covalent bond, (c) the coördinate covalent bond, and (d) the hydrogen bond. A proper and fluent use of chemical terms and formulae will aid in the evaluation of your answers.

2–64. What is the basic chemical nature of glasses?

2–65. How do the so-called heat-resistant glasses differ from ordinary glass?

2–66. Explain in some detail the chemistry of silicate materials. On what structural features do the properties of substances such as asbestos, mica, and feldspars depend?

2–67. Name two metals which are produced commercially by electrolysis of a fused electrolyte.

2–68. Name two metals which are important in industry but whose ores do not occur in the United States in material quantities.

2–69. What is the name of the most important iron ore that is mined in the United States? Write the formula for the iron compound in it.

2-70. The blast furnace used to produce pig iron uses four raw materials. What are they?

2-71. At the present time sea water is the source of one of the important metals of industry. What is this metal?

2-72. What metal forms the protective coating on galvanized iron?

2-73. Name three metals which are mined in the United States in the form of sulfide ores.

2-74. How is cast iron produced from pig iron?

2-75. What is one advantage of the Bessemer process over the open-hearth process for making steel?

2-76. What is one advantage of the-open hearth process over the Bessemer process for making steel?

2-77. Which of the following contains a material amount of slag? (a) Gray cast iron. (b) Wrought iron. (c) Low-carbon steel. (d) High-carbon steel. (e) Malleable cast iron.

2-78. Which of the commercial forms of iron listed in Prob. 2-77 has the lowest percentage of carbon?

2-79. If a steel is to be case-hardened, would a low-carbon or a high-carbon steel be used as the starting material? Why?

2-80. How do you explain the fact that high-carbon steel is hard when quenched and becomes softer after reheating to a relatively low temperature, while duraluminum is soft when quenched and becomes harder following heating to a relatively low temperature?

2-81. In a gaseous mixture collected over water at 14°C, the partial pressures of the components are hydrogen 300 mm, methane 100 mm, oxygen 50 mm, and ethylene 189 mm. The aqueous tension at 14° is 12 mm. (a) What is the total pressure of the mixture? (b) What is the volume per cent of hydrogen?

2-82. A gas analysis yields the following volumetric values: $CO_2=10.6$, $CO=1.4$, $O_2=8.2$, and $N_2=79.8$. (a) Convert the given volumetric analysis to an analysis by weight. (b) Compute the pounds of carbon in each 100 lb of gas.

2-83. When one mol (M) of nitroglycerin, $C_3H_5(NO_3)_3$, is detonated, carbon dioxide, steam, nitrogen, and oxygen are released. Write the chemical equation and balance it.

2–84. (a) What is the composition of the combustion products obtained when pure carbon is burned to CO_2 with the theoretical amount of dry air? (Air contains approximately 21 per cent by volume of O_2, and 79 per cent N_2 and other inerts). (b) What would be the composition of the combustion products when burning pure carbon in air if half of the carbon consumed were burned to CO and all of the oxygen in the air were consumed?

2–85. How many cubic ft of SO_2 measured at 760 mm mercury, and 500°F can be made by roasting 2000 lb of ZnS with oxygen?

2–86. How much water is required to set 100 lb of Plaster of Paris? Formulae: Plaster of Paris—$CaSO_4 \cdot \frac{1}{2}H_2O$. Set form of Plaster of Paris (gypsum)—$CaSO_4 \cdot 2H_2O$.

2–87. Chlorine may be prepared by oxidizing hydrochloric acid with manganese dioxide, MnO_2. The byproducts are water and manganous ion, Mn^{++}. What weight of MnO_2 will be required to produce 10 liters of chlorine, measured at standard temperature and pressure? It is understood that excess hydrochloric acid is present.

2–88. Compute the weights in grams of commercial sodium carbonate and hydrochloric acid required to produce 234 grams of pure sodium chloride. The commercial soda ash is 90 per cent pure and the commercial acid contains 30 per cent by weight of dissolved acid. Molecular weights of pure compounds are $Na_2CO_3=106$, $HCl=36.5$, and $NaCl=58.5$.

2–89. A steel mill is planning to heat treat certain grades of metal which must be protected from contact with the oxygen in air during such treatment. Tests have determined that a combustion gas mixture of carbon dioxide and nitrogen from which all water has been condensed, and the gas further dried over silica gel, would be satisfactory as an inert gas for use in the heat-treating furnace. It has been estimated that 10,000 cu ft/hr at standard conditions would be required of this inert gas mixture. Propane is to be used. (a) Write the balanced equation (reaction) for the combustion of propane with air. (b) How much propane in lb/hr would have to be burned to produce the desired amount of inert gas? (c) How much air in cu ft/hr at standard conditions must be supplied to the propane burner? Standard conditions, 32°F, 14.7 psia.

2–90. A sample of mercuric oxide ore weighing 1.362 grams was heated and the oxygen evolved was collected by the displacement of water from a calibrated tube. The resultant gas had a volume of 50.7 milliliters. The room temperature was 20°C. The barometer reading was 750 mm. What per cent of the ore was mercuric oxide? Vapor pressure of water at 20°C is 17.5 mm.

2–91. When a potassium permangante solution ($KMnO_4$) reacts with a ferrous salt (Fe^{++}) in the presence of an acid (HCl), a manganous salt (Mn^{++}), and a ferric salt (Fe^{+++}) are produced. (a) How would one prepare a 1 normal solution of potassium permanganate for use in this reaction? (b) How would one prepare a 1 normal solution of ferrous chloride? Atomic weights are as follows: K= 39.10, Mn=54.94, O=16.00, Fe=55.84, and C=35.46.

2–92. What volumes of 2N H_2CO_3 and 6N H_2CO_3 must be mixed to yield 700 ml of a 3N H_2CO_3 solution? Assume all volumes are additive.

2–93. A new organic compound has been prepared which is soluble in benzene. Addition of 1.20 gm of the compound to 40 gm of benzene raises the boiling point of the benzene 0.422°C. (The molal boiling point elevation of benzene is 2.53°). What is the molar weight of the compound?

2–94. A compound contains only carbon, hydrogen, and sulfur. One gram, when vaporized, occupies a volume of 269.22 ml at 150°C and 760 mm Hg. One gram burned in oxygen produced 0.5745 gr H_2O, 0.9363 gr CO_2, and an undetermined amount of SO_2. Calculate the simplest formula and the molecular formula.

2–95. Ammonia is made synthetically from pure hydrogen and nitrogen by the reversible reaction: $3H_2+N_2 \rightleftharpoons 2NH_3$. Due to equilibrium limitations, less than half of the raw materials will react in a batch reactor at high pressures. Determine the number of moles of ammonia formed by the time equilibrium is obtained (let $2x$ be the number of moles) if initially a mixture of 75 moles of hydrogen and 25 moles of nitrogen were placed in a closed container at 900°F and 1000 atmospheres. The equilibrium constant at 900°F for the reaction is 0.00000188 in terms of partial pressures in atmospheres.

2–96. A 0.1 M solution of NH_4OH also containing some ammonium chloride NH_4Cl is found to have an OH^- ion concentration of 2.5×10^{-6} M gram ions per liter. Determine the concentration of the NH_4^+ ion in this solution. The ionization constant of NH_4OH is 1.8×10^{-5}.

2–97. What is the normality (gram-equivalent/liter) of hydroxyl ion (OH^-) in pure water if the equilibrium constant for ionizing water is 1.9×10^{-16}? The equilibrium constant is defined in terms of concentrations in units of gram-equivalent/liter. The atomic weight of hydrogen is 1 and that of oxygen is 16.

2–98. Which values of *p*H represent acidity and which alkalinity of solutions? What weight of NaOH would be required to neutralize a solution containing 3 grains of H_2SO_4? (Na=23, O=16, S=32, H=1).

2–99. The passage of 4825 coulombs of electricity through a cell causes 3.95 grams of a metal (M) to be deposited from a water solution at the cathode. The electrolyte has the formula MCl_3. Avogadro's number is 6.02×10^{23}. One Faraday=96,500 coulombs. From these data calculate the atomic weight of the metal (M).

2–100. The common commercial preparation of magnesium metal is by electrolysis of a mixture of 70 per cent magnesium chloride and 30 per cent sodium chloride. (a) Would 5 kilograms of this mixture be enough to yield one kilogram of magnesium? Justify your answer. (b) Would you predict that a current of 8 amperes would be sufficient to produce one kilogram of magnesium metal in 24 hours? Justify your answer. (c) During an electrolytic production of one kilogram of magnesium metal, what volume of chlorine would be formed as a byproduct? This calculation should be precise to 3 significant figures. Assume a temperature of 127°C and a pressure of 740 mm Hg.

Statics 3

The statics problems in this chapter may be classified as Newtonian mechanics, in which space, time, and mass are independent. This is in contrast to relativistic mechanics, in which concepts of space, time, and mass are dependently related.

The study of mechanics is based upon the following fundamental principles which (within the realm of ordinary speeds) have held for more than two centuries: (1) the parallelogram law for addition of forces, (2) the principle of transmissibility, (3) Newton's three laws, and (4) Newton's law of gravitation.

The problems herein are resolved into five general types and, as far as possible, grouped accordingly: (1) statics of rigid bodies in two dimensions, (2) statics of rigid bodies in three dimensions, (3) centroids and moments of inertia, (4) friction, and (5) analysis of structures.

The unit vectors **i**, **j**, and **k** are designated as i, j, and k in example problems.

3–1. Determine completely the resultant of the force system shown.

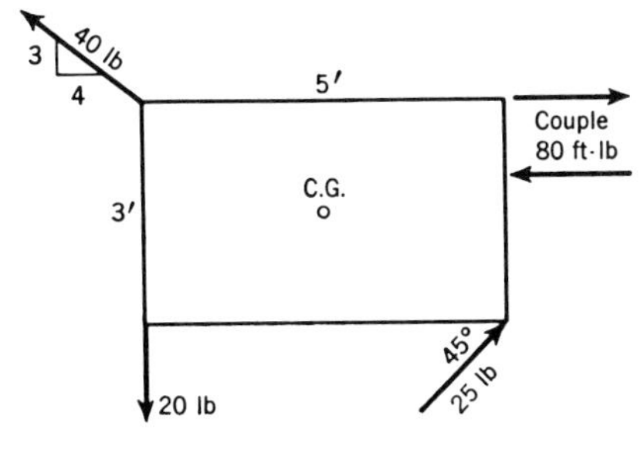

Problem 3–1.

Solution:

$$\Sigma F_X = 32 - 17.7 = 14.3 \text{ lb} \leftarrow$$

$$\Sigma F_Y = 24 + 17.7 - 20 = 21.7 \text{ lb} \uparrow$$

$$\Sigma M_{CG} = 80 + 24(2.5) - 32(1.5) - 20(2.5) - 17.7(1.5) - 17.7(2.5) = 28.8 \text{ ft-lb ccw}$$

$R = 14.3 \mathrel{+\!\!\rightarrow} 21.7 = 26$ lb at 56.6° from horizontal

$$d = \frac{28.8}{26} = 1.11 \text{ ft}$$

3–2. A 3-ft × 3-ft × 8-ft tank full of water is being held in a horizontal position, as shown in the diagram, by a force F and a roller hinged at H along the 3-ft bottom width of the tank. The force F is applied at the mid-point of the 3-ft width at the top of the tank. Assume that tank and water weigh a total of 4500 lb and the center of gravity is 4 ft from either end, 1.5 ft from either side, and 1.5 ft from the top and bottom. Determine (a) the required force at F when $\theta = 53°$, (b) the horizontal component of the reaction on the hinge H, (c) the vertical component of the reaction on the hinge H, (d) the resultant reaction and direction of reaction on the hinge at H.

Solution:

$\Sigma M_H = 0 = 4500(4) - 8.2F \qquad F = 2195$ lb

$\Sigma F_x = 0 = H_x - 0.602(2195) \qquad H_x = 1320$ lb →

$\Sigma F_y = 0 = H_y - 4500 + 0.8(2195) \qquad H_y = 2745$ lb ↑

$R_H = 1320 \mathrel{+\!\!\rightarrow} 2745 = 3050$ lb at 25.7° from vertical

Problem 3–2.

3–3. A 10-ft × 10-ft slab supports four columns which exert the forces shown on the slab. Determine the magnitude and point of application of the single force equivalent to the given system.

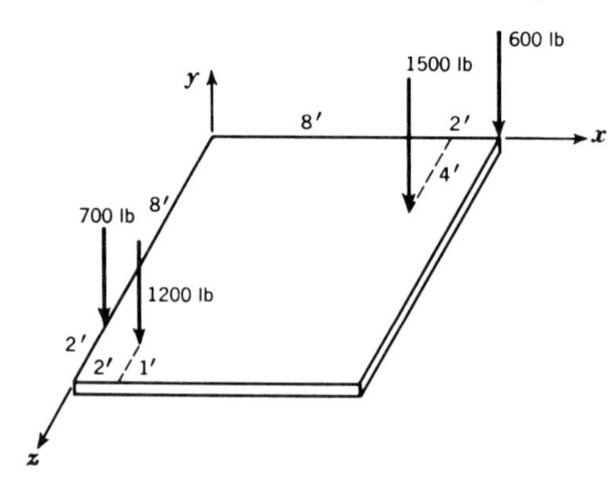

Problem 3–3.

Solution:

$$
\begin{aligned}
M_0 &= \Sigma(r \times F) = (10i) \times (-600j) + (8i + 4k) \times (-1500j) \\
&\quad + (8k) \times (-700j) + (2i + 9k) \times (-1200j) \\
&= -6000k - 12{,}000k + 5600i + 6000i - 2400k + 10{,}800i \\
M_0 &= 22{,}400i - 20{,}400k
\end{aligned}
$$

$$\Sigma F = -(700+1200+1500+600)j = -4000j$$
$$(\bar{x}i+\bar{z}k)\times(-4000j) = 22{,}400i - 20{,}400k$$
$$-4000\bar{x}k + 4000\bar{z}i = 16{,}400i - 20{,}400k$$
$$\bar{x} = 5.1 \text{ ft} \qquad \bar{z} = 5.6 \text{ ft}$$

3–4. A 5-ft × 5-ft table that weighs 40 lb is supported by three legs and has a 160-lb point load applied as shown. Determine the reactions at A, B, and C.

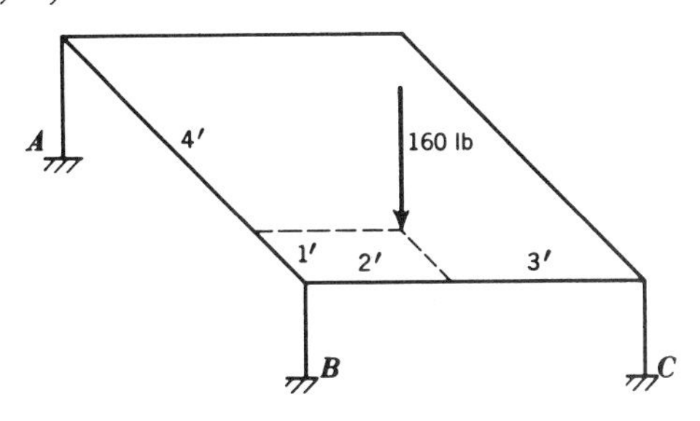

Problem 3–4.

Solution:

$$\Sigma M_{B-C} = 0 = 5A - 1(160) - 2.5(40) \qquad A = 52 \text{ lb} \uparrow$$
$$\Sigma M_{A-B} = 0 = 5C - 2(160) - 2.5(40) \qquad C = 84 \text{ lb} \uparrow$$
$$\Sigma F_y = 0 = B + 52 + 84 - 160 - 40 \qquad B = 64 \text{ lb} \uparrow$$

3–5. Determine the coordinates of the center of gravity of the section shown.

Solution:

$$\bar{x} = \frac{8(1)(0.5)+6(1)(4)+4(1)(7.5)}{8+6+4} = 3.22 \text{ in.} \qquad \bar{y} = 0$$

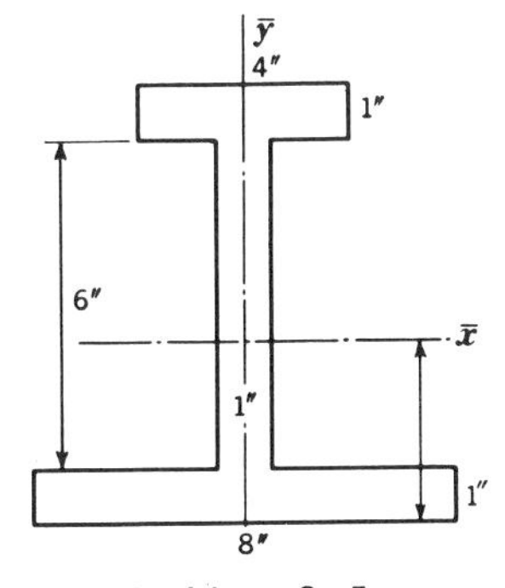

Problem 3–5.

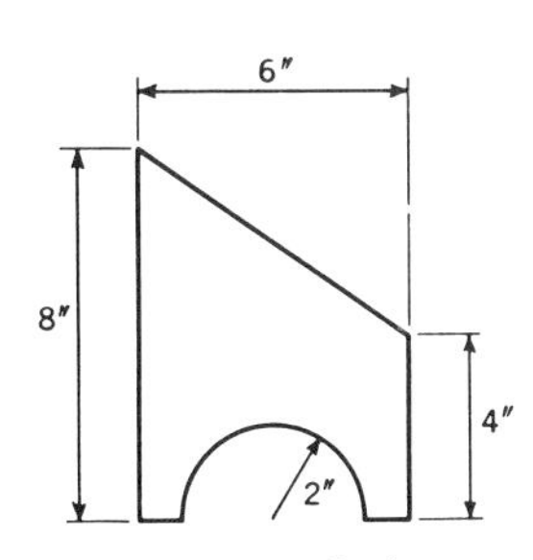

Problem 3–6.

3–6. Find the second moment (moment of inertia) of the area shown about its horizontal centroidal axis.

Solution:

$$\bar{x} = \frac{4(6)(2)+4/2(6)(16/3)-(3.14/2)(2)^2[8/3(3.14)]}{4(6)+4/2(6)-3.14(2)^2/2} = 3.58 \text{ in.}$$

$$I=\left[\frac{6(4)^3}{12}+24(1.58)^2\right]+\left[\frac{6(4)^3}{36}+12(1.75)^2\right]-\left[0.1098(2)^4+\frac{3.14}{2}(2)^2(2.814)^2\right]$$

$I=90.74$ in.^{4}

3–7. Find the horizontal force necessary to start a 400-lb block up a wooden chute at an angle of 10° with the horizontal if the coefficient of friction f equals 0.20.

Solution: $\Sigma F_x=P=69.5+78.8=148.3$ lb

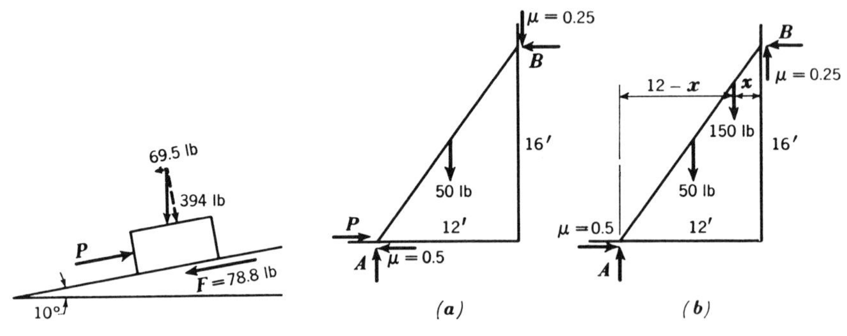

Problem 3–7. Problem 3–8.

3–8. A ladder weighing 50 lb leans to the right against a wall. Its top is 16 ft from the floor and its base 12 ft from the wall. The coefficient of friction for the ladder and vertical wall is 0.25, and for the floor and ladder 0.50. (a) Find the horizontal force at the floor that will cause motion to impend to the right. (b) Using coefficients of friction as given above [and neglecting horizontal force solved for in part (a)], how far up the ladder can a 150-lb man climb before motion impends?

Solution: (a) $\Sigma M_A=0=6(50)-16B_H+0.25(12)(B_H)$ $\quad B_H=23.1$ lb

$\Sigma F_y=0=A_Y-50-0.25(23.1)$ $\quad A_y=55.78$ lb

$\Sigma F_x=0=P-23.1-0.5(55.78)$ $\quad P=51$ lb

(b) $\Sigma M_A=0=(12-x)(150)+6(50)-16B-12(0.25)B$

$\Sigma M_B=0=6(50)+150x+16(0.5)A-12A$

$$-19B-150x=-2100$$

$$\frac{-4A \qquad +150x=\ -300}{-4A-19B \qquad =-2400}$$

$\Sigma F_y=0=200-A-0.25B$

$-4A-19B=-2400$ $\quad B=89$ lb

$-4A-\ \ B=-\ 800$ $\quad A=177.8$ lb

$$150x = -300 + 4(177.8) \qquad x = 2.73 \text{ ft}$$

$$\text{Distance} = \frac{9.72}{12}(20) = 15.45 \text{ ft up ladder}$$

3–9. Find the tensions T_{BD} and T_{BE} in the cables and the forces acting at the ball and socket connection A in the figure.

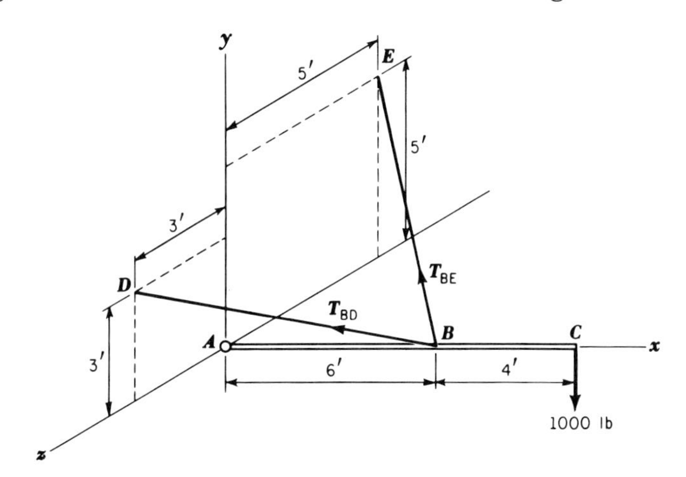

Problem 3–9.

Solution:

$$T_{BD} = \left(\frac{-6i+3j+3k}{7.33}\right)T_{BD} \qquad T_{BE} = \left(\frac{-6i+5j-5k}{9.26}\right)T_{BE} \qquad M_0 = \Sigma(r \times F)$$

$$M_0 = (6i) \times \left(\frac{-6i+3j+3k}{7.33}\right)T_{BD} + (6i) \times \left(\frac{-6i+5j-5k}{9.26}\right)T_{BE} + (10i) \times (-1000j)$$

$$= 2.46kT_{BD} - 2.46jT_{BD} + 3.24kT_{BE} + 3.24jT_{BE} - 10{,}000k = 0$$

$$\begin{cases} 2.46\ T_{BD} + 3.24\ T_{BE} = 10{,}000 \\ -2.46\ T_{BD} + 3.24\ T_{BE} = 0 \end{cases}$$

$$T_{BD} = 2030 \text{ lb} \qquad T_{BE} = 1540 \text{ lb}$$

$$\Sigma F = 0$$

$$= T_{BE} + T_{BD} + (-1000j) + Azk + Ayj + Axi = 0$$

$$= 1540\left(\frac{-6i+5j-5k}{9.26}\right) + 2030\left(\frac{-6i+3j+3k}{7.33}\right) - 1000j + Azk + Ayj + Axi = 0$$

$$(-1000 - 1680 + Ax)i \qquad (833 + 833 - 1000 + Ay)j \qquad (-833 + 833 + Az)k$$

$$Ax = 2680 \text{ lb} \qquad Ay = -667 \text{ lb} \qquad Az = 0$$

3–10. Determine the stresses in bars a, b, and c. State whether tension or compression. Assume that the weight of the truss can be neglected.

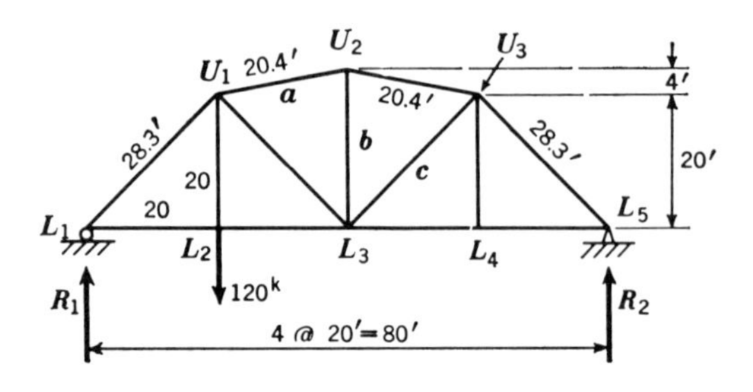

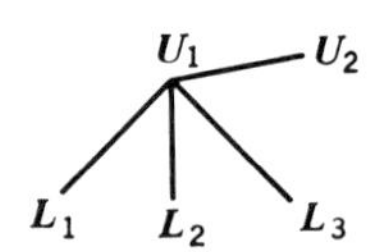

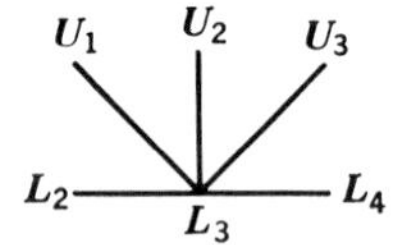

Problem 3–10.

Solution:

$$R_1 = \frac{60}{80}(120) = 90^k \qquad R_2 = \frac{20}{80}(120) = 30^k$$

$$L_1U_1 = \frac{28.3}{20}(90) = 127.3^k \text{ compression}$$

$$L_1L_2 = \frac{20}{28.3}(127.3) = 90^k \text{ tension} = L_2L_3$$

$$L_4L_5 = L_3L_4 = 30^k \text{ tension}$$

Joint U_1

$$\Sigma F_H = 0 = 90 - \frac{20}{20.4}(U_1U_2) - \frac{20}{28.3}(U_1L_3)$$

$$\Sigma F_V = 0 = 90 - 120 - \frac{4}{20.4}(U_1U_2) + \frac{20}{28.3}(U_1L_3)$$

$$a = U_1L_2 = 51.0^k \text{ compression}$$

$$U_1L_3 = 56.6^k \text{ compression}$$

Joint L_3

$$\Sigma F_H = 0 = 90 - 0.707\,(c) - 0.707\,(56.6) - 30$$

$$c = 28.3^k \text{ tension}$$

$$b = 40 - 20 = 20^k \text{ tension}$$

3–11. Three forces of 800 lb, 1000 lb, and 600 lb are acting on a boat. The first acts due north, the second due east, while the third acts 30° east of south. Find the magnitude and direction of the resultant force on the boat.

3–12. Three forces of 1050 lb, 700 lb, and 500 lb are acting upon a small boat on a lake. The first force acts due south, the second force acts due west, while the third acts 60° west of south. Determine (a) the magnitude of the resultant force on the boat and (b) the direction of the resultant force on the boat.

3–13. Give complete information on magnitude, sense, line of action, and position of the resultant in each of the three problems (a), (b), and (c). (a) Determine the resultant of a 10-lb force acting up along the left edge of a 4-ft × 4-ft board and a clockwise couple of 50 ft-lb acting in the plane of the board. (b) Determine the resultant of the 10-lb force described in part (a) and a force of 30 lb acting vertically down along the right-hand edge of the board. (c) Determine the resultant of the 10-lb force described in part (a) and a force of 20 lb acting to the right along the bottom edge of the board.

3–14. Find the magnitude, direction, and location of the resultant of the four vertical forces all in the same plane as shown.

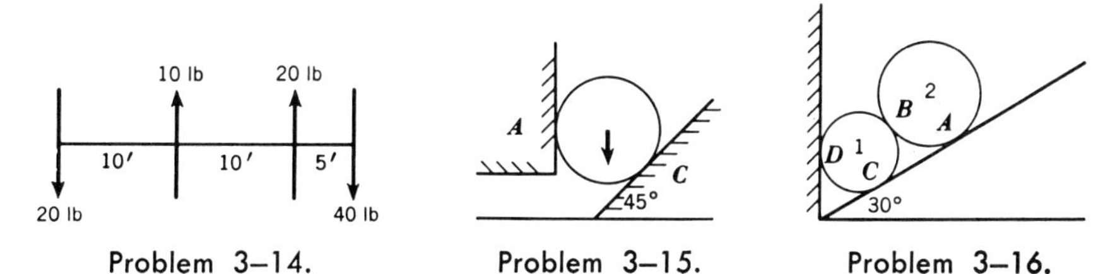

Problem 3–14. Problem 3–15. Problem 3–16.

3–15. (a) Write three fundamental equations which can be set up if the forces on the roller are in equilibrium, as shown. (b) What is the magnitude of the normal forces acting on the roller if the roller weighs 100 lb and has a radius of 6 in.? Assume the friction to be negligible.

3–16. Two cylinders, *1* and *2*, rest on a plane inclined 30° to the horizontal as shown. Cylinder *1* is in contact with a vertical wall at *D*. Cylinder *1* is 12 in. in diameter and weighs 1000 lb. Cylinder *2* is 24 in. in diameter and weighs 4000 lb. Determine the reactions at the four points of contact, *A*, *B*, *C*, and *D*.

3–17. A gate in a rectangular spillway 6 ft wide and 3 ft deep is held in position by a diagonal support which makes an angle of 30° with the spillway floor and is attached to the gate 2 ft above the floor. When the spillway is full of water, what is the force in the support? (All connections are pin-connected.)

3–18. The flow into a channel is controlled by a wooden gate 6 ft high and 2 ft wide. The water level is 6 ft above the top of the gate. The gate seats vertically against brass strips 2 in. wide. Assume the coefficient of friction of the gate against the strips as 0.2. How much force is required to lift the gate vertically?

3–19. A watertight gate *AB* is 2 ft square and has a hinge at its upper edge *A*. A cord, which makes an angle of 45° with the vertical gate, is tied to the lower edge of the gate *B*. What force will be required in this cord to just open the gate? Note the level of the water is 2 ft above the upper edge of the gate.

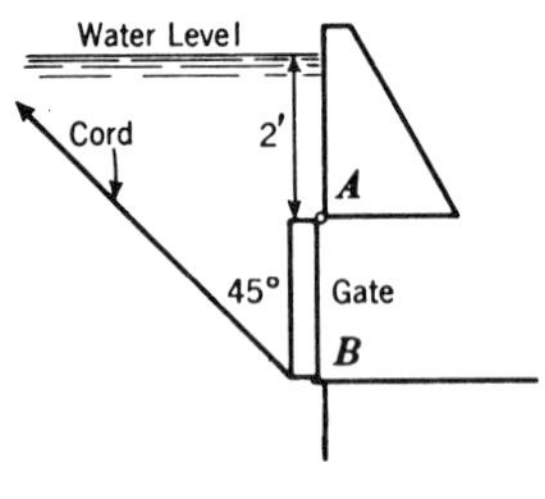

Problem 3–19.

3–20. A weight of 2000 lb is hung from a solid point of support by a cable 100 ft long. When the weight is held at a point 70.7 ft either to the right or left from a vertical line through the point of support, determine (a) the vertical reaction to the point of support, (b) the horizontal pull required to hold the weight at 70.7 ft from the vertical, and (c) the tension in the cable while in this position.

3–21. (a) A tractor is on level ground. What pull *X* will remove all weight from the front wheels? (b) Assume the same tractor is going up a slope 20° from the horizontal; what will *X* be, in pounds?

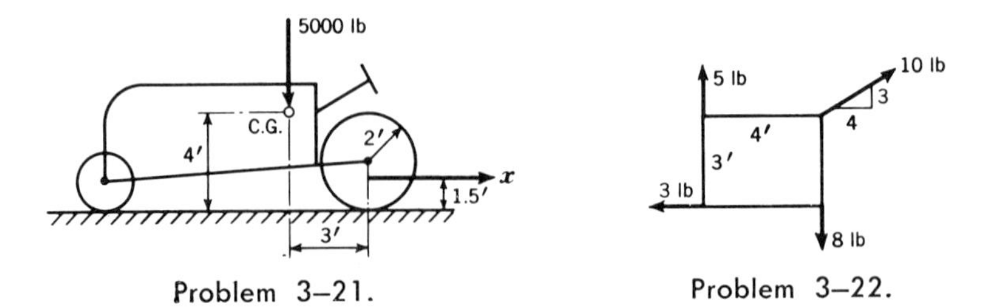

Problem 3–21. Problem 3–22.

3–22. Find the resultant of the system of forces indicated. All forces act in one plane.

3–23. The tractor shown can develop a drawbar pull of 2500 lb. Is it safe to operate the tractor hitched as shown? Prove your answer by suitable calculations.

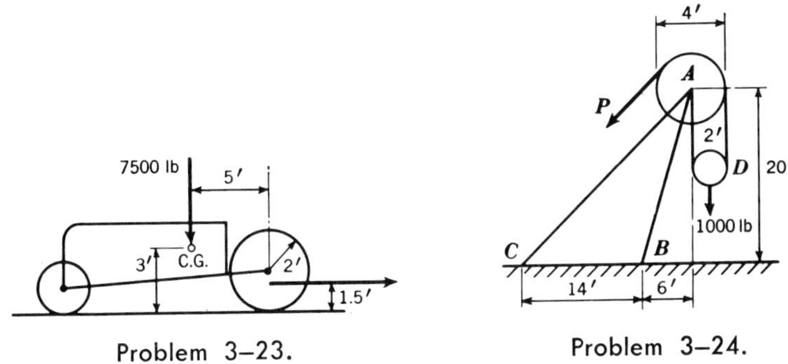

Problem 3–23. Problem 3–24.

3–24. The weight of 1000 lb is held in position by a flexible rope attached at A and running over the sheaves at D and A as shown, the force P applied at the end of the rope being parallel to AC. Find the stresses in the members AB and AC.

3–25. The weights A and B are supported by a continuous rope which is attached at points C and D and passes around frictionless pulleys as shown. Neglect the weight of the rope and pulleys. Find the position of pulley P relative to the point O for equilibrium.

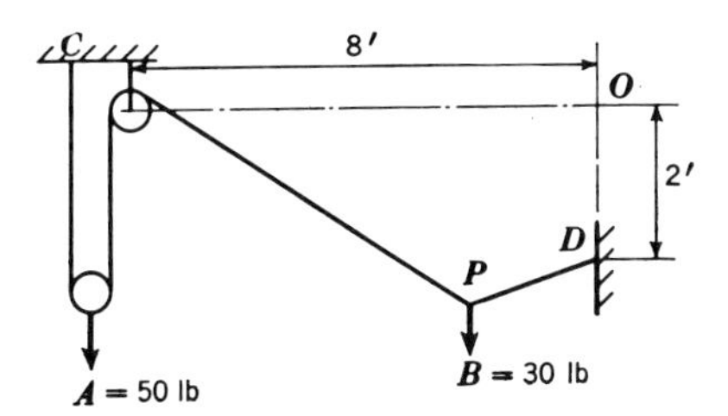

Problem 3–25.

3–26. A loaded concrete transfer bucket weighing 4500 lb is transported by an overhead cable and single-wheel trolley. The cable suspension points are 575 ft apart horizontally and the cable length is 600 ft. What is the tension in the cable when the bucket has been pulled to within 100 ft horizontally of a suspension point by a horizontal dragline fastened to the trolley? What is the pull on the dragline? Neglect weight of cable.

3–27. Two points are 6 ft apart horizontally and 3 ft apart vertically. A flexible cord 10 ft long is tied between the two points, and a weight is hooked over the cord so that it may slide until equilibrium is reached. Neglecting the weight and stretch of the cord, what is the position of the low point of the cord with respect to the ends?

3–28. The uniform boom of a crane is 40 ft long and weighs 400 lb. It is hinged at the bottom and held at an angle of 45° by a tie rope attached 10 ft from the upper end. The tie rope makes an angle of 60° with the vertical. A load of 3600 lb is supported at the end of the boom. Calculate the tension in the tie and the total reaction at the hinge.

3–29. A derrick boom is attached to a vertical mast at its lower end so that it makes an angle of 30° with the mast. Its upper end is held in position by a rope which makes an angle of 90° with the boom. Neglect the weight of the boom and calculate the tension in the rope and the thrust of the boom when a load of 900 lb is carried by the upper end of the boom.

3–30. One end of a beam is hinged to a wall. A 200-lb man stands on the beam 5 ft from the hinged end. The beam is 18 ft long and weighs 10 lb/ft. The end of the beam opposite the hinge is supported by a vertical rope which in turn is supported by a system of frictionless pulleys and pulled vertically downward by the man. How hard must the man pull to maintain his and the beam's position?

3–31. A horizontal steel plate weighing 150 lb rests on three vertical legs at A, B, and C. What weight does each leg support?

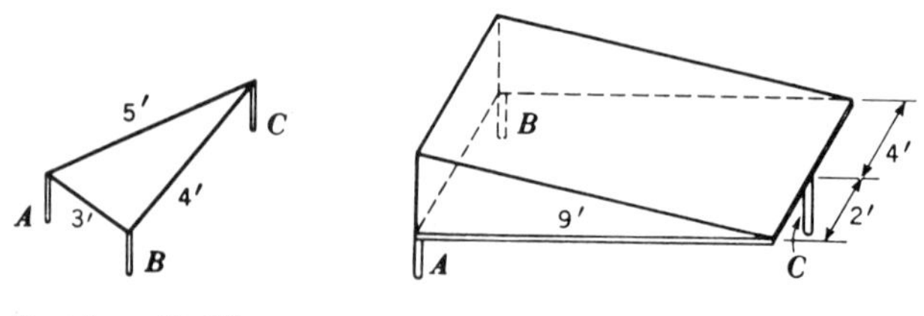

Problem 3–31. Problem 3–32.

3–32. A horizontal plate rests on three posts A, B, and C. Material of uniform density is piled on the plate at a depth increasing uniformly from zero at the right edge to a maximum at the left edge. If the total weight of the material is 1000 lb, what are the reactions at A, B, and C? Neglect the weight of the plate.

3–33. A surveying instrument weighing 15 lb is mounted on a tripod. The legs of the tripod are equally spaced and form an angle of 20° with the vertical. Find the reaction of the ground on each leg, neglecting the weight of its tripod and assuming (a) that the tripod is rigid and the ground is smooth and (b) that the screws connecting the legs to the instrument mount are loose but that the ground is sufficiently rough to keep the legs from sliding.

3–34. The crankpin pressures P_1 and P_2 on the crankshaft shown are 6000 lb and 4800 lb, respectively. Find the bearing reactions R_1 and R_2 and the resisting moment QQ required for equilibrium of the shaft.

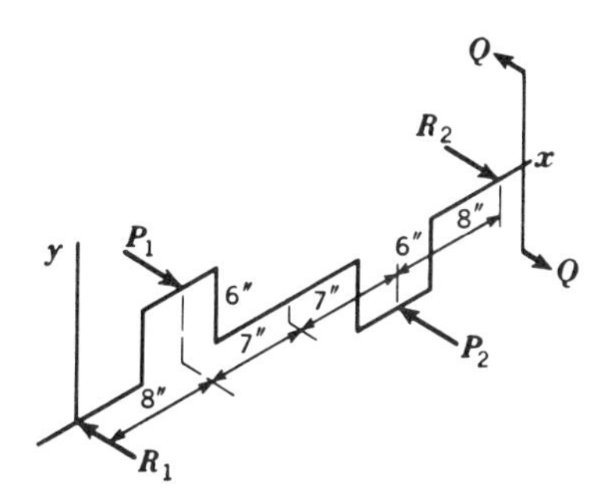

Problem 3–34.

3–35. The solid homogeneous block weighs 6000 lb. Determine the tension in the cord at C and the reaction of the ball bearings at B and D on the block.

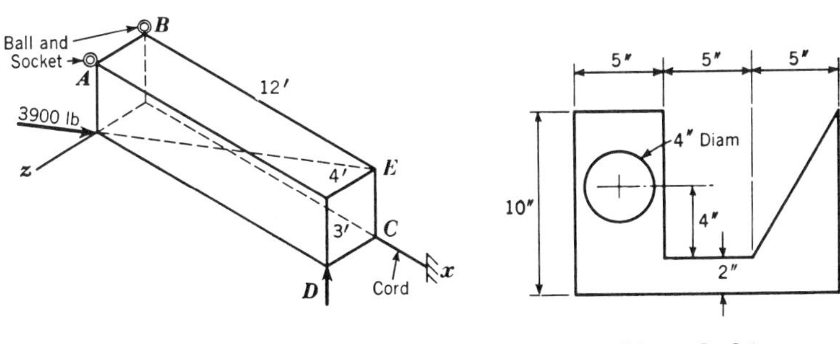

Problem 3–35.

Problem 3–36.

3–36. Determine the location of the centroid and the second moment of area ("moment of inertia") about an x axis through the centroid for the given figure.

3–37. A concrete aqueduct cross section is made up as shown. Locate the horizontal neutral axis of bending if it is to be analyzed as a beam of homogeneous material. What is the moment of inertia of the area about this neutral axis?

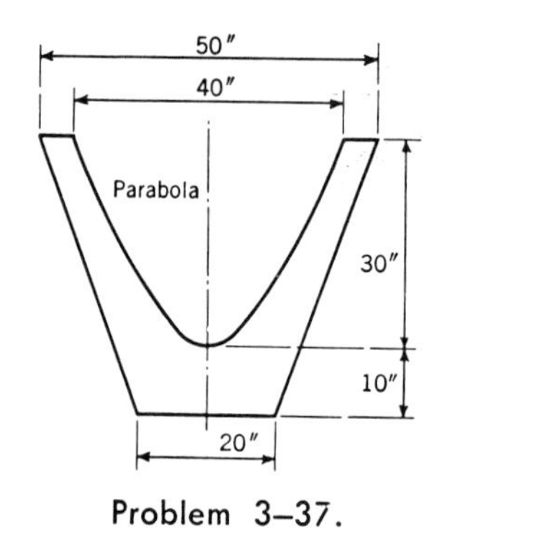

Problem 3–37.

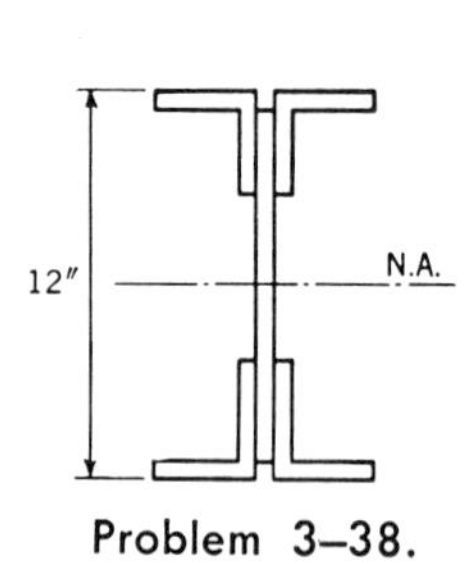

Problem 3–38.

3–38. What is the moment of inertia about its horizontal neutral axis of a section assembled from four 3-in. × 3-in. × 0.5-in. angles and an 11-in. × 0.5-in. plate as shown?

3–39. The side and base of a cylindrical drum are made of sheet metal of the same thickness. If r is the radius and h is the height of the drum, locate the center of gravity of the drum when empty and without a cover.

3–40. The end of a 1-in.-diameter rod, 10 in. long, is welded to a 3-in.-diameter sphere. The rod weighs 2.2 lb; the sphere weighs 4 lb. Locate the center of gravity.

3–41. A 7-ton concrete block is to act as an anchor for a guy rope from a derrick mast. The horizontal component of pull from the guy rope may be as much as 2.5 tons. The coefficient of friction at this place between the block and the ground is 85 percent. If a factor of safety of 1.6 is allowed, determine (a) the maximum angle of elevation at which the guy rope may leave the anchor. (b) Forgetting the factor of safety, what angle would just let the block move when the horizontal component of force becomes 2.5 tons?

3–42. A man weighing 180 lb climbs the wooden ladder shown, which weighs 75 lb. The ladder's center of gravity is at its mid-point. The coefficient of friction between the ladder and the floor is 0.25 and that between the ladder and the vertical wall is 0.16. How close to the wall can the man get before the ladder would start to slip?

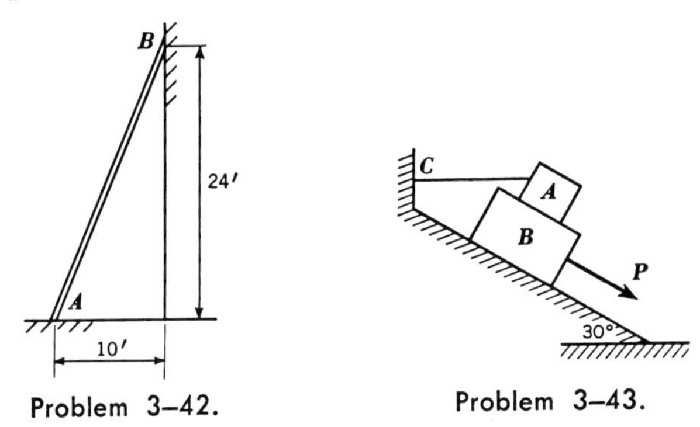

Problem 3–42. Problem 3–43.

3–43. Block A, weighing 80 lb, rests on block B, which weighs 100 lb. Block A is restrained from moving by a horizontal rope tied to the wall at C. What force P parallel to the plane inclined 30° with the horizontal is necessary to start B down the plane? Assume the coefficient of friction to be 0.3 for all surfaces.

3–44. The frictional resistance to sliding between the weight W_1 and the table in the figure shown is 0.4 of the net weight on the table. Cables are horizontal or vertical except as noted. Pulleys are assumed to be frictionless. Compute the weight W_2 which will cause motion of the three weights to impend.

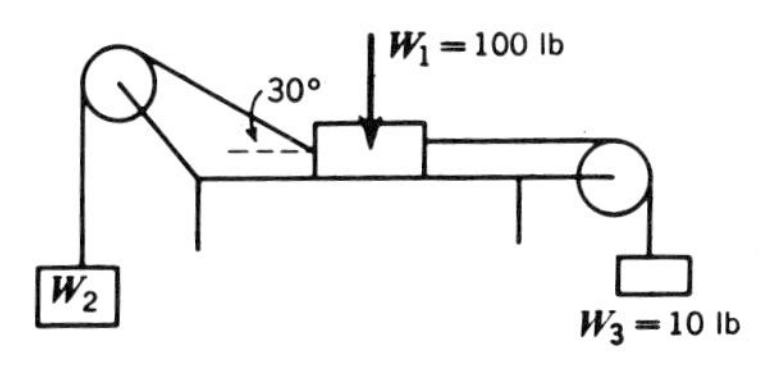

Problem 3–44.

3–45. A ladder 15 ft long weighs 3 lb/ft and is fixed at the lower end 5 ft from a vertical smooth wall. A weight of 150 lb is supported 10 ft from the lower end of the ladder. What are the components of the reactions at the top and bottom of the ladder?

3–46. What weight W is required to set the 100-lb block in motion? NOTE: The symbol μ represents the coefficient of friction.

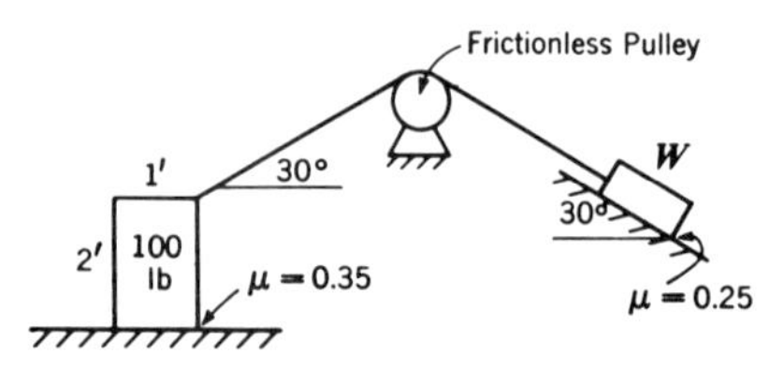

Problem 3–46.

3–47. Block A weighs 150 lb. The cord attached to A passes over a frictionless pulley. Solve for P if motion is impending toward the left. Clearly show free-body diagram and axes.

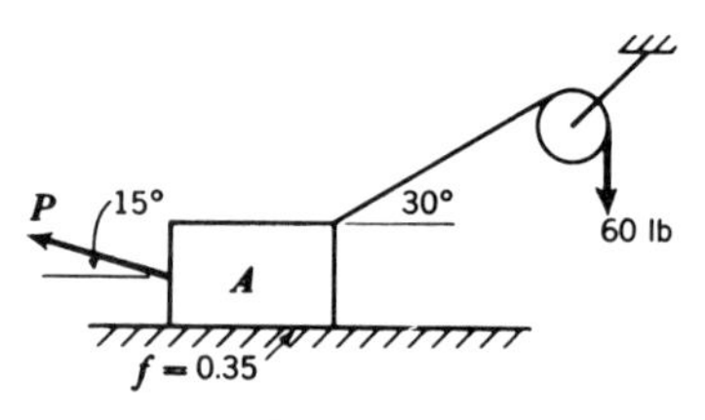

Problem 3–47.

3–48. A homogeneous rod weighing 50 lb is hinged at A and rests on a block at B. The block weighing 3 lb rests on a horizontal floor. If the coefficient of friction for all surfaces is $\frac{1}{3}$, find the horizontal force P necessary to cause the block to slide to the left. Consider the hinge at A to be frictionless.

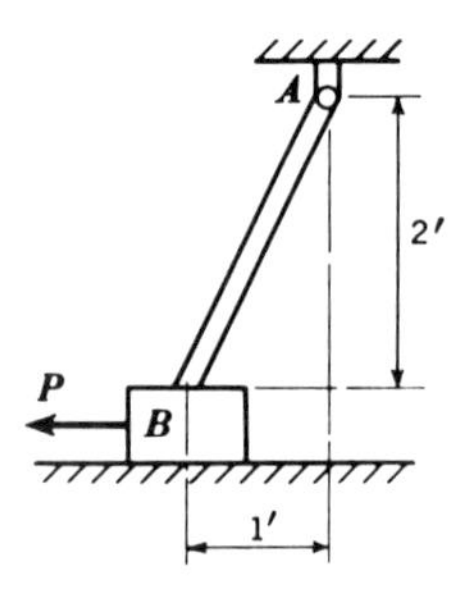

Problem 3–48.

3–49. A uniform ladder 16 ft long weighing W pounds is placed with one end on a horizontal plane and the other against a vertical wall. The angle of friction at all contact surfaces is 20°. Find the minimum angle θ at which the ladder can be inclined with the horizontal plane before slipping occurs.

3–50. A ladder rests on a pavement and has a roller (without friction) which rests against a wall. If a weight of 400 lb is hung from the middle of the ladder, find the least coefficient of friction which will maintain equilibrium.

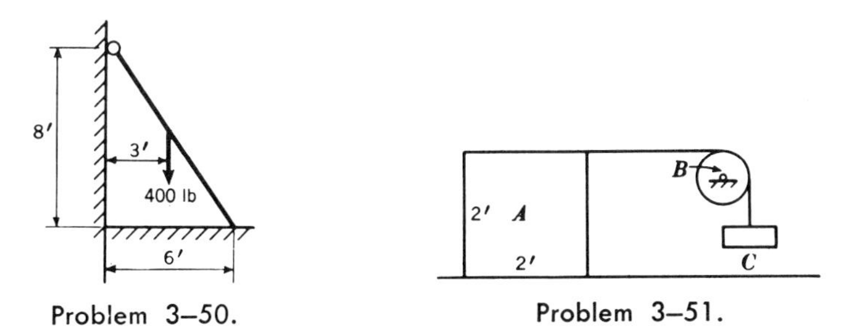

Problem 3–50.

Problem 3–51.

3–51. Determine the value for the weight of block C at which block A will start to tip over. Assume block A is a homogeneous cube which weighs 100 lb. Pulley B is a right circular cylinder of 1-ft diameter and weighs 50 lb. The connecting cord is weightless. The coefficient of friction between the block A and its support is 0.2. The coefficient of friction between the pulley B and the cord is 0.5, and the bearing at B is frictionless.

3–52. What is the maximum grade a loaded truck can climb if the coefficient of friction between tires and pavement is 0.7?

3–53. Blocks A and B weigh 60 and 200 lb, respectively. The plane is inclined 30° from the horizontal and the blocks are connected by a cord. Coefficient of friction for A is 0.2 and for B is 0.6. (a) Will bodies A and B slide down the plane? (b) What is the tension in the cord connecting them when motion is impending?

3–54. A block rests on a rough inclined plane 10 ft long and 6 ft high. The weight of the block is 80 lb and the coefficient of friction is 0.3. What force parallel to the plane is required (a) to move the block up the plane and (b) to lower the block down the plane?

3–55. A seaman can exert a force of 75 lb on the free end of a hawser. The coefficient of static friction between the hawser and the capstan head is 0.30. How many times should he wrap the hawser around the capstan head in order to resist a force of 3 tons?

3–56. A rope weighing 0.5 lb/ft is wound $2\frac{1}{2}$ times around a horizontal bar. What length X of rope should be left hanging if a load of 100 lb at the end of 10 ft of rope is to be supported? The coefficient of static friction between the rope and bar is 0.25.

3–57. A timber frame is connected by frictionless pins. The weights of the members are as follows: *RV*, 150 lb; *UW*, 200 lb; *SU*, 80 lb; *ST*, cable, neglect. The cable is attached to the pin at *S*. Find the horizontal and vertical components of the pin reactions at *R* and *S* on the member *RV* and show the pin reactions on member *RV* by a free-body diagram.

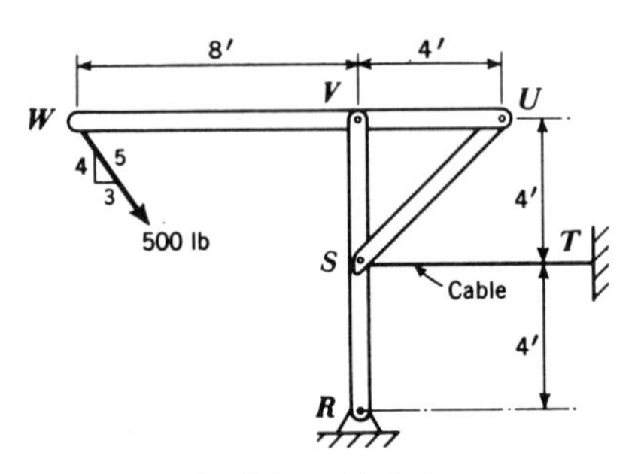

Problem 3–57.

3–58. Determine the reactions at *A* and *B* of the three-hinged arch for the live loads shown.

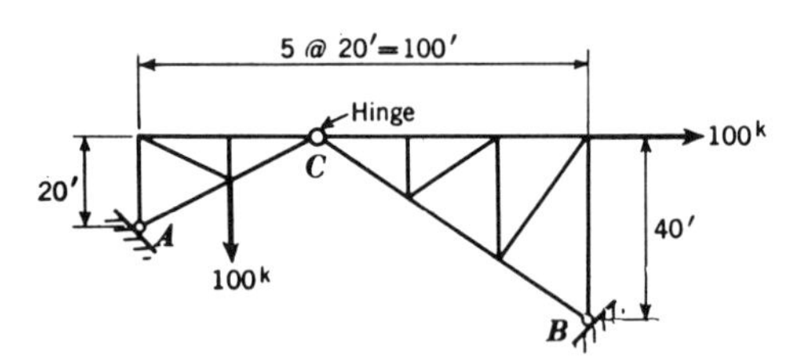

Problem 3–58.

3–59. A cantilever beam is hinged to the wall as shown. What are the amount and direction (compression or tension) of stress in members *A* and *B*?

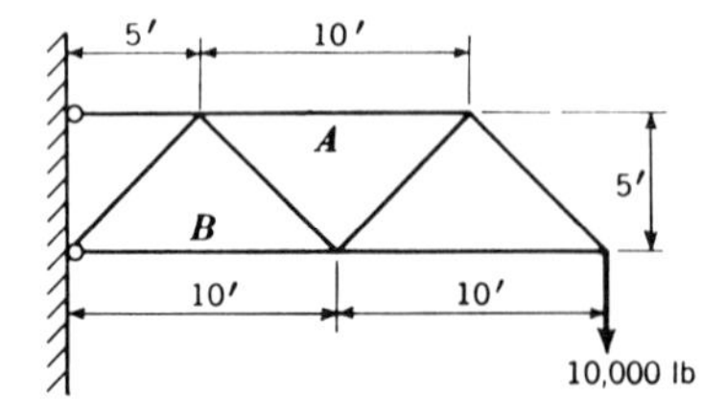

Problem 3–59.

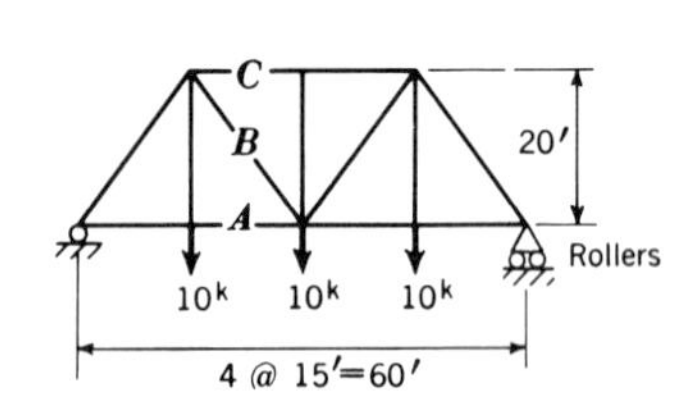

Problem 3–60.

3–60. Ignore the weight of the truss. Find the stresses in members *A*, *B*, and *C*. Be sure to state whether compression or tension.

3–61. Neglect weights of members. All joints are pin-connected. Find (a) tension in wire *A* and (b) stress in member *B*.

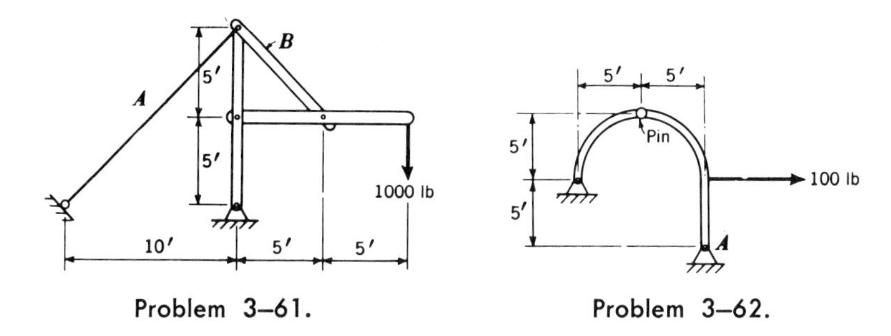

Problem 3–61. Problem 3–62.

3–62. Neglect weight of members. Find the magnitude of the horizontal and vertical reactions at pin *A*. All connections are pinned.

3–63. Neglecting the weights of the members of the pin-connected structure shown, determine B_x on member *BEF*.

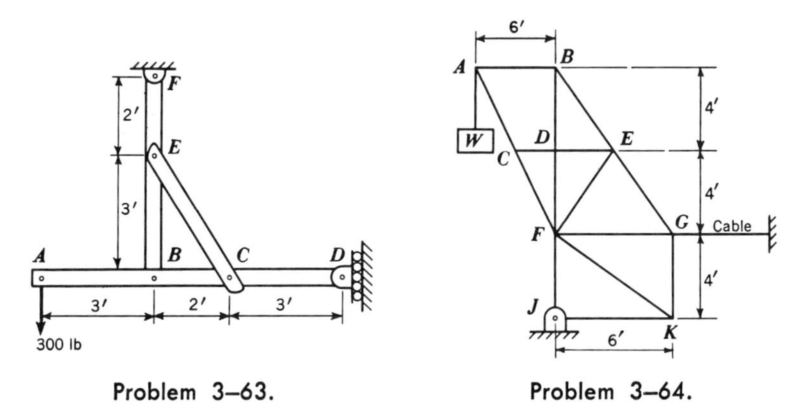

Problem 3–63. Problem 3–64.

3–64. In the pin-connected truss shown, determine the stresses in members *BE*, *DE*, and *DF*. The weight *W* is 10^k.

3–65. A 200-ft cable is hung between two supports *A* and *B* at the same elevation. With a sag of 40 ft, the maximum tension is found to be 500 lb. Determine the horizontal distance from *A* to *B* and the total weight of the cable.

3–66. Determine the total force in each of the members a, b, and c of the pin connected structure shown.

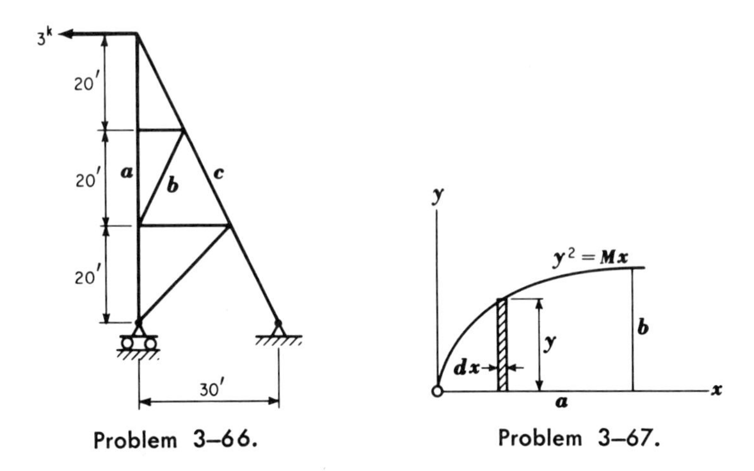

Problem 3–66. Problem 3–67.

3–67. Determine the moment of inertia with respect to the y axis of the area shown in the figure.

3–68. With reference to the coordinate axes x and y as shown, locate the centroid of the area of the plane figure.

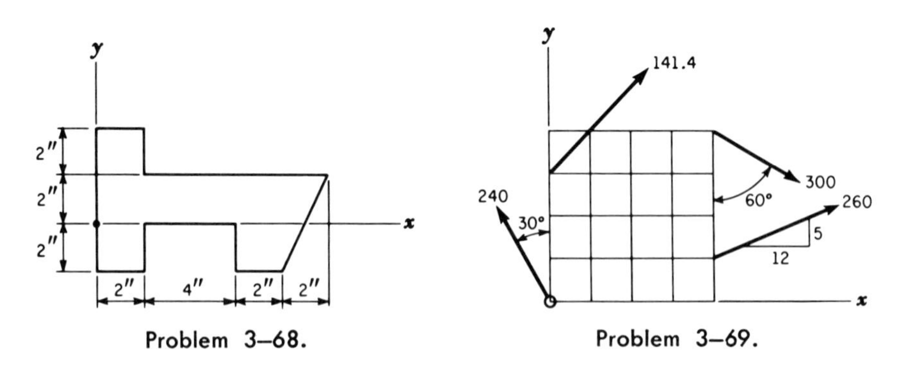

Problem 3–68. Problem 3–69.

3–69. From the figure, determine: (a) the magnitude and direction of the resultant of the forces shown, (b) the perpendicular distance from point "0" to the resultant force, and (c) where the resultant will intercept the y axis.

3–70. Find the magnitudes and directions of the resultant reaction at A and C due to the 100-lb force applied as shown. All surfaces and pins are smooth.

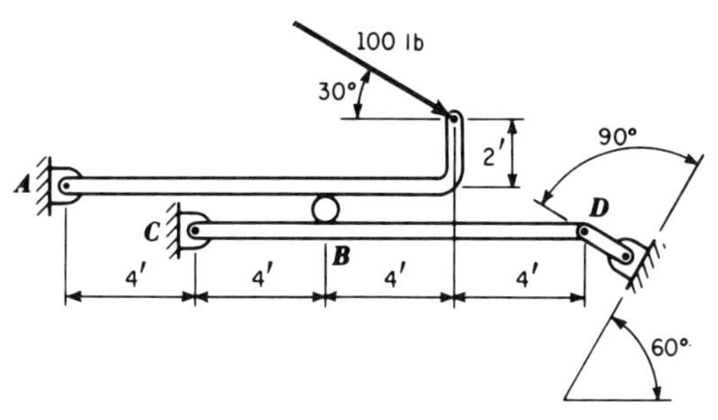

Problem 3–70.

3–71. The plane containing the members AB and BC is perpendicular to the plane containing the load and member BD. What are the forces in AB and BC?

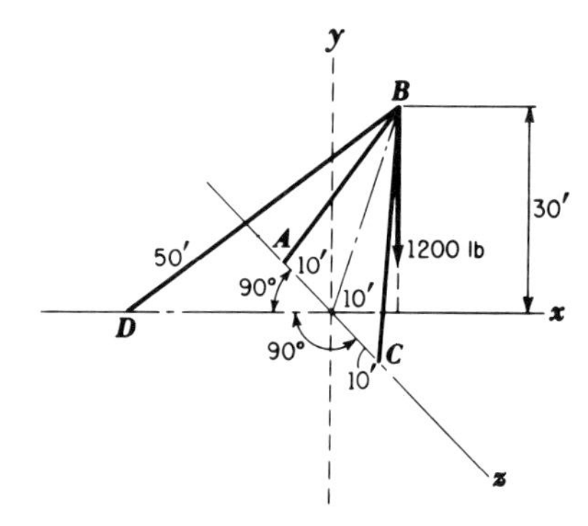

Problem 3–71.

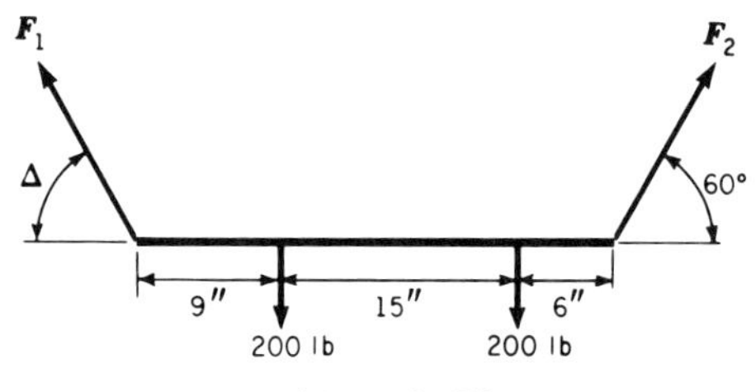

Problem 3–72.

3–72. The weightless beam shown is suspended at each end by cables. The beam carries two suspended loads. (a) Find the force F_2 that makes an angle of 60°. (b) Find the force F_1 and the angle Δ that it makes with the horizontal.

3–73. A 500-lb weight is supported by passing a cable over a horizontal member AB, and anchoring it at F. Neglect any friction at C. AB is supported by a ball-and-socket joint at A and by cables BD and BE. Find the stresses in the cables BD and BE and the components of the reaction at A.

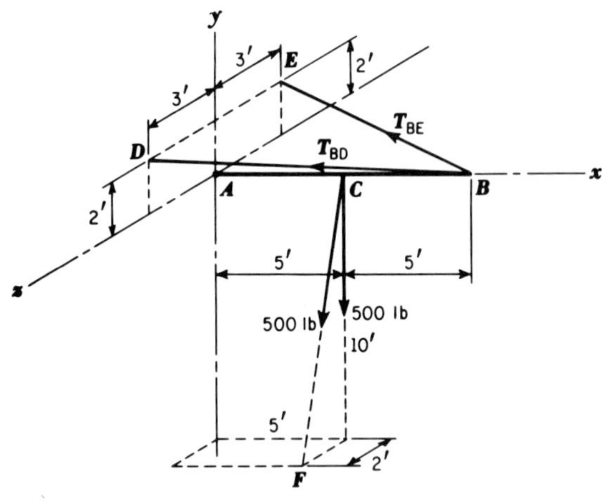

Problem 3–73.

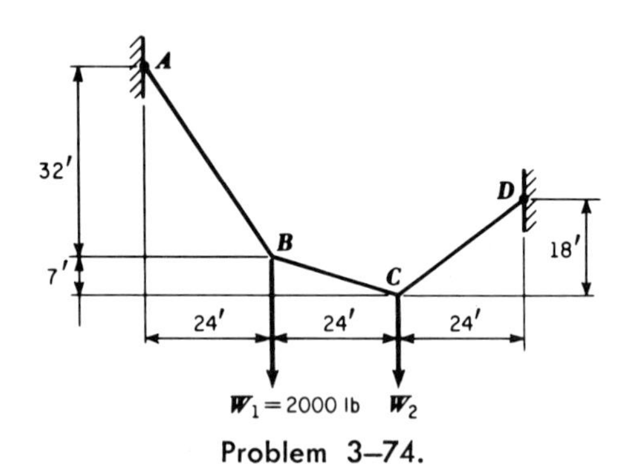

Problem 3–74.

3–74. The figure shows a cable, $ABCD$, supporting two loads. Find the magnitude of W_2 necessary to maintain the cable in the position shown if W_1=2000 lb.

3–75. Three men are carrying a homogeneous 18-ft long log that weighs 400 lbs. Its center of gravity is 0.60 of its length from the front end. One man carries the front end. Measuring from the front end, where must a bar be placed for the other two men, so that all three will be carrying equal weights?

3–76. A tripod whose legs are 6 ft, 7 ft, and 8 ft, respectively, has its "feet" at the vertices of a horizontal equilateral triangle whose sides are 9 ft. How high above the base is the vertex?

3–77. The truss shown is pinned at the top and at its two supporting points. Find the stress in members a and b.

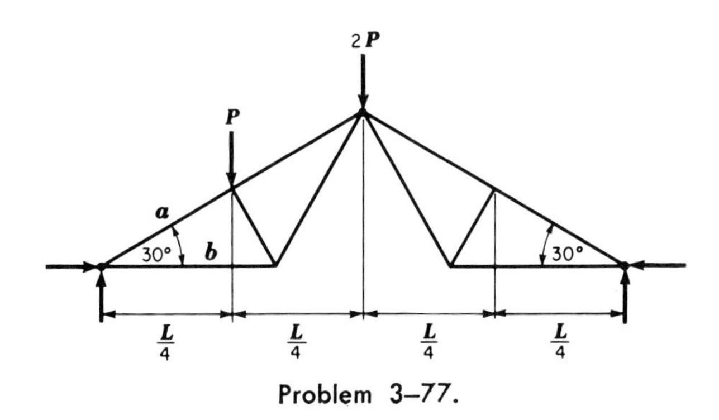

Problem 3–77.

3–78. The moment of inertia of the figure shown about the x-x axis is: (a) 420 in.^{4}, (b) 1230 in.^{4}, (c) 1260 in.^{4} (d) 1380 in.^{4}, (e) 2460 in.^{4}?

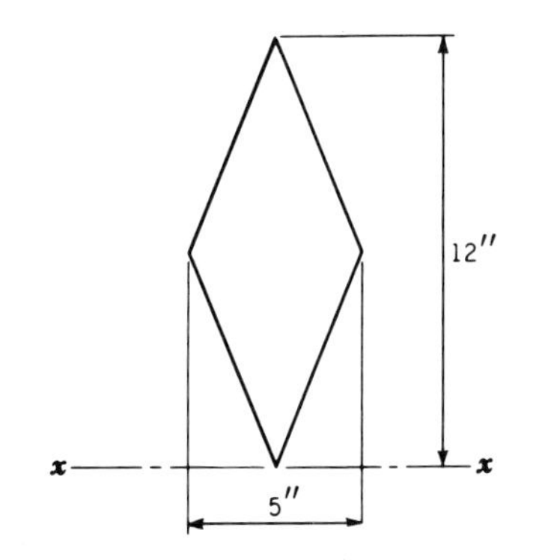

Problem 3–78.

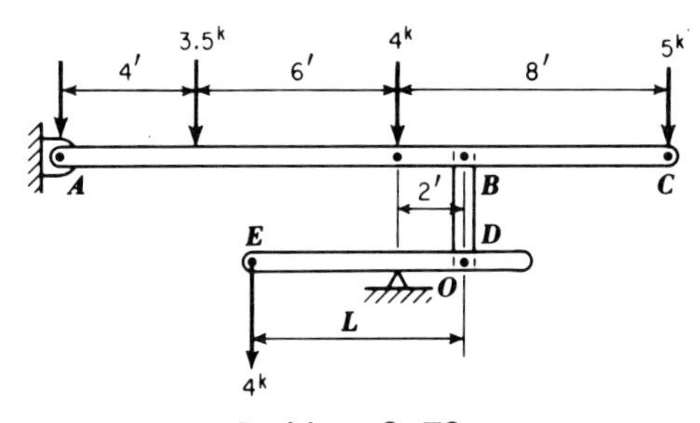

Problem 3–79.

3–79. The beam ABC is loaded as shown. The equilibrium is maintained by a weight of 4000 lb suspended from bar DE. Calculate the required length L of member DE. Neglect the weights of members.

3–80. In the diagram, Q represents a turnbuckle used to actuate a toggle press that pushes two plates E and G apart. If the links AB, BC, CD, and AD are of equal length, find the value of angle θ when the force against each wall is five times as great as the tension in the turnbuckle.

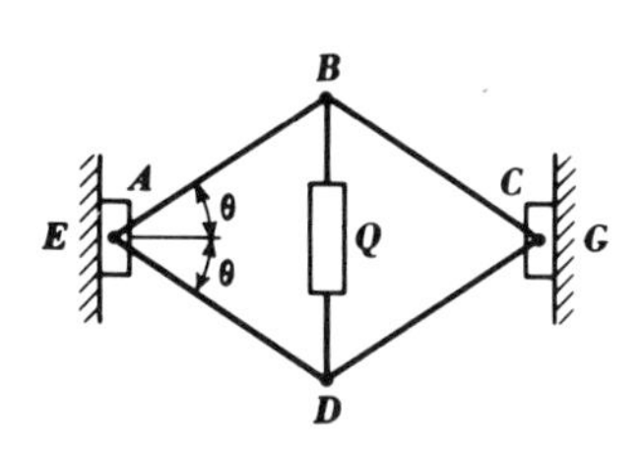

Problem 3–80.

Dynamics 4

Dynamics problems involve 1) force, mass, and acceleration, 2) work and energy, 3) impulse and momentum. In this chapter the problems are divided into two general types: 1) dynamics of particles and 2) dynamics of rigid bodies. The examples given illustrate the application of various methods of solution for different types of problem.

4–1. The velocity of a body starting from rest is $4t^2$ feet per second after t seconds. (a) How far will the body be from the starting point in 5 sec? (b) In what time will it reach a distance of 288 ft measured from the starting point?

Solution: (a)

$$v(t) = 4t^2$$

$$v = \frac{ds}{dt} = 4t^2$$

$$S = \frac{4t^3}{3} + C_1$$

Since $S = 0$ at $t = 0$, $C_1 = 0$.

$$S = \frac{4}{3}t^3 = \frac{4}{3}(125) = 166.7 \text{ ft}$$

(b)

$$288 = \frac{4}{3}t^3$$

$$t = 6 \text{ sec}$$

4–2. A descending cage and load weighing 10,000 lb in a mine shaft is being brought to rest. The rate of deceleration is 64.4 ft/sec^2. What is the tension in the cable holding the cage just before the downward motion is stopped?

Solution: $\Sigma F_y = 0 \qquad T - 10{,}000 - \dfrac{10{,}000(64.4)}{32.2} \qquad T = 30{,}000 \text{ lb}$

4–3. A dive bomber, moving 240 mph on a 60° dive, releases a bomb 3000 ft above point A. The bomb lands at point B. Neglecting air resistance, what is the distance AB?

Solution:

$$V_V = 0.866(240) = 208 \text{ mph} = 305 \text{ fps}$$

$$V_H = 0.5(240) = 120 \text{ mph} = 176 \text{ fps}$$

Vertical motion

$$S = V_y t + \frac{at^2}{2} \qquad 3000 = 305t + 16.1t^2 \qquad t = 7.14 \text{ sec}$$

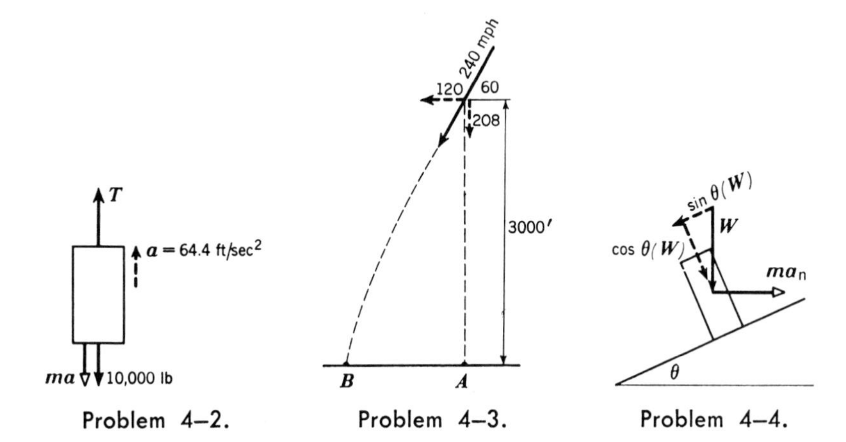

Problem 4–2. Problem 4–3. Problem 4–4.

Horizontal motion

$$S = BA = vt$$

$$BA = 7.14(176) = 1259 \text{ ft}$$

4–4. What superelevation is required on a highway for 55-mph traffic on a 2500-ft radius curve so that a 150-lb driver will exert no sidewise force on the car seat? What force perpendicular to the seat will be exerted by the driver?

Solution: $55 \text{ mph} = 80.6 \text{ fps} \quad a_n = \frac{v^2}{\rho} = \frac{(80.6)^2}{2500} = 2.60 \text{ fps}^2$

$$\tan\theta = \frac{V^2}{gr} = \frac{(80.6)^2}{32.2(2500)} = 0.0806$$

$$\theta = 4.61°$$

$$\text{Normal force} = W\cos\theta + Wa_n\sin\theta$$
$$= 150\ (0.9968) + (150/g)(2.6)(0.0806) = 150.5 \text{ lb}$$

4–5. A 40-lb block pulled by a rope passing over a frictionless pulley is connected to a 20-lb weight which falls vertically. If the coefficient of friction is 0.25, what is the tension in the rope while the blocks are in motion?

Solution:

$$T_1 = T_2 \qquad a_1 = a_2$$

$$\Sigma F_y = 0 = 20 - T - \frac{20}{32.2}(a)$$

$$\Sigma F_x = 0 = -10 + T - \frac{40}{32.2}(a)$$

$$a = 5.37 \text{ fps}^2$$

$$T = 10 + \frac{40}{32.2}(5.37) = 16.67 \text{ lb}$$

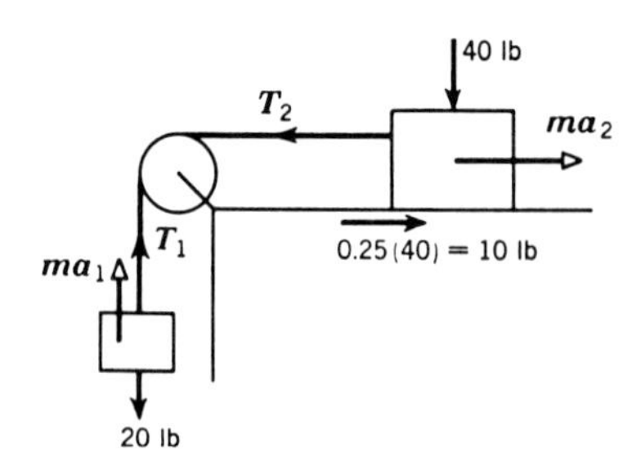

Problem 4–5.

4–6. A 5-lb object is held 1.00 ft above a spring of constant 50 lb-ft (i.e., a force of 50 lb will compress the spring 1.00 ft). The object is then dropped. How much is the spring compressed?

Solution:

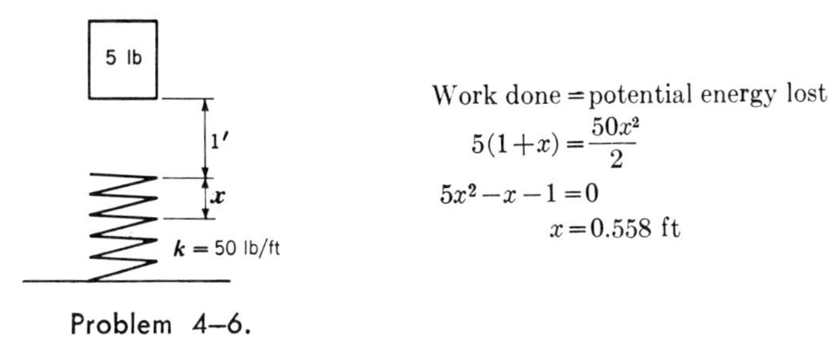

Problem 4–6.

Work done = potential energy lost

$$5(1+x)=\frac{50x^2}{2}$$

$$5x^2-x-1=0$$

$$x=0.558 \text{ ft}$$

4–7. Water falling from a height of 100 ft at the rate of 2000 cfm drives a water turbine connected to an electric generator at 120 rpm. If the total resisting torque due to friction is 400 lb at 1 ft radius and the water leaves the turbine blades with a velocity of 12 fps, find the horsepower developed by the generator.

Solution:

$$\omega=\frac{120}{60}(2\pi)=12.56 \text{ radians/sec}$$

$$\text{Friction loss}=400(1)(12.56)=5020 \text{ ft lb/sec}$$

$$\text{PE of water}=\frac{2000}{60}(62.4)(100)=208{,}000 \text{ ft lb/sec}$$

$$\text{KE of water leaving turbine}=\tfrac{1}{2}mv^2=\frac{2080}{64.4}(12)^2=4650 \text{ ft lb/sec}$$

$$\text{hp}=\frac{208{,}000-4650-5020}{550}=361$$

4–8. At the beginning of the drive, a golf ball has a velocity of 170 mph. If the club stays in contact with the ball for 1/25 sec, what is the average force on the ball? The weight of the ball is 1.62 oz.

Solution:

$$170 \text{ mph}=249 \text{ fps}$$

$$mv_1+F(\Delta t)=mv_2$$

$$\frac{0.1012}{32.2}(0)+F(0.04)=\frac{0.1012}{32.2}(249)$$

$$F=19.6 \text{ lb}$$

4–9. Three bodies, A, B, and C, whose weights are 40 lb, 10 lb, and 20 lb, respectively, rest on a smooth horizontal surface. If A is given a velocity of 20 fps to the right and B a velocity of 10 fps to the left, and C remains at rest until A and B come in contact with it, what will be the final velocity of the bodies, assuming that they remain in contact after impact?

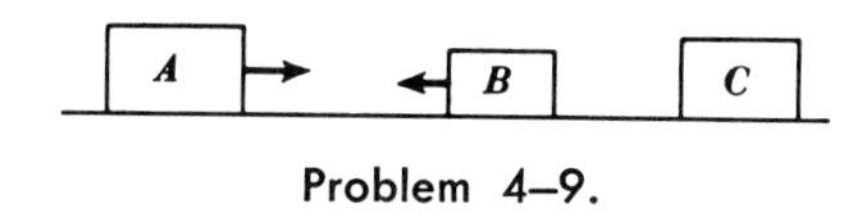

Problem 4–9.

Solution:

$$m_A v_A + m_B v_B = (mv)_{AB}$$

$$\frac{40(20)}{32.2} - \frac{10(10)}{32.2} = \frac{50}{32.2} V_{AB} \qquad V_{AB} = 14 \text{ fps} \rightarrow$$

$$(mv)_{AB} + m_C v_C = (mv)_{ABC}$$

$$\frac{50(14)}{32.2} + \frac{20(0)}{32.2} = \frac{70}{32.2} V_{ABC}$$

$$V_{ABC} = \frac{50(14)}{70} = 10 \text{ fps}$$

4–10. A rotating crankshaft of 1 ft radius rotates at 30 rpm. The connecting rod is 3 ft long. When the crank is as shown (i.e., at 45° with the horizontal) what is the velocity of point A?

Solution:

$$\omega_{BC} = \frac{30}{60}(2\pi) = 3.14 \text{ radians/sec}$$

$$v_C = 1(3.14) = 3.14 \text{ fps}$$

$$\frac{\sin 76.3°}{3.14} = \frac{\sin 58.7°}{v_A}$$

$$v_A = 2.76 \text{ fps} \rightarrow$$

Problem 4–10.

4–11. A flywheel 48 in. in diameter and 18 in. thick is made of steel plates. What torque, in foot-pounds, is required to bring the wheel from rest to 300 rpm in 1 min? Disregard any part of shaft external to the flywheel.

Solution:

$$V_{FW} = \frac{\pi d^2}{4} h = 18.85 \text{ cu ft}$$

$$W_{FW} = 490(18.85) = 9240 \text{ lb}$$

$$I = \tfrac{1}{2} m r^2 = \frac{9240}{64.4}(2)^2 = 573$$

$$w = w_0 + \alpha t \qquad 31.4 = 0 + 60\alpha$$

$$\alpha = 0.524 \text{ radians/sec}^2$$

$$T = I\alpha = 573(0.524) = 300 \text{ ft lb}$$

4–12. A 64-lb solid sphere, 1 ft in diameter, is released on a 30° slope. It does not slip. How far down the slope has it rolled in 5 sec? (Use $g=32$.)

Solution:

$$I=\frac{2}{5}mv^2=\frac{2}{5}\left(\frac{64}{32}\right)(0.5)^2=0.2$$

$$\Sigma M_C=0=w\sin 30°(0.5)-\frac{64}{32}(0.5)(0.5)\alpha-0.2\alpha$$

$$\alpha=22.85 \text{ radians/sec}^2$$

$$\bar{a}=r\alpha=0.5(22.85)=11.42 \text{ ft/sec}^2$$

$$S=\tfrac{1}{2}\bar{a}t^2=\frac{11.42}{2}(5)^2=143 \text{ ft}$$

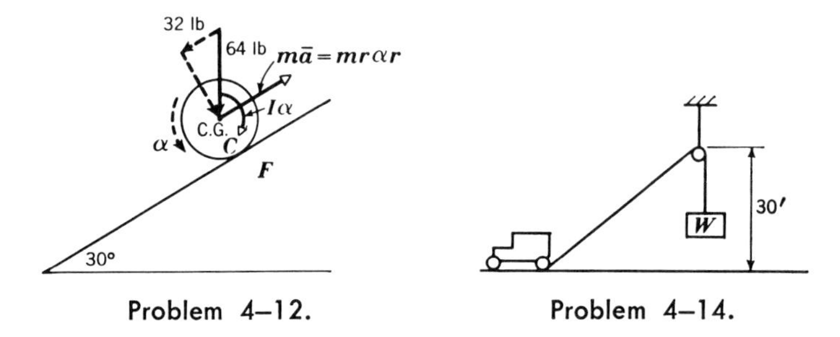

Problem 4–12. Problem 4–14.

4–13. An object, already moving in a straight line, undergoes a constant acceleration. During the first second of this acceleration, the object travels 12 ft. During the next 3 sec, it travels an additional 60 ft. What is the constant acceleration?

4–14. A truck is hoisting a weight, using a 70-ft length of rope over a pulley. The truck moves forward at 5 fps. When the weight is 10 ft above the ground, at what rate is it rising?

4–15. A section of a certain streetcar line is 50 blocks long, and the length of each block is 400 ft. The maximum speed between stops is 20 mph. The cars can accelerate and decelerate at 90 mph/min. If stops are 10 sec duration when stops are made every block and 15 sec duration when stops are made in alternate blocks, how much time can be saved in 50 blocks by stopping in alternate blocks instead of in every block?

4–16. A trailer truck passes station X at a speed of 10 mph increasing its speed to 35 mph in 1.5 min. At this time the truck's speed becomes constant and remains at 35 mph for 10 min. The speed is then decreased to zero in 3 min. (a) Draw a velocity-time diagram for the truck from station X to where it stopped. (b) What total distance did the truck travel? (c) What was its acceleration, in feet per second per second, in the first 1.5 min? (d) What was the truck's rate of deceleration during the last 3 min, in feet per second per second?

4–17. A ball is projected vertically upward from the ground with an initial velocity of 100 fps. Two seconds later another ball is projected in the same manner. Neglecting air resistance, calculate the elevation at which the two balls meet.

4–18. A skier on a mountain slope traveled 50 ft during a 2-sec interval and 40 ft during the next second. What constant acceleration did he have during the entire 3-sec interval?

4–19. A man stands on a spring-balance scale, which in turn rests on the floor of an elevator. When the elevator is stationary, the scale reads 200 lb. What will it read when the elevator is descending with an acceleration of 5 fps?

4–20. In an elevator a body of 8.0 lb weight at rest is suspended from the ceiling by an accurate spring balance which reads 7.0 lb. What is the acceleration of the system?

4–21. A railroad car is held on a 3 per cent grade by its brakes. The rolling resistance of the car is 6 lb/ton. The brakes are released, and the car is allowed to roll 100 ft down grade to a point where the track becomes level. How far will the car roll along the level track? Assume air resistance can be neglected. The car weighs 120,000 lb.

4–22. A train is hauled up a grade of 30 ft/mile along a straight track by an engine which is assumed to exert a constant tractive effort of 16,000 lb. If the weight of the engine and the train is 600 tons and the grade is 1 mile long and the velocity of the train at the bottom of the grade is 10 mph, determine the following, assuming that the frictional resistance is constant and equal to 10 lb/ton: (a) The velocity of the train at the top of the grade. (b) The time taken in going up the grade. (c) The total work done by the engine in going up the grade. (d) The horsepower the engine exerts at the bottom of the grade; also at the top. (e) The horsepower necessary to keep the train moving up the grade at a uniform speed of 20 mph.

4–23. A diesel locomotive pulls a train of 60 boxcars weighing 40 tons each over a level track at a constant speed of 50 mph.

Allow 8 lb/ton weight for frictional resistance and calculate (a) the constant drawbar pull, in pounds, and (b) the horsepower output of the diesel engine.

4–24. A "hotrod" traveling at a speed of 85 mph suddenly sees a deer standing on the highway just ahead. If it takes the driver 0.55 sec to apply the brakes and the brakes when applied will cause a deceleration of 16 ft/sec^2, determine (a) the distance, in feet, which he travels, from the instant he sees the deer, before reaching a complete stop and (b) the time, in seconds, which would elapse, from the instant he sees the deer, until he reaches a complete stop.

4–25. An observer at point A sights a car B moving along a highway at 30 mph. The line AB represents the line of sight. When angle θ is 30°, at what rate is θ changing? (That is, what is angular velocity of line AB?) Express in radians per second.

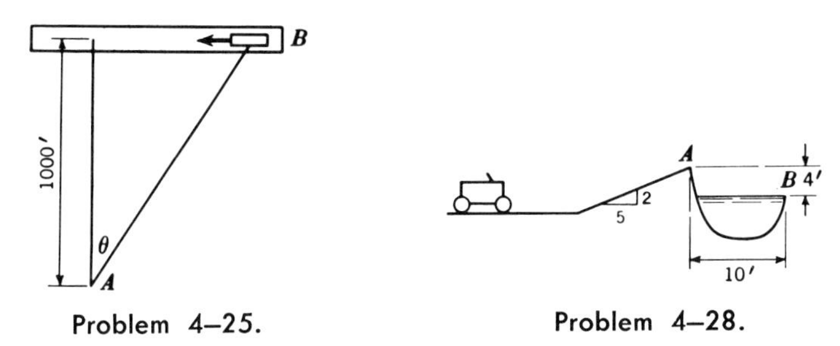

Problem 4–25. Problem 4–28.

4–26. An artillery shell has a muzzle velocity of 3000 fps and is fired at an angle of 15° above the horizontal. Neglect air resistance and find (a) initial horizontal velocity, (b) final horizontal velocity, (c) initial vertical velocity, (d) range, (e) maximum altitude shell attains, and (f) the time of flight.

4–27. A rifle is fired from the top of a 300-ft building. The initial velocity of the bullet is 1200 fps, and the rifle is pointed 15° above the horizontal. (a) When and where will the bullet strike the ground? (b) Determine the maximum height attained by the bullet and the time required to reach that height.

4–28. Determine the minimum speed a jeep must have at point A in order to clear the stream and land on the far bank at point B.

4–29. A 3000-lb automobile is rounding a curve of 500-ft radius at 50 mph without any tendency for the tires to slip sideways on the pavement. How much "banking" is provided on this curve? Does it represent safe curve design?

4–30. An automobile is moving around a circular curve on a highway pavement. Radius of the curve is 1000 ft. The curve is superelevated (outside edge of pavement higher than inner edge) at the rate of 1.0 ft of rise for each 10 ft of pavement width. (a) If coefficient of friction is 0.60 (equal on all tires), at what maximum speed may the automobile travel before it begins to slide off the pavement on the outside? (b) Under icy conditions the coefficient of friction on the curve is 0.05. What minimum speed must the automobile maintain to avoid slipping off the inside edge of pavement?

4–31. In an amusement park an aeroplane swing has six cars which when loaded weigh 1000 lb each. Cars are attached with vertical cables 30 ft long to the frame, which is 22 ft in diameter. (a) Determine speed, in radians per second, to swing cars out to an angle of 45° with the vertical. (b) What is the energy stored in each car at this speed?

4–32. A small flat object A weighs 15 oz and rests on a phonograph turntable. The coefficient of friction between A and the turntable is 0.40, and A is 6 in. from the center. (a) If the turntable is at rest, what instantaneous angular acceleration may be applied without causing slipping of the object A? (b) If the turntable is brought up to speed very slowly, what is the maximum revolutions per minute before the object A slips?

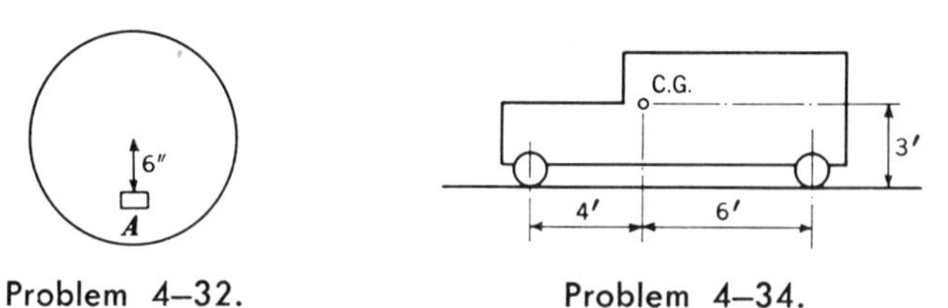

Problem 4–32. Problem 4–34.

4–33. An automobile with four-wheel brakes stops uniformly from 60 mph in a distance of 500 ft. The auto weighs 3200 lb and has a 10-ft wheel base; the center of gravity is 2 ft above the roadway and midway between the front and rear wheels. The maximum allowable coefficient of friction between the tires and roadway is 0.4. Calculate the reactions for front and rear wheels during the stopping period.

4–34. A 3200-lb car travels at 40 mph. Suddenly the driver locks the brakes on the rear wheels only. (It is an old-fashioned car with two-wheel brakes only.) Coefficient of friction between locked rear wheels and the pavement is 0.7. Neglecting any rotational effect of the wheels, what is the deceleration? (Use $g=32$.)

4–35. A truck with a gross weight of 6440 lb has a wheel base of 12 ft. Its center of gravity is 4 ft above the pavement and 5 ft ahead of the rear axle. When the truck is in motion, the brakes are applied, causing a total braking force of 3000 lb. (a) What is the acceleration of the truck? (b) What are the front and rear reactions of the truck? (c) Assuming another situation for the truck of part (a), the truck is traveling at the rate of 50 mph. What braking force would be required to bring it to a stop in a distance of 300 ft?

4–36. A homogeneous block 1 ft wide and 3 ft high rests on a truck bed. What is the maximum acceleration the truck can have without causing the block to move in relation to the truck bed if (a) coefficient of friction between block and bed is 0.2 and (b) coefficient of friction between block and bed is 0.5?

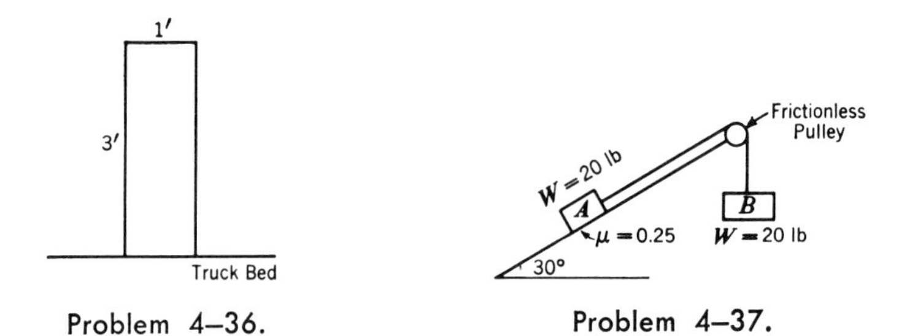

Problem 4–36. Problem 4–37.

4–37. This system is originally at rest. The coefficient of friction between A and the plane is 0.25. After B has fallen 10 ft, what is its velocity? (Use $g=32$.)

4–38. Bodies A and B are connected by a flexible cable over a weightless frictionless pulley. (a) Which way will body A move? (b) Compute tension in cable. (c) Compute acceleration of A.

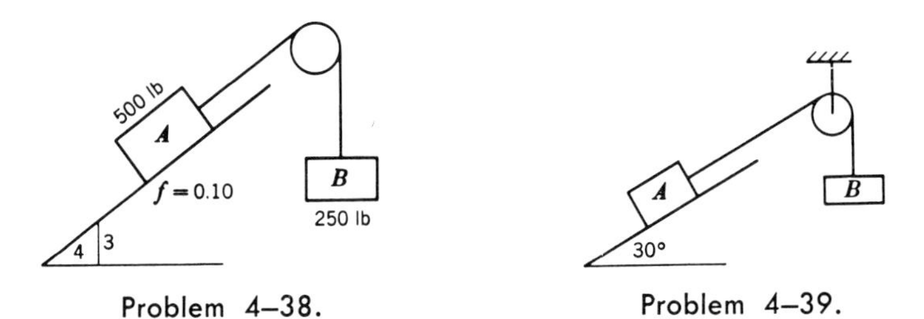

Problem 4–38. Problem 4–39.

4–39. In the figure, A and B represent 10-lb blocks joined by a rope over a smooth pulley. The plane surface is smooth. What is the tension in the rope?

4–40. A weight is projected up a plane inclined at 30° to the horizontal with an initial velocity of 40 fps and slides down again, arriving at the starting point with a velocity of 20 fps. Determine the coefficient of friction between the weight and the surface of the slope.

4–41. How much work is done in slowly compressing a coil spring a distance of 5 in. if the modulus of the spring is 250 lb/in.

4–42. A block that weighs 10 lb slides over a level surface ($f=0.2$) and strikes and compresses a spring. The block's velocity at instant of striking the spring is 50 fps. The spring has a rate or modulus of 100 lb/ft. The block rebounds and comes to rest. (a) How much is the spring compressed? (b) Where does the block finally come to rest?

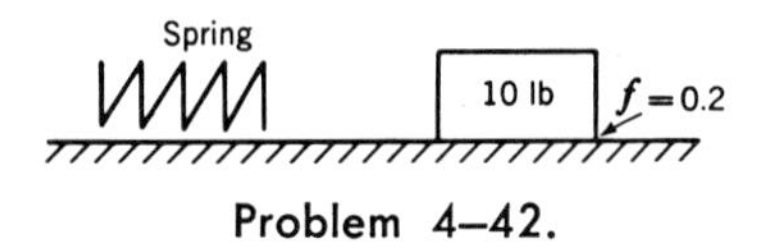

Problem 4–42.

4–43. A drop hammer of 1-ton dead-weight capacity is propelled downward by a 12-in. diameter air cylinder. At 100 psi air pressure, what is the impact velocity if the stroke is 28 in.? What is the impact energy?

4–44. If the velocity of water flowing from a water-turbine nozzle is 50 fps and the discharge is 20 cfs, what is the available horsepower from this one nozzle?

4–45. A concrete batch plant has a conveyor that lifts sand a total distance of 20 ft at the rate of 36 buckets per minute. Each bucket holds 2.50 cu ft of sand. When there is no sand being conveyed, the conveyor motor runs at 1760 rpm and operates against a torque of 3 ft-lb caused by the friction of the system. What is the total power required, in horsepower, to run the conveyor at the above rate if the sand being conveyed weighs 120 lb/cu ft? Assume the friction is the same loaded and empty.

4–46. A 1200-rpm motor is to drive a conveyor belt at 300 rpm through a triple-reduction gear system. Belt is 30 in. wide on a pulley 18 in. in radius. The gears on the first reduction gear set have 25 teeth and 75 teeth and on the second set 18 teeth and 54 teeth. (a) What must the gear ratio be on the third set of gears? (b) If difference in belt tension is 50 lb/in. of belt width and gear efficiency is 90 per cent, what is the motor brake horsepower?

4–47. A certain boat weighing 350 tons is regularly brought up to a full speed of 25 mph. Neglect all friction and windage and (a) determine the amount of kinetic energy, in foot-pounds, required to attain this speed of 25 mph. (b) If the engine propelling the boat delivers 1500 hp, how many seconds are required to attain the speed of 25 mph?

4–48. A car weighs 3000 lb, and it takes 5 hp at the shaft to maintain it at 30 mph on a level road. What horsepower is being developed at the shaft when the car is climbing a 30° slope at the constant speed of 30 mph?

4–49. A 75,000-lb freight car with a velocity of 4 mph collides and couples with a 50,000-lb car. Neglect friction, and compute their new final velocity.

4–50. In the figure, A represents a 5.00-lb ball at the end of a 2.00-ft string. It is at the same level as the string support. Then A is released and allowed to bump into B, which is a 5.00-lb block resting on a smooth, level table. Half of the energy is lost in the bumping process. With what speed does block B slide along the table?

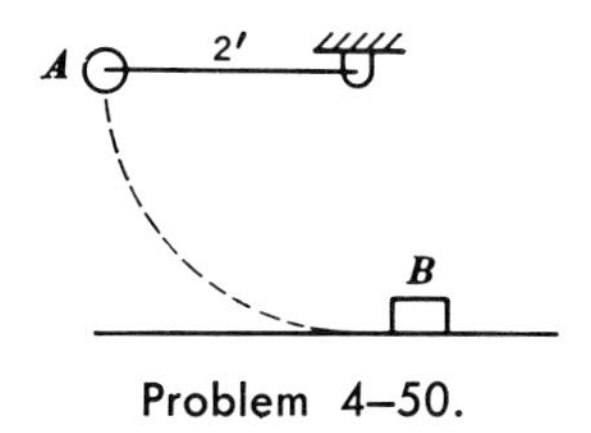

Problem 4–50.

4–51. An object of mass M is traveling with constant velocity when it makes an inelastic impact with a stationary mass $M/2$. After the impact, the resultant velocity of the two masses is in the same direction as the velocity of mass M before impact. (a) Does the momentum before impact equal the momentum after impact? (b) Is the kinetic energy of the masses before impact equal to the kinetic energy of the masses after impact? If not, what is the ratio of the kinetic energy of the masses before impact to that after impact? (c) Is the total energy of the system conserved? How?

4–52. Car A weighing 5000 lb travels 60 fps east, and car B weighing 3000 lb travels 40 fps north. They collide and lock together. Neglect any rotational effect of the wheels. For the instant immediately following impact, determine velocity (speed and direction) of the two cars. (Use $g=32$.)

4–53. Block A weighs 5 lb and travels north at 50 fps. Bullet B weighs 2 oz and travels east at 3000 fps. Both travel in horizontal paths. The bullet strikes block A squarely and imbeds itself at the center of gravity of A. (a) Determine the direction and magnitude of velocity of the system after impact. (b) Determine the final kinetic energy of the system.

4–54. The crank AB rotates at 600 rpm (clockwise). At the position shown, determine the velocity of the piston.

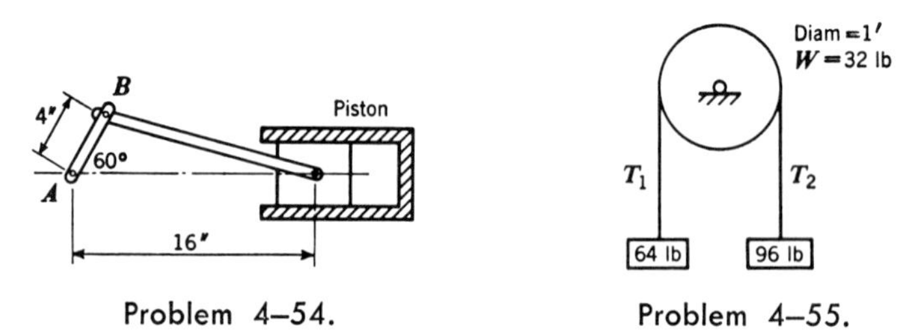

Problem 4–54. Problem 4–55.

4–55. In the figure shown, the pulley may be considered to be a homogeneous cylinder. Its axle is frictionless, and the cord does not slip on the surface of the pulley. Determine tensions T_1 and T_2. (Use $g=32$ fps.)

4–56. The belt which drives a 1600-lb flywheel of radius of gyration 2 ft passes over a pulley of 1-ft radius on the same shaft as the flywheel. The average pull of the tight side exceeds that of the slack side of the belt by 100 lb. Calculate the number of seconds that will be required for the flywheel to acquire a speed of 600 rpm if it starts from rest.

4–57. A wheel 4 ft in diameter weighs 320 lb and has a radius of gyration of 1.8 ft. What is the kinetic energy, in foot-pounds, when the rim of the wheel is moving with a speed of 48 fps?

4–58. A wheel 4 ft in diameter and weighing 150 lb is mounted on a fixed shaft and has imparted to it a speed of 300 rpm in 1 min by a constant horizontal force F applied tangent to the rim. The axis of the wheel is horizontal. Assume no friction at the shaft ($K=1.5$ ft). (a) Find the magnitude of the force F. (b) Find the pressure of the bearings on the shaft. (c) Find the kinetic energy at the end of 1 min, assuming that the wheel starts from rest. (d) Assuming that, when the speed is 300 rpm, the force F ceases to act and a brake is applied to the shaft whose moment is equal to 200 in.-lb, find the number of revolutions the wheel will make before stopping.

4–59. A 10-hp 1750-rpm motor is connected directly to a 30-lb-ft torque brake. The rotating system has a total inertia $\left(\frac{WR^2}{g}\right)$ of 10 lb-ft/sec². How long will it take the system to stop if the brake is set at the instant the motor is shut off? How much energy must be dissipated?

4–60. A 644-lb flywheel has a radius of gyration of 2 ft and is rotating with an angular velocity of 300 rpm when a force P of 200 lb is applied as shown. If the coefficient of kinetic friction between the brake shoe and wheel is 0.40, determine the number of revolutions that the flywheel will make before coming to rest.

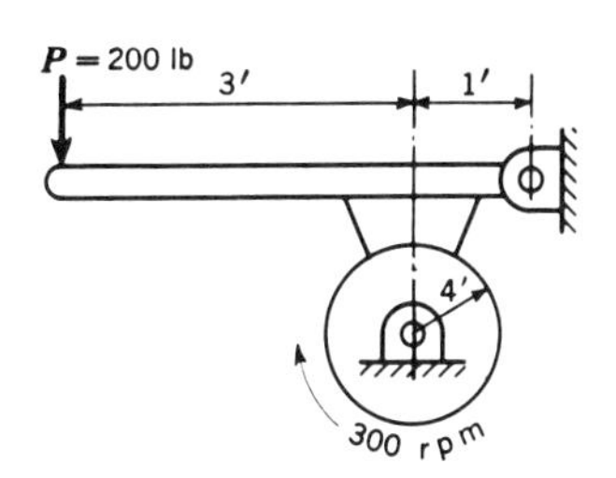

Problem 4–60.

4–61. A wheel, 4 ft in diameter and weighing 150 lb, is mounted on a fixed shaft and has imparted to it a speed of 300 rpm in 1 min by a constant horizontal force F, applied tangent to the rim. The axis of the wheel is horizontal, and the moment of inertia about the axis is 500. Assume no friction at the shaft. (a) Find the magnitude of the force F. (b) Find the pressure of the bearings on the shaft. (c) Find the kinetic energy at the end of 1 min, assuming that the wheel starts from rest. (d) Assuming that, when the speed is 300 rpm, the force F ceases to act and a brake is applied to the shaft whose moment is equal to 200 in.-lb, find the number of revolutions the wheel will make before stopping.

4–62. A cylinder 1 ft in diameter and 1 ft long and weighing 400 lb moves from rest down an incline having a slope 4 ft vertical to 12 ft horizontal. The coefficient of friction between material of cylinder and incline is 0.40. (a) What is total kinetic energy of cylinder when it reaches bottom of incline? (b) Did cylinder roll, slide, or both?

4–63. A solid cylinder of 2 ft radius and weighing 1000 lb starts from rest to roll down a 30° plane as shown. There is sufficient friction to prevent any slipping. With what velocity will the cylinder reach the bottom of the plane?

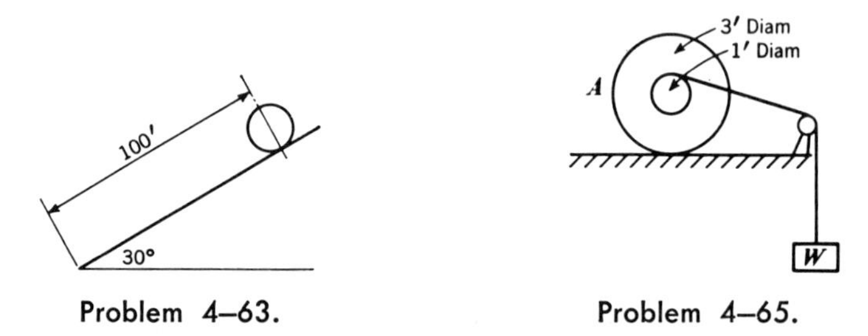

Problem 4–63. Problem 4–65.

4–64. A solid cylinder of 2.00 in. diameter and 1.50 lb weight is rolling on a plane with a speed of 3.00 fps. Find the kinetic energy of the cylinder.

4–65. The wheel *A* rolls without slipping along the level surface. The cord connecting *A* and the weight *W* is inextensible. Starting from a dead stop, the wheel rolls 50 ft to the left in 10 sec, undergoing a uniform acceleration. Determine (a) height through which the weight rises and (b) velocity of the weight at the end of the 10 sec.

4–66. In the four-bar mechanism of the figure, link *CD* has an angular velocity of 2 radians/sec counterclockwise. When the mechanism is in the position shown, determine: (a) the location of the instantaneous center of link *BC*, (b) the angular velocity of link *BC*, and (c) the velocity of point *B*.

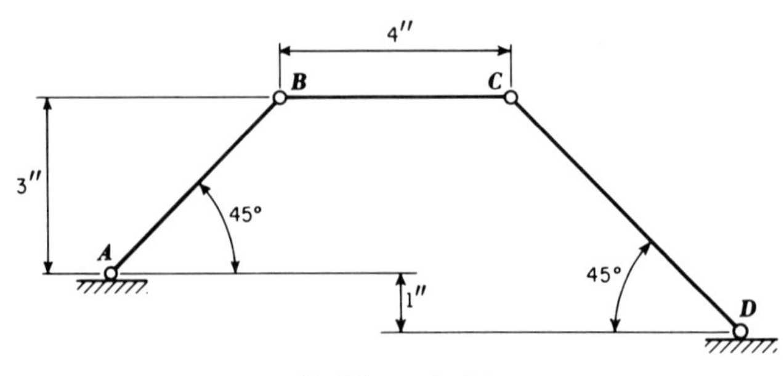

Problem 4–66.

4–67. If wheel D is rotating counterclockwise with an angular velocity of 6 radians/sec, what is: (a) the lineal velocity of B, and (b) the angular velocity of wheel A.

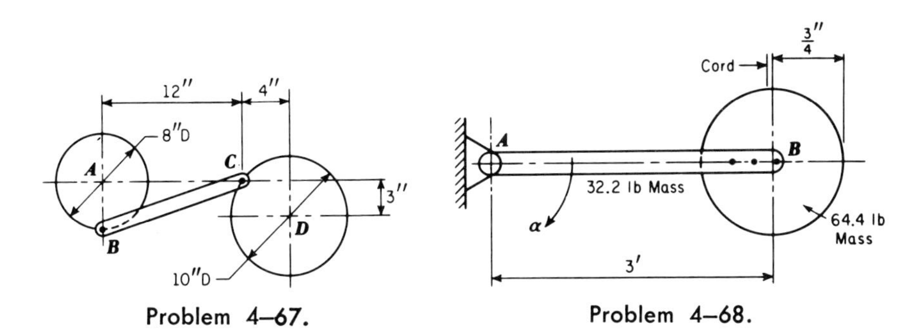

Problem 4–67.

Problem 4–68.

4–68. The long slender rod and disc are riveted together as shown in the figure and pivoted on the wall bracket at A. What will be the angular acceleration (α) an instant after the cord is severed?

4–69. In the figure, block A weighs 96.6 lb and block B weighs 64.4 lb. The coefficient of friction under A is 0.20 and under B is 0.25; P=200 lb. Determine the acceleration of A and B, and the tension T in the connecting rope.

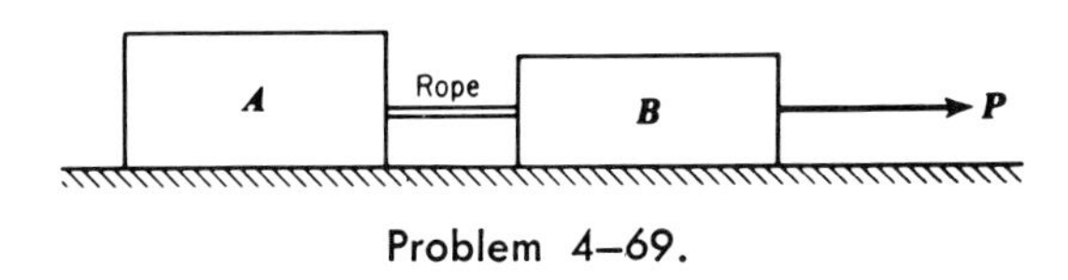

Problem 4–69.

4–70. What will be the tension in the rope?

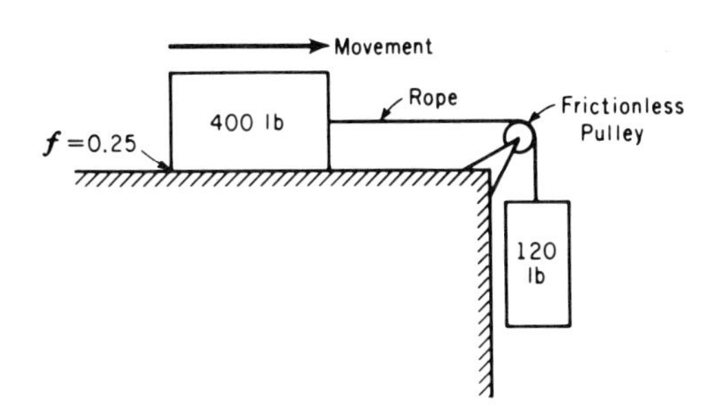

Problem 4–70.

4–71. A plumb line hangs from the dashboard of a car accelerating at the constant rate of 20 ft/sec^2. What angle does the string of the plumb line make with the vertical?

4–72. A baseball player throws a ball 200 ft from the outfield to home plate. Assume that he throws from ground level, and that the ball lands on home plate in 2 sec. What is the maximum height of the ball trajectory above ground?

4–73. Determine the tension in the cord before and immediately after the restraining force F is removed. Also, calculate the maximum kinetic energy attained by the weight.

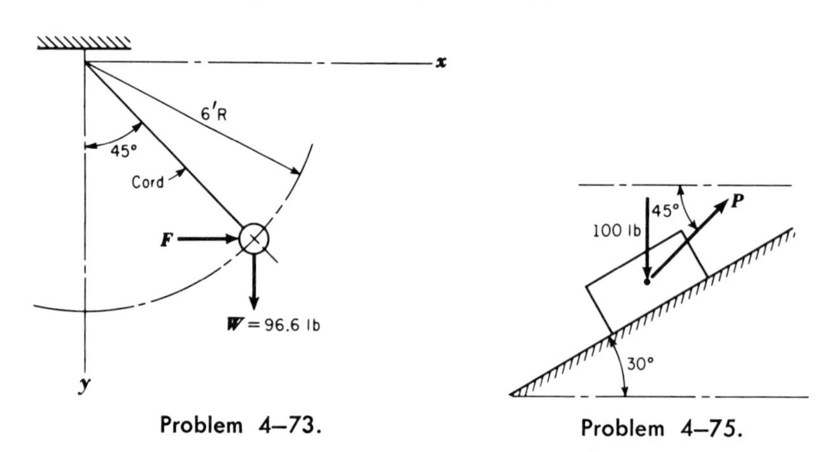

Problem 4–73.

Problem 4–75.

4–74. An automobile which weighs 3000 lb is traveling along a highway at 50 mph. Wind and friction resistance is 75 lb. The efficiency of the power transmission is 60 per cent (from engine to rear wheels). What is the required developed power of the engine if the automobile is moving up a 3 per cent grade (3 ft rise per 100 ft horizontal)?

4–75. Compute the force (P) which will be required to give the 100-lb block a velocity (v) of 10 fps up the plane in a time interval of 5 sec. The system is initially at rest.

4–76. A driver traveling at 55 mph sees a stop light. If it takes him 0.6 sec to apply the brakes, and the brakes give a deceleration of 15 ft/sec^2, how many feet does he travel before coming to a stop?

4–77. A 48,000-lb freight car rolling on a level track strikes a spring bumper at the end of a track spur. The spring constant of the bumper is 100,000 lb/in. When the car has been brought to a stop, the spring has been compressed 4 in. What was the speed of the car?

4–78. On icy roads the best coefficient of friction of a car with good tires drops to 0.15 or less. Assuming a one-second "reaction time," how far must a 4000-lb car travel while slowing to a stop from 60 mph (88 fps)? How far for a 3000-lb car? Assume icy, level roads.

4–79. A 6-oz egg drops 16 in. into a pan which is supported by a spring. If a force of 2 lb will break the eggshell, what is the maximum value of the spring constant that will prevent the production of scrambled eggs?

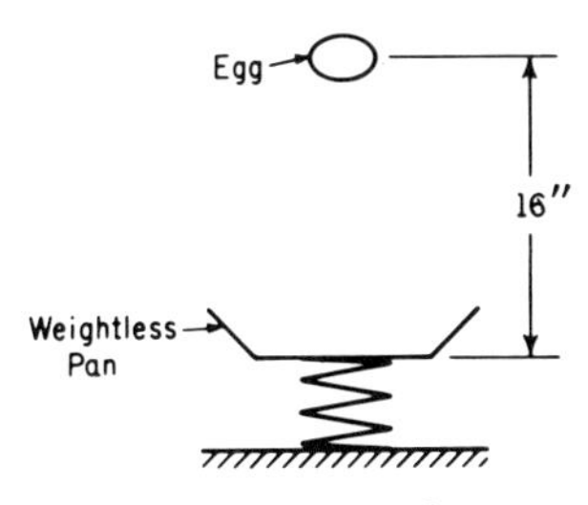

Problem 4–79.

4–80. A billiard ball moving at 8 fps strikes a stationary ball as shown. The balls weigh 15 oz each and the coefficient of restitution of ivory on ivory is 0.88. What is the velocity and direction of each ball after contact?

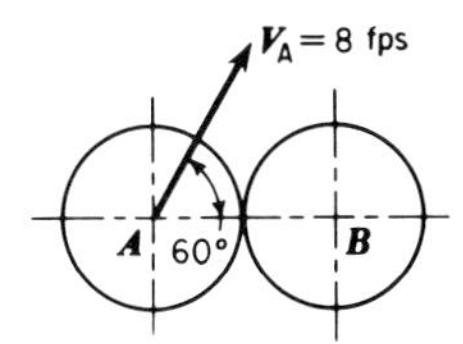

Problem 4–80.

4–81. A block that weighs (W) 16.1 lb slides over a level surface ($f=0.20$) and strikes and compresses a spring. The block's velocity at the instant of striking the spring is 40 fps. The spring has a modulus of 100 lb/ft. The block rebounds. How much is the spring compressed in inches?

4–82. A 20-lb steel ball is fired with a velocity of 25 fps at an angle of 30° with the horizontal into a container of loose sand weighing 100 lb resting on a smooth floor. The container, sand, and ball then hit a horizontal spring, the constant of which is 200 lb/in. What is the maximum force developed in the spring?

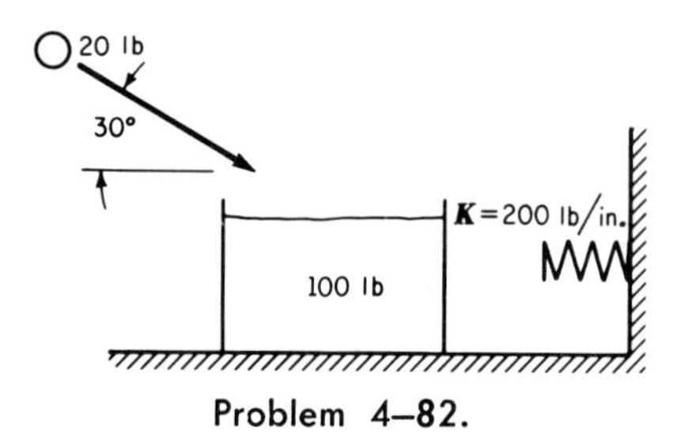

Problem 4–82.

4–83. A loaded ore car weighing 1 ton is being pulled up a 20 per cent grade at 15 mph when the coupling breaks. If the rolling resistance is 5 per cent of the car's weight, how far up the track will it travel before starting to roll back down?

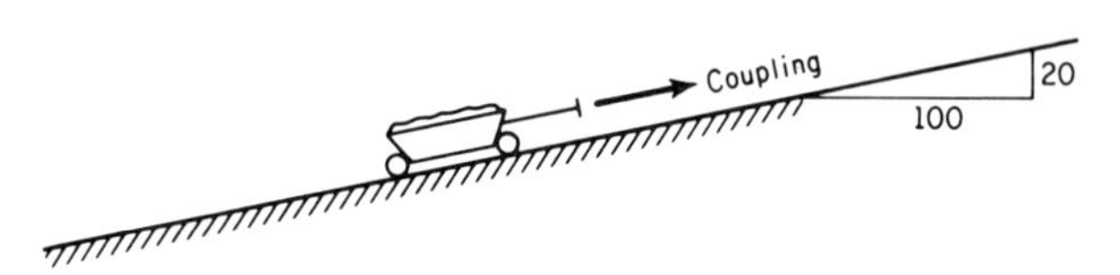

Problem 4–83.

4–84. A 3-lb block "C" is fastened to a shaft "AB" by a spring which has a free length of 20 in. and a spring modulus of 5 lb/in. The disk on which the block rests is smooth and rotates with a con-

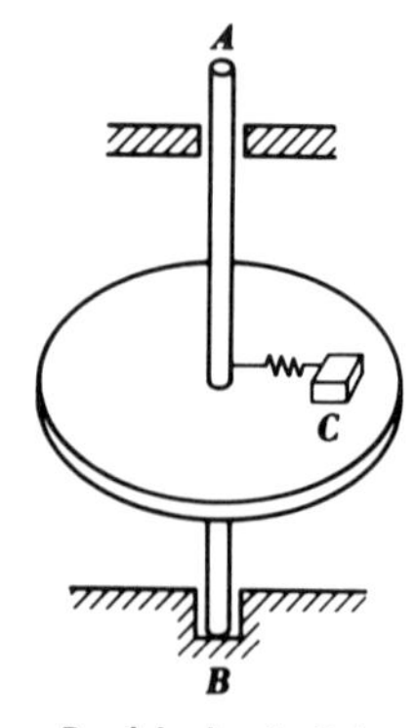

Problem 4–84.

stant angular velocity of 10 radians/sec. Determine the elongation of the spring.

4–85. Body I is a solid homogeneous cylinder, weighing 322 lb, which rotates about a fixed axis through O. Bearing friction is negligible. Determine the constant force P required to raise the 161-lb body (II) 10 ft in 3 sec, starting from rest.

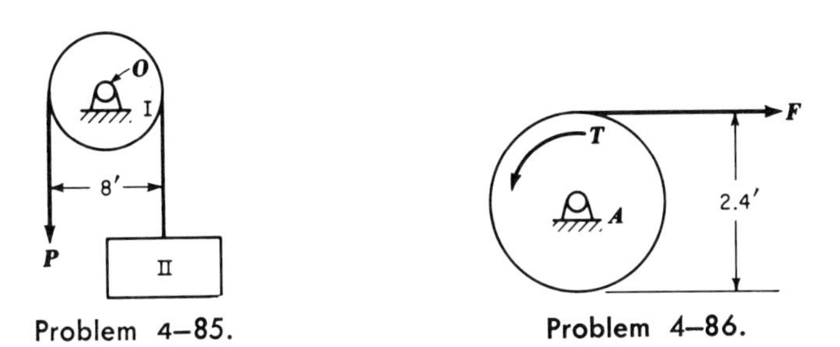

Problem 4–85. Problem 4–86.

4–86. The drum shown in the figure weighs 193.2 lb and rotates about the fixed axis "A". The radius of gyration of the mass with respect to the axis of rotation is 0.5 ft. Find the time required to change the angular velocity from 30 rpm clockwise to 90 rpm counterclockwise when the drum is acted upon by a constant force of 10 lb and a constant torque of 480 lb-in. as shown.

4–87. An unbalanced flywheel has its center of mass 4.00 in. from the axis of rotation. The radius of gyration of the flywheel with respect to an axis through the center of mass parallel to the axis of rotation is 16.00 in. The flywheel, which weighs 145.0 lb, is rotating clockwise about its axis at an angular speed of 3600 rpm when a counterclockwise torque $T = 18.00\ t^2$ is applied, where T is in lb-ft and t is in seconds. Neglecting friction, determine the angular speed in rpm of the flywheel when t is 10.00 sec.

4–88. Two rods, each weighing 4 lb/ft, are welded together and rotate about A. In the position shown, the angular velocity of the rods is 5 radians/sec clockwise. Determine (a) the angular acceleration of the rods, (b) the tangential and normal components of the reaction at A.

4–89. A homogeneous cylinder and block each weigh 64.4 lb and are connected by a link, AB, of negligible weight. The coefficient of friction between the cylinder and block and the plane is 0.2. The angle θ is 30° and the link is parallel to the incline. (a) What is the acceleration of the assembly? (b) What is the force in the link? (c) Does the cylinder slip on the incline?

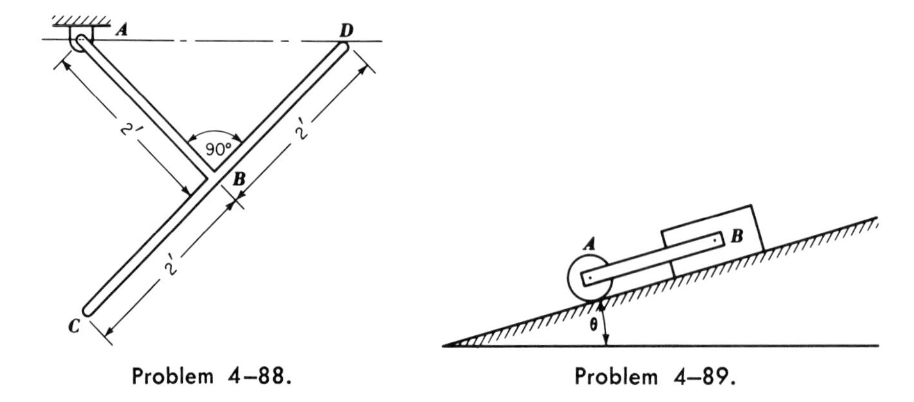

Problem 4–88.

Problem 4–89.

4–90. If the system shown in the figure is released from rest, compute the angular acceleration of the drum (B).

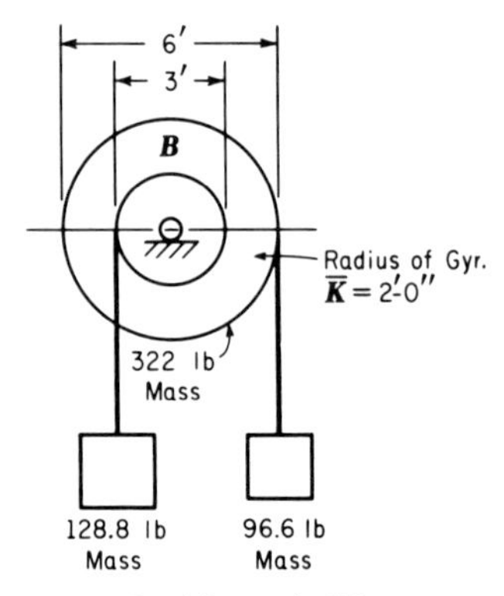

Problem 4–90.

Physics

5

The physics problems selected from numerous examinations have been classified arbitrarily into the following groups: mechanics, heat and thermodynamics, acoustics, light, and electromagnetism. Detailed solutions are given for one or two problems in each group, and the basic physical principle is stated in each solved problem.

5–1. Complete the following table, showing the fundamental units for each system (solution shown in italics):

Unit	Absolute System		Gravitational System	
	CGS	English	CGS	English
Time	*second*	*second*	*second*	*second*
Length	*centimeter*	*foot*	*centimeter*	*foot*
Force	*dyne*	*poundal*	*gram*	*pound*
Mass	*gram*	*pound*	*gram (mass)*	*slug*

5–2. A pull of 50 lb acting at 30° above the horizontal has a 200-lb weight just on the verge of sliding on a horizontal plane. What is the coefficient of friction between the body and the plane?

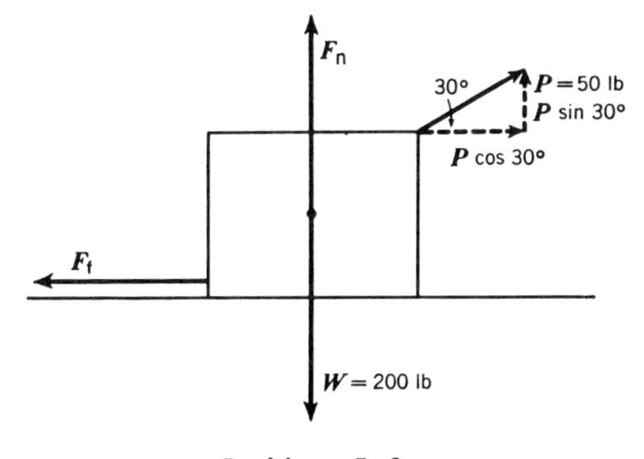

Problem 5–2.

Solution:

$\Sigma F_Y=0$

$$F_n+P \sin 30° - W = ma_y \qquad a_y=0$$

$$F_n = W - P \sin 30°$$

$\Sigma F_H=0$

$$P \cos 30° - \mu F_n = ma_x \qquad a_x=0$$

$$P \cos 30° = \mu F_n$$

$$P \cos 30° = \mu(W - P \sin 30°)$$

$$\mu = \frac{P \cos 30°}{W - P \sin 30°} = \frac{50(0.866)}{200-25} = 0.25$$

5–3. An automobile weighing 4000 lb can accelerate from 30 to 60 mph in 5 sec. (a) What is the average acceleration? (b) How many pounds thrust will be required at the rear wheels? (c) How many foot-pounds of work will be done? (d) How much kinetic energy will be gained? (e) What actual horsepower will be required to produce this acceleration?

Solution:

(a)
$$a = \frac{v_1 - v_0}{t} = \frac{88-44}{5} = 8.8 \text{ fps}^2$$

(b)
$$F = \frac{w}{g}a = \frac{4000}{32}8.8 = 1100 \text{ lb}$$

(c)
$$\text{Work} = Fs \cos\theta = \frac{1}{2}\frac{w}{g}v_1^2 - \frac{1}{2}\frac{w}{g}v_0^2 = \frac{1}{2}\frac{w}{g}(v_1^2 - v_0^2)$$

$$= \frac{1}{2}\left(\frac{4000}{32}\right)(88-44)(88+44) = 3.63\times 10^5 \text{ ft-lb}$$

(d)
$$\text{KE} = 3.63\times 10^5 \text{ ft-lb}$$

(e)
$$\text{Power} = \frac{dW}{dt} = \frac{F\,ds}{dt} = Fv$$

$$\text{Power} = Fv_1 = 1100(88) = 9.68\times 10^4 \text{ ft-lb/sec} = 176 \text{ hp}$$

5–4. Two balls of the same diameter roll toward each other on a smooth horizontal surface. Ball A has a mass of 1000 g and a velocity toward the right of 20 cm/sec; ball B has a mass of 250 g and a velocity toward the left of 10 cm/sec. Assume elastic impact to find the velocity of each ball after the collision.

Solution:

$$v_a = \frac{(m_a - m_b)u_a - 2m_b u_b}{m_a + m_b} \qquad v_b = \frac{(m_a - m_b)u_b + 2m_a u_a}{m_a + m_b}$$

$$v_a = \frac{(1000-250)(20) - 2(250)(10)}{1250} = 8.0 \text{ cm/sec}\rightarrow$$

$$v_b = \frac{(1000-250)(10) + 2(1000)(20)}{1250} = 38 \text{ cm/sec}\rightarrow$$

5–5. A 150-lb acrobat jumps from a height of 10 ft into a trampoline. If the trampoline gives 8 in., how far will it give if the man simply stands on it? What is its frequency of vibration? (Assume the motion to be simple harmonic, although this is not quite true.)

Solution:

$$\text{PE}=\int_0^{x_1} kx\,dx=\tfrac{1}{2}kx_1^2 \qquad \text{PE}_{\text{man}}=mgh=\tfrac{1}{2}kx_1^2 \qquad k=\frac{2mgh}{x_1^2}$$

$$W=kx \qquad x=\frac{W}{k}$$

$$x=\frac{W}{2Wh/x_1^2}=\frac{x_1^2}{2h}=\frac{(0.67)^2(12)}{2(10.67)}=0.25\text{ in.}$$

$$f=\frac{1}{2\pi}\sqrt{\frac{k}{m}}=\frac{1}{2\pi}\sqrt{\frac{2wh}{x_1^2w/g}}=\frac{1}{2\pi}\sqrt{\frac{2hg}{x_1^2}}=\frac{1}{2\pi}\sqrt{\frac{2(10.67)(32)}{(0.67)^2}}=6\text{ cps}$$

5–6. Starting from rest, a uniform sphere of mass m and radius R rolls without slipping down a plane which makes an angle θ with the horizontal. Find the linear speed of the center of the sphere when it has traveled a distance S.

Solution:

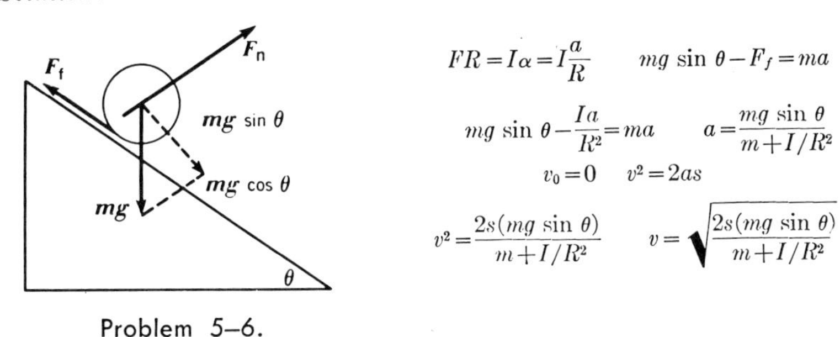

Problem 5–6.

$$FR=I\alpha=I\frac{a}{R} \qquad mg\sin\theta-F_f=ma$$

$$mg\sin\theta-\frac{Ia}{R^2}=ma \qquad a=\frac{mg\sin\theta}{m+I/R^2}$$

$$v_0=0 \qquad v^2=2as$$

$$v^2=\frac{2s(mg\sin\theta)}{m+I/R^2} \qquad v=\sqrt{\frac{2s(mg\sin\theta)}{m+I/R^2}}$$

5–7. How many kilograms of water at 100°C are required to melt 1000 g of ice at 0°C in a copper container weighing 1 kg and give a mixture of 20°C. Assume no heat loss.

Solution: $m_ih_f+m_ic_w(20-0)+m_cc_c(20-0)=m_wc_w(100-20)$

$$m_w=\frac{1000h_f+1000(c_w)(20)+1000c_c(20)}{80c_w}$$

$$m_w=\frac{1000h_f+20{,}000c_w+20{,}000c_c}{80c_w\ (1000)}\text{kg}=1.27\text{ kg}$$

5–8. A certain mass of air is expanding adiabatically according to the law, $pv^{1.4}$=constant. At a particular instant, the pressure is 40 psia, while the volume is 32 cu in. and increasing at the rate of 0.05 cu in./sec. Find the rate at which the pressure is changing.

Solution:

$$pv^{\gamma}=c \qquad \gamma p v^{\gamma-1}\frac{dv}{dt}+v^{\gamma}\frac{dp}{dt}=0$$

$$-\frac{1.4(40)(5\times10^{-2})}{32}=\frac{dp}{dt} \qquad \frac{dp}{dt}=-0.0875 \text{ psi/sec}$$

5–9. An automobile traveling at 50 mph sounds its horn during the period it is passing a pedestrian. Calculate the frequency shift of the tone heard by the pedestrian. Assume the frequency of the horn is 4000 cps.

Solution:

$$f_o=\frac{f/\mathbf{c}-\mathbf{v}_o/}{/\mathbf{c}-\mathbf{v}_s/} \qquad \mathbf{c}=\text{velocity of sound} \qquad \mathbf{v}_s=\text{velocity of source}$$

$$\mathbf{v}_o=\text{velocity of observer} \qquad c=1100 \text{ fps}$$

$$/\mathbf{c}-\mathbf{v}_s/=c-v_s \qquad \text{approaching}$$

$$f_{o_1}=f\frac{c}{c-v_s}$$

$$/\mathbf{c}-\mathbf{v}_s/=c+v_s \qquad \text{receding}$$

$$f_{o_2}=f\frac{c}{c+v_s} \quad \text{and} \quad f_{o_1}-f_{o_2}=f\frac{c}{c-v_s}-f\frac{c}{c+v_s}$$

$$\Delta f=fc\left(\frac{1}{c-v_s}-\frac{1}{c+v_s}\right)=\frac{2v_s fc}{c^2-v_s^2}=535 \text{ cps}$$

5–10. A taut steel wire, 0.30 in. in diameter and 80 ft long, drawn between rigid supports, is struck near one end with a stick, and the time elapsed until the pulse has returned five times to its starting point is measured (with a stop watch) to be 9.3 sec. At what frequencies would standing waves be set up in the wire? What must the tension be?

Solution:

$$n\frac{\lambda}{2}=L \qquad \lambda=\frac{2L}{n} \qquad v=f\lambda \qquad v=\frac{10L}{t}=\frac{2L}{n}f_n \qquad f_n=\frac{5n}{t}$$

$$f_1=\frac{5}{9.3}=0.54 \text{ cps} \qquad f_4=\frac{20}{9.3}=2.16 \text{ cps} \qquad \rho_s=\text{density of steel}$$

$$d=\text{diameter}$$

$$f_2=\frac{10}{9.3}=1.08 \text{ cps} \qquad f_n=\frac{5n}{9.3} \qquad n=1,2,3,4,\ldots,\infty$$

$$f_3=\frac{15}{9.3}=1.61 \text{ cps} \qquad T=\pi L^2\left(\frac{5}{9.3}\right)^2\rho_s d^2$$

5–11. (a) A 10-turn square coil, 5 cm on a side, rotates at 1200 rpm in a magnetic field with flux density of 1 weber/sq m. Calculate the maximum value of the emf generated in the coil. (b)

Calculate the total flux through a 100-turn air-core toroid carrying 10 amp and having a cross section of 10 sq cm and a mean length of 30 cm. State the name of the unit of flux.

Solution:

(a) $$e=\frac{Nd\phi}{dt}=N\frac{d}{dt}(BA\sin\omega t) \qquad \begin{array}{l}\theta=\omega t\\ \omega=2\pi\times\text{Frequency}\end{array}$$

$$e=NBA\omega\cos\omega t$$

$$e_{max}=NBA\omega=10(1)(25\times10^{-4})(2\pi)(1.2\times10^{3})/60$$
$$=3.2\text{ volts}$$

(b) Flux density $=B=\dfrac{\mu_0 Ni}{l}$

$$B=\frac{4\pi\times10^{-7}\times10^{2}(10)}{3\times10^{-1}}=\frac{4\pi}{3}\times10^{-3}=4.2\times10^{-3}\text{ webers/sq m}$$

$$\phi=BA=(4.2\times10^{-3})(10^{-3})=4.2\times10^{-6}\text{ webers}$$

5–12. The image of an object is formed by a double convex lens on a screen which is 8 ft from the lens. (a) If the object is 2 sq in. in size, where must it be placed with respect to the screen if the image is to be 4 sq ft? (b) Determine the focal length of the lens.

Solution:

(a) $$\frac{\text{Object distance}}{\text{Object height}}=\frac{\text{image distance}}{\text{image height}}$$

$$\frac{d}{\sqrt{2}}=\frac{8}{\sqrt{48}}$$

$$d=1.63\text{ ft}$$

(b) $$1/f=1/p+1/f$$

$$1/f=1/8+1/1.63=0.737$$

$$f=1.36\text{ ft}$$

5–13. Light with a wavelength of 6.0×10^{-5} cm passes through two optical slits 1 cm apart. How far is the third bright fringe line from the central bright line on a screen parallel to the slits and 1.0 m from the slits?

Solution:

$$\sin\theta=n\lambda/d$$

$$\frac{h}{100\text{ cm}}=\frac{(3)(6.0\times10^{-5})}{1.0\text{ cm}}$$

$$h=18.0\times10^{-3}\text{ cm}=0.018\text{ cm}$$

5–14. A black-body radiator is heated by electron bombardment using 250 volts and 200 ma. What temperature will it assume if it has 4 sq cm of radiating surface?

Solution:

$$P = VI = (250)(0.2) = 50 \text{ watts}$$

$$W = 5.672 \times 10^{-8} \frac{\text{watts}}{\text{m}^2(°\text{K})^4} T^4$$

$$\frac{50}{(0.01)^2 4 \text{ m}^2} = 5.672 \times 10^{-8} \frac{\text{watts}}{\text{m}^2(°\text{K})^4} T^4$$

$$T^4 = (1220)^4$$

$$T = 1220°\text{K}$$

5–15. A charge Q_2 of 0.05μ coulombs is moved to a distance of 1 m from a central fixed charge Q_1 coulombs. Find the force of Q_2, the electric field and potential at 1.0 m from Q_1.

Solution:

$$\text{Force} = 9 \times 10^9 \frac{\text{nt(m}^2)}{\text{coulombs}^2} \frac{Q_1 Q_2}{d^2} = 9 \times 10^9 \frac{\text{nt(m}^2)}{\text{coulombs}^2} \frac{(0.05\mu \text{ coulomb})(10\mu \text{ coulombs})}{(1.0)^2}$$

$$= 4.5 \times 10^{-3} \text{nt}$$

$$\text{Electric field} = \frac{\text{force}}{\text{charge}} = \frac{4.5 \times 10^{-3} \text{ nt}}{0.05 \times 10^{-6} \text{ coulombs}} = 90 \times 10^3 \text{ nt/coulombs}$$

$$\text{Potential} = \text{electric field} \times \text{distance} = 90 \times 10^3 \frac{\text{nt}}{\text{coulombs}} (1 \text{ m}) = 90{,}000 \text{ volts}$$

5–16. How much work is required to accelerate an electron to 0.8 the speed of light? The rest mass of the electron is 9.11×10^{-31} kg. Use $c = 3.0 \times 10^8$ m/sec.

Solution:

$$\text{Work} = \int F\, ds = \int mv\, dv = m_r \int_0^{0.8c} \frac{v\, dv}{[1-(v/c)^2]^{1/2}} = -m_r c^2(1 - v^2/c^2)^{1/2} \Big]_0^{0.8c}$$

$$= 9.11 \times 10^{-31}\text{kg } (9 \times 10^{16}\, m^2/\text{sec}^2)[-\sqrt{0.36} + 1]$$

$$= 32.8 \times 10^{-15} \text{nt (m)} = 2.05 \times 10^5 \text{ev}$$

5–17. Determine magnitude, direction, and line of action of the resultant of the two parallel forces shown in the figure.

5–18. Find the coordinates of the center of gravity of the uniform plate of sheet metal pictured in the diagram.

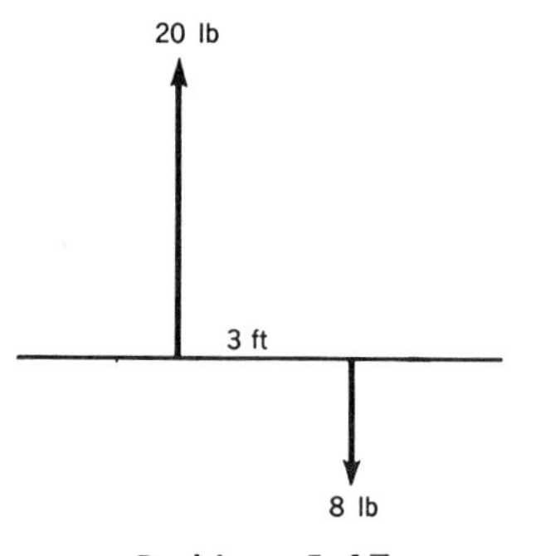

Problem 5–17.

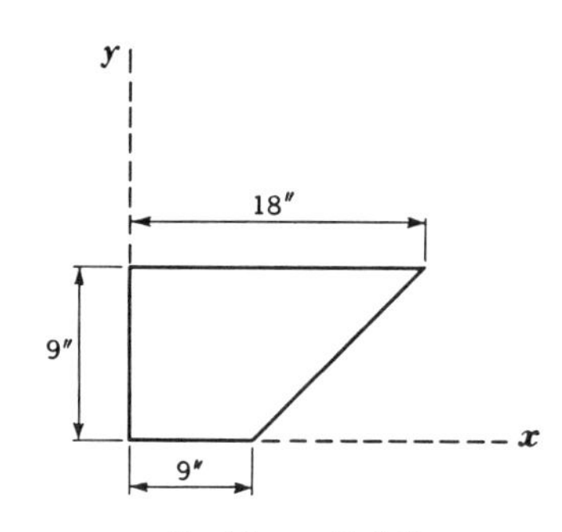

Problem 5–18.

5–19. A sled is moved horizontally 20 ft along a smooth (frictionless) icy surface in 4 sec, from rest. If the sled weighs 64 lb, (a) what is its acceleration, assuming it to be constant, and (b) what steady horizontal force is required?

5–20. A 64-lb block is pulled 16 ft along a smooth, horizontal surface by the application of a constant force of 20 lb at 60° above horizontal. Find (a) the work done by the given force, and (b) the magnitude of the acceleration of the block.

5–21. A 100-lb block of stone is being raised by means of a pulley arrangement as shown. The effects produced by the weight and friction of the system are negligible. (a) When a pull P of 60 lb is applied constantly to the rope, what is the acceleration of the stone? (b) If, while the system is at rest, the rope breaks suddenly, allowing the stone to fall freely, what is the kinetic energy of the stone when it reaches the ground level 20 ft below the starting point?

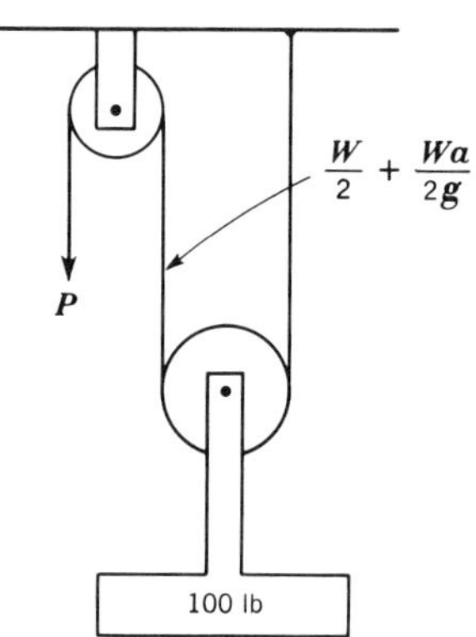

Problem 5–21.

5–22. How much energy, in foot-pounds, must be expended to bring a 300-ton train up to a speed of 30 mph? If the locomotive works at the rate of 1000 hp, how long will it take to bring the train up to speed? (The track is horizontal.)

5–23. A horizontal force is applied to a block moving in a horizontal guide. When the block is at a distance X from the origin, the force is given by the equation $F = X^3 - X$. What work is done by moving the block from 1 ft to the left of the origin to 1 ft to the right of the origin?

5–24. A driver traveling at 45 mph sees a stop light. If it takes him 0.6 sec to apply the brakes and the brakes give a deceleration of 15 ft/sec², how many feet does he travel before coming to a stop?

5–25. A boy pours 1 oz lead shot onto the platform of a spring balance from a height of 64 ft at a rate of 30 per second. If they do not bounce at all, but roll off the platform at once, what will the scale read, in pounds?

5–26. A block weighing 2 lb is forced against a horizontal spring of negligible mass, compressing the spring an amount $X_1 = 6$ in. Upon releasing the block, it moves on a horizontal table top a distance $X_2 = 2$ ft before coming to rest. The spring constant K is 8 lb/ft. What is the coefficient of friction between the block and table? HINT: Use conservation of energy principle. Assume constant frictional force.

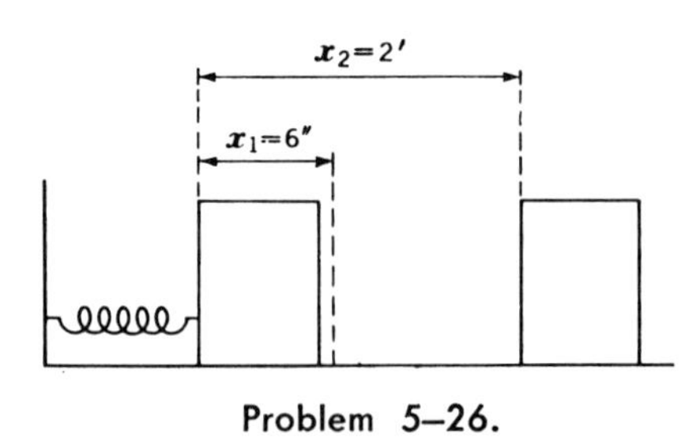

Problem 5–26.

5–27. A 16-lb body is pulled at constant speed along a horizontal surface by a cord making an angle of 30° above the horizontal. Assume a frictional drag of 2 lb along the surface. (a) What is the tension in the cord? (b) What is the vertical push of the surface on the body?

5–28. A 64-lb body is whirled in a horizontal circle at the end of a 10-ft rope fastened at the center of the circle. The body makes 1 rps. (a) What is the angular speed of the body, in radians per second? (b) What is the linear speed of the body? (c) What is the acceleration of the body? (Give magnitude and direction.) (d) What is the tension in the rope? (Take 32 ft/sec^2 as the value of the acceleration of gravity in this problem.)

5–29. An airplane weighing 10,000 lb is flying at 300 mph. What is the proper angle of bank if the pilot flies the plane into a turn of 300-ft radius? The angle that the wing makes with the horizontal plane is θ.

5–30. The relation between mass and energy as derived by Einstein is $E=MC^2$, where E=energy, M=mass, and C=speed of light. If 1 lb of uranium is caused to fission and there is a loss of 0.1 per cent of the mass in the process, how many kilowatt hours of energy are liberated?

5–31. A projectile traveling at the rate of 700 fps penetrates a homogeneous material to a depth of 2 in. With what velocity must the projectile travel to penetrate the same material a depth of 3 in.

5–32. What is the pressure, in pounds per square inch, in the ocean at a depth of 2000 ft? The density is 62.8 lb/cu ft.

5–33. A timber 1 ft $\times$ 1 ft $\times$ 10 ft weighing 40 lb/cu ft is submerged vertically in fresh water, the upper end being 1 ft below the surface of the water. What vertical force is required to hold it in position?

5–34. A certain piece of material weighs 200 lb in air at sea level and 137.5 lb in water. Determine (a) the volume of this material, in cubic feet, (b) the density of this material, in pounds per cubic feet, and (c) the specific gravity of this material.

5–35. A rectangular raft 10 ft $\times$ 10 ft $\times$ 2 ft is made of wood having a specific gravity of 0.6. It carries a uniformly distributed load over its entire area. What is the load, in pounds, if the water comes to within 6 in. of the top.

5–36. A solid insoluble object heavier than water weighs 18 lb in air. The same object when attached to a string completely submerged under water weighs 14.25 lb. The same object when completely submerged in a certain sample of oil weighs 15.3 lb. From these data determine (a) the specific gravity of the solid insoluble object, (b) the specific gravity of the oil, and (c) the weight of the oil per cubic foot.

5–37. A cylindrical barrel 2 ft in diameter and 4 ft in height stands half-filled with water. A piece of cast iron is submerged in the water and the water rises to 3 ft 6 in. What is the weight of the cast iron?

5–38. A vertical gate 8 ft wide and 6 ft high is hinged at the top and held closed by pressure of water standing 4 ft above the top of the gate. What force applied at the bottom of the gate and at right angles to the gate face will be required to open it?

5–39. A fire-hose nozzle $1\frac{1}{4}$ in. in diameter is delivering 250 gpm. Neglecting air friction, how high will the stream rise if directed vertically upward? (7.5 gal=1 cu ft)

5–40. The temperature as measured on a Fahrenheit thermometer is 80.6°. What would it be on a centigrade thermometer? At what temperature would the readings be the same on the two thermometers?

5–41. (a) How many Btu of heat are required to raise the temperature of 10 lb of ice at 10°F to steam at 212°F? (b) How many Btu of heat are required to raise the temperature of 12 lb of copper from 32°F to 212°F? (c) What is the thermal capacity of a copper calorimeter weighing 2.5 lb?

5–42. A cast-iron ball weighing 5 lb is heated in a furnace until its temperature is assumed to be the same as that of the furnace. The ball is removed from the furnace and dropped into a well-insulated tank containing 100 lb of water at 70°F. The temperature of the water rises 12°F. What is the temperature of the furnace?

5–43. The volume of gas at atmospheric pressure is 200 cu in. when the temperature is 20°C. What is the volume when the temperature is 50°C and the pressure is 80 cm of mercury?

5–44. The internal energy of a gas is given by $u=0.08t+0.002t^2$, where $t=$°F. The coefficient of t is 0.08 ft-lb/(lb)(°F). The coefficient of t^2 is 0.002 ft-lb/(lb)(°F^2). If 1 lb of this gas expands without heat flow but with a temperature drop from 300°F to 100°F, how much work is done?

5–45. A volume of gas having an initial entropy of 3000 Btu/°R is heated at a constant temperature of 1000°F until the entropy is 4500 Btu/°R. How much heat is added?

5–46. In drilling a hole in a block of iron whose weight is 1.6 lb, power is supplied at the rate of 0.80 hp for 3 min. If three-fourths of the energy supplied heats the iron, how much heat (Btu) is produced? Find its change in temperature. Specific heat of iron is 0.12 Btu/(lb) (°F).

5–47. A cylindrically shaped aluminum kettle has a uniform thickness of 0.25 in. with an inside diameter of 8 in. One gallon of water having a temperature of 20°C is placed in the kettle, and the kettle is placed on an electric stove. Assume that the stove is turned on and set to keep the temperature next to the kettle at 105°C while inside the kettle under the water the temperature is 103°C and remains constant. Determine (a) the depth of the water in the kettle, in inches, (b) the heat being conducted through the bottom of the kettle to the water, in Btu per second, (c) the time required to just bring the water to boiling.

5–48. In a scientific investigation an airplane attained an altitude where the atmospheric pressure was 13.73 in. of mercury and the temperature was minus 40°F. If the weight-density of air is 0.081 lb/cu ft at 29.92 in. of mercury and 32°F, what was the weight-density of the air at the altitude reached by the airplane? Assume the usual gas laws to apply.

5–49. Steam expands behind a piston doing 50,000 ft-lb of work. If 12 Btu of heat is radiated to the surrounding atmosphere during the expansion, what is the change of internal energy?

5–50. To measure the speed of a bullet, two cardboard disks mounted on a long straight shaft are rotated at 1200 rpm. The bullet is fired through the disks along a line parallel to the shaft. If the disks are 3 ft apart, and the holes made by the bullet have an angular displacement of 15°, find the speed of the bullet.

5–51. If steel rails 39 ft in length are placed when the temperature is 50°F, how much space must be left between two adjacent rails if the rails are to touch when the temperature rises to 130°F? Coefficient of expansion of steel is 6.5×10^{-6}/°F.

5–52. How much heat is conducted in 12 hr through a glass pane of 20 sq ft in area and ¼-in. thick if the surfaces are 60°F and 20°F? Conductivity of glass is 4.0 Btu in./hr ft^2°F.

5–53. A Carnot engine operates with reservoir temperatures of 212°F and 100°F. What is the efficiency of the engine?

5–54. A tuning fork of 512 frequency makes 2 beats/sec with a vibrating string. Tightening the string eliminates the beats so that the fork and the string vibrate in unison. Find in what proportion the tension in the string was increased?

5–55. It is desired to determine the depth of a vertical shaft sunk into the ground. A rock is released into the shaft from the ground level, and the sound of the rock striking the bottom is heard at the end of 4 sec. If the velocity of sound is 1100 fps, what is the depth of the shaft?

5–56. A sidewalk is to be illuminated by lamps 20 ft from the ground and spaced so that the light midway between the lamps on the sidewalk is one-fourth of that immediately beneath the lamps. Determine the spacing. For the purpose of this problem assume that reflectors are not used.

5–57. An aeroplane is flying toward a stationary point from which a sound at constant frequency of 420 cps is being broadcast. The frequency of the sound as received on the plane is 500 cps. Calculate the speed of the plane, in feet per second. The velocity of sound in air is assumed to be 1100 fps.

5–58. The weight-density of steel is 490 lb/cu ft, and Young's modulus for steel is 29×10^6 lb/sq in. What is the speed of sound, in feet per second, in steel rails?

5–59. An underwater explosion occurs at some distance from you but in a location which cannot be seen from your position. The sound of the explosion coming to you through the air is heard 16 sec after the same sound coming through the water. Assuming that sound travels 1100 fps in air and 4800 fps in water, how far away from you was the explosion, in miles?

5–60. An object is placed 2 ft to the left of a convex lens whose focal length is 6 in. Determine the location of the image and the magnification.

5–61. A converging lens has a focal length of 20 cm. Determine (a) the power of this lens, in *diopters,* (b) the location of the image of a small object placed 10 cm in front of this lens, (c) the relative size of the image to the object, and (d) whether the image is *real* or *virtual.*

5–62. A double convex lens of glass with an index of refraction of 1.574 has surfaces with radii of curvature of 50 cm and 100 cm. What is the focal length of the lens?

5–63. An object 1 in. tall is placed 2.5 in. away from a concave mirror whose radius of curvature is 10 in. Find the image distance and image size.

5–64. The apparent depth of an object below the water surface is one meter when viewed from above the surface at an incident angle of 30° from the vertical. What is the actual depth?

5–65. A certain drafting room table is illuminated by two 500-watt lamps, each having an output of 10,050 lumens. The lamps are 6 ft above the horizontal table-top level and are spaced 12 ft apart. Determine the illumination, in foot-candles, on the table (a) at a point directly beneath one of the lamps and (b) at a point midway between the lamps.

5–66. A light source of 16 candlepower is placed 20 ft from a screen. How far on the opposite side of the screen should a source of 36 candlepower be placed so that each side of the screen has equal illumination?

5–67. Find the current in the 20-volt generator in the circuit.

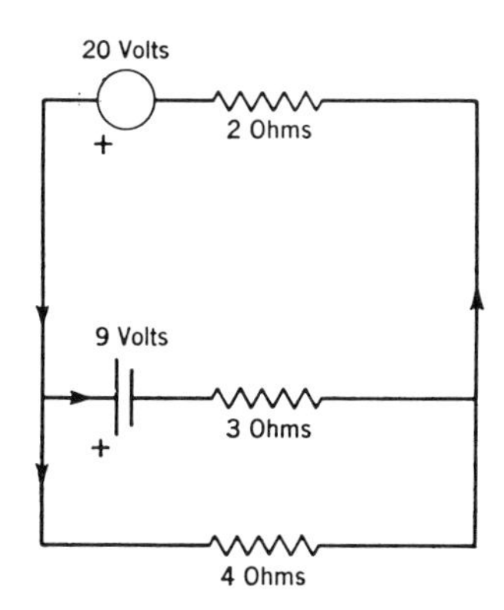

Problem 5–67.

5–68. Show diagrammatically how to connect (a) a 3-ohm, a 5-ohm, and a 6-ohm resistor in order for the combination to have a resistance of 7 ohms and (b) a 3-μf, a 5-μf, and a 6-μf capacitor in order for the combination to have a capacitance of 7 μf.

5–69. Calculate the cost per hour to light a room at 5 cents kwhr if six 60-watt lamps are used.

5–70. Two resistances of 6 and 8 ohms are connected in parallel across a line of unknown voltage. If the total current is 40 amp, what is (a) the current in each resistor and (b) the line voltage?

5–71. Find the resonant frequency of a series circuit consisting of a 0.005-μf capacitor and a 10-mh inductance.

5–72. When a certain coil is connected to a 60-volt battery, 2 amp of current flows. When the same coil is connected to a 50-

volt 60-cps a-c source, only 1 amp flows. What is the inductance of the coil, in henrys?

5–73. A 100-cm slide-wire bridge in which R_1 is a resistance of 120 ohms is found to balance when l_1=30 cm. What is the value of the resistance R_2?

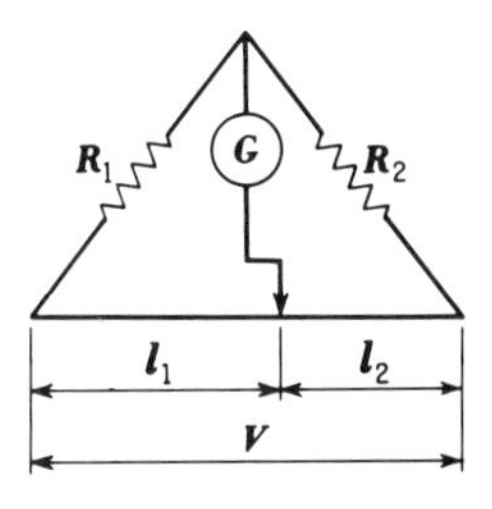

Problem 5–73.

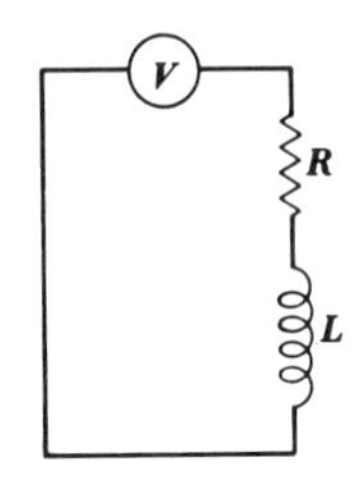

Problem 5–74.

5–74. In the circuit shown (Fig. 5-74) the applied voltage is 170 sin 120πt. The resistance R has a value of 100 ohms, and the inductance L has a value of 0.265 henrys. What is the reactance of the circuit? What is the phase angle?

5–75. A 60-plate condenser has plates 40 cm by 60 cm separated by glass plates 2 mm thick of dielectric constant 7.0. What is the capacitance in microfaradays?

5–76. A 2-volt, d-c source is placed across the terminals of a two-wire conductor which has been short-circuited. The two wires of the conductor have a resistance of 10.15 ohms/1000 ft. The current is measured in the circuit and found to be 1.0 amp. How far from the conductor terminals is the short circuit?

5–77. The photoelectric threshold of a metal is 273 mμ. Determine the maximum kinetic energy of the electrons ejected from the surface of this metal by ultraviolet light of wavelength 200 mμ.

5–78. If 50 cm of a straight conductor are at right angles to a uniform magnetic field of 0.5 webers/sq m, what current must flow in the conductor in order that the force on this section be 4 newtons?

5–79. A pulse of radiation is sent out by a radar set and a reflection received 60μ sec later. How far away is the object that produced the reflection?

5–80. A certain body has a surface with a reflectivity of 0.6 at 600°C. What is the emissive power of this body at 600°C?

Strength of Materials 6

Problem arrangement is generally in the following order, although some problems could not be assigned a definite classification because multiple answers were required: load, stresses and deformations, shear and moment diagrams, torsion, columns, trusses, beams, and bents. Standard design codes (AISC, ACI, etc.) were used when the conditions of the problems were not stated. When assumptions were necessary, every effort was made to note them in the solutions or answers. It must be remembered that in design problems several methods of solution are sometimes possible, although they may all arrive at the same or similar results. One method of solution is shown for 20 typical examples.

6–1. A steel rod in a given structure is 18 ft long and is to carry a 7-ton load. If the elongation of the steel rod is limited to 0.075 in. and the modulus of elasticity for steel is 33,000,000 psi, determine (a) the area of the rod which should be used and (b) the load which would cause the rod which was specified in part (a) to exceed its ultimate strength of 71,000 psi.

Solution: (a) $e=\dfrac{Pl}{AE}$ $\quad a=\dfrac{14{,}000(216)}{(0.075)(33\times10^6)}=1.22 \text{ sq in.}$

(b) $P=71{,}000(1.22)=86{,}600 \text{ lb}$

6–2. A load of 10,000 lb is hung on a steel block A, which hangs from a piercing block B, resting on blocks C and D. Block A is $1\frac{1}{4}$ in. × 3 in.; B is 1 in. × $1\frac{1}{2}$ in.; C and D are each $\frac{3}{4}$ in. × $1\frac{1}{2}$ in. Calculate the unit stresses, in pounds per square inch, for the (a) maximum tension in A, (b) maximum compression in A, (c) maximum shear in A, (d) maximum shear in B, (e) maximum compression in B.

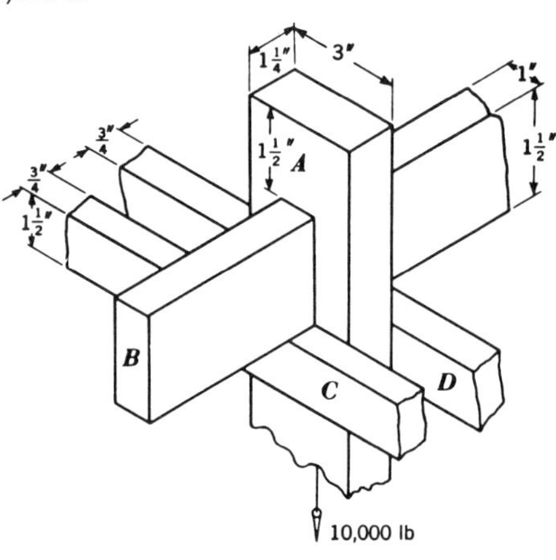

Problem 6–2.

Solution:

(a) $\sigma = \dfrac{10{,}000}{1.25(3) - 1.25(1)} = 4000$ psi

(b) $\sigma = \dfrac{10{,}000}{1(1.25)} = 8000$ psi

(c) $v = \dfrac{10{,}000}{2(1.5)(1.25)} = 2666$ psi

(d) $v = \dfrac{10{,}000}{2(1.5)(1)} = 3330$ psi

(e) $\sigma = \dfrac{10{,}000}{1.25(1)} = 8000$ psi

6–3. A slab of concrete is 20 ft long on a winter day when the temperature is −10°F. If this slab has an ultimate compressive strength of 3500 psi, a thermal coefficient of 6.2×10^{-6}, and a modulus of elasticity of 2.5×10^{6}, determine (a) the increase in length of this slab on a day when the temperature is 90°F and the slab is free to expand and (b) the compressive stress in the concrete slab if abutments at its ends permit only one-half of the previously determined expansion.

Solution:

(a) $e = nl\,(\Delta t) = (6.2 \times 10^{-6})(20 \times 12)(100) = 0.149$ in.

(b) $2\sigma = En(\Delta t) = (2.5 \times 10^{6})(6.2 \times 10^{-6})(100) \qquad \sigma = 775$ psi

6–4. A $3 \times 3 \times \frac{1}{2}\angle$ is to be welded to each side of a gusset plate as shown. Design the size and length of welds necessary to safely hold a total tension force of 88,000 lb. The allowable shearing stress in the weld is 11,300 psi; $x = 0.98$ in.

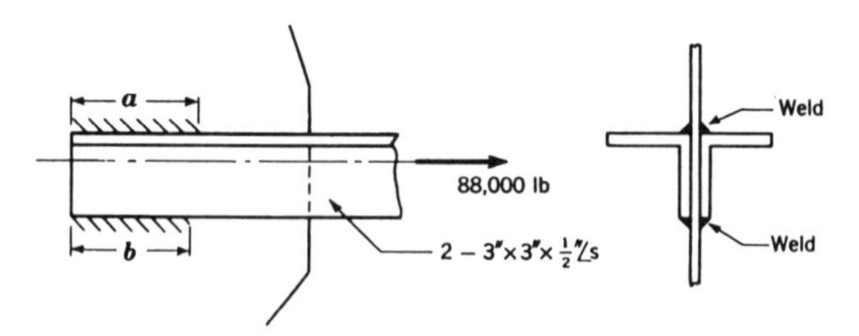

Problem 6–4.

Solution: $T = 0.707D$

$$s = 11{,}300(0.707D) = 8000D = \frac{3}{8}(8000) = 3000 \text{ lb/in.}$$

$$a = \frac{Px}{sc} = \frac{44{,}000(0.98)}{3000(3)} = 4.79 \text{ in.} + \text{returns}$$

$$b = \frac{P(c-x)}{sc} = \frac{44{,}000(2.02)}{9000} = 9.9 \text{ in.} + \text{returns}$$

6–5. A tension member is made up of 3/8 in. thick steel plates 9 in. wide and spliced by a lap joint made with three rows of 3/4-in. rivets arranged in the pattern shown. The permissible stresses in the rivets and plates are 20,000 psi for tension in the net section, 16,000 psi for shear, and 32,000 psi for bearing. (a) Find the maximum permissible tension in the plates. (b) Find the efficiency of the joint.

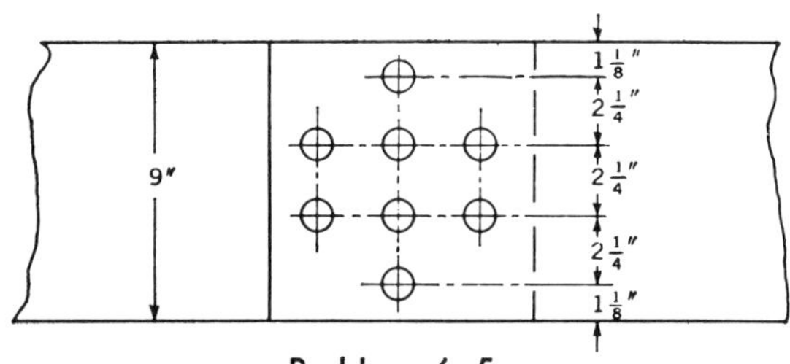

Problem 6–5.

Solution: Using 3/4 in. rivets and 7/8 in. design hole diameter,

(a) $$P_t = [9 - 2(0.875)](0.375)(20{,}000) = 54{,}300 \text{ lb (governs)}$$

$$P_s = 8\left(\frac{0.75^2}{4}\right)\pi(16{,}000) = 56{,}500 \text{ lb}$$

$$P_b = 8(0.75)(0.375)(32{,}000) = 72{,}000 \text{ lb}$$

(b) $$P_{\text{plate}} = 9(0.375)(20{,}000) = 67{,}500 \text{ lb}$$

$$\text{Efficiency} = \frac{54{,}300}{67{,}500} \times 100 = 80.5 \text{ per cent}$$

6–6. A 6-in.-diameter core (i.e., an axial hole of 3 in. radius) is bored out of a 9-in. solid circular shaft. What percentage of the torsional strength is lost by the operation?

Solution: $$J_s = \frac{\pi d^4}{32} = \frac{\pi(9)^4}{32} = 644 \text{ in.}^4 \qquad J_h = \frac{\pi}{32}(9^4 - 6^4) = 516 \text{ in.}^4$$

$$\text{Per cent reduction} = \frac{644 - 516}{644}(100) = 20$$

6–7. A steel shaft is to transmit 50 hp at 200 rpm. The modulus of elasticity in shear is 12,000,000 psi and the diameter of the shaft is 2 in. Find the maximum shearing stress in the shaft and the angle of twist per foot of length of the shaft.

Solution: $$50 = \frac{T(2\pi)(200)}{12(33{,}000)} \qquad T = 15{,}750 \text{ ft lb}$$

$$\tau_{\max} = \frac{Tc}{J} = \frac{15{,}750(1)(32)}{\pi(16)} = 10{,}000 \text{ psi}$$

$$\theta = \frac{Tl}{GJ} = \frac{15{,}750(12)(32)}{12(10^6)(\pi)(16)} = 0.01 \text{ radian}$$

6–8. A pulley 8 ft in diameter is mounted on a 2½-in. shaft. and rotates at 180 rpm, transmitting power to a belt. If the belt tensions are 1800 and 1200 lb, determine (a) horsepower transmitted, (b) maximum shearing stress in the shaft.

Solution:

$$T_{\text{net}} = 2400 \text{ ft lb}$$

(a)

$$\text{hp} = \frac{2400(12)(\pi)(180)}{198{,}000} = 82.2$$

(b)

$$J = \frac{\pi(39.1)}{32} = 3.84 \text{ in.}^4$$

$$\tau = \frac{2400(12)(16)}{\pi(2.5)^3} = 9390 \text{ psi}$$

6–9. A round column 24 in. in diameter has fourteen #11 bars placed in a circular pattern 18½ in. in diameter. The column carries an axial load of 300^k and a bending moment of $70'^k$. Find (a) the maximum unit stresses in the concrete and the steel and (b) the minimum stress in the concrete by using ACI tables.

Solution:

$$A_s = 14(1.56) = 21.8 \text{ sq in.} \qquad N = 300^k$$

$$A_g = 3.14(144) = 452 \text{ sq in.} \qquad M = 70'^k$$

$$t = 24 \text{ in.} \qquad g = \frac{18.5}{24} = 0.772 \qquad f_c' = 3000 \text{ psi}$$

$$e' = \frac{12M}{N} = 2.8 \text{ in.}$$

$$\frac{e}{t} = \frac{2.8}{24} = 0.117$$

$$np = \frac{10A_s}{A_g} = 0.483 \qquad g \cong 0.8$$

$$\frac{1000N}{f_c t^2} = 0.65 \qquad k > 1$$

$$f_c = \frac{1000(300)}{0.65(576)} = 800 \text{ psi}$$

$$f_s = 10(800)\left(\frac{1+0.772}{2} - 1\right) = 915 \text{ psi}$$

6–10. A 12-in.-ID pipe is made of 1.8-in. steel plate fastened by a single row of ½-in.-diameter rivets spaced 3 in. apart. There is sufficient end distance to prevent tearing of the plate, and the bending effects on the rivet are negligible. Allowable stresses are as follows: shear, 10,000 psi; tension, 16,000 psi; and bearing, 24,000 psi. What hydraulic pressure is allowable?

Solution:

P = rivet joint value, in pounds

p = unit pressure, in pounds per square inch

$A_R = 0.2$ sq in.

$P_s = 10{,}000(0.2) = 2000$ lb

$P_b = 24{,}000(0.125)(0.5) = 1500$ lb (controls)

$P_t = (3 - 0.625)(0.125)(16{,}000) = 4750$ lb

$\Sigma F_H = 0 \qquad 3(12)p = 2(1500) \qquad p = 83.3$ psi

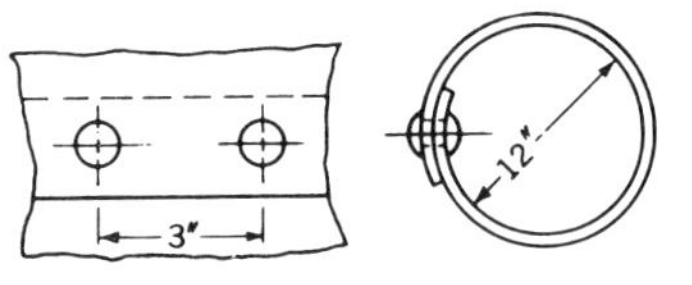

Problem 6–10.

6–11. Given the beam cross section shown. Total vertical shear on section is 40,000 lb. Bending moment at section is 120,000 ft-lb. What are the maximum and minimum unit stresses at point A? Point A is at the junction of flange and web, but in the web on the bottom of the beam.

Solution:

$$I_{\text{N.A.}} = 2\left[\frac{8(1)^3}{12} + 8(5.5)^2\right] + \frac{0.5(10)^3}{12} = 527 \text{ in.}^4$$

$$\sigma = \frac{Mc}{I} = \frac{120{,}000(12)(5)}{527} = 13{,}650 \text{ psi}$$

$$v = \frac{V}{t_w(d - 2tf)} = \frac{40{,}000}{0.5(12-2)} = 8000 \text{ psi}$$

$$v_{\max} = \frac{\sigma}{2} \leftrightarrow \tau = \frac{13{,}650}{2} \leftrightarrow 8000 = 10{,}500 \text{ psi}$$

$$\sigma_{\max \text{ or } \min} = \frac{\sigma}{2} \pm \left(\frac{\sigma}{2} \leftrightarrow \tau\right) = \frac{13{,}650}{2} \pm 10{,}500$$

$$= 17{,}325 \text{ psi maximum or } 3675 \text{ psi minimum}$$

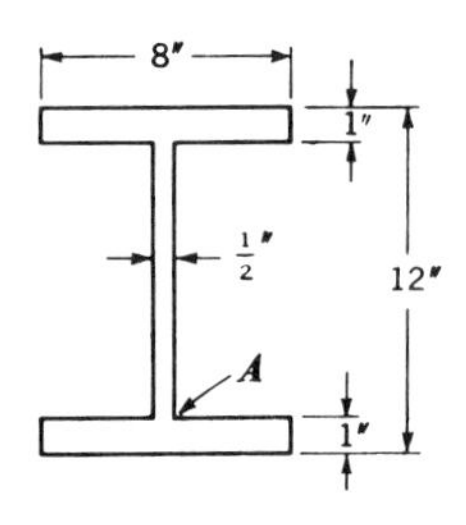

Problem 6–11.

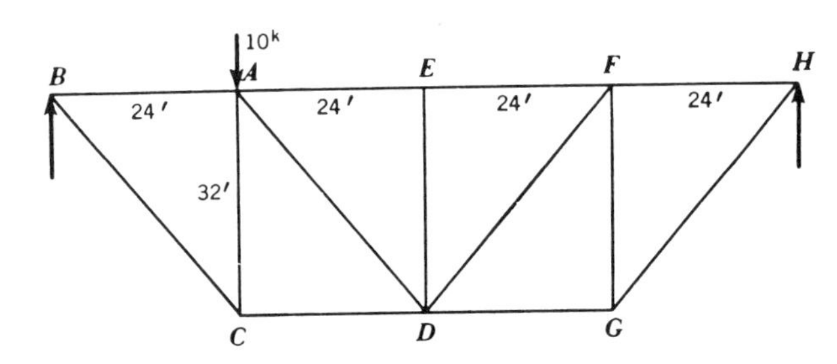

Problem 6–12.

6–12. Given a simple truss with loads and dimensions as shown. Find stresses in the members AC, AD, and AE.

Solution: $R_B = 7.5^k$ $R_H = 2.5^k$

$BC = {}^{40}/_{32}(7.5) = +9.38^k$ $AD = {}^{40}/_{32}(10 - 7.5) = -3.12^k$

$BA = {}^{24}/_{40}(9.38) = -5.63^k$ $AE = 5.63 - {}^{24}/_{40}(3.125) = -3.75^k$

$AC = {}^{32}/_{40}(9.38) = -7.5^k$

6–13. A pin-connected truss is loaded as shown. (a) Find the direction and magnitude of the reactions. (b) Solve for the force in each member. The length of each member is 10 ft.

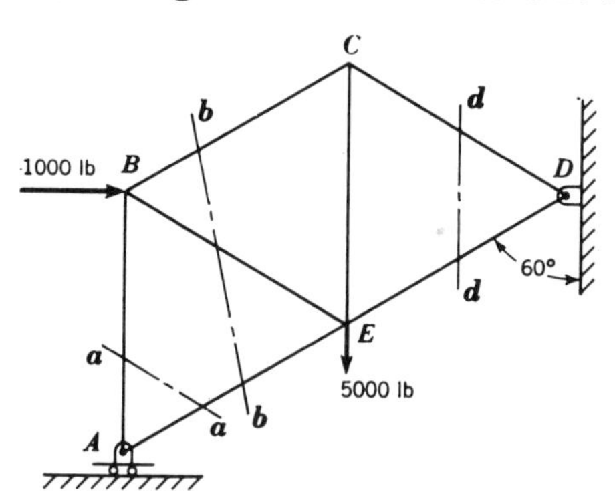

Problem 6–13.

Solution: (a)

$\Sigma M_D = 0$

$$17.32A_V = 8.66(5000) \qquad A_V = 2500 \text{ lb}$$

$\Sigma F_V = 0$

$$2500 + D_V - 5000 = 0 \qquad D_V = 2500 \text{ lb}$$

$\Sigma F_H = 0$

$$1000 - D_H = 0 \qquad D_H = 1000 \text{ lb}$$

(b) Section a–a

$\Sigma M_E = 0$

$(8.66)AB - 8.66(2500) = 0$

$AB = -2500$ lb

$\Sigma M_B = 0$

$8.66AE = 0$

$AE = 0$

Section b–b

$\Sigma M_E = 0$

$8.66BC - 5(1000) - 8.66(2500) = 0$

$BC = -3080$ lb

$\Sigma M_C = 0$

$8.66(2500) - 5(1000) - 8.66BE = 0$

$BE = +1915$ lb

Section d–d

$\Sigma M_C = 0$

$8.66ED + 5(1000) - 8.66(2500) = 0$

$ED = +1915$ lb

$\Sigma M_E = 0$

$8.66CD - 2500(8.66) - 5(1000) = 0$

$CD = -3080$ lb

Joint C

$CE = +3080$ lb

6–14. Where does the maximum bending moment occur in a beam with a 24-ft span that carries a load of 24,000 lb uniformly spread over its entire length and a further load of 12 tons uniformly spread over a section that starts 6 ft from the left support and extends 8 ft to the right? What is the maximum moment?

Solution:

$$R_R = 12{,}000 + 24{,}000(10/24) = 22{,}000 \text{ lb}$$
$$R_L = 12{,}000 + 24{,}000(14/24) = 26{,}000 \text{ lb}$$
$$M_6 = 26[6] - 1(6)(3) = 138'^{k}$$
$$M_{11} = M_{max} = 23(6) + 10(5) = 188'^{k}$$
$$M_{max} = 188'^{k}, \quad 11 \text{ ft from left end}$$

6–15. For the loaded beam shown, (a) calculate the magnitude of the reactions and (b) draw a shear and moment diagram with all principal points indicated. (c) What is the required section modulus of the beam if the maximum stress is 20,000 psi?

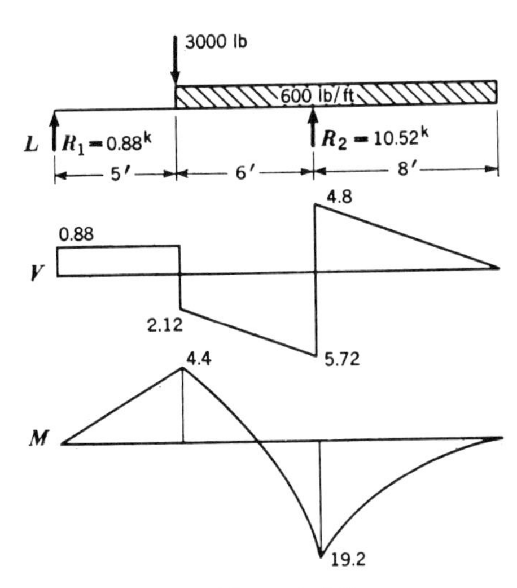

Problem 6–15.

Solution: (a)

$$11R_2 = 3(5) + 0.6(14)(12) \qquad R_2 = 10.52^{k}$$
$$11R_1 + 0.6(14)(1) = 3(6) \qquad R_1 = 0.88^{k}$$

(b)

$$M_{max} = +4.4'^{k} \qquad M_{max} = -19.2'^{k}$$

(c)

$$\frac{I}{C} = \frac{M}{\sigma} = \frac{19.2(12{,}000)}{20{,}000} = 11.52 \text{ in.}^3$$

6–16. A horizontal beam 30 ft long is simply supported at the right end and at a point 10 ft from the left end. It carries a concentrated load of 16^{k} located 10 ft from the right end and a load that varies uniformly from zero at the left end to 600 lb/ft at the right end. Neglect the beam weight. (a) Calculate the reactions. (b) Draw the shear and moment diagrams. (c) Determine position and the amount of maximum shear and moment.

Solution:

$$\text{Total load} = \frac{600(30)}{2} = W = 9000 \text{ lb}$$

$$R_A = R_B = \frac{9000}{2} + \frac{16{,}000}{2} = 12{,}500 \text{ lb}$$

$$M_{\max} = 98{,}334 \text{ ft lb midway between reactions}$$

$$V_{\max} = 12{,}500 \text{ lb at right reaction}$$

6–17. (a) Determine the reactions and draw the shear and moment diagrams for the beam shown. (b) Select an economical steel I beam to carry the loads. (c) Determine the deflection under the left 2000-lb load.

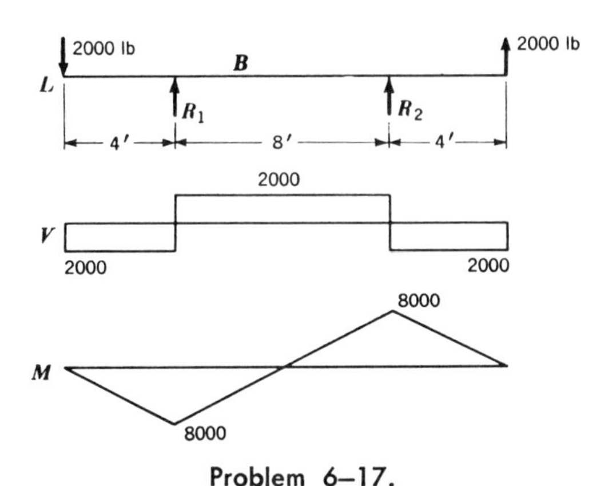

Problem 6–17.

Solution: (a) $R_1 = R_2 = 4^k \qquad M_{\max} = 8000$ ft-lb

(b)
$$\frac{I}{C}\text{required} = \frac{8000(12)}{20{,}000} = 4.8 \text{ in.}^3$$

5I10 lb $\quad \frac{I}{C} = 4.8$ not including beam weight

5I14.75 lb $\quad \frac{I}{C} = 6.0$

$$M = 8000 + 4(14.75) = 8059 \text{ ft lb}$$

$$\frac{M}{\sigma} = \frac{8059(12)}{20{,}000} = 4.84 < 6.0$$

5I10 lb $\quad \frac{I}{C} = 4.8 \sim 4.82$ required

(c)
$$EI\theta_B = \frac{32}{3}\left(\frac{12}{2}\right)\left(\frac{16}{3}\right)\left(\frac{1}{12}\right) - \frac{8(12)}{2}\left(\frac{2}{3}\right) = -3.6$$

$$EI\Delta_B = 3.6(4) + \frac{8(4)}{2}\left(\frac{2}{3}\right)(4) = 57.1$$

$$\Delta_B = \frac{57.1(1728)(1000)}{(30 \times 10^6)(12.1)}$$

$$\Delta_B = 0.27 \text{ in.}$$

6–18. Calculate the maximum deflection and the slope of the deflection curve at the ends for the following steel beam: It has a rectangular cross section 2 in. wide and 6 in. deep; assume that P is 3000 lb and w is 60 lb/ft.

Solution:

$$I = \frac{bd^3}{12} = \frac{2(216)}{12} = 36 \text{ in.}^4$$

$$M = \frac{wl^2}{8} + \frac{pl}{4} = \frac{60(100)}{8} + \frac{3000(10)}{4} = 8250 \text{ ft lb}$$

$$EI\theta_A = 750(5)(2/3) + \frac{7500(5)}{2} = 21{,}250$$

$$EI\Delta_C = 21{,}250(5) - 2500(5)(0.375) - 18{,}750(5/3)$$

$$EI\Delta_C = 70{,}360$$

$$\theta_A = \frac{21{,}250(144)}{(30 \times 10^6)(36)} = 0.00283 \text{ radian}$$

$$\Delta_C = \frac{70{,}360(1728)}{(30 \times 10^6)(36)} = 0.112 \text{ in.}$$

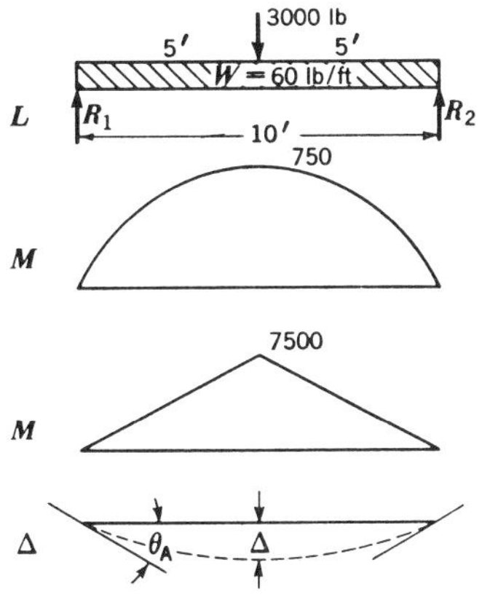

Problem 6–18.

6–19. A commercial 2 in. × 10 in. wooden beam has a 10-ft clear span and carries a concentrated load 2 ft from one support. Assume adequate bracing. Allowable stresses are 100 psi in shear and 1100 psi in bending. Find the allowable concentrated load P.

Solution:

$I_{2\times10} = 116 \text{ in.}^4$ $\quad A_{2\times10} = 15.4 \text{ sq in.}$ $\quad S_{2\times10} = 24.4 \text{ in.}^3$

$$M = \frac{P(2)(8)}{10} = 1.6P$$

$$\sigma = \frac{Mc}{I} = 1100 = \frac{1.6P_B(12)(4.75)}{116}$$

$$P_B = 1400 \text{ lb}$$

$$V_{max} = 0.8P$$

$$v_{avg} = \frac{0.8P}{15.4} = 100 \text{ psi}$$

$$P_s = \frac{15.4(100)}{0.8} = 1920 \text{ lb}$$

Problem 6–19.

6–20. A clamp is tightened until the force P is 5000 lb. The cross-section is T-shaped as shown. Find the maximum unit stress at this section.

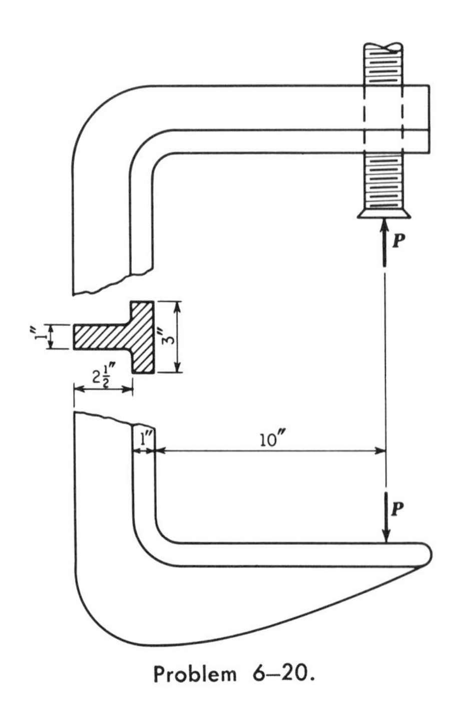

Problem 6–20.

Solution:

$$I_{NA}=5.37 \text{ in.}^4;\ A=5.5 \text{ in.}^2;\ e=11.3 \text{ in.}$$

$$\text{Direct } \sigma=\frac{P}{A}=\frac{5000}{5.5}=910 \text{ psi}$$

$$\text{Bending } \sigma=\frac{Mc}{I}=\frac{5000(11.3)(1.3)}{5.37}=+13{,}700 \text{ psi}$$

$$\sigma=\frac{5000(11.3)(2.2)}{5.37}=-23{,}200 \text{ psi}$$

$$\sigma_{\text{min}}=-22{,}290 \text{ psi}$$

$$\sigma_{\text{max}}=+14{,}610 \text{ psi}$$

6–21. In a loaded horizontal, homogeneous, rectangular beam, the horizontal shearing stresses at any cross section perpendicular to the neutral axis (a) has a maximum value at the outer fibers of the beam, (b) is equal to zero, (c) has a maximum value at the neutral axis and is equal to 1.5 times the average shearing stress at that section, (d) is constant across that section, (e) is none of these.

6–22. (a) Draw a stress-strain diagram for a mild steel. Indicate the following points on the curve: elastic limit; yield point; ultimate strength and approximate magnitude, in pounds per square inch; and failure. (b) For the mild steel used in (a) draw a stress vs. number-of-cycles curve and indicate the approximate endurance limit.

6–23. (a) A test bar of steel 0.50 in. in diameter is stressed to 40,000 psi. Compute the required load for the test. (b) Diameters of commercial steel bars vary by sixteenths of an inch. Allow a maximum stress of 22,000 psi and compute the commercial size which should be used to carry a load of 79,000 lb. (c) A concrete pier 30 in. in diameter carries a load of 300 tons. Compute the unit stress, in pounds per square inch and in tons per square foot.

6–24. A test specimen 0.505 in. in diameter by 2 in. gage length in a tensile machine shows an increase in length of 0.00187 in. with an increase in tension from 2000 to 5000 lb. Calculate the modulus of elasticity.

6–25. One mile of track is welded in one straight length, and the ends are restrained by similar lengths. What total compressive stress would result in each rail if the temperature were 50°F higher than when the rail was laid? The area of cross section is 12.8 sq in., the coefficient of expansion is 0.0000065, and the modulus of elasticity is 30,000,000 psi.

6–26. A rod exactly 10 in. long at 60°F is to be made in two parts, one brass and one aluminum, in such proportions that the length of the rod will change 0.000125 in. for each change of 1°F in temperature. Calculate the lengths of brass and aluminum.

6–27. A solid steel block weighs 49 kips. It rests on a level concrete slab. The block is 10 ft high, 10 ft wide and 1 ft deep. A horizontal force of 6 kips is applied to the top edge perpendicular to the 1-ft side. What are the maximum and minimum pressures under the base in psf?

6–28. A piece of flat steel $\frac{1}{2}$ in. thick is cut in the shape of a right triangle. The hypotenuse is 5 ft long, and one side is 4 ft long. Determine (a) the weight of this piece and (b) the weight of a piece of aluminum having the same dimensions as the steel. (c) Which has the greater tensile strength, aluminum or steel?

6–29. The strength of a beam with rectangular cross section is sd^2, where s is the width and d the depth of the beam. By means of mathematics determine the dimensions of the strongest rectangular beam that can be cut from a 21-in. log. (HINT: $s^2+d^2=D^2=441$.)

6–30. Two wires each 30 in. long and ⅛ in. in diameter support a 400-lb weight. One wire is copper, the other is aluminum. (a) Calculate unit stress in each wire. (b) Calculate the amount of displacement, horizontal and vertical, of the point A (from original taut position before weight was added) where weight is attached.

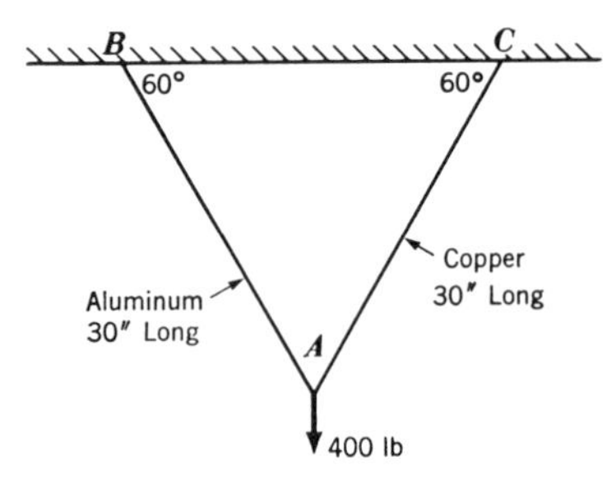

Problem 6–30.

6–31. Find the allowable load P that may be applied to the lever as shown. Pin C does not change its position.

Material	Working Stress (psi)	Area (sq in.)	E
A (aluminum)	20,000	0.200	10×10^6
B (bronze)	15,000	0.400	10×10^6

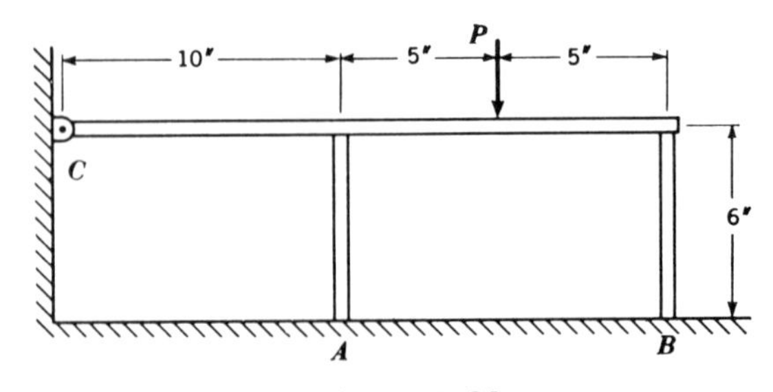

Problem 6–31.

6–32. Two plates 5 in. × ¼ in. are joined by a two-rivet lap joint placed in a single row parallel with the joint. The rivets are

¾ in. in diameter, inserted in punched holes. The allowable stresses are as follows: shear, 12,000 psi; bearing, 30,000 psi; tension, 20,000 psi. Determine the allowable load P for the joint.

6–33. Two rectangular plates, each having a rectangular cross section ½ in. thick by 10 in. wide, are joined by a riveted butt joint that has two cover plates. A load of 60,000 lb is transmitted from one plate to the other plate through rivets. The rivets are ¾ in. in diameter and have working unit stresses as follows: shear, 13,500 psi; tension, 18,000 psi; and bearing, 27,000 psi. (a) How many rivets are needed on each side of the joint? (b) What is the greatest number of rivets that may be placed in one row parallel to the joint?

6–34. A concrete beam is shown on a simple span of 15 ft. It was designed according to 1956 ACI specifications with 3000-lb concrete, $n=10$, and $f_s=18{,}000$ psi. Assuming that the web reinforcement is satisfactory, what concentrated live load may be carried at the center of the span if the deflection due to this load is not to exceed 1/800 of the span?

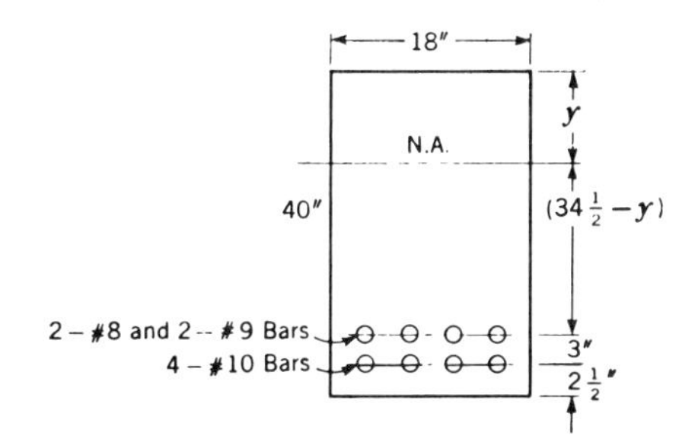

Problem 6–34.

6–35. A gusset plate ½ in. thick supports a 12,000-lb load by means of four rivets as shown. Compute the shearing stress in the least and heaviest loaded rivets.

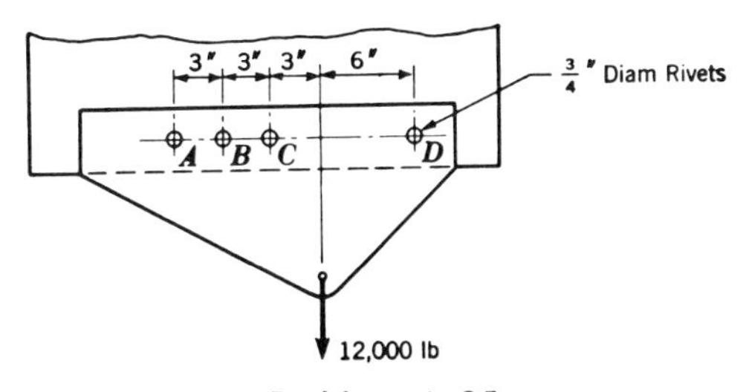

Problem 6–35.

6–36. An A4 standard beam connection is made up of two angles $4 \times 3\frac{1}{2} \times \frac{3}{8}$ in. with 4-in. legs outstanding. Rivets are $\frac{7}{8}$ in. in diameter. What is the tension in the top rivet under a maximum shear loading, assuming the end shear passes through rivet line in the web of the I beam? Shearing unit stress in rivets is 15,000 psi.

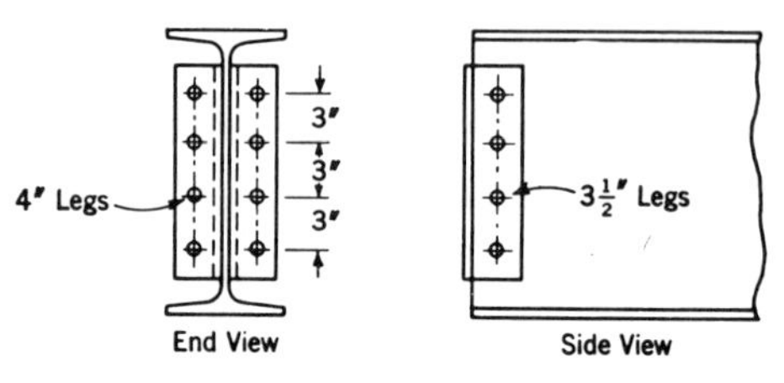

Problem 6–36.

6–37. A solid steel shaft, 8 ft long, is to transmit torque of 20.000 ft-lb. Modulus of elasticity is 12,000,000 psi, and the allowable shearing stress is 10,000 psi. (a) What diameter of shaft is required? (b) What is the angle of twist between the two ends?

6–38. Two line shafts are transmitting power. They are revolving at the same rate (100 rpm) and are subjected to the same maximum shearing stress. Line shaft A is hollow, 4 in. OD, 2 in. ID, and has an area of 9.43 sq in. Shaft B is solid, has a 3.5-in. diameter, and its area is 9.62 sq in. (a) Which shaft is transmitting the greater horsepower, (b) what horsepower is it transmitting? (c) Which shaft twists through the greater angle?

6–39. A hollow steel shaft BC is connected to a solid steel shaft AB. The system is properly supported so that there is no bending. (a) Determine the torque such that the maximum unit shear stress

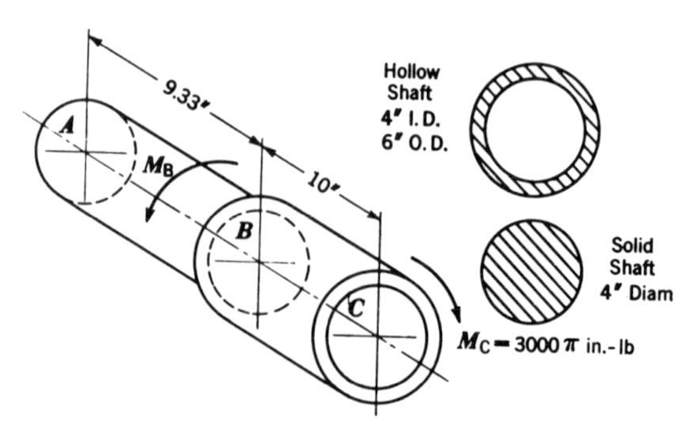

Problem 6–39.

is the same in both parts. Neglect stress concentrations. (b) Determine the angle of twist in *BC*.

6–40. (a) Find the maximum shearing unit stress, due to torque, in a 1-in.-diameter shaft 3 ft long when it is transmitting 5 hp at 1500 rpm, uniform rotation. The polar moment of inertia of a circle is $\pi d^4/32$. (b) Is the unit stress at a given radius, due to torque, constant over the length? (c) How does the unit stress, due to torque, vary from the center of the rod to the outer fiber at a given cross section?

6–41. A certain bearing sustains a load of 12,500 lb. The diameter of the steel shaft is 4.5 in. The speed at which the shaft is turning averages 500 rpm. If the coefficient of friction is 0.012, determine (a) the horsepower required to overcome friction and (b) the Btu of heat generated per hour of operation at the rubbing surfaces.

6–42. (a) What torque, expressed in foot-pounds, is exerted upon a revolving door by a force of 7 lb applied perpendicular to the door at a point 2 ft from its axis of rotation? (b) Two shafts are coupled by means of a belt around two pulleys. The drive shaft has a 20-in. pulley, while the driven shaft has a 30-in. pulley. The taut side of the belt is under 84 lb tension, while the slack side is under only 12 lb tension. What torque is exerted at each pulley? (c) In part (b), when the 30-in. pulley turns at 1000 rpm, what horsepower is being delivered to it?

6–43. A solid steel shaft subjected to torque only is designed for a shearing stress of 8 ksi. A hollow shaft, having the same outside diameter as the solid shaft with an inside diameter of 0.707 times the outer diameter, is subjected to the same torque. (a) What is the unit shearing stress in the hollow shaft? (b) What is the saving in weight?

6–44. A rounded-end steel bar, ½ in. square and 2 ft long, is subjected to an axial compressive load. The modulus of elasticity is 30×10^6 psi, and the proportional elastic limit is 40,000 psi. (a) How great a total load can be applied before the bar buckles? (b) If *E* remains the same, but if the proportional elastic limit were increased to 50,000 psi by means of an alloy, how would the buckling load change?

6–45. A steel column unbraced for a length of 20 ft is made up of a 14WF287 and two cover plates 22 in. × 2 in. Will this column carry a concentrated load of 1250^k placed on the axis of the web of the WF but acting on the inner face of one of the cover plates? Use AISC column formula and method of design. For the WF: $A=84.37$ sq in., $d=16.81$ in., $I_{1\text{-}1}=3912$ in.^{4}, $I_{2\text{-}2}=1466$ in.^{4}, $F_a=17{,}000-0.485(l^2/r^2)$, $F_b=20{,}000$ psi, and $f_a/F_a+f_b/F_b<1.0$.

6–46. A cubic, homogeneous crate weighing 30 tons rests on four supports, one at each corner, made as follows: a solid steel cylinder, 3 in. in diameter, is surrounded by an aluminum tube having an outside diameter of 5 in. and a wall thickness of ¾ in. If the aluminum tube is initially 12 in. long and the steel cylinder is 12.0001 in. long, calculate the load carried by each member, steel and aluminum.

6–47. Steel pipe is used to fabricate a truss. One diagonal member of the truss consists of a standard 1½-in.-diameter pipe (OD=1.900 in., ID=1.610 in.), and it is 5 ft long. Use a suitable column formula (state which is used) and determine the allowable compressive axial load on this pipe.

6–48. A column is to be inserted next to an existing column to take up some of the load. The new column is to be 10 ft long and is to be stressed to 10,000 psi. The column will be shortened sufficiently to be inserted in place by cooling with dry ice. Assuming normal temperature of 70°F, to what temperature should the column be cooled to provide a clearance of $\frac{1}{32}$ in. before insertion and yet to take up its load when brought up to room temperature? Modulus of elasticity is 30×10^6 psi, and the temperature coefficient is 0.0000076.

6–49. A water tank 12 ft in diameter and 10 ft high is constructed of vertical wooden staves held together by ½-in.-diameter steel rods, which are threaded and bolted at joints. The allowable stress in the steel rods is 20,000 psi. Determine the required spacing of the steel rods near the bottom of the tank.

6–50. Design a reinforced-concrete square footing by ACI code for a concrete column 12 in. × 12 in. and carrying a load of 200^k. The footing shall be at least 24 in. thick to provide for sufficient embedment of column dowels. Use deformed bars and an allowable soil bearing value of 2 tons/sq ft. Specifications 20,000–3000–10.

6–51. The stresses at a point in a stressed body are $s_x=20{,}000$ psi in tension, $s_y=8000$ psi compression. (a) Determine the maximum shear stress and the angle of the plane on which it acts measured from the x axis. (b) Determine the normal and shearing stresses on a plane inclined 30° to the x axis.

6–52. For the truss shown, determine values for reactions and stresses in the members under the loading noted. The members of the truss form equilateral triangles and the loads are perpendicular to the inclined member.

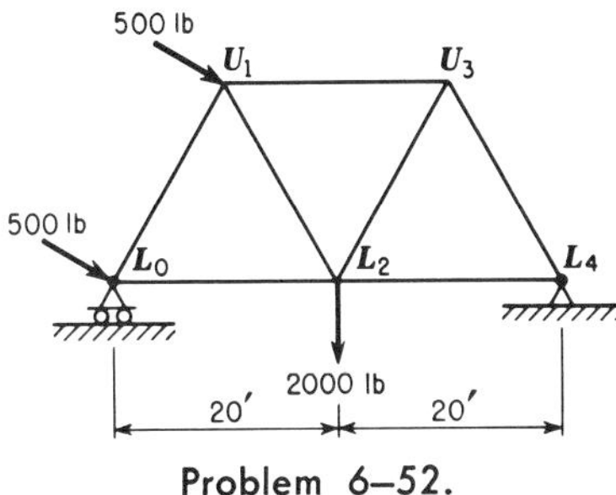

Problem 6–52.

6–53. The diagram shown is used to find the maximum shearing stress in a member that is in combined tension, torsion, and circumferential tension (i.e., a pipe under pressure with torsion and axial tension applied). (a) Derive the equation for the maximum shearing stress from this diagram in terms of $S_{s\max}$=maximum shearing stress, S_s=stress due to torsion, S_x=stress due to pure tension, S_y=stress due to circumferential tension. (b) Draw a stress diagram for a unit area of the external pipe surface.

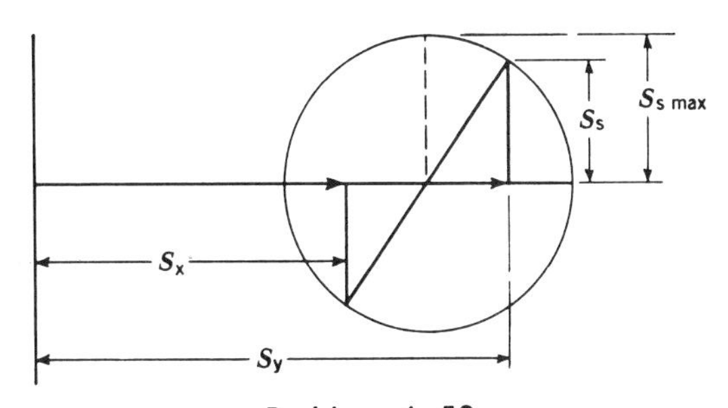

Problem 6–53.

6–54. A 4 ft long pipe made of steel has a 1-in. OD and a ½-in. ID. It acts as a spreader bar in the arrangement shown. If cables and connections are properly designed, what pull P may be safely applied to the assembly?

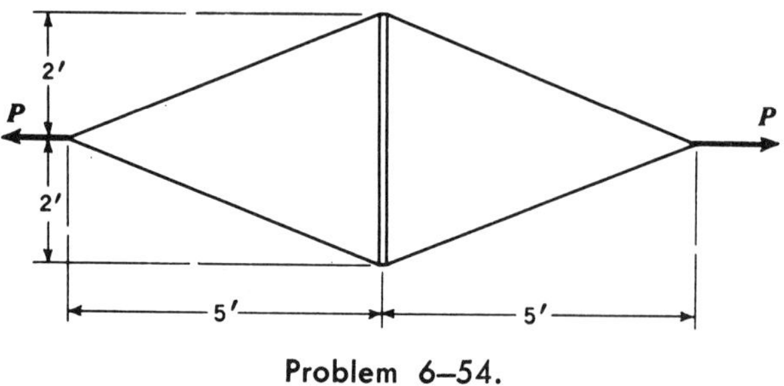

Problem 6–54.

6–55. A weight is supported on a bracket made from circular mild-steel rods as shown in the side and plan views. Calculate the diameter of the rods required for AB, BC, and BD for the following situation: $AB=12$ ft, $BC=BD=4$ ft. Distance between C and D is 4 ft.

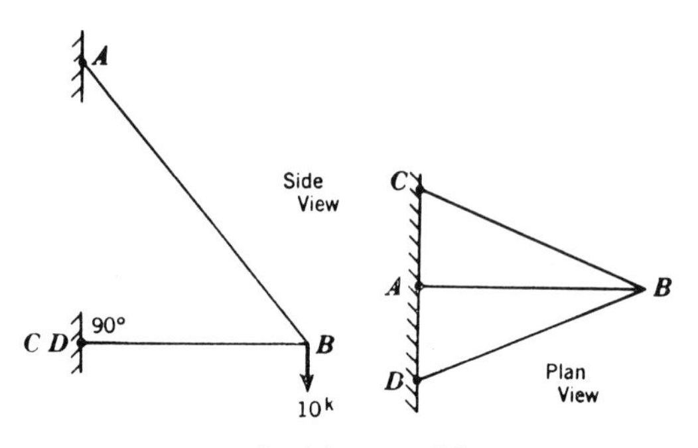

Problem 6–55.

6–56. Determine the force in each member of the frame shown and indicate whether in compression or tension.

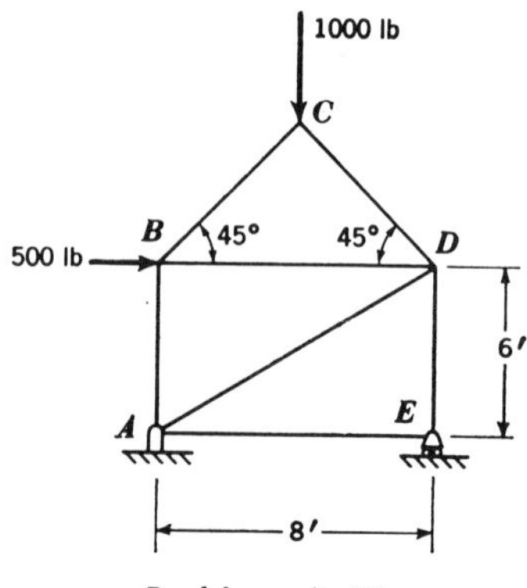

Problem 6–56.

6–57. Draw a sketch of the truss shown and indicate the bars in which there is zero stress under the loads given. Also indicate which bars are in tension and which are in compression without computing the magnitudes of the stresses.

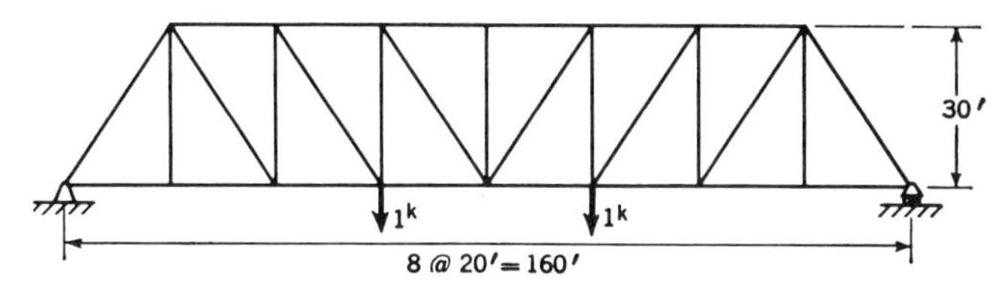

Problem 6–57.

6–58. Calculate the forces in *AB, BD,* and *CE,* indicating whether they are in tension or compression.

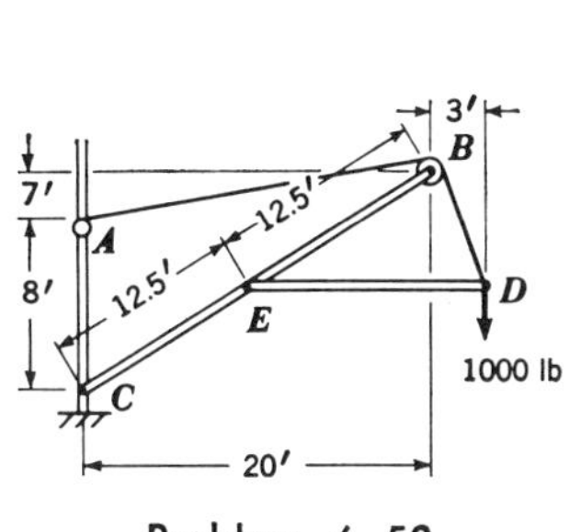

Problem 6–58.

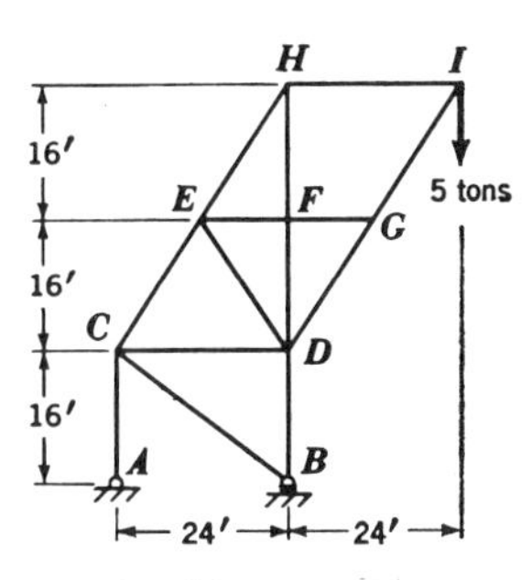

Problem 6–59.

6–59. A crane assembly consisting of pin-connected members is shown schematically. A 5-ton weight is supported by the pin at *I*. Assume the effect of the weight of the members to be negligible. Find the reactions at *A* and *B* and stresses in all members.

6–60. Find the stresses or components of stresses in all the members of the truss shown. Indicate compression or tension as the case may be.

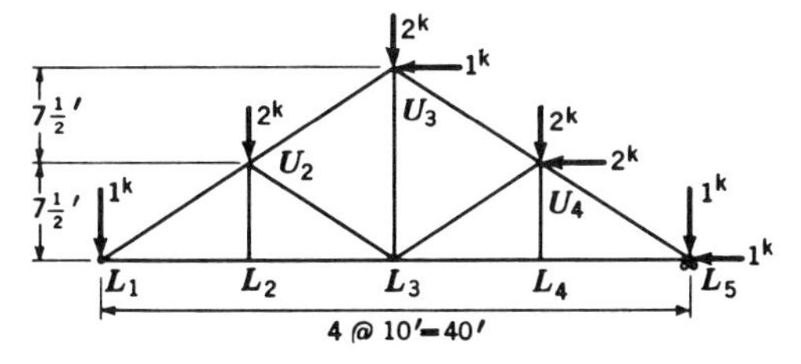

Problem 6–60.

6–61. A 20-in. I beam weighing 80 lb/ft rests on two supports 18 ft apart and is loaded as shown. Find the position of the resultant of all loads and compute the reactions.

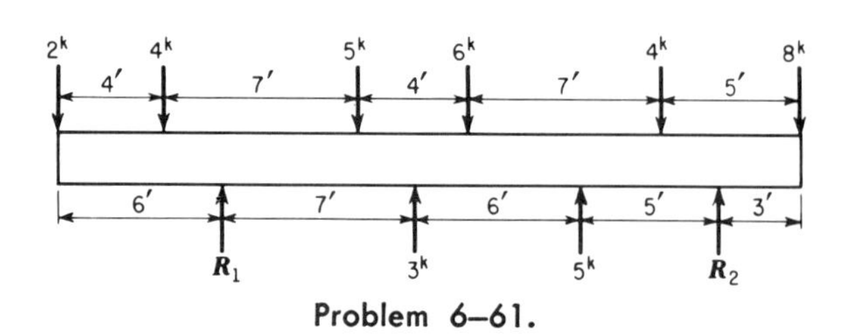

Problem 6–61.

6–62. Determine the magnitude and direction of stress in each member of the truss shown.

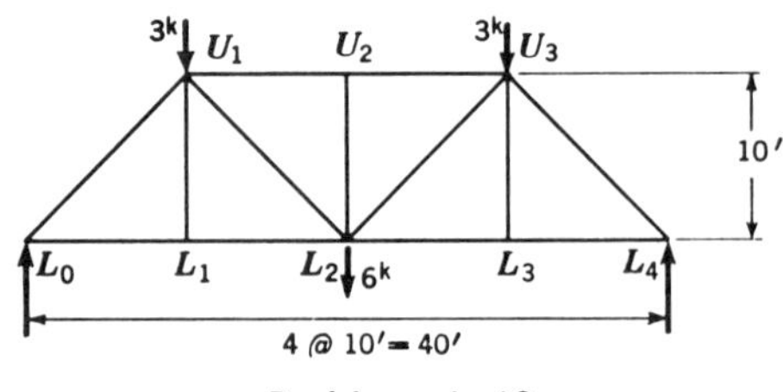

Problem 6–62.

6–63. Find the reactions for the beam, I being uniform.

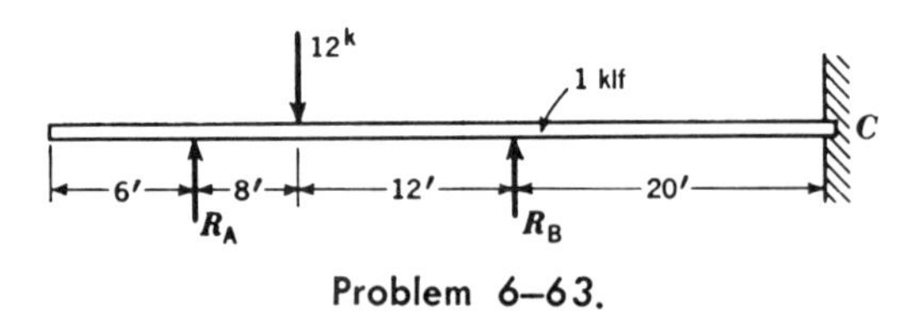

Problem 6–63.

6–64. A cantilever beam 15 ft long is fixed at the left end and carries a uniformly distributed weight of 200 lb/ft and a concentrated load of 3200 lb at a point 8 ft from the right end. (a) Draw the shear diagram. (b) Write two shear equations.

6–65. A beam 20 ft long has two supports, one 5 ft from the left and the other 3 ft from the right end. The beam is carrying a uniformly distributed load of 100 lb/ft and a concentrated load of 2000 lb 9 ft from the right end. (a) Draw the shear diagram and write equations or indicate method used to obtain values on the shear diagram. (b) Draw the moment diagram, pointing out inflection points, and show formulae to obtain points on the curve.

6–66. Which is the proper shape of the moment diagram for the cantilever beam loaded as shown?

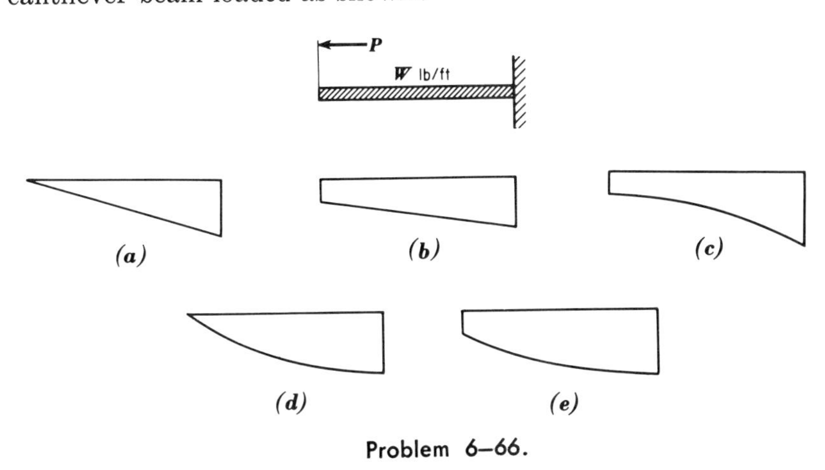

Problem 6–66.

6–67. Draw a shear and moment diagram, locating the points of zero and maximum moment, and determine the values of peak plus and minus moments for the beam described as follows: Loaded with a uniform load of 2 klf and supported 4 ft from the left end of the beam and 2 ft from the right end. The central portion of the beam between reactions is 14 ft long.

6–68. A certain beam 28 ft long is supported at points 6 ft from each end. It carries a uniformly distributed load of 300 lb/ft and a concentrated load of 6000 lb at each end. Write equations and determine (a) the reactions 6 ft from each end and (b) the shear. Draw complete shear diagram to scale.

6–69. A beam 16 ft long is simply supported at the left end and 4 ft from the right end. It carries a uniformly distributed load of 1 klf between supports and two concentrated loads of 3^k each, one at the right end and one 8 ft from the right end. Draw shear and moment diagrams to scale.

6–70. Draw shear and bending moment diagrams for the conditions shown. Give the necessary critical values.

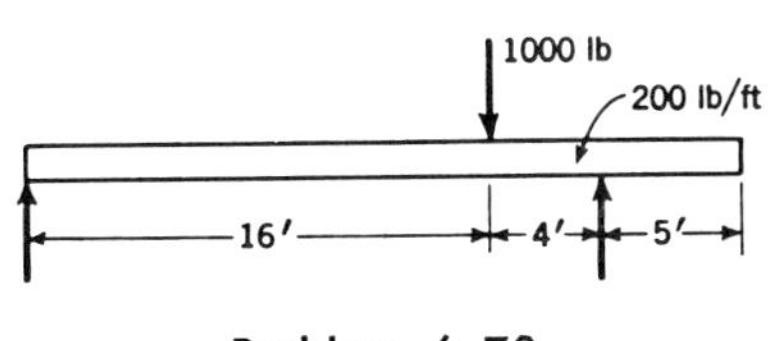

Problem 6–70.

6–71. (a) Draw the shear and moment diagrams for the beam shown. (b) Using a homogeneous steel beam with an allowable unit stress of 20,000 psi, compute the required section modulus.

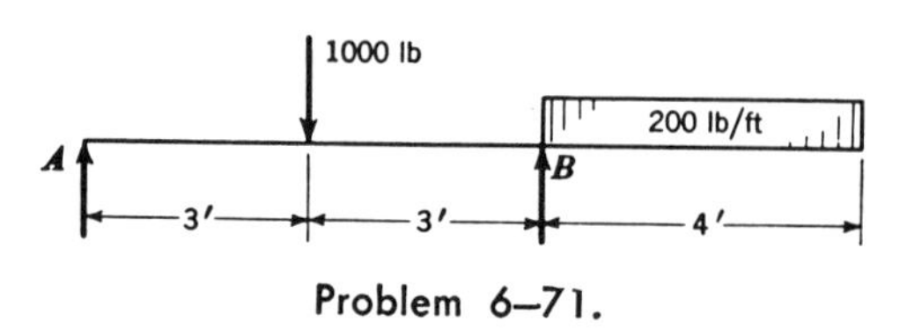

Problem 6–71.

6–72. For the loaded beam shown, (a) calculate the reactions and (b) draw shear and moment diagrams with maximum point values shown. (c) Determine section modulus of the beam if the maximum allowable stress is 20,000 psi.

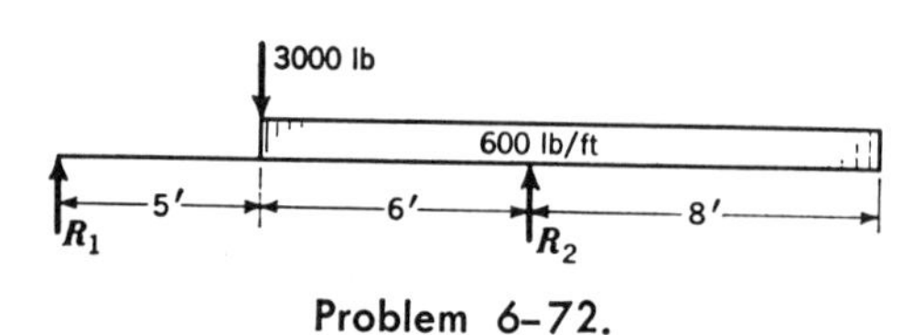

Problem 6–72.

6–73. Draw a moment diagram and a shear diagram for the beam loaded as shown. Indicate the magnitude of the maximum moment.

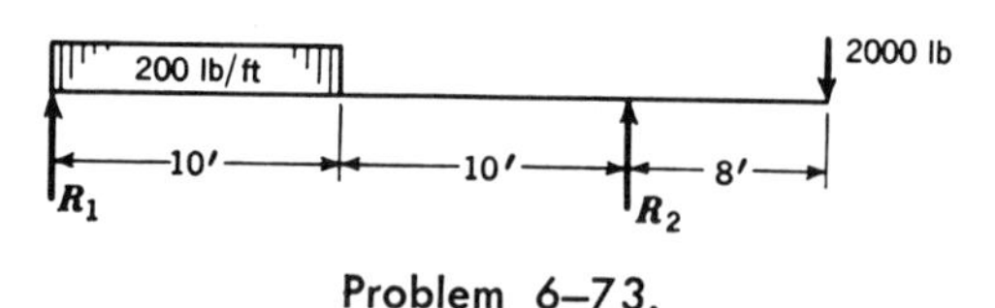

Problem 6–73.

6–74. Draw the shear and moment diagrams for a horizontal beam 30 ft long, supported at the right end and at a point 10 ft to the right of the left end. The loading consists of a uniform load of 1500 lb/ft over the entire length, a concentrated load of 15,000 lb at the center, a concentrated load of 1000 lb at the left end, and a concentrated load of 10,000 lb 2 ft to the left of the right reaction. Show values of the shear and moment at all controlling points.

6–75. Find the shear just to the right of the left reaction and the bending moment under the 5000-lb load.

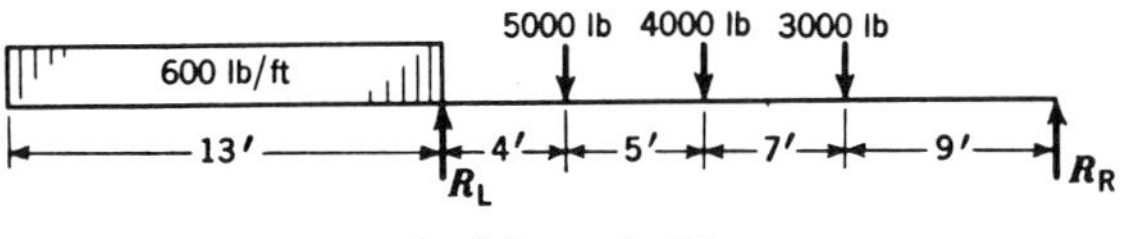

Problem 6–75.

6–76. The loading diagram for a beam is shown. The beam is a 6 in. × 12 in. timber (actual size) placed on edge with respect to the loads. Find the following values: (a) The magnitude of the reactions. (b) The location and the intensity of the maximum flexure stress. (c) The location and the intensity of the maximum shear stress.

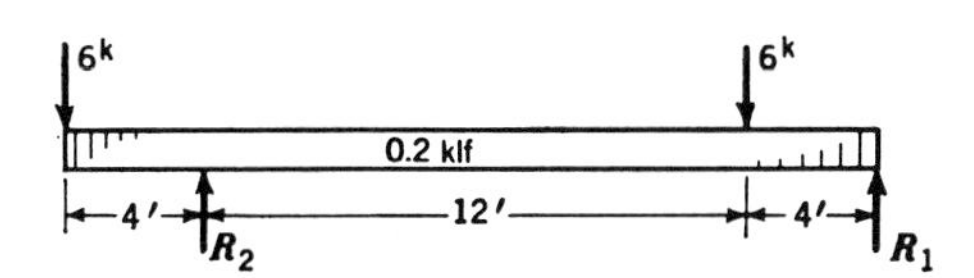

Problem 6–76.

6–77. Steel bars 1 in. in diameter (such as reinforcing bars) are supported at the quarter points. What maximum length may be thus supported without the bending stresses exceeding 18,000 psi?

6–78. Determine the required depth of a simply supported beam 8 ft long used to support a uniformly distributed load of 200 lb/ft. The design shear stress is 12,000 psi, and the design fiber stress is 20,000 psi. Assume the beam cross section to be rectangular with a width equal to one-half the depth. Disregard deflection.

6–79. A uniformly distributed load of 1 ton is to be supported by a wooden beam 5 ft long. The weight of the beam can be neglected. Allowable stresses are as follows: bending, 1000 psi; shear, 125 psi. Deflection will not govern. What is the most economical wooden beam of commercial size to use?

6–80. A beam is to be made up of four 2 in. × 8 in. planks. Using nominal dimensions, compute the maximum moment of inertia which can be obtained by the best symmetrical arrangement of the four planks to give maximum stiffness under a vertical load on the horizontal beam.

6–81. Wood joists, 3 × 10 in. in section, are to span 20 ft under a total load of 100 psf of floor. What would their spacing be at a permissible unit stress of 1200 psi? Make sure that your answer satisfies all criteria. Assume that allowable bearing stresses will not be exceeded at the supports. Include deflection and assume simple supports with $E=1{,}200{,}000$ psi.

6–82. A machine part is loaded as a cantilever beam. Two possibilities of design are being considered, utilizing different materials and different cross sections as shown. Show by your calculations which design will be the more rigid. Length of each is 6 in.

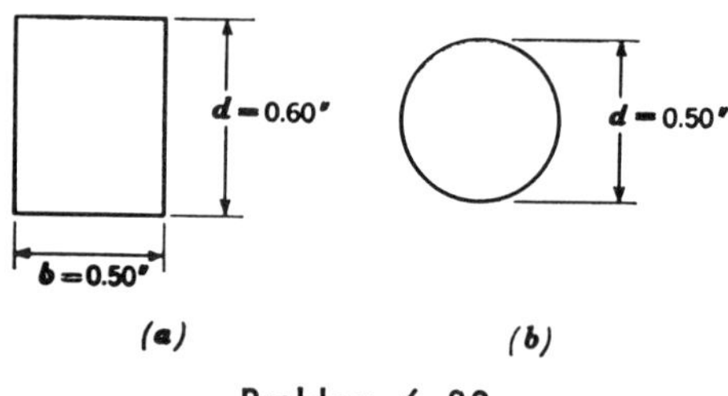

Problem 6–82.

6–83. A series of Douglas fir joists 16 ft long carries a uniformly distributed load of 50 psf plus a cross partition four ft from one end which carries a load of 400 lb/ft. If the joists are spaced 16 in. on center, what size of joist is needed if the stresses are limited to 1600 psi? $E=1{,}600{,}000$ psi and horizontal shear is limited to 100 psi.

6–84. A log is available from which a farmer may cut one of two cross-sections. Section *A* is 8 in. × 10 in. and Section *B* is 6 in. × 12 in. All are full dimension sections. (a) If the length is such that horizontal shear is not a factor, which section is the stronger section as a beam? (b) For an intermediate length column, which section will carry the greater load?

6–85. The plan of the floor framing for part of a mill building is shown. In the drawing, *A* and *D* are steel beams whose ends rest on walls 20 ft apart, *C* is a steel beam reaching between the beams *D*, and *B* is a beam with one end resting on the wall and the other on the cross beam *C*. A timber flooring of 2¾-in.-thick planks is laid on top of the steel beams. The floor carries a load of 150 psf. Beam *C* carries only the reaction of the beams *B* but no direct floor load. Neglect the weight of the flooring and the beams. Assume the working stress in flexure for the beams to be

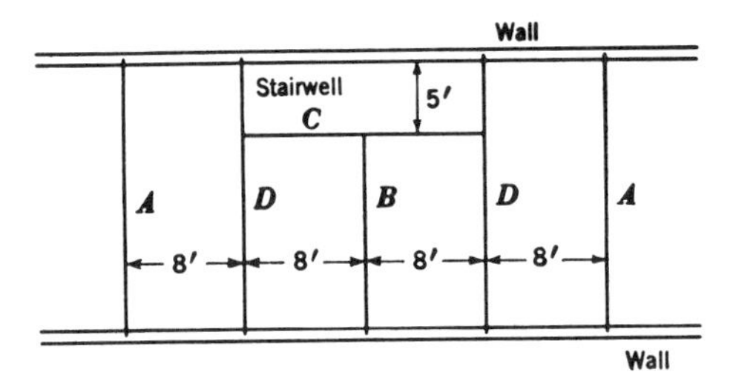

Problem 6-85.

20,000 psi. With lateral support for flanges, (a) find the required section modulus for beams, (b) select suitable WF sections, and (c) find the maximum fiber stress in the planks assuming them to be freely supported every 8 ft on the beams.

6-86. A cantilever steel beam is 12 ft long. Load is 6000 lb/ft extending for 6 ft from the support and $E=30\times10^6$ psi. Cross section of the beam is in the shape of a T with horizontal rectangle 6 in. wide by 2 in. thick and a vertical rectangle 12 in. deep and 1 in. thick. What is maximum deflection? Neglect weight of beam.

6-87. A 20-ft beam of I moment of inertia has top and bottom cover plates over the center 10 ft of beam giving a moment of inertia of $2I$ for the built-up section. The beam carries a 10^k concentrated load at the center. Find the deflection at the center due to the 10^k load in terms of EI.

6-88. A horizontal steel cantilever beam 21 in. long having a rectangular section 4 in. deep by 2 in. wide supports a distributed load varying linearly from 0 lb/in. at the wall to 500 lb/in. at the free end. Find the maximum combined stress on the particle 1 in. below the top surface. Calculate the force which must be applied upward at the free end to raise that end just in line with the beam at the wall.

6-89. A beam consists of two angles $2\frac{1}{2}$ in. $\times$ $2\frac{1}{2}$ in. $\times$ $\frac{1}{4}$ in. and 10 ft long. The two angles are welded together at the proper spacing with the outstanding legs on the top. The load is 100 lb/ft. The beam is simply supported. Find (a) the maximum unit bending stress in tension, (b) the maximum unit bending stress in compression, (c) the maximum unit shearing stress along the neutral axis.

6-90. A glued laminated timber I beam is made up of two 1 in. $\times$ 6 in. flanges with a 1 in. $\times$ 4 in. web. It is used on a simple span of 8 ft to support a uniformly distributed load of 300 lb/ft. Using full-dimension lumber, calculate the maximum bending stress produced. What is the maximum shearing stress on the glued surface?

6–91. Three boards, each 1 in. thick (full dimension), have been joined together to form the U-shaped section shown. What maximum safe uniformly distributed load W (in pounds per foot) can this beam safely carry if loaded as shown and if the working stress in tension=1400 psi, in compression=1000 psi, and in longitudinal shear=100 psi?

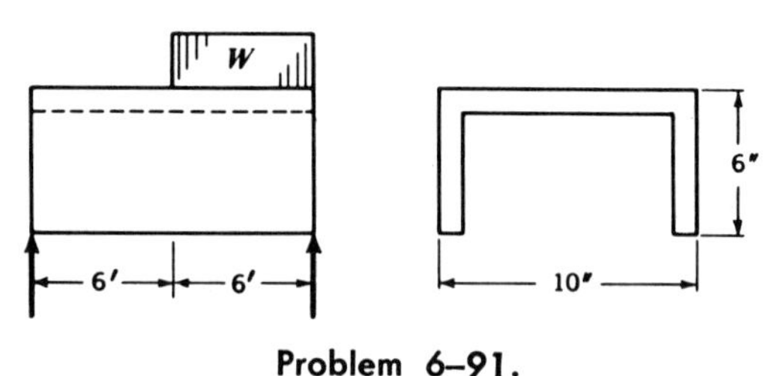

Problem 6–91.

6–92. Find the end moments of the frame shown either by slope deflection or by the moment-distribution method.

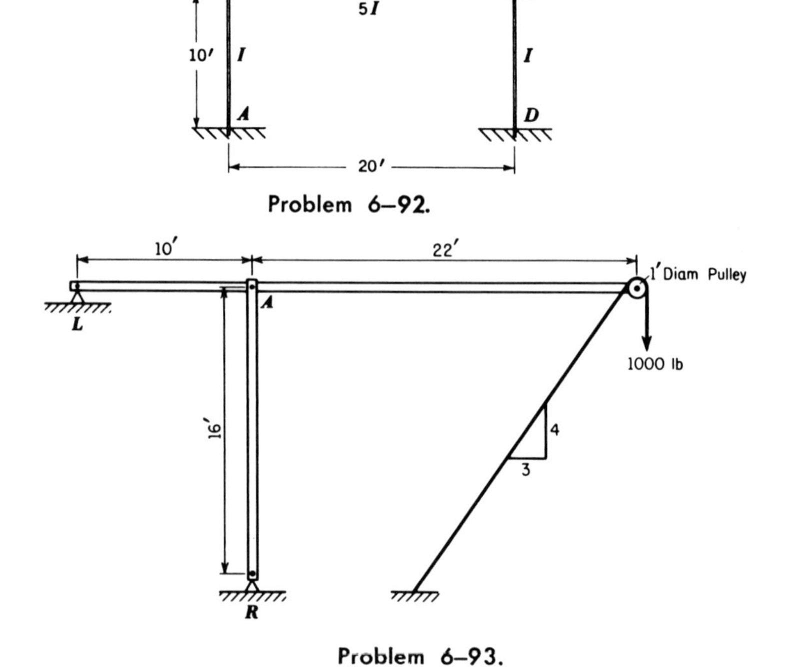

Problem 6–92.

Problem 6–93.

6–93. Calculate the reactions at L and at R and the bending moment at pin A. The radius of the pulley is 1 ft.

6–94. A cantilever beam carries a uniform load W (in pounds per foot) over one-half its length and has a couple applied at the free end as shown. Find the maximum deflection of the beam. Is this deflection up or down? Where does it occur?

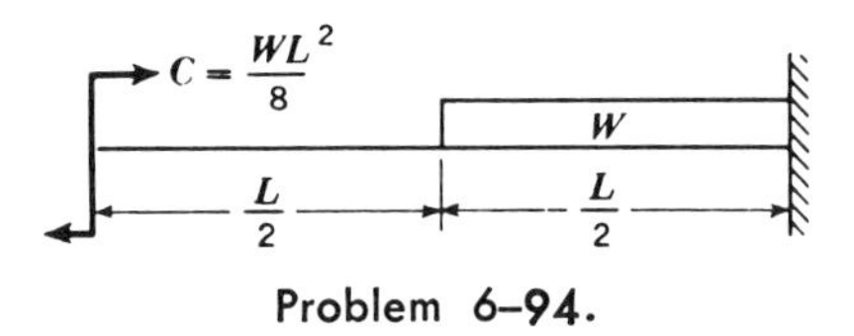

Problem 6–94.

6–95. What uniform load will cause a simple beam 10 ft long to deflect 0.3 in. if it is also supported at mid-span by a spring whose modulus K is 30,000 psi? Assume $I=100$ in.^{4}, $E=3\times10^7$ psi, and $d=10$ in. At zero load the spring just touches the beam.

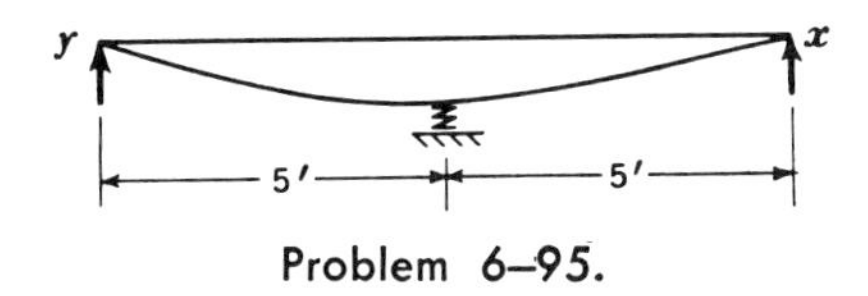

Problem 6–95.

6–96. A T-shaped lintel is made of steel plates. The flange (at the top) is 8 in. × ½ in., the web is 6 in. × ½ in. The flange and web are welded with intermittent fillet welds of proper sizes. It carries a uniform load of 4000 lb/ft on a 5-ft simple span. Find the maximum tensile and compressive unit stresses.

6–97. (1) The term $I=bd^3/12$ refers to (a) radius of gyration, (b) section modulus, (c) instant center, (d) moment of inertia, (e) product of inertia.

(2) In Euler's formula $P/A=\pi^2E/(L/r)^2$, the L/r is commonly known as (a) slenderness ratio, (b) proportional limit, (c) stiffness ratio, (d) rigidity factor, (e) Poisson's ratio.

(3) The chief difference between exterior grade plywood and interior grade plywood is (a) in the number of laminations used, (b) in the weight per square foot, (c) in the size of knotholes permitted, (d) that selected heart woods only are used for exterior grades, (e) that different types of glues are used.

(4) The moment curve for a simple beam with a concentrated load at midspan takes the shape of a (a) triangle, (b) semi-circle, (c) semi-ellipse, (d) parabola, (e) rectangle.

6–98. Indicate if the following statements are true or false.
(a) Concrete is stronger in compression than in tension.
(b) Aluminum is stiffer than mild steel.
(c) The ductility of steel increases rapidly as the carbon content increases.
(d) The strength of concrete decreases as the water-cement ratio increases.
(e) Phosphorus and sulfur are desirable constituents of structural steel.

6–99. What single test would you recommend to determine the
(a) quality of concrete in building construction,
(b) stiffness of a large wooden beam without destruction,
(c) approximate carbon content of a piece of steel if a machine shop is available,
(d) uniformity of case-hardened steel gears,
(e) strength of wire rope.

6–100. Using stress-strain diagrams and/or other pertinent sketches, explain the calculations for beam bending by both elastic and plastic theories.

Thermodynamics 7

Representative problems in thermodynamics involve processes of gases, processes of vapors, cycles and heat engines, mixtures of gases, and gas-vapor mixtures.

In the past few years, there has been a trend away from the applied thermodynamic-type problems such as heat transfer, internal combustion engines, and steam cycles. The problems tend toward the more fundamental, with greater emphasis on mixtures. Terms such as availability, entropy production, and equilibrium composition are beginning to appear.

Some examination problems furnish all information required, such as portions of steam tables, specific heats and molecular weights. If not supplied in the problem, references with this information will be necessary. Symbols used in giving answers to these problems are compatible with most thermodynamics textbooks.

7–1. A Carnot engine utilizes a perfect gas as the medium. At the beginning of the isothermal expansion the pressure is 120 psia and the volume is 1 cu ft. At the end of adiabatic expansion the pressure is 20 psia and the volume is 3 cu ft. What is the efficiency?

Solution: From $PV=wRT$, $T_1=P_1V_1/wR$, $T_2=P_2V_2/wR$, where point *2* is the end of adiabatic expansion. Then

$$e=\frac{T_1-T_2}{T_1}=1-\frac{T_2}{T_1}=1-\frac{P_2V_2}{P_1V_1}=1-\frac{20(3)}{120(1)}=0.5, \quad \text{or} \quad 50 \text{ per cent}$$

7–2. Five pounds per minute of air are compressed in a steady-flow process from 100 psia and 40°F to 200 psia and 240°F. (a) Neglecting kinetic energy changes and assuming air to be a perfect gas, what would be the power required to compress the air in an irreversible adiabatic compression? Express answer in Btu per minute. (b) Compute the entropy change during the irreversible adiabatic compression of part (a). Is the entropy increased or decreased during this change of state?

Solution: (a) From a steady-flow energy balance, $H_1+Q=H_2+W$. For adiabatic compression, $Q=0$ and the work, $W=H_1-H_2$. $W=5(0.24)(40°-240°)=-240$ Btu/min, work being done on the air.

(b) The change in entropy can be found by using a reversible constant-pressure process and a reversible constant-volume process to connect the initial and final state points.

$$\Delta S = wc_p \ln \frac{P_1 T_2}{T_1 P_2} + wc_v \ln \frac{P_2}{P_1}$$

$$= 5(0.24) \ln \frac{100(700)}{500(200)} + 5(0.1716) \ln \frac{200}{100} = 0.166 \text{ Btu/°R, an increase}$$

7–3. A large tank contains gaseous hydrogen at a pressure of 1000 psia and a temperature of 60°F. A smaller tank which contains 1 lb of hydrogen is located on the inside of the larger tank. Ten pounds of gas occupy the space outside the small tank and inside the larger one. The gas in the smaller tank is at a pressure of 300 psia and a temperature of 200°F. A valve in the smaller tank is then opened and part of the 10 lb of hydrogen flows into the smaller tank until the pressures in the two are equal. Consider that during the process, the gas surrounding the small tank remains at constant temperature and that no heat is transferred through the walls of the small container. Determine the final temperature of the gas in the small tank and the amount of gas that flowed into it during this process. Specific heat of hydrogen = 3.5 Btu/lb m°F and molecular weight = 2.

Solution:

$$R = \frac{1545}{M} = \frac{1545}{2} = 772 \frac{\text{ft-lb}_f}{\text{lb}_m\text{°}R}$$

$$C_v = C_p - \frac{R}{J} = 3.5 - \frac{772}{778} = 2.51 \frac{\text{Btu}}{\text{lb}_m\text{°}R}$$

$$V_L = \frac{m_L R T_L}{P_L} = \frac{10(772)(520)}{1000(144)} = 27.9 \text{ cu ft}$$

$$V_s = \frac{m_s R T_s}{P_s} = \frac{(772)(660)}{(300)(144)} = 11.8 \text{ cu ft}$$

Choose the small tank as an open system and let m_i be the mass entering. With no heat transfer to or from the system, the energy balance gives

$$m_i h_i = (1 + m_i) u_{s2} - u_{s1}$$

$$m_i C_p T_i = (1 + m_i) C_v T_{s2} - C_v T_{s1}$$

$$m_i (3.5)(520) = (1 + m_i)(2.51) T_{s2} - 2.51(660)$$

$$1820 m_i = 2.51 m_i T_{s2} + 2.51 T_{s2} - 1655 \quad (1)$$

$$V_{L1} + V_{s1} = V_{L2} + V_{s2}$$

and using $PV = mRT$,

$$\frac{10(R)(520)}{1000(144)}+\frac{R(660)}{300(144)}=\frac{(10-m_i)(R)(520)}{P(144)}+\frac{(1+m_i)(R)T_{s2}}{P(144)}$$

$$7.4=\frac{5200-520m_i+T_{s2}+m_iT_{s2}}{P} \quad (2)$$

Considering the large tank, $P=\frac{mRT}{V}$

$$P=\frac{(10-m_i)(772)(520)}{27.9(144)}=1000-100\,m_i \quad (3)$$

Solving equations (1), (2), and (3), $m_i=1.63$ lb_m, $T_{s2}=700°R$

7–4. Steam is condensed in a surface condenser at 1 in. Hg abs. Cooling water is supplied at 68°F, and 80,000 lb of steam enters the condenser per hour at 1 in. Hg abs and with a quality of 90 per cent. Assume no subcooling of condensate. The over-all coefficient of heat transfer $U=490$ Btu/(hr) (sq ft) (°F), where °F is a degree Fahrenheit of temperature difference. Calculate the square feet of condenser surface required.

Solution:

Enthalpy of steam = 991 Btu/lb

Enthalpy of condensate = 47 Btu/lb at 79°F

Heat from steam = 80,000(991 − 47) = 7.55×10^7 Btu/hr

$Q=UA(\Delta t_m)$, assume 71°F exit-water temperature

$$\Delta t_m=\frac{(79-68)-(79-71)}{\ln(11/8)}=9.4°F$$

$$A=\frac{7.55\times10^7}{490(9.4)}=16{,}400 \text{ sq ft of surface}$$

7–5. An air-conditioner operates to reduce both the temperature and the relative humidity by first cooling the inlet mixture to the dewpoint of the required outlet condition and second, by adding heat to the cooled mixture until the required condition is reached. Any liquid water condensed during the cooling process is removed before the subsequent heating. The entire steady-flow process occurs at a constant total pressure of 12 psia. If the inlet mixture is 120°F with a 100 per cent relative humidity and the required outlet condition is 65°F with a 50 per cent relative humidity, find, in pounds mass per hour, (a) the air flow rate that can be handled, (b) the condensed water-flow rate from the cooling unit. Assume the cooling unit that produces the first effect is rated at 5 tons. (One ton of refrigerating effect = 200 Btu/min.)

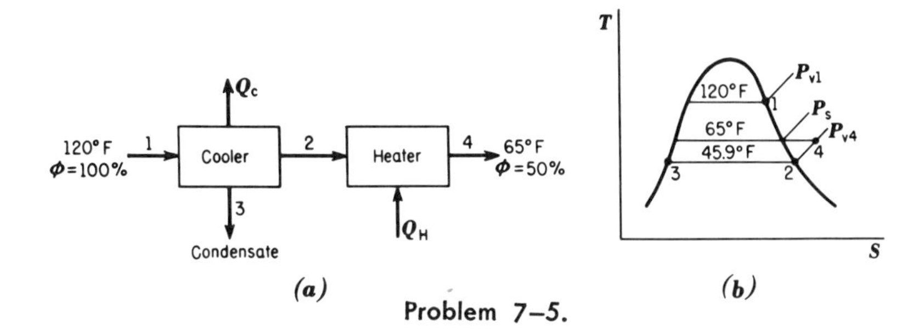

Problem 7–5.

Solution:

$$P_{v4}=\phi P_s=(0.5)(0.3055)=0.1525 \text{ psia}$$

t_2 is saturation temperature for $P_{v4}=45.9°\text{F}$

$$\omega_1=\frac{0.622\ P_{v1}}{P_m-P_{v1}}=\frac{(0.622)(1.692)}{12-1.692}=0.1021 \text{ lb}_\text{m} \text{ vap}/\text{lb}_\text{m} \text{ da}$$

$$\omega_2=\frac{0.622\ P_{v2}}{P_m-P_{v2}}=\frac{0.622(0.1525)}{12-0.1525}=0.00801$$

Choose the cooler as an open system and write an energy balance

$$H_1=H_2+H_3+Q_c \text{ where } Q_c=1000 \text{ Btu/min}$$

$$H_1=m_1c_pt_1+m_1\omega_1h_{v1} \text{ where } m_1 \text{ is lb}_\text{m} \text{ da/min}$$

$$H_3=m_1(\omega_1-\omega_2)h_{f3}, \text{ the Btu/min in the condensate}$$

$$m_1(0.24)(120)+m_1(0.1021)(1113.2)=m_1(0.24)(45.9)+m_1(0.00801)(1081.1)$$
$$+m_1(0.1021-0.00801)(14.06)+1000$$

Solving, $m_1=8.23$ lb$_\text{m}$ da/min
The mass of air is $1+\omega$ lb$_\text{m}$ air/lb$_\text{m}$ da
(a) $m=(8.23)(1+0.1021)(60)=545$ lb$_\text{m}$ air/hr
(b) $m_w=(8.23)(0.1021-0.00801)(60)=46.5$ lb$_\text{m}$ water/hr

7–6. One thousand cubic feet of moist air are drawn through a column containing an absorbent to remove water vapor. The air is at 68°F and one atmosphere. The absorbent increases in weight in the amount of 1.06 lb for every thousand cubic feet of moist air. Assuming that water vapor removal is complete and that the ideal gas laws hold, determine the partial pressure of water vapor in the untreated air and the volume of dry air obtained per thousand cubic feet of moist air. The effluent air is at 68°F and one atmosphere.

Solution: The humidity ratio of the incoming stream is

$$\omega = \frac{1.06 \text{ lb}_m\ v}{1000 \text{ cu ft} \left(\rho_{da} \dfrac{\text{lb}_m}{\text{cu ft}}\right)}$$

$$\rho_{da} = \frac{P_{da}}{R_{da}T}$$

$$\omega = \frac{\rho_v}{\rho_{da}} = \frac{0.622\ P_v}{P_{da}}$$

Therefore,

$$\frac{0.622\ P_v}{P_{da}} = \frac{1.06\ R_{da}T}{1000\ P_{da}(144)}$$

$$0.622\ P_v = \frac{1.06(53.3)(528)}{1000(144)}$$

$$P_v = 0.334 \text{ psia}$$

$$v_{da} \text{ in} = \frac{(53.3)(528)}{(14.7-0.334)(144)} = 13.6 \text{ cu ft/lb}_m \text{ da}$$

$$v_{da} \text{ out} = \frac{(53.3)(528)}{(14.7)(144)} = 13.3 \text{ cu ft/lb}_m \text{ da}$$

$$\text{Volume of dry air out} = \frac{(1000)(13.3)}{13.6} = 977 \text{ cu ft}$$

7–7. A completely airtight cylinder 300 cm long is divided into two parts by a freely moving, airtight, heat-insulating piston. When the temperatures in the two compartments are the same and equal to 27°C, the piston is located 100 cm from one end of the cylinder. How far will the piston move if the gas in the smaller part of the cylinder is heated to 74°C, the temperature of the larger section remaining constant? Assume that perfect-gas laws hold and neglect the thickness of piston.

7–8. A closed tank is divided into two compartments by a thin diaphragm. One compartment contains 2 cu ft of oxygen at 14.7 psia and 70°F. The other compartment contains 8 cu ft of nitrogen at 14.7 psia and 70°F. If the diaphragm is removed and the gases are allowed to mix, calculate the partial pressure of each gas in the mixture.

7–9. (a) The temperature of a gas sample is increased from 80°F to 135°F with a volume increase of 10 per cent. If the pressure before heating was 2 atm, calculate the new pressure. (b) A cylinder contains 3 cu ft of nitrogen at 15 psia and 60°F.

The gas is compressed reversibly and isothermally to a pressure of 100 psia. Compute the heat transferred and the work done. The R for nitrogen is 55.1.

7–10. The specific heat of a gas at constant pressure is 0.2025 Btu/(lb)(°F) and at constant volume is 0.1575 Btu/(lb)(°F). What is the final volume of 10.0 cu ft of gas at an initial pressure of 25 in. of mercury and a final pressure of 5 atm? Assume the process to be adiabatic. (Mercury weighs 0.49 lb/cu in.)

7–11. The internal energy of a gas is given by $u=0.08t+0.002t^2$, where $t=°F$. If 1 lb of this gas expands without heat flow but with a temperature drop from 300°F to 100°F, how much work is done?

7–12. One pound of air initially at 30 psi and 40°F is adiabatically compressed to 120 psi. Determine (a) initial volume, internal energy, and enthalpy, using 0°F as datum, and (b) final volume and temperature and work done on air, using 0°F as datum.

7–13. A cylinder-and-piston machine expands air according to the law PV=constant from 50 psia and 70°F to 15 psia. Compute the work done and the heat transfer during the process.

7–14. You are working with L Air Products Company and are given a customer's order for a 3-cu ft cylinder of oxygen under a gage pressure of 5000 psi at 60°F and at a barometric pressure of 28.5 in. of mercury. A partially filled cylinder of this capacity contains oxygen under a pressure of 400 psig and at 80°F. You use this cylinder and add oxygen to meet the customer's requirement. What weight of oxygen must be added to the cylinder? What would be the "free air" volume (barometric pressure and 70°F) of the oxygen added?

7–15. Four pounds of air are under a pressure of 136 psig and at a temperature of 60°F. The barometric pressure is 28.5 in. of mercury. In each of the following cases start with these initial conditions and analyze these procedures. (a) The air expands with no change in temperature to 14 psia. What will be the resulting volume? (b) The air expands under constant pressure to a volume of 100 cu ft. What will be the resulting temperature? (c) The volume remains constant while the pressure is reduced to 14 psia. What will be the resulting temperature?

7–16. A mixture of 60 per cent nitrogen, 10 per cent carbon dioxide, and 30 per cent hydrogen by volume is heated from 40°F to 250°F at a constant pressure of 1.0 atm. The volume of the total mixture at 40°F is 5.0 cu ft. (a) What is the total weight of the mixture? (b) What is the specific heat of the mixture? (c) How much energy is added to the mixture? (d) How much energy is available for external work during the process?

PHYSICAL PROPERTIES

Gas	Specific Heat C_p [Btu/(lb) (°F)]	Gas Constant R [ft-lb/(lb) (°F)]
Nitrogen	0.2485	55.3
Carbon dioxide	0.2175	35.0
Hydrogen	3.140	762.0

7–17. Ten pounds of air (consider as a perfect gas) are compressed isentropically from 15 psia and 60°F to 120 psia. (a) What is the final temperature? (b) What is the final volume? (c) How much work was required to compress the air?

7–18. If we have 4 lb of air at a pressure of P_1 equals 180 psia, and a volume of V_1 equals 5 cu ft, and let it expand adiabatically and reversibly to a pressure of 30 psia, what is the change in temperature? The change in internal energy? The change in enthalpy? The work done? The heat exchange?

7–19. One pound of fluid is confined in a cylinder and is compressed by a piston from 15 psia to 60 psia while the volume decreases from 8.0 cu ft to 2.8 cu ft. During the compression process, the enthalpy of the fluid increases by 36.1 Btu, and 22.8 Btu is transferred from the fluid as heat. If this compression process is completed in $\frac{1}{20}$ min, determine the horsepower being delivered by the piston to the fluid.

7–20. Three cubic feet of air at 100 psia expand adiabatically to 30 psia. Find (a) final volume of air, (b) amount of work done, and (c) change in internal energy during expansion.

7–21. A transformer at a temperature of 60°F has a 2.5 cu ft volume of gas sealed in above the oil at 2 psig. When heated by load to a temperature of 150°F, the oil has expanded and compressed the gas to 1.5 cu ft volume. Calculate the gas pressure, in pounds per square inch gage. Assume a perfect gas and no absorption of gas by the oil.

7–22. The volumetric analysis for a gas mixture shows that it consists of 70 per cent nitrogen, 20 per cent carbon dioxide, and 10 per cent carbon monoxide. If the pressure and temperature for the mixture are 20 psia and 100°F, respectively, compute (a) the partial pressures and (b) the weight analysis.

7–23. Five pounds of liquid H_2O at 32°F are in a cylinder. The weight W is such that the resultant pressure on the H_2O is 5 psig. (Atmospheric pressure is 15 psia.) (a) If 500 Btu of heat are added, what is the new temperature and volume of the H_2O? (b) If 500 Btu more (total of 1000 Btu) are added, what is the new temperature and volume? (c) If 4000 Btu more (total 5000 Btu) are added, what is the new temperature and volume. (d) If 1000 Btu more (total 6000 Btu) are added, what is the new temperature and volume?

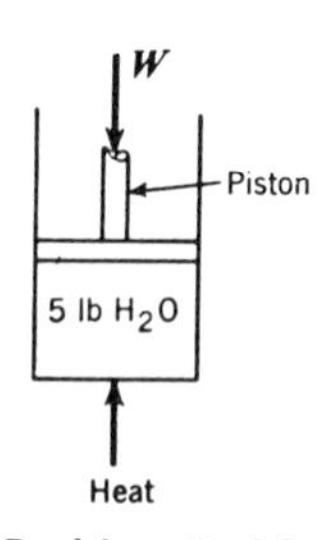

Problem 7–23.

7–24. A steam boiler, on test, evaporated 907,500 lb of water in 24 hr. Gage reading, 244 psi; atmospheric pressure, 14.5 psia; feed-water temperature, 238°F; superheat, 145°F. How much heat was given to the water per hour?

7–25. Saturated steam at a pressure of 150 psia flows through an orifice whose area is 0.32 sq in. Find the discharge, in pounds per minute, (a) when the back pressure is 110 psia and (b) when the back pressure is 30 psia.

7–26. A small steam generating plant burns oil as a fuel. The oil has a specific gravity of 1.008 and costs $2.50 per barrel. The heating value of the oil is 18,250 Btu/lb. The boiler operates at 75 per cent thermal efficiency when taking in feed water at 180°F and delivering dry saturated steam at 100 psig. What is the fuel cost per 1000 lb of steam on this basis? (1 barrel=42 gal)

Absolute Pressure (psi)	Temperature (°F)	Specific Volume (cu ft/lb)		Enthalpy or Heat Content (Btu/lb)		Entropy [Btu/(lb)(°F)]	
		Sat'd Liquid	Sat'd Vapor	Sat'd Liquid	Sat'd Vapor	Sat'd Liquid	Sat'd Vapor
14.7	212.0	0.0167	26.82	180.0	1150.2	0.312	1.756
85.3	316.5	0.01758	5.150	286.5	1183.6	0.459	1.615
100.0	327.8	0.01771	4.426	298.3	1186.6	0.474	1.602
114.7	337.8	0.01782	3.889	308.8	1189.0	0.487	1.591

7–27. Steam flowing at the rate of 40,000 lb/hr enters a turbine with a velocity of 700 fps and enthalpy of 1400 Btu/lb. Leaving the turbine, the steam has a velocity of 1600 fps and enthalpy of 1000

Btu/lb. Heat lost in the turbine is 30 Btu/lb. Determine the work done per pound, in Btu.

7–28. Per pound of coal fired a boiler evaporates 8 lb of steam at 250 psia and 97 per cent quality. The feed-water temperature is 100°F and the coal has 13,000 Btu/lb. Compute the over-all efficiency of the boiler.

7–29. (a) One pound of saturated steam at 400°F expands isothermally to 60 psia. Determine (1) change of entropy, (2) heat transferred, (3) change of enthalpy, (4) change of internal energy, and (5) work. (b) One pound of steam at 400 psia and 600°F expands isentropically to a final temperature of 200°F. Determine (1) initial a) enthalpy, b) entropy, c) volume, and d) internal energy; (2) final a) pressure, b) quality, c) volume, d) enthalpy, and e) internal energy; (3) heat transferred; (4) change of internal energy; and (5) work done during the process.

7–30. A steam boiler produces 100,000 lb of steam an hour at 400 psia and 700°F. This steam goes through a turbine (which in turn drives a generator) and then into a condenser at a pressure of 2 in. Hg abs. There is no "extraction" of steam. Turbine efficiency is 90 per cent and generator efficiency is 90 per cent. How many kilowatts can be produced?

7–31. Steam enters a horizontal nozzle at a pressure of 100 psia, temperature of 500°F, and velocity of 500 fps. It is discharged from the nozzle at 4 psia and 96 per cent quality. What is its discharge velocity?

7–32. A 20,000-kw turbogenerator, operating at full load, receives steam at 228 psia and 550°F, and it exhausts at 0.25 psia. The combined steam rate is 11.2 lb/kwhr. (a) For the corresponding Rankine engine, find the work per pound of steam, the thermal efficiency, and the steam rate. (b) For the actual unit, find the combined thermal efficiency and the combined engine efficiency.

7–33. A Carnot engine operates between a high temperature of 500°F and a low temperature of 100°F. If the engine is to produce 1 hp, how much heat is required per minute?

7–34. An open-cycle gas turbine receives air at 15 psia and 60°F. The compressor discharges at 75 psia. The temperature entering the turbine is 1250°F. Calculate (a) the heat added in the combuster, in Btu per pound, and (b) the efficiency of the cycle, in per cent.

7–35. (a) Draw a temperature-entropy diagram for a Carnot cycle. (b) What is the thermal efficiency if the cycle operates between 900°F and 350°F?

7–36. An internal-combustion engine runs at a speed of 250 rpm and produces a torque of 700 lb-ft. In a separate run at the same speed, friction horsepower is found to be 15. Find the mechanical efficiency of the engine.

7–37. A Carnot engine operates between a source at 1200°F and a receiver at 70°F. If the output of the engine is 100 hp, compute the heat supplied, heat rejected, and the efficiency of the engine.

7–38. (a) Tests of a six-cylinder 4-in.-bore and 3⅛-in.-stroke aircraft engine at full throttle show a brake horsepower of 79.5 at 3400 rpm. The compression ratio is 8:1, the specific fuel consumption is 0.56 lb/brake hp-hr. The higher heating value of the fuel is 19,800 Btu/lb. Determine (1) the brake mean effective pressure, (2) the brake torque, (3) the brake thermal efficiency, (4) the brake engine efficiency based on cold air standard if the ideal efficiency e is $e = 1 - 1/r_k^{k-1}$, where r_k = compression ratio. (b) An exhaust gas has the following volumetric analysis in per cent: $CO_2 = 12$, $CO = 2$, $O_2 = 4$, and $N_2 = 82$. Find the corresponding gravimetric (by weight) analysis.

7–39. An air compressor receives air at 14.4 psia and a specific volume of 13.7 cu ft/lb. The discharge pressure and specific volume are 100 psia and 2.74 cu ft/lb. The initial and final internal energy values of the air are respectively 12 Btu/lb and 47 Btu/lb. The cooling water around the cylinder removes 33 Btu/lb of air passing through. Neglect changes of kinetic and potential energy; calculate the shaft work per pound of air handled.

7–40. A Carnot engine requires 200 Btu/min from the "hot source." It produces 2 hp. The temperature of the "cold sink" is 40°F. (a) What is its thermal efficiency? (b) What is the temperature of the "hot source"?

7–41. A power plant is designed with a boiler capacity of 50,000 lb of steam per hour at 800 psia and 750°F. The turbogenerator exhausts to a condenser at 1.5 Hg abs. Exhaust steam to the condenser has a dryness factor of 90 per cent. (a) Compute the Carnot efficiency of the cycle. (b) Compute the steam rate and the combined thermal and electrical efficiency of the turbogenerator if the electrical output is 3500 kw using 50,000 lb/hr of steam. (Assume no heat loss between boiler and turbine.) (c) Compute the actual thermal efficiency of the cycle assuming the condensate is returned to the boiler at 88°F. Neglect pump work. (d) Compute the gallons per minute of cooling water required for the condenser, assuming a cooling-water temperature rise of 10°F and operation at 3500 kw. (e) What is the most common method of increasing the efficiency of the plant cycle without increasing the steam pressure and temperature or condenser vacuum? What is the cycle called? (f) Compute the pounds of coal required per hour with a boiler load of 50,000 lb/hr. The as-fired heating value of the coal is 12,200 Btu/lb and the boiler efficiency is 84.0 per cent.

7–42. An open-type deaerating feed-water heater has an output of 70,000 lb of water at 220°F. Supplied to the heater is 50,000 lb/hr of condensate at 160°F, make-up water at 60°F, and saturated steam at 20 psia. Determine the amount of make-up water and the amount of steam that must be added to the condensate each hour.

7–43. We have a 10-ton ammonia refrigerating machine and would like to check its operating characteristics. Assume dry isentropic compression between 150 psia and 30 psia and no subcooling of the refrigerant. (a) Find the pounds of refrigerant circulated per minute. (b) Find the work of compression per minute. (c) Find the pounds of cooling water required per minute, allowing 12 deg temperature rise. (d) Find the quality after the expansion valve. (e) Find the coefficient of performance.

7–44. An engine operating on the Carnot cycle uses 10 lb/sec of steam as the working substance. During the heat addition process the steam goes from a saturated liquid to a saturated vapor state. Heat addition takes place at 200 psia and heat rejection at 15 psia. (a) Sketch the cycle to *PV* and *TS* coordinates and show the saturation lines. (b) Determine the heat addition, in Btu per second. (c) Determine the heat rejection, in Btu per second. (d) Determine the net horsepower output. (e) Determine the pumping horsepower input. (f) Determine the thermal efficiency.

7–45. One pound of air completes a reversible cycle consisting of the following three processes: 1) From a volume of 2 cu ft and temperature of 40°F the air is compressed adiabatically to half the original volume. 2) Heat is added at constant pressure until the original volume is reached. 3) The air is returned isometrically to its original state. (a) Show cycle on *PV* and *TS* coordinates. (b) Calculate the heat transfer, work, and internal energy change for each process, and show *signs* of results.

7–46. An air compressor with a clearance of 4.5 per cent is to handle 1000 cfm of free air when the atmospheric pressure is 14.6 psia and the atmospheric temperature is 76°F. At the end of the suction stroke, the temperature and pressure of the air in the cylinder are 95°F and 14 psia. For a discharge pressure of 75 psia and $n=1.33$, what should be the displacement of the compressor?

7–47. A refrigerating plant uses 14,220 lb/hr of cooling water in the ammonia condenser. The cooling water enters the condenser at a temperature of 50°F and leaves at 76°F. The refrigerating compressor is water-cooled and uses 900 lb/hr of water. The water enters the compressor water jackets at 50°F and leaves at 60°F. The indicated horsepower of the compressor is 30. Determine the plant's load, in tons of refrigeration, and the coefficient of performance.

7–48. Indicator cards from a 5 in. × 4 in. 500-rpm air compressor are 2.9 in. long. The area of the head-end card is 1.30 sq in. and that of the crank end is 1.37 sq in., using a 60 lb/(sq in.)(in.) indicator spring. If the piston-rod diameter is ⅞ in., calculate the head- and crank-end mean effective pressure and the total indicated horsepower.

7–49. A certain internal-combustion engine connected to an electric dynamometer when operated at full load gives these data: 1000 rpm; 52.5 lb on the dynamometer scale at the end of a 2-ft brake arm; at 1000 rpm and no load except the dynamometer, the scale is adjusted to read zero so there is no tare. Fuel has 7000 Btu/lb and is used by this engine at the rate of 0.50 lb/min. Friction and windage losses are 2.5 hp. Determine (a) the horsepower delivered to the dynamometer, (b) the mechanical efficiency of the engine, and (c) the thermal efficiency of the engine at this load.

7–50. A two-cylinder steam locomotive engine has a 32-in. stroke, with piston diameters of 24 in. The engine when pulling a certain load operates at 300 rpm. Under these conditions the mean effective pressure is 100 psi. The wheels known as the "drivers" are 5 ft in diameter, and the total losses from piston to rails amount to 10 per cent. From these data determine (a) the indicated horsepower of the two-cylinder steam engine, (b) the output horsepower of the engine to the rails, (c) the speed of the train, in miles per hour, and (d) the tonnage of load being hauled if drawbar pull is 8 lb/ton.

7–51. One hundred cubic feet per minute of saturated air at 40°F are heated to a temperature of 70°F. (a) What is the resultant relative humidity? (b) How much heat per minute is required to heat this air?

7–52. A wall consists of 2.00 in. of insulation and 1.00 in. of wood. Thermal conductivities are as follows: insulation, 0.30 Btu-in./(sq ft)(hr)(°F); wood, 1.00 Btu-in./(sq ft)(hr)(°F). The inside surface of the insulation is at 70°F, and the outside surface of the wood is at 0°F. (a) What is the heat loss through this wall? (b) What is the temperature at the junction of the insulation and wood?

7–53. The relation between mass and energy as derived by Einstein is $E = MC^2$, where E=energy, M=mass, and C=speed of light. If 1 lb of uranium is caused to fission and there is a loss of 0.1 per cent of the mass in the process, how many kilowatthours of energy are liberated?

7–54. Steam in the amount of 7 lb at atmospheric pressure, superheated to 242°F, is introduced simultaneously with 8 lb of ice at 25°F into a copper calorimeter which weighs 5 lb and which contains 50 lb of water at 60°F. The heats of fusion and of vaporization for water are 144 and 970 Btu/lb, respectively. The thermal capacities in Btu per pound per degree Fahrenheit may be taken as follows: steam, 0.48; ice, 0.50; copper, 0.093. Calculate the resulting temperature of the mixture, neglecting heat losses to all bodies other than the calorimeter itself.

7–55. Atmospheric air has a dry-bulb temperature of 85°F and a wet-bulb temperature of 64°F. The barometric pressure is 14.10 psia. Calculate (without the use of the psychrometric chart) (a) specific humidity, in grains per pound of dry air, (b) relative humidity, (c) dew-point temperature, (d) enthalpy of mixture, in Btu per pound of dry air.

7–56. Air in steady flow expands from a pressure of 200 psia to 20 psia in a turbine following a non-reversible adiabatic process for which $PV^{1.37}$ = a constant (C) in the nozzle and an efficiency of 93 per cent in the blades. The initial temperature is 540°F. Constant pressure specific heat = 0.24. Find (a) the velocity leaving the nozzle in feet per second, (b) the work in foot pounds per pound of air, (c) the kw output of the turbine for a 97 per cent mechanical efficiency, and a flow rate of 1,000 lb/hr.

7–57. A Carnot engine operates on 0.1 lb of air. The pressure and volume at the beginning of the reversible isothermal expansion are 200 psia and 0.2 cu ft respectively. The volume at the beginning of the adiabatic expansion is 0.3 cu ft. Assuming the air follows the ideal gas law, and that the temperature of the receiver is 100°F, compute, (a) the temperature of the source, (b) the efficiency of the cycle, (c) the pressure at the end of the isothermal expansion, (d) the heat rejected to the receiver during each complete cycle.

7–58. A fluid at 100 psia has a specific volume of 4 cu ft/lb and enters an apparatus with a velocity of 500 ft/sec. Heat radiation losses in the apparatus are equal to 10 Btu/lb of fluid supplied. The fluid leaves the apparatus at 20 psia with a specific volume of 15 cu ft/lb and a velocity of 1000 ft/sec. In the apparatus, the shaft work done by the fluid is equal to 195,000 ft-lb. Does the internal energy of the fluid increase or decrease, and how much is the change?

7–59. A perfect gas is contained in a piston-and-cylinder machine. The arrangement is such that, at all times, the pressure of the gas is directly proportional to its volume. Initially, the gas is at a pressure of 15 psia and a volume of 1 cu ft. Heat is transferred reversibly to the gas until its pressure is 150 psia. It may be assumed that movement of the piston is frictionless. Determine the work done by, or on, the gas. Express your answer in Btu.

7–60. Since most gases do not behave ideally (i.e. $PV=RT$) over a large range of pressures, Van der Waals modified the ideal gas law to represent the pressure-volume-temperature relationship of one mole of a real gas.

$$\left(P + \frac{a}{V^2}\right)(V - b) = RT$$

where R is the gas constant (10.73 psia − cu ft/lb mole − °R). If the constant $b=1.32$ cu ft/lb-mole for propylene, and 1 mole of propylene occupied 50 cu ft at 390°F and 175 psia, what pressure does 1 mole of propylene exert if placed in a 3-cu-ft vessel at 150°F?

7–61. One pound of air at 300°F and 14.7 psia is mixed with one pound of air at 100°F and 14.7 psia in a non-flow process. The pressure remains constant. What is the decrease in availability of the energy in the two quantities of air referred to surroundings at 14.7 psia and 77°F?

7–62. A client is considering the installation of a heat pump arrangement. He has a low temperature source of river water at 35°F. The high temperature discharge temperature is to be 150°F. Assuming the most ideal (Carnot) system, how many Btu's can be delivered to the discharge by using one kwhr of electricity driving the pump?

7–63. Four pounds of ammonia are in a steel tank of 2 cu ft volume. The temperature is 60°F. What is the pressure in the tank?

7–64. An ideal nozzle allows methane (CH_4) at the rate of 1.6 lb/sec to expand from a region where the velocity (v_s) is 400 fps, the pressure (P_i) is 100 psia, and the temperature (t_i) is 80°F to a region where (P_2) is 80 psia. Calculate for this nozzle (a) the exit temperature t_2 (°F), (b) the exit specific volume (V_2), (c) the exit velocity (v_s) in feet per second, (d) the exit area (A) in square feet, (e) the stagnation temperature (t_x), (f) if it is convergent or convergent-divergent.

7–65. How many cubic feet of air, at 85°F, 760 mm mercury, and 50 per cent relative humidity, are required in a furnace burning 1000 cu ft of dry natural gas, (CH_4), per hour, (measured at 60°F, 14.7 psia) with 25 per cent excess air?

7–66. A gas mixture (M) composed of 10 lb nitrogen and 8 lb oxygen at (P_1) 15 psia and 150°F is compressed isentropically to a pressure of 60 psia. Find (a) final temperature (T_2), (b) final volume (V_2), (c) work done during the process (Btu).

7–67. A reversed cycle (refrigerating) has been proposed which uses a gas. The gas is first compressed isothermally to a given pressure. It is then expanded ideally and adiabatically to the initial pressure. Finally, heat is absorbed at constant pressure until the initial temperature is reached. Assuming the pressure ratio of the initial compression process is 10 and that the initial temperature is 60°F, determine the coefficient of performance (COP) for this cycle and compare this value with that of a reversed Carnot cycle that uses the same hot and cold body temperatures. Let the gas be CO_2 which has a specific heat at constant pressure of 0.22 Btu/lb mass°F and a molecular weight of 44.

7–68. A sealed 10,000-gallon tank contains 1.5 lb of H_2O in the gaseous state; no other medium is present. The pressure in the tank is 1 psia. As the tank and H_2O are cooled, determine (a) the temperature where condensation begins, and (b) the cooling effect in Btu required to cool the H_2O to produce: (1) The condition where the maximum possible liquid is present in the tank; (2) the condition where the minimum ice and no liquid is present in the tank.

7–69. How much water will condense out of 1000 cu ft of air at 70°F, 760 mm pressure, and 50 per cent relative humidity if it is cooled to 40°F?

7–70. Two 3½-in. × 12-in. ducts supply warm air at a temperature of 140°F to a room with the temperature in the room maintained at 70°F. The velocity in the ducts is 450 ft/min, $C_p = 0.24$. (a) Determine the Btu's per hour supplied to the room. (b) If the relative humidity in the room is 30 per cent, at what temperature of the inside glass surface will condensation occur on the glass?

7–71. A block of copper weighing 200 lb is heated to 200°F and then plunged into a tank containing 100 lb of liquid water at 60°F. Neglecting thermal radiation and the thermal capacity of the tank material, determine the change of entropy. Specific heat of copper is 0.0915 Btu/lb°F.

7–72. Two identical bodies of constant heat capacity originally at temperatures T_1 and T_2, respectively, are used as heat reservoirs for a heat engine operating in infinitesimal cycles. If the bodies remain at constant pressure, show that (a) the work obtained is $C_p(T_1+T_2-2T_f)$, where T_f is the final temperature and C_p is the specific heat in Btu/lb°F, and (b) the final temperature T_f is $T_f=\sqrt{T_1 T_2}$.

7–73. A system involving a flowing fluid has an engine (or a pump), X. It also has a heat transfer device, Y. Both X and Y are located between points A and B in the fluid system. The fluid flows from A to B through X and Y. Point B is 250 ft higher than point A. The enthalpy of the fluid at A is 25 Btu/lb higher than B. The fluid velocity at A is 1000 fps, while at B it is 300 fps. There is a transfer of heat from the system through Y at the rate of 20,000,000 Btu/hr. (a) If the rate of flow of the fluid in the system is 1,000,000 lb/hr, what is the fluid horsepower of X? (b) Does X transmit power from the system, or does it absorb power from an external source?

7–74. One pound of a mixture of steam and water at 160 psia is contained in a rigid vessel. Heat is added to the vessel until the contents are at 560 psia and 600°F. Determine the quantity of heat, Btu, added to the tank contents.

7–75. One pound of air, to be considered a perfect gas, is contained in a cylinder and piston machine at an initial volume of 1.0 cu ft and at a pressure of 100 psia (state 1). The gas is expanded reversibly at a constant temperature to a volume of 2.0 cu ft (state 2). The gas is then compressed reversibly and adiabatically to a volume of 1.0 cu ft (state 3). It is then returned to its initial state (state 1) by a reversible constant-volume process. (a) What is the net entropy change for the complete cycle? (b) What is the net amount of heat transfer? State your answer in Btu and indicate whether it is into or out of the system. (c) What is the net amount of work? State your answer in Btu and indicate whether work has been done on, or by, the air.

Fluid Mechanics

8

The fluid mechanics problems in this chapter have been classified and arranged in the following order: hydrostatics, fluid meters, pipe friction, pumps and turbines (including horsepower), open channels, and hydrodynamics. A solution is given for each type. The specific weight of water is taken as 62.4 lb/cu ft. If the selection of a coefficient is necessary, it is noted in the solution or answer.

8–1. If the hinged gate is 5 ft wide, calculate the force P required to keep the gate closed.

Solution:

$$F_L = w\bar{h}A = 62.4(5.5)(25) = 8580 \text{ lb}$$

$$e_L = I_G/\bar{y}A = \frac{bh^3}{12\bar{y}A} = \frac{5(5)^3}{12(5.5)(25)} = 0.379 \text{ ft}$$

$$F_R = w\bar{h}A = 62.4(1.5)(15) = 1405 \text{ lb}$$

$$e_R = \frac{I_G}{\bar{y}A} = \frac{5(3)^3}{12(1.5)(15)} = 0.50 \text{ ft}$$

$$\Sigma M_{\text{hinge}} = 0 \qquad 8580(2.12) - 1405(1) - P(5) = 0$$

$$P = 3360 \text{ lb}$$

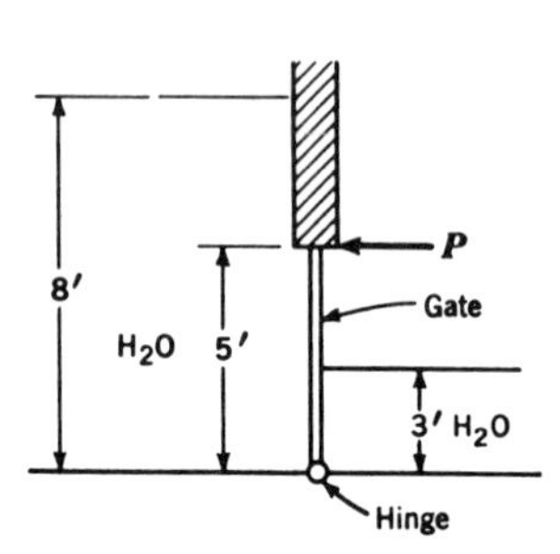

Problem 8–1.

8–2. The venturi meter shown is set up to measure the flow of water in the 6-in. pipeline. With a pressure difference of 16 in. as indicated by the mercury manometer, what is the rate of flow, in gallons per minute? Assume meter coefficient is equal to 1.0.

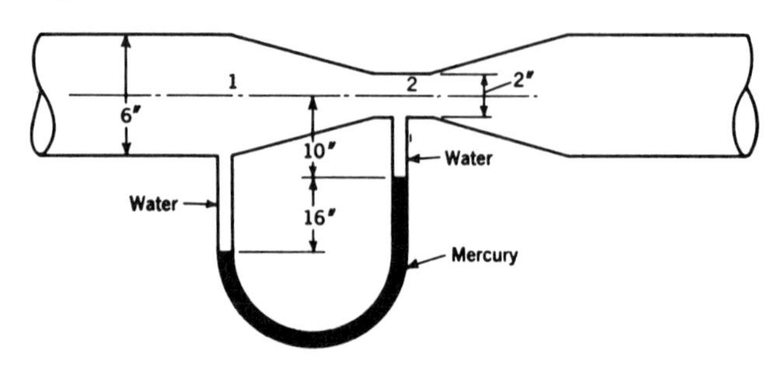

Problem 8–2.

Solution:

$$\frac{P_1}{w}-\frac{P_2}{w}=-\frac{16}{12}+\frac{16}{12}(13.6)=16.8 \text{ ft} \qquad \frac{V_2^2}{2g}=81\frac{V_1^2}{2g}$$

$$\frac{P_1}{w}-\frac{P_2}{w}=\frac{80V_1^2}{2g}=16.8 \text{ ft} \qquad V_1=\sqrt{\frac{16.8(64.4)}{80}}=3.68 \text{ fps}$$

$$Q=C_mQ_T=1(3.68)(0.785)(0.5)^2=0.722 \text{ cfs}=324 \text{ gpm}$$

8–3. Find the horsepower required to overcome pipe friction with a flow of 100,000 gpd of heavy fuel oil (specific gravity=0.95) at a temperature of 90°F through 3000 ft of new 4-in. diameter steel pipe. The kinematic viscosity of the oil is 8.36×10^{-4} sq ft/sec.

Solution:

$$N_R=\frac{VD}{\nu}=\frac{0.1545(144)(4/12)}{0.785(16)(8.36\times10^{-4})}=707$$

$$f=\frac{64}{N_R}=\frac{64}{707}=0.0905$$

$$h_f=f\frac{L}{D}\frac{V^2}{2g}=\frac{0.0905(3000)(1.77)^2}{4/12(64.4)}=39.6 \text{ ft of oil}$$

$$\text{hp}=\frac{Qwh_f}{550}=\frac{0.1545(62.4)(0.95)(39.6)}{550}=0.66$$

8–4. A centrifugal pump is to operate against a total head of 135 ft and is to discharge 250 gpm of water. If the pump has an efficiency of 65 per cent, calculate (a) the water horsepower, and (b) the brake horsepower required. (c) When 180,000 gpd is the average output, the electric motor which drives the pump has an efficiency of 85 per cent and the cost of kilowatthours is $0.018. What is the monthly cost of operation?

Solution:

(a) $$\text{whp}=\frac{Qwh}{550}=\frac{250(62.4)(135)}{449(550)}=8.52$$

(b) $$\text{bhp}=\frac{\text{whp}}{E}=\frac{8.52}{0.65}=13.1$$

(c) $$\text{Cost}=\frac{13.1(0.746)(360)(0.018)}{0.85}=\$74.50 \text{ for September}$$

8–5. (a) Find the hydraulic radius of the section shown when the water is flowing at a depth of 5.0 ft from the bottom of the V notch. (b) What quantity of water, in cubic feet per second, will flow through this section, at the above-mentioned depth, if the slope is 1.0 ft/100 ft and the coefficient of roughness is 0.013? Manning's equation for velocity is $V=1.486R^{2/3}S^{1/2}/n$.

Solution:

(a)

$$R=\frac{A}{P}=\frac{8(4)+1(2)/2}{8+6+2/0.707}=1.96$$

(b)

$$V=\frac{1.486(1.96)^{2.3}(0.01)^{1/2}}{0.013}=17.9 \text{ fps}$$

$$Q=VA=17.9(33)=590 \text{ cfs}$$

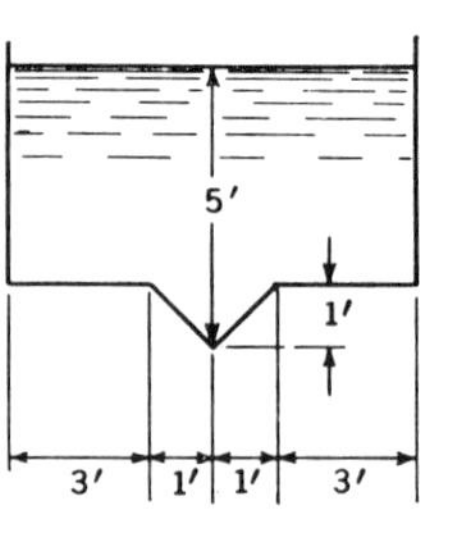

Problem 8–5.

8–6. A 60° pipe bend reduces from a diameter of 8 in. to a diameter of 6 in. The static pressure at the 8-in. diameter is 20 psi. If the flow is 3.0 cfs, and the fluid is water, find, (a) the dynamic force on the bend, (b) the static force on the bend, and (c) the total force on the bend. The centers of the 6-in. and the 8-in. apertures lie in the same horizontal plane.

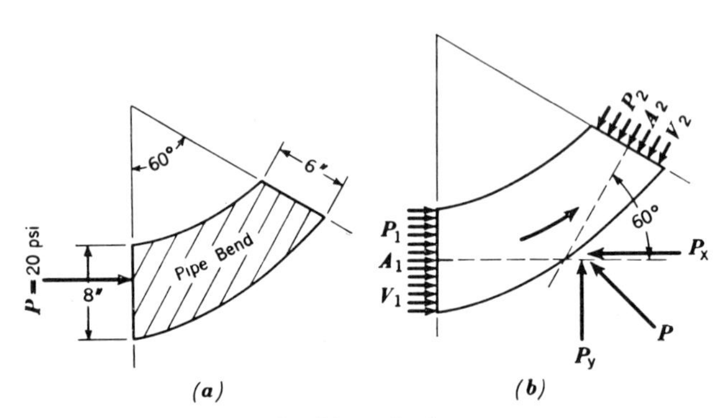

Problem 8–6.

Solution:

(a)

$$P_{xd}=\frac{Qw}{g}(V_1-V_2\cos\theta)=\frac{3(62.4)}{32.2}(8.6-15.3\cos 60°)$$

$$\underset{\leftarrow}{P_{xd}=5.52 \text{ lb}} \quad \text{[see Fig. 8-6}b\text{]}$$

$$P_{yd}=\frac{Qw}{g}V_2\sin\theta=5.81(15.3)(\sin 60°)=77 \text{ lb} \uparrow$$

$$P_d=77 \text{ lb} \quad 85.9° \qquad R_d=77 \text{ lb} \quad 85.9°$$

(b)

$$\frac{P_1}{w}+\frac{V_1^2}{2g}=\frac{P_2}{w}+\frac{V_2^2}{2g} \qquad \frac{20(144)}{62.4}+\frac{(8.6)^2}{64.4}=\frac{P_2}{w}+\frac{(15.3)^2}{64.4}$$

$$\frac{P_2}{w}=43.7 \text{ ft} \qquad P_{xs}=A_1P_1-A_2P_2\cos\theta$$

$$P_{xs}=0.349(20)(144)-0.197(43.7)(62.4)(\cos 60°)=\overleftarrow{736}\text{ lb}$$

$$P_{ys}=A_2P_2\sin\theta=0.197(43.7)(62.4)(\sin 60°)=466\text{ lb}\uparrow$$

$$P_s=872\text{ lb}\quad 32.3°\searrow \quad R_s=872\text{ lb}\quad 32.3°\searrow$$

(c) $$P=543\uparrow \ \leftrightarrow \overleftarrow{742}=920\text{ lb}\quad 36.2°$$

Total force on bend $R=920$ lb $36.2°$

8–7. A vertical gate 8 ft wide and 6 ft high is hinged at the top and held closed by pressure of water standing 4 ft above the top of the gate. What force applied at the bottom of the gate will be required to open it?

8–8. A vertical 4 ft × 4 ft gate is submerged with the level top 2 ft below the water surface. The gate is exposed to hydrostatic pressure on one side. Find the magnitude and location of the resultant of these hydrostatic forces.

8–9. Find the dimensions of a concrete (150 lb/cu ft in air) cube sized to have the minimum weight to hold the gate closed. The gate opening is 3 ft wide and 10 ft high and is closed by a weightless gate which is hinged as shown. Pulley is frictionless.

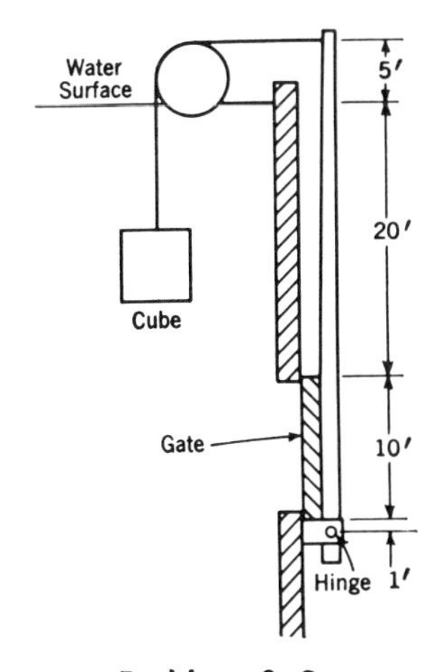

Problem 8–9.

8–10. A rectangular opening in a dam is 6 ft wide and 3 ft deep. If the top of the opening is 12 ft below the surface of the water, what is the total force on the gate which closes the opening and how far from the top of the gate is the center of pressure?

8–11. A storage vat is 25 ft long, 14 ft deep, and its width at the bottom is 10 ft and at the top 15 ft. (Trapezoidal cross section.) The ends of the vat are vertical. Petroleum crude flows into the vat at a rate of 400 gpm. Determine (a) the time required to fill the vat to a depth of 10 ft, (b) the weight of the petroleum crude being held by the vat when filled to a depth of 10 ft, and (c) the pressure against one end of the vat tending to push it out.

8–12. Assume that one of the outlet pipes through Grand Coulee Dam is 10 ft in diameter and the top of the pipe is 200 ft below the water surface. (a) What is the total pressure on the shutoff valve? (b) Where is the center of pressure with respect to the center of the pipe?

8–13. A cylindrical wooden-stave tank with its axis vertical is 10 ft in diameter and 6 ft high. It is held together by two steel hoops, one at the top and the other at the bottom. What is the tension in each of the hoops when the tank is full of fluid having a specific gravity of 0.8?

8–14. The gate shown covers a 3-ft diameter circular opening. It is held down by a 300-lb weight made of 2 cu ft of concrete, submerged in the water. How high in the standpipe will the water be when the gate is dislodged?

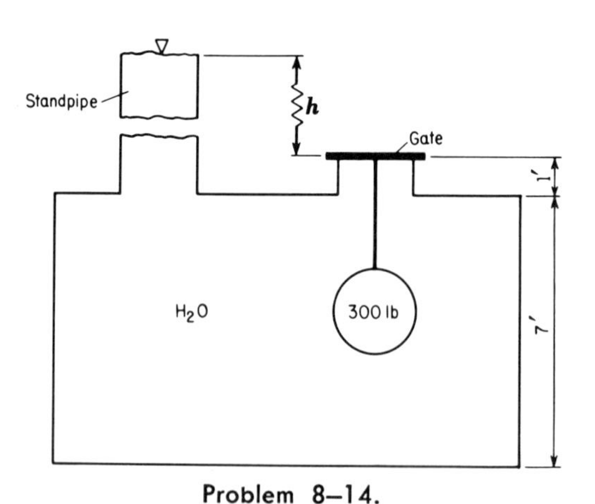

Problem 8–14.

8–15. A rectangular barge 25 ft wide × 46 ft long × 8 ft deep floats in a canal lock which is 32 ft wide × 60 ft long × 12 ft deep. With no load on the barge, other than its own weight, the bottom of the barge is 3 ft beneath the water surface, and the depth of water in the lock is 7 ft. What is the new water depth in the lock if a load of steel which weighs 75 tons is added to the barge?

8–16. Compute the absolute pressure at the center line of the pipe shown in the figure. The local atmospheric pressure is 15.0 psia. The temperature of all fluids is 60°F.

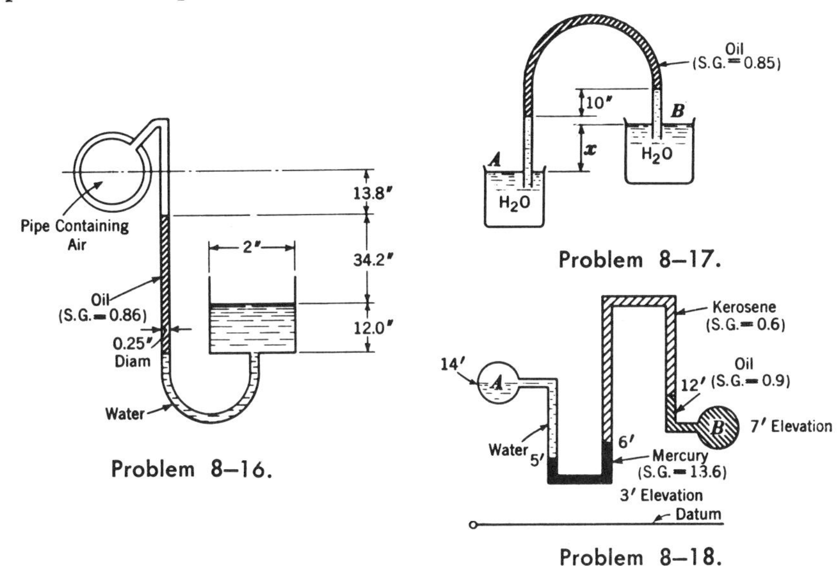

Problem 8–16.

Problem 8–17.

Problem 8–18.

8–17. Determine the distance x between the two free surfaces A and B.

8–18. If the pressure in pipe A is 100 psi, determine the pressure in pipe B.

8–19. A hydrometer bulb and stem displace 0.5 cu in. when immersed in fresh water. The stem has an area of 0.05 sq in. What is the distance on the stem between the graduations for 1.00 and 1.10 specific gravity?

8–20. State Bernoulli's equation for the relation between the heads at two points on a closed channel running full of fluid, in words and in algebraic form. Define each symbol and give an example of an engineering problem involving the use of this equation.

8–21. The sketch shows a transition section of a pipeline from a 20-in. diameter at B to a 12-in. diameter at A. The flow of water through the line is 6 cfs. A pressure gage at A reads 16 psi, and at B, a pressure gage indicates 10 psi. The center line of the pipe at B is 25 ft above the center line of the pipe at A. Determine (a) the direction of the flow of the 6 cu ft of water per second,

(b) the loss in head between the sections A and B, and (c) the velocity of the water at A and at B.

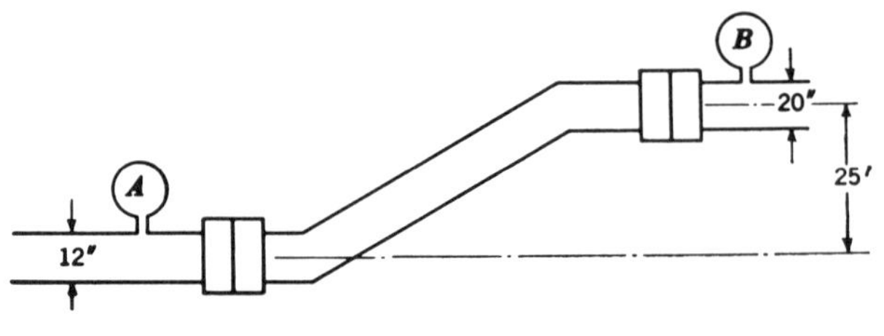

Problem 8–21.

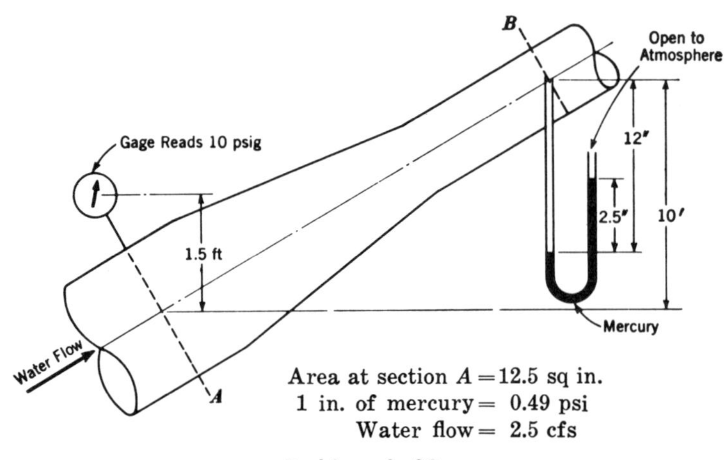

Problem 8–22.

8–22. From the information shown on the schematic diagram, calculate the velocity of the fluid at section B, in feet per second.

8–23. A horizontal venturi meter in a 6-in. pipe has a 4-in. throat. The meter constant is 0.96. A differential manometer using mercury as a fluid shows a 7-in. differential between the throat and the approach pipe. Calculate the water discharge of the meter.

8–24. A venturi meter with a 2-in. throat is placed in a 4-in. pipeline (2 in. and 4 in. are actual inside diameter). When the throat pressure is 4 ft less than the line pressure at the same elevation, what are the gallons per second flowing through the meter?

8–25. What is the flow through a venturi meter with a throat 2 in. in diameter and with an entrance diameter of 4 in. if the difference in level of an attached mercury manometer is 25 in.? Assume that there are no losses, that the venturi tube is horizontal, and that the connecting lines to the manometer are filled with water.

8–26. A 1-in. diameter nozzle on the end of a 2-in. diameter hose is required to throw a stream of water to a height of 100 ft. Neglecting friction, what is the required pressure in the hose and the rate of flow, in cubic feet per second?

8–27. A certain water-turbine nozzle discharges 25 cfs and delivers 100 hp to the turbine. What is the velocity of the water flowing from the nozzle?

8–28. How high will the jet rise and what will be the flow, in cubic feet per second, through the 6-in. vertical orifice shown? Use $C_c=0.65$, $C_v=0.95$.

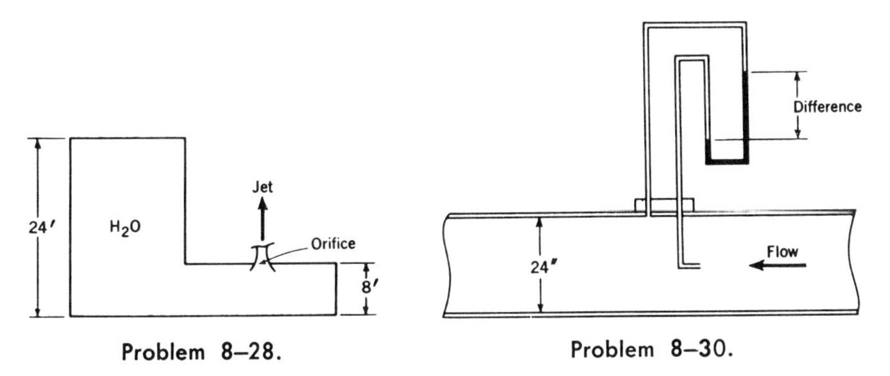

Problem 8–28. Problem 8–30.

8–29. Water issues from a circular orifice 4 in. in diameter. The height of water above the center of the orifice is 30 ft. Assuming a coefficient of discharge of 0.72, what is the discharge, in cubic feet per minute?

8–30. A pitometer is inserted in a new 24-in. cast-iron main carrying 2 mgd and is placed at a point on the diameter where the velocity is equal to the average velocity of the pipe. What should be the difference in elevation of mercury in the two limbs of the manometer?

8–31. The sketch shows cold water discharging horizontally from a nozzle (2.0 in. ID) at the end of a pipe. A small L-shaped tube is inserted into the jet. One open end points squarely upstream; the other open end extends some distance vertically. The water flows into the L-shaped tube and fills it to a height of 1.0 ft above the lower end. Estimate the discharge, in cubic feet per second. The tube is not small enough for capillary effects to be important.

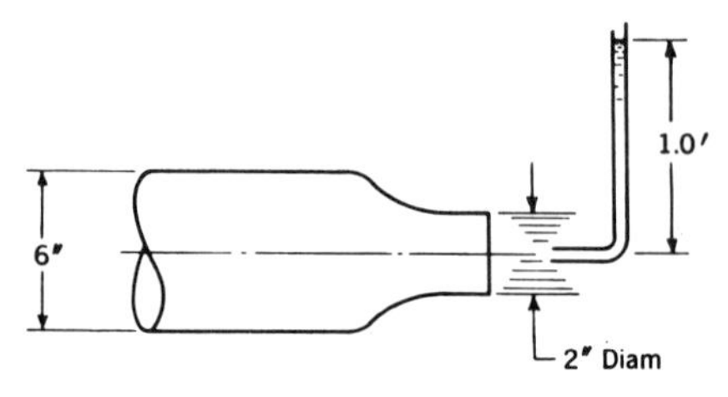

Problem 8–31.

8–32. A 6-in. diameter pipe to which is attached a 3-in. nozzle is inclined at an angle of 30° with the horizontal. At a point 100 ft horizontally from the point of discharge through the 3-in. nozzle, the water has reached a height of 50 ft above the nozzle. Neglecting all losses, compute the flow rate.

8–33. The jet, from a sharp orifice in a vertical surface, falls in a trajectory. The liquid passes through a point 5.0 ft out from the surface and 2.5 ft below the level of the orifice. What is the velocity of the jet?

8–34. An oil, with kinematic viscosity=0.001 sq ft/sec and with uniform steady flow through a circular pipe 3 in. in diameter, has a flow rate. of 0.2 cfs. The pipe is horizontal. The oil weighs 70 lb/cu ft. Find the drop of pressure per 1000 ft of pipe.

8–35. An oil pipeline is 10 in. ID and 100 miles long and is made of welded steel. The discharge end is 500 ft above the intake. The rate of flow is 4 fps. What is the total pressure, in pounds per square inch gage, at intake when the entire length is full of gasoline at 60°F and 0.68 specific gravity?

8–36. A Pelton water turbine with an efficiency of 80 per cent is installed where a flow of 10 cfs is available under a total head of 750 ft. The water is conveyed to the turbine through a 12-in.-diameter penstock 4000 ft long having a friction factor f of 0.020. What horsepower output may be expected?

8–37. From the sketch shown, determine the following: (a) the total loss of head, in feet, from A to B due to fluid friction in the pipe and fittings, (b) the head loss due to pipe friction, and (c) the head loss due to valves and fittings.

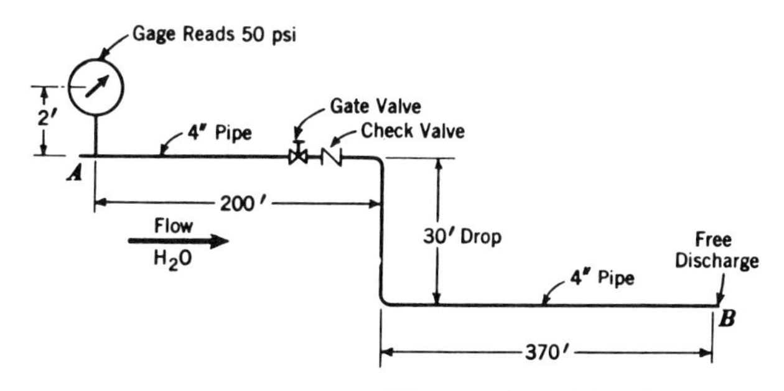

Flow at A = 1.25 cfs
Actual inside diameter of pipe = 4.02 in.
Actual inside area of pipe = 12.7 sq in.
Friction factor for 4-in. pipe = 0.024

Problem 8–37.

8–38. Water is pumped through 10,000 ft of 24-in. new steel pipeline at the rate of 20.0 cfs. The intake end of the pipe is at elevation 1000.0 ft and the discharge end (where discharge pressure is 10 psi) is at elevation 1400.0 ft. The water is pumped by a centrifugal pump that is 85 per cent efficient, and power is supplied to the pump by an electric motor that is 90 per cent efficient. How much power will be required to pump the water?

8–39. A 36-in. water main, carrying 60 cfs, branches at point X into two pipes, one 24 in. in diameter and 1500 ft long and the other 12 in. in diameter and 3000 ft long. They come together at Y and continue as a 36-in. pipe. If the factor f is equal to 0.022 in all pipes, find the rate of flow in each of the branches.

8–40. A 6-in. pipe connects two points in a water system which are some distance apart and at different elevations. When the system is full of water with no velocity, the pressure at the second point is 12 psi lower than that at the first point. When 8 cfs flows from the first to the second point, the pressure at the latter is 33 psi less than that at the first. If the 6-in. pipe should be replaced by an 8-in. pipe, what would be the pressure drop between the two points when the same flow of 8 cfs takes place?

8–41. Two reservoirs with a difference in elevation of 100 ft are connected by 10,000 ft of clean cast-iron pipe of 12-in. internal diameter. Compute the probable instantaneous rate of discharge from the upper reservoir to the lower one.

8–42. A centrifugal pump is located at point x at elevation 720.0 ft. A pipeline carrying the water from the pump discharges at point y at an elevation of 820.0 ft. The head loss due to friction as the water flows through the pipe is 40 ft. (a) Find the approximate length of the pipe if the diameter is 12 in., the pipe is new cast iron, and the discharge is 3.93 cfs. (b) If the quantity delivered at point y is 1000 gpm and the speed of the pump is 875 rpm, what would be the theoretical capacity and total dynamic head developed by this pump if the speed is increased to 1750 rpm?

8–43. Calculate the head loss in 1000 ft of new 6-in. cast-iron pipe discharging $\frac{1}{2}$ cfs of water.

8–44. A 10-in. steel pipeline leaves a reservoir, water surface elevation of 550 ft, at elevation 300 ft and drops to elevation 100 ft where it terminates in a 2-in. diameter nozzle. If the head loss in the line and nozzle is 50 ft, compute the rate of flow (Q) in cfs when the reservoir is full. Assume the coefficient of discharge for the system is 0.92.

8–45. Water is flowing in a 5-ft diameter pipeline at the rate of 500 cfs. The pipe line is 2000 ft long and is horizontal. The friction factor is 0.018. Determine the head loss due to friction and the power necessary to force the water through the pipe.

8–46. What is the discharge in cfs from a 12-in. pipe for which $C = 110$, if the loss of head per 1000 ft is 3.4 ft?

8–47. Two reservoirs are connected by 5000 ft of 12-in. diameter average cast iron pipe. Calculate (a) the discharge rate in cfs when the difference in surface elevation of the reservoirs is 200 ft, (b) the horsepower which must be supplied to a pump by a motor in order to increase the discharge rate to double that found in part (a). Assume a pump efficiency of 70 per cent.

8–48. In a test of a centrifugal pump driven by an electric motor, the suction pipe is 10 in. in diameter and its gage indicates a partial vacuum of 2.5 ft of water. The discharge pipe is 5 in. in diameter, 2 ft higher than the suction gage, and shows a pressure of 50 ft of water. If the pump is discharging 1.6 cu ft of water per second, and the electrical power input is 12kw, what efficiency is indicated?

8–49. A centrifugal pump of 90 per cent efficiency is pumping salt water (20 per cent NaCl at 60°F) against a static head of 100 ft at 300 gpm through 1000 ft of 8-in. ID galvanized-iron pipe. What is the total head, in feet?

8–50. The flow in a river is 300 cfs at a point where it would be possible to build a dam which would allow a drop of 50 ft for water flowing through a turbine. Assuming a turbine efficiency of 85 per cent, what horsepower might be developed?

8–51. A pump delivers 12 gpm to an overhead storage tank where it is discharged at atmospheric pressure. The pump is located 10 ft above the water in the well and the point of discharge is 30 ft above the pump. (a) Neglecting friction in the pipe, what is the horsepower output of the pump? (b) If the efficiency of the pump is 60 per cent, what size electric motor is required?

8–52. A centrifugal pump is used to pump crude oil up to a tank through a net vertical distance of 50 ft. The specific gravity of the oil is 0.92, and the pump unit delivers 690 gpm. The efficiency of the pump unit is 80 per cent and that of the electric motor 81 per cent. Determine (a) the horsepower input to the pump, (b) the kilowatt input to the electric motor, and (c) the monthly electric bill for the motor when it operates at this load 200 hr/month and the average rate is $0.025/kwhr plus a monthly demand charge of $1.20/kw.

8–53. Determine the input horsepower required by a pump operating at 60 per cent efficiency to reverse a flow of 5 cfs through a long pipe connecting two reservoirs. The difference of surface elevations of the reservoirs is 50 ft. The final flow shall be from the lower to the upper reservoir.

8–54. (a) What horsepower could (theoretically) be developed from a stream of water carrying 25 cfs if the available fall is 250 ft? (b) What horsepower is represented by a jet of water 1 ft in diameter traveling at 100 fps?

8–55. A new riveted steel culvert 2 ft in diameter is running half full of water. The gradient is 0.0004. What is the discharge, in cubic feet per second?

8–56. A wood flume, of cross section as shown, is to carry 200 cfs of water. What slope, in feet per 1000 feet, is required?

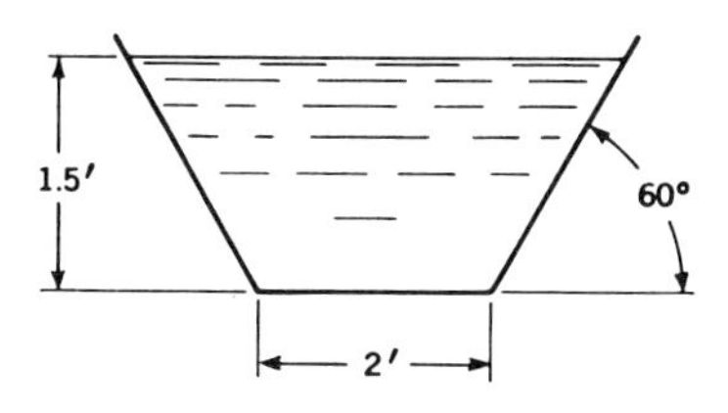

Problem 8–56.

8–57. A rectangular open channel has a bottom width of 6 ft and a slope of 2 ft/mile; it is lined with concrete with a Manning's n equal to 0.013. Calculate the capacity of the channel when the water has a uniform depth of 4 ft.

8–58. What factors must be known in order to calculate the flow, in cubic feet per second, in an open concrete-lined channel? Assume a steady uniform flow condition.

8–59. For a constant-flow cross-sectional area, flowing full, which one of the following will give the least hydraulic radius? (a) Circle. (b) Square. (c) Rectangle with width twice the height. (d) Trapezoid with 45° sides and a base two times the altitude. (e) Equilateral triangle.

8–60. Twenty-eight thousand board feet of 2-in. tongue and grooved plank are available to line a rectangular flume 1000 ft long. Determine the dimensions of the flume to give the best hydraulic properties if the water surface is to be 1 ft below the top of the side walls. Use nominal dimensions of planks.

8–61. The hydraulic properties of a concrete-lined, trapezoidal irrigation canal have deteriorated because of algae growths. The canal has a bottom width of 6 ft, side slopes of 1 on 1, and a water surface width of 12 ft. The channel slope is 0.015. Weir measurements indicate that the channel is carrying 370 cfs. Determine the roughness coefficient n under these conditions. What flow might be expected if the concrete lining were thoroughly cleaned?

8–62. A 2-in. diameter jet of water created by a net head of 100 ft impinges on a flat plate. (a) What is the velocity of the jet? (b) What force is required to hold the plate normal to the jet?

8–63. An impulse water wheel is driven by a water jet 2 in. in diameter under a 500-ft effective head. What force P is required at right angles to the jet as it leaves the nozzle on a vane to deflect the jet 15°?

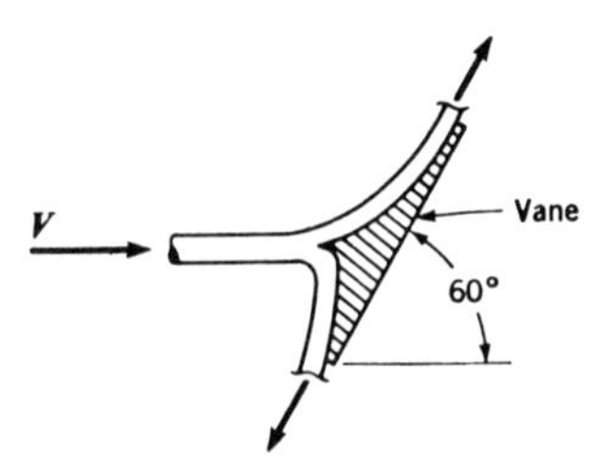

Problem 8–64.

8–64. A jet strikes a stationary vane, and half of it is deflected in each direction, as shown. The jet diameter is 6 in. and the jet velocity is 80 fps. Calculate the horizontal and vertical components of the force with which the vane resists the jet.

8–65. Water flows at the velocity of 12 fps through a 10-in. pipe and then through a conical reducer to form a jet 6 in. in diameter which is discharged horizontally into the atmosphere. If the pressure in the pipe near the reducer is 6.58 psi and the effect of friction may be neglected, what is the thrust of the water on the reducer?

8–66. Water flows through a 12-in. diameter pipeline containing a 60° bend in a horizontal plane at the rate of 15.70 cfs. The pressure is 40.0 psi at the entrance to the bend. Neglecting head losses through the bend, determine the force components parallel and normal to the approach velocity, to be provided for by an anchor that holds the bend in place.

8–67. A nozzle at the end of a 6-in. pipe discharges a jet 2 in. in diameter. The pressure in the pipe is 55 psia and the velocity of the water in the pipe is 10 fps. The discharge takes place in air. Find (a) the resultant force acting on the water in the nozzle, and (b) the axial component of the force exerted on the nozzle.

8–68. A rectangular plate, weight 12 lb, is suspended vertically by a hinge on the top horizontal edge. The c.g. of the plate is 4 in. from the hinge. A horizontal jet of water 1 in. in diameter whose axis is 6 in. below the hinge impinges normally on the plate with a velocity of 18.5 fps. Find the horizontal force applied at the c.g. required to hold the plate in its vertical position.

8–69. A 1-in. diameter jet of water having a velocity of 80 fps strikes a curved vane having a deflection angle of 160° and traveling with a velocity of 30 fps in the direction of the jet. Determine the resultant force which the water exerts on the vane. Neglect friction.

8–70. A horizontal 12-in. pipe is reduced to 8 in. The pipeline is conveying 4 cfs of oil, specific gravity 0.89, and the pressure in the smaller pipe is 40 psi. What resultant force is exerted on the contraction, neglecting friction?

Electricity 9

The problems on electricity are grouped generally in the following sequence: direct-current circuits, including direct-current meters, resistance computations, and direct-current machinery; alternating-current circuits; alternating-current machinery, and electronics. A complete solution for each representative type of problem is given. Most engineering problems can be solved by more than one method; hence, each of the solutions given illustrates only one of several possible methods of approach.

9–1. What size resistor should be used in parallel with a 100-ohm resistor to give a parallel resistance of 98 ohms? What size third resistor, in parallel with the other two, will cause the parallel resistance of the three to be 96 ohms?

Solution:

$$R\text{ (equivalent)}=\frac{R_1R_2}{R_1+R_2}\qquad 98=\frac{100R_2}{100+R_2}\qquad R_2=4900\text{ ohms}$$

$$96=\frac{98R_3}{98+R_3}\qquad R_3=4704\text{ ohms}$$

9–2. Refer to the electrical circuit *abcd* in the figure and determine (a) the direction and amperes of current through each resistance and (b) the voltage between points *a* and *c*.

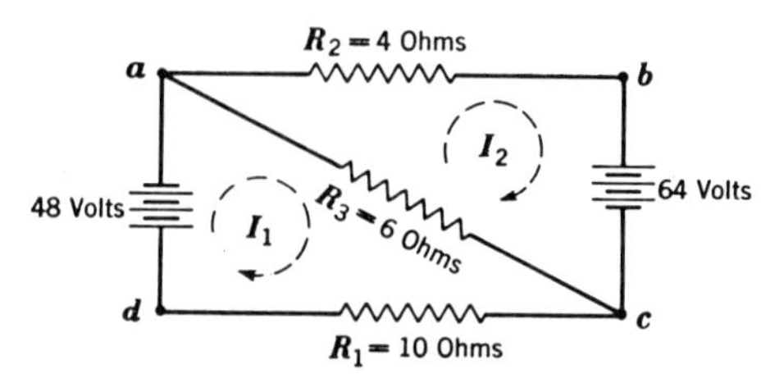

Problem 9–2.

Solution: (a) By using the loop currents I_1 and I_2 as shown above, the following loop-current equations can be written:

(1) $$-48=16I_1-6I_2$$

(2) $$-64=-6I_1+10I_2$$

By solving these simultaneous equations,

$$I_1 = -6.97 \text{ amp} \qquad I_2 = -10.58 \text{ amp}$$

Therefore

$$I_{R1} = 6.97 \text{ amp } (d \rightarrow c) \qquad I_{R2} = 10.58 \text{ amp } (b \rightarrow a)$$

$$I_{R3} = I_1 - I_2 = -6.97 + 10.58 = 3.61 \text{ amp } (a \rightarrow c)$$

(b)

$$\underset{+\,-}{V_{ac}} = (I_1 - I_2)R_3 = 3.61(6) = 21.7 \text{ volts}$$

9–3. All of the electrical energy supplied to an electric water heater is converted to heat. Due to the loss of heat through the walls of the heater, only 90 per cent of the electrical energy supplied to the heater is used in raising the temperature of the water. With an applied voltage of 115 volts the heater takes a current of 9 amp. (a) How long will it take to raise the temperature of a gallon of water from 20°C to the boiling point? (b) At a rate of 5 cents/kwhr, determine the cost of heating the water.

Solution:

(a)

$$\frac{(1\ \cancel{\text{gal}})\left(\frac{8.33\ \cancel{\text{lb}}}{1\ \cancel{\text{gal}}}\right)(80\ \cancel{^\circ\text{C}})\left(\frac{180\ \cancel{^\circ\text{F}}}{100\ \cancel{^\circ\text{C}}}\right)\left(\frac{1\ \cancel{\text{Btu}}}{\cancel{\text{lb}\text{-}^\circ\text{F}}}\right)\left(\frac{1054\ \cancel{\text{joules}}}{1\ \cancel{\text{Btu}}}\right)}{(0.90)(115)(9)\ \cancel{\text{watts}}}\left(\frac{\cancel{\text{watt}}\text{-sec}}{\cancel{\text{joule}}}\right) = 1360 \text{ sec}$$

(b)

$$[115(9) \times 10^{-3}\ \cancel{\text{kw}}](1360\ \cancel{\text{sec}})\left(\frac{1\ \cancel{\text{hr}}}{3600\ \cancel{\text{sec}}}\right)\left(\frac{5 \text{ cents}}{\cancel{\text{kw-hr}}}\right) = 1.95 \text{ cents}$$

9–4. It is necessary to measure the voltage across a line which is known to be about 220 volts. Two voltmeters are available: (a) one has a 150-volt scale and a 15,000-ohm internal resistance and (b) another has a 100-volt scale and a 12,000-ohm internal resistance. If the line voltage is actually 225 volts, what will be the reading of each meter if the two are connected in series across the line?

Solution:

$$I = \frac{V}{R} = \frac{225}{15{,}000 + 12{,}000} = 8.33 \times 10^{-3} \text{ amp}$$

$$V_{(a)} = 15{,}000(0.00833) = 125 \text{ volts}$$

$$V_{(b)} = 12{,}000(0.00833) = 100 \text{ volts}$$

9–5. Given a 10-hp 1750-rpm 230-volt 38-amp d-c shunt motor which has a field-circuit resistance of 384 ohms and an armature resistance, not including brush effect, of 0.3 ohms. A constant brush drop of 2 volts may be assumed. Calculate the number of ohms necessary in a controller to cause this motor to operate at half rated speed when delivering half rated torque. The effects of armature reaction may be neglected.

Solution:

$$T = K_1 \phi I_a$$

Since ϕ = constant,

$$T = K_2 I_a \qquad \frac{T}{2} = K_2\left(\frac{I_a}{2}\right)$$

$$I_f = \frac{V_T}{R_f} = \frac{230}{384} = 0.596 \text{ amp} \qquad I_a = I_L - I_f = 38 - 0.596 = 37.4 \text{ amp}$$

$$\frac{I_a}{2} = 18.7 \text{ amp} \qquad V_T = E_g + I_a R_a + 2 \qquad 230 = E_{gR} + 37.4(0.3) + 2$$

For rated speed and torque

$$E_{gR} = 217 \text{ volts}$$

$Eg = K_3 \phi N = K_4 N$; then

$$\frac{E_{g(1/2)}}{E_{gR}} = \frac{\frac{1}{2} N_R}{N_R} \qquad \frac{E_{g(1/2)}}{217} = \frac{1}{2} \qquad E_{g(1/2)} = 108 \text{ volts} \qquad \text{for } \tfrac{1}{2} \text{ speed}$$

For half speed, half torque (with controller in armature circuit):

$$230 = 108 + 2 + 18.7(0.3 + R_c) \qquad R_c \text{ (controller)} = 6.09 \text{ ohms.}$$

9–6. The resistance of the armature of a 50-hp 550-volt shunt-wound d-c motor is 0.35 ohm. The full-load armature current of this motor is 76 amp. (a) What should the resistance of the starter be in order that the initial armature current be 150 per cent of the full-load armature current? (b) If the field current under full load is 3 amp, what is the over-all efficiency of the motor when the motor is delivering 50 hp? (c) Compute the stray power losses at 50-hp load.

Solution:

(a) $$I_a = \frac{V_T}{R_a + R_s} \text{ (for initial } I_a) \qquad 1.50(76) = \frac{550}{0.35 + R_s} \qquad R_s = 4.47 \text{ ohms}$$

(b) $$P_{\text{in}} = \frac{[550(76+3) \text{ watts}]}{}\left(\frac{1 \text{ hp}}{746 \text{ watts}}\right) = 58.2 \text{ hp}$$

$$\text{Per cent efficiency} = \frac{P_{\text{out}}}{P_{\text{in}}} \times 100$$

$$= \frac{50}{58.2} \times 100 = 85.9 \text{ per cent}$$

(c) $$\text{Losses} = P_{\text{in}} - P_{\text{out}} = I_a^2 R_a + V_T I_f + (\text{SP}) + P_{SL}$$

where SP = stray power and P_{SL} = stray load losses = $0.01\ P_{\text{out}}$

$$(58.2 - 50)(746) = (76)^2(0.35) + 550(3) + 0.01(50)(746) + (\text{SP}) \qquad \text{SP} = 2070 \text{ watts}$$

9–7. When a certain coil is connected to a 60-volt battery, 2 amp of current flows. When the same coil is connected to a 50-volt 60-cycle a-c source, only 1 amp flows. What is the inductance of the coil, in henrys?

Solution:

$$R=\frac{V_{dc}}{I_{dc}}=\frac{60}{2}=30 \text{ ohms} \qquad Z=\frac{V_{ac}}{I_{ac}}=\frac{50}{1}=50 \text{ ohms}$$

$$Z^2=R^2+X^2 \qquad X=\sqrt{(50)^2-(30)^2}=40 \text{ ohms}$$

$$X_L=2\pi fL \qquad 40=2\pi(60)L \qquad L=0.106 \text{ henry}$$

9–8. What will the ammeter read in the circuit shown?

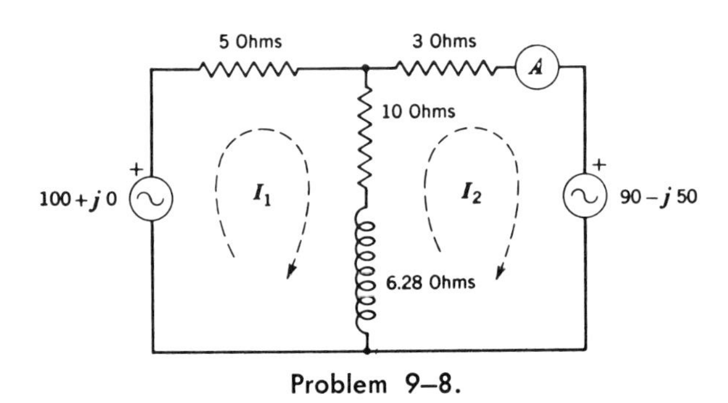

Problem 9–8.

Solution: Writing the loop-current equations:

(1) $$100+j0=(15+j6.28)I_1-(10+j6.28)I_2$$

(2) $$-(90-j50)=-(10+j6.28)I_1+(13+j6.28)I_2$$

(1) $$100\underline{/0^\circ}=16.27\underline{/22.72^\circ}I_1-11.81\underline{/32.12^\circ}I_2$$

(2) $$-102.8\underline{/-29.08^\circ}=-11.81\underline{/32.12^\circ}I_1+14.42\underline{/25.80^\circ}I_2$$

$$I_2=\frac{\begin{vmatrix} 16.27\underline{/22.72^\circ} & 100\underline{/0^\circ} \\ -11.81\underline{/32.12^\circ} & -102.8\underline{/-29.08^\circ} \end{vmatrix}}{\begin{vmatrix} 16.27\underline{/22.72^\circ} & -11.81\underline{/32.12^\circ} \\ -11.81\underline{/32.12^\circ} & 14.42\underline{/25.80^\circ} \end{vmatrix}}=\frac{-1671\underline{/-6.36^\circ}+1181\underline{/32.12^\circ}}{234.6\underline{/48.52^\circ}-139.6\underline{/64.24^\circ}}$$

$$I_2=\frac{-1659+j185.2+1000+j628}{155.4+j176.0-60.6-j125.8}=\frac{-659+j813}{94.8+j50.2}=\frac{1047\underline{/129.03^\circ}}{107.2\underline{/27.92^\circ}}=9.75\underline{/101.11^\circ}$$

Therefore, the ammeter reads 9.75 amp rms

9–9. Blocks *1, 2,* and *3* in the figure represent parallel loads connected to a 60-cycle power circuit. Load *1* is a pure resistance of 10 ohms and draws 4 kw. Block *2* is an inductive load of 2.5 kw and 0.8 power factor. Block *3* is a capacitive load of 2 kw and 0.6 power factor, and Z is the line impedance. Calculate the input voltage V.

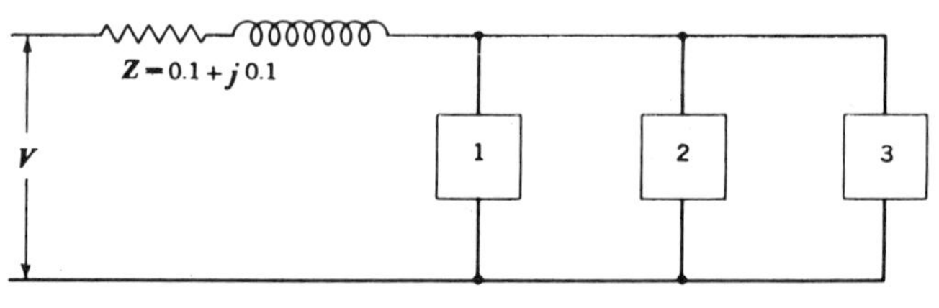

Problem 9–9.

Solution:

$$P=\frac{V^2}{R} \qquad 4000=\frac{V_1^2}{10} \qquad V_1=V_2=V_3=200 \text{ volts} \qquad I_1=\frac{V_1}{R_1}=\frac{200\underline{/0^\circ}}{10}$$

$$I_1=20\underline{/0^\circ} \text{ amp} \qquad P=|V|\cdot|I| \cos \theta <\frac{V}{I}$$

$$2500=200(|I_2|)(0.8) \qquad |I_2|=15.62 \qquad \cos \theta_2=0.8 \text{ (inductive)}$$

$$\theta_2=-36.9^\circ \qquad I_2=15.62\underline{/-36.9^\circ} \text{ amp}$$

$$2000=200(|I_3|)(0.6) \qquad |I_3|=16.67 \qquad \cos \theta_3=0.6 \text{ (capacitive)}$$

$$\theta_3=53.1^\circ \qquad I_3=16.67\underline{/53.1^\circ} \text{ amp}$$

$$I_T=I_1+I_2+I_3=20\underline{/0^\circ}+15.62\underline{/-36.9^\circ}+16.67\underline{/53.1^\circ}$$

$$I_T=20+12.50-j9.38+10.00+j13.32=42.50+j3.94=42.6\underline{/5.32^\circ} \text{ amp}$$

$$V=V_1+I_TZ=200\underline{/0^\circ}+42.6\underline{/5.32^\circ}(0.1414\underline{/45^\circ})=200+6.04\underline{/50.32^\circ}$$

$$V=200+3.86+j4.65=203.9+j4.65; \qquad |V|=204 \text{ volts}$$

9–10. A certain two-element polyphase watthour meter is properly connected into a 240-volt three-wire three-phase supply circuit. Its disk constant is 3.6 watthours per revolution. When operating on one element alone, its disk makes 15 revolutions in 2 min 42 sec, and when operating on the other element alone its disk makes 7 revolutions in 2 min 31.2 sec. In both cases the disk rotates in the "forward" direction. Calculate the load current.

Solution:

$$P_1=\left(\frac{15 \text{ rev}}{162 \text{ sec}}\right)\left(\frac{3.6 \text{ watt-hr}}{\text{rev}}\right)\left(\frac{3600 \text{ sec}}{\text{hr}}\right)=1200 \text{ watts}$$

$$P_2=\frac{7 \text{ rev}}{151.2 \text{ sec}}\left(\frac{3.6 \text{ watt-hr}}{\text{rev}}\right)\left(\frac{3600 \text{ sec}}{\text{hr}}\right)=600 \text{ watts}$$

Assuming a balanced load $P_1=VI\cos(\theta_p-30^\circ) \qquad P_2=VI\cos(\theta_p+30^\circ)$

$$1200=240\, I \cos(\theta_p-30^\circ) \qquad 600=240\, I\cos(\theta_p+30^\circ)$$

$$\frac{1}{I}=\frac{240}{1200}\cos(\theta_p-30^\circ)=\frac{240}{600}\cos(\theta_p+30^\circ) \qquad \theta_p=30^\circ$$

$$1200=240\, I\cos(30^\circ-30^\circ) \qquad I=\frac{1200}{240}=5.00 \text{ amp rms}$$

9–11. A certain 200-hp three-phase four-pole 60-cycle 440-volt squirrel-cage induction motor operates at full load with an efficiency of 95 per cent, a power factor of 91 per cent, and a slip of 3 per cent. For this full-load condition determine (a) the speed, in revolutions per minute; (b) the torque delivered to the load, in pound-feet; and (c) the line current fed to the motor.

Solution:

(a) $$N_s = \frac{120f}{P} = \frac{120(60)}{4} = 1800 \text{ rpm}$$

$$N = N_s(1-s) = 1800(1-0.03) = 1747 \text{ rpm}$$

(b) $$T = \frac{33{,}000P}{2\pi N} = \frac{33{,}000(200)}{2\pi(1747)} = 602 \text{ lb ft}$$

(c) $$P = \sqrt{3}V_L I_L \text{ (pf)}; \quad \frac{200 \text{ hp}}{0.95}\left(\frac{746 \text{ watts}}{\text{hp}}\right) = \sqrt{3}(440)I_L(0.91)$$

$$I_L = 226 \text{ amp rms}$$

9–12. In the circuit shown, part (*a*), R_1 is 5000 ohms, R_2 is 2000 ohms, and C is 4 μf. Also, E_s is a 1-kc sinusoidal source of 10 mv peak value, and E_{cc} and E_{bb} are selected to provide class A operation of the tube. In this case an E_{bb} of 250 volts and an E_{cc} of 45 volts will provide such operation. The tube characteristics show that for this class A operation the values of the 2A3 tube constants are $\mu = 4.2$, $r_p = 800$ ohms, and $g_m = 5250$ μmhos. What is the effective (rms) value of the output voltage, E_{out}?

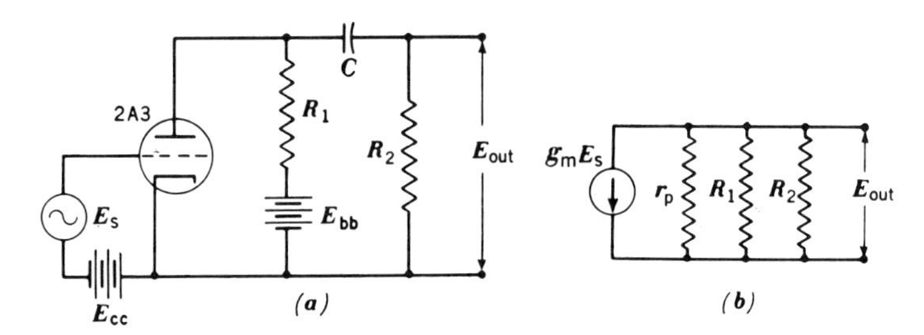

Problem 9–12.

Solution:
$$X_c = \frac{1}{2\pi fC} = \frac{1}{(2\pi\times 10^3)(4\times 10^{-6})} = 39.8 \text{ ohms}$$

$2000 - j39.8 \sim 2000$; therefore, the reactance of the capacitor may be neglected, and the equivalent circuit of part (*b*) can be drawn, converting the tube to an equivalent current generator of output

$$I = gmE_s = (5.25\times 10^{-3})(0.707)(10\times 10^{-3})$$

$$I = 3.71\times 10^{-5} \text{ amp rms}$$

$$E_{out} = IR_{||} = \frac{I}{G_{||}} \qquad G_{||} = \frac{1}{800} + \frac{1}{5000} + \frac{1}{2000} = 1.95 \times 10^{-3} \text{ mhos}$$

$$E_{out} = \frac{3.71 \times 10^{-5}}{1.95 \times 10^{-3}} = 19.0 \text{ mv rms}$$

9–13. Shown in the figure is the T-equivalent circuit for a small signal, common-emitter transistor amplifier. It drives a 10,000 ohm load from a 0.020 volt (rms) voltage source having 1200 ohms of internal resistance. The transistor constants are: $r_e = 30$ ohms, $r_b = 140$ ohms, $r_c = 10^6$ ohms and $r_m = 9.6 \times 10^5$ ohms. Determine the output voltage (V_{ce}) across the load, the power gain (PG) and the required load for maximum power transfer.

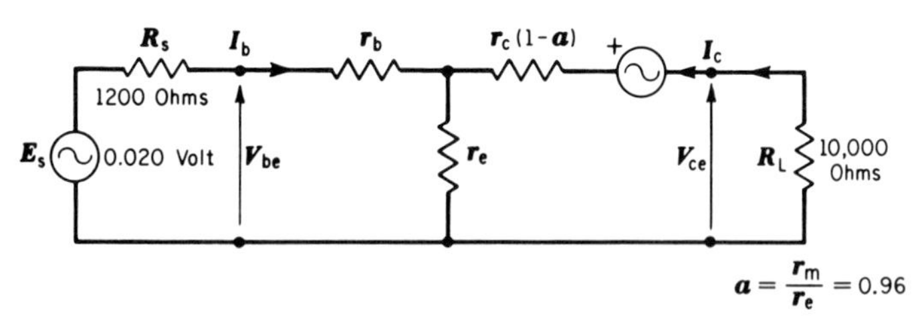

Problem 9–13.

Solution: From the equivalent circuit, the following loop equations are obtained:

(a) $V_{be} = (r_b + r_e)I_b + r_e I_c$

(b) $V_{ce} = (r_e - r_m)I_b + [r_e + r_c(1 - a)I_c]$

(c) $V_{be} = E_s - I_b R_s$

(d) $V_{ce} = -I_c R_L$

The output voltage and power gain are

$$V_c = E_s A_{ve} \qquad \text{PG} = /A_{ve} A_{ie}/$$

where A_{ve} and A_{ie} are the voltage and current gain respectively. A_{ve} and A_{ie} are found by solving the above equations for V_c/E_s and I_c/I_b respectively:

$$A_{ve} = \frac{V_c}{E_s} = \frac{-R_L(r_m - r_e)}{(r_b + r_e + R_s)[r_e + v_c(1 - a) + R_L] + r_e(V_m - r_e)}$$

$$A_{ve} \cong \frac{-a\,R_L}{r_e + (r_b + R_s)(1 - a)} = \frac{-(0.96)(10^4)}{30 + (140 + 1200)(1 - 0.96)} = -115$$

Since $R_e \gg R_L < r_c\,(1 - a)$, $R_s \gg R_e$

$$A_{ie} = \frac{r_m - r_e}{r_e + V_c(1 - a) + R_L} \cong \frac{a}{1 - a} = \frac{0.96}{1 - 0.96} = 24$$

Therefore,

$$V_c = E_s A_{ve} = (0.020)(-115) = -2.3 \text{ volts (phase reversal)}$$
$$\text{PG} = /A_{ve} A_{ie}/ = /(-115)(24)/ = 2760$$

For maximum power transfer, $R_L = R_o$ where R_o is the output resistance of the amplifier. By definition, $R_o = V_c/I_c$ with the independent voltage and current sources shorted and open, respectively.

After substituting equation (c) for V_{be} in (a) with $E_s = 0$, equations (a) and (b) can be solved for V_c/I_c:

$$R_o = \frac{V_c}{I_c} = r_e + r_c(1 - a) - \frac{r_e\,(r_e - r_m)}{r_b + r_e + R_s}$$

Therefore, for maximum power transfer:

$$R_L = R_o \cong r_c(1 - a) + \frac{r_e r_m}{r_b + r_e + R_s}$$

$$= 10^6(1 - 0.96) + \frac{30(9.6 \times 10^5)}{30 + 140 + 1200} = 21{,}000 \text{ ohm}$$

9–14. The hybrid-parameter equivalent circuit of a common-base transistor amplifier is shown in the figure. The amplifier drives a 10,000 ohm resistive load from a 200-microampere current source having an internal conductance of 0.01 ohms. Determine the input current (I_e) and the output voltage (V_{cb}) of the amplifier. The h-parameters of the transistor are: $h_{ib} = 30$ ohm, $h_{rb} = 5 \times 10^{-4}$, $h_{fb} = -0.978$, and $h_{ob} = 0.6 \times 10^{-6}$ mhos.

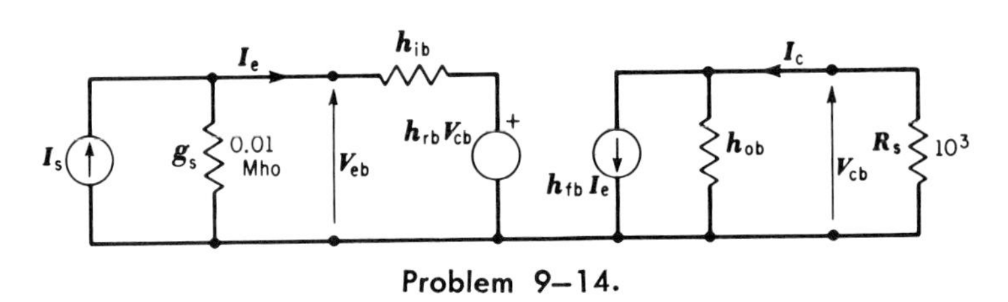

Problem 9–14.

Solution: Based on the above equivalent circuit, the following loop and nodal equations are obtained:

(a) $V_{eb} = h_{ib}I_e + h_{rb}V_{cb}$ (c) $I_s = g_sV_{eb} + I_e$
(b) $I_c = h_{fb}I_c + h_{ob}V_{cb}$ (d) $V_{cb} = -I_cR_L$

The input current I_e is

$$I_e = V_{eb}/R_{ib}$$

where R_{ib} is the input impedance to the transistor. R_{ib} is found solving equations (a) and (b) for the ratio V_{eb}/I_e

(e) $$R_{ib} = \frac{V_{eb}}{I_e} = \frac{R_L\Delta + h_{ib}}{h_{ob}R_L + 1}$$

where

$$\Delta = h_{ib}h_{ob} - h_{rb}h_{fb} = (30)(6 \times 10^{-7}) - (5 \times 10^{-4})(-0.978) = 5.07 \times 10^{-4}$$

Therefore,

$$R_{ib} \cong R_L\Delta + h_{ib} = 10^4(5.07 \times 10^{-4}) + 30 \qquad R_{ib} = 35.1 \text{ ohm}$$

From equations (c) and (e)

$$\text{(f)} \qquad I_e = \frac{I_s}{1 + g_s R_{ib}} = \frac{2 \times 10^{-4}}{1 + (0.01)(35.1)} = 1.48 \times 10^{-4} \text{ amp}$$

From equations (b), (d), and (f)

$$V_{bc} = \frac{-h_{fb} I_e}{h_{ob} + \dfrac{1}{R_L}}$$

$$V_{bc} \cong -h_{fb} I_e R_L = -(-0.978)(1.48 \times 10^{-4})\, 10^4 = 1.45 \text{ volts}$$

9–15. A cubical framework is put together as shown below. Each member is identical and has an electrical resistance of R. What is the equivalent resistance across the diagonal AB?

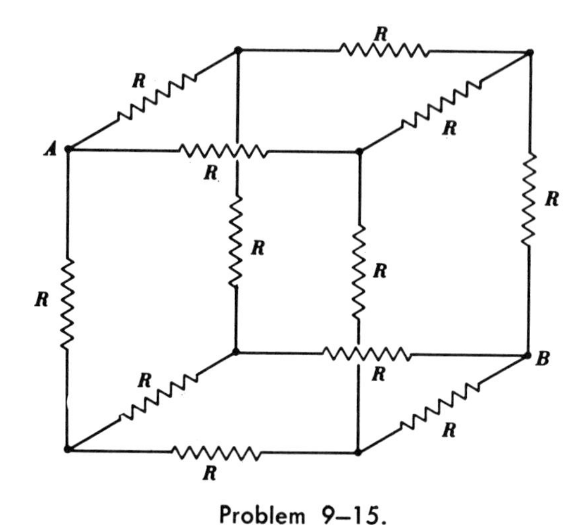

Problem 9–15.

9–16. What voltage must be impressed on the circuit shown in the accompanying illustration in order to have a current of 8 amp in the 5-ohm resistor?

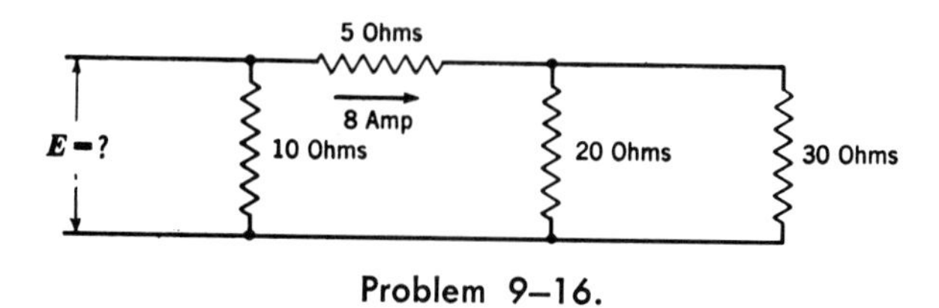

Problem 9–16.

9–17. (a) In the circuit of the figure what is the required resistance of X so that $V_1=0$? (b) With the value of X found above and 120 volts of direct current applied, what is the voltage V_2?

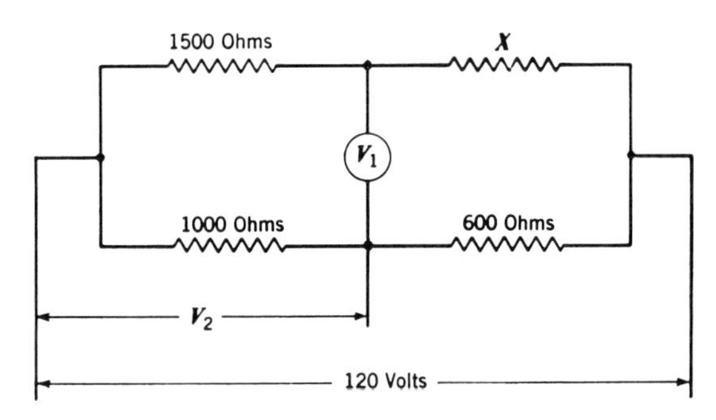

Problem 9–17.

9–18. A 72-volt 150-amp-hour storage battery has an internal resistance of 0.20 ohm. (a) What terminal voltage is required to charge this battery at a 15-amp rate? (b) If the charging source is a 120-volt generator, what series resistance will maintain the 15-amp charging rate?

9–19. Calculate the power consumed by the 6- and 8-ohm loads in the circuit shown.

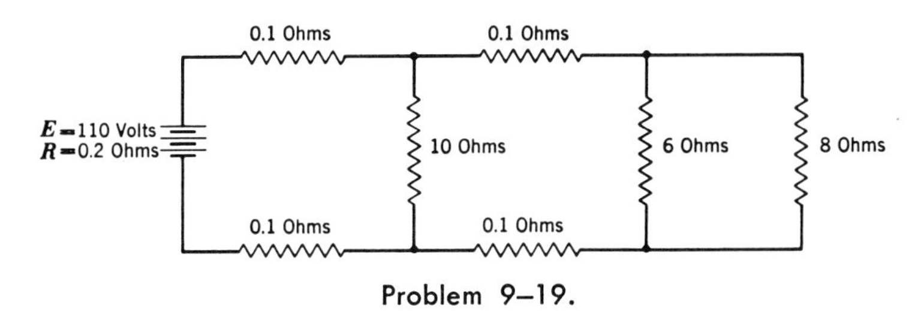

Problem 9–19.

9–20. The voltages and internal resistances of two batteries are 26 volts, 0.3 ohm and 23 volts, 0.6 ohm, respectively. These batteries are paralleled (positive terminals connected) to supply a common load. What is the resistance of the load that will draw maximum power, and what will be the terminal voltage of the batteries?

9–21. Two storage batteries of 10- and 15-volt internal emfs and 1- and 2-ohm internal resistances, respectively, are paralleled (positive terminals connected) to a common load. Find the resistance of the load that will draw the same current from each battery.

9–22. A storage battery for farm lighting produces 64 volts across its terminals on open circuit. The battery has 0.035 ohms internal resistance and is connected through a pair of copper wires, which have a resistance of 1.835 ohms/1000 ft, to a load 200 ft distant. The load draws 15 amp under the above conditions. Determine (a) the voltage at the load 200 ft from the battery, (b) the voltage across the battery terminals when delivering this load, and (c) the voltage regulation at the load.

9–23. A trouble lamp designed for plugging into the cigarette-lighter receptacle of an automobile has a 50-ft cord of AWG #18 copper wires. The lamp is rated for 60 watts at 10 volts. Assuming that 12 volts are maintained at the receptacle and that the resistance of the lamp does not change with temperature, what is the wattage input to the lamp?

9–24. A 220-volt electric water heater has a resistance of 11 ohms. What is the rated load, in kilowatts, and how much would it cost to operate it for 5 hr at 1 cent/kwhr?

9–25. The wiring diagram for a d-c voltmeter is shown in the figure. When a 0.588-volt potential is applied across *AB*, the meter registers a full-scale deflection. The scale is graduated from 0 to 15. What should the meter read when a 20-volt potential is applied across *OP*?

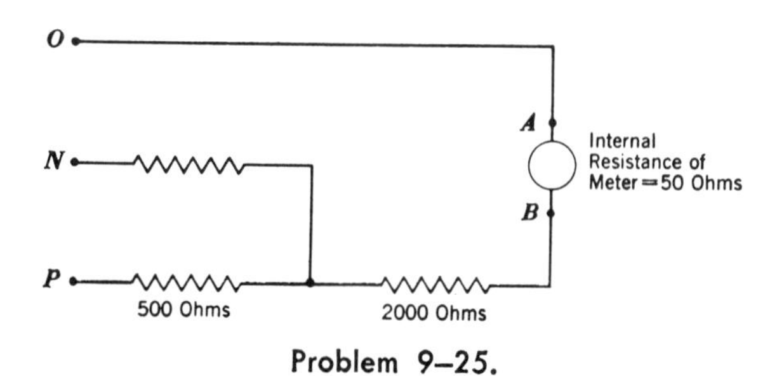

Problem 9–25.

9–26. A 300-scale voltmeter, having a resistance of 60,000 ohms, reads 250 volts when connected across a well-regulated d-c supply. It is then connected in series with an unknown resistance, across the same 250-volt supply line, and reads 25 volts. What is the value of the resistance?

9–27. A 60,000-ohm voltmeter is used to measure the insulation resistance of a motor. A 40,000-ohm resistor is connected across the voltmeter terminals. This combination is then connected in series with the insulation resistance and a 550-volt battery. The voltmeter deflection is 12 volts. Determine the value of the insulation resistance, in ohms.

9–28. The temperature coefficient of resistance for a particular conductor is defined at the temperature t_1 as $\alpha_1 = [(215 + t_1)\,°C]^{-1}$. A length of the wire has a resistance of 12 ohms at −25°C. Determine the resistance at 50°C.

9–29. A ribbon of copper having a resistivity of 10.4 ohm-cir mil/ft is 4 m long, 0.06 in. wide, and 0.02 in. thick. Compute the resistance between the ends of the ribbon.

9–30. The electrical resistance of copper wire varies directly with the length and inversely as the square of the diameter. If a certain copper wire has a resistance of 10 ohms, determine (a) the resistance, in ohms, for a second wire whose length is 70 per cent greater and whose diameter is 40 per cent greater than the first wire mentioned and (b) the resistance of the third wire whose length is the same as the first wire mentioned but whose diameter is twice that of the first wire.

9–31. A 230-volt source is to supply power to a heating load of 2.5 ohms. The distance from the source to the load is 1000 ft. The maximum permissible voltage drop is to be 3 per cent. Weatherproof copper wire is to be used. (a) Determine the wire size to be used. (b) If the load is used 800 hr/year and the electric rate is 2.0 cents/kwhr, how much money would be saved per year in line loss by using the next larger size conductor?

9–32. A 24-volt battery is used to run a small d-c shunt motor. The field resistance is 50 ohms, and the armature resistance is 30 ohms. (a) Determine the back emf generated by the motor when the battery current is 750 ma. (b) If the load is reduced so that the battery current is only 500 ma, how much has the motor speed changed?

9–33. Given a 100-volt 20-hp d-c shunt motor. (a) Explain how you would limit the current during the starting period. (b) Approximately how much added resistance would you use? (c) Where would you place this added resistance in the circuit? Why?

(d) Why is it desirable to limit the current? (e) To what value would you limit it?

9–34. The rated horsepower of an electric motor is (a) the horsepower delivered to the drive shaft at twice rated current, (b) the horsepower of the electric power necessary to operate the motor at full load, (c) the horsepower output which causes a specific rise in temperature when the motor is run continuously under a given ambient temperature, (d) the horsepower necessary to twist the shaft to the yield point, or (e) none of these.

9–35. Find the efficiency of a shunt motor if the supplied voltage is 110 volts and the supplied current is 35 amp. The armature resistance is 0.20 ohms, and the constant brush drop is 2 volts. The armature current is 30 amp, and the stray power loss is 55 watts.

9–36. A series d-c motor is delivering 100 hp. The efficiency is 85 per cent, and the supply voltage is 230 volts. Calculate the supply current, in amperes.

9–37. An electric truck is propelled by a d-c motor connected to a 110-volt storage battery. The truck is required to exert a tractive effort of 200 lb at a speed of 5 mph. If the over-all efficiency of the motor and drive is 70 per cent, what is the current taken from the battery?

9–38. A d-c generator has two poles, with each pole face having an area of 12 sq in.; pole face=0.6 of pole span (radial projection). The flux density of the air gap is 40,000 lines/sq in. (a) Compute the average emf for one turn on the armature when the machine is running at 1200 rpm. Assume that there is no stray flux outside the pole-face area. (b) What is the relation between the average voltage, maximum voltage, and rms voltage?

9–39. The operating coil of an electromagnet must operate from a 24-volt d-c supply. In what way should the coil be changed (a) to develop more pull and (b) if the coil runs too hot?

If the coil must operate from a 110-volt a-c supply, in what way should it be changed (c) to develop more pull (d) if the coil runs too hot?

9–40. A circular-cross-section magnetic chuck made of steel, used to hold flat pieces of steel for machining operations requires 240-lb attractive force. The holding surface is 24 sq in. and the air gap is approximately 0.30 in. The magnetization curve for the steel may be taken as follows:

Kilolines per square inch	10	30	40	60	80	100
Ampere-turns per inch	1.1	1.8	2.4	4.4	10.2	80

Allow 16 in. for the mean length of flux path through the chuck and the flat piece being worked and determine (a) the flux density required, in lines per square inch, (b) the ampere-turns for the steel and chuck, and (c) the ampere-turns for the air gap.

9–41. The admittance of an a-c circuit is given as $Y=4-j3$. (a) What is the simplified complex expression for the impedance? (b) What is the magnitude of the pure resistance in the circuit?

9–42. A circuit consisting of resistance, inductance, and capacitance in series is connected to a variable-frequency oscillator of a constant 15-volt output. At 1000 cps the current is a maximum at 10 ma; at 2000 cps the current decreases to 1.0 ma. Find the resistance, inductance, and capacitance in this circuit.

9–43. What is the total impedance Z_t for the circuit shown below. What is the magnitude of the absolute impedance?

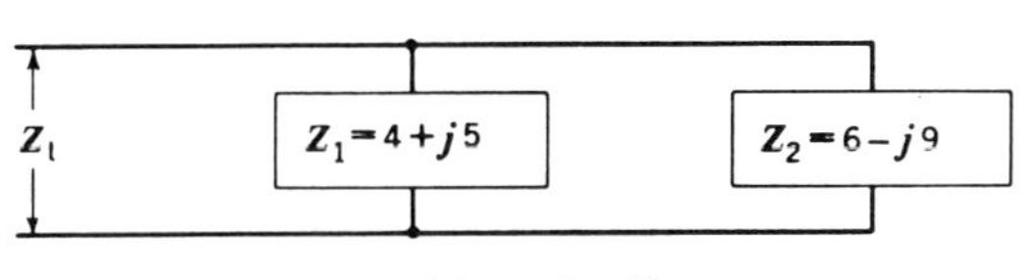

Problem 9–43.

9–44. A certain inductance coil takes 6 amp and 360 watts from a 120-volt 60-cycle single-phase line. (a) For this coil determine (1) the resistance; (2) the impedance; (3) the reactance; and (4) the inductance, in henrys. (b) Draw the complete vector diagram for this condition showing the power-factor angle. (c) If a condenser, having a negligible loss, takes 8 amp when connected in parallel with the inductance coil, what total current, in amperes, will the single-phase line supply to the combined load?

9–45. A three-wire three-phase line with 100 volts between wires has three resistances of 10 ohms each connected between wires. Find the line currents and their phase relations to the line voltages.

9–46. An alternating current has a maximum (peak) value of 10 amp; the waveshape is triangular with both quarter- and half-wave symmetry. What is the effective, or rms, value of the current?

9–47. Calculate, for the a-c circuit shown below, the value of (a) the current I_2, (b) the current I_1, (c) the voltage across the capacitor, (d) the current I_t, (e) the voltage E, (f) the power factor of the system, and (g) the inductance L_1.

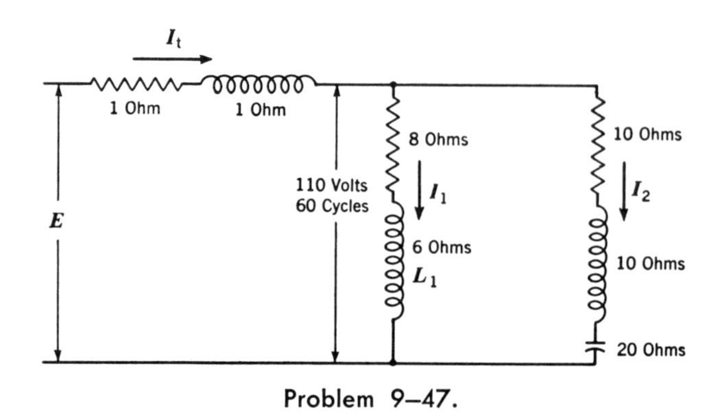

Problem 9–47.

9–48. A company has a 200-kva synchronous motor which is operated at 0.8 power factor, leading. How much load (kilovolt-amperes) at 0.6 power factor lagging can be added to give an over-all power factor of 0.9 lagging?

9–49. A 60-cycle single-phase motor draws 8.5 amp at 120 volts and has an inductive power factor of 87 per cent at this load. (a) How much power, in watts, is the motor using? (b) If a 150-μf capacitor is connected in parallel with the motor, what will the new power factor be?

9–50. A certain single-phase 60-cycle feeder is supplying 20 amp lagging current at 220 volts and 87 per cent power factor to the terminals of a small motor. The feeder from the supply line to the motor has a total resistance of 0.2 ohm and a reactance of 0.8 ohm. For this set of conditions determine (a) the horsepower being delivered to the motor, (b) the voltage input to the feeder, and (c) the efficiency of the feeder.

9–51. (a) State what is meant by a three-phase power system. (b) State what is meant by the Edison three-wire distribution system. (c) State two advantages of a three-phase power system over a single-phase system. (d) Describe a power transformer, briefly and with the aid of a sketch, and explain its function in the power system. (e) Explain the advantages gained by connecting banks of capacitors at various points in electric power systems.

9–52. Calculate the horsepower output of a three-phase 220-volt a-c motor when it is drawing a line current of 50 amp and operating at 85 per cent power factor and 90 per cent efficiency.

9–53. A 1000-hp three-phase 2200-volt induction motor is loaded to rated capacity. The efficiency is 92 per cent, and the power factor is 87 per cent. (a) What is the current input to the motor? (b) What total kvar of capacitors is required connected in parallel with the motor to bring the power factor to 100 per cent?

9–54. The following loads are connected to a 208-volt three-phase four-wire distribution system. A three-phase induction motor operating at 90 per cent efficiency and 85 per cent power factor is delivering 15 hp. A three-phase synchronous motor operating at 85 per cent efficiency and 80 per cent power factor leading is delivering 10 hp. A balanced three-phase, 20-kw lighting load is connected from line to neutral. Calculate (a) the induction motor current, (b) the synchronous motor current, (c) the lighting-load voltage and phase current, and (d) the power factor of the total load.

9–55. A three-phase 440-volt squirrel-cage induction motor draws a line current of 200 amp and produces a starting torque of 150 lb-ft when supplied at rated voltage. If 220 volts were applied, what would be (a) the starting torque and (b) the starting current?

9–56. What changes in internal or external connections are required to change the direction of rotation of the following motors: (a) three-phase induction motor, (b) single-phase a-c capacitor-start motor, (c) d-c shunt motor, and (d) d-c series motor.

9–57. The transformer shown below is rated 2400 volts to 120/240 volts with four high-voltage taps, two of them $2\frac{1}{2}$ per cent above and two $2\frac{1}{2}$ per cent below normal. On what taps should the primary be connected to a 2280-volt circuit, and how should the secondary be connected to deliver full current capacity at 120 volts?

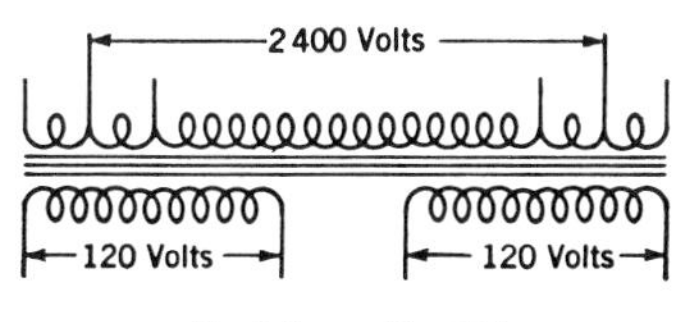

Problem 9–57.

9–58. A triode has a plate resistance of 3000 ohms and an amplification factor of 5.0 when operated with a plate supply voltage of 250 volts and a grid bias of —30 volts. (a) What is the voltage gain of this tube when supplying a load resistance of 5000 ohms? (b) What a-c voltage is produced across the load resistance when an a-c voltage of 15 volts rms is applied to the grid? (c) What is the a-c power supplied to the load resistance?

9–59. A diagram of a basic amplifier circuit and the tube characteristic curves are given in the figure; the load line for the amplifier circuit is indicated on the tube characteristic curves. With no signal on the input, the grid voltage is $e_c = -4$ volts. (a) If a sinusoidal a-c signal of 2 volts rms is applied to the input, what will the voltage be across the output? (b) What would happen if a signal of 20 volts rms were applied to the input? (c) What is the magnitude of R_L?

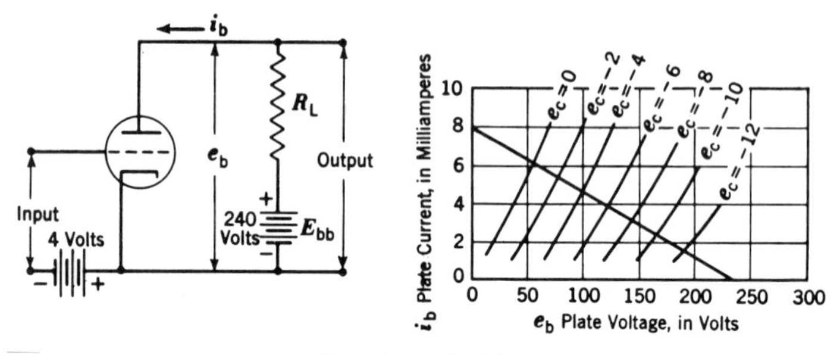

Problem 9–59.

9–60. In a vacuum tube (commonly called a triode) consisting of a filament, grid, and plate, (a) the grid is usually given a positive charge to attract electrons, (b) there must be current flowing in the grid circuit to operate the tube as an amplifier, (c) electrons flow from the plate to the filament and are accelerated by the potential between the plate and grid, (d) the grid can be made to control the flow of electrons from the filament to the plate, or (e) none of these.

9–61. The characteristics of a given triode may be represented by the expression $i_b = 8.8 \times 10^{-3} \, (e_b + 16e_c)^{1.5}$ ma. It is to be operated at a plate potential $E_b = 250$ volts and a grid-bias potential $E_c = -9$ volts. (a) Calculate the plate resistance and the amplification factor of the tube. (b) If this tube is to be used in the circuit shown with a load resistance of 10 kilohms, determine the plate supply potential necessary for the tube to operate under the specified conditions. (c) Assuming that $R_o = 20{,}000$ ohms and

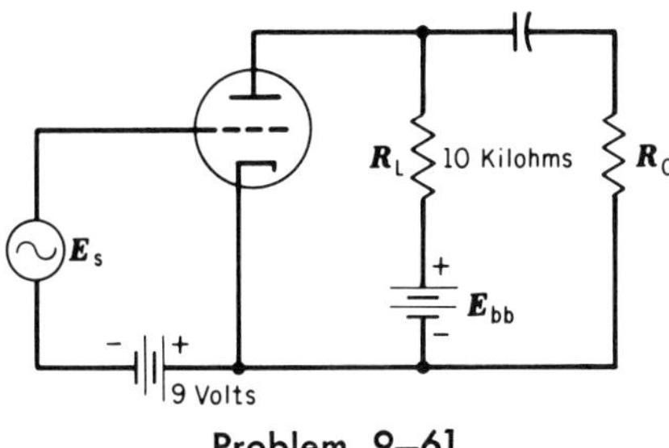

Problem 9–61.

neglecting the reactance of the coupling capacitor, determine the small signal voltage gain. (d) Neglecting a-c loading, calculate the percentage of second harmonic distortion of the a-c potential across the load resistance if $E_s = 8 \sin \omega t$.

9–62. For a given common-emitter transistor stage, the transistor constants are $r_e = 30$ ohms, $r_b = 140$ ohms, $r_c = 1.3$ megohms, $r_m = 1.25$ megohms. Connected to the input of the stage is a voltage source of 10 millivolts, and the effective a-c resistance load is 2000 ohms. What is the (a) voltage gain of the stage and the magnitude of that output voltage, (b) input resistance of the transistor stage, (c) output resistance of the transistor stage, (d) current gain of the stage, (e) power gain of the stage, and (f) input resistance if R_L is infinite?

9–63. The h-parameters for an NPN transistor are given as $h_{ib} = 35$ ohms, $h_{rb} = 1.3 \times 10^{-4}$, $h_{fb} = -0.94$, and $h_{ob} = 1.2$ micromho. Find the power gain possible when this transistor is connected as a common-emitter amplifier, and it is used to drive an effective a-c resistive load of 20,000 ohms with a voltage source having an internal resistance of 250 ohms.

9–64. Three resistors, $R_1=0.2$ ohms, $R_2=0.3$ ohms, and $R_3=0.6$ ohms, are connected in parallel across the terminals of a storage battery having an internal resistance of 0.02 ohm and an emf of 6-volts on open circuit. With this circuit closed determine (a) the total current supplied by the battery to the three resistors; (b) the terminal voltage of the battery to this load; (c) the total power, in watts, supplied to the three resistors; and (d) the current, in amperes, through the 0.2-ohm resistor.

9–65. (a) Show how two 100-watt and one 200-watt 120-volt lamps can be connected to a 240-volt supply to give normal illumination. (b) What current will flow through each lamp when connected as you have them in (a)? (c) What current will be supplied to the three as you have them connected in (a)?

9–66. Referring to the figure, the resistors R_1 and R_2 have the following respective ratings: the resistance of $R_1 = 22.5$ ohms and its maximum permissible power dissipation is 1000 watts; the resistance of $R_2 = 40$ ohms and its maximum permissible power dissipation is 360 watts. The resistance of each is constant, and R_3 is an adjustable resistor which represents an adjustable load in the circuit shown. Determine the minimum and maximum resistance of R_3 (in ohms) permissible without exceeding the power ratings of either R_1 or R_2.

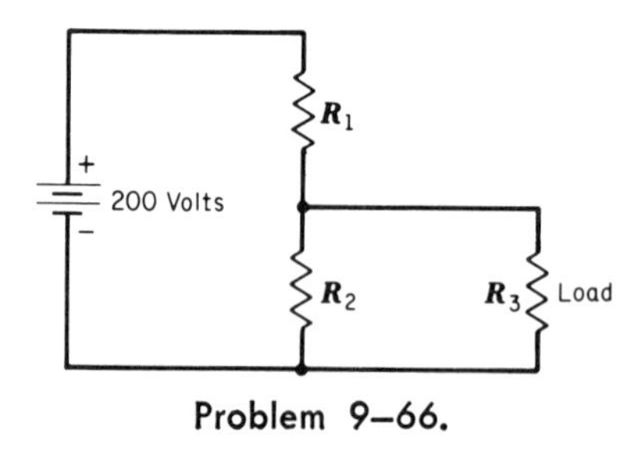

Problem 9–66.

9–67. For the circuit shown, find: (a) The current in all branches of the circuit, (b) the power delivered to the circuit or stored in each battery, and (c) the power dissipated in the 2-ohm resistor.

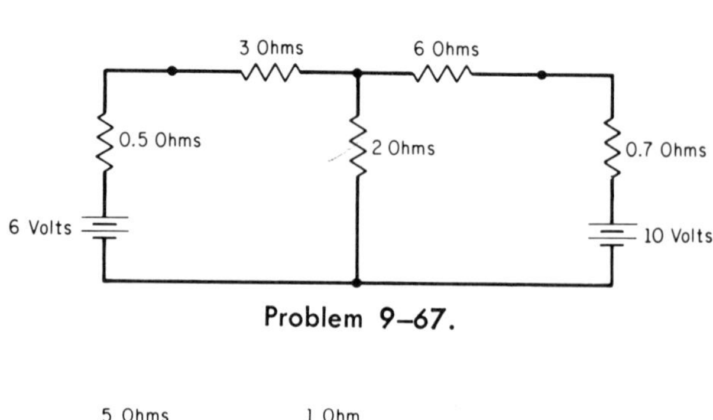

Problem 9–67.

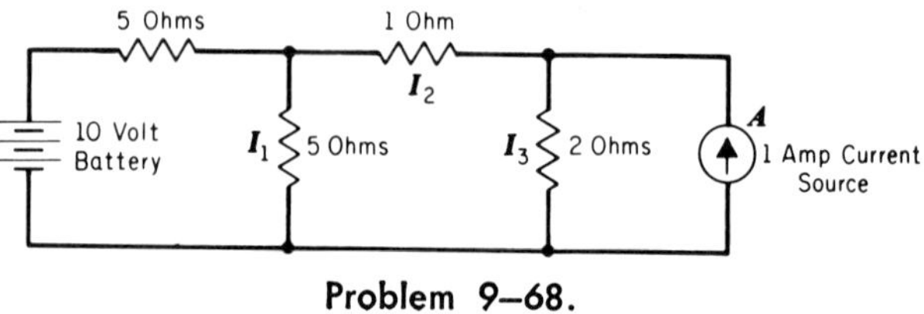

Problem 9–68.

9–68. Find the currents I_1, I_2 and I_3 in the d-c resistive circuit shown.

9–69. Show by a sketch and a circuit diagram: (a) the construction of a voltmeter for a 1 ma meter movement with 100 ohms internal resistance to read 30 volts full scale; (b) for the same movement, construction of an ammeter to read full scale as 15 amp total current; (c) for the same movement and a 30-volt battery, construction of an ohmmeter.

9–70. A storage battery consists of 120 cells, connected in series. Each cell has an emf of 2.10 volts and an internal resistance of 0.0015 ohm. Determine: (a) voltage necessary to charge battery at a 60-amp rate, (b) total power delivered to the battery and power lost in the battery, and (c) terminal voltage when battery is disconnected from charging source and a resistor of 2.5 ohms is connected across terminals.

9–71. Given a 2-hp d-c shunt-wound motor rated: 1725 rpm, 115 volts, 15.8 amp. Field resistance = 230 ohms. Armature resistance = 0.5 ohms. If we wish to operate this motor as a d-c generator at 115 volts and receive the same output line current as the input line current of the motor, at what speed must the machine run?

9–72. A series circuit consists of the following: a pure resistance of 32 ohms, a pure inductance of 0.24 henry, and a pure capacitance of 80 μf. These are connected to a power supply of 240 volts, 60 cycle, alternating current. Calculate the following: (a) the circuit current, (b) the power supplied from the source, (c) the load reactance, and (d) the size capacitor required for unity power factor.

9–73. For the circuit shown, find (a) the input impedance of

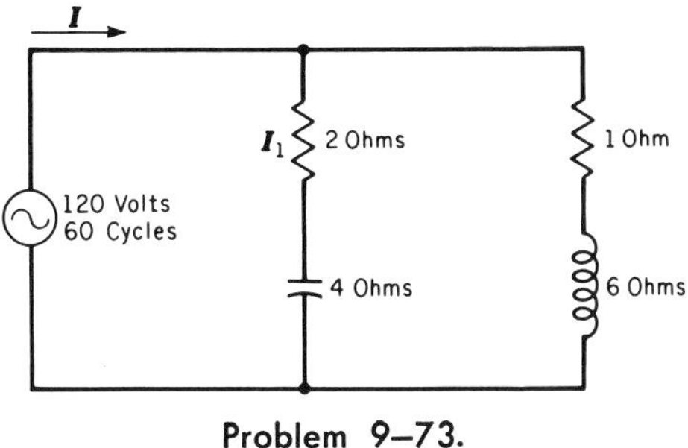

Problem 9–73.

the circuit, magnitude, and angle; (b) the current that will flow in the branches and line: (c) the power consumed by the circuit; and (d) the parallel impedance required for unity power factor.

9–74. A coil with an inductance of 1 henry and a resistance of 50 ohms is connected in series with a 0.01 μf capacitor and a variable frequency supply. (a) At what frequency will the maximum voltage appear across the capacitor if the supply voltage is held constant as the frequency is varied? (b) What is the maximum value of supply voltage which may be used in this circuit if the capacitor voltage rating is 200 volts? The frequency is that found in part (a).

9–75. The voltage $e(t)$ has the periodic waveform indicated in the figure. How much power is dissipated in resistor R_3 in the resistive circuit shown in part (b) of the figure?

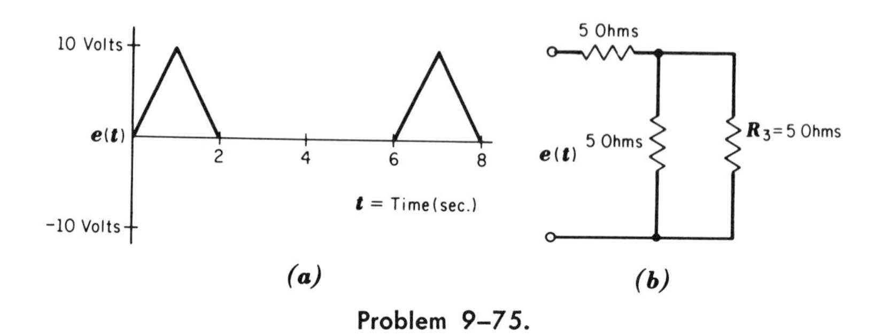

Problem 9–75.

9–76. Referring to the diagram, $L = (1/1.1)\,(10^{-1})$ henry and $C = (1/1.1)\,(10^{-5})$ farads. A d-c constant current generator of 1 amp is applied to the circuit shown. At time $t=0$, the switch is opened. Specify the conductance g in mhos so that the circuit will oscillate with an angular velocity of 1000 radians/sec. The amplitude of node voltage a relative to node b will be attenuated.

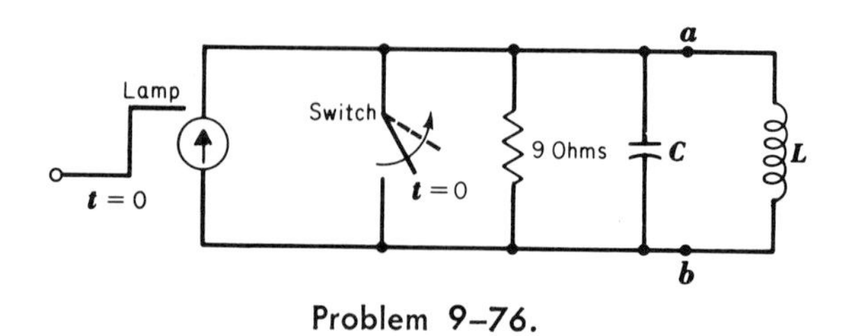

Problem 9–76.

9–77. A single phase, 60 cps, a-c distribution circuit supplies a 1000 volt 70.7 kw, 70.7 per cent power lagging load as shown. Compute the required quantities.

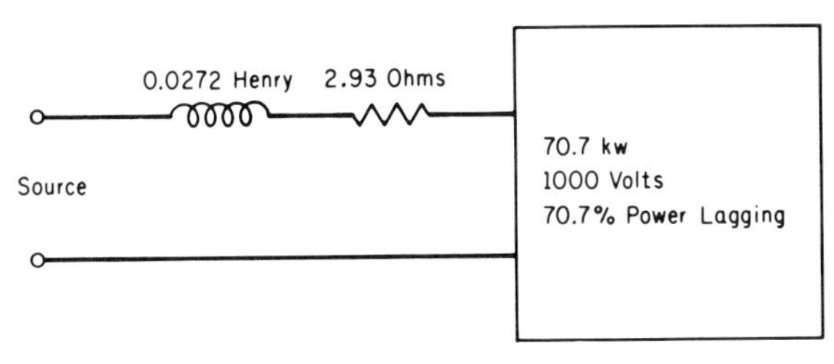

Problem 9–77.

For the source:	For the line:	For the load:
$I =$ _____amp	$I =$ _____amp	$I =$ _____amp
$V =$ _____volts	$kw_{loss} =$ _____	$V = 1000$ volts
$pf =$ _____%	$kvar_{loss} =$ _____	pf = 70.7%
kw = _____	Reg = _____%	kw = 70.7
kvar = _____	eff = _____%	kvar = _____
kva = _____		kva = _____

9–78. A three-phase 2400-volt pump motor lifts 3000 gal/min from a mine. The water is lifted 300 ft. The pump and motor system is 50 per cent efficient. If the power factor of the circuit is 0.8, what would it cost per day at 1.5 cents/kwhr, for each day of operation?

9–79. (a) Indicate terminals of like polarity in the iron-core transformer shown in the figure. Describe two methods of finding transformer polarity of an enclosed power current transformer. Explain what is meant by "additive" and "subtractive" polarity in a power transformer. (b) What will be the secondary voltage E_s with no load? If the transformer is considered as loss free, what

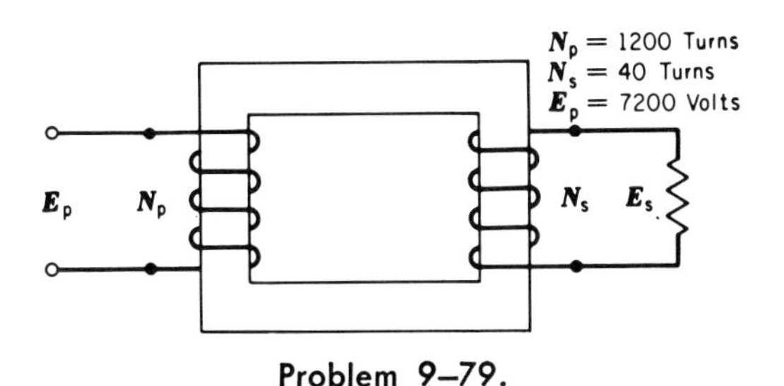

Problem 9–79.

will be the secondary current with 4 ohms resistive load? What would be the primary current with no losses and 4 ohms resistive load? (c) In a real transformer, the loss gives rise to a term "per cent impedance." If the transformer shown were listed as 24 kva and 3 per cent impedance, what would be the full load secondary voltage? Show work.

9–80. A microwave radiator having a wavelength (L) of 0.10 meters is used as a radar to measure the speed of an oncoming automobile. The measured frequency shift (Δf) is 600 cps. Compute the speed (in mph) of the car. Velocity of light is assumed to be 3.0×10^8 m/sec.

Engineering Economy 10

Most problems in engineering economy require computations to determine the time value of money. Such calculations are facilitated by the use of interest tables given in standard textbooks. If reference to such tables is not permitted, the following formulas must be used:

$$S = P(1+i)^n \tag{10–1}$$

$(1+i)^n$ is the single payment compound amount factor *caf′* and $1/(1+i)^n$ is the single payment present worth factor *pwf′*.

$$R = S\left[\frac{i}{(1+i)^n - 1}\right] \tag{10–2}$$

$\dfrac{i}{(1+i)^n - 1}$ is the sinking-fund deposit factor *sff*. The reciprocal is the uniform series compound amount factor *caf*.

$$R = P\left[\frac{i(1+i)^n}{(1+i)^n - 1}\right] \tag{10–3}$$

$\dfrac{i(1+i)^n}{(1+i)^n - 1}$ is the uniform series capital recovery factor *crf*. If the formula is reversed, the reciprocal factor is the uniform series present worth factor *pwf*.

$$i' = (1+i)^n - 1 \tag{10–4}$$

in which i = interest rate per interest period;
i' = effective interest rate per year;
n = number of interest periods;
P = present sum of money;
S = a sum of money at the end of n interest periods, as given in formula 10–1;
R = end-of-period payment in a uniform series running for n periods, as given in formula 10–3.

Fundamentally, problems normally fall into two types which involve cost comparisons for alternatives based upon (1) annual cost or (2) present worth and capitalized cost. Depreciation, break-even and increment costs, and bond calculations are common ingredients. Occasional questions requiring definitions or discussion without numerical calculations are also used. Relatively short economy problems are given in the engineering fundamentals section; longer ones, such as 10–54 and 10–55, in the professional sections.

10–1. With interest at 6 per cent compounded annually, (a) what sum of money will be required 5 years hence to repay $950 deposited today with a savings and loan company? (b) If a down payment of $5000 is made on a house and $750 per year for the next 12 years is required by the contract, what was the price of the house?

Solution: (a) From formula 10–1

$$\text{caf}' = 1.338$$

$$S = \$950(1.338) = \$1271$$

(b) From formula 10–3

$$\text{pwf} = 8.384$$

$$\text{Price} = \$5000 + \$750(8.384) = \$11{,}288$$

10–2. A company sells an issue of $1,000,000 of 4 per cent noncallable bonds on which interest is paid semiannually. The bonds are to be retired in 20 years by means of a sinking fund in which deposits are made annually. The sinking fund earns interest at the rate of 3 per cent. What are the annual charges for bond interest and sinking-fund deposits?

Solution:	$1,000,000(0.04)	= $40,000
sff formula 10–2	$1,000,000(0.03722) =	37,220
	Annual charges	= $77,220

10–3. A piece of equipment for a concrete batching plant costs $10,000 and has a life expectancy of 20 years. At the end of 20 years, the salvage value is estimated to be $2000. Taxes and insurance are $250 per year. Maintenance costs are estimated to be $15 per month. Calculate the yearly cost of the equipment on the basis of 6 per cent interest using (a) straight-line depreciation and average interest, and (b) the exact capital recovery method.

Solution:

(a)	Annual depreciation	$= \dfrac{\$10{,}000 - \$2000}{20}$	= $ 400
	Average interest	$= \$8000(0.06/2)21/20 + \$2000(0.06) =$	372
	Taxes		= 250
	Maintenance	$= \$15(12)$	= 180
	Annual cost		= $1202

(b) Capital recovery (from Formula 10–3)

(\$10,000 − \$2000) (0.08718) + \$2000(0.06)	= \$ 817
Taxes	= 250
Maintenance = \$15(12)	= 180
Annual cost	= \$1247

The straight-line depreciation and average interest method therefore tends to underestimate the annual cost.

10–4. A section of roadway pavement costs \$400 a year to maintain. What expenditure for a new pavement is justified if no maintenance will be required for the first 5 years, \$100 per year for the next 10 years, and \$400 a year thereafter? Assume money to cost 4 per cent.

Solution:

By pwf formula 10–3

pw \$400 for 5 years	= \$400(4.452)	= \$1781

Formulas (10–3, 10–1)

pw \$300 saving for 10 years = \$300(8.111)(0.8219)	= 2000
Expenditure justified	= \$3781

10–5. A \$10,500 truck has an estimated life of 6 years and a scrap value of \$500. At the end of 3 years it is wrecked so badly that the remains are worth only \$100. How much money would have to be raised to purchase a new truck of the same first cost if an amount equal to the annual depreciation charge had been invested as follows: (a) Depreciation calculated by the straight-line method and funds invested at zero per cent interest; (b) in a sinking-fund at 5 per cent annual compound interest.

Solution:

(a) Annual depreciation for 3 years $= \frac{\$10{,}500 - \$500}{6}(3) = \$5000$

Actual salvage value	= 100
Available	= \$5100
Amount required for new truck = \$10,500 − \$5100	= 5400

(b)

From formula 10–2, sff for $n = 6$ and $i = 5$ per cent is 0.14702.

Sinking fund charge, first year, (10,500 − \$500)(0.14702)	= 1470
Available in sinking fund after 3 years (using the caf) \$1470(3.153)	= 4635
Actual salvage value	= 100
Available	= \$4735
Amount required for new truck = \$10,500 − \$4,735	= \$5765

10–6. A certain machining job can be done on six existing lathes if $120 is spent on each lathe for special tool equipment. It is estimated that 25 min time will be required per piece machined with labor at $1.20 per hour. The job could also be done on automatic machines which will have to be purchased for $3640 each, including tools. Time per piece on these machines will be 4 min, and labor will be charged at the rate of $0.20 per hour because one man can tend 6 machines. What size of order for such pieces would justify purchasing automatic machines, assuming the cost of the special tools or the automatic machines to be written off on the job?

Solution: Let x = size of order

Existing Lathes — Automatic Machines

$$6(\$120)+(\$1.20)\left(\frac{25}{60}\right)x=(\$3640)+\$0.20\left(\frac{1}{15}\right)x$$

$$x=6000 \text{ units}$$

10–7. As a consulting engineer, you are asked to choose between two methods of supplying water for perpetual service: (1) A pipeline with first cost of $150,000, perpetual life, and annual operation and upkeep of $2000; or (2) an aqueduct with initial cost of $30,000, 10-year life, salvage value of $5000, and annual operation and upkeep of $4000. Interest rate is 5 per cent.

Solution:

Pipeline	
First cost	= $150,000
pw of perpetual annual disbursements = $2000/0.05	= 40,000
Total capitalized cost	= $190,000
Aqueduct	
First cost	= $ 30,000
pw of infinite series of renewals = ($30,000 − $5000) (sff − 0.05 − 10)/0.05 = $25,000(0.07950)/0.05	= $ 39,750
pw of perpetual annual disbursements = $4000/0.05	= 80,000
Total capitalized cost	= $149,750

The aqueduct would be the more economical choice.

10–8. The manager of a warehouse has been advised that his insurance rate will be decreased from $0.75 per $100 of coverage to $0.40 per $100 of coverage if he installs an adequate sprinkler system. The warehouse and its contents are insured for $600,000. The sprinkler system proposed can be installed for $20,000, will have an annual maintenance cost of $382, and an estimated life of

20 years with no salvage value at the end of that period. Property taxes are 0.9 per cent of the cost of warehouse, equipment, and contents. The manager wants to know what rate of return, if any, investment in the sprinkler system will produce.

Solution:

Annual costs attributable to the sprinkler system

Initial cost = \$20,000 (crf − 1 − 20)	= \$20,000crf
Maintenance	= 382
Property taxes = \$20,000 (0.009)	= 180
Additional insurance = \$20,000 × \$0.40/\$100	= 80
Annual cost = \$20,000 (crf − 1 − 20) + \$642	
Annual savings resulting from installation of the sprinkler system	
\$600,000 (\$0.75 − \$0.40)/100	= \$ 2100

To solve for rate of return, Costs = Savings

\$20,000 (crf − 1 − 20) + \$642 = \$2100

From formula 10–3, rate of return = 4 per cent

10–9. A manufacturing company plans to improve its operations and considers it profitable to make all expenditures for this purpose that result in a return of 30 per cent or more on its investment. Four alternate and mutually exclusive plans are advanced for improvements in a certain operation. On the basis of the following data, determine which plan is most desirable.

Plan	Cost	Annual Return
A	\$10,000	\$4000
B	\$12,000	\$4560
C	\$15,000	\$5600
D	\$17,000	\$6000

Solution:

Rate of return on total investment:

A = \$4000/\$10,000 = 40 per cent
B = \$4560/\$12,000 = 38 per cent
C = \$5600/\$15,000 = 37 per cent
D = \$6000/\$17,000 = 35 per cent

While it appears that all plans would qualify, with D the plan most likely to be selected, the important question is whether or not the incremental investment made beyond Plan A returns at least 30 per cent.

Rate of return on incremental investment:

B = (\$4560—\$4000)/(\$12,000—\$10,000) = 28 per cent
C = (\$5600—\$4000)/(\$15,000—\$10,000) = 32 per cent
D = (\$6000—\$4000)/(\$17,000—\$10,000) = 29 per cent

Plan C is the most desirable.

10–10. What do you understand by the term (a) profit, (b) capitalization, (c) interest, (d) the point of diminishing return?

10–11. (a) Discuss the difference between retiring a funded debt by issuing serial bonds and by employing the sinking-fund method, touching on the relative effects of possible future changes in interest rates, maintenance of loan security, and flexibility in budgeting. (b) What is a construction cost index? Name at least one and describe the method used in determining it. What important factors are not included in such determinations, and how do such omissions affect the use of these indices?

10–12. Point *B* is 12 miles east of point *A* and point *C* is 9 miles south of point *B*. A road from *A* to *B* carries 500 cars per day between these two points only. The road from *B* to *C* carries 400 cars per day between these two points only, while 1400 cars per day travel between *A* and *C*.

A new road is to be constructed between *A* and *C*, which is 15 miles long. The right-of-way for this road is to be 82.5 ft wide and will cost $300 per acre. Paving will cost $30,000 per mile. The old road as well as the new is to be paved. Saving in car operation on the new road is to be assumed as 2.6 cents per mile.

The county proposes to issue bonds bearing interest at 3½ per cent which will all mature at the same date. To pay the bonds when due, the county will deposit the annual savings in car operation in a sinking fund with interest at 3½ per cent until the amount still due on the bonds is accumulated. What is the life of the bonds, and what is the last payment?

10–13. In planning a state police radio system, it is desired to maintain a specified minimum signal strength at all points in the state. Two plans for accomplishing this are proposed for comparison. Plan I involves the establishment of six transmitting stations of low power. The investment for each of these in buildings, ground improvements, piping and tower—all assumed to have a life of 25 years—is estimated as $35,000. The investment in transmitting equipment for each station—assumed because of the probability of obsolescence, to have a life of 8 years—is estimated as $25,000. The monthly disbursements for operation of each station are estimated as $1050.

Plan II involves the establishment of only two transmitting stations of much higher power. The investment in buildings, etc. for each of these stations is estimated as $45,000, and the useful life of the facilities is estimated as 25 years. The investment in transmitting equipment at each station is estimated as $220,000, and the life of the equipment is estimated as 8 years. The monthly operating cost is established as $1400 per station.

Compare the annual costs of these plans, using straight-line depreciation plus average interest with an interest rate of 6 per cent per year.

10–14. A city must convey sewage through or over a rock ridge to its treatment plant. Plan A calls for a 5000-ft-long gravity sewer in rock tunnel at a cost of $175 per linear foot. Plan B calls for the construction of a pumping station for $500,000 and a 5000-ft-long force main at a cost of $50 per linear foot. The pumping station will have an annual operating and maintenance cost of $15,000. Capital costs in each case will be financed by 30-year 3 per cent bonds retired by equal annual payments combining interest and principal. Ignoring salvage value and replacement, compute the annual cost for *each* plan, state which is more economical, and show the difference in annual costs.

10–15. Two possible routes for a power line are under consideration. Route A is around a lake, 15 miles in length. First cost will be $5000 per mile, yearly maintenance $200 per mile, and the salvage value at the end of 15 years will be $3000 per mile. Route B is a submarine cable across the lake 5 miles long. The first cost will be $30,000 per mile, the annual upkeep $400 per mile, and the salvage value at the end of 15 years will be $5000 per mile. The yearly power loss will be $500 per mile for both routes. Interest rate is 4 per cent, taxes 2 per cent of the first cost. Compare the two routes on the basis of annual costs and capitalized costs.

10–16. To undertake the production of a new item, an inventor purchased a simple machine that required much hand labor. The machine cost $4400 and was estimated to have a useful life of 5 years, at the end of which time there would be no salvage value. Annual operating and maintenance costs, exclusive of depreciation and interest, were $2600. At the end of the first year he was urged to purchase a semiautomatic machine for $6200 which could match production of the first machine and which would have an annual operating and maintenance cost, exclusive of depreciation and interest, of $800. Trade-in value of the first machine would be $1600. The new machine is estimated to have a life of 4 years and no salvage value. Using an interest rate of 8 per cent, calculate the difference in equivalent annual cost for the two machines, and state which machine should be used for the next 4 years.

10–17. A refinery can provide for water storage with a steel tank on a steel tower adjacent to the plant, or a concrete standpipe on a hill some distance away. The elevated tank is estimated to cost $82,000, while the standpipe and extra length of service line are estimated to cost $60,000. The standpipe installation will require an additional capital expenditure of $6000 for pumps and controls. Operating and maintenance costs for the pumps and standpipe are estimated at $500 per year. The maintenance cost of the elevated tank is estimated to be $150 per year. Using an interest rate of 5 per cent, a life of 30 years, and assuming no salvage value, compute the equivalent annual cost for each plan.

10–18. Two alternative plans are proposed for a portion of an aqueduct. Plan A involves a short tunnel and 4 miles of flume. The tunnel is estimated to cost $200,000 and to be permanent. Its estimated annual upkeep is $500. The flume will cost $23,000 per mile and will have an estimated life of 20 years. Its estimated annual upkeep cost is $500 per mile.

Plan B involves 5 miles of concrete-lined earth canal and 2 miles of pipeline. The earth canal will cost $18,000 per mile and will be permanent. It is estimated that the upkeep costs on it will be $1000 per mile for the first 5 years until the earth is well consolidated and $200 per mile thereafter. The concrete lining has a first cost of $8000 per mile, an estimated life of 25 years, and annual maintenance costs of $50 per mile. The pipeline has an estimated first cost of $35,000 per mile, an estimated life of 50 years, and an estimated annual maintenance cost of $300 per mile.

Compare these two plans on the basis of annual cost, using the exact method for calculating *capital recovery*, with interest at 5 per cent. (Straight-line depreciation plus average interest not acceptable.)

10–19. A small city provides power with a diesel plant. The total annual cost of operation is $12,000. The existing plant has an estimated remaining life of 8 years. A hydroelectric plant can be built for $100,000 and will have an estimated life of 30 years and an operation cost of $6000. The old diesel plant has a present salvage value of $15,000 now but will have a zero value in 8 years. A new diesel plant would cost $45,000 and have an estimated life of 20 years. With money at 4 per cent, what should be done about the power supply?

10–20. The owner of a 20-year old asphalt plant is studying two alternatives. (a) He can continue with the old equipment for possibly 5 years more, at which time there will be no salvage value.

Its present salvage value is $4000. Annual repairs cost $1000. Annual output is 10,000 tons. Operating costs are $2 per ton. (b) He can sell the equipment for salvage now and purchase new equipment of the same annual output. This will cost $50,000. It is estimated that operating costs will be about $1.60 per ton and annual repairs about $500. The estimated life of the new unit is 20 years. If interest is at 6 per cent, which of these alternatives should be selected?

10–21. A furniture-manufacturing company is considering the installation of an automatic machine for boring holes to replace two machines which now provide the same total capacity. The proposed machine will cost $3000 installed. Annual expenditures for its operation are estimated as follows: Labor required will be one operator at $55.00 per week for the entire year. Power required will be 4000 kwhr per year at 3 cents per kwhr. Annual repairs and supplies are estimated at $120.00. Taxes and insurance are each estimated at 1 per cent of first cost.

The present machines cost $700 each and are 5 years old. As their life was originally estimated as 10 years, their present book value is $350 each. Their present net realizability value is only $100 each. Annual expenditures are as follows: Labor required is two operators at $45 each per week for the entire year. Power required is 2500 kwhr per machine per year at 3 cents. Annual repairs and supplies are $70 per machine. Taxes and insurance are each 1 per cent of present book value.

Compare the automatic machine with the two present machines on the basis of annual cost. Assume a 5-year pay-off period for the new machine and a 5-year remaining life for the old ones. Assume zero salvage value at the end of 5 years for all. The minimum attractive return is 8 per cent. Compute recovery by straight-line depreciation. Recommend course of action.

10–22. A company is considering adding storage space by constructing a steel building or a wood-frame building. The first cost of the metal building would be $60,000 with an estimated life of 60 years. The wood-frame building is expected to last 15 years and have a first cost of $35,000. Insurance for the steel building would be $0.75 per thousand per year and for the wood-frame building, $0.80 per thousand per year. On the basis of straight-line depreciation and negligible salvage value, what are the following: (a) the annual cost of each building with interest at 4 per cent and (b) the interest rate at which the buildings would have the same annual cost?

10–23. For a report to be submitted to the city council on the probable cost of a pumping and purification works for a proposed water supply, the following estimated values have resulted from the studies. The project if built will be financed by 3½ per cent 40-year serial bonds, the face value being equal to the estimated first cost. (1) The average amount of water to be delivered is 30 mgd. (2) Total first cost is $2,000,000. (3) Estimated life, 40 years. (4) Insurance, $2000. (5) Maintenance, $20,000. (6) Operation, $150,000. (7) Taxes, $10,000. (8) Salvage value, $200,000. (a) Determine the average cost per million gallons delivered when depreciation is computed by the straight-line basis. (b) What would be the necessary annual contribution to a sinking fund bearing 3½ per cent interest which would provide sufficient money, assuming that this cost would be $1,800,000, to reconstruct the plant at the expiration of the bond issue?

10–24. Fourteen years ago a 1200-kw steam electric plant was constructed at a cost of $220 per kilowatt. Annual operating expenses have been $31,000 to produce the annual demand of 5,400,000 kw-hr. It is estimated that the annual operating expenses and demand for current will continue. The original estimate of a 20-year life with a 5 per cent salvage value at that time is still considered correct.

The company is contemplating the replacement of the old steam plant with a new diesel plant. The old plant can be sold now for $75,000, while the new diesel plant will cost $245 per kilowatt to construct. The diesel plant will have a life of 25 years with a salvage value of 10 per cent at the end of that time and will cost $23,000 annually to operate. Annual taxes and insurance will be 2.3 per cent of the first cost of either plant.

Using an interest rate of 5 per cent, determine whether the company is financially justified in replacing the old steam plant now.

10–25. Compute each of the following, accurate to three places: (a) The present worth of $5000 per year for the next 20 years, using an interest rate of 5 per cent compounded annually. (b) The present worth of a $10,000 single payment to be made 30 years from now, using an interest rate of 4 per cent compounded annually. (c) The present worth of $3000 per year for the past 15 years, with interest at 6 per cent compounded annually. (d) The amount required to be invested per year at 2 per cent per annum to produce a sum of $400,000 at the end of 10 years.

10–26. In the purchase of land for the construction of a manufacturing plant, the question arises regarding the possibility of purchasing certain adjoining unimproved land for possible use in future plant expansion. The land is available now for $20,000. Assume that the land will not be used for 10 years and that average taxes are 2 per cent. (a) If money is worth 7 per cent, what must be the prospective price of the land 10 years hence to make it worthwhile to purchase now? (b) What additional information should enter a decision on such a matter?

10–27. Three different types of bridges are being considered for construction across a greatly fluctuating stream. Cost data on the structures have been found to be as shown in the table. Assume

Type	Construction Time (days)	First Cost	Maintenance
Steel	270	$302,000	$2000
Reinforced concrete ..	365	$358,000	300
Prestressed concrete ..	290	$325,000	500

a useful life of 30 years and interest on all money at 4 per cent. Determine the most economical structure. What other factors would you consider when deciding which structure to choose?

10–28. A certain firm wishes to invest some funds in a new manufacturing plant which according to best estimates will show a net income of $75,000 per year for 25 years. If 8 per cent return is desired on the investment, and a sinking fund can be established at 3 per cent compounded annually to recover the investment, determine the maximum cash price which can be paid for the plant. What rate of return would be earned if the price paid were $100,000?

10–29. The ABC Construction Company agreed to pay $5000 for a new dozer with an expected life of 20 years. After delivery, it was found that the dozer had only 85 per cent of the guaranteed horsepower. If a more efficient machine would increase the earnings of the company by an estimated $1000 annually, what would the company be willing to pay for the more efficient machine if the interest rate is 6 per cent?

10–30. A manufacturing concern owns a building on which there is a $100,000 mortgage which earns 6 per cent per annum. The mortgage is to be paid for in 20 equal year-end payments. After making eight payments, the concern desires to reduce its annual overhead by refinancing the balance of the debt with a 30-year mortgage at 5 per cent, also to be retired by equal annual payments. By how much would the annual charges be reduced?

10–31. An engineer decides to set aside funds for his newborn son's college education. He estimates the needs will be $2000 on the son's 18th, 19th, 20th, and 21st birthdays. The fund is to receive the deposit of a fixed amount on the son's 1st to 17th birthdays, inclusive. If the fund earns 3 per cent per annum, what should be the annual deposit in the fund?

10–32. A standard pumping installation costs $15,000 installed and has an estimated life of 12 years. By the addition of certain auxiliary equipment, an annual saving of $200 in operating costs can be obtained and the estimated life of the installation can be doubled. Neglecting any salvage value for either installation and with interest at 6 per cent, what present expenditure is justified for the auxiliary equipment?

10–33. The Central School District has under consideration two alternative plans for school construction. Plan A proposes the construction of a small building immediately and the construction of a second building of the same size at the end of 15 years. Each building will cost $1,000,000. Plan B proposes the construction of a larger building at a cost of $1,500,000, requiring no future capital expenditure.

The district proposes to finance the capital cost of each school by selling, at the time of construction, 30-year bonds bearing an interest rate of 3½ per cent per annum. Debts are to be retired by uniform annual payments combining principal and interest. Depreciation of each structure is by straight line over 50 years with no salvage value at the end of that period. Maintenance cost per year in plan A is estimated at $20,000 per year per structure, and in plan B, $30,000 per year.

Compare the present worth of each plan.

10–34. With interest at 4 per cent compounded annually, determine the following: (a) If a down payment of $7500 was made on a piece of real estate and $1500 at the end of each of the succeeding 5 years was required, what was the cash price of the property? (b) What payment 10 years hence is equivalent to a payment of $5000 five years hence?

10–35. A water tank cost $45,000 ten years ago and is expected to be useable for another 20 years, when it will be worth $2000 as scrap. Assuming the sinking-fund method of depreciation to apply with interest at 3¾ per cent annually, what is the present value of the tank?

10–36. An engineer is asked by a client to recommend a method of construction for a pier. Concrete piles have a life of 20 years, a maintenance cost of $500 per year, and a first cost of $30,000. Pressure-treated timber piles have a life of 15 years, a maintenance cost of $1000 per year, and a first cost of $20,000. It is probable that the total structural life will be 60 years. The client can get 4 per cent for his money in outside investments and considers risk in the pier venture to be worth an extra 2 per cent. If you were the engineer, what would you recommend?

10–37. A new machine which costs $10,000 is estimated to have a life of 5 years and a salvage value of $400. If the interest rate is 4 per cent, compare the annual depreciation costs by the (a) straight-line method, (b) sinking-fund method, and (c) declining-balance method.

10–38. A new water line must be constructed from an existing pumping station to a tank 1500 ft away. An analysis of costs for these sizes of pipe has been made as shown in the table. The annual

Pipe Size (in.)	Cost per Hour for Pumping	Estimated Construction Cost
8	$1.60	$15,000
10	$1.20	$30,000
12	$0.60	$50,000

cost is to be computed on the basis of straight-line depreciation and average interest, using a life of 15 years with no salvage value and an interest rate of 6 per cent per year. (a) Determine the most economical pipe size for pumping 4000 hr/year. (b) How many hours per year pumping would be required to make the 8- and 10-in. pipes equally economical?

10–39. A manufacturer offers an inventor the choice of two contracts for the exclusive right to manufacture and market the inventor's patented article. Plan A calls for the immediate single lump-sum payment of $30,000. Plan B calls for an annual payment of $1000 plus a royalty of $0.50 for each unit sold. The remaining life of the patent is 10 years. Assuming interest compounded annually at 5 per cent, what must be the uniform annual sale of the article to make plan B as attractive to the inventor as plan A? (Disregard income-tax considerations.)

10–40. Two 100-hp motors are under consideration for an intermittent service. Motor A costs $1600 and has an efficiency of 90 per cent. Motor B costs $1300 and has an efficiency of 87 per cent. If all charges for depreciation, maintenance, insurance, etc., are a total of 15 per cent of the initial cost, and if power costs 1.1 cents/kwhr, how many hours of full-load operation per year are necessary to justify purchase of motor A? (Assume each motor has a life of 25 years with no salvage value and that money can be borrowed for 6 per cent.)

10–41. What cash price should be paid for a business store to be equivalent to an annual rental of $3600 if the store will have a life of 20 years and average annual maintenance is $270, taxes and insurance are $180, and the interest rate is 4 per cent compounded annually?

10–42. The complete cost of a new all-season hotel is $980,000, of which the land costs $300,000 and is considered not to depreciate in value. Fixtures cost $150,000, and a working capital of 30 days' gross income at 100 per cent capacity is required. The investment in fixtures should be recovered in 7 years, that in the structure in 25 years. When operating at 100 per cent capacity, the gross income is $1200 per day. Operating expenses, exclusive of capital recovery and interest, amount to a fixed cost of $115,000 per year and a variable cost, varying in direct proportion to the level of operation, of $78,000 per year for 100 per cent capacity. If interest is taken at 6 per cent compounded annually, at what per cent of capacity must the hotel operate to break even?

10–43. A company may furnish a car for use of its salesman, or the company may pay for the use of his car at a rate of $0.11 per mile. The following estimated data apply to company-furnished cars: A car costs $1800 and has a life of 4 years with a trade-in value of $700 at the end of that time. Monthly storage cost for the car is $3, and the cost of fuel, tires, and maintenance is $0.028 per mile. What annual mileage must a salesman travel by car for the cost of the two methods of providing transportation to be equal if the interest rate is 8 per cent?

10–44. An asphalt plant purchases a certain grade of petroleum for processing purposes in 50-gal drums and uses 6000 gal/year.

The purchase price per gallon delivered to the door is $0.30. Annual storage costs are $0.20 per drum, and at least 500 gal are kept on hand at all times as emergency insurance. Annual carrying charges are 16 per cent on the complete inventory. The bookkeeping and clerical costs are $20 per purchase order regardless of the size of the order. What is the most economical order size, in number of drums, for purchase purposes?

10–45. It is necessary to replace ties on a railroad. Untreated ties, costing $1.50 in place, have a life of 6 years. What expenditure per tie is warranted for creosoting if the life of the tie is thereby increased to 9 years? Interest rate is 6 per cent.

10–46. A certain type of industrial building having 18,000 sq ft of floor space can be constructed for $65,000 on land costing $5000. Money can be obtained at 4 per cent with annual compounding for this venture. Taxes and insurance are 2.5 per cent; annual maintenance is $950. The building when finished can be leased for 10 years at $13,860 per year. If the total cost of the building and the land is to be written off in 10 years, determine the per cent profit over and above the 4 per cent which will be realized if the 10-year program is completed.

10–47. A contract is let for $10,000. It is to be completed in 4 weeks time, subject to a penalty of $240 per day if that time is exceeded. At the end of 3 weeks the work is 60 per cent complete. Labor costs were initially estimated to be $4000 when working 40 hr/week. If overtime labor must be compensated at double time, (a) would it be cheaper to take the penalty or to complete the job by working overtime? (Give cost figures.) (b) By what per cent would the estimated labor cost be increased by the cheaper plan?

10–48. A manufacturing plant has been purchasing the energy required for plant operation. It is considering building a power plant to supply a load estimated at 1000 kw (24 hr/day, 365 days/year). Purchased power will cost $0.023 per kilowatt-hour. The cost of the required plant is $1,000,000, and total operating expense including interest on investment is estimated at $95,000 per annum. Assuming 8 per cent sinking-fund depreciation, 15-year life, and zero scrap value, determine whether energy should be purchased or supplied by the new power plant.

10–49. You are currently renting a house and paying $90 per month. You can build a house for $10,000 which you estimate will have a life of 25 years. Taxes and insurance will be $300 per year. Assuming that you have sufficient capital and using straight-line depreciation, determine whether or not you should build. You can invest your money elsewhere at 4 per cent.

10–50. A certain piece of equipment costs $30,000 and will serve 16 years. A better piece of equipment can be had to perform the same service for 22 years. Neither piece of equipment will have any salvage value at the end of its life. Use the sinking-fund method for depreciation, assuming annual compounding of interest. Assume maintenance and operating costs will be the same for either piece of equipment and determine how much can be paid for the better equipment when the interest rate is 6 per cent.

10–51. Two offers are received for a piece of property: (a) $8000 cash, and (b) $2000 in cash plus $4000 at the end of 2 years and $2500 at the end of 4 years. Which is the better offer if money is worth 5 per cent?

10–52. You have developed a new product and are contemplating renting a building, purchasing equipment, and manufacturing the product. Your estimates are as follows: investment, $35,000; annual out-of-pocket expenses, $76,000; annual sales, $100,000. You believe that sales will hold up for only 3 years and that the special equipment to be used will have no resale value; therefore, it should be depreciated in 3 years to zero. The capital you will require is now invested in stocks which are returning 6 per cent. To manage the project, it will be necessary to give up a job paying $6000 per year. Compute the difference in dollars between your present income and your future income if you embark on this project.

10–53. It is necessary to determine whether to use insulation 1 in. thick or 2 in. thick for a steam pipe. The heat loss from the pipe without insulation would cost $1.50 per year per foot of pipe. The 1-in. insulation will eliminate 89 per cent of the loss and will cost $0.40 per foot. Two-inch insulation will stop 92 per cent of the loss and will cost $0.85 per foot. Compare the annual cost per 1000 feet for the two thicknesses of insulation, using a life of 10 years for the insulation with no salvage value. Assume straight-line depreciation, average interest, and an interest rate of 6 per cent.

10–54. In studying a proposed highway location, two possible routes appear feasible. Final choice will be determined by the economics. The ADT for a 30-year service life of the road is estimated to be 3000 passenger cars and 500 trucks and busses. It is assumed that traffic is equally divided in both directions. A summary of the location details and estimated costs is given in the table. Determine which of these two locations is the more eco-

Type of Alignment and Grade	Location A (miles)	Location B (miles)	Curvature Operating Cost Index Values
	Location Details		
Length of ±3% grade......	6	1	Curvature 3° to 5° = 1.02
Length of ±6% grade......	...	4	Curvature 5° to 8° = 1.05
Length of curvature of 3° to 5°	2	...	...
Length of curvature of 5° to 8°	2	...	...
Comparatively level and straight	2	5	...
Total length	12	10	...
	Estimated Costs		
Initial investment cost	$1,140,000	$910,000	...
Annual maintenance cost ...	$ 3,400	$ 3,300	...
Salvage value	$ 100,000	$100,000	...

Variable Vehicle Operating Costs (dollars per 1000 vehicle miles)

Grade	Passenger Cars	Trucks and Busses	Grade	Passenger Cars	Trucks and Busses
Level	42	120	−6%	37	140
+6%	61	300	−3%	35	105
+3%	50	183			

nomical, using a service life of 30 years, an interest rate of 3 per cent, and the vehicle operating cost data given. Ignore possible time saving and accident costs.

10–55. Elimination of a railroad grade crossing is being considered. A new installation would cost $600,000, and the capital recovery period is assumed to be 30 years on the theory that either the railroad or the highway under it will be relocated by then.

Salvage value of the bridge at that time is estimated at $100,000. A return of 6 per cent is to be used.

Average highway traffic is 1000 vehicles per day, consisting of 40 per cent trucks and 60 per cent other vehicles. Time for truck drivers is valued at $3.00 per hour and for other drivers at $1.20 per hour. Average time saving per vehicle will be 2 min. No time saving occurs for the railroad, nor is any extra profit anticipated from new customers attracted by the grade-crossing elimination.

The installation will save the railroad an annual expense of $10,000 now spent in guarding the crossing. During the 10-year preceding period, the railroad has paid out $300,000 in accident cases, but the proposed project will give a 100 per cent reduction in the accident rate. The state estimates that the new overpass will save it about $2000 per year in expenses directly due to the accidents. The railroad offers to pay 60 per cent of the project's cost and the state has countered with an offer to pay 10 per cent.

On the basis of the information given, compare the two offers.

10–56. A general construction contract is advertised by a municipality for the construction of a new road 5000 feet long. Two low bids having the same total are received, the unit prices and quantities being as shown in the table. Bonds have been sold for $500,000, and the full amount is placed on deposit at 2.4 per cent per annum, payable at year's end on the average monthly balance. It will take 12 months to complete the project. Work is

Item	Quantity	Bidder A	Bidder B
Clearing	Lump sum	$ 25,000.00	$100,000.00
Grading and subgrade preparation	5000 ft	40.00	50.00
Drainage structures	Lump sum	50,000.00	50,000.00
Paving	5000 ft	40.00	19.00
Guardrails	1000 ft	2.00	1.00
Sodding and seeding	Lump sum	23,000.00	4,000.00
Totals, extended	......	$500,000.00	$500,000.00

required to proceed in the order given above and on the following schedule: item 1, first month; item 2, second through fifth month; item 3, sixth month; item 4, seventh through tenth month; item 5, eleventh month; and item 6, eleventh and twelfth months. The contractor is to be paid at the end of each month for the work performed that month. Assume that items of work to be done in more than one month are completed in direct proportion to the time specified. What would be the value to the municipality at completion of the work if the contract is awarded to bidder A instead of to bidder B? Show all computations.

10–57. A general contractor is required to install and operate a temporary well-point system during a 6-month phase of construction of a riverside powerhouse, from April through September, 1960. The necessary equipment will cost $800.00 per month to rent. A pump operator will have to be in attendance continuously, and he must be paid an hourly wage of $3.00 for each 8-hour weekday shift, $4.50 for each 8-hour Saturday shift, and $6.00 for each 8-hour Sunday and legal holiday shift. Payroll taxes and insurance are 13 per cent of wages. Fuel is estimated at $20.00 per day. Overhead and maintenance charges are 15 per cent of wages, fuel, and rental charges.

Payment for successful completion of the well-pointing operation will be in one lump sum at the end of the 6-month period. If financing costs the contractor 6 per cent per annum and he desires a profit and contingency of 10 per cent of his costs, what would be his lump-sum bid for the well-pointing operation?

10–58. Present average hourly traffic over a certain inadequate two-lane road is 500 cars. Traffic is expected to increase at the rate of 300 cars per hour per year for at least 20 years. It is estimated that conversion to a three-lane road will cost $100,000 per mile; to a four-lane road, $150,000 per mile; to a freeway, $350,000 per mile. It is further estimated that later changes from a three-lane road to a four-lane road will cost $100,000 per mile and that to convert the four-lane road to a freeway will cost $200,000 per mile. The capacities of the three-lane road, the four-lane road, and the freeway are 1500 cars hourly, 3000 cars hourly, and 4500 cars hourly, respectively. On the basis of 3 per cent compound interest, which road would you recommend for construction now if economy is the prime consideration?

10–59. An old plant manufacturing a certain article cannot expand because of lack of available land at its present site. What data would you collect and what phases of the problem would you investigate and study if you were called upon to make a complete report on the advisability of buying a new site and building a new plant?

10–60. Enumerate all of the items which an engineer must take into consideration in estimating whether or not a certain improvement can be justified from a purely economic point of view. If you wish, you may select a particular case in order to make your answer more clearly understood.

10–61. A certain bus-line company purchased 15 busses costing $20,000 each, upon an agreement of 15 per cent cash and the balance in 10 equal year-end installments. Determine the annual year-end installment when interest is 4 per cent.

10–62. What amount must be donated to build an institution having an initial cost of $500,000, to provide an annual upkeep of $50,000, and to have $500,000 at the end of each 50-year period to rebuild the institution? Assume that invested funds return 4 per cent.

10–63. When buying an automobile on the installment plan, the purchaser is required to pay interest at the rate of 6 per cent per annum on the amount of the original loan. If the loan is repaid in 12 monthly installments, beginning at the end of the first month, what is the average rate of interest paid for the use of the money?

10–64. A company is considering the purchase of a machine that will save $2000 per year in maintenance costs. It is estimated that the machine will be used for 10 years and then can be sold for $3000. If money is worth 6 per cent, how much can the company afford to pay for this machine?

10–65. Two types of storage batteries are being considered for use in a fleet of industrial lift trucks. Type A costs $690 per truck and will have an estimated life of 8 years. Type B has a first cost of $530 with an estimated life of 5 years. Operation and maintenance costs will be about the same for the two types. The salvage value of each will be $20. Minimum attractive rate of return is 10 per cent. (a) Compare the true equivalent annual costs. (b) Make annual cost comparisons using straight-line depreciation plus average interest.

10–66. A Diesel locomotive engine will run 1, 2, 3, or 4 years between overhauls but the maintenance labor cost per year between overhauls (P_1) increases each year. If a new set of replacement parts costs $10,000 installed and the labor cost (P_2) for maintenance each year from past records is: first year $1000, second year $3000, third year $5000, and fourth year $8000. How often should the locomotive diesel be overhauled for greatest economy?

10–67. A yearly expenditure of $1000 is needed to keep a certain pavement in repair. It is believed that a new surface will reduce the annual maintenance cost to $200 a year for the first 5 years, $600 a year for the next 5 years, and that after 10 years the annual maintenance cost will again be $1000. Considering only the prospective saving in maintenance cost, what investment is justified for the new surface? Assume interest at 5 per cent.

10–68. The total cost of an item being designed is made up of 3 parts: The first part of the cost, C_1 dollars per item, varies directly with a design parameter, P, and the constant of proportionality is K_D so that $C_1 = K_D P$ dollars per item. The second part of the cost, C_2 dollars per item, varies inversely with the same design parameter, P, and the constant of proportionality is K_i with $C_2 = K_i/P$ dollars per item. The third part of the cost, C_3 dollars per item, is constant for all values of the design parameter, P. (a) Derive the value of the design parameter, P, that will result in the minimum total cost per item. (This value of P is to be given in terms of K_D, K_i and C_3). (b) Compute the minimum total cost per item.

10–69. The prepaid premium of insurance policies covering loss to buildings by fire and storm for a 3-year period is usually 2.5 times the premium for one year of coverage. What interest does a purchaser of this type of insurance receive on the additional present cash investment if he purchases a 3-year policy now rather than three 1-year policies at the beginning of succeeding years?

10–70. Friendly Finance Ltd. will arrange a loan of $100 for payments of only $6.23 per month for 24 months. What are the (a) nominal and (b) effective interest rates actually being charged for the loan?

10–71. The economy of country A is now twice as large as that of country R. However, R's economy is growing at a rate of 7 per cent per year, while A's economy is growing only at the rate of 3 per cent per year. Assuming that these growth rates continue to apply, how long will it be until the two economies are the same size?

10–72. A machine costing $10,000 has an estimated economic life of 10 years and an estimated salvage value of $1000. Maintenance expenses are estimated at zero for the first 5 years and $500 for each of the last 5 years. Property taxes and insurance are estimated to be $300 the first year and decrease by $20 per year. Space and other costs are expected to be $700 per year. Use a before-tax return rate of 20 per cent to find the annual cost of the machine.

10–73. Five mutually exclusive alternatives are under consideration with each having a life of 10 years and zero salvage value. The required investment and estimated after-tax reduction in annual disbursements are given for each alternative. For what minimum attractive rate of return is alternative C the best?

Alternative	Required Investment	After-Tax Reduction In Annual Disbursements
A	$10,000	$2070
B	20,000	3700
C	30,000	5690
D	40,000	6920
E	50,000	8550

10–74. In the determination of costs of public hydroelectric power projects, the following items were included as costs: (1) Interest on first cost of the project; (2) depreciation by the straight-line method based on estimated life of the project; (3) an annual deposit in an amortization sinking fund sufficient to equal the first cost of the project at the end of 50 years (or at the end of the life of the project if that should be less than 50 years); (4) where money is borrowed, the annual disbursements for bond interest and bond repayment; and (5) all actual annual disbursements for operation and maintenance of the project. Is the annual cost properly considered as the sum of these items? If not, why not? In any case, explain specifically.

10–75. The following estimates are made for two alternative plans to provide a given service. The minimum attractive return is 5 per cent. The service period is 8 years.

	Plan A	Plan B
First cost	$14,000	$30,000
Salvage value after 8 years	2000	4000
Annual operating cost	3000	1000

Compare the two plans on the basis of annual cost, using straight-line depreciation plus average interest.

10–76. A new snow removal machine costs $50,000, and will operate at a reputed saving of $400 per day over the present equipment in terms of time and efficiency. For interest at 5 per cent and a machine life of 10 years with zero salvage, how many days per year must the machine be used to make the investment economical?

10–77. A manufacturing company has been discharging too much smoke from its chimney. A survey has determined that the installation of a precipitator will remove the solids from the hot gases before they leave the chimney and thereby alleviate the smog condition. Four precipitators are being considered and the estimates for installation and maintenance are as follows:

	Precipitator			
	A	B	C	D
First cost	$3000	$3800	$4500	$4750
Life, years	10	10	10	10
Salvage	0	0	0	0
Anual operating costs				
Power and water	$ 640	$ 640	$ 500	$ 480
Cleaning	400	400	290	265
Maintenance	300	250	300	250
Labor	400	400	290	265
Taxes and insurance, 2% of first cost	60	76	90	95
	$1800	$1766	$1470	$1355

If all precipitators are the same capacity, which would you recommend assuming that the minimum attractive rate of return before income taxes is to be 10 per cent?

10–78. A contractor wishes to establish a special fund by making uniform semi-annual deposits for 20 years. The fund should provide $10,000 per year for each of the last 5 years of the 20-year period. With interest at 4 per cent compounded semi-annually, how much must the semi-annual deposit be?

10–79. A market analysis estimates that the sales of a new product will be as follows: First year, 1,000,000 lb at 50 cents per lb; next 4 years, 6,000,000 lb at 50 cents per lb; and next 5 years, 5,000,000 lb at 30 cents per lb. Research shows the product can be produced for 20 cents per lb plus overhead and fixed charges on the required investment. Overhead is estimated at $100,000 per year. If the interest rate is 6 per cent and the company wants a profit before taxes of 10 per cent on its sales income, how much can it afford to invest in a plant to produce this product?

10–80. A company faces the decision of whether to lease or purchase a piece of manufacturing equipment. Purchase price is $250,000 and installation costs will be $25,000. The equipment can be expected to have a useful life of 5 years after which it can be sold as scrap with a net return of $25,000. Estimated maintenance is $3000 per year, taxes and insurance $1200. Assume outlays occur at the beginning of each year.

The machine can be leased for 5 years at an annual rental fee of $58,000 in 5 equal installments at the beginning of the respective years. The lessor agrees to install the equipment so it is ready for use, to remove it at the end of 5 years, and to keep it in working order. The lessee will have to spend about $1000 per year for ordinary maintenance and $500 per year for insurance. If alternative investment opportunities would produce a 5 per cent return to the company, should the management lease or buy? Use the present value comparison method.

Ethics and Practice, Contracts and Specifications 11

Answers to questions in this chapter are less definite than the numerical values available for the problems of preceding and succeeding chapters. Differences in state laws affect questions involving contracts and specifications (and to some extent, engineering practice also), making it impossible to provide an explicit and unique answer. The Cannons of Ethics of the Engineers' Council for Professional Development offer the best fundamental review material for many of the questions in this chapter.

11–1. A statement that has often been heard is: "An ethical man almost never has any 'brushes' with the 'law'." Is this statement true? Explain.

11–2. A friend comes to you and asks for advice in making a formal complaint against a man who is offering to perform engineering services. (a) If the alleged violation was apparently a violation of the registration law, to whom should he address his complaint? (b) If the alleged violation was apparently a violation of the Cannons of Ethics, to whom should he address his complaint?

11–3. Recently, a man who was a graduate of an engineering college, but who was not legally qualified to practice because he was not registered, sued a contractor for payment for "professional services rendered." The court denied the plaintiff on the grounds that "an illegal contract is unenforceable," which decision is similar to many other like cases.

An unregistered engineering graduate approaches you to apply your seal to his plans and specifications for a project. Would his contract with his client be enforceable? Explain. (NOTE: Assume that you are a properly registered engineer, that you make a complete and thorough review of the plans and specifications, and that you affix your seal and signature to the plans and specifications only.)

11–4. Assume that you have correctly analyzed your client's problems and have logically proceeded to an adequate, serviceable, yet economical solution. You wish to prepare plans and specifications that will (a) attract the most favorable bids from the better contractors, (b) facilitate prompt initiation and rapid progress of the work, (c) minimize arguments between trades and the need for extras and change orders, and (d) assure a finished project of intended caliber. List 10 major characteristics required of your plans and specifications.

11–5. When is it ethical and in the client's interest to specify a material or product flatly?

11–6. As a practicing professional engineer, what is your relationship to an architect also retained by the owner to handle related work?

11–7. List four methods of computing charges to a client for professional engineering services. Discuss each method briefly, listing advantages and disadvantages for both the client and the engineer.

11–8. A certain engineer has been engaged to make an investigation and to report upon a specific matter relating to the client's business. During the investigation period, discoveries unrelated to the specific engagement were made which, if disclosed to the client, might well be of great importance to the business. The engineer mentioned these discoveries in his report. Later, at his own expense, the engineer studied these discoveries more thoroughly, and they seemed to have considerable industrial and scientific value. (a) Would the ethical relation of the engineer to his former client permit him to develop these discoveries for his own personal benefit or profit? (b) Should the engineer publish an account of the new discoveries for the benefit of science?

11–9. Engineering commissions or committees usually submit a written report of their findings, conclusions, and recommendations to the proper authorities in due time. Before such a report has been properly submitted, would it be an infraction of professional ethics for a member of the commission or committee to divulge or publish any or all of the findings of the committee?

11–10. Discuss the display of the professional engineer's license as it pertains to the lawful practice of consulting engineering in your state.

11–11. Discuss knowledge of illegal practice by others as it pertains to the practice of consulting engineering in your state.

11–12. A realty company is considering the erection of a steel-frame office building. An engineer proposes to take responsibility for the design, check the fabricator's shop plans, and supervise erection for a price considerably below the prevailing rate if a certain fabricator is used. Discuss the aspects of the situation.

11–13. You have advised a client that your fee for doing certain professional work is 6 per cent. The client informs you that one of your competitors has offered to do the work for a fee of 5½ per cent. What are your actions?

11–14. Discuss briefly the ethics of engineer A's action in each of the following cases: (a) Engineer B, on request of a company, is in the process of negotiating with the company for the performance of professional engineering services on a fee basis. Engineer A, hearing of this, on his own initiative makes a proposal to do the work. (b) Engineer A, hearing that several other engineers are negotiating with a company to perform professional engineering services on a fee basis, on his own initiative makes a proposal to do the work.

11–15. A client is considering overruling your engineering judgment by accepting the word of a nontechnical authority in a case where you are responsible for the technical adequacy of the engineering work. What would you tell the client?

11–16. Discuss the ethics of the following hypothetical situations: (a) Engineer A has been asked to prepare, without a fee, an estimate of the cost for a project with the understanding that, if the cost is acceptable, the project design will be done by A and the cost of the estimate will be paid for at that time. (b) A town council asks three engineers to submit designs and specifications for a project with the understanding that the best of the three as selected by the council will be given the contract.

11–17. Discuss the ethics of the following hypothetical situations: (a) An engineer revises his original design of a structure to take advantage of a particularly generous discount on a certain product. The general cost of the project by either design remains the same to the owner. (b) An engineer called in as a consultant by engineer B on a $1,000,000 job charged a larger fee than he had just charged for a similar service on a $500,000 job, although the time spent in arriving at his conclusions was exactly the same for both cases.

11–18. Discuss the ethics of the following hypothetical situations: (a) An engineer deliberately arranges his bid data and invitations such that of nine contractors seemingly invited to bid only five could submit bids. (b) An owner asks engineer C to review and make any changes deemed necessary in the design and specifications of a project prepared by engineer D. Engineer D's fee has been paid by the owner.

11–19. You have undertaken to do a large job. A manufacturer's representative advises you that his company will do the bulk of your engineering work for you at no charge if you will specify his equipment and will not allow any substitutions of like and equal equipment. What action would you take?

11–20. A certain contractor, who advertises himself as an engineering contractor, has neglected to make application and qualify for registration as a professional engineer. He did a job for a client for which he sent a bill to the client. The client felt that the bill was unreasonable and refused to pay. (a) What recourse does the practicing contractor have in your state courts? (b) If you are duly registered as a professional engineer and this contractor approaches you for professional help in this case, what can you do legally and ethically?

11–21. Comment briefly on the propriety of an engineer's conduct under the following actions: (a) Participating in competitions for the adoptions of plans according to merit. (b) Obtaining gratuitously plans and specifications from prospective bidders for insertion in contract plans and specifications. (c) Specifying a product when he holds the patent rights for the product.

11–22. (a) Discuss briefly and specifically just what legal registration of an engineer in any state certifies. (b) You are engaged by a client to examine the designs of another engineer and to report upon whether or not they are full and complete, as to the cost of same, and in general advise the client as to whether the plans are adequate for the purpose desired. Would you consider accepting the job, and make the report without the knowledge of the original engineer?

11–23. A certain registered professional engineer contracted to do the engineering work on a construction job. In writing the contract, standard engineering fees were specified. The owner claims that the engineer agreed verbally upon a reduced figure. After partially finishing the job he decided to move from this state to another state. Before leaving he billed the owner of the new building under construction for the proportion of the engineering work he had completed and turned the engineering contract over to another engineer, who agreed to finish the job as per the contract in writing. The owner wishes to recover the difference between the written contract and the verbal figure mentioned originally. (a) What legal recourse has the owner? (b) Discuss the ethics involved in this contract.

11–24. A certain engineer was interviewed by a personnel representative from a company in Chicago. Subsequently he was requested to come to Chicago at the company's expense for further interviews. The engineer was also interested in another company near Chicago, and wished to interview it on the same trip. (a) What ethical procedure should have been taken on this one trip and two interviews? (b) If you had been that engineer, would you have allowed the first company to pay the total expense and said nothing? (c) If you had allowed the first company to pay your expenses and the second company which had not shared in your expense of the trip made you the more attractive offer, what then should have been your procedure?

11–25. Discuss briefly in not more than 150 words the ethics of the following situation: Engineer A, in the employ of a large corporation finds, in preparing drawings on which his company holds a contract, inherent errors of design in the drawings prepared by the consulting engineers for the project.

11–26. A certain engineering contractor is offered a contract containing the provision "all work must be done to the satisfaction of the owners." (a) In what ways is this "provision" unethical? (b) Suggest a substitute "provision" which would be fair to both parties.

11–27. Explain the difference between (a) legally right or wrong and (b) ethically right or wrong. Use an example, if necessary, to answer the question clearly.

11–28. (a) What are the essential elements of a contract? (b) Discuss the reason for the difference between a voidable contract and a void contract.

11–29. Discuss the filing of drawings and reports with public officials as it pertains to the lawful practice of engineering in your state.

11–30. (a) What is a mechanic's lien? (b) Can a professional engineer or architect obtain a mechanic's lien?

11–31. What is the status of the professional engineer under the Taft-Hartley Law?

11–32. Discuss partnerships, sole ownerships, and corporations as they pertain to the lawful practice of consulting engineering in your state.

11–33. What is meant by (a) performance bond, (b) bid bond, (c) workmen's compensation insurance, (d) public liability insurance, and (e) escalator clause.

11–34. A municipal building is to be constructed in 12 months under the following four separate, simultaneously awarded contracts: (1) General construction, (2) heating and ventilating, (3) plumbing, and (4) electrical wiring and equipment. Describe briefly the general provisions you would include in *each* contract relative to the furnishing of the following: (a) Temporary heat, (b) temporary electric light and power, (c) temporary water service, (d) temporary sanitary facilities, (e) masonry chases. openings, and apertures for electric conduits, ventilating ducts, and water pipes, and (f) performance bond.

11–35. Discuss briefly (150 to 200 words) your opinion as to the unionization of professional engineering.

11–36. Write a code of ethics by which you would govern yourself as a practicing professional engineer.

11–37. A municipality hires the services of an engineer on an annual salary basis. Is the engineer justified in doing private work during his spare time and keeping the pay therefrom for his own private use?

11–38. Is it proper for an engineer employed in the Municipal Engineer's office to make property surveys on his own time at a reduced cost, since he has access to information which reduces his office research time? Evaluate this statement and substantiate with facts.

11–39. Many engineering educators engage in private consulting work. Usually the justification for such activity is the necessity for the educator to keep abreast of actual practice and thereby be a better teacher. Discuss the ethical questions connected with such an activity.

11–40. Should engineers make themselves available for service to the public for work on committees or commissions without charge? Explain in detail.

11–41. What methods of advertising are considered ethical for a registered professional engineer?

11–42. Discuss the professional issues involved in the offering of engineering services through the corporate form of organization.

11–43. An engineer for a government agency has the responsibility for purchasing expensive and exotic equipment for a laboratory. One of the equipment suppliers gives the engineer an expensive attache case as a gift. The questions to be answered are: (a) Was it proper for the engineer to keep the case? (b) Should the engineer's immediate supervisor be told of the gift? (c) Should there be a top limit on the value of gifts which can be accepted?

11–44. For what practices or violations of the state's statutes may an individual be penalized by the State Board of Professional Engineers and Land Surveyors?

11–45. Under what conditions may an individual, not licensed as a professional engineer or as a land surveyor in this state, practice professional engineering or land surveying in this state?

11–46. A non-registered competent engineer has designed and prepared specifications for a dam. Discuss the ethical and non-ethical aspects of having a registered engineer certify the work.

11–47. Give a succinct answer to the following questions but do not use just "yes" or "no." (a) Is it ethical for engineers to submit competitive bids for a portion of work requiring only engineering services? (b) Is it proper for an engineer to guarantee an engineering estimate or give bond for its accuracy? (c) If an inspector on a job saved a contractor money by showing him a more efficient method or short cut in doing some work, would the inspector be justified in receiving remuneration in money or other items of value from the contractor?

11–48. Contract law is intricate and a simple "yes" or "no" answer is not usually applicable but in the following situations, considerable precedent has been established and is accepted. Comment on the individual cases and ramifications if any. (a) The plans and specifications are in conflict. Which will prevail? (b) A contractor is being sued for infringement of patent rights on a component constructed by him. The contract documents contain the usual "save harmless" clause. The engineer believing that it was common knowledge the product was patented had not informed the contractor. Would the contractor be correct in assuming the engineer is legally at fault and liable? (c) Does a letter sent by registered mail to the construction job constitute written notice to the contractor doing the job?

11–49. For the same conditions as in Problem 11–48, (a) must the contractor comply with the engineer's request that he return all drawings and specifications? The job was completed 30 days prior to the request. (b) Is the contractor responsible to the owner for a delay in job completion caused by an electrical subcontractor?

11–50. A section of state highway is to be constructed along an existing route through a built-up municipality containing the normal utilities. Due to the new alignment in grade, these utilities will affect the construction operation. Relative to handling the utilities, what are the respective responsibilities of the following: (a) Municipality, (b) private utilities, (c) State Highway Department, (d) the contractor.

part two

APPLIED ENGINEERING

Aeronautical Engineering 12

Problems in this chapter are grouped as follows: Aircraft performance, boundary layer theory and heat transfer, hypersonic aerodynamics, vibrations, aircraft and missile propulsion, aircraft structures, aircraft stability, and general. Solutions are shown for five typical problems.

12–1. Suppose the C_D vs. C_L^2 for an airplane is a straight line such that $C_L=0$ when $C_D=0.02$ and $C_L=1.0$ when $C_D=0.10$. (a) Write the equation for the drag curve. (b) Find the aspect ratio if it is an elliptical wing with efficiency factor unity. (c) Find the minimum gliding angle. (d) Find the L/D maximum. (e) If the angle of attack for zero lift is $-5°$ and $C_L=1.0$ for $\alpha=10°$, write the equation for the lift curve.

Solution:

(a) $$C_D=0.02+0.08C_L^2$$

(b) $$\frac{dC_D}{dC_L^2}=\frac{1}{\pi A}=0.08 \qquad A=3.99$$

(c) $$\text{Gliding angle}=2\sqrt{0.02(0.08)}=0.08\text{ radian}=4.58°$$

(d) $$\frac{L}{D}=12.5$$

(e) $$C_L=\frac{dC_L}{d\alpha}(\alpha-\alpha_L=0) \qquad C_L=\frac{1.0}{15}(\alpha+5)$$

12–2. Assume that a body of revolution has the general shape $r=x^n$, where r is the radius and x is the axial distance. Using simple impact theory of hypersonic flow, find the shape of the body (the value of n) that gives minimum drag at zero angle of attack.

Solution:

$$C_D=4\delta^2\int_0^1 FF'^3\,dx=4\delta^2n^3\int_0^1 x^{4n-3}\,dx$$

$$C_D=\frac{4n^3}{4n-2} \qquad \text{thus } \frac{dC_D}{dn}=0 \text{ gives } n=\frac{3}{4}$$

12–3. Suppose a weight of 75 lb is connected to a spring with a modulus of $K=25$ lb/in. Attached to the weight is a piston moving in a dashpot filled with a viscous fluid. The damping force is directly proportional to the velocity of the weight and is 40 lb when the velocity is 3 fps. Find (a) the damping constant, (b) the natural frequency of damped vibration, (c) the natural frequency of the undamped vibration, and (d) the logarithmic decrement.

Solution:

(a)
$$\frac{40}{36}=r=1.11 \text{ lb-sec/in.}$$

(b)
$$\frac{W}{g}\frac{d^2y}{dt^2}+r\frac{dx}{dt}+Kx=0 \qquad f=\frac{1}{2\pi}\sqrt{\frac{Kg}{W}-\left(\frac{rg}{2w}\right)^2}=1.747 \text{ cps}$$

(c)
$$f=\frac{1}{2\pi}\sqrt{\frac{Kg}{W}}=1.805 \text{ cps}$$

(d)
$$e^{\pi rg/W}=e^{\delta} \qquad \delta=1.633$$

12–4. Suppose that the combustion gases in a rocket motor are such that the stagnation temperature is 5520°R and the stagnation pressure is 300 psia. If the molecular weight of the combustion gases is 25.4, the static pressure is standard, and the ratio of specific heats is 1.25, calculate the velocity and temperature for the gases flowing through the throat of the rocket nozzle.

Solution:
$$V_t=315.3\left(\frac{\gamma}{\gamma+1}\right)^{1/2}\left(\frac{T_c}{m}\right)^{1/2}$$
$$=315.3(0.745)(14.8)=3480 \text{ fps}$$
$$t_s=\left(\frac{2}{\gamma+1}\right)T_c=0.889(5520)=4910°\text{R}$$

12–5. Find the ultimate column strength of a round 24SR-T aluminum alloy tube, 1×0.049 in., with a length of 20 in. and an end fixity of 1.5. Assume critical slenderness ratio is 66.7.

Solution: The properties of the cross section can be determined from a handbook or can be calculated easily: $A=0.1464$, $\rho=0.3367$, and $D/t=20.4$. The effective length is $L_1=L/\sqrt{c}=16.34$ in. The slenderness ratio is $L_1/\rho=48.5$. Since critical slenderness ratio is 66.7, the short-column formula must be used:

$$F_c=70{,}000-700\frac{L_1}{\rho}=36{,}000 \text{ psi}$$

The allowable load is

$$P=F_cA=5270 \text{ lb}$$

12–6. A rectangular monoplane wing has a span of 43 ft and a chord of 6 ft. (a) What is the induced angle of attack and induced drag coefficient when $C_L=0.8$? (b) What is the induced drag when the velocity is 100 fps?

12–7. For a particular airfoil of infinite aspect ratio at 6° angle of attack, $C_L=1.01$ and $C_{D0}=0.063$. Using these values, find the characteristics for a finite aspect ratio of 8.

12–8. An airplane weighing 2000 lb has a span of 38 ft. (a) Find the induced drag at 10,000 ft altitude if the airspeed is 80 mph. (b) What horsepower is required to overcome the induced drag?

12–9. Describe the minimum drag wing for the low-speed (incompressible) range.

12–10. Consider two steady, concentric rotating cylinders moving at different rotational speeds. The fluid between the two cylinders of inner and outer radius r_1 and r_2, respectively, is flowing due to two angular velocities ω_1 and ω_2. If the Navier-Stokes equations are (in plane polar coordinates)

$$\rho\frac{u^2}{r}=\frac{dp}{dr} \qquad \text{and} \qquad \frac{d^2u}{dr^2}+\frac{d}{dr}\left(\frac{u}{r}\right)=0$$

where p is the static pressure and u is the circumferential velocity, (a) find the general expression for u if the boundary conditions are $u=r_1\omega_1$ at $r=r_1$, $u=r_2\omega_2$ at $r=r_2$. (b) If the inner cylinder is at rest while the outer cylinder rotates, find the torque transmitted by the outer cylinder to the fluid.

12–11. If the flow through a tube of circular cross section is governed by the Navier-Stokes equation (cylindrical coordinates)

$$\mu\left(\frac{d^2u}{dy^2}+\frac{1}{y}\frac{du}{dy}\right)=\frac{dp}{dx}$$

where μ is the coefficient of viscosity, u is the velocity along the pipe, p is the static pressure, and x is the axial distance, prove that the velocity is distributed across the pipe in a parabolic fashion.

12–12. Show that the ratio of the inertia force to the friction force in the laminar boundary layer gives one of the most important dimensionless numbers in boundary layer theory.

12–13. In the theory of heat transfer for the laminar boundary layer, reference is often made to the Reynolds analogy. Explain.

12–14. For the aerodynamic heating in the stagnation region, what is the one parameter over which the designer has some control?

12–15. Assuming in general that the body shape in hypersonic flow is $y=x^n$, compare the n values for two-dimensional and axially symmetric flow that give finite drag.

12–16. Find the lift coefficient for half a circular cylinder in hypersonic impact flow.

12–17. Assuming the ratio of specific heats $\gamma=1.2$, find the density ratio across a normal shock at a Mach number of 10. Find the density ratio if $\gamma=1$. Compare these results for the limiting case of Mach number infinity.

12–18. Find the location of the zero pressure coefficient and the drag coefficient for a hemisphere when centrifugal force effects are taken into account. The flight is considered to be in the true hypersonic speed range.

12–19. An unknown weight has a natural frequency of 94 cycles/min when attached to the end of spring with unknown spring constant. When a 1-lb weight is added, the natural frequency is 76.7 cycles/min. Find the weight and spring constant.

12–20. List and discuss at least six factors that should be considered in selecting a liquid propellant suitable for a high-performance liquid rocket engine.

12–21. Suppose that a liquid-propellant rocket motor burns liquid oxygen at a combustion pressure of 500 psia. If the combustion temperature is 5400°R and the molecular weight of the combustion gases is 30, find the area of the throat of the nozzle. Calculate the thrust coefficient and the characteristic velocity. Assume weight flow is 20 lb/sec, $C_d=0.96$, and $\gamma=1.25$.

12–22. Suppose a certain rocket discharges gases at a rate of 1000 lb/sec so that the final gross weight is 4000 lb at the end of 20 sec. If the initial gross weight is 24,000 lb and the relative discharge velocity is 3000 fps, find (a) the thrust and (b) the final velocity of the rocket at the burnout.

12–23. Consider a concentrated load P acting on a simply supported uniform beam so that the load is a distance b from the right end of the beam. If the length of the beam $L=a+b$, assume elastic deflections and find a general expression for the deflection of the beam. You may use the beam-deflection equation:

$$\delta=\int\frac{Mm}{EI}dx$$

12–24. Suppose that the characteristic equation for the lateral oscillation of a given airplane is $\lambda^2+2.97\lambda+38.36=0$. Find the period in τ seconds and the time to damp to one-half amplitude (or double amplitude) in τ seconds if $\tau=b\mu/V$, where the span b is 40 ft, the velocity is 200 fps, and the airplane density factor $\mu=10$.

12–25. Name at least five well-known men who have either directly or indirectly contributed to our knowledge of aeronautical engineering. Describe very briefly the contribution of each.

Chemical Engineering 13

The chemical engineering problems in this chapter cover the various phases of thermodynamics, fluid flow, combustion, heat transfer, mass transfer, process dynamics, reactor kinetics, and material balance with recycle. Process dynamics, reactor kinetics, and material balance with recycle are new additions on recent examinations so an example solution is shown for each type. Unit operations which are common in the applicant's state should be reviewed in preparing for the registration examination.

13–1. Calculate the change in entropy when water at 0°C is converted to steam at 14.7 psia and 50°F superheat. Assume the average specific heat of water is 1 Btu/(lb) (°F); the latent heat of vaporization is 973 Btu/lb at 212°F, 14.7 psia; and the specific heat of water vapor is $C_p = 6.89 + 3.283 \times 10^{-3} T - 0.343 \times 10^{-6} T^2$; $C_p = \text{cal/(g mole) (°K)}$; $T = \text{°K}$.

Solution: Basis, 1 lb mole water.

$$\Delta S = \int_{T_1}^{T_2} \frac{C_p}{T}\, dT + \frac{\lambda}{T_2} + \int_{T_2}^{T_3} \frac{C_p}{T}\, dT$$

$$= \int_{492}^{672} \frac{18}{T}\, dT + \frac{17{,}500}{672} + \int_{373.2}^{401} \left(\frac{6.89}{T} + 3.283 \times 10^{-3} - 0.343 \times 10^{-6} T\right) dT$$

integrating gives

$$\Delta S = 5.58 + 26.05 + 0.6037 = 32.234 \text{ Btu/(lb mole) (°R)}$$

13–2. (a) Plot a typical head-capacity curve for a centrifugal pump, using assumed values for head and capacity. (b) On the same graph plot new curves for (1) two of the same pumps in series and (2) two of the same pumps in parallel. (c) If the impeller diameter remains unchanged, what is the relation of each of the following to speed? (1) Quantity of water delivered. (2) Head. (3) Power.

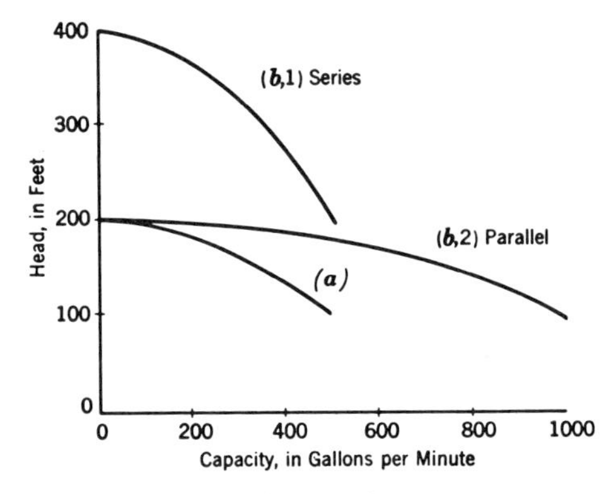

Problem 13–2.

Solution: (a) See illustration. (b) See illustration. (c) (1) Quantity varies directly as speed. (2) Head varies as the square of speed. (3) Horsepower varies as the cube of speed.

13–3. A fuel gas has the following volumetric analysis, in per cent: CH_4, 40.0; C_2H_6, 20.0; CO, 30.0; N_2, 10.0. The gas is burned with dry air in an amount 25.0 per cent in excess of that theoretically required to burn the gas. (a) What is the composition of the hot stack gas if combustion is complete? (b) Assuming that the perfect-gas law holds, what is the dew point of the stack gas at a pressure of 1 atm?

Solution: Basis, 100 lb moles fuel gas.

Composition	Pound Moles	Moles Theoretical O_2 Required	Combustion Products	
			Moles CO_2 Formed	Moles H_2O Formed
CH_4	40	80	40	80
C_2H_6	20	70	40	60
CO	30	15	30	..
N_2	10	..	..	..
Total	100	165	110	140

Moles O_2 (25% excess) $=165(1.25)=206$

Moles O_2 in flue gas $=206-165=41$

Moles N_2 in with $O_2=206\left(\frac{79}{21}\right)=774$

Total moles $N_2=774+10=784$

(a) Stack-gas analysis

Composition	Pound Moles	Mole Per Cent
CO_2	110	10.23
N_2	784	72.93
O_2	41	3.82
H_2O	140	13.02
Total	1075	100.00

(b) Dew point of stack gas:

$$\text{Partial pressure of } H_2O \text{ in stack gas} = \frac{140(29.92)}{1075} = 3.9 \text{ in. Hg}$$

Therefore the dew point (from steam tables) = 125°F

13–4. Cold water is to be heated from a temperature of 45°F to a temperature of 185°F by means of steam condensing at 215°F. The water is to be pumped through a bundle of #14 bwg tubes surrounded by a shell containing the condensing steam. How many square feet of heat-transfer area (based on inside area) are required to heat 35 gal of water per minute if the following data apply?

Tube characteristics: Outside diameter, 0.500 in.; inside diameter, 0.370 in.; material, copper [thermal conductivity=218 Btu/(hr) (sq ft) (°F/ft)].

Film coefficients [Btu/(hr) (sq ft) (°F)]: steam (based on outside area), 1500; water (based on inside area), 350.

Fouling factors [Btu/(hr) (sq ft) (°F)]: steam, 600; water, 500.

Solution: Basis, 1 hr operation.

$$\text{LMTD} = \frac{\Delta t_1 - \Delta t_2}{\ln(\Delta t_1/\Delta t_2)} = \frac{170-30}{\ln(170/30)} = 80.9°\text{F}$$

Over-all heat-transfer coefficient $= u_i$

$$u_i = \cfrac{1}{\cfrac{1}{500} + \cfrac{1}{350} + \cfrac{[0.130/2(12)](0.370/12)}{218\left[\cfrac{0.500-0.370}{\ln(0.500/0.370)}\right]} + \cfrac{0.370/12}{1500(0.500/12)} + \cfrac{0.370/12}{(0.500/12)600}}$$

$= 151$ Btu/(hr)(sq ft)(°F)

$$\text{Duty} = Q = 35(8.33)(1.0)(140)(60) = 2.45 \times 10^6 \text{ Btu/hr}$$

$$A = \frac{Q}{U\Delta_t} = \frac{2.45 \times 10^6}{151(80.9)} = 202 \text{ sq ft}$$

13–5. The spent acid from a nitrating process contains 43 per cent H_2SO_4, 36 per cent HNO_3, and 21 per cent H_2O, by weight. This acid is to be strengthened by the addition of concentrated sulfuric acid containing 91 per cent H_2SO_4 and concentrated nitric acid containing 88 per cent HNO_3. The strengthened mixed acid is to contain 40 per cent H_2SO_4 and 43 per cent HNO_3. Calculate the quantities of spent and concentrated acids which should be mixed together to yield 1000 lb of the desired mixed acid.

Solution: Basis, 1000 lb mixed acid. Let X=weight spent acid, in pounds; let Y=weight sulfuric acid, in pounds; and let Z=weight nitric acid, in pounds.

Over-all weight balance: $X+Y+Z=1000$

Water balance: $0.21X+0.09Y+0.12Z=0.17(1000)=170$

Nitrogen balance: $0.222(0.36)+0.222(0.88)Z=1000(0.43)(0.222)$

$$0.08X+0.196Z=95.6$$

Solution of the above equations by substitution results in:

Spent acid required = 608 lb

Sulfuric acid required = 152 lb

Nitric acid required = 240 lb

13–6. A triple-effect evaporator is set up and operated as shown below. The following assumptions may be utilized: (1) Boiling point elevation=0; (2) specific heats of all solutions=1.0; (3) condensates leave at condensing temperatures; and (4) all vapors are saturated and at condensing temperatures.

Material Balance (basis, 1 lb solids)

In 95/5	$=19.000$ lb H_2O/lb solids
Out 55/45	$=\ \ 1.222$ lb H_2O/lb solids
Evaporation	$=17.778$ lb H_2O/lb solids
Total evaporation	$=60{,}000\ (0.05)(17.778)=53{,}334$ lb/hr

Evaporation per effect $=53{,}334/3=17{,}778$ lb/hr

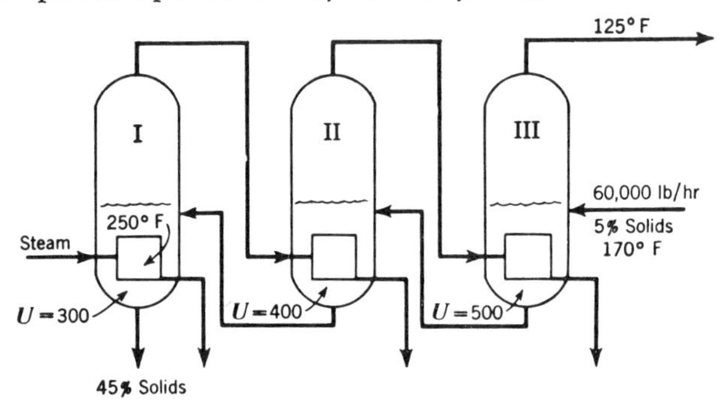

Problem 13–6.

Find (a) area required for evaporation per effect and total and (b) steam economy.

Solution: Basis, 1 hr operation. Since there is no boiling-point elevation, $\Delta t_{\text{true}} = 250 - 125 = 125°\text{F}$ and

$$u_1 \; \Delta t_1 = u_2 \; \Delta t_2 = u_3 \; \Delta t_3$$

$$\Delta t_1 + \Delta t_2 + \Delta t_3 = \Delta t = 125°\text{F}$$

or

$$300\Delta t_1 = 400\Delta t_2 = 500\Delta t_3$$

Upon solution of the equations above, we obtain:

$$\Delta t_1 = 53°\text{F} \qquad \Delta t_2 = 40°\text{F} \qquad \Delta t_3 = 32°\text{F}$$

Weight balance:

$$w_3 = \text{liquid from III to II} = 60{,}000 - 17{,}778 = 42{,}222 \text{ lb}$$

$$w_2 = \text{liquid from II to I} = 42{,}222 - 17{,}778 = 24{,}444 \text{ lb}$$

$$w_1 = \text{liquid from I} = 24{,}444 - 17{,}778 = 6666 \text{ lb}$$

The following information is obtained from steam tables

Stream	Temp. (°F)	Latent heat (Btu/lb)
Steam to I	250	$\lambda_s = 945.3$
Liquid in I, steam to II	197	$\lambda_1 = 979.6$
Liquid in II, steam to III	157	$\lambda_2 = 1003.8$
Liquid in III	125	$\lambda_3 = 1022.4$

Heat balance:

$$Q_1 = 17{,}778\lambda_1 + w_2 c_{p_2} \Delta t_2 = 17{,}778 \; (979.6) + 24{,}444(1.0)(40) = 1.828 \times 10^7 \text{ Btu/hr}$$

$$Q_2 = 17{,}778\lambda_1 = (w_2 - w_1)\lambda_1 = 17{,}778 \; (979.6) = 1.730 \times 10^7 \text{ Btu/hr}$$

$$Q_3 = (w_3 - w_2)\lambda_2 = 17{,}778(1003.8) = 1.785 \times 10^7 \text{ Btu/hr}$$

$$\text{Pounds of steam required} = w_s = \frac{1.828 \times 10^7}{945.3} = 19{,}300 \text{ lb/hr}$$

(a) Area required per effect:

$$A_{\text{I}} = \frac{1.828 \times 10^7}{300(53)} = 1150 \text{ sq ft}$$

$$A_{\text{II}} = \frac{1.730 \times 10^7}{400(40)} = 1082 \text{ sq ft}$$

$$A_{\text{III}} = \frac{1.785 \times 10^7}{500(32)} = 1115 \text{ sq ft}$$

Total area required = 3347 sq ft

(b)

$$\text{Steam economy} = \frac{53{,}333}{19{,}300} = 2.76 \text{ lb/lb steam}$$

13–7. Given a system of two tanks where inflow m is the manipulated variable; inflow u is the load variable; head h_1 in tank I is the controlled variable; R_1 and R_2 are resistances; and A_1 and A_2 are cross-sectional areas of tanks I and II respectively. (a) If the resistance to flow is linear (flow directly proportional to head), derive the process equation relating the head h_1 in tank I to inflow

m and load u, both of which change with time. (b) Draw the block diagram of the process.

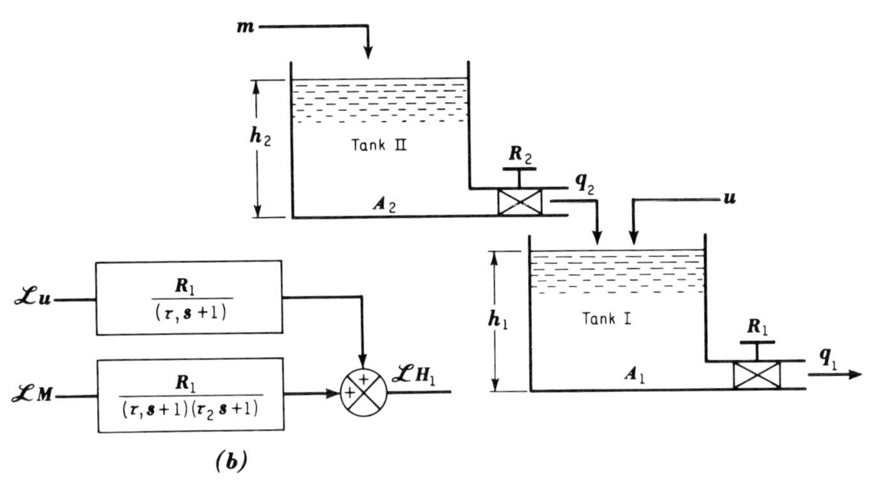

Problem 13–7.

Solution: (a) Write a material balance for tank II and tank I and combine the two equations. Σ inputs $-$ Σ outputs $=$ accumulation.

Tank II:

$$m - q_2 \equiv A_2 \frac{dh_2}{dt}$$

where t = time, in hours, q_2 is obtained from the relation, rate = driving force/resistance, $q_2 = h_2/R_2$ (laminar flow). Then

$$m - \frac{h_2}{R_2} \equiv A_2 \frac{dh_2}{dt} \tag{1}$$

Tank I:

$$q_2 + u - q_1 \equiv A_1 \frac{dh_1}{dt}$$

However, $q_1 = h_1/R_1$ (laminar flow). Then

$$\frac{h_2}{R_2} + u - \frac{h_1}{R_1} \equiv A \frac{dh_1}{dt} \tag{2}$$

At steady state,

$$m_s - \frac{h_{2s}}{R_2} = 0 \tag{3}$$

$$\frac{h_{2s}}{R_2} + u_s - \frac{h_{1s}}{R_1} \equiv 0 \tag{4}$$

Subtracting equations (3) and (4) from equations (1) and (2), respectively, and using the deviation variables $H_2 = h_2 - h_{2s}$, $H_1 = h_1 - h_{1s}$, $M = m - m_s$, and $U = u - u_s$, followed by application of Laplace transform, gives

$$R_2 \mathfrak{L}M = (\tau_{2s} + 1)\mathfrak{L}H_2 \tag{5}$$

$$\frac{R_1}{R_2}\mathfrak{L}H_2 + R_1\mathfrak{L}U = (\tau_{1s} + 1)\mathfrak{L}H_1 \tag{6}$$

Elimination of H_2 by algebraic means using equations (5) and (6) gives

$$\frac{R_1}{(\tau_{1s} + 1)(\tau_{2s} + 1)}\mathfrak{L}M + \frac{R_1}{(\tau_{1s} + 1)}\mathfrak{L}U = \mathfrak{L}H_1 \tag{7}$$

This is the desired process equation in the s-domain describing the deviation variable H_1 as a function of the deviation variables M and U. Unless initial conditions and the time-variation of M and U are known, the solution cannot be evaluated.

(b) The block diagram is obtained directly from equation (7).

13–8. Consider a chemical A which decomposes by the following two mechanisms to form a product mixture: (1) A→B+D and (2) A→R+S. Analysis of the mixture for a run at 327° C indicated a composition of 14.3 mole per cent R, 27.2 mole per cent B, 14.7 mole per cent S, and 26.6 mole per cent D. At what temperature should this reaction be run if R is the only desired product and thus the desired ratio of R to B is at least 4 to 1? The activation energy (in cal/gm mole of A) is 44,000 for reaction (1) and 50,000 for reaction (2).

Solution: 1. Assume Arrhenius law applies, $k = k_0e^{-E/RT}$. From law of mass action for elementary reactions (1) and (2), $r_1 = k_1[\mathrm{A}]$ and $r_2 = k_2[\mathrm{A}]$, $r_2 = 4\,r_1$. Therefore

$$k_2 = 4\,k_1 \qquad \text{and} \qquad k_{02}e^{-E_2/RT} = 4\,k_{01}e^{-E_1/RT} \tag{1}$$

Evaluate the frequency factor ratio based on data at 327° C (600° K). The production of R is described by

$$\frac{dn_R}{dt} = \gamma_R r_2$$

where γ_R = stoichiometric coefficient = +1 and the production of B is

$$\frac{dn_B}{dt} = \gamma_B r_1$$

where $\gamma_B = +1$.

2. Assume the analysis contains experimental error and use the average mole fraction for the two reactions. Basis: 1 mole initial charge of A; no R, B, D, S.

$$\frac{1}{\gamma_R}\frac{dn_R}{dt} = r_2 = 0.145 \text{ moles/unit time}$$

$$\frac{1}{\gamma_B}\frac{dn_B}{dt} = r_1 = 0.269 \text{ moles/unit time}$$

$$r_2/r_1 = 0.145/0.269 = 0.539$$

$$\frac{k_{02}\, e^{-E_2/R(600)}}{k_{01}\, e^{-E_1/600R}} = 0.539$$

$$\frac{k_{02}}{k_{01}} = (0.539)\left(e^{\frac{-44,000+50,000}{600R}}\right) = 0.539\,(e^{6000/600R})$$

$$= (0.539)\,(e^{10/1.98}) = 0.539(155)$$

$$k_{02} = 83.5\, k_{01}$$

Solving equation (1) for $T°$ K,

$$e^{-E_2/RT+E_1/RT} = \frac{4\, k_{01}}{83.5\, k_{01}} = 0.0479$$

$$e^{(-50,000+44,000)/RT} = 0.0479$$

$$-6000/RT = ln\, 0.0479 = -3.04$$

$$(3.04)(1.98)T = 6000$$

$$T = 995° \text{ K} = 722° \text{ C}$$

13–9. In the Haber process of ammonia synthesis from nitrogen and hydrogen, the fresh gas mixture containing nitrogen, hydrogen, and argon feeds to the reactor system. The gas mixture leaving the reactor contains ammonia, unreacted nitrogen and hydrogen, and argon. This mixture passes through an absorption tower where the ammonia is absorbed. The unabsorbed gases leave the top of the absorption tower. A portion of this mixture is purged from the system and the remainder is recycled to the reactor inlet where it is mixed with the fresh gas mixture. The fresh mixture contains 75.1 per cent hydrogen, 24.6 per cent nitrogen, and 0.3 per cent argon. The mixture of fresh gas and recycle gas entering the reactor contains 79.5 per cent hydrogen. The gas mixture leaving the top of the absorber contains 80.0 per cent hydrogen.

The net reaction may be represented by $1/2\,N_2+3/2\,H_2 \rightarrow NH_3$. Gas compositions are given on a volume or mol per cent basis, and only ammonia is absorbed in the absorber column.

(a) What is the molar ratio of recycle gas to fresh gas? (b) What per cent of fresh gas hydrogen entering the reactor is converted?

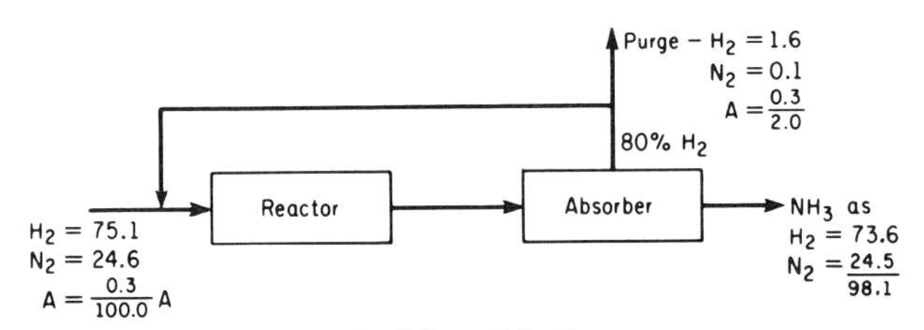

Problem 13–9.

Solution: Assume no NH_3 in recycle gas stream. Let x = moles of recycle, y = moles of fresh feed. Work on basis of 100 moles of total feed to reactor.

$$(24.6)(3) = 73.8$$

Therefore there is an excess of H_2 in the fresh feed.

$$0.751y + 0.800x = 0.795(100) = 79.5$$

and $x + y = 100$. Then $x = 89.8$ and $y = 10.2$.

(a) $x/y = 89.8/10.2 = 8.81$ molar ratio of recycle gas to fresh gas. Let u = mole per cent N_2 in recycle, v = mole per cent A in recycle. On the basis of 100 moles to reactor, the table shown is constructed.

Component	Fresh Feed		Recycle Gas		Total Gas to Reactor	
	Mole Per Cent	Total Moles	Mole Per Cent	Total Moles	Mole Per Cent	Total Moles
N_2	24.6	2.51	u	$0.898u$	$0.898u + 2.51$	$0.898u + 2.51$
H_2	75.1	7.66	80.0	71.8	79.5	79.5
A	0.3	0.03	v	$0.898v$	$0.898v + 0.03$	$0.898v + 0.03$
	100.0	10.20	100.0	89.8	100.0	100.0

Let α = moles produced per 100 moles of total reactor feed. Then moles into reactor

$$(0.898u + 2.51)_{N_2} + (79.5)_{H_2} + (0.898v + 0.03)_A = 100 \quad (1)$$

Moles out of reactor

$$\alpha NH_3 + \left[(0.898u + 2.51) - \frac{\alpha}{2}\right] N_2 + \left[79.5 - \frac{3\alpha}{2}\right] H_2 + [0.898v + 0.03]\, A = 100 - \alpha \quad (2)$$

After absorption: $100 - 2\alpha$ = moles out of absorber.

$$\frac{79.5 - 3\alpha/2}{100 - 2\alpha} = 0.80$$

and $\alpha = 5$ per cent per pass through reactor.

Solving for u and v, by equation (1),

$$0.898u + 0.898v = 100 - 79.5 - 2.51 - 0.03 = 17.96$$

and $u + v = 20$. Material balance around entire plant, on basis of 100 moles of fresh feed: Let β = moles of NH_3 produced and γ = moles of purge,

$$N_2 + 3H_2 = 2\,NH_3 \qquad 100 = 2\beta + \gamma$$

Component material balance: Hydrogen, $75.1 = 1.5\beta + 0.8\gamma$; Nitrogen, $24.6 = 0.5\beta + u\gamma$;

and Argon, $0.3 = v\gamma$. Substituting $\gamma = 100 - 2\beta$ and substituting in hydrogen balance equation,

$$75.1 = 1.5\beta + 0.8(100 - 2\beta)$$

and $\beta = 49$ moles, $\gamma = 100 - 2(49) = 2$, and $2\beta = 98$ moles = per cent of fresh gas hydrogen converted to ammonia. By argon balance: $0.3 = v(2)/100$ and $v = 15$ per cent argon in recycle; $u = 20 - v = 5$ per cent N_2 in recycle.

13–10. A plant consumes a 6000-gal tank car of ethylene chloride ($ClCH_2CH_2Cl$) each week. The solvent is pumped to storage tanks which are vented to the atmosphere and located in an area which averages 75°F. What is the vent loss during pumping, calculated as per cent of solvents pumped? (Ethylene chloride vapor pressure: 300 mm at 75°F).

13–11. Calculate, from the information given, the heat of combustion of carbon monoxide at 500°F, 1000°F, and 2000°F. The reaction is

$$CO + \tfrac{1}{2}O_2 \rightarrow CO_2$$

The heat of combustion of carbon monoxide at 18°C is −67,410 cal/g mole and the average molal heat capacities for the reactants and products are given below.

Temperature Range	C_p, CO	C_p, O_2	C_p, CO_2
18°C– 500°F	7.1 Btu/lb mole	7.25 Btu/lb mole	9.95 Btu/lb mole
18°C–1000°F	7.25	7.6	10.8
18°C–2000°F	7.7	8.0	12.1

13–12. One lb mole of air is subjected to the following series of processes: (a) an expansion process from an intial temperature of 140°F to 240°F, (b) a constant-pressure cooling process from 240°F to 100°F, (c) a constant-volume heating process from 100°F to 300°F, and (d) a constant-pressure cooling process from 300°F to 140°F. The state of the air at the end of this process is the same as that at the beginning of step (a). The total heat absorbed by the air in all four processes is 750 Btu. Calculate Q, W, ΔE, and ΔH for each of the processes and for the cycle as a whole. Assume that air behaves as a perfect gas and that the molal heat capacity at constant pressure remains constant at 7 Btu/(lb mole) (°F).

13–13. For the equation $CH_3OH(g) + HCl(g) \rightarrow CH_3Cl(g) + H_2O(g)$, calculate the equilibrium constant at 150°C from the following data:

	CH_3OH	HCl	CH_3Cl	H_2O
H^0 kg-cal/mole	−48.10	−22.06	−24.0	−59.56
S^0 cal/(mole) (°K)	56.8	44.62	70.86	47.38
C_p cal/(g) (°C)	0.68	0.21	0.26	0.47

13–14. A plant requiring 8000 gal of acetone per day has been purchasing the solvent in tank-truck quantities delivered to the plant site. It has been suggested that the relative costs of railroad delivery in 8000-gal cars might be advantageous, even though this would require construction of a 1-mile pipeline from the siding to the tank farm. As a basis for the economic study determine (a) the size of standard-weight steel pipe you would select for this pipeline and (b) the pumping head required to overcome friction in the pipeline during pumping.

13–15. A Venturi meter with a 2-in. throat is measuring the flow of water in a pipe having an inside diameter of 4 in. The difference in pressure between the throat and the upstream pipe is 6 in. of mercury. Calculate (a) velocity through the throat, in feet per second; (b) velocity through the pipe, in feet per second; and (c) number of gallons of water flowing per minute.

13–16. A furnace uses an otherwise high-grade petroleum fuel oil containing 5.2 per cent sulfur. The flue gas is analyzed carefully over mercury without prior removal of SO_2 (which is therefore reported along with the CO_2), showing 13.9 per cent CO_2 (plus SO_2), 0.4 per cent CO, 0.1 per cent H_2, 2.4 per cent O_2, and 83.2 per cent inerts. What is the analysis of the fuel?

13–17. A producer gas has the following analysis:

Atomic Weights	Components	Volume Per Cent
C = 12	CO	27.5
O = 16	CO_2	5.0
H = 1	H_2	14.0
N = 14	N_2	50.0
	O_2	0.5
	CH_4	3.0
	Total	100.0

Calculate the Orsat analysis of the flue gas when this is burned with 25 per cent excess air.

13–18. Two types of slab insulation are available for a certain installation. The slabs have the same dimensions, each being ¾ in. thick. Slab A insulation costs $0.08 per square foot and has a thermal conductivity of 0.8. Slab B insulation costs $0.40 per square foot and has a thermal conductivity of 0.075. An insulating wall is to be built in which one side of the wall will be exposed to a temperature of 1000°F and the other side to a temperature of 100°F. Assume that both types of insulation are equally capable of withstanding these temperatures. Assume also, for simplicity and for these particular conditions, that the most economical thickness of insulation will be reached when the cost of an additional slab is greater than the value of the heat saved per year by its use. Heat is valued at $0.40 per million Btu. From these data calculate the most economical thickness of wall (a) if only insulation A is used and (b) if only insulation B is used.

13–19. The plane wall of a furnace consists of two layers: 4½ in. of firebrick ($k=1.0$) and 9 in. of red brick ($k=0.4$). In steady operation, the flame side of the firebrick was at 1365°F and the outside of the red brick was at 300°F. To reduce the heat loss, the outside surface of the red brick was covered with a 1½-in. layer of magnesia ($k=0.049$); when steady conditions had been attained, the temperature of the outer surface of the magnesia was 200°F and the temperature of the flame side of the brick was 1425°F. Assume all conductivities independent of temperature. (a) Calculate the heat flux, in Btu per hour per square foot, before and after insulating. (b) For the insulated wall, calculate the temperatures at the junction of the firebrick and the red brick and at the junction of the red brick and the magnesia.

13–20. The apparent over-all coefficient of heat transfer U is 735 Btu/(hr) (sq ft) (°F) for a forced-circulation evaporator concentrating sulfite liquor under certain specified conditions. How long will it take to concentrate, to a final concentration of 15 per cent, 10 tons of such a feed liquor containing 5 per cent solids if the steam temperature is 230.8°F and the temperature corresponding to the pressure in the vapor space is 210.7°F? The heating surface is 100 sq ft. Tabulate any assumptions made in solving this problem.

13–21. Many salts when crystallized from water solution form crystals containing water of crystallization. If sodium sulfate is crystallized, the formula of its crystals is $Na_2SO_4 \cdot 10\ H_2O$ (Glauber's salt). If an aqueous solution containing 7.3 per cent Na_2SO_4

is evaporated, calculate the per cent of the water initially present which must be removed to have 80 per cent of the Na_2SO_4 crystallized as Glauber's salt when the evaporated residue is cooled to 20°C. The solubility of Na_2SO_4 at this temperature is 19.4 parts by weight per 100 parts of water. Atomic weights: Na=23, S=32, O=16, H=1.

13–22. Caustic soda is required in concentrations of 10 and 54 per cent NaOH. It can be purchased as 50, 73 or 100 per cent solid at $0.018, $0.019, and $0.022 per pound, respectively, of pure 100 per cent NaOH contained. Freight costs are $0.008 per liquid pound and $0.0082 for the solid including all containers. Handling and diluting costs for any concentration are $0.004*C* per pound of final diluted mixture, where *C* is the fractional concentration as purchased. What are the costs using each purchased material for the final required concentrations of 10 and 54 per cent NaOH?

13–23. (a) If 954 lb of copper were completely converted to cupric oxide, CuO, using 300 lb of oxygen, how much excess oxygen was present in the reaction kettle? (b) What percentage of excess is this?

13–24. A quantity of 100 moles of a solution that is 10 mole per cent *A* and 90 mole per cent *B* is subjected to simple distillation until the composition in the still pot is 95 mole per cent *B*. The distillation is carried out at atmospheric pressure, and it may be assumed that Raoult's law holds in the range of compositions involved. The ratio of the pressure of the pure component *B* to the pressure of the pure component *A* in this range is 0.5. Determine the number of moles removed in the distillation.

13–25. An atmospheric rotary drier handles 10 tons of a wet crystalline salt per day, reducing the moisture content from 10 to 1 per cent by means of countercurrent flow of hot air entering at 225°F dry-bulb, 110°F wet-bulb temperature and leaving at 150°F dry-bulb. Calculate (a) humidity of air entering and leaving the drier, (b) number of pounds of water removed from the salt per hour, and (c) number of tons of dry product per 24 hr.

13–26. A plant wishes to dry the filter cake from a filter press. To determine the drying characteristics, a sample of the cake 1 ft square was placed on a screen, suspended in a laboratory cabinet dryer, and exposed to a current of hot, dry air. The initial moisture content was 70 per cent. The cake lost weight at the constant rate of 0.5 lb/hr until the moisture content fell to 56 per cent, after which the rate fell off. Further tests showed that the equilibrium moisture content was 12 per cent and that the sample weighed 4.8 lb with this moisture content. The thickness of both cake and sample was 4 in. Compute the time required to dry 4 ft × 4 ft sections of the cake to 20 per cent water.

13–27. A packed tower has been designed to recover acetone from an acetone-air mixture. When the entering gas stream contains 2 per cent by volume of acetone, and water (pure) is used as a solvent, the recovery is 80 per cent. If the acetone concentration in the inlet gas drops to 1 per cent by volume and the gas rate, water rate, and temperature remain constant, determine the relationship between HTU and number of transfer units in the two sets of operation conditions. The equilibrium curve on a mole/mole basis is linear in this concentration range.

13–28. The vapor-liquid equilibria of the acetone–acetic acid system (at 1 atm) are as shown in the table.

Temp (°C)	Mole Per Cent Acetone		Temp (°C)	Mole Per Cent Acetone	
	Liquid	Vapor		Liquid	Vapor
118.1	0	0	74.6	50	91.2
110.0	5	16.2	70.2	60	94.7
103.8	10	30.6	66.1	70	96.9
93.1	20	55.7	62.6	80	98.4
85.8	30	72.5	59.2	90	99.3
79.7	40	84.0	56.1	100	100.0

A distillation column is to take a saturated liquid feed of 40 mole per cent acetone and produce a distillate product of 98 mole per cent acetone and a bottoms product of 95 mole per cent acetic acid. Determine (a) moles of distillate product per mole of feed, (b) moles of bottoms product per mole of feed, (c) number of theoretical plates to produce the separation at total reflux, and (d) minimum reflux ratio.

13–29. For the closed loop control system diagrammed,

$$G_1 = K_c,\ G_2 = R_1/T_1 s(T_2 s+1),\ \text{and}\ N = R_1/T_1 s(T_2 s+1)$$

where s is the argument of the Laplace transform, i.e., $L\{f(t)\} = F(s)$. (a) Calculate the proportional sensitivity K_c for a condition of critical damping (numerical result not required). (b) What is the static error following a unit step change in set point?

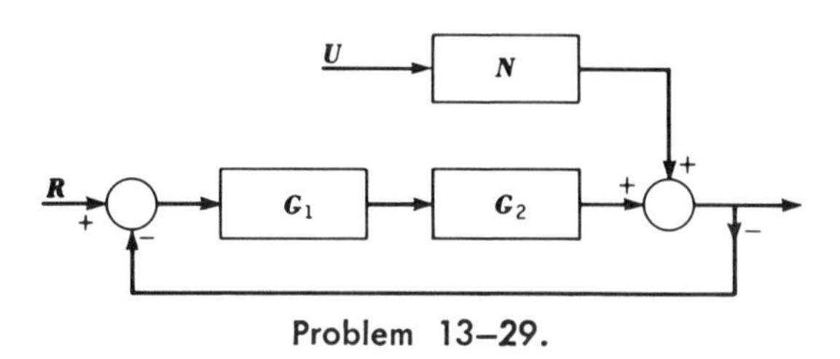

Problem 13–29.

13–30. It is desired to design an adiabatic heat exchanger to cool continuously 110,000 lb/hr of a solution from 150° F to 103° F using 100,000 lb/hr of cooling water, available at a temperature of 50° F. Specific heat of the solution is 0.91, and the over-all coefficient of heat transfer may be assumed to be 400. Calculate the heat transfer area for each of the following proposals: (a) Parallel flow, (b) counter flow, (c) reverse current exchanger with 2 shell passes and 4 tube passes, with the hot solution flowing through the shell and the cold water flowing through the tubes, and (d) cross flow with one tube pass and one shell pass.

13–31. A filter cake is to be dried in a tray dryer from an initial moisture content of 200 per cent (dry basis), to a final moisture content of 2 per cent (dry basis). The wet cake will be loaded in stainless steel trays to an average depth of 1.0 in. The trays in the dryer are 30 in. × 48 in. and are 2.0 in. apart. Shrinkage during drying is insignificant.

A test drying curve is not available but it is estimated that the critical moisture content will be 50 per cent (dry basis), and the equilibrium moisture will be zero per cent. Air will be circulated in the dryer at 225° F and 5.0 per cent relative humidity. During constant-rate drying, a velocity over the trays of 800 ft/min will be employed. After surface drying, to avoid dusting, this velocity must be reduced to 400 ft/min. For estimating purposes, assume a true surface temperature 9° F above the air wet bulb temperature, resulting from heat conduction and radiation. Dry cake density is 60 lb/cu ft and thermal conductivity is 1.0 Btu/(hr)(sq ft)(°F/ft).

Determine the approximate necessary drying cycle time.

13–32. The mercury-filled stainless steel bulb of an industrial thermometer has a mass of 3.8 lb, an outside surface area of 6.3 sq in., and a heat capacity of 0.032 Btu/lb° F. It is immersed in flowing water in a pipe, and under these conditions the film heat transfer coefficient from water to the bulb is 200 Btu/hr sq ft° F. (a) Calculate the time constant of this first-order measuring element in seconds. (b) Sketch the response of this bulb (as shown on a perfect recorder) to a sudden change at time zero from 75° F to 200° F.

13–33. A plate-type column is to be designed to produce continuously a primary distillate product containing 95 per cent (mol) benzene, a secondary or side-stream product containing 25 per cent (mol) benzene removed as a saturated liquid, and a bottoms product containing 5 per cent (mol) benzene. The feed contains 40 per cent (mol) benzene and 60 per cent (mol) toluene and will be introduced on the proper plate. The feed is at the bubble point, is 25 per cent vapor, and is fed at the rate of 1750 mols per 24-hour day. It is desired to obtain 500 mols of the secondary or side-stream product per 24-hour day. Vapors will be generated in a steam-heated still attached to the base of the column, and the residue is to be withdrawn continuously from the still. The column will be operated at normal atmospheric pressure with a total condenser, reflux at its bubble point being returned to the top plate.

Calculate (a) the quantity (mols per 24-hour day) of distillate and bottoms product obtained; (b) the minimum reflux ratio (L/D) at the top of the column; and (c) for a reflux ratio of twice the minimum, (1) the number of theoretical plates required, (2) the location of feed plate, and (3) the location of the side-stream draw-off. The equilibrium and bubble point data for Benzene-Toluene at 760 mm Hg are listed, x = mol fraction of benzene in liquid, y = mol fraction of benzene in vapor.

x	y	b.p. C	x	y	b.p. C	x	y	b.p. C
0.000	0.000	110.40	0.380	0.600	95.90	0.740	0.878	86.00
0.060	0.132	107.90	0.460	0.679	93.35	0.820	0.922	84.10
0.100	0.209	106.20	0.500	0.714	92.20	0.900	0.959	82.30
0.220	0.404	101.40	0.580	0.776	90.05	0.940	0.976	81.45
0.300	0.507	98.50	0.660	0.831	88.00	1.000	1.000	80.30

13–34. Methyl acetoxypropionate decomposes irreversibly in the gas phase on heating by the following one-step mechanism:

$$CH_3\,COOCH\,(CH_3)\;COOCH_3 \rightarrow CH_3COOH + CH_2CHCOOCH_3$$

When the reaction is carried out in an isothermal tubular flow reactor at 4 atmospheres and 1100° F, a reactor volume of 1.0 cu ft is required to produce a 65 per cent decomposition of methyl acetoxypropionate with a feed rate as follows: Feed stream, $CH_3COOCH(CH_3)COOCH_3$—5 lb moles/hr, inert gases—5 lb moles/hr. What reactor volume would be required for the following cases, all other conditions being the same as noted: (a) 10 atmospheres? (b) 10 lb moles/hr of feed of both inert and methyl acetoxypropionate? (c) 90 per cent decomposition?

13–35. An irreversible chemical reaction $A+B \rightarrow C$ has a specific reaction rate constant at 760° R of 3.1 ft^3/lb mole sec. Compute the time required for 95 per cent of A to react. The reaction occurs at a constant pressure of 5 atmospheres and a constant temperature of 760° R. Initially we have 5 moles of A, 6 moles of B, 1 mole of C, and 4 moles of an inert, D. All species are gaseous and follow the ideal gas law.

In principle, it would be possible to conduct a homogeneous reaction of this kind in a flow process in a series of several large tanks, or in a long tubular reactor. Which type of reactor would require the least reaction volume? Justify your answer on theoretical grounds.

13–36. Water is flowing in a circular pipe with a velocity of 1 ft/sec and temperature of 60° F at the beginning. These properties are constant over the entire cross-section. The tube wall is hotter than the water. Some distance along the pipe the water takes on a parabolic velocity distribution (maximum velocity at the centerline and decrease of velocity with the square of the radius until it is zero at the wall). At this point the temperature also varies with the radius as follows: $(T-T_w) = (T_{℄}-T_w)\{1-(r/R)^2\}$ where T_w = wall temperature = 200° F, $T_{℄}$ = centerline temperature = 100° F, r = radius to any point in inches, and R = radius of pipe = 1 in. How much heat has been added to the fluid between the entrance and the section specified?

13–37. Oil is flowing from an oil field to a refinery through a circular conduit. The conduit runs only ½ full. A pitot tube is inserted in the conduit 6.7 in. below the surface of the oil. Chloroform is used in the manometer arm of the pitot tube and gives a reading of 5.34 in. of chloroform. What is the flow rate of oil in lb/hr? Given data: density of chloroform = 92.5 lb/ft^3, density of oil = 56.5 lb/ft^3, viscosity of oil = 140 centipoises, ID of conduit = 2 ft.

13–38. A pump, powered by a 5-hp motor, is to be used to deliver 300 gal/min of a carbonate solution to an open tank through a horizontal pipe whose equivalent length is 500 ft of pipe. The efficiency of the motor-pump combination is 74 per cent, the inlet pressure is atmospheric, and the carbonate solution has a specific gravity of 1.10 and a viscosity of 2.5 centipoise. (a) What is the minimum-size standard schedule-40 pipe that can be used? Neglect kinetic energy effects and assume turbulent flow where the Fanning friction factor can be represented by $f = 0.046 (Du\rho/\mu)^{-0.2}$. (b) Check the two assumptions made in part (a).

13–39. Acetic acid and ethyl alcohol are to be esterified under conditions of catalyst and temperature such that the specific rate constant is 0.005 liters/(min) (g-mole) and the rate of the reverse reaction is negligible. The density of the reaction mixture may be taken as constant at 8.33 lb/gal. The raw materials, a 90 wt per cent aqueous solution of acetic acid (10 per cent H_2O) and a 95 wt per cent aqueous alcohol solution (5 per cent H_2O) are to be mixed in a weight ratio of 2 lb alcohol solution per pound acid solution.

A 90 per cent conversion of the acid is specified and the plant is to be designed to produce 50,000 lb of ester per day (24-hour basis). In the preliminary calculations, two different methods of operating the plant are to be considered: batch and tubular flow. (a) Batch operation. Allowing 2¼ hr per cycle for dead time (filling, bringing to reaction temperature, emptying, cleaning, etc.), how large a reactor will be required, in gallons? (b) Tubular flow operation. If 1-in. ID tubes are used and a minimum linear velocity of 1 ft/sec is maintained to provide adequate mixing and heat transfer, how long will the flow path have to be? (The tubes can be either coiled or doubled back and forth like a multipass heat exchanger). How many tubes will be needed in parallel? The two feed streams will be blended as they enter the reactor in both cases, so do not allow any reactor time or volume for this.

$$HA_c + \epsilon t OH \xrightarrow{k_1} \epsilon t OA_c + H_2O.$$

13–40. Calculate the bubble point temperature and dew point temperature, at one atmosphere total pressure, of a 2-phase mixture of tuolene and water containing 57 mole per cent water. Assume that toluene and water are completely insoluble in each other. Vapor pressures are given by the following expressions, with pressure in mm Hg and temperatures in °K:

Water $\log_{10} P = 8.70 - 2{,}170/T$ Toluene $\log_{10} P = 7.74 - 1{,}870/T$

Civil Engineering 14

The chapter on civil engineering is divided into five parts comprising plain concrete and asphalt, fluids, sanitary engineering, soils, and structural engineering. Typical problems with solutions, followed by similar problems, will be found under each heading. As far as possible, problems of a similar type are grouped together. Many problems are of a design nature and require an individual approach; solutions and answers could not be shown for all of these. If assumptions are needed, they are generally noted in the solution or in the answers. In some states, surveying, contracts, and ethics are included in the civil engineering portion of examinations. These have been covered elsewhere in the book.

PLAIN CONCRETE AND ASPHALT

14–1. The engineer has called for a 1:2:3½ concrete mix for construction of an airport concrete wearing slab. There is a water content of 235.4 lb/cu yd. If necessary for the solution of the problem, assume that 587 lb of cement are required per cubic yard. (a) How many pounds of sand and how many pounds of coarse aggregate are required for a 1 cu yd batch? (b) How many sacks of cement does the mix contain for the 1 cu yd batch? (c) What is the water-cement ratio of the mix, in gallons per sack of cement? (d) What is the absolute volume of the cement plus the water in each cubic yard batch, expressed in cubic feet? (e) If there were 5 per cent free water in the fine aggregate, what changes in the weights of the materials would you make? (f) If there were 1 per cent absorption in the coarse aggregate, which changes in weights would you make?

Solution: Assuming specific gravities of 3.15 for the cement and 2.6 for the aggregates:

(a) 1 part cement = 587 lb/cu yd
2 parts sand = 1174 lb/cu yd
3½ parts gravel = 2054 lb/cu yd

(b) 587/94 = 6.24 sacks

(c) Water/cement = 235.4/6.25 = 37.7 lb water/sack
Gallons per sack = 37.7/8.33 = 4.53

(d) Cement = 587 lb/yd, abs vol $= \frac{587}{62.4(3.15)} = 2.98$ cu ft

Water = 235.4 lb/yd, abs vol = 235.4/62.4 = 3.78 cu ft

Total = 6.76 cu ft

(e) Increase sand and decrease water.

(f) Decrease gravel and add water.

14–2. A batch of concrete contains the following weights of materials having the indicated specific gravities:

Water	50 lb, sp gr 1.00	Sand	200 lb, sp gr 2.60
Cement	94 lb, sp gr 3.15	Gravel	390 lb, sp gr 2.65

The concrete was found to weigh 144 lb/cu ft and the slump measured 3 in. Compute (a) the water content, (b) the cement content, (c) the weight of aggregate, all in pounds per cubic yard. (d) Determine the water-cement ratio by weight. (e) Find the number of gallons of water per sack of cement. (f) What is the air content, in per cent?

Solution: (a), (b), (c)

Material	Weight (lb)	Absolute Volume (cu ft)	Volume per Cubic Yard	Weight per Cubic Yard (lb)
Water ...	50	50/62.4 = 0.80	4.43	4.43(62.4) = 276
Cement ..	94	94/3.15(62.4) = 0.48	2.66	2.66(62.4) (3.15) = 523
Sand	200	200/62.4(2.6) = 1.23	6.81	6.81(62.4) (2.6) = 1105
Gravel ...	390	390/62.4(2.65) = 2.36	13.07	13.07(62.4) (2.65) = 2161
	734	4.87		

Yield per 1-sack batch = 4.87 cu ft Sacks/yd = 27/4.87 = 5.54

(d) Water to cement ratio by weight = 276/523 = 0.53

(e) Water = 50/8.33 = 6.13 gal/sack cement

(f) Weight = 734 lb for 4.87 cu ft or 150.7 lb Per cent air $= \frac{150.7 - 144}{150.7} = 4.45$ per cent

14–3. The proportions of a mix by volume and the properties of the materials are listed as follows. Determine the amount of cement and fine and coarse aggregate (sand and gravel) to be ordered for 3000 cu yd of concrete. Assume that 5 per cent of the aggregates will be wasted in handling the materials.

Mix (dry-rodded) 1:2.4:3.6
Water .... 6 gal/sack
Dry-rodded gravel ..... 96 lb/cu ft
Dry-rodded sand ..... 102 lb/cu ft
Specific gravity gravel 2.70
Specific gravity sand 2.65
Specific gravity cement 3.14
Bulking factor gravel 1.05
Bulking factor sand 1.17

Solution:

Mix		Weight per 1-Sack Mix (lb)	Absolute Volume (cu ft)
Cement	1	94	$\frac{94}{3.14(62.4)}=0.48$
Sand	2.4	2.4(102) = 245	$\frac{245}{2.65(62.4)}=1.48$
Gravel	3.6	3.6(96) = 345.6	$\frac{345.6}{2.70(62.4)}=2.05$
Water	6 gal/sack	6(8.33) = 50	$\frac{50}{62.4}=0.80$
		734.6	Yield = 4.81

One sack yields 4.81 cu ft concrete $\quad$ Cement/cu yd $=\frac{27}{4.81}=5.61$ sacks

For 3000 cu yd:

$$\text{Sand}=\frac{5.61(3000)(2.4)(1.17)(1.05)}{27}=1839 \text{ cu yd}$$

$$\text{Gravel}=\frac{5.61(3000)(3.6)(1.05)(1.05)}{27}=2468 \text{ cu yd}$$

$$\text{Cement}=5.61(3000) \qquad =16{,}830 \text{ sacks}$$

14–4. In order to find the compacted density of an undisturbed sample of asphalt pavement, the following procedure was used: A sample weighing 560.0 g was selected and completely coated with paraffin having a specific gravity of 0.864. The sample and the coating weighed 582.8 g. The sample suspended in water weighed 312.9 g. What is the specific gravity and unit weight, in pounds per cubic foot, of the pavement sample?

Solution:

Wt mixture = 560 g

Wt (mixture + paraffin) = 582.8 g

Wt paraffin = 582.8 − 560 = 22.8 g

$$\text{Vol paraffin}=\frac{22.8}{0.864}=26.4 \text{ cc}$$

Loss of wt in water = 582.8 − 312.9 = 269.9 g

$$\text{Density}=\frac{560}{269.9-26.4}=2.30$$

Wt/cu ft = 2.30(62.4) = 143.5 lb/cu ft

14–5. It is proposed to cement-treat native material in place as a base for bituminous surfacing. The maximum dry weight of soil-cement mixture is 122.4 lb/cu ft with 10 per cent cement by weight. Find the number of barrels of cement per station for base 24 ft wide and a compacted thickness of 6 in.

Solution:

Vol per station = 24(0.5)(100) = 1200 cu ft

Assuming material compacted to the maximum density:

$$\text{Wt cement} = 1200(12.24) = 14{,}690 \text{ lb}$$

$$\text{Number of 376-lb barrels needed} = 14{,}690 \div 376 = 39$$

14–6. The following concrete design for a 1 cu yd batch was made assuming that the aggregates would be saturated surface-dry. However, the stockpiles show that the sand contains 3.8 per cent and the gravel 1.1 per cent free moisture, by saturated surface-dry weight. Adjust the batch quantities to account for the free moisture. The design calls for 6 sacks cement, 1230 lb sand, 1980 lb gravel, and 36 gal water.

Solution:

Weights per Cubic Yard SSD (lb)	Weight Surface Moisture (lb)	Final Batch Weights (lb)
Cement = 6(94) = 564	... ...	564
Sand = 1230	0.038(1230) = 46.7	1230 + 46.7 = 1276.7
Gravel = 1980	0.011(1980) = 21.8	1980 + 21.8 = 2001.8
Water = 36(8.33) = 300	... ...	300 − 68.5 = 231.5
	Wt Water = 68.5	

14–7. Materials and their conditions as used in a batch of paving concrete are as shown in the table. For the mix shown,

Material	Batch Quantities	Sp. Gr. Agg. on SSD Basis	Moisture Content, Based on Oven-Dry Weights	
			For SSD Conditions	As Used
Cement	7.5 bags	3.15	...	...
Sand	1420 lb	2.70	1.2	5.0
Crushed rock ...	2470 lb	2.66	0.8	1.4
Water	30.0 gal	1.00	...	...

calculate (a) the cement factor on an air-free basis and (b) the water-cement ratio, in gallons per sack, on the basis of saturated surface-dry aggregates. (c) If the actual weight of a cubic foot of wet concrete is 147.0 lb, what is the percentage of entrained air?

14–8. Calculate the volume of concrete produced per batch from a mixer using the following batch weights: stone, 2500 lb; sand, 1600 lb; cement, 720 lb; and water, 437 lb. The specific gravities are 2.70, 2.66, and 3.15, respectively.

14–9. A concrete mix is to contain 2.20 cu ft of sand and 3.30 cu ft of stone for each bag of cement. The sand weighs 95 lb/cu ft and the stone weighs 92 lb/cu ft, dry-rodded weights. The mix is to contain 5.75 gal water per sack of cement. The specific gravity of both aggregates is 2.55. The specific gravity of the cement is 3.10. Find the volumes of cement, sand, stone, and water required to produce 2½ cu yd of concrete.

14–10. An aggregate has a bulk specific gravity on a saturated surface-dry basis of 2.70. The absorption is 1 per cent. In a test for free moisture, 2045 g of wet aggregates are placed in an overflow-type pycnometer and displace 836 g of water. (a) What is the weight of the free water per cubic foot of wet aggregate? (b) What is the weight of the oven-dry aggregate per cubic foot?

14–11. The proportions by weight and the specific gravities of each of the constituents of a sheet asphalt paving mixture are as shown in the table. A cylindrical specimen of the mixture was

Material	Specific Gravity	Per Cent by Weight
Asphalt	1.04	10.0
Filler	2.82	16.5
Sand	2.66	73.5

molded in the laboratory and weighed in air and in water with the following results:

Weight of dry specimen in air = 111.95 g
Weight of SSD specimen in air = 112.09 g
Weight of saturated specimen in water = 61.20 g

(a) Calculate the bulk specific gravity of the compacted specimen. (b) Compute the maximum theoretical specific gravity of the sheet asphalt paving mixture. (c) Determine the percentage of voids in the laboratory-molded specimen. (d) When this mixture was placed and rolled on the street, a core was removed and its specific gravity was found to be 2.13. Does this meet the requirement of 95 per cent of the density obtained on a standard laboratory specimen? (e) Calculate the weight of a square yard of 1½-in. wearing surface composed of this sheet asphalt mixture.

14–12. An asphaltic mixture with the ingredients listed when compacted in place had a specific gravity of 2.32. Determine (a) maximum theoretical density, (b) percentage of voids, (c) weight (in tons) for a 3-in surfacing on a section of road 21 ft wide and 3000 ft long, and (d) if the specific gravity of a sample compressed in the laboratory was 2.40, compare the efficiency of the rolling operation with the density obtained in the laboratory.

	Specific Gravity	Percentage by Weight
Graded stone	2.70	54
Sand	2.67	36
Limestone dust	2.70	4
Asphaltic cement	1.04	6

14–13. A carload of RC 3 consisting of 10,250 gallons with a specific gravity of 0.95 is pumped from the tank car at a temperature of 150° F. (a) Determine the value upon which payment will be based. (b) What tests would you perform to determine if the material is actually an RC 3? Give reasons for your answer.

14–14. The following materials were used for a mix design in asphaltic concrete: 52.0 per cent coarse aggregates with a specific gravity of 2.58; 34.6 per cent fine aggregate with a specific gravity of 2.72; 7.4 per cent mineral filler with a specific gravity of 2.70; and 6.0 per cent asphalt cement with a specific gravity of 1.02. (a) Determine the theoretical density, and the per cent voids in the compacted mix. (b) Determine the bulk density of the specimen if the weight in air is 1174.7 g and in water is 668.4 g.

14–15. An asphalt paving sample weighs 1610 g in air and 945 g when immersed in water. The mixture had the composition by weight shown in the table. (a) Determine the per cent voids in the sample. (b) Determine the per cent total voids filled with asphalt. (c) Will this mixture make a high quality highway pavement? Explain your answer.

	Per Cent	Specific Gravity
Sand	50.0	2.65
Stone	40.0	2.78
Dust	4.0	2.70
Asphalt	6.0	1.02

14–16. Determine the thickness of flexible pavement required by the conditions listed. Use any method you desire, but check your answer by a second method.

Subgrade Information	Wheel Load and Traffic
Passing No. 200 sieve 67%	9000-lb wheel load
Liquid limit 45%	Area of contact . . . . 90 sq in.
Plastic limit 37%	Traffic-passenger cars . . . . 300 vpd/lane
Calif. bearing ratio . . . . CBR 5	Trucks . . . . 20 vpd/lane
Shearing resistance, q . . . . 20 psi	

14–17. Shown below are the gradations for two aggregates, neither of which meets the specifications for a particular paving mix. (a) Determine the full range of blends for the two aggregates that will meet the specifications. (b) If both aggregates are available at equal cost, what blend should be used?

Size	Aggregate A (per cent passing)	Aggregate B (per cent passing)	Specifications (per cent passing)
1 in.	96	100	96–100
½ in.	71	93	75–85
#4	32	62	40–50
#16	15	36	20–30
#50	2	19	5–10
#100	0	5	0–3

14–18. A stockpile of sand on a job contains 6 per cent free moisture. A gravel stockpile is completely dry and will absorb 1 per cent moisture. What weight of water, sand, and gravel should be added to a batch of concrete so that the combination will equal 50 lb of water, 200 lb of SSD sand, and 390 lb of SSD gravel?

14–19. Outline the precautions to be taken in pouring concrete and protecting freshly poured concrete in freezing weather.

14–20. Discuss the effect of −200 mesh material in the aggregate which is to be used in asphaltic paving mixtures.

14–21. Define (a) pozzolith, (b) prestressing, and (c) fly ash. (d) Explain the use of each of the above in the construction industry and list the advantages and disadvantages of each.

14–22. In what respects does the use of air-entraining agents in portland cement concrete pavements improve the concrete? What is the principal detrimental effect of air entrainment?

14–23. Describe each of the following tests and explain its use: (a) Sieve analysis. (b) Colorimetric test. (c) Slump test. (d) Compression test.

14–24. (a) Give three methods which may be used to keep fresh concrete moist when exposed to rapid-drying conditions. (b) If a pile-driver crew had a timber pile only partly driven at quitting time, would you allow the crew to stop work and resume driving the next morning? (c) What are the advantages and the disadvantages of using mechanical internal vibrators in placing concrete? (d) A new highway will have a 20-ft deep embankment. Describe three methods of compacting the fill. (e) For reinforced concrete made with type I portland cement, placed and maintained at an average temperature of 55°F, give the time limit, in days, before you would remove the forms from the floor slab, the beam sides, the girder bottom, and long-span bridge arch centering.

14–25. The statements which follow are not necessarily true. Discuss each one. (a) Concrete made with air-entraining cement has improved workability and resistance to deterioration by freezing and thawing. (b) Sea water may be used in place of fresh water to build a satisfactory reinforced-concrete structure. (c) The chlorides of potassium, sodium, and calcium added in dissolved form to the mixing water act as an accelerator to concrete. (d) Asphalt or magnesium sulfate employed as an admixture in portland cement concrete piles improves impact resistance and prevents shattering. (e) Linseed oil and sodium silicate are both effective agents to use on concrete floors which are dusting badly.

14–26. (a) What is a tie bar as used in concrete pavement construction? (b) What diameter and center-to-center spacing of tie bars are normally used? (c) For best results, should a structural concrete be proportioned by weight or volume? Why?

14–27. Answer or describe each of the following: (a) How would you place concrete under water? (b) By schematic diagram explain the operation of a pneumatic caisson. (c) How are the heads of timber and concrete piles protected during driving? (d) Describe briefly the three types of pile-driving hammers and give the advantages and the disadvantages of each type.

14–28. Several defects have developed in a portland cement concrete paving. They are spalling, pumping, and map cracking. For each defect state (a) the possible causes, (b) how it might have been prevented in the original construction, (c) what remedial action may be taken.

14–29. (a) Outline the procedure which should be followed in constructing a bituminous macadam road. (b) On what does the strength and durability of a bituminous macadam road depend? (c) What are the principal maintenance problems of this type of road?

14–30. (a) Write specifications for a concrete to be used in the walls and floor of a sedimentation basin for a water treatment plant. (b) Sketch a watertight expansion joint to be used in this basin.

14–31. A concrete mix is to be made according to the following proportions by weight: Cement 94 lb, sand 250 lb (bone dry basis), gravel 300 lb (bone dry basis), and water 65.8 lb. If the sand is found to contain 3 per cent total moisture and the gravel 2.5 per cent total moisture, what corrected amounts of sand, gravel and water must be used with 94 lb of cement?

14–32. The following are concerned with the use of portland cement concrete as a construction material. Indicate whether each is true or false. (a) The 28-day strength at 70°F will be measurably reduced if 7 gal water per sack of cement are used in place of 6 gal water. All other conditions remain unchanged. (b) Heavy mineral oil in the amount of 4 per cent of cement by weight will improve the water tightness of the concrete without significantly impairing its strength. (c) Coloring obtained by grinding mineral pigments will not impair the strength of the concrete in which it is used. (d) Air entrainment permits a reduction of the amount of mixing water without a loss of workability or without a significant reduction in strength. (e) The compressive strength of concrete increases directly with the time allowed for mixing up to initial set.

14–33. How many sacks of cement will be required per 100-ft station for a soil-cement mixture containing 12 per cent cement by volume if the base is 24 ft wide and 7 in. thick?

14–34. Given the following specifications: Minimum 6 sacks of cement per cu yd of concrete, minimum w/c ratio 7 gal/sack, air content 3—7 per cent, minimum per cent C.A. by volume of total aggregate 67 per cent. Two aggregate sources available with specific gravities and costs per ton.

	C.A.	F.A.	Cost/ton
Source I	2.68	2.65	$4.35
Source II	2.64	2.67	$4.50

When correcting for air content, reduce only volume of F.A. and water. Reduce sand volume by 65 per cent of total volume of air. Find (a) cost of aggregate for most economical mix to produce 10,000 cu yd, (b) batch weights of most economical mix.

14–35. A batch of concrete consists of 200 lb of fine aggregate, 310 lb of coarse aggregate, 94 lb of cement, and 5.1 gal water. Specific gravity of the sand and gravel may be assumed as 2.6 and that of cement as 3.1. What is the volume of the batch? How much by weight of each ingredient is required to produce one cu yd of concrete?

14–36. Calculate the quantities of materials in one cu yd of concrete for a mixture having the following properties:

One sack of cement. . . . . .sp gr 3.14
350 lb of fine aggregate. . . . . .sp gr 2.62
300 lb of coarse aggregate. . . . . .sp gr 2.58
6 gal water

14–37. A concrete mix design is needed for a large sidewalk project. Working with the basic information listed, determine the weight of each ingredient to be used for a one cu ft trial batch of concrete.

Coarse Aggregate Available

Maximum size. . . . . .1 in.
Minimum size. . . . . .No. 4
Apparent specific gravity. 2.64

Fine Aggregate Available

Maximum size. . . . . .No. 4
Fineness modulus. 2.78
Apparent specific gravity. 2.70

14–38. Design a trial mix for a concrete pavement using a cement factor of 5.5 sacks per cu yd and 6 per cent air. The fine aggregate has 1.0 per cent absorption and 8.0 per cent free moisture; coarse aggregate has 0.5 per cent absorption and 0.2 per cent free moisture. The coarse aggregate is 2 in., angular, with specific gravity of 2.60 and unit weight of 100 lb/cu ft. The fine aggregate has a specific gravity of 2.65, unit weight of 105 lb/cu ft, and a fineness modulus of 2.60. Use the material crushed stone P.C.A. or A.C.I. method for your design. Indicate the method used.

14–39. (a) Given sieve analyses and specifications shown, within what limits may material B be combined with existing material A so that the mixture will conform to the specifications? Using the lower limit of material B, show the sieve analysis percentages for the mixture.

Sieve	Per Cent Passing (by weight)			
	Existing Material A	Specifications	Material B Borrow	Material C Borrow
1 in.	100	100	100	100
3/8 in.	75	50–85	52	64
No. 4	54	35–65	30	45
No. 10	51	25–50	17	28
No. 40	35	15–30	6	15
No. 200	22	5–15	2	5

(b) It is desired to combine the minimum amount of B or C with the existing material so that the mixture will conform to the specifications. If material B is available at \$0.50 per cu yd and material C at \$0.40 per cu yd, which borrow material would be more economical to use? Assume that the existing material is available at no cost.

14–40. A 4-lane concrete highway is to be built as an access road to a large industrial plant. All shipping will be done by truck. The highway slab will be of uniform thickness and will be poured one lane at a time. Subgrade soil description is as follows:

Passing No. 40 .... 60%
Passing No. 10 .... 84%
Liquid Limit—for portion passing No. 40 .... 45%
Plasticity Index—for portion passing No. 40 .... 5%

Discuss the design of this pavement covering (a) purpose and spacing of transverse joints and reinforcement of these joints;

(b) purpose of reinforcement of longitudinal joints; (c) thickness of slab; (d) purpose and amount of slab reinforcement; and (e) purpose, type, and thickness of sub-base if used.

FLUIDS

14–41. A gas main 10 in. in diameter has open-water manometer gages provided at points A and B. Point B is 500 ft higher than A. If the height of the (fresh) water column at A is 10 in., what would be the height of the water column at B? (Assume no flow in pipe. Specific weight of gas is 0.035 lb/cu ft; specific weight of air is 0.075 lb/cu ft.)

Solution:

$$\frac{P_A}{w}=\frac{14.7(144)}{0.035}+\frac{10(62.4)}{12(0.035)}=61{,}942 \text{ ft of gas}$$

Atmospheric pressure at $B=14.7(144)-500(0.075)=2078.5$ psf

Let h = height of water column at B, in inches

$$\frac{2078.5}{0.035}+\frac{h(62.4)}{12(0.035)}=61{,}442 \qquad h=13.84 \text{ in.}$$

Check:

$$h_B=10+\frac{500(0.04)(12)}{62.4}=13.84 \text{ in.}$$

14–42. Find the horsepower required to overcome pipe friction with a flow of 90,000 gpd of fuel oil of specific gravity 0.925 at a temperature of 65°F through 2500 ft of new 4-in. diameter steel pipe. Kinematic viscosity of the oil is 0.000836 sq ft/sec.

Solution:

$$V=\frac{Q}{A}=\frac{90{,}000(144)(4)}{24(3600)(7.49)(\pi)(4)^2}=1.59 \text{ fps}$$

$$N_R=\frac{VD}{\nu}=\frac{1.59(4)}{12(0.000836)}=633 \text{ laminar flow}$$

$$f=\frac{64}{N_R}=\frac{64}{633}=0.101$$

$$h_f=\frac{fL}{D}\frac{V^2}{2g}=\frac{0.101(2500)(12)(1.59)^2}{4(64.4)}=29.6 \text{ ft of oil}$$

$$\text{Power}=\frac{Qwh_f}{550}=\frac{0.139(0.925)(62.4)(29.6)}{550}=0.432 \text{ hp}$$

14–43. A 12-in. circular vitrified-clay sewer is laid on a 2 per cent grade and carries sewage 8 in. deep in uniform flow. Calculate the flow, in gallons per minute. What head will develop on a rectangular weir, fully contracted, 1.00 ft long when discharging 275 gpm of water?

Solution:

$$\frac{d_8}{d_{12}}=\frac{8}{12}=0.667 \qquad Q_{12}=4.90 \text{ cfs (from nomograph } n=0.013)$$

From hydraulic elements chart $\frac{Q_8}{Q_{12}}=0.8$

$$Q_8=0.8(4.90)(449)=1760 \text{ gpm}$$

$$\text{Cone formula}-Q=3.247LH^{1.48}-\left(\frac{0.566L^{1.8}}{1+2L^{1.8}}\right)H^{1.9}$$

$$0.613=3.247H^{1.48}-\left(\frac{0.566}{1+2}\right)H^{1.9}$$

$$H=0.332 \text{ ft}$$

14–44. A pump test is made with the following apparatus: A simple U-tube mercury manometer is attached to a piezometer ring on the suction line of the pump. The left leg of this manometer is attached to the piezometer ring of the suction line, and the right leg is open to the atmosphere. A Bourdon pressure gage is attached to piezometer ring of the discharge line. The discharge line is 6.00 in. in diameter and is 1.00 ft higher in elevation than the suction line. The suction line is 8.00 in. in diameter. The pressure gage reads 32.5 psi. The mercury level in the left leg of the manometer is 3.421 ft below the center line of the suction line, and in the right leg it is 3.957 ft below the center line of the suction line. The discharge measured by an orifice is 1020 gpm. The pumped fluid is water at 58°F. What is the power output of the pump?

Solution: Energy equation from suction to discharge

$$\frac{V_s^2}{2g}+\frac{P_s}{w}+Z_s+H_p=\frac{V_D^2}{2g}+\frac{P_d}{w}+Z_d$$

$$\frac{42.2}{64.4}-7.26+0+H_p=\frac{134.5}{64.4}+75+1 \quad \text{(datum at suction)}$$

$$H_p=75.0+2.09+10.7+1.00-0.656=88.1 \text{ ft of water}$$

$$\text{Power}=\frac{QwH_p}{550}=\frac{2.27(62.4)(83.69)}{550}=22.7 \text{ hp}$$

14–45. One side of a U tube containing mercury is connected through the bottom of a tank in which water stands 15.00 ft deep. The other side of the U tube is connected through the side of the same water tank at a point 2.00 ft below the water surface. If water fills the connecting tubes and the U tube down to the mercury, compute the difference in mercury levels in the two legs of the U tube.

14–46. A timber 12 in. × 12 in. × 10 ft long, having a specific gravity of 0.6, is to be used as a buoy in salt water (64.0 lb/cu ft).

How many cubic feet of concrete (145 lb/cu ft) should be fastened to one end so that just 2 ft of timber will float above the surface of the water?

14–47. A rectangular caisson is to be sunk for the foundation for a bridge pier. It is in the form of an open box 50 ft × 20 ft in plan and 25 ft deep. If it weighs 80 tons, how deep will it sink when launched? What additional load will sink it 20 ft to the bottom?

14–48. It is proposed to raise a concrete gravity dam 4 ft as shown by the dotted lines in the sketch. Maximum depth of water over the dam will be 3 ft with a resulting tail-water depth of 4 ft. The structure is founded on rock, with a coefficient of friction between the two materials of 0.45. Uplift pressure head will vary from $0.6h_1$ at the heel to h_2 at the toe. (a) Determine the location of the new resultant of forces and comment on whether or not the revised dam is safe from overturning. (Neglect the weight of water on the downstream sloping face of the dam.) Weights of concrete and water equal 150 and 62.5 lb/cu ft, respectively. (b) Determine whether the revised dam is safe from horizontal sliding. Show all calculations.

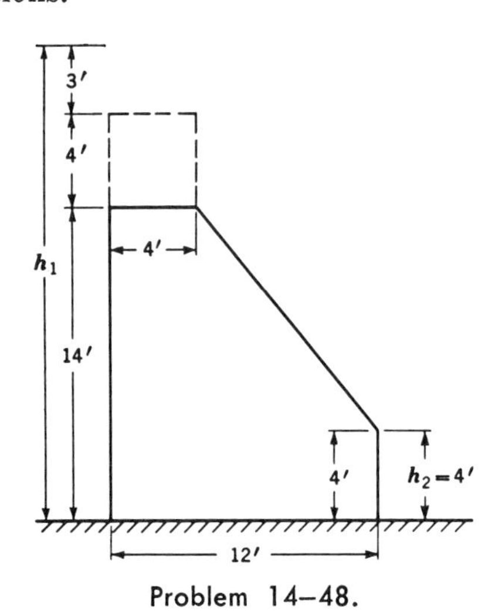

Problem 14–48.

14–49. A cubical box 4 ft on a side contains water to a depth of 3 ft and air above the water under a pressure of 2 psi. Find the total force on one side of the box.

14–50. A sluice gate, 4 ft high and 6 ft wide, is set in the vertical face of a dam. The top of the gate is 20 ft below the water surface and the coefficient of friction is 0.3. (a) What force is required to raise the gate, neglecting its weight? (b) If the gate were hinged at the top, what force at an angle of 45° applied at its base would be required to open the gate?

14–51. Points C and D, at the same elevation, are 500 ft apart in an 8-in. pipe and are connected to a differential gage by means of small tubing. When the flow of water is 6.31 cfs, the deflection of the gage is 6.43 ft. Determine the friction factor f.

14–52. Determine the power required to convey 8.0 cfs of water through 5000 ft of 12-in. diameter, welded-steel pipe, if it is discharged 100 ft above its inlet.

14–53. Three pipes, each 6440 ft long and 10-in. in diameter, meet at a common junction at elevation 100.0 ft. Each pipe leads from an open storage tank containing water. The water surface elevations in the tanks are 140.0 ft, 120.0 ft, and 80.0 ft. At what rate, in feet per hour, is the water surface changing in the tank where the surface elevation is 120.0 ft if this tank is 40 ft in diameter? Assume $f = 0.025$ for all pipes.

14–54. A conical water tank is 8 ft in diameter at the top and 6 ft deep. The tank is full of water when a 6-in. in diameter valve at the bottom is opened. How long will it take for the water level to drop 2 ft? Neglect energy losses in valve.

14–55. The required pressure at a hydrant is 100 psi at an elevation of 70 ft. A dam 20 miles away from this point has an elevation at the base of the dam of 760 ft. Assuming a pipe loss of 4 ft/1000 ft, is the elevation of the dam satisfactory to produce the required pressure for a gravity system?

14–56. (a) Given $V = 1.318Cr^{0.63}s^{0.54}$, develop the expression for the number of gallons of water flowing per minute through a filled pipe whose diameter is d inches. The values of C and s are the same as in the original formula (7.48 gal=1 cu ft). (b) A centrifugal pump discharges 300 gpm against a head of 125 ft when turning at 1100 rpm and receiving 12.0 hp. Estimate the head, discharge, and horsepower if the speed is increased to 1800 rpm.

14–57. A swimming pool is being cleaned by a rubber hose 2 in. in diameter with a brush fixture on the end through which the water is drawn by a vacuum pump. The hose is 50 ft long, leading to the pump 12 ft above the bottom of the pool. If the water in the pool is 8 ft deep, what suction, in pounds per square inch, would be required at the pump to draw 60 gpm through the hose? (Assume a loss coefficient at the brush of $0.5V^2/2g$, where V is the velocity in the hose; assume kinematic viscosity of water $= 1.2 \times 10^{-5}$ sq ft/sec.)

14–58. For the given section of a pipe network shown, determine the flow in each pipe due to the inputs and discharges shown. Assume f of each pipe is 0.02.

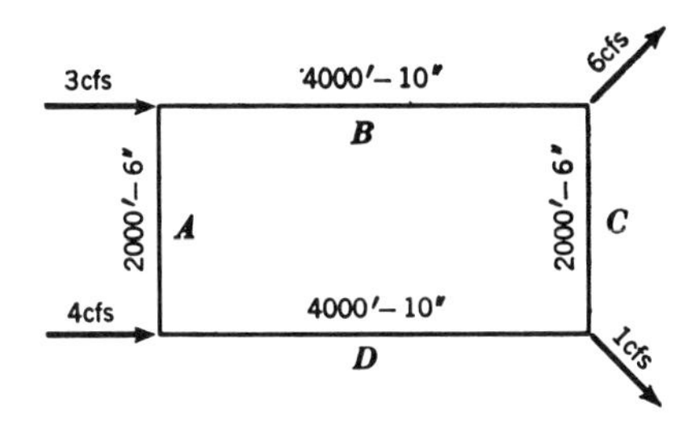

Problem 14–58.

14–59. Three pipelines 1, 2, 3, each 1000 ft long and constructed of 6-in.-, 8-in.-, and 12-in.-diameter pipe, respectively, leave reservoir A, converge, and join a 24-in. line (line 4) which is 3000 ft long and which feeds reservoir B. Lines 1, 2, and 3 have C coefficients of 120; line 4 has a C coefficient of 120. Reservoir B is 50 ft below reservoir A and the pipe junction is 10 ft below reservoir A. Using the Hazen and Williams formula, compute the division of flow in lines 1, 2 and 3. Express the division as percentages of flow in line 4.

14–60. A water supply canal is excavated in sandy earth, 120 ft wide at the bottom with side slopes of 1 vertical on 2 horizontal. If the slope of the water surface is 3 in./mile, how much water is flowing through the canal? (Depth of water $=$ 15 ft.)

14–61. The combined discharge from two 18-in.-diameter concrete storm sewer pipes, each flowing one-half full on a 1.25 per cent grade, is to be carried by a cement-lined open rectangular channel on a 1.0 per cent grade. (a) Design the rectangular channel so that it will have a depth of flow equal to one-half of its width when carrying the above discharge. (b) How much additional depth of channel will be required so that the channel will carry the combined discharge when the two pipes are flowing just full?

14–62. A vitrified-clay sanitary sewer is to carry the discharge from an area with 2500 present population to a trunk sewer for a distance of 500 ft. The sewer will be laid on a uniform slope and will drop a total distance of 0.5 ft. There is free discharge into the trunk sewer. Select a pipe with capacity, when flowing full, of not less than 400 gpcd for the total future population, assuming an anticipated increase of 50 per cent in population. (Velocity when flowing half full must equal or exceed 2.0 fps. Use n of 0.013 for Kutter's or Manning's formula.)

14–63. A canal is to be constructed in earth which is stable on a slope of 1 vertical to 2 horizontal. It is required to carry 470 cfs at a velocity of 3 fps. The canal is to be lined with a bituminous material. What gradient would be required and what are the dimensions of the cross section that would use the least amount of lining material?

14–64. A ditch of trapezoidal cross-section has a slope of 1 ft /1000 ft. The bottom width is 5 ft; the depth of water is 4 ft; side slopes are 1:1.5; and $n = 0.030$. Determine the discharge through the ditch. What size concrete storm sewer would be required to carry the same discharge, at the same slope, flowing full, with $n = 0.013$?

14–65. A concrete-lined canal excavated in rock has a rectangular cross-section 10 ft wide, and is built to a slope of 0.528 ft per mile. How deep must water flow to deliver 100 cfs if n for the canal is 0.0149?

14–66. A stream carrying 30 cfs per foot of width, with a velocity of 19.9 fps, is discharged from the toe of a dam into a channel whose bed has a negligible slope. What will be the height of the accompanying hydraulic jump, and what amount of energy will be absorbed in the jump?

14–67. A 36-in. vitrified-clay sewer is installed on a 0.5 per cent slope. Calculate the discharge in gal/min when uniform flow occurs in it at a depth of 27 in. Assume $n = 0.013$.

14–68. A centrifugal pump driven by an electric motor lifts water through a total height of 160 ft from a reservoir to discharge. The pump efficiency is 75 per cent and motor efficiency is 80 per cent. The lift is through 1000 ft of 4-in. diameter cast-iron pipe and the pumping rate is 30 gal/min. If electrical energy costs 6 mills per kilowatt-hour, what is the cost of pumping one million gallons of water? (1 cu ft of water = 7.48 gal; water at 59° F; 1 hp-hr = 0.746 kwhr.)

14–69. In testing a centrifugal pump, the inlet and outlet pressures were found to be minus 2 psi and plus 20 psi respectively. Both pipe diameters were 1.0 ft. Under these conditions, the flow of fresh water was 6.0 cfs. What was the water horsepower developed?

14–70. A centrifugal pump is used to force water through a pipeline from a ground storage reservoir to an elevated storage tank. The pipeline is 6-in. ductile cast iron with a cement lining which is enamel coated. The ID of this pipe is 6.02 in., and the length of line is 8456 ft. Water surface level in the ground storage reservoir is 846 ft MSL; in the elevated storage tank it is 896 ft. Pump characteristics are as follows:

Q (gpm)	0	100	200	300	400	500	600	700	800
Head produced by pump, ΔH in ft.	300	296	284	267	246	222	200	166	110

What will be the discharge, Q, with the conditions as specified?

14–71. In connection with a water turbine test, the discharge water goes into a flume 3 ft wide. At the end of this flume it is measured by a sharp-crested weir 3 ft high with no end contractions. If the head on the weir is 3.5 ft, what is the flow, in cubic feet per second, that is used in the test? (The water in the flume has a normal velocity distribution.)

14–72. In a circular sewer 10 ft in diameter, flowing nearly full, the water surface has a width of 5 ft. (a) Compute the hydraulic radius. (b) The sewer is laid on a grade of 1 ft/mile. The mean velocity is measured by current meter and is found to be 2.90 fps. Compute the discharge, in cubic feet per second. (c) For flow as in (b), compute the value of C in Chézy's formula. (d) For flow as in (b), compute by table and check by diagram the value of Kutter's n, interpolating as necessary. (e) For depth of flow and grade as in (b), what would be the velocity if n were 0.017? (f) Compute velocity and discharge for sewer flowing just flush full. (g) If another circular sewer of the same diameter and laid on the same grade flows nearly empty with surface width of water again 5 ft and is masonry with well-laid brickwork, compute the discharge.

14–73. Carbon tetrachloride weighing 98.7 lb/cu ft and having a viscosity of 0.000021 lb-sec/sq ft is to be pumped from one open tank to another in which the liquid is 75 ft higher. The delivery rate is 65 gpm; the pipe is 2 in. galvanized and is 290 ft long.

If the pump efficiency is 80 per cent, what horsepower is required to drive it?

14–74. A highway culvert 2 ft in diameter with a friction factor f of 0.015 discharges 50 cfs. The pipe is 100 ft long, and both ends are square-edged and submerged. Find the difference in water level on each side of the roadway.

14–75. A turbine-driven generator is fed through a 30-in.-diameter penstock 4000 ft long leading from a reservoir whose water surface elevation is 640 ft. In the penstock the velocity of flow is 8 fps, with a Hazen-Williams coefficient C of 120. The tail-race water surface elevation is 400 ft and the residual velocity head is 0.5 ft. If the efficiency of the turbine is 90 per cent and that of the generator is 96 per cent, how many kilowatts of electricity can be generated?

14–76. Each of two variable-speed centrifugal pumps to be used in a water pumping station has the characteristic curve shown when operating at a rated speed of 400 rpm. The pumps are to be arranged for series or parallel operation. Compute the following: (a) The brake horsepower input for *each* pump when the pump is operating at the point of maximum efficiency at 50 per cent of its rated speed. (b) The total discharge when both pumps are operated in parallel at rated speed and when the total head is 40 ft. (c) The total discharge when both pumps are operated in series at rated speed and when the total head is 50 ft.

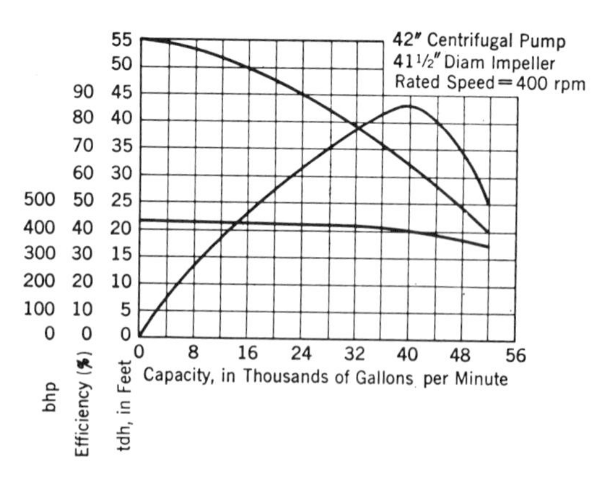

Problem 14–76.

14–77. (a) A centrifugal pump delivers 700 gpm at 1800 rpm against a tdh of 120 ft and requires 25 brake hp for its operation.

If the speed is reduced to 1450 rpm, what would be the pump's probable discharge, developed head, and required brake horsepower? (Assume the same efficiency at both speeds.) (b) If the impeller of this pump is reduced in diameter from 9 to 8 in. and the speed is maintained at 1800 rpm, what would be the resulting capacity, head, and required brake horsepower? (Assume the efficiency remains relatively constant.) (c) If this pump, as first described, was designed as a two-stage pump, what would be the specific speed?

14–78. A nozzle 2 in. in diameter is held on the end of a 4-in. pipe by means of four bolts. Neglecting head loss in the nozzle, find the tension in each bolt when the pressure in the pipe is 100 psi.

14–79. Compute the length of a sharp-edged, vertical, rectangular weir 3 ft high with two end contractions, to be installed at the end of a rectangular channel 12 ft wide and 4 ft high to pass a discharge of 10 cfs, keeping the depth of water in the canal at 3.5 ft?

14–80. A sluice gate is used to regulate the depths of flow in a horizontal open channel. The channel is rectangular, with a width of 7.0 ft. The depth a few feet upstream from the sluice gate is 4.84 ft. Depth at the vena contracta is 1.0 ft and Manning n is 0.0149. The channel terminates abruptly at a brink, and there is no tailwater. The water surface downstream from the brink is below the bottom of the channel. (a) What is the depth at the brink if the distance from the gate to the brink is 50 ft? (b) What is the depth at the brink if the distance from the gate to the brink is 200 ft? Answers to the nearest 0.1 ft are satisfactory.

SANITARY ENGINEERING

14–81. (a) Determine the required usable reservoir capacity, in acre-feet, to give dependable regulated flow of 950 cfs for the stream flow pattern given below. (b) Determine for this same record period the dependable flow that can be obtained with 430,000 acre-ft of usable reservoir capacity.

Month	Avg Flow (cfs)	Month	Avg Flow (cfs)	Month	Avg Flow (cfs)
April	2000	August	2500	December	750
May	3000	September	1500	January	700
June	4500	October	1000	February	800
July	3500	November	800	March	1100

Month	Avg Flow (cfs)	Month	Avg Flow (cfs)	Month	Avg Flow (cfs)
April	1500	September ...	1200	February	750
May	2000	October	900	March	1000
June	3000	November ...	800	April	1500
July	2500	December	700	May	2500
August	1800	January	600		

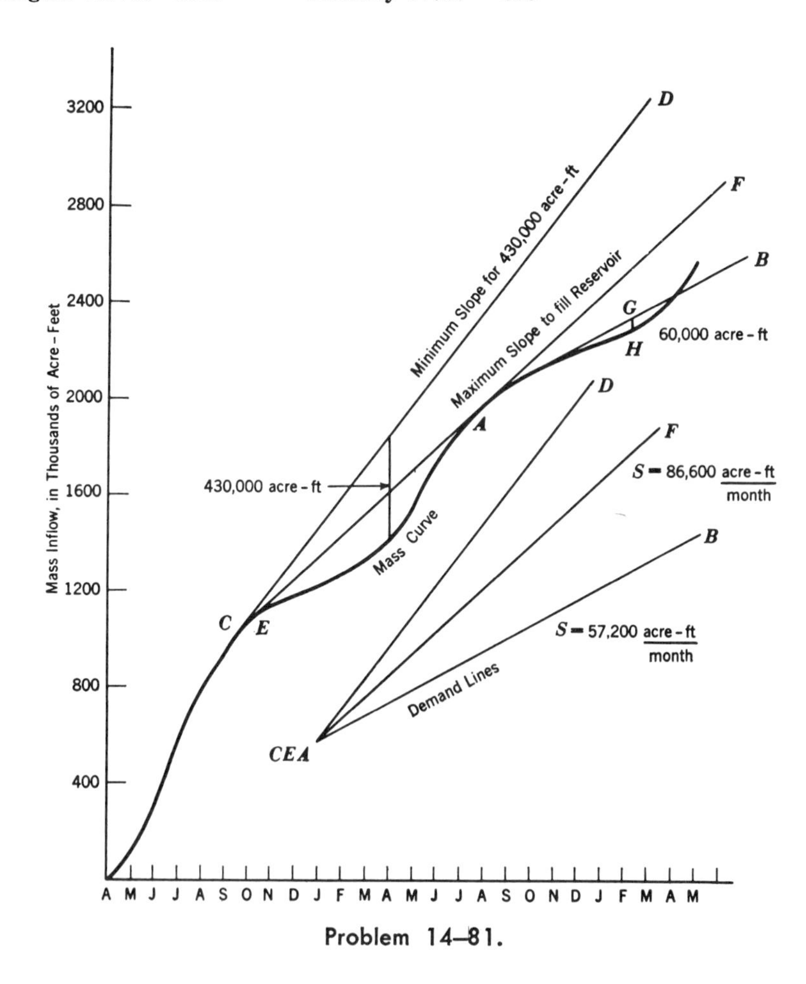

Problem 14–81.

Solution: (a) Convert cfs to acre-ft/month and accumulate stream flow. Plot mass curve as shown in the figure. From high points of the mass curve draw tangents at slope equal to demand rate (57,200 acre-ft/month). The maximum vertical distance between tangents and the mass curve is the required reservoir capacity ($GH = 60{,}000$ acre-ft). (b) Draw tangents from high points of mass curve at various slopes to obtain a vertical distance of

430,000 acre-ft between the tangents and mass curve. The slope of the flattest tangent which intersects the mass curve is the dependable demand. In this case, the flattest tangent does not intersect the mass curve. Therefore, the maximum slope of tangents drawn from the high points of the mass curve which will intersect the mass curve again is determined. This slope is the dependable demand. Slope of $EF = 86{,}600$ acre-ft/month, or 1440 cfs.

14–82. A city with an expected future population of 150,000 is to provide complete water treatment facilities consisting of rapid mix, flocculation, sedimentation, filtration, and chlorination. Determine and prepare a table showing the design criteria, design capacities, dimensions, and number of units required to give this treatment. Also state chemicals used and potential points of application. The average per capita consumption is assumed to be 150 gpcd.

Solution: Design flow $= 150{,}000(150) = 22{,}500{,}000$ gpd

Settling basins

Design criteria: 4 hr detention, overflow rate = 700 gpd/sq ft, length = 2 × width, weir overflow rate < 15,000 gpd/ft, 4 basins

$$\text{Capacity each basin} = \frac{5{,}625{,}000(4)}{24(7.5)} = 125{,}000 \text{ cu ft}$$

$$\text{Surface area} = \frac{5{,}625{,}000}{700} = 8040 \text{ sq ft}$$

$$\text{Water depth} = \frac{125{,}000}{8040} = 15.5 \text{ ft}$$

$2w^2 = 8040 \qquad w = 63.2$ ft $\qquad L = 126.4$

Dimensions each basin $= 63 \times 126 \times 15\frac{1}{2}$ ft

Length of weir per unit = 375 ft

Flocculators

Design criteria: 4 tanks, 1 hr detention

$$\text{Capacity of each} = \frac{5{,}625{,}000(1)}{24(7.5)} = 31{,}250 \text{ cu ft}$$

Width of tank = 63 ft, water depth = 15.5 ft

$$\text{Length} = \frac{31{,}250}{63(15.5)} = 32 \text{ ft}$$

Dimensions of each: $63 \times 32 \times 15\frac{1}{2}$ ft

Rapid mix

Design criteria: 1 min detention, square tank

$$\text{Capacity} = \frac{22{,}500{,}000}{24(7.5)(60)} = 2090 \text{ cu ft}$$

Assume water depth = 13 ft

$13w^2 = 2090 \qquad w = 12.7$, or 13 ft

Dimensions: $13 \times 13 \times 13$ ft

Filters

Design criteria: 8 units, filter rate = 2 gpm/sq ft, wash-water rate = 15 gpm/sq ft, backwash water applied for 5 min each day, filters out of service for 10 min once a day

Capacity: let x = square feet of filter area; then

$$x(2)(60)(23.83) - x(15)(5) = 22{,}500{,}000$$

$$x = 8080 \text{ sq ft} \qquad \text{Surface area/unit} = 1010 \text{ sq ft}$$

Distribution and waste-water channel each unit, 2 ft wide (4-in. channel walls and 6-in. unit walls)

$$(31.25 - 2.67)L = 1010 \qquad L = 35.3 \text{ ft}$$

Depth (water level to bottom) = 9 ft

Dimension of unit: $31.25 \times 35.30 \times 9$ ft

Elevated storage: capacity to wash two units for 5 min

Capacity = 15[(28.58)(35.3)](2)(5) = 151,000 gal

Ground storage: one-third daily output

$$\text{Capacity} = \frac{22{,}500{,}000}{3} = 7{,}500{,}000 \text{ gal}$$

Chlorination

Design criteria: maximum capacity of chlorinators is equal to 150 per cent of maximum dosage expected; dosage = 15 ppm

Capacity = 22.5(8.34)(15)(1.5) = 4230 lb/day, that is, three 1200-lb/24 hr chlorinators and one 600-lb/24 hr chlorinator

Chemicals	Point of Application
Alum	Before rapid mix
Ferric sulfate	Before rapid mix
Lime	Before rapid mix
Activated carbon	Before rapid mix and filters
Chlorine	Before mixer, flocculation, filters, ground storage, and distribution

Unit	Number	Design Criteria	Capacity	Dimensions (ft)
Rapid mix	1	1 min detention	2090 cu ft	13 × 13 × 13
Flocculator	4	1 hr detention	31,250 cu ft	63 × 32 × 15½
Settling basin	4	4 hr detention, 700 gpd/sq ft	125,000 cu ft	63 × 126 × 15½
Filter	8	2 gpm/sq ft	1010 sq ft	31.25 × 35.3 × 9
Elevated storage	1	2 units for 5 min	151,000 gal	......
Ground storage	..	⅓ daily capacity	7,500,000 gal	......
Chlorinators	4	150% max dosage	3–1200 lb/24 hr 1– 600 lb/24 hr	

NOTE: All depths are water depths.

14–83. A small town with a population of 3000 has an average domestic sewage of 80 gpcd. Find the required dimensions of a high-rate trickling filter to reduce the 5-day BOD by 85 per cent for the raw sewage influent if the 5-day BOD of the influent to the filter is 210 ppm.

Solution:

BOD of final settling tank effluent (35 per cent reduction in primary) $= \dfrac{210(0.15)}{0.65}$

$= 48.5$ ppm

Required efficiency of filter and final settling tank $= E$

$E = \dfrac{(210 - 48.5)(100)}{210} = 77$ per cent   Recirculation ratio $= 1$

No. of passages, $F = \dfrac{1+R}{(1.0+0.1R)^2} = \dfrac{1+1}{[1+(0.1)(1)^2]} = 1.65$

Pounds per day of BOD to filter, $w = 0.24(8.34)(210) = 420$

$E = \dfrac{100}{1+0.0085\sqrt{w/VF}}$ $77 = \dfrac{100}{1+0.0085\sqrt{420/V1.65}}$ $V = 0.207$ acre − ft, or 9000 cu ft

Assume a 6-ft depth of filter media

$V = \dfrac{\pi D^2}{4}(d)$ $9000 = 0.785(D^2)(6)$ $D = 43.6$ ft

Filter: 44 ft in diameter, 6 ft media depth

14–84. An industrial-waste treatment plant receives 500,000 gpd of raw waste having a 5-day BOD at 20°C of 500 ppm. The treatment plant provides a BOD reduction of 60 per cent. Plant effluent is discharged into a large, slow stream having, during minimum flow periods, a dissolved-oxygen content of 9.2 ppm, a temperature of 20°C, and a 5-day BOD at 20°C of 2.0 ppm. What minimum stream flow, in million gallons per day, is required to maintain a dissolved-oxygen content in the stream of not less than 4.0 ppm at any point, giving consideration to the effects of oxygen sag and reaeration?

Solution:

$t_c = \dfrac{1}{K_1(f-1)} \log \left\{ f\left[1 - (f-1)\dfrac{D_A}{L_A}\right]\right\}$ Assume $D_A = 0$, $f = 1.8$, $K_1 = 0.1$

$t_c = \dfrac{1}{0.1(1.8-1)} \log \left\{ 1.8\left[1 - (1.8-1)\dfrac{0}{L_A}\right]\right\}$ $t_c = 3.19$ days

$D_c = \dfrac{L_A}{f} 10^{-K_1 t_c}$ $D_c = 5.2$ ppm $5.2 = \dfrac{L_A}{1.8} 10^{-0.1(3.19)}$ $L_A = 19.5$ ppm

$X_5 = 0.68(19.5) = 13.25$ ppm $200\ (0.5) + 2Q = 13.25\ (Q + 0.5)$

$Q = 8.29$ mgd; but D_A, not 0.0, so Q must be greater than 8.29 mgd.

Try $Q = 8.6$ mgd $\quad 200(0.5) + 8.6(2.0) = X_5(9.1) \quad X_5 = 12.87$ ppm

$$L_A = \frac{12.87}{0.68} = 18.95 \text{ ppm} \qquad 0.5(0.0) + 8.6(9.2) = 9.1\, DO_A \qquad DO_A = 8.7 \text{ ppm}$$

$$D_A = 9.2 - 8.7 = 0.5 \text{ ppm} \qquad t_c = \frac{1}{0.1(1.8-1)} \log \left\{1.8\left[1 - (1.8-1)\frac{0.5}{18.95}\right]\right\}$$

$$t_c = 3.06 \text{ days} \qquad D_c = \frac{18.95}{1.8} 10^{-0.1(3.06)} = 5.2 \text{ ppm}$$

$DO_c = 9.2 - 5.2 = 4.0$ ppm (OK) $\qquad$ Answer: $Q = 8.6$ mgd

14–85. What average surface runoff over a period of 30 days would be required just to replenish evaporation losses from a 4.06 sq mile impoundment if the following climatological averages existed for one month: water temperature, 72°F; air temperature, 79°F; wind velocity, 6 mph; and relative humidity, 52 per cent.

14–86. A reservoir has a water surface of 1200 acres and an available storage of 4000 million gal. The watershed contributing to the reservoir covers 30 sq miles. If the runoff for the area amounts to 20 in./year and the evaporation from the water surface is 8 in., compute the yield available, in million gallons per day. (If needed, the coefficient of variation for the area is 0.24.) State clearly the method used and indicate not only the reference but also the edition.

14–87. Determine the mean and the standard deviation from the following monthly rainfall totals which were obtained from a certain watershed: January 1.2, February 2.0, March 3.2, April 5.5, May 6.4, June 5.0, July 2.2, August 1.0, September 3.0, October 2.7, November 2.0 and December 3.0.

14–88. A watershed has an area of 100 square miles. Determine the maximum rate of runoff by at least two empirical formulas and the frequency of occurrence of maximum floods from this watershed in a 100-year period if the predetermined constant c is 100.

14–89. Using any rational method, determine the expected runoff from an area of 900 acres, made of 10 per cent bituminous pavement, 10 per cent gravel and the remaining 80 per cent of impervious turf. Assume that the design intensity is 2.5 in./hr.

14–90. A drilled well is to be used as a water supply for a small municipality. The well is 8 in. in diameter and is 350 ft deep. The casing and the screen extend to the bottom of a sand and gravel water-bearing stratum. (a) Explain the purpose and a method of "developing" this well. (b) What is the purpose of the pumping test? Explain how this is done.

14–91. Assume that rapid sand filters are required to supply 10 mgd net from a river to a city: rate, 2 gal/(sq ft)/(min) of filtering area; wash water, 10 gal/(sq ft)/(min) for 15 min per day; 1 hr out for washing, rewashing, etc.

(a) Compute the total area of filtering surface required. (b) If the filter units are 24 ft × 18 ft, how many are required? (c) What amount of wash water is used, in per cent of total? (d) If total supply, including wash water, is to be chlorinated with 0.8 ppm, how many pounds of chlorine are required?

14–92. The filtration plant for a community is the rapid sand type and consists of 10 units with a nominal capacity of 20 mgd. Wash water is supplied from an elevated storage tank capable of washing two units at a time. The filtration rate is 2 gal/(sq ft)/(min); the wash water rate is 2 cu ft/(min)/(sq ft); the wash period is 6 min. Find the required capacity of the storage tank.

14–93. A rapid sand filter plant treats 10 mgd of water. The water has a hardness of 300 ppm. It is estimated that this can be reduced to 90 ppm by softening at a cost of $1.50 per million gallons for each grain per gallon of hardness removed. If the saving in soap will amount to 3 cents per person per day, what will be the net annual savings to the people of the city? The population is 110,000.

14–94. A new water treatment plant of nominal capacity of 200 mgd is being designed for the year 2000 to treat a source of supply from a river. Superchlorination of the raw water will be given. Past experience with the source of supply has shown chlorine demands require chlorine applications varying on a daily basis from 1.5 ppm to a maximum of 10 ppm with an average of 3 ppm of liquid chlorine to satisfy these demands and maintain a free chlorine residual. However, the trend in pollution of the supply is upward because of increased development on the watershed and indications are it will continue. It must be assumed that public awareness of pollution and its effect on water resources will increase and act to inhibit or hinder rapid deterioration of the stream.

What chlorine dosage in ppm would you design for and how many gas chlorinators would you provide for ultimately if such chlorinators are available in capacities for feeding liquid chlorine of 2000 lb/day, 4000 lb/day, and 6000 lb/day? The record of maximum daily chlorine dosage for the year is given as follows:

Year	1937	1942	1947	1952	1957	1962	1965
Dosage—ppm	0.5	1.0	1.5	2.5	5.0	8.0	10.0

14–95. The water at a certain treatment plant is disinfected with the addition of one pound of chlorine gas per million gallons of water. Satisfactory results are obtained with this dose. During plant alterations, disinfection is to be accomplished by adding calcium hypochlorite. How much should be added? Compute for 100 per cent pure compound with formula $Ca(OCl)_2$.

14–96. To induce chemical coagulation, Alum (aluminum sulfate) $Al_2(SO_4)_3$ is added to water. If bicarbonates are present in the water, give the important chemical equations for the resulting action. How many parts of alkalinity will be destroyed by 600 parts of alum?

14–97. A water treatment plant is treating 3 mg of water per day. If it is using 1.25 gpg of alum, compute the number of pounds of coagulant used per day. How many ppm natural alkalinity expressed as $CaCO_3$ will be required to act with the alum? If there is no natural alkalinity, compute the theoretical dosage of 85 per cent lime as CaO in pounds per day.

14–98. One million gallons of water per day pass through a sedimentation basin which is 20 ft wide, 50 ft long, and 10 ft deep. (a) Find the detention time for this basin. (b) What is the average velocity of flow through the basin? (c) If the suspended solids content of the water averages 40 ppm, what weight of dry solids will be deposited every 24 hr, assuming 75 per cent removed in the basin?

14–99. A cast-iron pipe 3 ft in diameter is subjected to an internal pressure of 100 psi. Assume a safe working stress of 11,000 psi in tension and a modulus of rupture of 31,000 psi. (a) Calculate the thickness of the shell necessary to resist the bursting pressure only. (b) If the pipe is buried in backfill which brings an equivalent three-edge bearing load of 1000 lb per foot of length upon it, what must be the thickness of the shell to withstand this load when the internal pressure is zero? (c) In determining the final thickness of the shell, would it be safe to assume that the thickness required to resist the stress caused by the external load would also care for the bursting pressure? Why?

14–100. A municipality is required to increase the capacity of the water transmission facilities from a continuous flow of 7 mgd to 10 mgd. The water surfaces of the impounding reservoir and distribution reservoir are at elevation 2000 ft and 1900 ft, respectively. It is proposed either to construct additional 24-in. pipe in parallel with the existing 10 miles of 24-in. main or to construct a booster pumping station along the line to increase the capacity to 10 mgd. Assuming 25-year bonds retired by equal annual payments combining principal and interest, determine the first year's cost for each of the two projects. Use the following data:

Project cost to construct 24-in. main...........	$20 per foot
Project cost to construct the pumping station....	$1700/ft tdh
Cost of electrical power........................	2 cents/kwhr
Annual maintenance cost of new pipeline.......	$15 per 100 ft
Annual maintenance cost of pumping station....	$2000
Wire to water efficiency of pumps..............	75 per cent

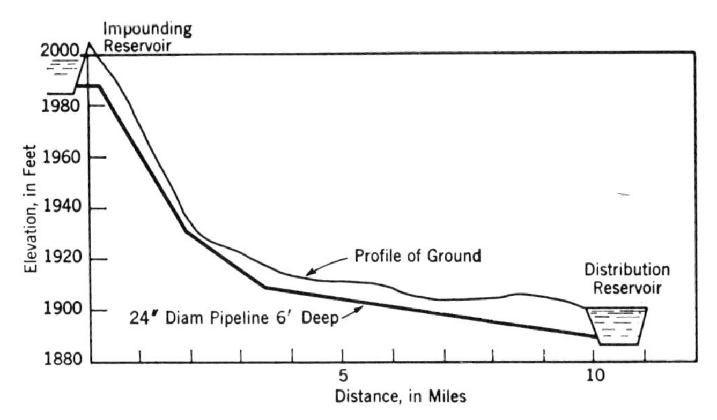

Problem 14–100.

Life of pipeline................................	100 years
Life of pumping station........................	25 years
Interest rate..................................	5 per cent
Coefficient C (Hazen-Williams)................	120
Head loss through pumping station............	5 ft

14–101. Design a radial-flow primary sewage clarifier to be used prior to standard trickling filters to handle a flow of 2.0 mgd. With a 2-hr detention period and a 10-ft side-water depth determine (a) the clarifier diameter, (b) surface loading, and (c) weir overflow rate. Is either (b) or (c) in excess of normally acceptable standards? Cite references. Neglect sludge storage capacity. If the same clarifier were used in a water treatment plant, are (b) and (c) acceptable?

14–102. By sketches and words describe the principles and recommended use of an Imhoff tank in sewage disposal.

14–103. A sewage treatment plant provides primary treatment for 25 mgd of sanitary sewage having a suspended solids content of 220 ppm, 60 per cent of which is removed in the clarifier. The solids are pumped daily to separate digesters in a sludge containing 3 per cent dry solids, 70 per cent of which are volatile. Mesophilic digestion at 90°F reduces volatile solids 60 per cent and provides gas having a heat value of 550 Btu/cu ft at the rate of 14 cu ft/lb of volatile matter destroyed. All of the gas is used as fuel in engines. Heat recovered from engine jackets and exhaust gas is 45 per cent of input and is used to heat the digesters in a system having an efficiency of 70 per cent. Compute the additional heat, in Btu per hour, required from other sources if digestion tank losses are 900,000 Btu/hr and primary sludge has a temperature of 50°F. Assume the sludge has a specific gravity of 1.00.

14–104. Design a standard-rate trickling filter installation to treat 2 mgd of domestic sewage with no recirculation. Raw sewage has a 5-day BOD of 200 ppm of which the clarifier removes 40 per cent. If the allowable BOD loading is 600 lb BOD per acre-foot per day, what will be the filter diameter if a 6.0 ft depth of filter media is used? Local conditions will not allow a diameter greater than 100 ft. If two filters are required, design both the same size.

14–105. A community with an estimated future population of 10,000 is contemplating the construction of a sewage treatment plant. It is a typical community having the usual variety of commercial and industrial establishments. What would be the reasonable number of trickling filters in this plant (a) if standard (low-rate) filters designed for a loading of 400 lb of 5-day BOD per acre-foot were to be provided and (b) if high-rate filters designed for a loading of 3000 lb of 5-day BOD per acre-foot and a recirculation ratio of 1 were to be provided?

14–106. The following excerpt from a set of specifications for a sewage treatment plant contains errors. Indicate on your answer sheet the changes you would make by line number and the change to be made.

EXAMPLE:

1 A century consists of 99 years. Each year contains
2 13 months most of which are of 28 days duration.
3 One day contains 24 hours.

ANSWER:

Line 1 Change 99 to 100.

Line 2 Change line to read 12 months, one of which is 28 days long.

Line 3 No change.

1 Bars in bar screens shall be spaced a minimum of 6
2 in. and the screening chamber shall be designed to
3 provide a velocity of not less than 8 fps.
4 Sludge storage space in digestion tanks shall be not
5 less than 2 cu ft/capita in unheated tanks.
6 Coagulants in solid form proportional to flow shall
7 be applied to the sewage. No mixing shall be permitted
8 during the detention period after the application of
9 coagulants. Detention periods of 2 to 3 hr shall be
10 provided for flocculation. Flocculation tanks shall be
11 fully watertight with no openings such as entries or
12 drains except on top. Several sources of power for
13 control of all pumps shall be provided.
14 Where sprinkling or trickling filters are used,
15 the minimum effective depth of the filtering medium
16 shall not be less than 2 ft. No maximum depth limit
17 is required. No sizes larger than ½ in. shall
18 be used in the filtering medium. Adequate protection
19 against complete flooding of filters shall be provided.
20 Primary sedimentation is to be bypassed, and sprinkling
21 filter treatment to be used immediately whenever the
22 average 5-day BOD exceeds 600 ppm.
23 Where intermittent sand filters are provided, the
24 minimum depth shall be at least 6 in. and contain
25 a minimum of 20% loam and 15% clay well mixed. All
26 underdrains shall be protected with tar paper or other
27 approved waterproofing material. Ventilators in sand
28 beds shall be spaced one per 400 sq ft of surface.
29 Detention periods in Imhoff tanks shall be not less
30 than 1 hr.

14–107. Raw sewage entering a treatment plant contains 350 ppm of suspended solids. If 55 per cent of these solids are removed in sedimentation, find the volume of raw sludge produced per million gallons of sewage. Assuming the sludge has a moisture content of 96 per cent and the specific gravity of the solids is 1.2, find the unit weight of raw sludge. If 40 per cent by weight of the suspended solids in the raw sludge is changed to liquid and gas in the digester, find the volume of digested sludge per million gallons of sewage. Assume the moisture content of the digested sludge is 90 per cent.

14–108. A standard-rate trickling filter receives settled sewage with a 5-day BOD of 95 ppm. Flow is 2.0 mgd. Average temperature is 10°C. Average daily flow is 2 mg/acre/day and loading is 400 lb/acre-ft/day. Determine the volume, area, and depth of the filter.

14–109. A proposed sewage treatment plant that is to treat the wastes from a typical small residential city having no major industrial plants has the following flow diagram: Screens, grit chambers, parshall flume, primary sedimentation, dosing siphons, standard rate trickling filters, final sedimentation, heated sludge digestion, and sludge drying beds. Making the necessary assumptions, compute the volume, and give the inside dimensions of the sludge digestion tank or tanks you would design for the plant.

Raw Sewage analysis:

Design flow	2.5 mgd	Oxygen consumed	100 mg/l
Total solids	500 mg/l	Dissolved oxygen	0
Susp. solids	260 mg/l	Nitrogen, total	50 mg/l
BOD (5 day 20°C)	225 mg/l	Fats	15 mg/l

14–110. A municipality of 100,000 people must utilize the resources of a stream for disposal of domestic sewage. At low water the discharge of the stream is 500 cfs, and the stream is 100 ft wide with an average depth of 10 ft. Time of flow from point of introduction of sewage to a large river with ample dilution is 2 days. Will plain sedimentation provide sufficient treatment if fish life is to be preserved in the stream used for disposal? The following data are provided:

(a) Average 5-day 20°C BOD—non-settleable solids in domestic sewage—23 grams/capita daily. (b) Average 5-day BOD—Dissolved solids—12 grams/capita daily. (One gram per capita = 2.2 lb/1000 population.) (c) Daily rate of BOD exerted at 20°C as per cent of first stage BOD remaining to be satisfied at beginning of day—32 per cent. (d) 5-day BOD as per cent of first stage BOD at 20°C—86 per cent. (e) Oxygen absorbed from atmosphere at 20°C through the water surface at constant oxygen deficiency of:

100 per cent oxygen saturation— 0 lb per acre/day.
90 per cent oxygen saturation— 6 lb per acre/day.
80 per cent oxygen saturation—12 lb per acre/day.

70 per cent oxygen saturation—18 lb per acre/day.
60 per cent oxygen saturation—24 lb per acre/day.
50 per cent oxygen saturation—30 lb per acre/day.

(f) Minimum dissolved oxygen required to support fish life is 4 ppm, preferably 5 ppm.

14–111. In determining the size of a concrete storm sewer, the following data are obtained: Area of watershed = 30 acres; Runoff coefficient = 0.40; Time of concentration = 50 minutes; Rainfall intensity = 4 in. in 15 min once in 5 years, 3 in. in 30 min once in 5 years, 2.5 in. in 40 min once in 5 years, 2.2 in. in 50 min once in 5 years. Increase these intensities by 25 per cent for once in 10 years, 40 per cent for once in 15 years, 50 per cent for once in 20 years, and 60 per cent for once in 30 years. What size sewer should be used if the grade is 1 per cent and the coefficient of friction, n, in the Manning formula is 0.013?

14–112. (a) Estimate the runoff in cfs for a 700-acre drainage area with an average slope of 2 per cent for an hourly rainfall of 4 in. One-half of the drainage area is wooded, and the remaining area is under cultivation. The soil is pervious. It may be assumed that the duration of the rainfall exceeds the time of concentration for the drainage area. (b) Calculate the uniform flow in an earth-lined (n=0.020) trapezoidal canal having a bottom width of 10 ft, sides sloping 1:2, laid on a slope of 0.0001 and having a depth of 6 ft. (c) If the slope of the above canal is increased to 0.001, what velocity will result?

14–113. With regard to flow in sewer pipes: (a) In a closed conduit flowing full, at what point in the cross-section is the velocity of flow at its maximum value? (b) In a circular conduit, at what depth of flow does the pipe deliver the maximum discharge? (c) In a circular conduit, at what depth of flow does the maximum velocity occur? (d) In a circular conduit, at what depth of flow is the discharge equal to the discharge when flowing full? (e) What factors determine the minimum grade of a sewer?

14–114. On the basis of Marston's theory of loads on underground conduits, (a) compute the load on a 24-in. pipe with 3-in. wall thickness in a trench 16 ft to the sewer invert. The trench has a clearance of 5 ft 6 in. between faces of 2-in. sheeting. Sheeting will be pulled as backfill is made. The excavation will be made in sand and gravel weighing 125 lb/cu ft. Select type of pipe and type of bedding to support this load, allowing a factor of safety of 1.5. (b) Compute the total load on the above pipe under similar conditions with a trench depth of 6 ft 6 in. to sewer invert and a 10,000-lb wheel load superimposed over the center of the pipe. (Assume conduit length 3.0 ft.)

14–115. The following are elevations on 6-ft offset stakes between two manholes in a 15-in. vitrified-clay sewer in a sewerage system:

Manhole 1	Sta. 0+00—525.2
	Sta. 0+50—526.5
	Sta. 1+00—526.8
	Sta. 1+50—527.5
Manhole 2	Sta. 2+00—529.5

The following are invert elevations at the manholes, manhole 1, 520.0; manhole 2, 524.0. Make a complete cut sheet showing the cut at each 50-ft station.

14–116. An existing storm-drain system was laid out to serve a territory that was suburban-residential in character. That portion of the area tributary to manhole *2* is being developed into a retail shopping center, with off-street parking. What are the recommended modifications to the storm drain system because of change in character of land use in drainage area *2*? The storm drain is located in a former ravine that has been improved as a parkway, with bridle paths, etc. Given: $r = 9/\sqrt{t}$, where r designates rainfall in inches per hour and t is the rainfall duration in minutes (20 min is minimum for design).

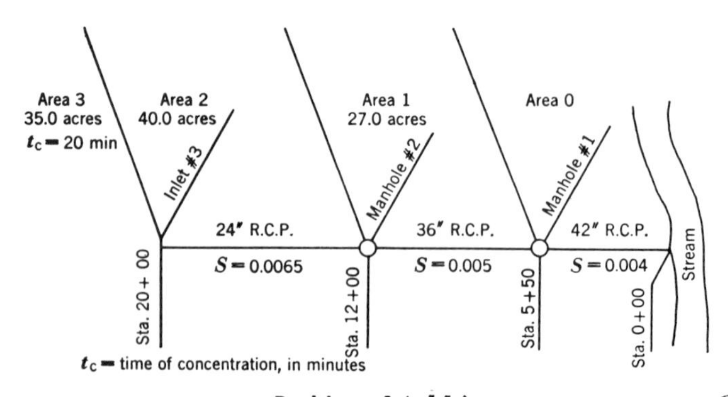

Problem 14–116.

14–117. The following refers to sewerage and sewage treatment:

A. You find that the standards being used at a plant require the number of *E coli* to be less than 100 per 100 cc, full removal of all floating solids, and at least 60 per cent removal of suspended solids. You conclude that the discharge area is intended for (a) drinking water use, (b) bathing, (c) irrigation purposes, (d) industrial use, or (e) none of the above.

B. You enter a storage area at a plant and find the floor covered with an oily brown liquid spilling out of a broken rubber-lined tank. What is the liquid and for what use was it intended?

C. What conclusions would you draw from seeing light, hollow, metal balls being dropped into a sewer at a manhole?

D. What would you decide if you saw copper sulfate being dumped into a sewer?

E. What would you infer if you saw a lighted candle being lowered into a manhole?

14–118. Determine the population equivalent of an industrial waste that has a flow of 0.7 mgd and a 5-day 20°C BOD of 1000 ppm. The normal per capita oxygen demand for the domestic sewage is 0.18 lb/day with a sewage flow of 100 gpcd.

14–119. As city engineer for a city of 20,000 population providing complete treatment of its sewage by means of an activated sludge type of plant, what local treatment would you require of (a) a meat packing plant, (b) a large dairy, and (c) a metallurgical plant discharging copper-bearing wastes, before permitting discharge of wastes from these plants into the city's sewer system?

14–120. (a) What is public health engineering and why is it so called? (b) What diseases are prevented by protecting a dairy herd and what measures are applied in such protection? (c) Discuss briefly modern methods used in the control of malaria. (d) Discuss briefly methods used in the control of murine typhus fever. (e) Give the method of transmission of bubonic plague. (f) Of the following organisms, name three that may be undesirable in a water supply and state what would result from their presence: *Diatoma, Anabaena, Protococcus, Dasmidium, Crenothrix, Synura.* (g) What are the three main classes of bacteria from the viewpoint of morphology? (h) In investigating a typhoid fever outbreak in a county of 10,000 population, what steps would you take and what type data would you collect in determining the source of the infection? (i) Name two methods of municipal sanitary garbage disposal applicable to a city or town. Compare the two methods, giving the application of each with advantages and disadvantages.

NOTE: Open refuse dumps and feeding of garbage to hogs are not to be considered. (j) What is meant by hydrogen-ion concentration? (k) A state has a population of 2,000,000. For the year 1943 the physicians of the state reported 2891 cases of tuberculosis with 1304 deaths from this disease. Compute (1) case rate, (2) death rate, and (3) fatality rate.

SOIL MECHANICS

14–121. Triaxial compression tests are run on two samples of the same soil. The results are as follows:

	σ_1	σ_3
Test 1	55.2 psi	18.6 psi
Test 2	118.0 psi	49.6 psi

Find the angle of internal friction and the cohesion.

Solution:

$\theta = 20°$

$c = 6$ psi

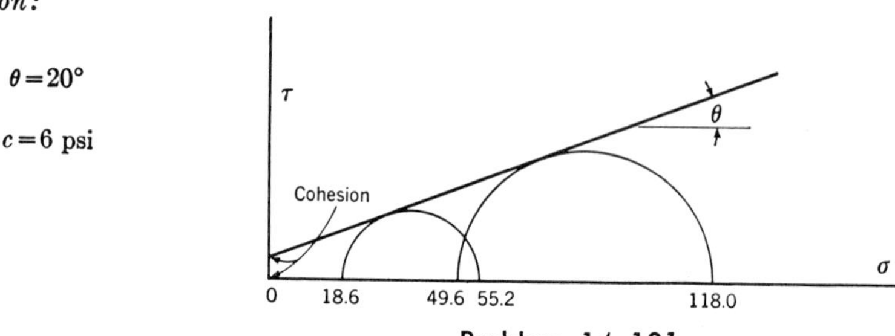

Problem 14–121.

14–122. The foundation soil at the toe of a masonry dam has a porosity of 41 per cent and a specific gravity of grains of 2.68 to assure safety against piping. The specifications state that the upward gradient must not exceed 25 per cent of the gradient at which a quick condition occurs. What is the maximum permissible upward gradient?

Solution:

$$n = 41 \text{ per cent} \qquad G = 2.68$$

$$e = \frac{n}{100-n} = \frac{41}{59} = 0.695$$

$$i_c = \frac{G-1}{1+e} = (0.25)\frac{2.68-1}{1.695} = 0.248$$

14–123. A sample of moist soil has a volume of 0.75 cu ft and weighs 96 lb. After drying, its weight is 85 lb. The soil particles have a specific gravity of 2.68. Calculate the water content on a dry-weight basis, the void ratio, and the degree of saturation.

Solution:

$$dw = \frac{96}{0.75} = 128 \text{ lb/cu ft} \qquad \text{Weight water} = 96 - 85 = 11 \text{ lb}$$

$$d_d = \frac{128}{1.1295} = 113.5 \text{ lb/cu ft} \qquad m = \frac{11}{85}(100) = 12.94 \text{ per cent}$$

$$V_s = \frac{113.5}{62.4(2.68)} = 0.679 \text{ cu ft} \qquad V_e = 1 - 0.679 = 0.321 \text{ cu ft}$$

$$e = \frac{0.321}{0.679} = 0.472 \qquad S = \frac{128 - 113.5}{62.4(0.321)} = 72.3 \text{ per cent}$$

14–124. A clay layer 12 ft thick rests beneath a deposit of submerged sand 26 ft thick. The top of the sand is located 10 ft below the surface of a lake. The saturated unit weight of the sand is 125 lb/cu ft and of the clay 117 lb/cu ft. Compute (a) the total vertical pressure, (b) the pore-water pressure, (c) the intergranular vertical pressure at mid-height of the clay layer.

Solution:

(a) $$P_T = 10(62.4) + 26(125) + 6(117) = 4576 \text{ psf}$$

(b) $$P_P = 42(62.4) = 2620 \text{ psf}$$

(c) $$\text{Effective stress} = 4576 - 2620 = 1956 \text{ psf}$$

14–125. A compressible soil layer is 30 ft thick and its initial void ratio is 1.038. Tests indicate that the final void ratio of this soil after construction of a building will be 0.981. What will be the probable total settlement of the building over a long period of time?

Solution:

$$S = 30\left(\frac{1.038 - 0.981}{2.038}\right) = 0.84 \text{ ft}$$

14–126. A retaining wall 12 ft high is to support granular earth which weighs 115 lb/cu ft. The surface of the earth slopes upward at 10° above the horizontal from the top of the wall. The angle of internal friction for the earth is 28° and the face of the wall exposed to the earth is vertical. Find the resultant earth pressure and its location on each linear foot of the wall.

Solution: Coulomb method (angle of wall friction assumed = 0°):

$$P_R = \frac{115(144)}{2}\left[\frac{\sin^2(90° - 28°)}{\sin^2 90° \sin(90° + 0°)\left(1 + \sqrt{\dfrac{\sin 28° \sin 18°}{\sin 80° \sin 90°}}\right)^2}\right]$$

$P_R = 3890$ lb acting 4.0 ft above base and parallel to backfill surface

14–127. The following questions refer to accepted practice in foundation engineering and soil mechanics. In each case, supply the best word or phrase which, in your opinion, is being defined. (a) The locus of points obtained from a standard liquid limit test and plotted on a graph representing water content as ordinates and plotted on an arithmetic scale, and the number of blows as abscissas on a logarithmic scale. (b) The ratio between a given volume change, expressed as a percentage of the dry volume, and the corresponding change in water content above the shrinkage limit, expressed as a percentage of weight of the oven-dried soil. (c) The ratio of the volume of intergranular space to the volume of solid particles in a given soil mass without regard to the proportions of liquid, air, or gas which may occupy the space. (d) The ratio, expressed as a percentage, of the weight of water in a given soil mass to the weight of solid particles. (e) The total lateral force, externally applied, which a given mass of earth is capable of resisting over a given area. (f) The ratio of the volume change to the developed pressure in a soil mass of unit volume. (g) Total pressure per unit area of soil in the pore water at a given time. (h) The slope of the pressure-void ratio diagram obtained from a consolidation test. (i) The ratio, expressed as a percentage, of the volume of water in a given soil mass to the total volume of the soil mass.

14–128. (a) How is overdriving of wooden piles evidenced? (b) What functions do piles serve? (c) What are the advantages and disadvantages of the use of precast as compared to cast-in-place concrete piles? (d) To what kinds of attack, decay, or erosion are the various types of piles subject? (e) What factor must be considered in selecting the type of pile to be used?

14–129. (a) Name and describe five properties of soils which are of particular interest to the highway engineer. (b) How can the supporting power of sand subgrades be increased? Can the supporting power of soft clay be increased by the same means? (c) Describe the condition called "pumping action" of concrete pavements. What can be done to correct this situation?

14–130. A triaxial compression test is conducted on three identical samples of soil with the following results. (Pressures given are failure stresses, in pounds per square foot.) Draw the Mohr diagram, and determine the cohesion and the angle of friction of the soil.

Specimen	Lateral Pressure (psf)	Axial Load (psf)
1	1000	4800
2	2000	7600
3	3000	9800

14–131. The accompanying figure shows the subsurface conditions under a concrete diversion dam. By use of a flow net, roughly estimate the seepage under a dam 200 ft long if the material is isotropic and has a coefficient of permeability, $k=20$ ft/day.

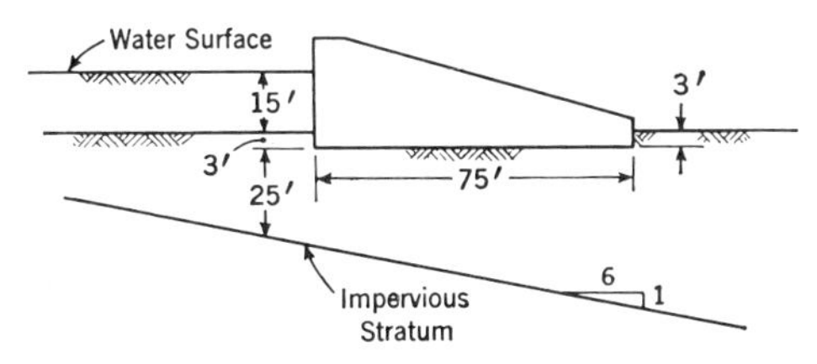

Problem 14–131.

14–132. The weight of an undried specimen of clay was 33.62 g. The oven-dry weight of the same specimen was 20.36 g. Before drying, the specimen was immersed in mercury and its volume found to be 24.36 cc. If the specific gravity of the solids is 2.7, what were the water content, the void ratio, and the degree of saturation of the material?

14–133. A dry soil has a void ratio of 0.65 and its grains have a specific gravity of 2.80. (a) Determine the unit weight, in pounds per cubic foot. Sufficient water is added to the sample to give a degree of saturation of 60 per cent. (b) Assuming no change in void ratio, determine the water content and the unit weight. (c) The sample is next placed below water. Neglecting buoyancy, calculate the unit weight by assuming the degree of saturation becomes 95 per cent. (d) Again neglecting buoyancy, calculate the unit weight by assuming the sample becomes completely saturated. (e) Determine the percentage error involved in the value obtained for the true weight if the sample actually is 95 per cent saturated but is assumed completely so.

14–134. A bulkhead is to be constructed of sheet-steel piling and tie rods as shown. Using Rankine's theory, determine the tension in the tie rod per linear foot of bulkhead. Assume there is no friction between the piling and earth. Use the following data: angle of internal friction = angle of repose = 30° for both dry and submerged earth; weight of dry earth = 100 lb/cu ft; weight of submerged earth = 65 lb/cu ft.

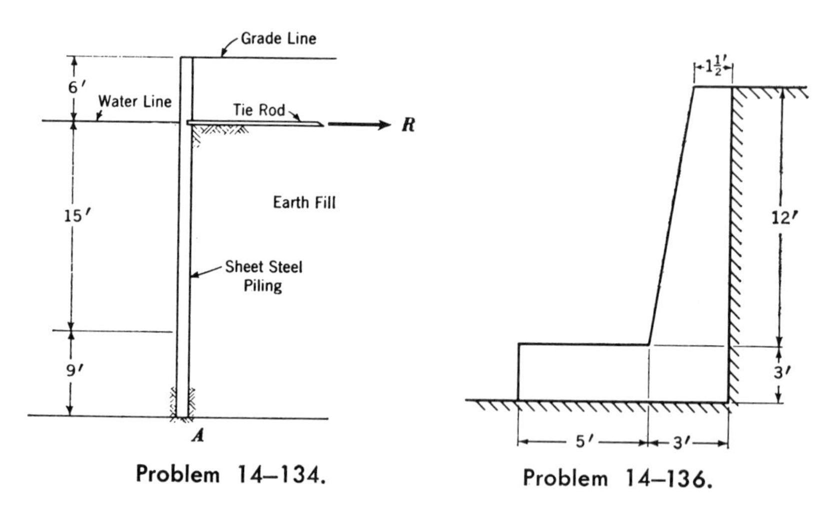

Problem 14–134.

Problem 14–136.

14–135. A sheet-piling wall is to be driven into sand to support an embankment of the same material. The sand has a unit weight of 100 lb/cu ft and an internal friction angle of 30°. The height of the embankment is 20 ft. The sheet piling is supported at a point 5 ft from the top by a wale beam and anchor rods spaced at 5-ft intervals. What is the minimum penetration of the sheet piling into the same to maintain stability?

14–136. An L-shaped retaining wall supports a cohesionless backfill weighing 130 lb/cu ft and having an internal friction angle of 35°. Find the active earth pressure on the wall, assuming no backwall friction, and the pressure on the toe and the heel of the footing.

14–137. A retaining wall 15 ft high forms the rear wall (ground floor) for a manufacturing plant two stories high. On the front of the building the ground floor is at grade, but on the rear a deep cut was necessary. The second floor wall and floor will rest on the top of the retaining wall. The wall will be backfilled with sand weighing 120 lb/cu ft dry and 132 lb/cu ft saturated. The maximum anticipated ground-water level will be 10 ft above the bottom of the wall. The angle of internal friction of the sand is 33°.

(a) Compute the total pressure the retaining wall will have to support if its face is vertical. (List the method used and reference.) (b) How could the pressure be reduced? (c) What provisions are necessary regarding the time the backfill is placed, compared to the time the second-story wall and floor are constructed, to avoid damage to the floor and wall?

14–138. The concrete in this dam weighs 150 lb/cu ft. Compute the foundation pressure, in tons per square feet, at the heel and toe, assuming a straight-line variation and neglecting hydrostatic uplift.

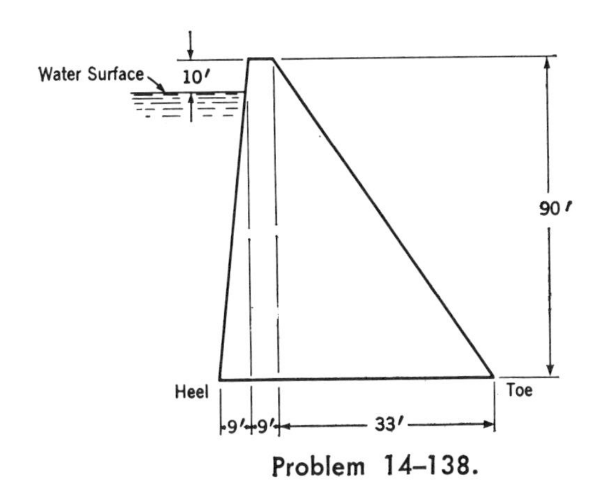

Problem 14–138.

14–139. A concrete dam is 12 ft high, 4 ft thick at the base, and 2 ft thick at the top, with the upstream face vertical. Is it stable against overturning when full?

14–140. Test borings at a building site disclose the soil profile in the tabulation. The structure will be 100 ft wide by 400 ft long

Depth (ft)	Soil Description	Penetration Resistance (blows/ft)
0–8	Loose fine sand	5–6
8–12	Soft black clay	2–3
12–18	Stiff silty clay (sandy)	18–20
18–25	Firm gray highly plastic clay	6–8
25–35	Dense brown clayey sand	20–25
35–	Refusal, apparently rock (boring stopped)	

NOTE: 8-ft water table.

and made of reinforced concrete; column loads of 350^k are spaced 25 ft on centers. (a) Is the boring deep enough? If not, how deep should it go? (b) What additional soil data, if any, are necessary in order to prepare a rational foundation design or to make an intelligent choice between foundation types which might be used? (Be specific, stratum by stratum.) (c) On the basis of the data available, what types of foundation could be employed? Give their possible advantages and disadvantages for this structure and site.

14–141. A multistory building is being designed with a reinforced-concrete frame. Because of the low soil bearing value, metal-cased concrete piles will be used for the foundations. The ground floor will be supported by the columns, leaving a clear space of 3 ft between the bottom of the floor beam and the ground surface. The concrete piles have a maximum bearing value of 60^k each and a minimum diameter of 15 in. at point of cutoff; they will be spaced a minimum of 3 ft center to center. Use uniform building code stresses for concrete having an ultimate strength of 3000 psi at 28 days and deformed reinforcing bars of intermediate-grade steel. Design the pile foundation for a typical interior column which is 16 in. square at the base with a total design load (LL and DL) of 270^k, including all reductions allowed, as follows: (a) Show number and arrangement of piles with dimension. (b) Design and detail the pile cap. (c) Design foundation ties, assuming adjacent footings are not loaded to exceed 270^k.

14–142. A mat-type foundation for a large structure is to rest upon coarse sand that is overlain by 3 ft of volcanic clay and then 12 ft of medium sand. The water table for the entire area is 3 ft below the ground surface. You are approached by the contractor, who wishes to know if he may excavate the area with a cat and scraper unit and control the ground water with shallow sumps as the depth of excavation increases. Make a full analysis of the contractor's request and state if it should or should not be approved, with supporting reasons. If the proposed procedure is not acceptable, give at least two alternate procedures that would be acceptable.

14–143. A raft 60 ft $\times$ 40 ft in plan rests on a clay that has an unconfined compressive strength of 1.2 tons/sq ft. The factor of safety against a bearing-capacity failure must be 3. What total weight of building and foundation can safely be supported by the raft?

14–144. What measures may be taken to prevent or minimize frost heave in a highway subgrade?

14–145. A test sample of soil had a natural weight of 1010 g and a weight when dried of 918 g. Its volume was 558 cc. Find (a) the natural water content and density of the soil and (b) the void ratio and degree of saturation if the specific gravity of the soil solids is 2.67.

14–146. From the following information, classify each of the soils by either the AASHO Unified Soil Classification or any other system.

Sample No.	Sieve Analysis Per Cent Passing			L.L.	P.I.
	−10	−40	−200		
1	100	100	98	33	11
2	37	20	9	15	NP
3	93	81	44	44	17
4	100	100	90	69	37
5	75	37	28	42	7

14–147. A trench with vertical walls is to be made in clay with the following characteristics: Material density = 110 lb/cu ft, Angle of Internal Friction = 9°, Unit cohesion = 300 lb/sq ft. Determine the maximum depth of such a trench, using a safety factor of slightly over 1.

14–148. A stratum of clay 30 ft deep lies with its upper surface 25 ft below ground surface. Ground water level is 8 ft below ground surface. The material above and below the clay layer is uniform sand. Laboratory analysis shows:

Sand—above water table—wet unit weight = 118 pcf
Sand—below water table—wet unit weight = 130 pcf
Clay—Wet unit weight = 114 pcf
Clay—Water content = 38 per cent
Clay—Specific gravity of particles = 2.65
Clay—Void ratio at pressure of 4000 psf = 0.961
Clay—void ratio at pressure of 3500 psf = 0.977

A structure 60 ft square in plan is to be placed with the bottom of its footings 5 ft below ground surface. The weight of the structure is 2100 psf. Estimate the settlement due to consolidation of the clay layer.

14–149. The following information was obtained in the laboratory using the Standard Proctor Compaction Method. Determine the optimum moisture and maximum density for this soil. Weight of Mold = 2075 grams, Volume of Mold = 1/30 cu ft.

Trial No.	1	2	3	4	5	6	7
Weight of Compacted Soil plus mold (gr.)	3741	3800	3868	3982	4004	3968	3936
Moisture Content— Per cent	5.6	7.0	8.9	11.0	13.9	16.0	17.9

Draw the moisture-density curve and determine optimum moisture and maximum density for this soil.

14–150. A main rural route carrying wheel loads of 15,000 lb has a section of construction over a sandy clay subgrade with a CBR value of 8. The tire pressure is 60 psi. Determine the required thickness of base course and pavement by the CBR method. Estimate the actual subgrade pressure if an 8-in. thickness of base course and pavement is used.

14–151. A 14-in. square concrete pile 30 ft long is driven to full penetration by a Vulcan single-acting steam hammer. The average penetration per blow for the last 10 blows was ¼ in. The weight of the free-falling hammer mass is 5000 lb falling through a distance of 3 ft. (a) Compute the safe load which may be applied to this pile by an empirical or semi-empirical formula of your choice and designate reference used. (b) If the coefficient of restitution between the hammer and the pile is 0.4, determine by the fundamental principles of dynamics, a safety factor encompassed in the empirical formula used in part (a).

14–152. A building is to be founded on a very thick stratum of clay. The results of a plate bearing test, using a 12-in. × 12-in. square plate, showed the coefficient of subgrade reaction to be 8 TSF/in. and the ultimate bearing capacity to be 4 TSF. The building will contain two column loads of 20,000 and 40,000 lb. Select the size of square spread footing that should be used for each column if no differential settlement is to exist.

14–153. A soil sample weighing 58 lb was taken from an embankment. The volume of the sample, as determined by filling the mold with dry sand, was 0.5 cu ft. After oven drying, the sample weighs 50 lb. Assuming a specific gravity of the soil particles of 2.65, what was the original moisture content and void ratio of this soil?

14–154. A pile foundation is used to support a bridge pier. The foundation consists of 4 rows of piles with 10 piles in each row spaced 3 ft, center-to-center, in both directions. The loading consists of a vertical load of 400 tons uniformly distributed along the long centerline of the pile cap, and a moment of 450 ft-tons acting about the long centerline of the pile cap. The maximum load that any one pile can support is 20 tons. Investigate the foundation to determine if any of the piles is overstressed.

14–155. A two-story shopping center building 200 ft × 400 ft is to be built on a site consisting of two small knobby hills separated by a small creek. The difference in elevation between the tops of the hills and the creek is 40 ft. It is proposed to cut 20 ft from the hill tops and fill the creek valley to provide a level site for the building and its adjacent parking lots and walkways. The building would be supported on shallow spread footings. 1. From the point of view of soils and foundations, what are the primary considerations in the feasibility of this proposal? (a) List the considerations of factors to be adjudged. (b) What effect could each have on the success or failure of this proposal? (c) How would each be investigated? 2. Assuming that each of the factors listed in (1a) can be evaluated, outline a specification that would insure the necessary construction precautions and/or steps for a satisfactory foundation for the building and its parking lots.

14–156. An excavation 30 ft deep is to be made 5 ft from the outer edge of the continuous wall footings of an old store building. The soil is a medium density sand with a unit weight of 120 pcf and an angle of internal friction of 36°. The footing is 4 ft wide with its base 3 ft below the ground surface (27 ft above the excavation bottom) and supports a load of 8000 plf. The excavation must be made while the building is occupied and the contractor is responsible for any damage to the building. The contractor elects to drive a line of steel sheet piling 5 ft from the wall footing and excavate in front of the sheeting, leaving the building untouched behind the sheeting.

(a) Compute the earth pressure diagram that must be used for the design of the sheet piling bracing system. Give references used. (b) Sketch a plan and cross section of a bracing system for such a project. (c) Show briefly the sequence of the principal steps in the installation. (d) What alternative procedure to this bracing might be considered to protect the building?

14–157. Assume that you have been given the responsibility of designing a 2-story industrial building 36 ft × 196 ft in plan in an area where the subsoil conditions are unknown to you. (a) Describe briefly the type and indicate the approximate number and depth of any exploratory subsoil explorations which you deem desirable in this situation. (b) Itemize the information that should be obtained as a result of this subsoil exploration.

14–158. List several alternate methods for performing field density tests on fill material being placed in a highway embankment. To what type of soil is each method best suited? What are the shortcomings of each method?

14–159. Discuss the basic principles, advantages, and limitations of the following methods for determining the bearing capacity of a pile: (a) Load test, (b) dynamic formula, (c) static analysis.

14–160. A foundation consisting of a cluster of piles fails even though a load test on one of the piles of the group indicated adequate safe capacity. Discuss why this could occur.

STRUCTURAL

14–161. How many ⅞-in. rivets are needed for the joint shown based upon their shearing strength? How many if bearing governs?

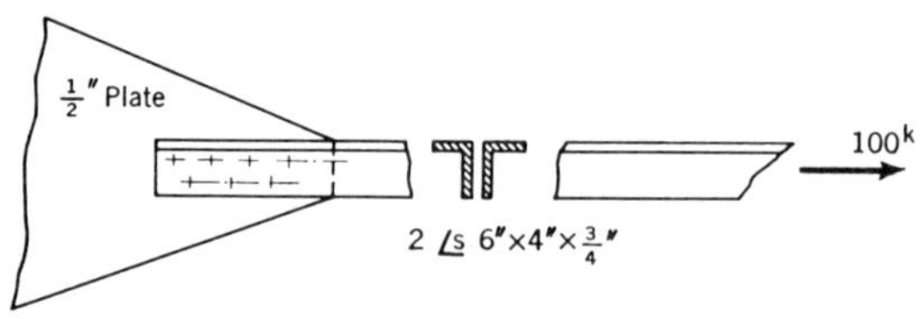

Problem 14–161.

Solution:

AISC specifications: ⅞-in. rivet, ½-in. plate Load/rivet = 18.04ᵏ (shear)

$$N_S = \frac{100}{18.04} = 5.5 \qquad 6 \text{ required}$$

Load/rivet = 17.5ᵏ (bearing)

$$N_B = \frac{100}{17.5} = 5.7 \qquad 6 \text{ required}$$

14–162. Find the length of a ½-in. fillet weld at the top and bottom to develop the tensile strength of the member shown without any eccentricity.

Solution:

$$P_{\text{angle}}=4.75(20{,}000)=95{,}000 \text{ lb} \qquad s_{1/2\text{ weld}}=4800 \text{ lb/in.}$$

$$a=\frac{Px}{sc}=\frac{95{,}000(1.99)}{4800(6)}=6.58 \text{ in. (+returns)}$$

$$b=\frac{P(c-x)}{sc}=\frac{95{,}000(4.01)}{4800(6)}=13.22 \text{ in. (+returns)}$$

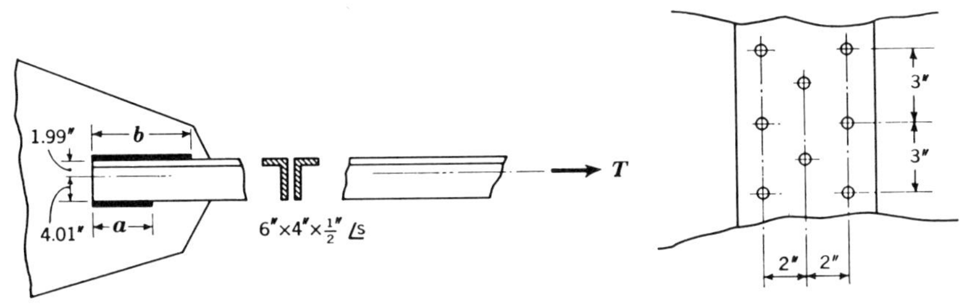

Problem 14–162. Problem 14–163.

14–163. A pressure tank has a shell ¼ in. thick and is spliced by a lap joint with three rows of ½-in.-diameter rivets as shown. If the tank is 12 ft in diameter, what is the maximum pressure, in pounds per square inch? Allowable unit stresses are as follows: tension, 20,000 psi; shear, 15,000 psi; and bearing, 32,000 psi.

Solution: Holes are ⅝-in.-diameter for tension in 12-in. section.

$$P_T=20{,}000[12-4(0.625)]0.25=47{,}600 \text{ lb}$$

$$P_B=32{,}000[12(0.5)(0.25)]=48{,}000 \text{ lb}$$

$$P_S=15{,}000(12)(0.196)=35{,}200 \text{ lb (controls)}$$

$$\text{Pressure}=\frac{2(35{,}200)}{144(12)}=40.6 \text{ psi}$$

14–164. A 14WF61 column is 20 ft long with no lateral supports for the strong axis but laterally supported at the mid-point for the weak axis. Calculate the safe axial load using AISC specifications.

Solution: $\frac{l}{r}<120$

$$\text{Strong } f=17{,}000-0.485\,\frac{(240)^2}{(5.98)^2}=16{,}225 \text{ psi} \qquad P=\frac{15{,}838(17.94)}{1000}=284^{k}$$

$$\text{Weak } f=17{,}000-0.485\,\frac{(120)^2}{(2.45)^2}=15{,}838 \text{ psi}$$

14–165. Design a square reinforced-concrete tied column 20 ft long to carry a concentric load of 900^{k} using 3750-psi concrete and 16,000-psi steel.

Solution: ACI plastic method and 4 per cent steel assumed.

$$A_g = \frac{900{,}000}{0.8[0.225(3750)+16{,}000(0.04)]} = 760 \text{ sq in.} \qquad b = \sqrt{760} = 27.5 \text{ in.}$$

Use 28 in. × 28 in. column with $A_g = 784$ sq in.

$$A_s = 0.04(784) = 31.4 \text{ sq in.} \qquad 20 \ \#11 \text{ bars furnish } 31.2 \text{ sq in.}$$

$$\text{Ties} = 0.02(4)(1.56) = 0.49 \text{ sq in.} \qquad \text{Use } \#6 \text{ ties at 16 bar diameter} = 22 \text{ in.}$$

14–166. A camel-back truss has four 25-ft panels on a span of 100 ft. The vertical member at mid-span is 30 ft high. The vertical members at the quarter-points are 20 ft high. The truss carries three 40^k vertical loads, one at each lower panel point. Cut a vertical section through the panel left of midspan and calculate the stresses in this panel.

Solution:

$$\Sigma M_O = 0 \qquad 25(60) - 50(40) - 46.8(U_1L_2) = 0 \qquad U_1L_2 = -10.7^k$$

$$\Sigma M_{U_1} = 0 \qquad 25(60) - 20L_1L_2 = 0 \qquad L_1L_2 = 75^k$$

$$\Sigma M_{L_2} = 0 \qquad 27.8(U_1U_2) + 25(40) - 60(50) = 0 \qquad U_1U_2 = 71.9^k$$

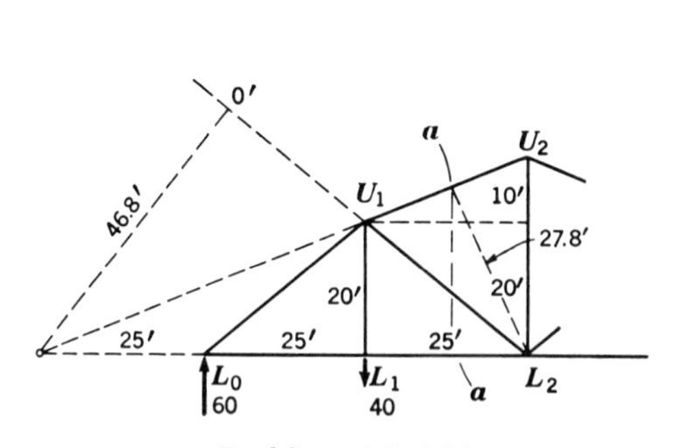

Problem 14–166.

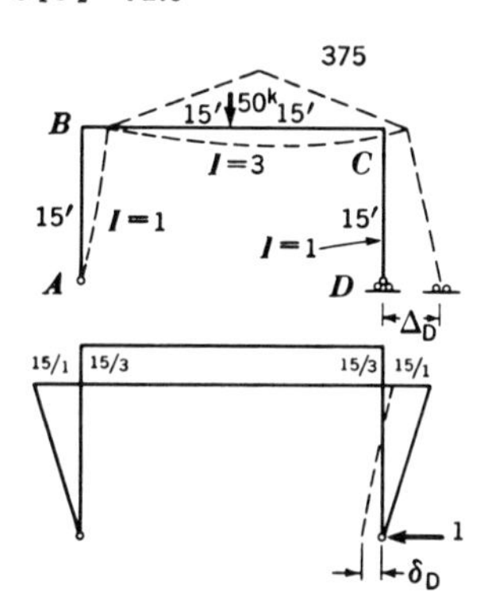

Problem 14–167.

14–167. A single-span symmetrical rigid frame has a beam span of 30 ft and a column height of 15 ft. The columns are hinged at the base and have moments of inertia equal to one-third that of the beam. Calculate the horizontal reactions due to a vertical load of 50^k applied at the mid-point of the beam.

Solution:

$$M = \frac{30(50)}{4} = 375'^k \qquad E\theta_B + E\theta_C = \frac{375(30)}{3(2)} = 1875$$

$$E\Delta_D = 1875(15) = 28{,}200 \qquad E\delta_D = 2\left[\frac{15}{1}\left(\frac{15}{2}\right)(10)\right] + \frac{15}{3}(30)(15) = 4500$$

$$D_H = A_H = \frac{28{,}200}{4500} = 6.25^k$$

14–168. A truss carries a dead load of 1200 lb/ft and a moving live load as shown. Determine the maximum combined stress in members A, B, and C. Loads are applied to the bottom chord.

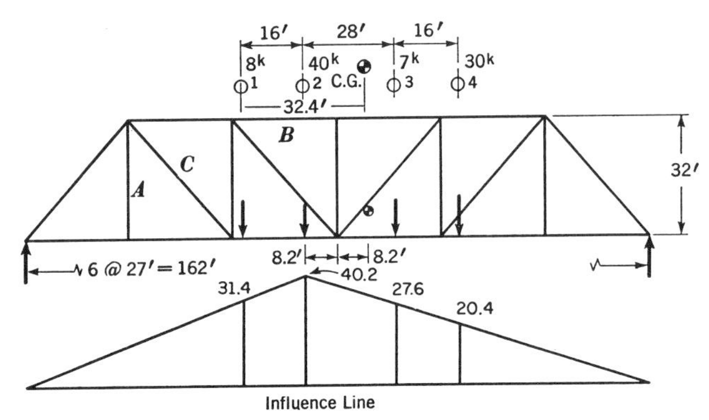

Problem 14–168.

Solution: Panel DL = 32.4^k; by index stresses, $A = 32.4^k$, $B = -123^k$, $C = 63.7^k$; by criteria method, wheels in position shown for M_{max} at 40^k wheel.
From influence line,

$$M_{max} = 8(31.4) + 40(40.2) + 27.6(7) + 30(20.4) = 2666'^k$$

$$\sigma_B = \frac{2666}{32} = 83.2^k \qquad \text{LL stress, partial answer}$$

with 40^k load at center,

$$\sigma_B = 81.8^k \qquad \text{LL stress}$$

14–169. The continuous beam shown is 50 ft long, and it is supported at the ends and at a point 30 ft from one end. It is to be designed to carry a uniformly distributed load of 3000 lb/ft over its entire length. Use AISC specifications and assume lateral support at the reactions. Select the lightest WF section that could be used.

Solution: Removing M_B

$$M_L = \frac{3000(900)}{8} = 338{,}000 \qquad M_R = \frac{3000(400)}{8} = 150{,}000$$

$$\theta_{AB} = 338{,}000(15)(2/3) = 3{,}380{,}000 \qquad \theta_{BC} = 150{,}000(10)(2/3) = 1{,}000{,}000$$

$$\theta_B = 4{,}380{,}000 \qquad d\theta_B = \frac{30(1)}{2}(2/3) + \frac{20(1)}{2}(2/3) = 16.67$$

$$M_B=\frac{4.38\times10^6}{10^3(16.67)}=262'^{k} \qquad R_A=36.3^k \qquad R_B=96.8^k \qquad R_C=16.9^k$$

$M_{max}=+219'^{k}$ 12.08 ft to right of R_A

$M_{max}=-262'^{k}$ at R_B

$$\frac{I}{C}\text{ required}=\frac{262{,}000(12)}{20{,}000} \qquad \text{Check stress with } \frac{12\times10^6}{ld/bt}$$

(Figure shows solution by Hardy-Cross)

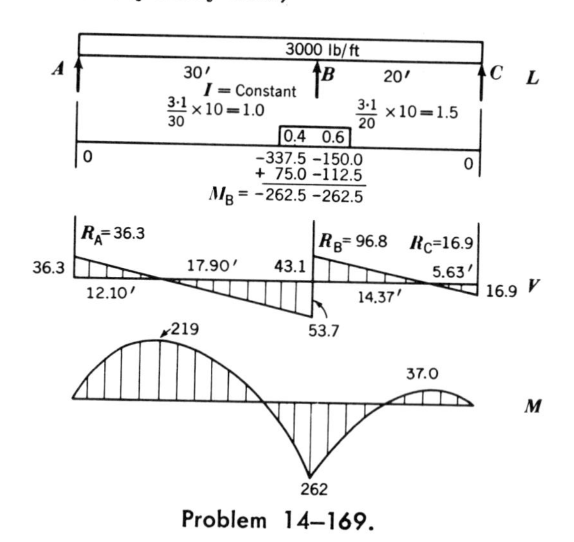

Problem 14–169.

14–170. Calculate the moments of inertia and radii of gyration about both axes of a 10WF49 with 1 in. × 10 in. cover plates riveted to each flange.

Solution:

$$I_{yy}=93\text{ in.}^4 \qquad I_{xx}=272.9\text{ in.}^4 \qquad A=14.4\text{ sq in.} \qquad d=10\text{ in.}$$

$$I_{xx}=272.9+2\left[\frac{10(1)^3}{12}+10(5.5)^2\right]=878.56\text{ in.}^4$$

$$I_{yy}=93+\frac{2(1)(10)^3}{12}=259.7\text{ in.}^4$$

$$r_{xx}=\sqrt{\frac{878.56}{34.4}}=5.05\text{ in.} \qquad r_{yy}=\sqrt{\frac{259.7}{34.4}}=2.74\text{ in.}$$

14–171. Calculate the absolute maximum moment on a 30-ft simple beam loaded with a uniform dead load of 2 klf and a moving load system consisting of a 10^k load followed by a 20^k load located 8 ft behind it.

Solution: $$M \text{ of uniform load} = \frac{2000(900)}{8} = 225{,}000 \text{ ft-lb}$$

M of moving load with 20^k load at center and influence line $= M_{ML}$

$$M_{ML} = 20(15/2) + 10(7/2) = 185'^k \qquad M_T = 410'^k$$

14–172. Given an 8 in. × 18 in. wooden beam on a 10 ft simple span, find the safe concentrated load that can be placed at the center of the beam if the maximum allowable bending stress is 1400 psi and the maximum horizontal shearing stress is 90 psi. Neglect the weight of the beam and use full dimensions.

Solution: $$M_{max} = \frac{P(10)(12)}{4} = 30P \qquad I = \frac{8(18)^3}{12} = 3890 \text{ in.}^4$$

Bending $$\sigma = \frac{Mc}{I} \qquad 1400 = \frac{30P(9)}{3890} \qquad P = 20{,}200 \text{ lb}$$

Shear $$90 = \frac{0.5P(72)(4.5)}{3890(8)} \qquad P = 17{,}300 \text{ lb (controls)}$$

14–173. A glued laminated timber I beam is made up of two 1 in. × 6 in. flanges with a 1 in. × 4 in. web. It is used on a simple span of 8 ft to support a uniformly distributed load of 300 lb/ft. (a) Calculate the maximum bending stress produced. (b) What is the maximum shear stress on the glued surface?

Solution: Without beam weight, $M = 300(8)^2/8 = 2400$ ft-lb.

(a) $$I = \frac{1(4)^3}{12} + 2\left[\frac{6(1)^3}{12} + 6(2.5)^2\right] = 81.33 \text{ in.}^4 \qquad \sigma = \frac{28{,}800(3)}{81.3} = 1062 \text{ psi}$$

(b) $V = 1200$ lb, $A = 6$ sq in.

$$v = \frac{VAy}{It}$$

$$v = \frac{1200(6)(2.5)}{81.33(1)} = 222 \text{ psi}$$

14–174. A simple beam AB is 20 ft long. It carries a uniformly distributed load of 2 klf and a concentrated load of 20^k at the center. (a) Find the slope at A, in radians. (b) Find the center deflection, in inches, if $E = 10{,}000$ ksi, $I = 1440$ in.^{4}

Solution:

$$M_C = \frac{20(20)}{4} + \frac{2(400)}{8} = 200'^k$$

$$EI\theta_A = \frac{100(10)}{2} + 100(10)(2/3) = 1167$$

$$EI\Delta_C = 500(10) + 667(10) - 500(10/3) - 667(10)(3/8) = 7503$$

$$\theta_A = \frac{1167(10^3)(12^2)}{(10 \times 10^6)(1440)} = 0.01167 \text{ radian} \qquad \Delta_C = \frac{7.503(10^6)(12^3)}{(10 \times 10^6)(1440)} = 0.9 \text{ in.}$$

14–175. A cantilever beam 12 ft long is to support a uniform load of 2500 lb/ft. (a) Draw and dimension shear and moment diagrams. (b) Select the best steel I or WF beam. The allowable flexural stress is 19,000 psi. (See diagram on opposite page.)

Solution:

$$M=\frac{2500(144)}{2}=180{,}000 \text{ ft-lb}$$

$$\frac{I}{c}=\frac{180{,}000(12)}{19{,}000}=113.8 \text{ in.}^3$$

Try 21WF 62 $\quad M_{\text{beam}}=\dfrac{62(144)}{2}=4460 \qquad M_T=184{,}460 \text{ ft-lb}$

$$\frac{I}{c}\text{ required}=\frac{184{,}460(12)}{19{,}000}=116.4<126.4$$

Lightest I beam = 20 I 65.4

14–176. A rectangular beam of reinforced concrete is simply supported and has $b=15$ in. and $d=22$ in. A uniformly distributed load of 2850 lb/ft including the beam weight is carried on a simple span. Find the required area of tensile steel. The span is 20 ft, $f_s=20{,}000$ psi, $j=0.866$, $k=0.433$.

Solution:

$$M=\frac{2850(400)}{8}=142{,}500 \text{ ft-lb}$$

$$p=\frac{M}{f_s jbd^2}=\frac{142{,}500(12)}{20{,}000(0.866)(15)(484)}=1.36 \text{ per cent}$$

$$A_s=pbd=0.0136(15)(22)=4.47 \text{ sq in.}$$

14–177. A pair of 6 in. × 3½ in. × ⅜ in. angles are used to make up the web member of a truss which will have a ½-in. gusset plate. The member is subject to fluctuating loads which vary from 90^k in compression to 60^k in tension. Using AISC specifications, design the end connections by (a) using fillet welds, (b) using rivets, (c) using high-tensile-strength bolts.

14–178. A member is composed of one 8 in. × 4 in. × ⅞ in. angle to be welded to a ⅞-in. gusset plate. The member is to carry a tensile load of 180^k. Design the length of welds. Use ⅝-in. fillet welds at 6^k per inch continuous around the end of the angle. The 8-in. leg is welded to the gusset plate. The distance from the back of the outstanding leg to the neutral axis of the 8-in. leg is 3 in.

14–179. Design a heavy riveted bracket connection to both flanges of a 14WF287 column to resist a crane girder reaction of 100^k. The girder reaction has an eccentricity of 22 in. from the axis through the web of the column. Use AISC specifications.

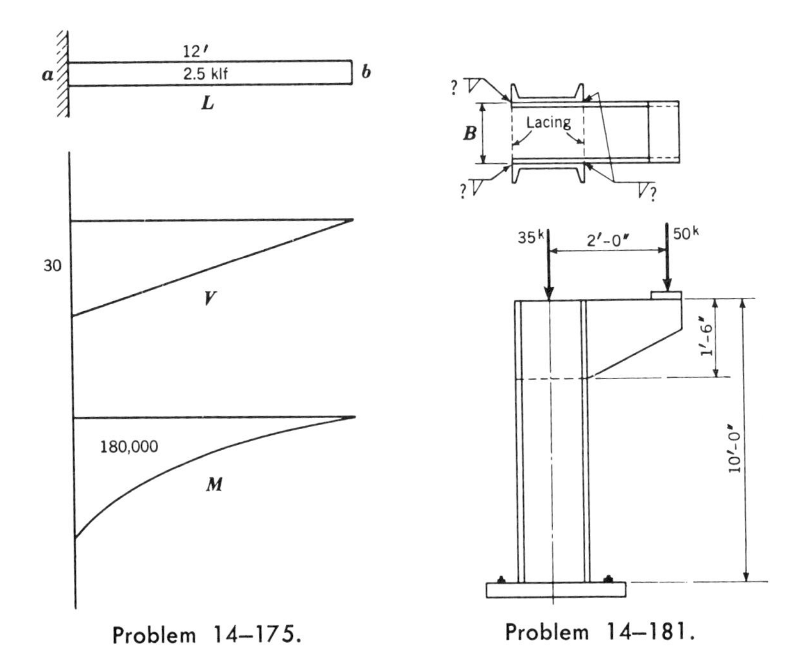

Problem 14–175.

Problem 14–181.

14–180. A concrete column is 12 ft long and composed of 3750-lb concrete with hard-grade steel reinforcing as follows: The main reinforcing is eight #11 bars tied with ¼-in. ties. The column size is 20 in. × 20 in. Find the allowable axial load on this column.

14–181. Using AISC specifications, select channels and find the distance B and the weld size for the structure shown. The top of the column is not supported in the horizontal plane.

14–182. A circular reinforced-concrete column has spiral reinforcement. Find the safe axial load. The diameter of the column is 16 in. Area of the steel is 10.0 sq in., $f_s=16{,}000$ psi, $f'_c=3750$ psi. Column formula: $P=A_g(0.225f'_c+f_sp_g)$.

14–183. Design a 12WF steel column 24 ft long to carry an axial load of 200^k and a bending moment about the major axis of $1000''^k$. Use AISC specifications.

14–184. A reinforced-concrete square-tied column with a length of 24 ft between lateral supports carries a vertical load of 245^k with an eccentricity of 1.25 in. about the x–x axis and a 2.25-in. eccentricity about the y–y axis. The vertical reinforcing consists of twelve #9 bars. Specifications: 18,000-3000-10. Determine whether the column is adequate for the given loading conditions and allowable stresses.

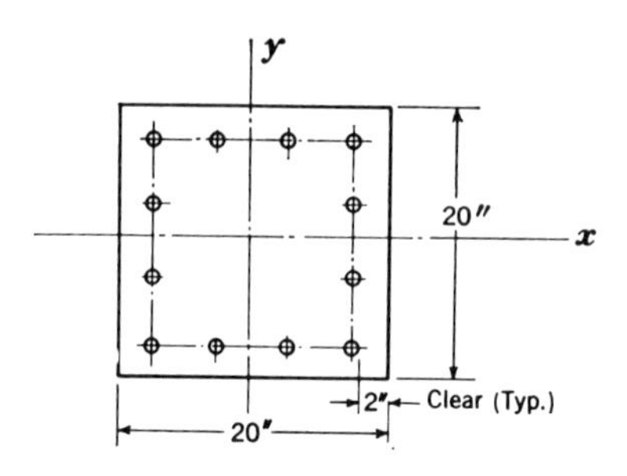

Problem 14–184.

14–185. Find algebraically the stress, in kilopounds, for members *7, 8, 9,* and *10* of the truss shown.

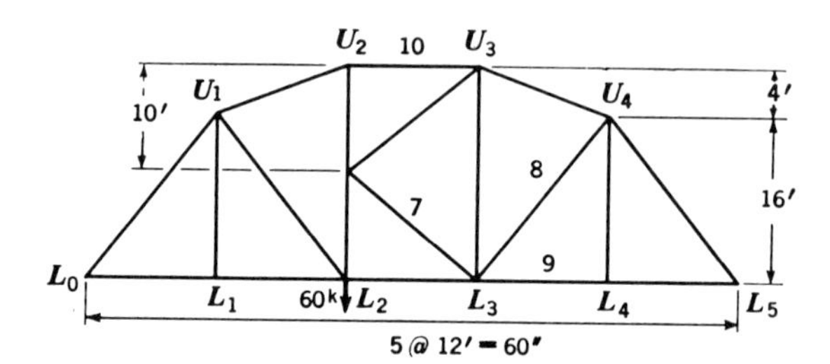

Problem 14–185.

14–186. During erection, the truss is supported as shown. Members *cD* and *Cd* are designed to take tension only. If the weight carried by this truss is 10 tons per linear foot, compute the stresses in each member intersecting at *D*.

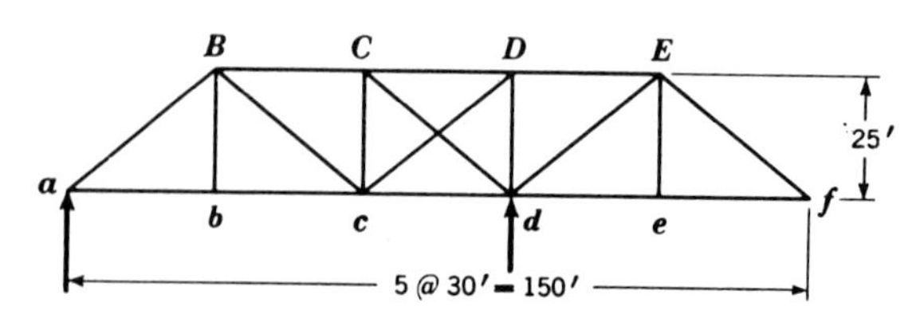

Problem 14–186.

14–187. Draw and label the Maxwell diagram for the Fink truss shown. Find stresses in members *b-1*, *4-5*, and *2-3*.

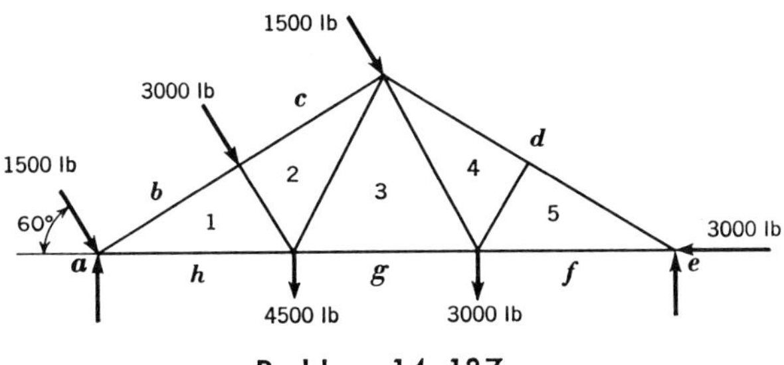

Problem 14–187.

14–188. Draw the shear and moment diagrams for both members of the structure shown.

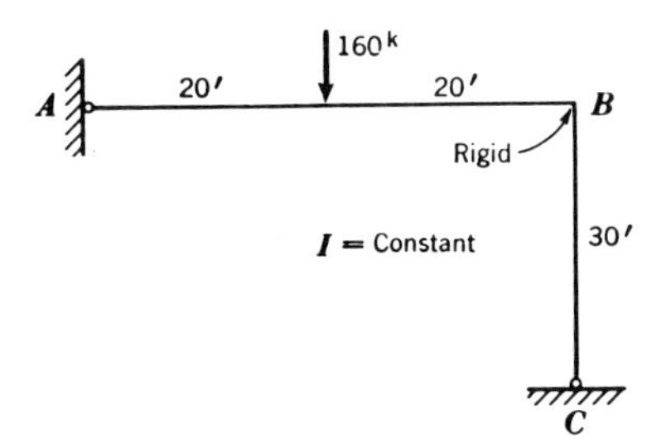

Problem 14–188.

14–189. Compute the amount and kind of stresses in a stiff-leg derrick having the dimensions shown.

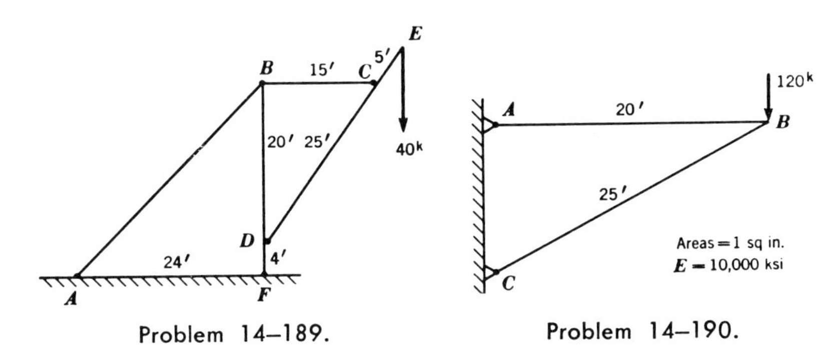

Problem 14–189. Problem 14–190.

14–190. Using the method of virtual work, find the vertical and horizontal deflection of *B*, in inches.

14–191. Determine the maximum bending, axial, and shear stresses in the frame which is fixed at A. Neglect the weight of frame.

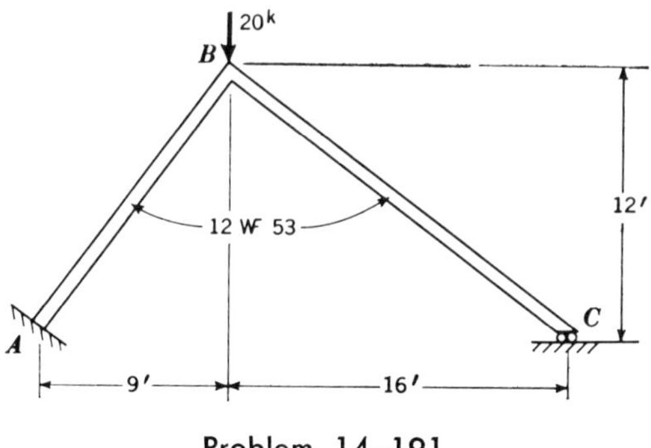

Problem 14–191.

14–192. A column has a total load of 344.5^k and a soil bearing pressure of 2 tons/sq ft. Design a reinforced-concrete column footing to carry a 25 in. square column as shown.

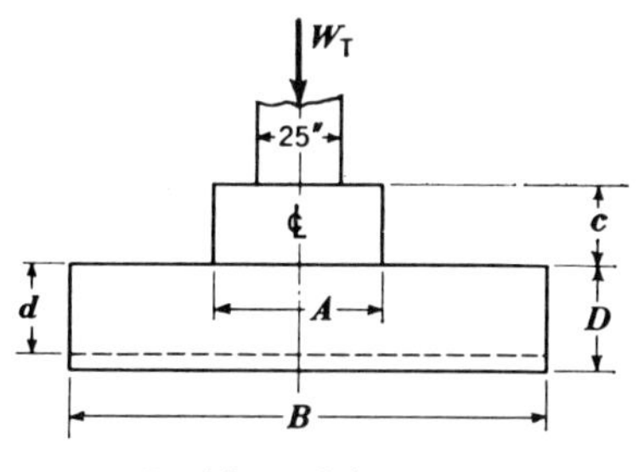

Problem 14–192.

14–193. A spread footing is 14 ft 10 in. square with an effective depth of 32½ in. The footing supports a column 30 in. square carrying a load of 1,000,000 lb. The soil pressure may not exceed 5000 psf. Find the required steel area; select the bars; check bond; and find the shearing stress. Specifications: 20,000-1350-10.

14–194. A beam simply supported at two points 25 ft apart carries a uniform load of 250 lb/foot in addition to two moving loads. The moving loads are 10^k and 20^k, respectively, and are placed 8 ft apart along the beam. (a) Find the maximum bending moment, in inch-pounds. (b) What is the maximum vertical shear at the center of the beam? (c) What is the maximum vertical shear on the beam, and where does it occur?

14–195. Using plastic design theory, select a WF section for the continuous beam shown. Use a load factor of 2.0 and steel with a yield stress of 33 ksi.

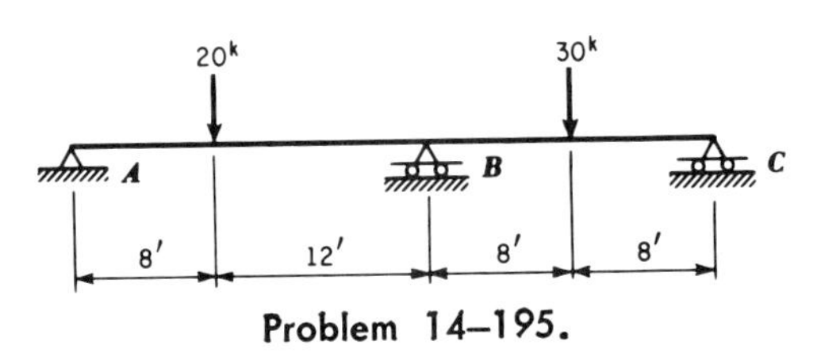

Problem 14–195.

14–196. In a mill building the track girders supporting a bridge crane have a simple span of 25 ft without lateral bracing. The maximum crane load on the girder consists of two wheel loads of 25^k each, spaced 10 ft on centers. The maximum weight of lifted load and trolley is 20^k. Allow 80 lb/ft for the weight of rail and girder and comply with AISC specifications. Design typical crane track girder using WF section with standard channel cover on top flange.

14–197. A fully braced plate girder on a 60-ft span carries a total uniform load of 5000 lb/ft. At the ends, the girder consists of a 54-in. × ½-in. web plate and four angles 6 in. × 4 in. × ½ in. The 4-in. legs are vertical. What cover plates should be added at the center of the girder? Use AISC specifications.

14–198. Find the maximum tension and/or compression stress in members *a*, *b*, and *c* of the truss shown. The uniform load may be partial or discontinuous. Loads are applied at the top chord.

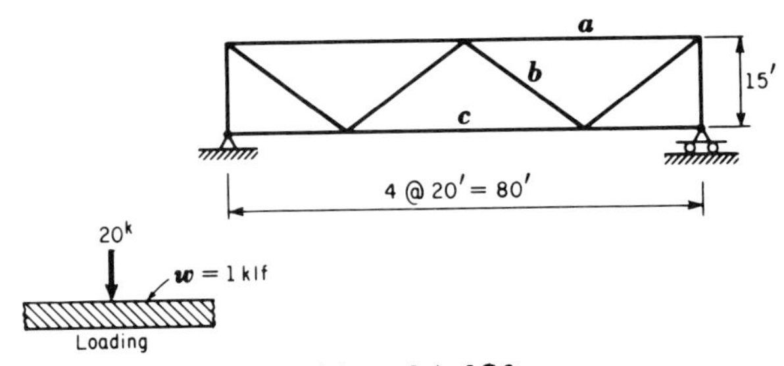

Problem 14–198

14–199. Compute the reactions of the three-hinged arch as shown.

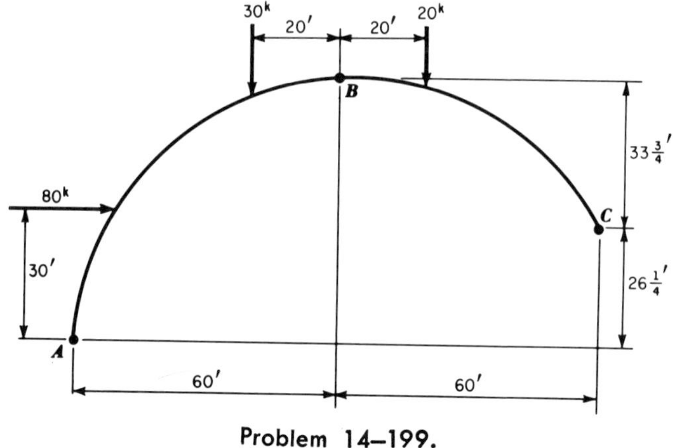

Problem 14–199.

14–200. (a) Find the fiber stress in the beam shown with no jack. (b) Find the load on the jack required to reduce the maximum fiber stress to 20,000 psi.

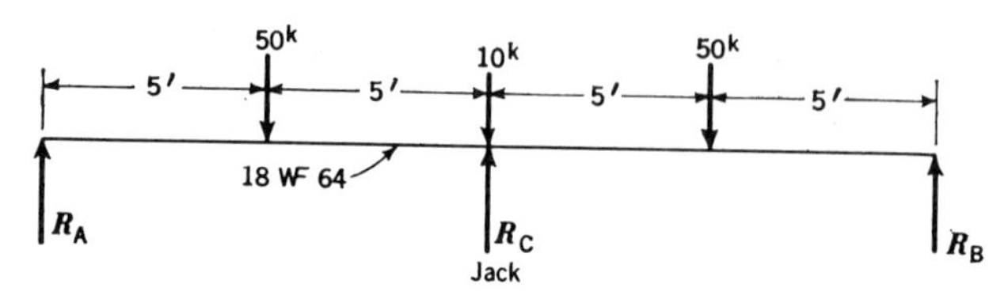

Problem 14–200.

14–201. A beam is continuous over two spans of 20 ft and 30 ft. The 20-ft span carries a uniform load of 2 klf. The 30-ft span is not loaded. Calculate the moment at the interior support and all reactions.

14–202. The cross section at the center line of a welded-plate girder is shown. (a) Compute the maximum allowable uniform live load that can be placed on the girder if it is a simple span of 60 ft. (b) At what point could the outside cover plate be discontinued? Indicate any specifications used.

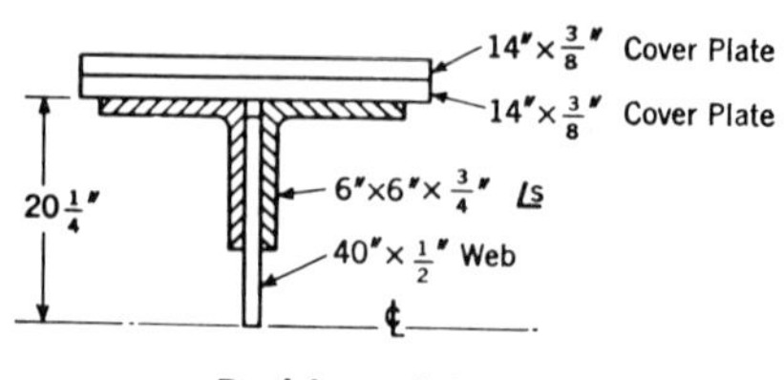

Problem 14–202.

14–203. Write the three necessary moment equations for solution of the beam shown by the moment-area method.

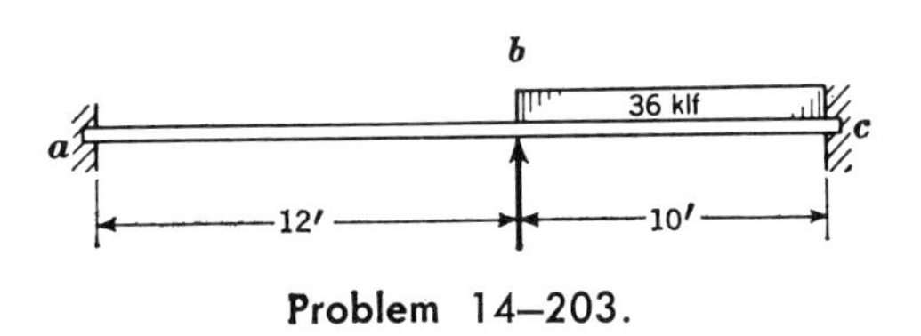

Problem 14–203.

14–204. A 1-ft-wide section of a concrete slab has an effective depth of 5.5 in. and an area of steel equal to 0.75 sq in. Find the permissible bending moment the section may carry. Specifications: 20,000-1350-10.

14–205. (a) Determine the maximum allowable moment on the concrete T beam shown when used as a simple span. (b) If the end shear is 15,000 lb, will web reinforcement be required? Use the following stresses: $f'c = 2500$ psi, $fc = 1125$ psi, $n = 12$, $fs = 20{,}000$ psi, shear $= 75$ psi without web reinforcement.

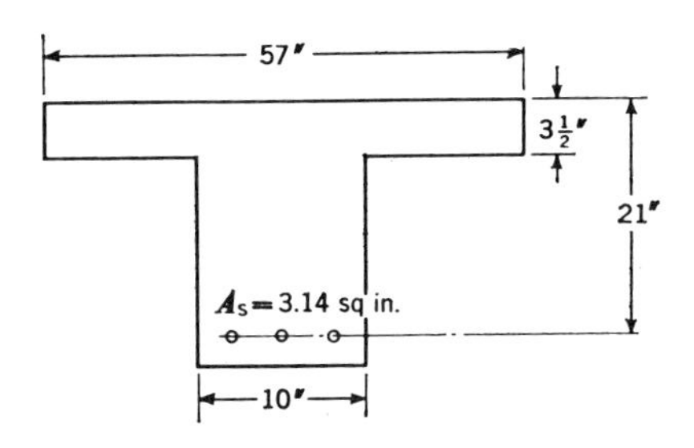

Problem 14–205.

14–206. Determine the value of the distance, e, so that the shearing stress will not exceed 12,000 psi on the cross-section of any rivet in this 5-rivet combination. Assume ⅞ in. diameter rivets.

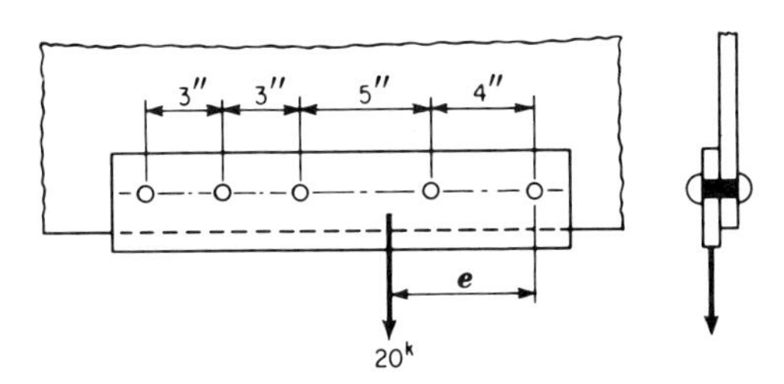

Problem 14–206.

14–207. A 16WF45 simple beam with a 20-ft span is laterally unsupported. Find the safe uniform load, in pounds per foot. Allowable stresses are $f=20{,}000$ psi, if ld/bt is less than 600, and $f=\dfrac{12{,}000{,}000}{ld/bt}$ psi, if ld/bt exceeds 600.

14–208. An 11½ in. × 17½ in. wooden beam is to be replaced with an equivalent reinforced-concrete beam of 12-in. width. The beam is in a warehouse and must carry its maximum uniform load. The span is 18 ft, and the allowable flexure stress is 1400 psi. The concrete beam is to be designed on the basis of 18,000-800-12 specifications. Draw a section of the new concrete beam to scale, and show reinforcing.

14–209. A steel pipe 8.625 in. outside diameter with 0.322 in. wall thickness is used as a 20-ft long compression member. For the entire length as the effective length, what is the maximum allowable concentric load it can carry?

14–210. A concrete beam is simply supported, and it has a span of 20 ft and a cross section composed of four #8 bars located 2 in. from the bottom of the beam. The over-all dimensions are 12 in. × 20 in. The allowable stress in steel is 20,000 psi; that in concrete is 1300 psi in flexure; and $n=11$. The beam carries a uniform live load of 400 lb/ft and a concentrated load of P pounds at midspan. Find the maximum allowable value of P, using a concrete density of 150 lb/cu ft.

14–211. Given a simple one-way slab with an effective depth of 7 in., reinforced with #4 straight deformed bars 6 in. on centers. Find the safe superimposed uniformly distributed loads due to flexure, shear, and bond. Assume anchorage is sufficient to develop bond. The span is 16 ft. Specifications are 20,000-3000-10.

14–212. A 6 in. × 8 in. deep wooden beam has a steel plate 2 in. wide and ½ in. thick fastened to the lower surface. Find the maximum fiber stress in each material if the modulus of elasticity of the steel is 20 times as great as that of the wood and the bending moment is 150,000 in.-lb.

14–213. Find the slope at C and the deflection at B and C.

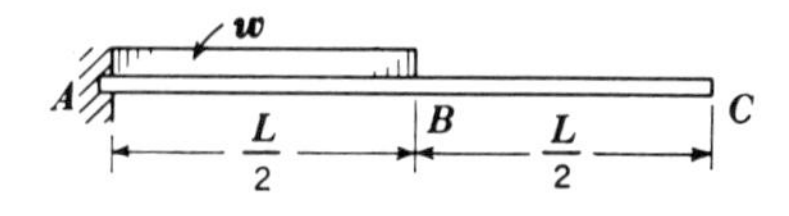

Problem 14–213.

14–214. A 36WF160 is cut as shown and welded together as in the second part of the figure. What is the comparative strength of the resultant beam, based solely on section modulus as compared with the original beam?

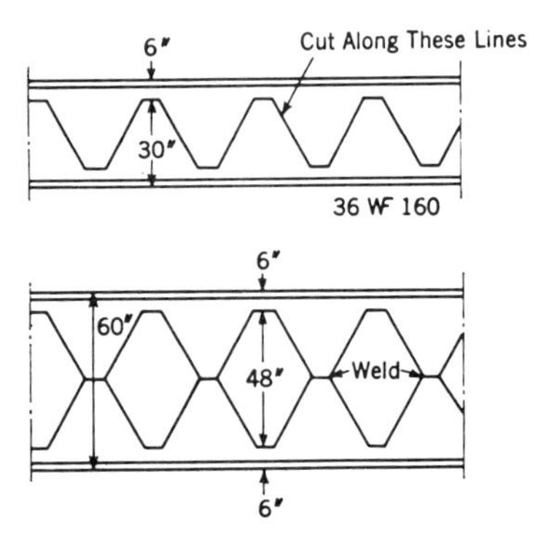

Problem 14–214.

14–215. Determine the deflection of points A, C, and E caused by the concentrated load of 20^k at A in the beam shown.

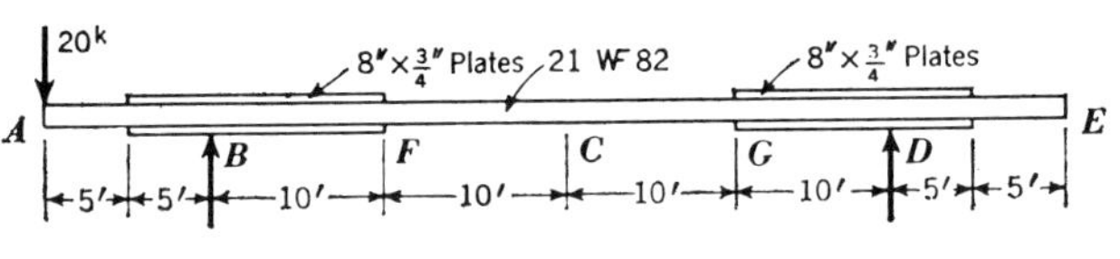

Problem 14–215.

14–216. A beam 15 ft long is supported at the left end and 10 ft from the left end. It carries a concentrated load of 2^k at the right end. Calculate the deflection under the load and at a point midway between the supports if $I = 60$ in.^{4} and $E = 30 \times 10^6$ psi.

14–217. A 6 in. × 10 in. Douglas fir beam (1600-lb stress grade) is reinforced by the addition of two 10 in. American Standard 15.3-lb channels properly bolted vertically to the sides of the wood beam. What is the relative strength in bending of the reinforced beam to the original wood beam? Use full-dimension lumber.

14–218. A simply supported one-way reinforced concrete slab has an effective span of 10 ft and supports a live load of 300 psf. Find the effective depth d and the spacing of #4 bars, using 2500-psi concrete and intermediate-grade steel.

14–219. A simple reinforced-concrete beam is used on a 10-ft span to carry a uniformly distributed load including its own weight of 3200 lb/ft and a concentrated load of 20,000 lb at the center of the span. Design the beam using $b=2/3d$ and 20,000-3000-10 specifications.

14–220. A rectangular wood beam is twice as deep as it is wide and is simply supported at points 14 ft apart. It supports a uniformly distributed load of 200 lb/ft, including beam weight, and a concentrated load of 500 lb at mid-span. (a) If the maximum bending stress is 2000 psi, find the theoretical dimensions of the cross section. (b) What is the maximum horizontal shearing stress, and where does it occur?

14–221. Select the lightest steel section for this beam and live load. The compression flange is laterally supported.

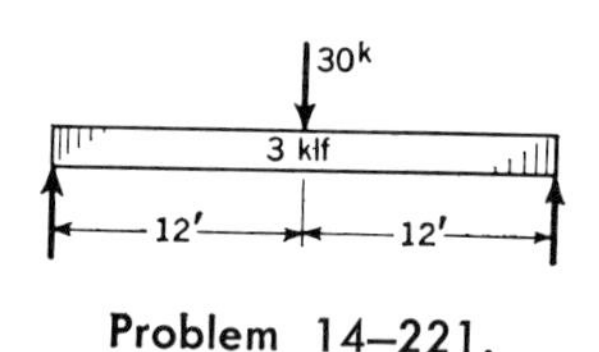

Problem 14–221.

14–222. A continuous T beam with a stem width of 11.5 in. and a depth of 20.5 in. to the steel must provide for the following unit shears: $f_y=40{,}000$, $f'c=3000$ psi. Design and space the necessary stirrups. Use ACI specifications.

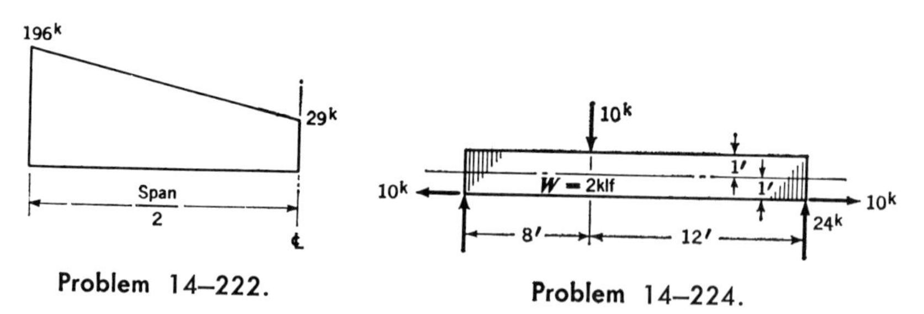

Problem 14–222.

Problem 14–224.

14–223. A reinforced-concrete beam section 12 in. wide is 25 in. deep to the steel. The main steel consists of three #8 bars. Use 3000-lb concrete and intermediate-grade steel. (a) Find k, j, and the resisting moment M_r, in kilopounds per foot. (b) Find the bond stress upon the bars at a point in the beam where the external shear V is 45^k. (c) Find the required spacing of #3 U stirrups at the same point in the beam.

14–224. For the beam shown draw the shear and moment diagrams and record values at breaks in the curves.

14–225. Draw the shear and moment diagrams for a simply

supported beam with 20 ft between supports and a 5 ft overhang at the right end (total beam length is 25 ft). The beam carries a uniformly distributed load of 2 klf over its entire length and a concentrated load of 10^k midway between the supports.

14–226. In the beam shown, determine the maximum moment that would be used and select a WF section for the design.

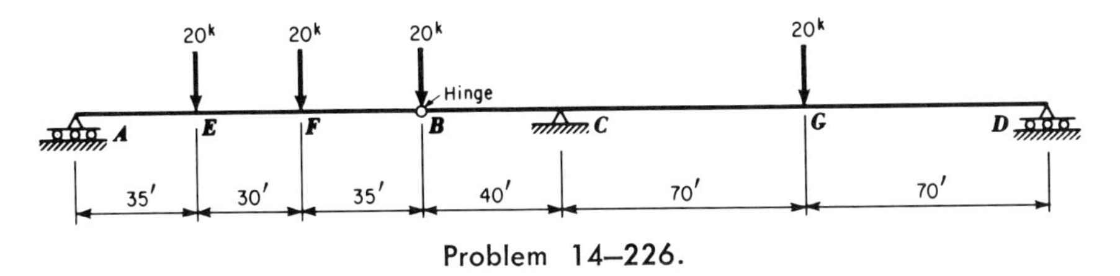

Problem 14–226.

14–227. Texanium, a new structural metal, is about to be put on the market. The stress-strain curve of Texanium compared with the curve for ASTM A-7 structural steel is shown in the figure. Allowable working stress values of A-7 steel are given below for four loading conditions. For each of these conditions and approximately the same factor of safety, state whether the stress values for Texanium should be (a) larger or smaller, (b) what numerical value, approximately, and (c) the reason for your decision.

Loading Condition	A-7 Allowable
A. Tension	$f = 20{,}000$ psi
B. Compression	$f = 17{,}000 - 0.485\,(l/r)^2$
C. Shear	$v = 13{,}000$ psi
D. Compression on beam flanges	$f = \dfrac{12{,}000}{ld/bt}$

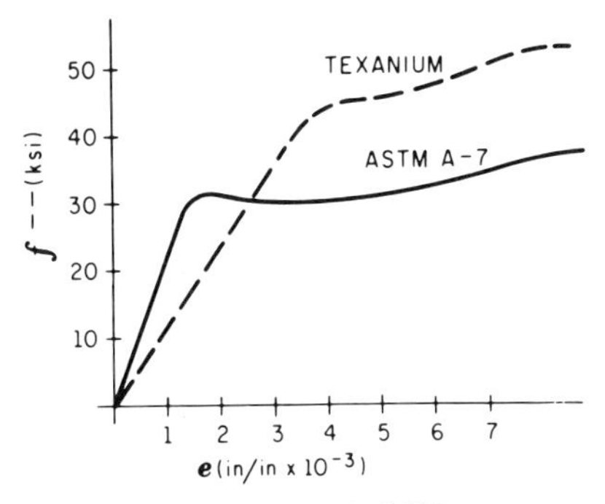

Problem 14–227.

14–228. The officials of a small city have asked you over the telephone, to advise them on the replacement, modification, or repair of a 50-ft clear span bridge over a river. The existing bridge deck is in poor condition and is rated as not more than H-10 capacity. (a) Describe your actions after accepting the assignment. (b) List and discuss at least nine factors to which you would give consideration before making recommendations to the city. (These may be in the form of questions to which you would seek answers before making recommendations.)

14–229. For each of the structures listed, give briefly at least two major advantages and two disadvantages of the types of construction used, and your first choice of type.

A. *The roof of a large supermarket.*
1. Wood plank on laminated timber beams.
2. Light-weight concrete panels on bar joists.
3. Metal decking on steel purlins.
4. A thin shell hyperbolic paraboloid.

B. *A multi-story high school classroom building.*
1. Concrete beam and joist framing.
2. Steel frame with curtain walls.
3. Concrete lift slab.

C. *A 100-ft R.R. bridge over a river.*
1. Steel deck truss.
2. Through-truss, with curved top chord.
3. Through plate-girder.
4. Deck plate-girder.

D. *Fireproof 3-story warehouse.*
1. Concrete, beam and girder framing.
2. Concrete, flat slab.
3. Concrete-block bearing walls with timber, mill construction framing.

14–230. A tractor-trailer of 120,000 lb total weight will be moved across a single-span bridge of 80 ft with the wheel loading shown. The bridge is designed for a maximum live loading at the center of 810,000 ft-kip. Is the bridge overloaded, and if so, what is the percentage of overstress?

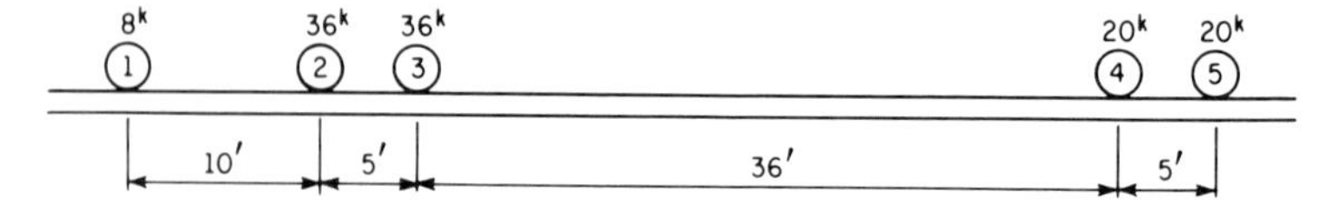

Problem 14–230.

Electrical Engineering 15

Where it is possible the problems are arranged as follows: (1) circuits including a-c circuits, single and 3-phase a-c circuits and networks; (2) electronics including vacuum tube and transistor amplifiers, rectifiers, feedback control and communication; (3) illumination; (4) machinery including induction motors; (5) power transmission including low and high frequency lines, wave-guides, and electromagnetic propagation. The greatest change in recent examinations is the increased emphasis on transistors.

CIRCUITS

15–1. Calculate the current in branch *b-c* of the circuit shown in the diagram when $E = 100$ volts, and the branch resistances are expressed in ohms, as indicated.

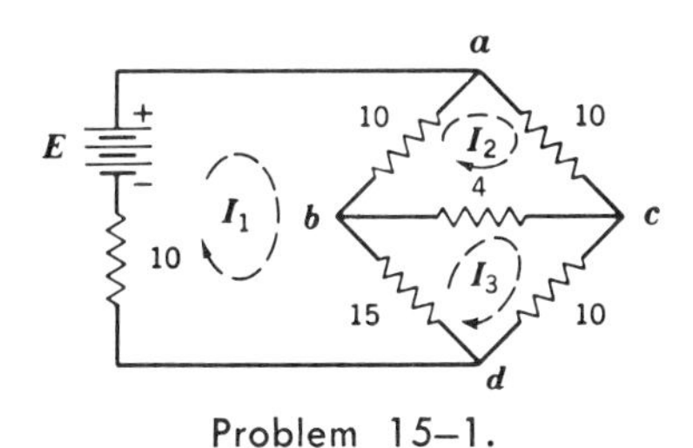

Problem 15–1.

Solution: Writing the loop-current equations from the loop currents suggested in the illustration,

(1) $100 = 35I_1 - 10I_2 - 15I_3$

(2) $0 = -10I_1 + 24I_2 - 4I_3$

(3) $0 = -15I_1 - 4I_2 + 29I_3$

$$\Delta = \begin{vmatrix} 35 & -10 & -15 \\ -10 & 24 & -4 \\ -15 & -4 & 29 \end{vmatrix} = 14{,}300$$

$$I_2 = \frac{\begin{vmatrix} 35 & 100 & -15 \\ -10 & 0 & -4 \\ -15 & 0 & 29 \end{vmatrix}}{\Delta} = 2.45 \text{ amp} \qquad I_3 = \frac{\begin{vmatrix} 35 & -10 & 100 \\ -10 & 24 & 0 \\ -15 & -4 & 0 \end{vmatrix}}{\Delta} = 2.80 \text{ amp}$$

$$I_{bc} = I_3 - I_2 = 2.80 - 2.45 = 0.35 \text{ amp}$$

15–2. The diagrammatic circuit represents the components of a coil and a capacitor. The coil has an inductance of 0.001 h and a time constant of 10^{-6} sec. The time constant of the capacitor is $\sqrt{2}\times10^{-6}$ sec. The product LC is 10^{-12}. Determine (a) the values of R, C, and r, (b) the frequency of series resonance of this circuit, and (c) the effective resistance of this circuit at resonance.

Solution: (a) $LC=10^{-12}=0.001C$; $C=10^{-9}$ f; $rC=\sqrt{2}\times10^{-6}=r(10^{-9})$; $r=\sqrt{2}\times10^{3}$ ohm.

$$\frac{L}{R}=10^{-6}=\frac{0.001}{R}\qquad R=1000\text{ ohm}$$

(b)

$$Z_C=\frac{r(-jX_c)}{r-jX_c}\cdot\frac{r+jX_c}{r+jX_c}=\frac{rX_c^2-jr^2X_c}{r^2+X_c^2}$$

At resonance

$$X_L=\frac{r^2X_c}{r^2+X_c^2}$$

$$\omega L=\frac{r^2/\omega C}{r^2+1/\omega^2C^2}=\frac{r^2\omega C}{r^2\omega^2C^2+1}=\omega L$$

$$\omega^2r^2LC^2+L-r^2C=0$$

Problem 15–2.

$$\omega=\sqrt{\frac{r^2C-L}{r^2LC^2}}=\sqrt{\frac{(2\times10^6)(10^{-9})-0.001}{(2\times10^6)(0.001)(10^{-18})}}$$

$$\omega=7.07\times10^5=2\pi f\qquad f=1.13\times10^5\text{ cps}$$

(c) At resonance,

$$X_L=\omega L=(7.07\times10^5)(0.001)=707\text{ ohm}$$

$$X_C=\frac{1}{\omega C}=1/(7.07\times10^5)(10^{-9})=1414\text{ ohm}$$

$$Z_T=1000+j707+\frac{1414(-j1414)}{1414-j1414}$$

$$=1000+j707+707-j707$$

$$Z_T=1707\text{ ohm}$$

15–3. Find the three line currents to an unbalanced delta-connected load as indicated in the diagram.

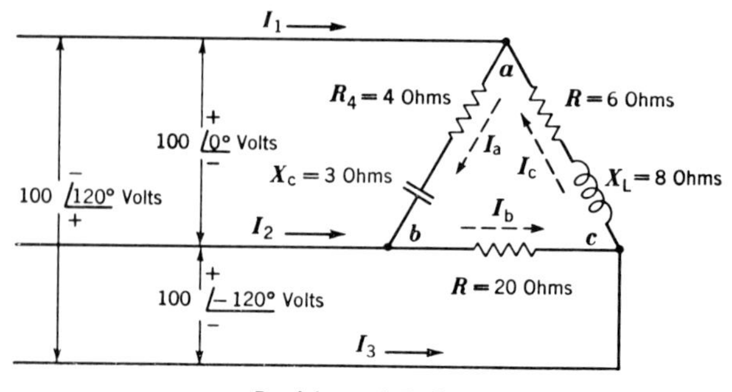

Problem 15–3.

Solution:

$$I_a=\frac{100/\underline{0^\circ}}{4-j3}=\frac{100/\underline{0^\circ}}{5/\underline{-36.9^\circ}}=20/\underline{36.9^\circ}=16+j12 \text{ amp}$$

$$I_b=\frac{100/\underline{-120^\circ}}{20/\underline{0^\circ}}=5/\underline{-120^\circ}=-2.5-j4.33 \text{ amp}$$

$$I_c=\frac{100/\underline{120^\circ}}{6+j8}=\frac{100/\underline{120^\circ}}{10/\underline{53.1^\circ}}=10/\underline{66.9^\circ}=3.94+j9.20 \text{ amp}$$

$$I_1=I_a-I_c=16+j12-3.94-j9.20=12.06+j2.80=12.4/\underline{13.1^\circ} \text{ amp}$$

$$I_2=I_b-I_a=-2.5-j4.33-16-j12=-18.5-j16.33=24.7/\underline{-138.5^\circ} \text{ amp}$$

$$I_3=I_c-I_b=3.94+j9.20+2.5+j4.33=6.44+j13.53=15.0/\underline{64.6^\circ} \text{ amp}$$

15–4. A 40-ohm load is to receive power at 10 kc from a 1000-ohm generator. The coupling network will be a T network of pure reactances, the horizontal elements of which must be equal. In addition to providing perfect coupling between its terminations, the T network must include tuning in its vertical element which will prevent any third-harmonic power present in the output of the generator from reaching the load. Draw the simplest network which will meet these specifications, and calculate the values of its elements.

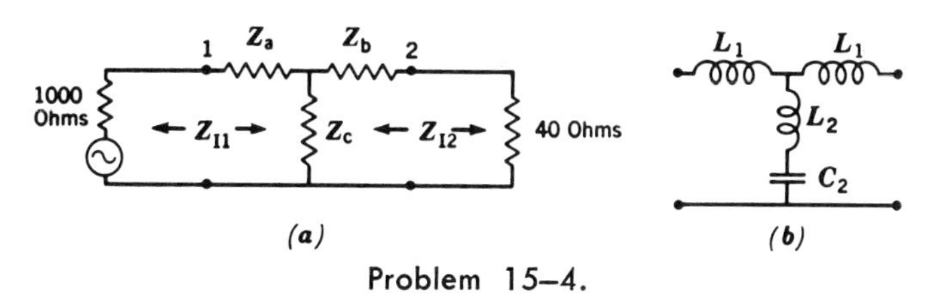

Problem 15–4.

Solution: The network will have the basic configuration shown in (*a*) of the diagram. For perfect coupling, $Z_{I1}=1000$ ohms and $Z_{I2}=40$ ohms, where Z_{I1} and Z_{I2} are the image impedances for the respective terminals. Since $Z_{I1}\neq Z_{I2}$, the equations for the unsymmetrical T will be used:

$$Z_c=\frac{\sqrt{Z_{I1}Z_{I2}}}{\sinh\theta} \qquad Z_a=\frac{Z_{I1}}{\tanh\theta}-Z_c \qquad Z_b=\frac{Z_{I2}}{\tanh\theta}-Z_c$$

The term θ is defined in the expression

$$\epsilon^\theta=\sqrt{\frac{E_1I_1}{E_2I_2}} \qquad \theta=\alpha+j\beta,$$

where α is the attenuation, in nepers, and β is the phase shift, in radians. According to filter theory, one characteristic of the passband ($\alpha=0$) is that the image impedances are purely resistive. Since Z_{I1} and Z_{I2} are resistive, $\alpha=0$ and $\theta=j\beta$.

$$\sinh\theta=\sinh(j\beta)=j\sin\beta \qquad \tanh\theta=\tanh(j\beta)=j\tan\beta$$

Since $Z_a = Z_b$ (given),

$$\frac{1000}{j \tan \beta} - Z_c = \frac{40}{j \tan \beta} - Z_c$$

For this equality to be true, $\beta = \pm 90°$. For reasons to be obvious later, $\beta = +90°$ will be used. Then

$$Z_c = \frac{\sqrt{1000(40)}}{j \sin 90°} = -j200 \text{ ohms} \qquad \text{and} \qquad Z_a = Z_b = -Z_c = +j200 \text{ ohms.}$$

For the network to fullfill the imposed conditions, the components would be reduced to those shown in (*b*) of the illustration. At 10 kc,

$$X_{L1} = 200 = 2\pi(10^4)L_1 \qquad L_1 = 3.18 \times 10^{-3} \text{ h}$$

Also at 10 kc,

$$X_{C2} - X_{L2} = 200 = \frac{1}{(2\pi \times 10^4)C_2} - (2\pi \times 10^4)L_2.$$

At 30 kc,

$$X_{L2} = X_{C2} \qquad 2\pi(3 \times 10^4)L_2 = \frac{1}{2\pi(3 \times 10^4)C_2} \qquad \text{or} \qquad C_2 = \frac{1}{(36\pi^2 \times 10^8)L_2} \text{ f}$$

Substituting into the previous equation,

$$\frac{(36\pi^2 \times 10^8)L_2}{2\pi \times 10^4} - (2\pi \times 10^4)L_2 = 200 \qquad L_2 = 3.98 \times 10^{-4} \text{ h}$$

$$C_2 = \frac{1}{(36\pi^2 \times 10^8)(3.98 \times 10^{-4})} = 7.08 \times 10^{-8} \text{ f}$$

Had $\beta = -90°$ been picked, then $Z_c = +j200$ ohms and it would have been impossible for $Z_c = 0$ with an increase in frequency to 30 kc.

15–5. The movement of a D'Arsonval meter has a resistance of 0.1 ohm and requires 20 millivolts for full-scale deflection. The meter scale is uniformly divided from 0 to 100. If this movement is equipped with a 0.001-ohm shunt, what will be the deflection of the meter when it is used to measure a 10-amp current?

15–6. The magnetic core shown in the diagram is made of transformer steel for which the *B-H* data are as follows:

B, kilolines per square inch....	20	40	60	70	80	85	90	95
H, ampere-turns per inch......	2	3	5	7	13	20	34	70

The core has a stacking factor of 0.92. A current of 0.56 amp is

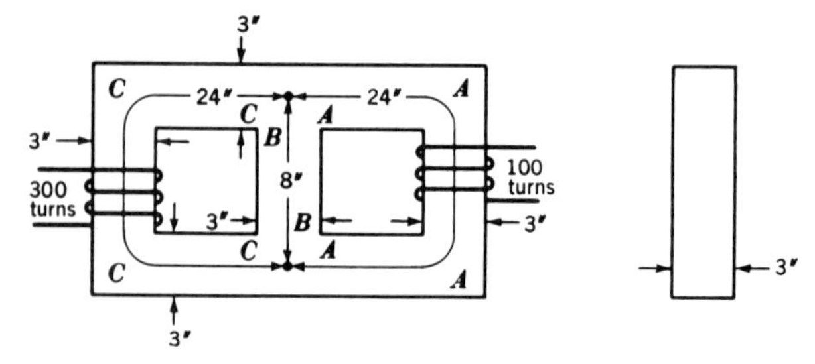

Problem 15–6.

entering the top terminal of the coil on the right. It is desired that there be no flux in the portions of the magnetic circuit marked *A*. (a) Should the current enter or leave the top terminal of the coil on the left to attain the desired result? (b) What should be the magnitude of the current in the coil on the left?

15–7. It is proposed to heat electrically the water for a pool requiring 15×20×3.5 cu ft of water. When the water is changed, it is heated from 55°F to 70°F. Between changes the water is reheated once from 65°F to 70°F. If all the electric energy supplied to the heater is considered transferred to the water and the cost of electricity is 1.5 cents/kwhr, calculate the total cost of one heating and one reheating of the water.

15–8. A current wave flows in a circuit consisting of a resistance, *R*, an inductance, *L*, and a capacitance, *C*, in series. The current has a cycle as follows: it increases linearly from −5 amp to +5 amp in 0.01 sec then decreases linearly to −5 amp in 0.02 sec. Sketch the voltage across each element.

15–9. A current varies as shown in the diagram. (a) What is the effective value of the current? (b) What is the d-c component value of the current?

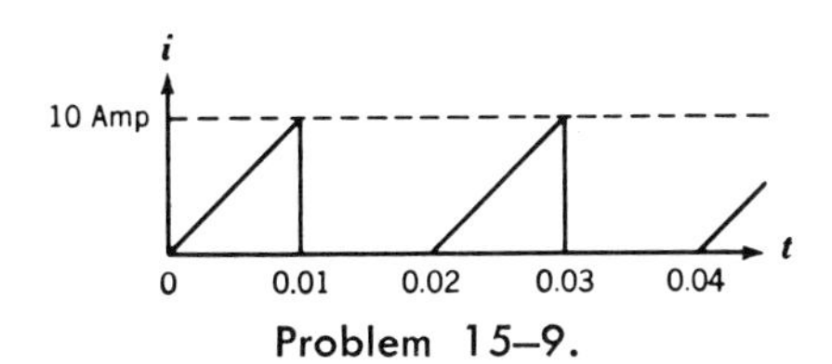

Problem 15–9.

15–10. A series circuit of *R*, *L*, and *C* is to resonate at $\omega_r = 10^6$ radians/sec, have a band width between half-power points of $0.1\omega_r$, and draw 10 watts from a 100-volt source at resonance. (a) Calculate the necessary values of *R*, *L*, and *C*. (b) What is the band width of this circuit, between quarter-power points, as a fraction of ω_r?

15–11. The circuit shown in the diagram includes a generator with variable frequency, an internal resistance $R_g = 1000$ ohms, and an emf of constant magnitude $E = 150$ volts. The coil in the tank circuit has an inductance $L = 200$ μh and a *Q* factor $Q = 10$, which may be considered constant. The tuning capacitor is fixed at $C = 10^{-10}$ f. Calculate (a) the frequency of parallel resonance, (b) the voltage E_o across the tank at parallel resonance, and (c) the power delivered to the tank coil at parallel resonance.

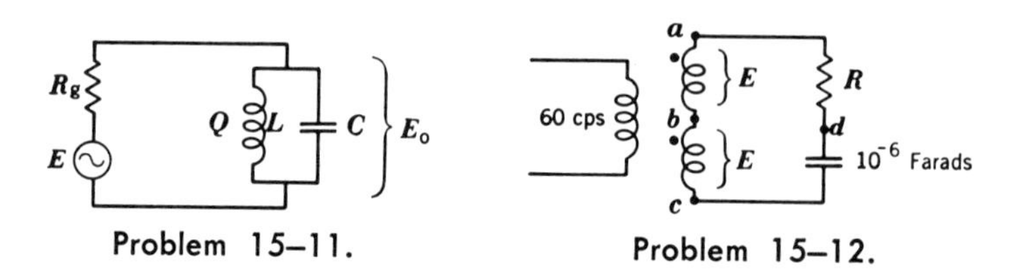

Problem 15–11. Problem 15–12.

15–12. The phase-shifting network shown in the diagram is used as a control circuit. (a) Calculate the value of R which will yield a voltage E_{bd} which leads E_{ac} by 60°. (b) What is the magnitude of E_{bd} as compared with E?

15–13. The circuit shown in the diagram presents an incomplete bridge for the measurement of the parallel combination of R_x and L_x. (a) Specify the appropriate missing arm such that the expressions for R_x and L_x are independent of the frequency of E. (b) Determine the expression for R_x and L_x when the complete bridge is balanced.

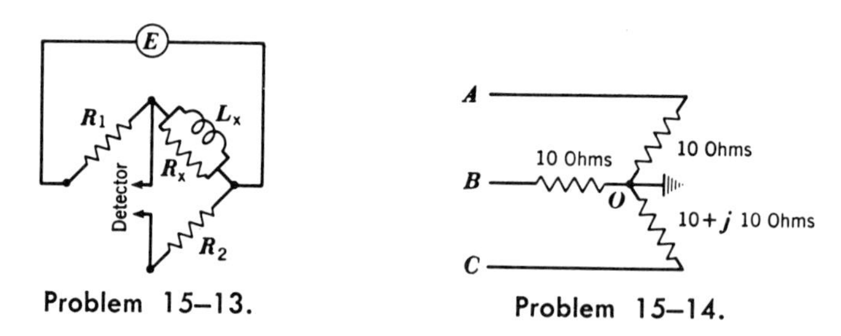

Problem 15–13. Problem 15–14.

15–14. A three-phase wye-connected power system with grounded neutral supplies energy to a three-phase wye-connected load shown in the diagram. The line voltages are $E_{AB}=2200\underline{/0°}$, $E_{BC}=2200\underline{/120°}$ and $E_{CA}=2200\underline{/-120°}$. Calculate the potential difference between O and ground when the ground connection at O is accidentally opened.

15–15. Each phase of a delta load has 6 ohms resistance and 9 ohms capacitive reactance in series. Each phase of the wye load has 8 ohms resistance and 6 ohms inductive reactance in series. The two loads are connected in parallel across three-phase line voltages of 100 volts. Calculate the resultant line current, the total power consumed, and the power factor of the combination.

15–16. A manufacturing plant served by a 2400/4160-volt three-phase 60-cycle four-wire distribution circuit has an induction motor load of 1500 kw at a power factor of 0.65. Determine the total kilovoltamperes of 2400-volt capacitors required to correct the power factor of this load to 0.9. Discuss the advantages which accrue to the power consumer and the power company from the installation of static capacitors.

15–17. Power is supplied by a three-phase four-wire 120/208-volt source to a balanced three-phase lighting load which draws (a) 25 amp per phase at unity power factor for incandescent lamps and (b) 75 amp per phase at 0.95 power factor for fluorescent lamps. The current drawn by the fluorescent lamps contains a third harmonic which is 20 per cent of the fundamental. Calculate the current in the neutral wire.

15–18. A balanced three-phase load of 50 kw and 0.707 power factor is measured by the two-wattmeter method. What are the two wattmeter readings?

15–19. A three-phase source with balanced line voltages of 240 volts supplies power to the circuit shown below. The phase order is 12, 31, 23. Calculate the reading of the wattmeters.

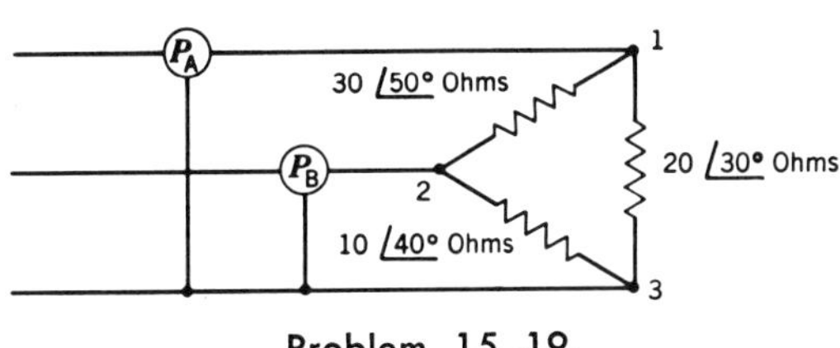

Problem 15–19.

15–20. A circuit consisting of a resistance of 10 ohms and an inductance of 0.1h is in parallel with another circuit consisting of a resistance of 5 ohms and an uncharged capacitor of 10 μf. This parallel combination is then to be connected through a switch to a 100-volt battery of negligible internal resistance. (a) At the instant the switch is closed, what is the battery current? (b) A long time after the switch is closed, what is the battery current?

15–21. (a) In the circuit shown in the diagram the current through the inductance has reached steady state. Now the line switch is opened (assume no arcing). What will be the maximum voltage between *a* and *b*? (b) Explain what would happen, when the switch is opened, if the 200-ohm resistance were replaced by a coil having 100 ohms resistance and 1h inductance, other conditions remaining the same as before.

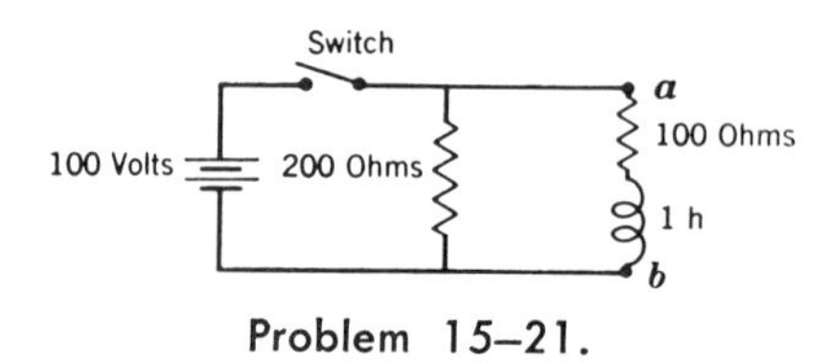

Problem 15–21.

15–22. A d-c source with a pure resistance of 60 ohms feeds a pure resistance load of 60 ohms. A T network of resistances is to be inserted between the source and load to produce a 5-db attenuation in power. The resistance as seen from the source or from the load must remain equal to 60 ohms. What should be the value of each of the three resistances in the T?

15–23. (a) Design the constant-K T section of the low-pass filter which matches a 500-ohm circuit and has a cutoff at $\omega=1000$ radians/sec. (b) Calculate the attenuation, in decibels, of this section at $\omega=2000$ radians/sec.

15–24. The network shown in the diagram is a T section of an m-derived low-pass filter. Determine (a) the cutoff frequency, (b) the frequency of infinite attenuation, and (c) the attenuation at $\omega=10{,}000$ radians/sec.

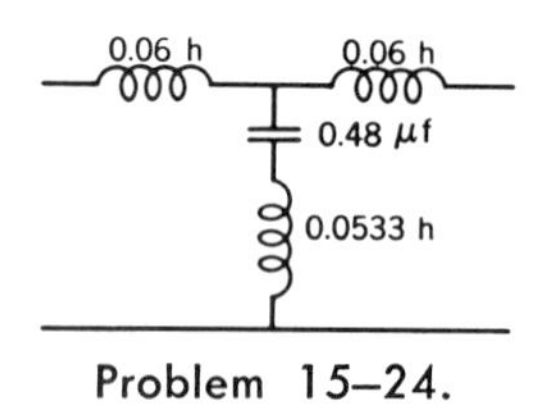

Problem 15–24.

15–25. In the circuit shown in the diagram the generator has an internal impedance of 1000 $(1+j)$ ohms and an internal emf of 100 volts, both at $f=10^4/2\pi$ cps. This generator is matched to the

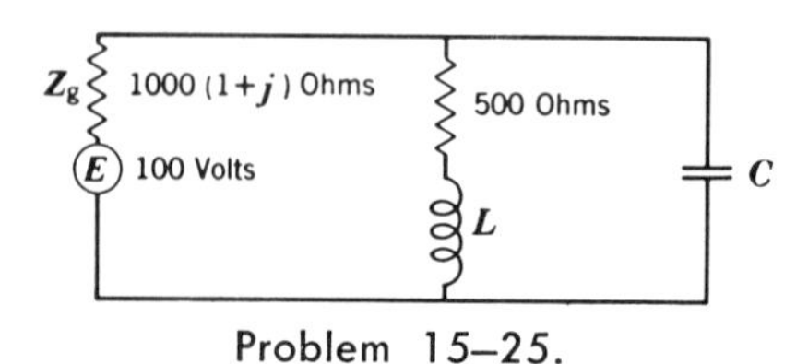

Problem 15–25.

500-ohm load by means of L and C. Calculate the necessary values of L and C which will yield maximum power in the 500-ohm load.

15–26. In the circuit shown, the switch is closed at time zero when all currents and charge are zero. Write the equation for current as a function of time, employing numerical coefficients, and indicate the steady-state and transient terms.

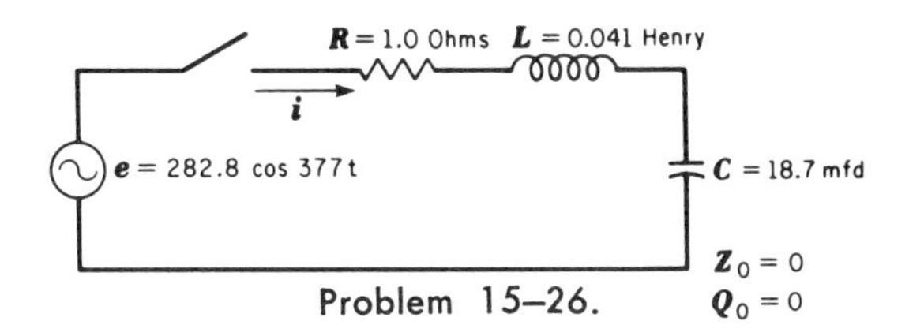

Problem 15–26.

15–27. Given that the input impedance in a passive circuit is $Z = (s^3 + 16s)/(s^2 + 4)$. Synthesize a circuit of the conformation shown which will have the given input impedance.

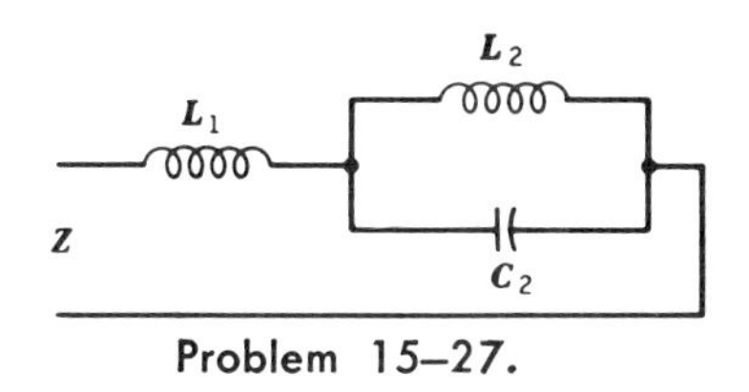

Problem 15–27.

15–28. Find the output response $e_3(t)$ of the 4-terminal network shown to a unit-step constant-current driving function $i(t)$.

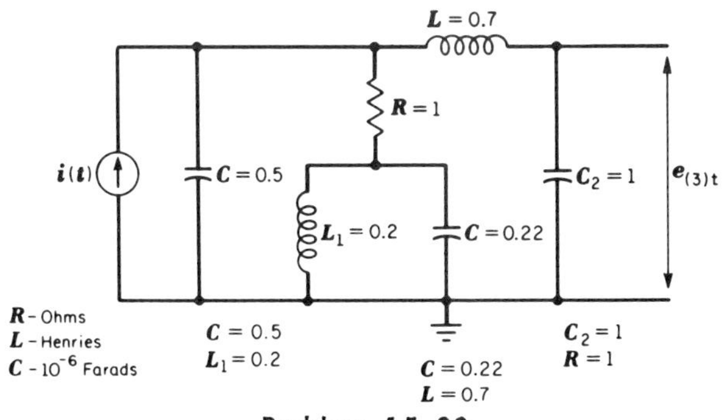

Problem 15–28.

15–29. For the wave shape shown determine: (a) the root-mean-square value, (b) the amplitude of the fundamental, (c) the amplitude of the third harmonic.

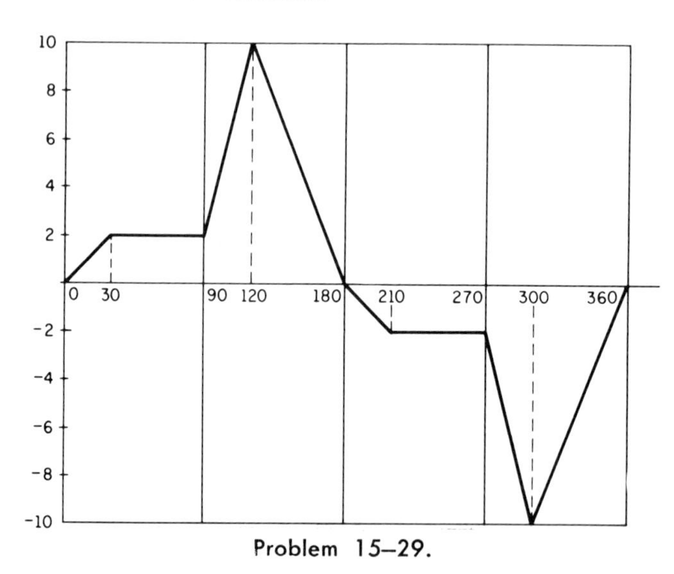

Problem 15–29.

15–30. A certain pulse generator puts out a positive pulse of amplitude +1 volts, followed by a negative pulse of amplitude −1 volts, followed by another positive pulse of amplitude +1 volts, etc, as shown in the figure. The duration of each pulse is a random variable; the transition points are Poisson distributed, i.e., the probability that there are n transitions in a time t is:

$$Pn(t) = 1/n! \left[(\lambda t)^n e^{-\lambda t}\right]$$

(a) Find the autocorrelation of the generator output. (b) Sketch the autocorrelation. (c) Find the power density spectrum of the generator output. Give all units.

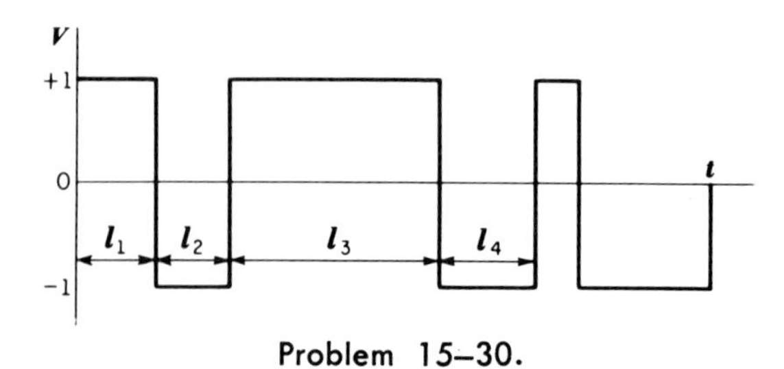

Problem 15–30.

ELECTRONICS

15–31. A pair of triodes, the plate currents of which obey the 3/2-power law, are used with ideal input and output transformers to form a push-pull amplifier. Plate power is supplied at 200 volts. The grid bias is fixed at $-E_c$ volts. The plate current per tube is I_m at zero grid voltage and zero when the grid voltage is $-2E_c$. The μ factor of each tube is 4 and may be considered constant over the range of operation. The output transformer has a turns ratio of N_1/N_2, where N_1 and N_2 are the total turns in the primary and secondary windings, respectively. A resistive load of 100 ohms is connected to the secondary. If the peak signal voltage on each tube is E_c volts and I_m is 0.15 amp, calculate (a) the maximum power this amplifier can deliver, (b) the proper value of the bias E_c, and (c) the proper value of the turns ratio N_1/N_2.

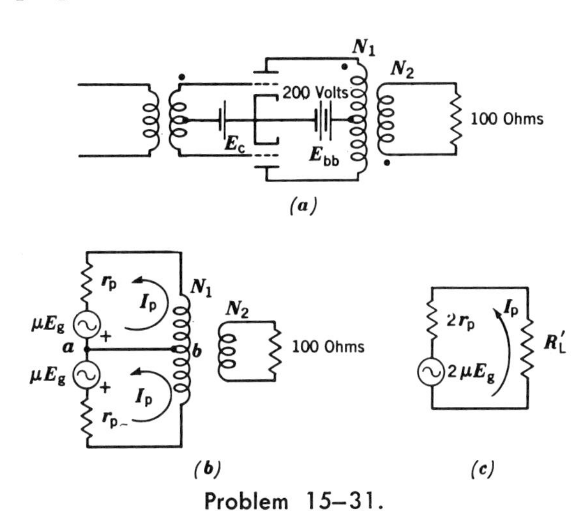

Problem 15–31.

Solution: The push-pull circuit is shown in (*a*) of the diagram. The equivalent a-c circuit is shown in (*b*), after replacing each tube with an emf source μE_g in series with a resistance r_p, the dynamic plate resistance of the tube. Since the left part of the circuit is symmetrical about conductor *a-b* in (*b*) of the diagram, $I_{ab} = 0$ and the equivalent circuit then further reduces to that shown in (*c*). The 3/2 power law:

$$i_b = k(e_c + e_b/\mu)^{3/2}$$

When $e_c = 0$,

$$i_b = 0.15 \text{ amp} \qquad 0.15 = k(0 + 200/4)^{3/2} \qquad k = 4.25 \times 10^{-4}$$

(b) When $e_c = -2E_c$

$$i_b = 0 \qquad 0 = k(-2E_c + 50)^{3/2} \qquad E_c = 25 \text{ volts}$$

(a) Solving the 3/2 power law for e_b,

$$e_b = \mu\left[\left(\frac{i_b}{k}\right)^{2/3} - e_c\right] \qquad r_p = \frac{\partial e_b}{\partial i_b} = \frac{2}{3}\left(\frac{1}{k}\right)\mu\left(\frac{i_b}{k}\right)^{-1/3}$$

To find the quiescent point,

$$I_b = (4.25\times10^{-4})\left(-25+\frac{200}{4}\right)^{3/2} \qquad I_b = 0.0531 \text{ amp}$$

To find the value of r_p corresponding to the quiescent point,

$$r_p = \frac{2}{3}\left(\frac{1}{4.25\times10^{-4}}\right)(4)\left(\frac{0.0531}{4.25\times10^{-4}}\right)^{-1/3} = 1257 \text{ ohms}$$

It will be noted that r_p will vary as a function i_b. The r_p for the quiescent point was found as a nominal value for r_p. For maximum power transfer to the load,

$$R_L' = 2r_p = 2514 \text{ ohms}$$

$$2\mu E_g = 2(4)(25)(0.707) = 141.4 \text{ volts rms}$$

$$I_p = \frac{141.4}{5028} = 0.02816 \qquad P_{\text{max}} = (0.02816)^2(2514)$$

$$P_{\text{max}} = 1.99 \text{ watts}$$

(c)

$$2514 = \left(\frac{N_1}{N_2}\right)^2(100) \qquad \frac{N_1}{N_2} = 5.01$$

15–32. The circuit in (*a*) below shows a small triode amplifier arranged to employ inverse feedback. Calculate the voltage output E_o, considering the reactances of the capacitors as negligible.

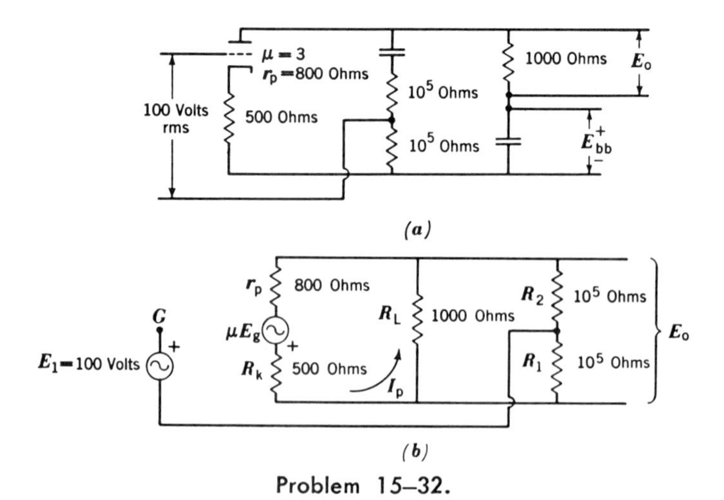

Problem 15–32.

Solution: Referring to the equivalent circuit in (*b*) of the diagram,

$$\mu E_g = I_p(r_p + R_k + R_L) = \mu\left(E_1 - I_pR_k - \frac{I_pR_LR_1}{R_1+R_2}\right)$$

$$I_p(800+500+1000) = 3(100 - 500I_p - 500I_p)$$

$I_p = 0.0566$ amp rms

$E_o = I_p R_L = 0.0566(1000) = 56.6$ volts rms

This was assuming a negligible loading effect of $R_1 + R_2$ on R_L. If R_L' is substituted for R_L in all the above expressions, where $R_L' = 1000(2 \times 10^5)/(1000 + 2 \times 10^5) = 995$ ohms, $E_o = 56.4$ volts rms.

15–33. For the complementary symmetry amplifier shown in part (*a*) of the figure, determine (a) the output power to the resistive load R in terms of the input current I_1, (b) the value of R for maximum power transfer, (c) the maximum power output. Assume identical transistor characteristics, class A operation, and that the transistor input impedances are much smaller than the biasing resistors R_B.

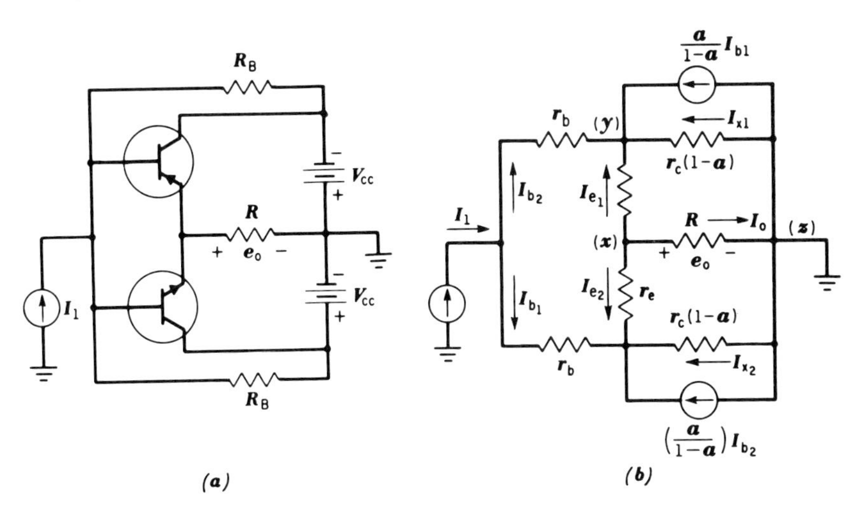

Problem 15–33.

Solution: (a) The common-collector equivalent circuit is shown in part (*b*) of the diagram. Because of symmetry conditions,

$$I_{b_1} = I_{b_2} = I_1/2;\ I_{e_1} = I_{e_2} = -I_o/2 \tag{1}$$

It is sufficient to work with the upper half of the circuit. The nodal and loop equations at (x) and at (x-y-z) are

$$I_{b_1} + I_{e_1} + I_{x_1} + \frac{a}{1-a} I_{b_1} = 0 \tag{2}$$

$$I_{e_1} r_e - r_c(1-a) I_{x_1} - e_o = 0 \tag{3}$$

From equations (1) and (2) an expression for I_x in terms of I_1 and I_o is

$$I_x = \frac{1}{2} I_o - \frac{1}{2(1-a)} I_1 \tag{4}$$

Substituting into equation (3) equations (1) for I_{b_1} and I_{e_1}, equation (4) for I_{x_1}, e_o for I_oR, and solving for I_o:

$$I_o = \frac{r_c I_1}{r_c(1 - a) + r_e + 2R} \tag{5}$$

The output power P is

$$P = I_o^2 R = \frac{r_c^2 R I_1^2}{[r_c(1 - a) + r_e + 2R]^2} \tag{6}$$

(b) The conditions for maximum transfers are $dP/dR = 0$. Taking the derivative of equation (6) with respect to R and equating the result to zero yields the required value of R for maximum power transfer:

$$R = \frac{r_c(1 - a) + r_e}{2} \tag{7}$$

(c) Substituting equation (7) in (6) for R, the maximum power input is

$$P = \frac{1}{8} \frac{r_c^2 I_1^2}{[(1 - a)r_c + r_e]} \cong \frac{1}{8} \frac{r_c}{(1 - a)} I_1^2$$

since $(1 - a)r_c \gg r_e$.

15–34. It is proposed to assemble a single-phase, bridge-connected battery charger to charge 12.6-volt batteries. The available elements for the bridge have the following ratings: full-load current=10 amp d-c; full-load forward voltage drop per element=2 volts rms; and permissible inverse peak voltage=22 volts. (a) Assuming that the rectifier is ideal within the limits of its rating, calculate (1) the rms input voltage required for full-load operation of the bridge and (2) the maximum inverse peak voltage to which each element in the bridge would be subjected in normal operation. (b) State whether you approve or disapprove this proposal.

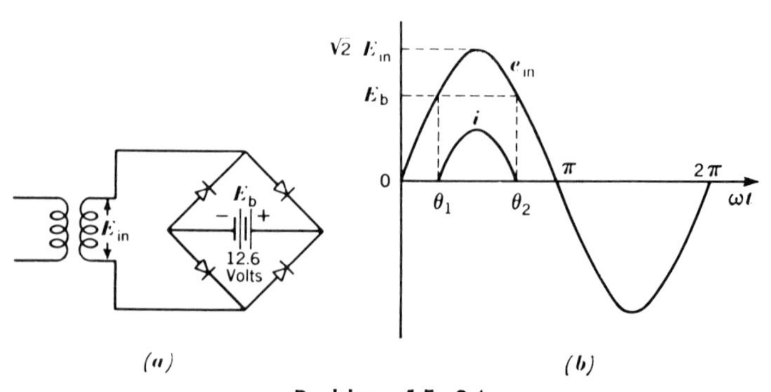

Problem 15–34.

Solution: (a) The circuit is shown in (*a*) above. Since the forward voltage drop

V_f is given in rms terms, V_f will not be assumed constant; however, the forward resistance R_f will be assumed constant.

$$I_{dc} = (2/\pi)I_m, \quad 10 = (2/\pi)I_m, \quad \text{and} \quad I_m = 15.71 \text{ amp, peak.}$$

Then

$$I = \frac{15.71}{\sqrt{2}} = 11.11 \text{ amp rms} \qquad R_f = \frac{V_f}{I} = \frac{2}{11.11} = 0.180 \text{ ohm}$$

The internal resistance of the battery will be assumed negligible. The waveform of e_{in} and the current wave for one pair of the elements is shown in (*b*) above, where $\sin\theta_1 = \sin\theta_2 = E_b/\sqrt{2}E_{in}$, where $\theta_2 = \pi - \theta_1$. For each cycle:

$$i = \frac{\sqrt{2}E_{in}\sin\omega t - E_b}{2R_f} \quad \text{when } \theta_1 \leq \omega t \leq \theta_2 \qquad i = 0 \text{ when } \theta_1 \geq \omega t \geq \theta_2$$

$$I_{dc} = \frac{1}{2\pi}\int_{\theta_1}^{\theta_2} \frac{\sqrt{2}E_{in}\sin\omega t - E_b}{2R_f}\,d(\omega t) = \frac{1}{4\pi R_f}\left[\sqrt{2}E_{in}(-\cos\omega t)\Big|_{\theta_1}^{\theta_2} - E_b(\omega t)\Big|_{\theta_1}^{\theta_2}\right]$$

$$I_{dc} = \frac{1}{4\pi R_f}\left\{\sqrt{2}E_{in}[-\cos(\pi - \theta_1) + \cos\theta_1] - E_b(\pi - \theta_1 - \theta_1)\right\}$$

$$I_{dc} = \frac{1}{4\pi R_f}\left\{2\sqrt{2}E_{in}\cos\left[\sin^{-1}\left(\frac{E_b}{\sqrt{2}E_{in}}\right)\right] - E_b\left[\pi - 2\sin^{-1}\left(\frac{E_b}{\sqrt{2}E_{in}}\right)\right]\right\}$$

$$10 = \frac{1}{4\pi(0.18)}\left\{2\sqrt{2}E_{in}\cos\left[\sin^{-1}\left(\frac{12.6}{\sqrt{2}E_{in}}\right)\right] - 12.6\left[\pi - 2\sin^{-1}\left(\frac{12.6}{\sqrt{2}E_{in}}\right)\right]\right\}$$

$$E_{in} = 20.2 \text{ volts rms}$$

$$V_{f\,max} = I_{max}R_f = \tfrac{1}{2}(\sqrt{2}E_{in} - E_b) = \frac{\sqrt{2}(20.2) - 12.6}{2} = 8.00 \text{ volts}$$

$$V_{R\,max} = E_b + V_{f\,max} = 12.6 + 8.00 = 20.6 \text{ volts}$$

the maximum inverse peak voltage on each element.

(b) Approved, because the maximum inverse peak voltage is less than the maximum rating.

15–35. Consider a simple electronic voltage-regulator circuit consisting of a resistor R in series with a cold-cathode gaseous glow tube connected across a d-c supply whose voltage varies from 275 to 380 volts; the load, connected across the tube, requires 40 ma at 150 volts. The normal operating current range of the tube is 5 to 40 ma, and the nominal tube drop is 150 volts. Can the circuit be made to function properly under the stated conditions? If so, between what limits must R lie, and if not, why?

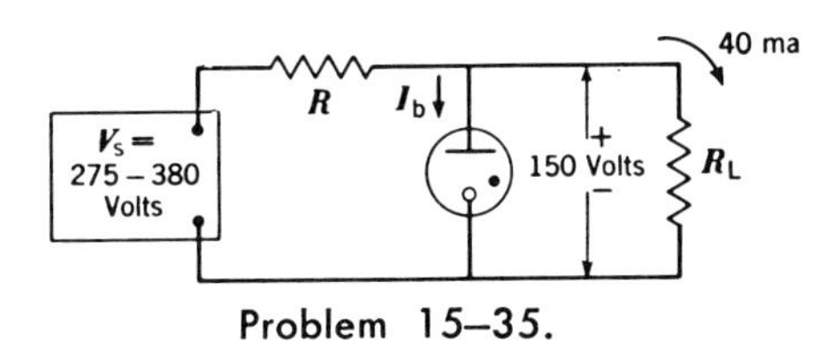

Problem 15–35.

Solution: The circuit is as shown above. The lower current limit of the tube should be reached when the lower limit of the supply voltage occurs for maximum utilization of the operating range of the tube. That is, $I_b = 5$ ma when $V_s = 275$ volts. To find R for these conditions, $275 = 150 + [(40+5) \times 10^{-3}]R$; $R = 2780$ ohms. To check the necessary tube current to maintain 150 volts across the load when the supply voltage reaches the maximum limit, $380 = 150 + (2780)\ (0.040 + I_b)$; $I_{b\text{-max}} = 42.8$ ma. Since the necessary range of the tube current to maintain 150 volts across the load is greater than the operating range of the tube, this circuit will not function properly.

15–36. A vacuum tube is to be operated in a grounded-cathode amplifier circuit with a d-c plate voltage E_b of 250 volts, a grid bias of -10 volts (obtained by a cathode resistor adequately bypassed by a large capacitor), and a d-c plate current of 2.5 ma. The tube "constants" under these conditions are $\mu = 20$, $r_p = 10{,}000$ ohms, and $g_m = 2000$ μmhos. The impedance in the plate circuit is $4000 + j10{,}000$ ohms at the frequency corresponding to that of the impressed signal voltage E_g of 1.0 rms volt. Compute (magnitudes only) the a-c signal output voltage E_o and the d-c plate-supply voltage E_{bb}.

15–37. A triode voltage amplifier has a transconductance of 900 μmhos, a plate resistance of 10,000 ohms, a load resistor of 25,000 ohms, and an output capacitance of 15 $\mu\mu$f. Determine (a) the amplification at a frequency of 100 kc and (b) the high frequency where the amplification is 12 db below the maximum to be found as a function of frequency.

15–38. The connections of a two-stage, resistance-coupled, audio amplifier are shown in the diagram. Both tubes have an amplification factor of 20 and a dynamic plate resistance of 10,000 ohms. Determine (a) the mid-frequency voltage gain, (b) the voltage gain for an audio frequency of 100 cps (assuming the cathode bypass capacitors to have zero reactance at this frequency), and (c) the mid-frequency gain if 1/200 of the output voltage is introduced into the input circuit 180° out of phase with E_{in}. Will the feedback in part (c) have any effect on the output impedance of the amplifier?

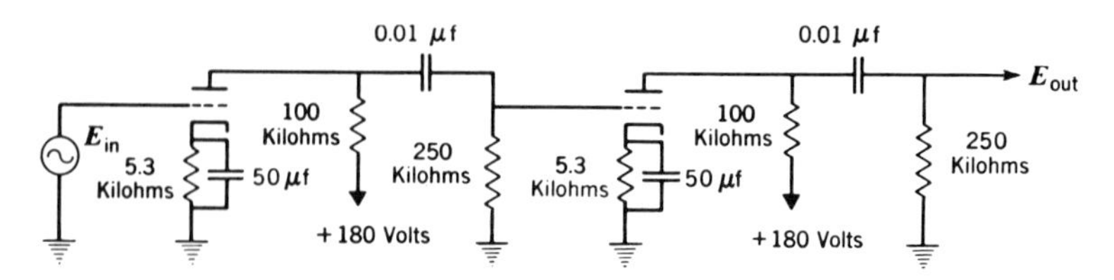

Problem 15–38.

15–39. The load line of a triode for a load resistance of 5000 ohms and an E_{bb} of 500 volts passes through the static plate characteristic curves at the following points:

E_g, volts....	0	−30	−60
E_p, volts....	249	387	492

Operation is such that $E_c = -30$ volts, and E_g is a sine wave having an rms value of 21.2 volts with $E_{bb} = 500$ volts. Determine (a) the second-harmonic component in the a-c plate-current output, (b) the plate dissipation in the triode, (c) the power supplied to the load, and (d) the amplification, or gain.

15–40. Diagram a class C r-f amplifier using a resonant circuit in the plate circuit; include provisions for neutralizing the feedback that occurs through the grid-plate capacitance. Assuming a sinusoidal grid-excitation voltage, sketch the waveform of plate current and output voltage. Justify the waveform relationship that exists between plate current and output voltage.

15–41. The r-f amplifier stage shown in the figure employs a pentode having a mutual conductance of 1200 μmhos and a plate resistance of 1 megohm. The tuning inductance L has a value of 1500 μh and a Q factor of 50 at the operating frequency, $f = 10^6/2\pi$ cps. The capacitor C_1 has a value of 0.002 μf, and C is the variable tuning capacitor. All the other capacitors shown have negligible reactances. The resistor R_1 has a value of 50,000 ohms. Calculate the gain of this stage when it is tuned to the operating frequency.

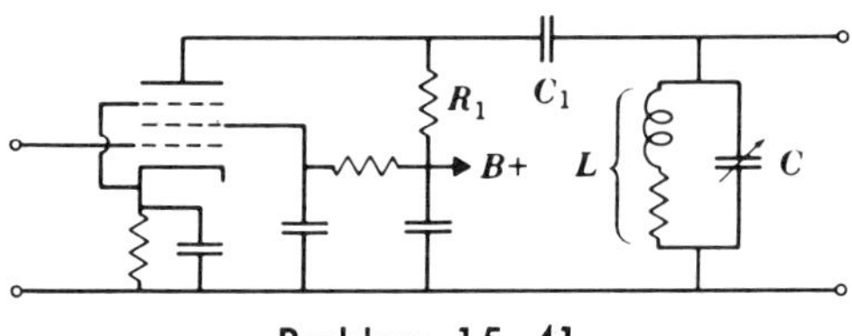

Problem 15–41.

15–42. (a) The gain of an amplifier is 60 with the feedback circuit in shunt with the plate circuit but no feedback voltage injected into the grid circuit. When the feedback voltage is injected into the grid circuit, the gain drops to 10. What is the percentage feedback? (b) In another amplifier the feedback is 50 per cent. What is the approximate gain?

15–43. In the triode circuit diagram shown, the capacitors C have negligible reactance at the operating frequency. The μ factor of the tube is 5, and its plate resistance is 3000 ohms. Calculate the rms open-circuit voltages E_{oa}, E_{ob}, and E_{ba} when the input voltage e is 50 volts rms and the operation of the circuit is class A.

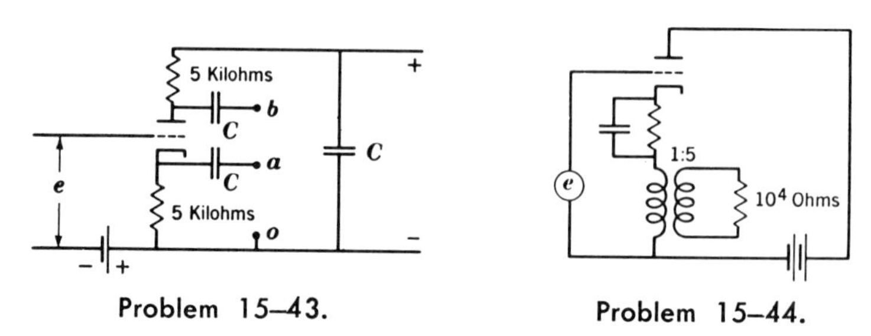

Problem 15–43.

Problem 15–44.

15–44. The power amplifier shown in the diagram is to deliver 5 watts to the 10,000-ohm load by way of the output transformer, which has a turns ratio of 1:5 and may be considered as ideal. The amplification factor of the tube is 3, and its plate resistance is 800 ohms. Calculate the rms value of the input voltage e under the conditions of class A operation.

15–45. In the amplifier shown in the diagram the tube used is a linear triode having a μ factor of 8 and a plate resistance of 1800 ohms. The quiescent current of this tube is 0.050 amp. The output transformer is ideal and has a turns ratio N_1/N_2 of 25. The reactance of C, at the frequency of the signal, is negligible. Neglecting distortion and its effects, calculate (a) the power delivered to the 8-ohm load, (b) the power dissipation in each resistor, and (c) the plate dissipation.

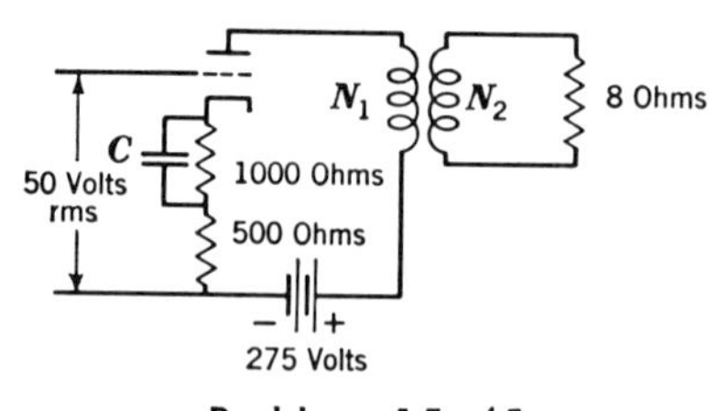

Problem 15–45.

15–46. What should be the rms current ratings of the Y-connected secondary windings of a transformer supplying a three-phase half-wave rectifier supplying I d-c amperes to a load? Neglect losses.

15–47. A half-wave, grid-controlled thyratron rectifier is supplied directly from a 440-volt line, and the load is a pure resistance. Firing of the tube is delayed, by grid action, 90° after the anode voltage passes through zero in the positive direction. Carefully sketch, one above the other to compare phase relationships, the waveforms of (a) the voltage across the load and (b) the voltage across the tube. What is the average (d-c) voltage across the load?

15–48. Given a phase-shift control circuit for a thyratron as shown in the diagram. (a) Using a circle diagram explain how the average value of plate current I_b can be changed by adjusting R. (b) What happens if R and L are interchanged? Explain.

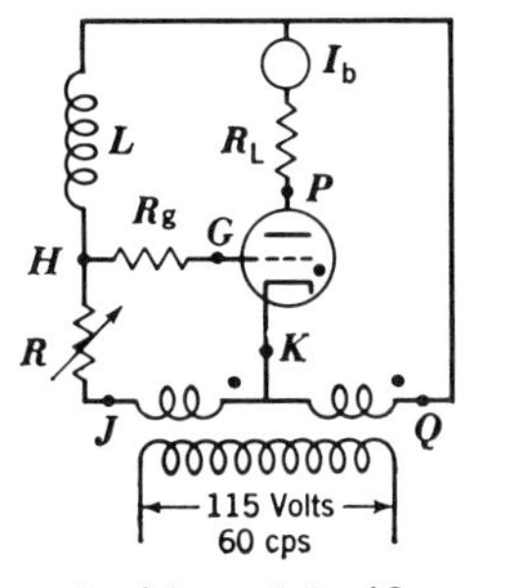

Problem 15–48.

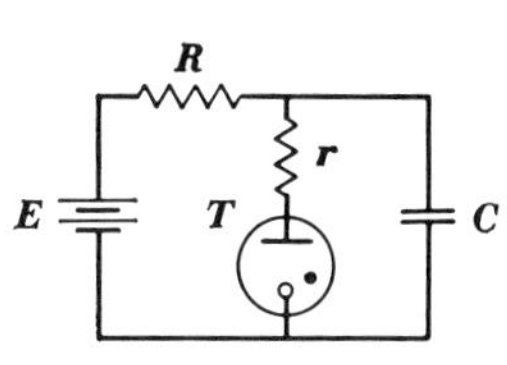

Problem 15–49.

15–49. The gas regulator tube T shown in the diagram ceases to conduct when the current through it falls below 0.001 amp. For currents higher than this value, the tube drop is constant at 15 volts. In order to initiate conduction in T, 100 volts across it is required. Calculate the frequency of the sawtooth wave available across the capacitor C when the circuit constants are $E=200$ volts, $R=0.5$ megohm, $r=100$ ohms, and $C=0.1$ μf.

15–50. The equation of an amplitude-modulated wave is $e=100(1+0.85 \sin 628{,}320\, t)(\sin 2{,}200{,}000\, t)$. Determine the per cent modulation, the carrier frequency, the frequency of the upper side band, the frequency of the lower side band, the maximum magnitude, and that of the upper side band.

15–51. (a) Consider a 60-cps sinusoidal voltage to be applied to the vertical-deflection amplifier of a cathode-ray oscilloscope and a 180-cps sinusoidal wave to be applied to the horizontal-deflection amplifier; sketch the resulting trace that appears on the tube face. (b) Consider the sinusoidal waves of the same frequency to be applied to the vertical- and horizontal-deflection amplifiers of the cathode-ray oscilloscope; if these voltages are approximately 45° out of phase with each other, sketch the resulting trace that appears on the tube face.

15–52. The equivalent circuit of the transistor shown has the following characteristics: Emitter resistance (r_e) 20 ohms, base resistance (r_b) 500 ohms, collector resistance (r_c) 1 megohm, $a =$ 0.98. Calculate the hybrid parameters in the following equations: $v_e = h_{11}\, i_e + h_{12}\, v_c$; $i = h_{21}\, i_e + h_{22}\, v_c$.

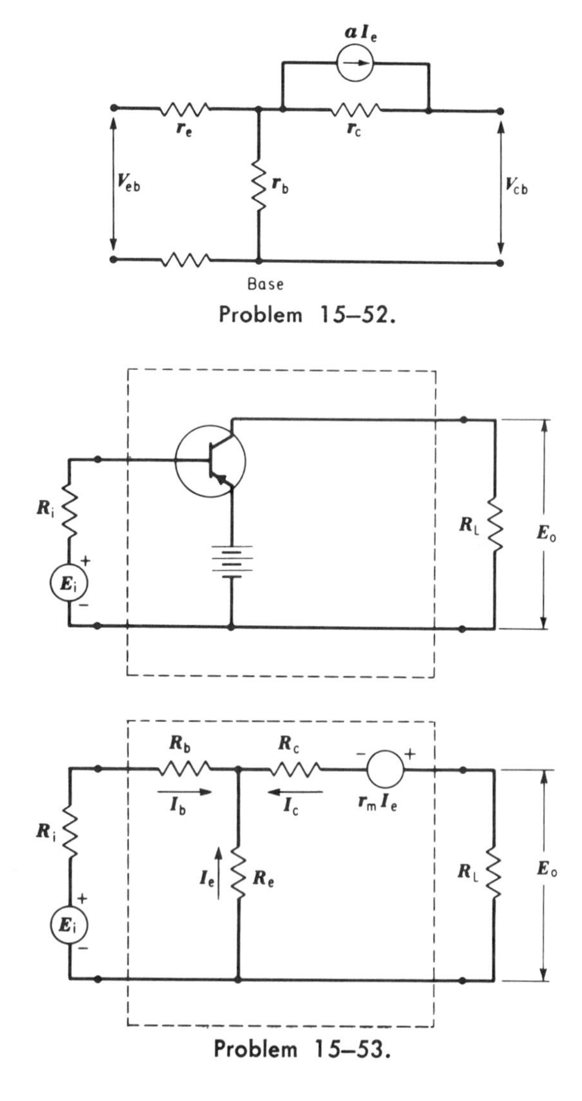

Problem 15–52.

Problem 15–53.

15–53. The transistor amplifier shown in the first figure is represented by the equivalent circuit of the second figure. The a-c signal source, E_i, is assumed to have zero internal impedance. The equivalent circuit omits quiescent conditions, and treats only the a-c components. In the equivalent circuit, $r_m I_e$ is a dependent voltage source. Derive the voltage gain of the amplifier.

15–54. For the npn junction-type transistor having characteristics as listed, and for common-collector type application, find the numerical values for the: (a) incremental input resistances when the incremental load resistance is zero and when it is infinity; (b) incremental output resistances when the incremental resistance of the signal-voltage sources is zero and when it is infinity; (c) matched input resistance; (d) maximum available power gain. $I_e = -1.0$ ma, $I_c = 1.0$ ma, $V_e = -0.1$ volt, $V_e = 4.5$ volt, $r_e = 25.9$ ohms, $r_c = 13.4 \times 10^6$ ohms, $r_b = 240$ ohms, $r_m = 13.1 \times 10^6$ ohms.

15–55. Calculate the power gain of the two-stage amplifier shown. Give the gain of the two individual stages, the interstage losses and the pre-first stage losses. The common-base h parameters for the transistors used in both stages are $h_{ib} = 50$ ohms; $h_{rb} = 5 \times 10^{-4}$; $h_{fb} = -0.97$; and $h\ _b = 10^{-6}$ mho.

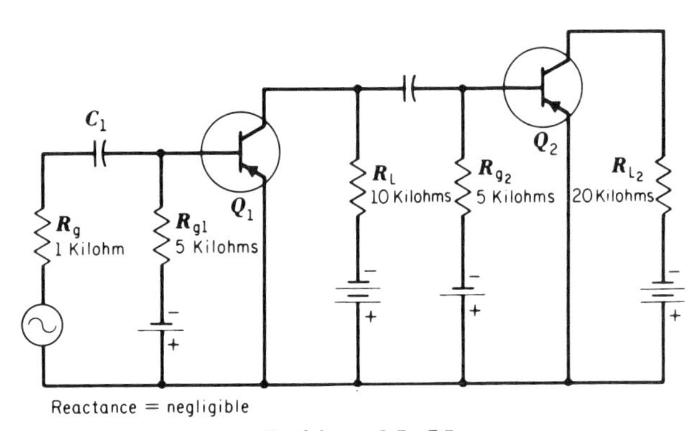

Problem 15–55.

15–56. Using the equivalent circuit for the transistor shown in the diagram, develop an expression for the mid-frequency voltage gain e_o/e_i of the amplifier also shown in the diagram.

15–57. In a simple feedback circuit shown, all capacitors may be considered short-circuited for a-c voltage. Give an incremental model of this circuit, using the low frequency current-source representation for the tube. Assume e_s is given. Solving the node equations for the equivalent circuit found above, calculate the gain (e_o/e_s) and the input conductance (i_s/e_s) for tube parameters $g_m = 5000\ \mu$mohs, $r_p = 10$ kilohms, and resistances $R_1 - 50$ kilohms, $R_2 = 200$ kilohms, and $R_3 = 50$ kilohms.

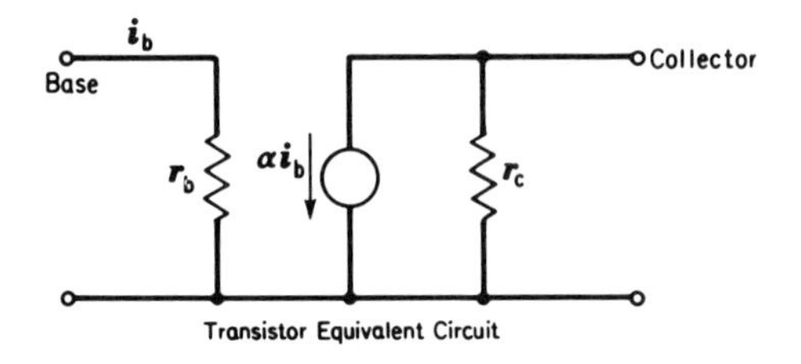

Transistor Equivalent Circuit

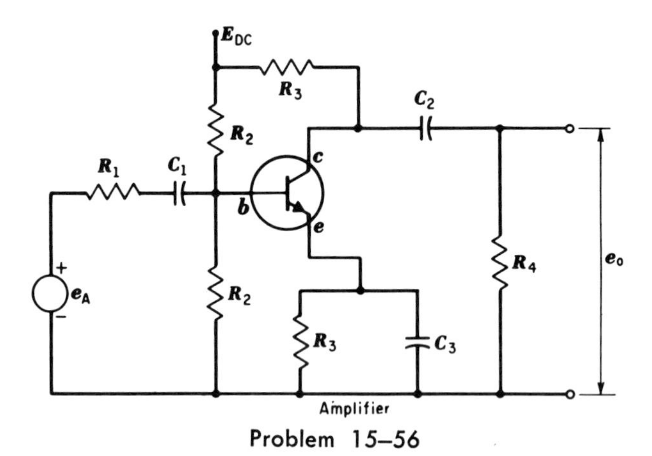

Amplifier

Problem 15–56

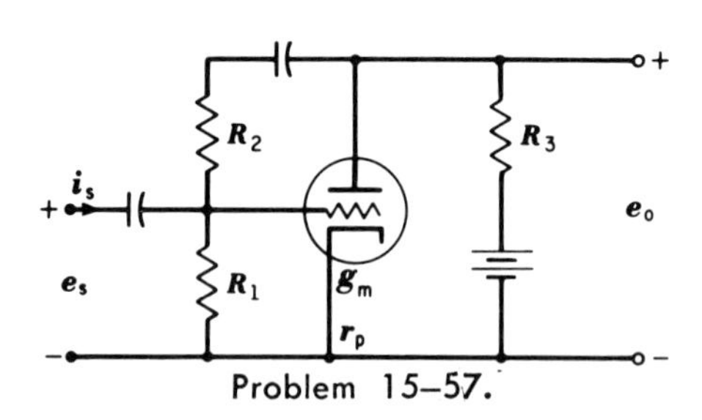

Problem 15–57.

15–58. In the circuit shown, capacitor C is large enough to short-circuit the resistor R_E effectively at the oscillating frequency. (a) Determine the minimum value of R_B to produce oscillation. (b) What is the frequency of oscillation in the circuit as shown? (c) If all other values remain the same, what is the minimum value of R_B to produce oscillations if: (1) R_c is changed to 10 kilohms? (2) R_c is changed to 100 kilohms? (c) $h_{12} = 10^{-2}$? Amplitude of oscillation is not required; therefore linear calculations may be used for all solutions. Point contact resistor data: $r_e = 120$ ohms, $r_b = 16$ ohms, $r_c = 13{,}000$ ohms, $\alpha = 2.5$.

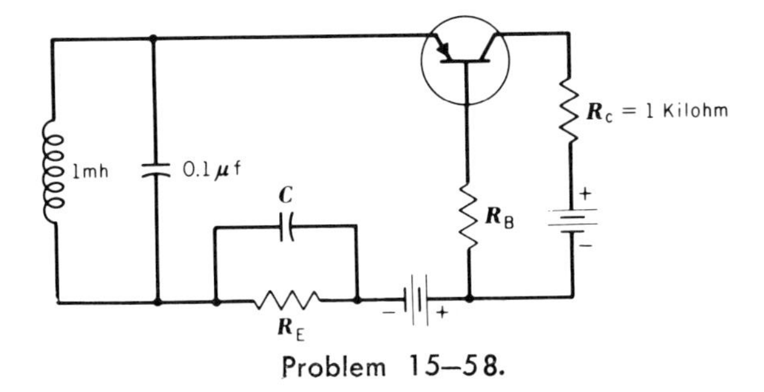

Problem 15–58.

15–59. A silicon-controlled rectifier (SCR) is to be installed to supply an inductive d-c load of 20 amp at 10kv through a 3-phase, full-wave bridge. (a) What is the required average current rating of each leg of the SCR? (b) What is the a-c input line voltage without allowance for loss? (c) What is the forward blocking voltage required of the SCR? (d) Assuming the device is supplied by 275-kva, 20 per cent impedance transformer, what is the required one-cycle surge rating of the SCR?

15–60. Find the thermal and plate shot-effect noise voltage across R_L in the figure for $R = 0$ and 5000 ohms, $R_L = 20{,}000$ ohms, $r_p = 7700$ ohms, $g_m = 2600$ μmhos, bandwidth $= 10$ kc, temperature $= 25°$C, and noise parameter $= 0.75$.

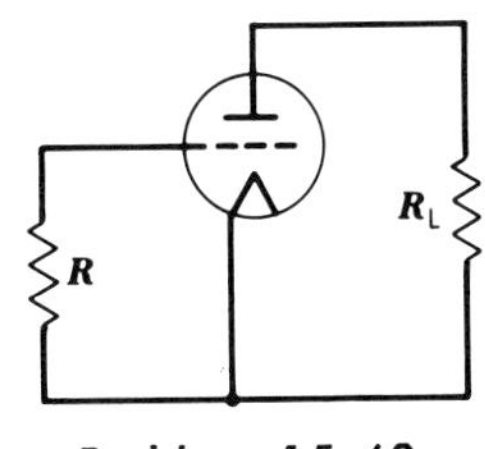

Problem 15–60.

15–61. A suppressed carrier amplitude-modulated signal has the expression: $e = (100 \cos 50t)(\cos 1000t)$. What is the carrier-level injection needed to produce a 50 per cent modulated amplitude-modulated signal?

15–62. The circuit shown is used to supply d-c power to a resistance and a capacitance in parallel. (a) What transformer ratio is necessary to produce an output voltage of 300 volts d-c? (b) What are the peak and average diode currents? (c) What is the ripple factor across the load?

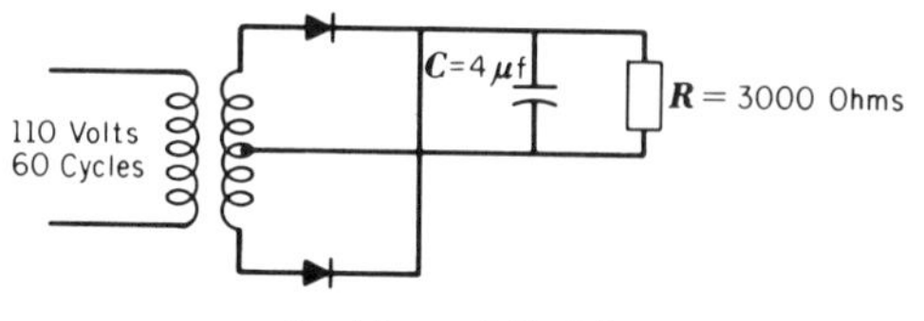

Problem 15–62.

15–63. A 96-MC carrier, whose peak amplitude is 100 volts, is frequency-modulated by a 10,000 cycle sinusoid so that the frequency deviation is 70 kc. (a) Determine the peak amplitudes of all side frequencies up to the 11th pair. (b) Determine the overall bandwidth. (c) Make a rough sketch of the frequency spectrum. (d) Calculate the phase angle of the FM carrier.

15–64. The open loop transfer function for a control system is approximated by $G(s) = \frac{C(s)}{E(s)} = K\frac{s-3}{(s-0.5)\,(s+7)}$. It is desired to make the output signal C correspond as nearly as possible to some input signal R in steady state, at the same time keeping the system stable. (a) Sketch a block diagram for a feedback control system to accomplish the given objective. Carefully label the summation polarity of all signals coming into the feedback junction summing point. (b) Select a value of K which assures system stability and at the same time brings the ratio C/R in steady state as close to 1.0 as possible. [Note the properties of $G(s)$ are such that it is advisable to make a check on the requirements for closed-loop system stability.]

15–65. For the block diagram shown, (a) find the closed-loop transfer function $C(s)/R(s)$. (b) What type of system is this? (c) What is the velocity-error constant K_1 ? (d) If the input to the system $r(t) = t$ radian, what will be the steady-state error? Solve for your answer by use of K_1 . (e) Sketch the root locus for this control system. Do not compute the breakaway point, just estimate it. Use a scale of 1 in. = 2 units for the root-loci sketches.

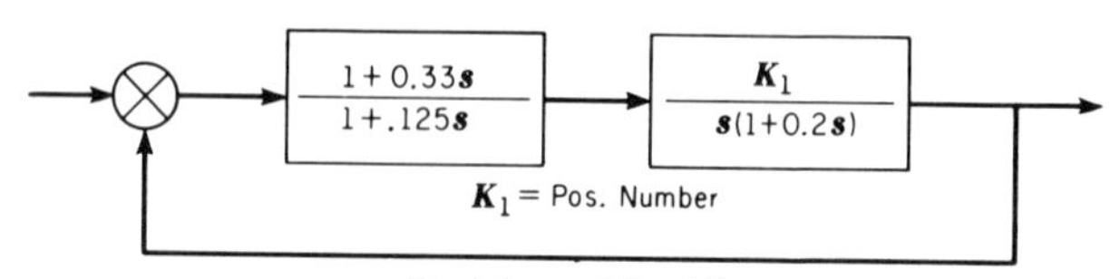

Problem 15–65.

ILLUMINATION

15–66. The dimensions of a drafting room are 62 ft × 25 ft with a ceiling height of 12 ft. The fixtures are to be suspended 2 ft below the ceiling (center line of lamps 10 ft above the floor). The tops of the drafting tables are 4 ft above the floor. The intensity of illumination on the working surface is to be 80 foot-candles. Assume the use of two-lamp fluorescent lighting fixtures with a utilization factor of 0.57 and a maintenance factor of 0.7; use 40-watt lamps with a lumen output rating of 2600 lumens. (a) How many lighting fixtures are required? (b) Make a scale layout (⅛″=1′-0″) of the floor plan showing fixture locations, branch-circuit wiring, and switching.

Solution: (a)

$$\text{Foot-candles (avg)} = \frac{\dfrac{\text{lumens}}{\text{lamp}}\left(\dfrac{\text{lamps}}{\text{fixture}}\right)(\text{no. of fixtures})(\text{coef. of util.})(\text{main. factor})}{\text{area (sq ft)}}$$

$$80 = \frac{2600(2)(\text{no. of fixtures})(0.57)(0.7)}{62 \times 25}$$

No. of fixtures = 60

(b) The floor plan is shown in the accompanying diagram.

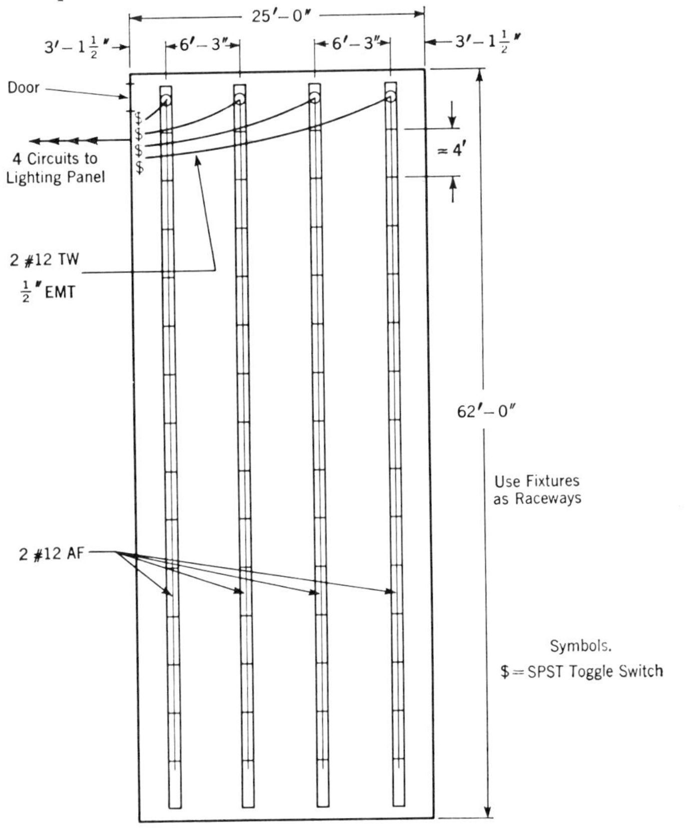

Problem 15–66.

15–67. Four lamps are located outdoors in a row with a horizontal separation of 32 ft between adjacent lamps. The ground level is horizontal. The lamps are all 12 ft above the ground. The candle power of each lamp may be taken as 1000 in any pertinent direction. Determine the horizontal illumination at a point on the ground midway between the two center lamps and directly under the row of lamps.

15–68. A certain point A is illuminated by a spotlight and a floodlight located as shown in (*a*) of the illustration and having candlepower curves as given on the graph in (*b*) of the illustration. What is the illumination on the horizontal surface at A, in foot-candles?

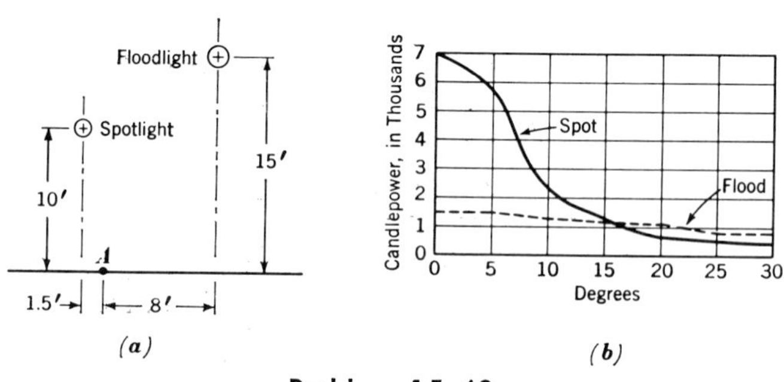

Problem 15–68.

15–69. A floodlighting system was designed to produce a certain average illumination. The projectors were to have clear lenses, and clear 1000-watt lamps were to be used on a circuit voltage of 115 volts. In the actual installation, 750-watt 120-volt lamps were used, and these were the only changes. Determine the resulting illumination in percentage of the design value. Assume that 1000-watt lamps give 21,500 lumens and that 750-watt lamps give 15,500 lumens, both at rated voltage.

15–70. An incandescent lamp which radiates light approximately uniformly in its lower hemisphere is located 12 ft directly above a foot-candle meter, which is facing upward and is reading 26 foot-candles. If the meter is moved horizontally 9 ft and continues to face upward, what will it read? Assume no other source of light and negligible reflection.

15–71. An aircraft assembly room is 200 ft × 300 ft × 40 ft. Fluorescent light reflectors with two lamps each are mounted 35 ft from the floor. Lamps are rated 5050 initial lumens. Part of the data on the fixture includes: Efficiency = 79 per cent, average maintenance factor = 65 per cent (RLM Standard Industrial Reflector). Determine the number of luminaires to give a time-average illumination of 40 footcandles 3 ft above the floor.

15–72. When tested in a distribution photometer, a luminaire gave the following results:

Lower Hemisphere		Upper Hemisphere	
Degrees	Candlepower	Degrees	Candlepower
0 (nadir)	100	90	59 (checkpoint)
10	98	100	56
20	95	110	58
30	89	120	64
40	82	130	70
50	77	140	74
60	68	150	80
70	64	160	81
80	60	170	82
90	58	180	80

What is the lumen output of the luminaire?

15–73. Design a lighting system for a room 50 ft × 100 ft with a 9-ft ceiling. Reflector factor of the ceiling is 75 per cent, walls 50 per cent. Use semi-direct fluorescent luminaires, louvered type with luminous side panels on ceiling, with 40-watt T-12 cool-white (2800 lumens). Maintenance conditions are good. Level of illumination to be 50 foot-candles 30 in. from floor. Determine the lumens required, lamps required, and an arrangement.

MACHINERY

15–74. The saturation curve at 1200 rpm of a certain self-excited, shunt-wound, d-c generator may be approximated, for the purposes of this problem, by the two lines shown in the figure. At

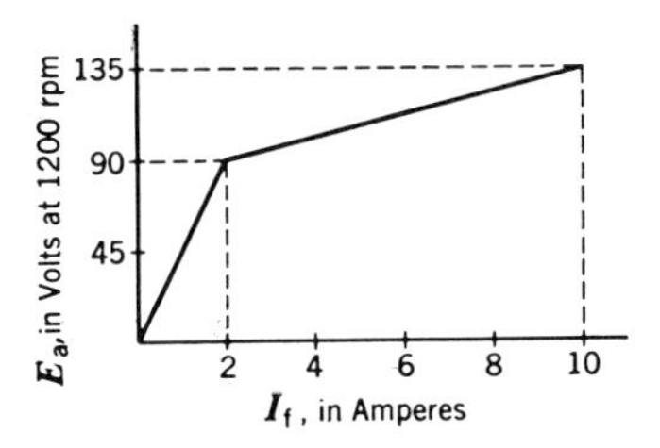

Problem 15–74.

what speed must this machine be operated in order to yield an open-circuit voltage of 130 volts when the resistance of the shunt field circuit is 21.67 ohms?

Solution: On open circuit $E_a \approx V_T$. If the generator is to build up to 130 volts, then the field current $I_f = 130/21.67 = 6.00$ amp. According to the saturation curve, $E_a = 113$ volts when $I_f = 6.00$ amp at 1200 rpm. If $E_a = K\phi N$, then $E_a = K'N$ if ϕ is constant as it is on a constant I_f line. Therefore,

$$\frac{E_{a1}}{E_{a2}} = \frac{N_1}{N_2} \qquad \frac{113}{130} = \frac{1200}{N_2} \qquad N_2 = 1380 \text{ rpm}$$

15–75. A 230-volt shunt motor runs at 1600 rpm at both full load and no load. Under full-load conditions the armature current is 50.0 amp. There are 1000 turns on each of four poles in the shunt-field winding. The armature is lap-wound, and the measured terminal-to-terminal armature resistance is 0.15 ohm with full-load armature current. The interpole circuit has a resistance of 0.05 ohm. At 1600 rpm the magnetization curve is given by the following:

E_a, volts.......	200	210	220	230	240	250
I_f, amperes.....	0.80	0.88	0.97	1.10	1.22	1.43

(a) How is it possible that the full-load speed equals the no-load speed? (b) A cumulative series field having five turns per pole and a total resistance of 0.05 ohm is to be added to the machine. A long-shunt connection is to be used. What will be the new full-load speed at rated voltage?

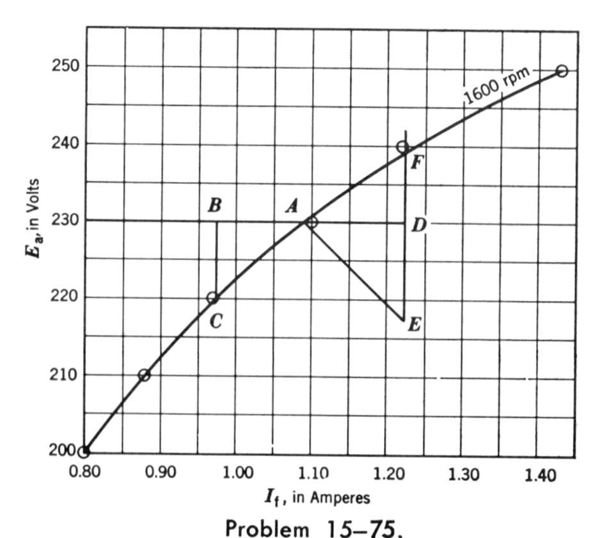

Problem 15–75.

Solution: (a) This is possible owing to a certain amount of demagnetization in the magnetic field. The amount of demagnetization necessary can be found as follows: At full load the total voltage drop in the armature is $I_a(R_a+R_i)=50(0.15+0.05)=10$ volts. This determines the vertical side BC of the load triangle ABC shown in the figure. The horizontal side AB represents the demagnetization and measures 0.117 amp with respect to the I_f scale. Since there are 1000 turns per pole in the shunt field, this is equivalent to $1000(0.117)=117$ amp-turns of demagnetization per pole.

(b) The full-load armature drop is $I_a(R_a+R_i+R_s)=50(0.15+0.05+0.05)=$ 12.5 volts; this is side DE of load triangle ADE. At full load the increase in excitation due to the 5 turns per pole of cumulative series field is $5(50)=250$ amp-turns. The net increase is

$$\frac{(250-117)\text{ amp-turns}}{1000\text{ turns}}=0.133\text{ amp}$$

referred to the I_f scale. This is side AD of triangle ADE. Point E represents the E_a ($=217.5$ volts) necessary to satisfy the voltage equation at full load; point F represents the E_a ($=239.3$ volts) generated at 1600 rpm and with the same excitation as point E. Therefore,

$$\frac{217.5}{239.3}=\frac{N}{1600} \qquad N=1454\text{ rpm}$$

15–76. A 100-kva 60-cycle 2400/240-volt transformer yields the following test data when excited on the low side:

	V	I	P
(1) High side open	240	32	600
(2) High side short-circuited....	15	417	800

Determine (a) efficiency and (b) voltage regulation when operating at full load and 0.8 power factor lag.

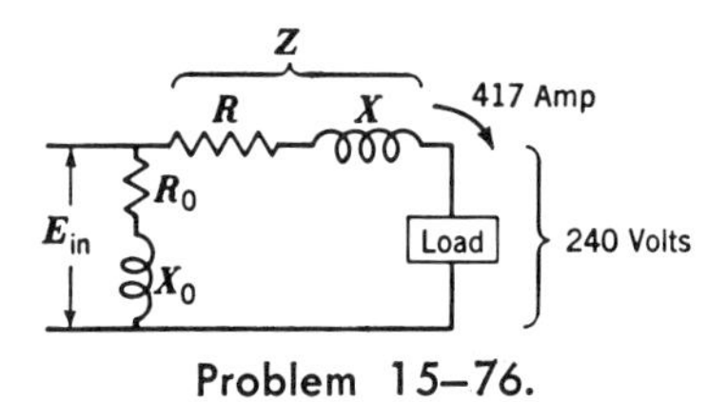

Problem 15–76.

Solution:

(a) Low side $I_{FL}=10^5/214=417$ amp. From measurement 1, core loss $=600$ watts (assumed constant for all loads); from measurement 2, full-load copper loss $=800$ watts. Total full-load losses $=1.4$ kw.

$$P_{out}=(100\text{ kva})(0.8)=80\text{ kw} \qquad \text{Efficiency}=\frac{P_{out}}{P_{in}}$$

$$P_{in}=P_{out}+\text{losses}=81.4\text{ kw} \qquad \text{Efficiency}=\frac{80}{81.4}=98.3\text{ per cent}$$

(b) To find R and X of the equivalent circuit shown in the diagram, the data of measurement 2 are used:

$$I^2R=P \qquad (417)^2R=800 \qquad R=0.00460 \text{ ohm}$$

$$|Z|=\frac{V}{I}$$

$$|Z|=\frac{15}{417}=0.0360 \text{ ohm} \qquad \cos^{-1}\left(\frac{0.00460}{0.0360}\right)=82.66°$$

$$Z=0.0360\underline{/82.66°} \text{ ohm}$$

$$E_{\text{in}}=240\underline{/0°}+(417\underline{/-36.9°})(0.036\underline{/82.66°})$$

$$E_{\text{in}}=V_L+IZ$$

$$|E_{\text{in}}|=251 \text{ volts}$$

$$\text{Regulation}=\frac{(E_{\text{in}} \text{ at full load})-(\text{rated } E_{\text{in}})}{\text{rated } E_{\text{in}}}$$

$$\text{Regulation}=\frac{251-240}{240}=4.6 \text{ per cent}$$

15–77. A turboalternator is Y-connected and rated at 40,000 kw, 0.8 power factor, and 13,800 volts. It has a synchronous reactance of 3.0 ohms per phase and a resistance of 0.4 ohm per phase. (a) How much excitation is required to deliver its name-plate rating? (b) If the excitation found in part (a) is not changed, how much current would be delivered to a three-phase short circuit at the terminals?

Solution: $P=\sqrt{3}V_LI_L(\text{pf})$, $4\times10^7=\sqrt{3}(13{,}800)I_L(0.8)$, $I_L=I_a=2090$ amp. $V_P=V_L/\sqrt{3}=13{,}800/\sqrt{3}=7970$ volts.

(a)
$$E_g=V_P+I_aZ=7970\underline{/0°}+(2090\underline{/-36.9°})(0.4+j3.0)$$

$$|E_g|=13{,}200 \text{ volts/phase}$$

(b)
$$I_s=\frac{13{,}200}{0.4+j3.0} \qquad |I_s|=4360 \text{ amp/line}$$

15–78. A 15-kva 230-volt 6-pole 60-cycle three-phase Y-connected synchronous motor has the following constants: effective armature resistance per phase, 0.15 ohm; armature leakage reactance per phase, 1.2 ohms. Determine the counter emf of the motor at rated current (a) when the power factor is unity, (b) when the power factor is 0.80 lagging, and (c) when the power factor is 0.80 leading.

Solution: $V_T=E_g+I_aZ_a \qquad E_g=V_T-I_aZ_a \qquad VA=\sqrt{3}V_LI_L$

$$I_a=I_L=\frac{1.5\times10^4}{\sqrt{3}(230)}=37.6 \text{ amp} \qquad V_T=\frac{230}{\sqrt{3}}=132.8 \text{ volts/phase}$$

(a)
$$E_g=132.8\underline{/0°}-(37.6\underline{/0°})(0.15+j1.2)=132.8-5.6-j45.1 \qquad |E_g|=135 \text{ volts/phase}$$

(b) $E_g = 132.8\underline{/36.9°} - 5.6 - j45.1$ $|E_g| = 106$ volts/phase

(c) $E_g = 132.8\underline{/-36.9°} - 5.6 - j45.1$ $|E_g| = 160$ volts/phase

15–79. A 10-hp 550-volt 60-cps three-phase induction motor has a starting torque of 160 per cent full-load torque and a starting current of 425 per cent full-load current. (a) What voltage is required to limit the starting current to full-load value ? (b) If the motor is used on a 440-volt 60-cps system, what is the starting torque and starting current expressed in per cent of full-load value?

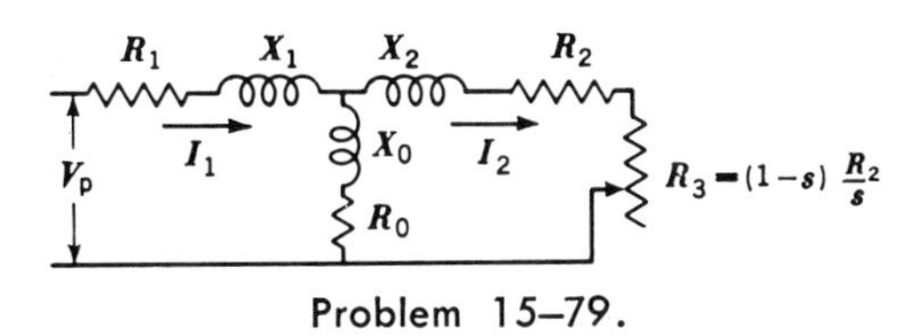

Problem 15–79.

Solution: Referring to the equivalent circuit diagram shown, it can be seen that the starting current will be directly proportional to the phase voltage, V_p since the starting value of slip s is unity. $I_{1s} = KV_p$.

(a) $\dfrac{550}{\sqrt{3}(4.25I_{FL})} = \dfrac{V_L}{\sqrt{3}(1.00I_{FL})}$ $V_L = 129$ volts, line-to-line

(b) $\dfrac{550}{\sqrt{3}(4.25I_{FL})} = \dfrac{440}{\sqrt{3}(I_{FL})}$ $\bar{X}_L = 3.40$, 340 per cent full-load current

Since torque is directly proportional to rotor input, $T_s = KI_2{}^2(R_2 + R_3)$. If the voltage drop across the primary impedance, $R_1 + jX_1$, is assumed negligible, $T_s = KV_p{}^2$.

$\dfrac{1.60T_{FL}}{(550/\sqrt{3})^2} = \dfrac{XT_{FL}}{(440/\sqrt{3})^2}$ $X = 1.02$, 102 per cent full-load torque

15–80. A six-pole 250-kw 250-volt d-c generator has a simplex lap winding on its armature. It is reconnected as a duplex lap winding. (a) Give the voltage, current, and kilowatt rating under the new conditions. (b) What changes, if any, would have to be made in the shunt-field connections?

15–81. The shunt-field winding of a six-pole 125-volt d-c generator has 500 turns per pole and carries 12.5 amp; the resistance of the field winding is 7.5 ohms and the resistance of the field rheostat is $(125/12.5) - 7.5 = 2.5$ ohms; and the flux per pole is 6.3×10^6 lines. Determine the following: (a) the inductance of the field winding, (b) the time taken by the current to reach one-tenth full value and one-half full value, after the field switch is closed, (c) the initial rise of voltage, if the field circuit carrying a current of 12.5 amp is instantaneously closed through a resistance of 25 ohms, (d) the energy stored in the magnetic field when the current is 12.5 amp.

15–82. (a) Sketch speed and torque curves for d-c shunt, cumulative compound, and differential compound motors. (b) Discuss three methods of speed control for d-c motors. (c) A 220-volt 10-hp 1200-rpm d-c shunt motor has an armature resistance of 0.05 ohms (including brush-contact resistance). With an applied voltage of 220 volts and a total shunt-field circuit resistance of 150 ohms, the motor delivers 10 hp at 1175 rpm. Under this load its efficiency is 88 per cent. Calculate the motor speed when the load is decreased to a value such that the motor draws 12 amp from the line. (Neglect armature reaction.)

15–83. The resistance of the armature of a 250-volt series motor is 0.18 ohm, and the resistance of the field is 0.10 ohm. When the motor takes 80 amp from the line, the speed is 600 rpm. Determine the speed when the current is 40 amp. Neglect saturation and the demagnetizing effect of armature reaction.

15–84. Each pole of a four-pole d-c machine covers 16 armature slots, each of which contains 8 conductors arranged in 2 layers. The armature is a simplex lap winding. The average distance of the conductors from the axis of the armature is 10 in. The effective length of each conductor is 20 in. The average flux density under each pole is 50,000 lines/sq in. Neglecting the effects of fringing and of armature reaction, calculate the torque, in pound-feet, developed by this armature when the total input to it is 100 amp.

15–85. A 500-kva 13,200/2400-volt, 60-cycle single-phase transformer has a 4.0 per cent reactance and a 1.0 per cent resistance. The leakage reactance and the resistance of the low-voltage winding are 0.250 and 0.055 ohm, respectively. The core loss under rated conditions is 1800 watts. Calculate (a) the leakage reactance and the resistance of the high-voltage winding, in ohms, and (b) the efficiency of this transformer at full load and 85 per cent power factor.

15–86. When 2200 volts at 60 cycles are impressed on a certain transformer at no load, the total iron loss is 200 watts. When the frequency of the impressed voltage is changed to 25 cycles and the magnitude of the voltage is made such as to maintain the same maximum flux density as before, the iron loss falls to 75 watts.

Neglect the impedance drop at no load and calculate (a) the magnitude of the impressed voltage necessary at 25 cycles and (b) the eddy current loss and the hysteresis loss at 60 cycles.

15–87. Two identical transformers are operating in open delta to supply a balanced three-phase load of 60 kva and 0.866 power factor lagging. At what power factors are the transformers operating?

15–88. The self-reactance of each winding of a typical 1:1 60-cycle transformer is 100 ohms. Approximately what would be the reactance (a) if the two windings were connected in series aiding, (b) if the two windings were connected in parallel aiding, and (c) for one winding if the other is short-circuited?

15–89. An autotransformer is connected as shown in the diagram. For the purposes of this problem the losses in the transformer and its exciting current may be neglected, and the coupling among the various coils may be considered perfect. The turns ratios are $N_2/N_1=2$ and $N_3/N_1=3$. Calculate the value and sign of X_x in order that the input to the primary N_1 be at unity power factor.

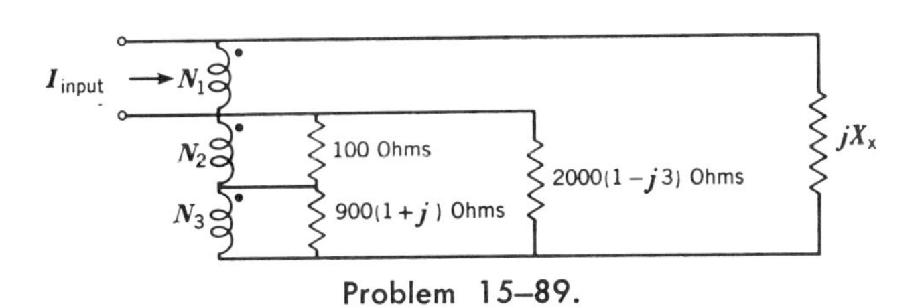

Problem 15–89.

15–90. A two-pole 60-cycle Y-connected three-phase turboalternator is rated to deliver 5000 kva at 0.8 lagging power factor, when the terminal voltage between lines is 6600 volts and the field current is of normal value. For the same field current, but at no load, the sinusoidally distributed magnetic flux per pole is equal to 24×10^6 lines. The armature winding of this machine consists of a total of 78 turns in series per phase, distributed into three slots per pole per phase, each coil having a pitch of 8/9. Calculate (a) the no-load voltage between line terminals and (b) the per cent voltage regulation.

15–91. A 5000-kva alternator and a 2500-kva alternator operate in parallel. The speed-load characteristic of the 5000-kva alternator is such that its frequency drops uniformly from 61 to 59 cycles from no load to 4500-kw load. The frequency of the 2500-kva alternator drops from 60.5 to 58 cycles from no load to 2500-kw load. Determine (a) the division of load when the combined load is 5000 kw and (b) the maximum unity power factor load which can be supplied without overloading either alternator.

15–92. A 2500-kva three-phase 60-cycle 6600-volt alternator has a field resistance of 0.43 ohms and an armature resistance of 0.072 ohms between each terminal and the neutral. The windings are Y-connected. The field current at full-load unity power factor is 200 amp and at full-load 0.80 pf lagging is 240 amp. The friction loss is 35 kw, and the core loss is 47.5 kw. Assume friction and core loss constant at either unity power factor or 0.80 pf lagging. Calculate (a) the full-load efficiency at unity power factor and (b) the full-load efficiency at 0.80 pf lagging.

15–93. A three-phase 6600-volt 6000-hp, Y-connected synchronous motor is to be operated under rated conditions with full load and a leading power factor of 0.5. The rotational losses under these conditions are 130 kw and may be taken as constant. The effective resistance and synchronous reactance, per phase, are 0.085 and 2.90 ohms, respectively. What is the current drawn by this machine and the excitation voltage under these conditions?

15–94. A three-phase three-wire transmission line has an input voltage of 2300 volts with a current of 225 amp at a power factor of 0.88 leading. The resistance and reactance per conductor are 0.6 ohm and 0.8 ohm, respectively. At the receiving end there is a synchronous motor that has a no-load input to the stator of 17.0 kw with negligible no-load copper losses. The motor is Y-connected and has a resistance and synchronous reactance of 0.16 and 2.1 ohms, respectively. Determine (a) the power output of the motor and (b) the receiving-end voltage of the line.

15–95. An industrial plant draws 500 kw at 0.6 power factor from a three-phase system. In order to raise the power factor to 0.866 lagging and to supply needed additional power, a synchronous motor is added. This motor draws 300 kw, bringing the new total plant load to 800 kw. Neglecting the losses of the synchronous motor, calculate its exact required kilovoltampere rating.

15–96. If resistance is added to the rotor circuits of an induction motor, how will the following quantities be affected: (a) starting current, (b) starting torque, (c) starting power factor, (d) speed regulation, (e) stalling torque, and (f) full-load speed?

15–97. A 230-volt three-phase six-pole 60-cycle induction motor is loaded by means of a Prony brake, the length and dead weight of which are 2 ft and 2 lb, respectively. The power input to this motor is measured by two wattmeters, P_1 and P_2, according to the two-wattmeter method. With 230 volts impressed on this motor, the total force delivered by the Prony brake is 30 lb, P_1 and P_2 indicate 3.5 and 7.0 kw, respectively, and the slip is 10 per cent. Calculate (a) the horsepower output of the motor, (b) its efficiency, and (c) its power factor.

15–98. A belt conveyor which moves at 150 fpm requires a pull of 330 lb at full load. The driving pulley has a diameter of 2 ft. The mechanical efficiency of the pulley and its associated gear reduction system is 0.75, and the speed reduction is 47.6:1. (a) Calculate the exact horsepower and speed of the motor required for this conveyor. (b) If the motor selected is a three-phase 208-volt induction motor operating at full load with an efficiency of 0.80 and a power factor of 0.80, calculate the full-load power and current required.

15–99. When a 50-kva, 2300/230 volt, 60-cycle transformer is operated at no load on rated voltage, the input is 200 watts at 0.15 power factor. When it is operating at rated load, the voltage drops and the total resistance and leakage reactance are 1.2 and 1.8 per cent of rated voltage respectively. Determine the input power and power factor when the transformer delivers 30 kw at 0.80 power factor lagging and 230 volts to a load on the low-voltage side.

15–100. You are to check the design of the solenoid shown. Find the electro-magnetic force on the plunger when the operating current is 1 amp, and the gap is 0.25 in. Neglect the mmf drop around the iron part of the magnetic circuit, the fringing of the flux in the air-gap and the effects of magnetic leakage.

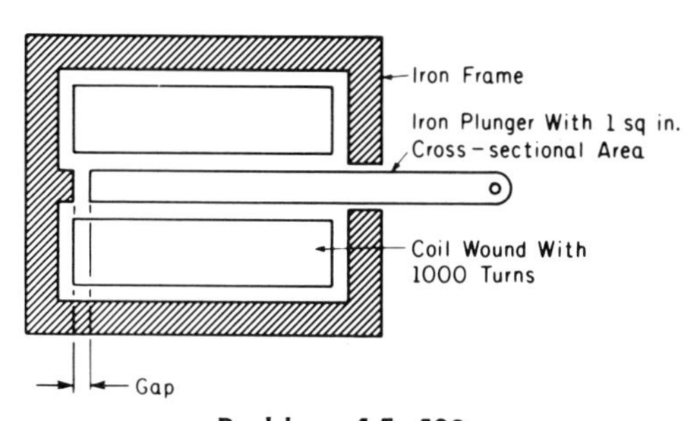

Problem 15–100.

15–101. The 230-volt winding of a 50-kva, 2300/230 volt, 60-cycle transformer is connected to 230-volt mains, the 2300-volt winding being open. The meters indicate the following readings: $P = 187$ watts, $E = 230$ volts, $I = 6.5$ amps. On short-circuit test with the low-tension winding short-circuited the transformed yields the following readings: $P = 620$ watts, $E = 87$ volts, $I_2 = 21.7$ amps. When measured, the resistance of the low-tension winding was found to be 0.06 ohms. Find: (a) Core losses, (b) angle between the exciting current and the impressed voltage, (c) percent exciting current, (d) regulation at unity power factor, (e) regulation at 0.80 power factor, current leading, (f) efficiency at full load and (g) efficiency at half load. Assume unity pf for (f) and (g).

POWER TRANSMISSION

15–102. At the sending end of a 20-mile three-phase transmission line the power input is 100,000 kw and the line-to-line voltage is 120 kv. The power factor at the sending end is 0.8 lagging, and the transmission-line impedance is $0.2+j1$ ohms per mile per phase. Determine (a) the power consumed by the concentrated load at the end of the transmission line, (b) the load voltage, and (c) the power factor of the load.

Solution: The total series impedance of each phase, $R+jX$, is

$$(0.2+j1)\,\frac{\text{ohm}}{\text{mile}}\,(20 \text{ miles}) = 4+j20 \text{ ohms}$$

$$P_{\text{in}} = \sqrt{3}V_L I_L \,(\text{pf}) \qquad I_L = \frac{10^8}{\sqrt{3}(1.2\times 10^5)(0.8)} = 601 \text{ amp}$$

(a) $$P_L = P_{\text{in}} - 3(I_L)^2R = 10^8 - 3(601)^2(4) = 95{,}660 \text{ kw}$$

(b) $$V_L = V_{\text{in}} - I_L Z = \frac{1.2\times 10^5}{\sqrt{3}}\underline{/36.9^\circ} - (601\underline{/0^\circ})(4+j20) \text{ per phase}$$

$$V_L = 60{,}700\underline{/29.2^\circ} \text{ volts, phase voltage}$$

$$|V_L| = \sqrt{3}(60{,}700) = 105 \text{ kv, line-to-line}$$

(c) $$Pf_L = \cos 29.2 = 0.872 \text{ lagging}$$

15–103. An open-wire, dissipationless transmission line has a characteristic resistance of 200 ohms. When a certain load is connected to this line and power is supplied at 600 megacycles, a voltage minimum results at a point 22.5 cm from the load, and the voltage–standing-wave ratio is 2.16. (a) Calculate the impedance of the load. (b) If a short-circuited stub is used to match the load to the line, calculate the length of the shortest stub and its nearest position to the load.

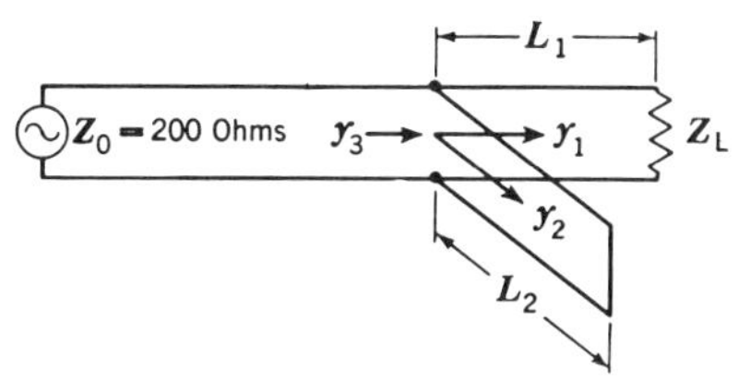

Problem 15–103.

Solution: A Smith Chart (SC) will be used. $\lambda = V/f = (3\times10^8)/(6\times10^8) =$ 0.5 m, or 50.0 cm

(a) Since VSWR=2.16, enter SC at $2.16+j0$. Then rotate 180° around a constant-K (coefficient of reflection) circle to the other side of the r axis. Rotate from that point around the same constant-K circle a distance of $22.5\lambda/50.0 = 0.450\lambda$ toward the load (counterclockwise). At this point read $0.50+j0.25$, which is the normalized load impedance. Then the load impedance will be $200(0.50+j0.25) = 100+j50$ ohms.

(b) Enter SC at the normalized load impedance, $0.50+j0.25$. Rotate 180° around a constant-K circle; this point is the normalized admittance of the load. From this point rotate around a constant-K circle toward the generator to the intersection of that constant-K circle with the circle corresponding to $r=1$. There are actually two such intersections; in this case pick that intersection of positive susceptance to yield the shortest stub. The distance traveled around the constant-K circle is the distance L_1 shown in the diagram, or the distance from the load to the stub.

$$L_1 = \frac{0.3547\lambda 50\text{ cm}}{\lambda} = 17.74\text{ cm}$$

The last point just described on SC is Y_1, the admittance looking toward the load from the connecting point of the stub. $Y_1 = 1+j0.78$. Let Y_2, the input admittance of the stub, be $Y_2 = -j0.78$. The terminating admittance for the stub is infinite. Rotate from infinity on SC around a constant-K circle toward the generator to $-j0.78$. The distance traveled is L_2, the length of the stub.

$$L_2 = \frac{0.1442\lambda 50\text{ cm}}{\lambda} = 7.21\text{ cm}$$

The total admittance at the connecting point of the stub is $Y_3 = Y_1 + Y_2 = 1+j0.78-j0.78 = 1$. The line is now terminated with its characteristic impedance.

15–104. A three-wire three-phase 60-cycle transmission line has an impedance, per conductor, of $1+j10$ ohms. The input to this line is at 13,200 volts between conductors. The power taken by the load is 1000 kw at 100 amp and a lagging power factor. Calculate (a) the efficiency of transmission, (b) the voltage at the load, and (c) the power factor of the load.

15–105. A load of 6000 kva 0.8 lagging pf is received at 7200 volts on the low-voltage bus of a substation. The power is transmitted over a 33-kv cable at each end of which identical transformations from 7500 volts line-to-line with delta connection to 33,000 volts line-to-line with star connection are employed to step up the voltage at the power station and to step down the voltage at the receiving end. Each transformer has an impedance of $1+j6$ ohms referred to the high-voltage winding, and the cable wires each have an impedance of $6+j3$ ohms. Neglecting the capacitance of the cable, calculate the sending-end voltage of the low-voltage bus.

15–106. A three-phase cable is employed to supply power to a three-phase transformer at 2200 volts. The primary of the transformer is delta-connected; the secondary is Y-connected and delivers power at 208/120 volts. The transformer supplies 100 kva to a motor load operating at 0.80 pf lagging and 50 kva to a lighting load of unity power factor. Both loads are balanced. The transformer losses are negligible. Calculate the current in the cable.

15–107. A 20-mile three-wire three-phase transmission line has an impedance of $0.1+j0.4$ ohms per wire mile. (A small capacitive component is neglected.) A regulator maintains 111,000 line volts at the input. The line terminates at the primary of a delta-wye transformer bank. Each transformer has a voltage ratio of 110,000/13,600. A load impedance on each leg of the Y is $100+j60$ ohms. Neglect transformer impedance and calculate (a) the load voltage phase-to-neutral and (b) the power loss in the line.

15–108. A 100-mile telephone line has the following parameters per mile of line: $R=10$ ohms, $L=0.004$ h, $C=0.008\times10^{-6}$ f, and $g=10^{-6}$ mho. (a) Calculate the impedance of the termination which will match this line at a frequency $f=5000/2\pi$ cps. (b) If this line included no repeaters, what would be the ratio, at this frequency, of the voltage at the input to that at the termination?

15–109. A quarter-wave section of radio-frequency transmission line is to be used to match a 50-ohm source delivering 50 kw to a 120-ohm resistive antenna. What should be the characteristic impedance of the quarter-wave section? What will be the voltage on the antenna input?

15–110. (a) State what is meant by a "long" transmission line. (b) Define the term "characteristic impedance" as applied to a transmission line. (c) State a procedure for measuring the characteristic impedance of a transmission line. (d) Define the term "standing wave ratio." (e) What are the objections to operating a line with a large standing wave ratio? (f) State the equivalent lumped circuits of the following transmission lines: (1) open circuit, less than quarter wavelength; (2) short circuit, quarter wavelength; (3) open circuit, half wavelength. (g) State a procedure and give numerical values for matching a 500-ohm line to a 72-ohm line.

15–111. Sketch curves of voltage and current distribution on a low-loss transmission line for the following load impedance conditions. In each case, calculate amplitude and location of minima and maxima accurately and show these minima and maxima in correct position in 1 wavelength from the receiving end of the line. (a) Reflection coefficient at load $= 0.2\underline{/0^\circ}$. (b) Reflection coefficient at load $= 1.0\underline{/-45^\circ}$.

15–112. A generator having a frequency of 6×10^6 cps, is supplying two loads over an open-wire line, which has a characteristic impedance of $50/0^\circ$ ohms, and each load has an impedance of $50/0^\circ$ ohms. The line has negligible attenuation, and its two loads are separated by ⅛ of a wavelength along the 50 ohm line. Find the location and length (in wavelengths) of a short-circuit matching stub which will match these loads to the line and make the line flat for as great a distance as possible. Use a 50-ohm characteristic impedance for the stub.

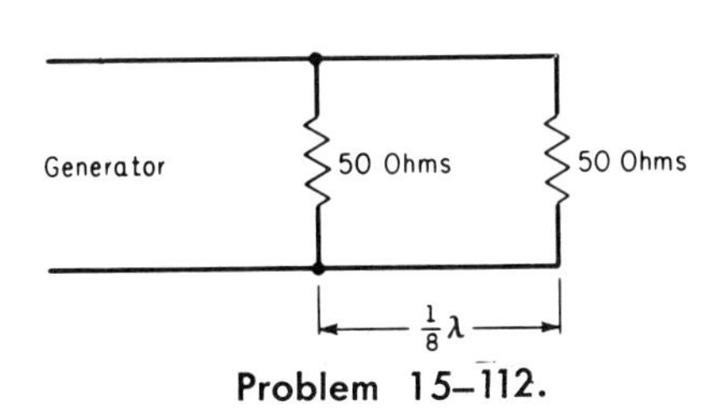

Problem 15–112.

15–113. A certain antenna is fed through a slotted line into which a voltage probe is inserted. With the antenna short-circuited the probe is moved until a minimum is located. The short is then removed and energy fed into the antenna. The probe is moved again until a new voltage minimum is located at a point 24 cm closer to the signal source. If the frequency is 100 megacycles per second, Z_o of the line and slotted line = 50 ohm, and the VSWR at the second location = 2.0, find the input impedance of the antenna in ohms.

15–114. A microwave system uses a rectangular cross-section wave guide to couple a load to a transmitter. The inside cross-section is 1 cm by 2 cm. (a) What is the lowest possible operating frequency? (b) What is the highest frequency at which waves at only one possible mode can be propagated by the wave guide?

15–115. A microwave system is to be designed for communication between points A and B. (a) The distance between the sites is 25 miles. Calculate the change in vertical distance in ft from a horizontal reference line for a point 10 miles from one end using an equivalent earth radius factor $k = 4/3$. (b) Calculate the free space attenuation in db for a 6800-megacycle signal between isotropic antennas 25 miles apart. (c) Calculate the first Fresnel zone radius f at the point described in (a) for a 6800 megacycle signal. (d) Calculate the receiver noise power for a microwave receiver with an intermediate frequency bandwidth of 8 megacycles, a noise figure of 14 db, and 60 db of available power gain.

Industrial Engineering 16

The following problems and those in Chapter 20, Examination K, are representative of the industrial engineering problems given in professional registration examinations by various states. Since industrial engineering is a growing field, it must be realized that questions on new developments will become more frequent. For example, actual problems on control charts and sampling as part of statistical quality control are now being given in place of general questions found in earlier examinations. PERT techniques, work sampling, and operations research must be studied in preparing for present-day examinations.

Solutions are shown for problems requiring computation of standard time, work sampling, quality control, plant layout, break-even point, and engineering economy.

16–1. A proposed method for operating a mechanical finishing machine involves three elements: 1) carefully adjusting the piece in a fixture, clamping, and placing in the machine; 2) automatic finishing by the machine; and 3) removal from the machine, unclamping piece, checking surface, and placing finished piece in tray. A time study was made of this operation *using the continuous method,* and the observer recorded the following stopwatch readings, in hundredths of minutes. Operator rating 90 per

Cycle	Put in Machine	Automatic-Machine Time	Remove from Machine	Cycle	Put in Machine	Automatic-Machine Time	Remove from Machine
1	40	105	25	6	55	715	35
2	67	231	50	7	74	837	58
3	92	360	82	8	901	63	85
4	422	87	508	9	1023	87	1105
5	44	99	618	10	41	99	1222

cent. Total allowances 15 per cent. Compute standard time for the job.

Solution:

Cycle	Put in Machine	Element Time	Automatic-Machine Time	Element Time	Remove from Machine	Element
1	40	40	105	65	125	20
2	167	42	231	64	250	19
3	292	42	360	68	382	22
4	422	40	487	65	508	21
5	544	36	599	55	618	19
6	655	37	715	60	735	20
7	774	39	837	63	858	21
8	901	43	963	62	985	22
9	1023	38	1087	64	1105	18
10	1141	36	1199	58	1222	23
Totals	....	393	....	624	....	205

Mean $= \dfrac{\Sigma x}{n}$ 39.3 62.4 20.5

(No leveling required) (Leveled time)

Rating 0.90........ 39.3 (0.90) = 35.4 20.5 (0.90) = 18.5

Allowance, 15%.... 35.4 (0.15) = 5.3 9.4 2.8

Standard time = 40.7 + 71.8 + 21.3 = 133.8

Total standard..... 133.8 min/piece

NOTE: The common practice in recording readings is to abbreviate the minute value for repeated readings as indicated by the full values shown.

Allowances can also be computed on standard time basis:

$$35.4 + 62.4 + 18.5 = \frac{116.3}{1.00 - 0.15} = \frac{116.3}{0.85} = 136.8 \text{ min/piece}$$

16–2. By use of the appropriate work sampling (ratio delay) and time study techniques, determine the following: (a) The unavoidable delay allowance to be applied to normal time if 2029 observations were taken over a 20-day period; 453 observations occurred during set-ups, 1227 during normal operations, 151 during personal time, and 198 during unavoidable delay time. (b) How many observations would be necessary in (a) to give ±5 per cent accuracy for the unavoidable delay element at 95 per cent confidence interval. (c) The allowances for unavoidable delay if the following data were obtained from an all-day stopwatch time study: Running time 300 min; set-ups, 30 min; avoidable delay, 30 min; personal time, 20 min; unavoidable delay, 100 min. (d) Briefly explain the differences (if any) in (a) and (c). Discuss the accuracy of each method.

Solution: (a) $\frac{198}{2029}=0.0976$ Use 10 per cent

(b) From H. B. Maynard (ed.), *Industrial Engineering Handbook* (New York: McGraw-Hill Book Company, Inc., 1956), p. 3–73:

$$N=\frac{Z^2(1-p)}{(\text{accuracy})^2(p)}=\frac{2^2(0.90)}{(0.05)^2 0.10}=\frac{36}{0.0025}=14{,}000$$

(c) $300+30+30+20+100=480$ $100/480=0.208$ use 21 per cent

(d) The all-day study may not be representative. The ratio-delay study covers 20 days and is more likely to be representative.

16–3. By the proper quality control techniques and tables, solve the following: (a) After taking 50 samples of 4 from a production process, the grand average is 55 and the average range is 3.5. Calculate the standard upper and lower control limits for average and range. (b) For the process in (a), the specifications are 54±3. Assuming normality, what percentage of the observations will be above the upper specification limit? (c) A process has run 7 per cent defective for some time. Establish the control limits for samples of 50. (d) A continuous strip of material has an average of eight defects per unit of length. Establish the control limits for the number of defects per unit. (e) Select a double-sampling plan for an acceptable quality level of 2.0 per cent, a lot size of 700, and a normal inspection level II (Military Standard 105A).

Solution:

(a) $N=50$, $\bar{\bar{X}}=55$, $n=4$, $\bar{R}=3.5$, $A_2=0.73$, $A_2\bar{R}=2.55$.

For $\bar{X}$ $\text{UCL}=55+2.55=57.55$ $\text{LCL}=55-2.55=52.45$

For R $\text{UCL}=D_4\bar{R}=2.28(3.5)=7.98$ $\text{LCL}=D_3\bar{R}=0(3.5)=0$

(b) $\sigma'=\frac{\bar{R}}{d_2}=\frac{3.5}{2.059}=1.70$ Upper specification $=54+3=57$

$$Z=\frac{57-54}{1.7}=\frac{3.0}{1.7}=1.76 \qquad P=1-0.9608=0.0392, \text{ or } 3.92 \text{ per cent}$$

(c) $$\sigma_p=\sqrt{\frac{p(1-p)}{n}}=\sqrt{\frac{0.07(0.93)}{50}}=0.036$$

$\text{UCL}=0.07+0.036=0.106$ $\text{LCL}=0.07-0.036=0.034$

(d) $c=8$ $\quad$ $UCL=8+\sqrt{8}=10.82$ $\quad$ $LCL=8-\sqrt{8}=5.18$

(e) Use Military Standard 105A: from Table I use AQL=2.5; from Table III use code J.

Double Sampling Plan

$n_1=50 \quad c_1=2$

$n_2=100 \quad c_2=6$

16–4. There are two general kinds of plant layout: that for the flow type of production where continuous or repetitive operations are carried on, and that for the intermittent type of production where special orders are the only kind of jobs put through. Designate what kind of layout would be best adapted to the two types of production mentioned above. Describe with sketches the arrangement of machinery in each kind of layout to produce items A, B, and C:

OPERATION SEQUENCES

Product	Operation 1	Operation 2	Operation 3
A	Lathe	Drill	Lathe
B	Drill	Mill	
C	Lathe	Mill	Drill

Solution: See James Apple, *Plant Layout and Materials Handling* (New York: The Ronald Press Company, 1950), p. 27.

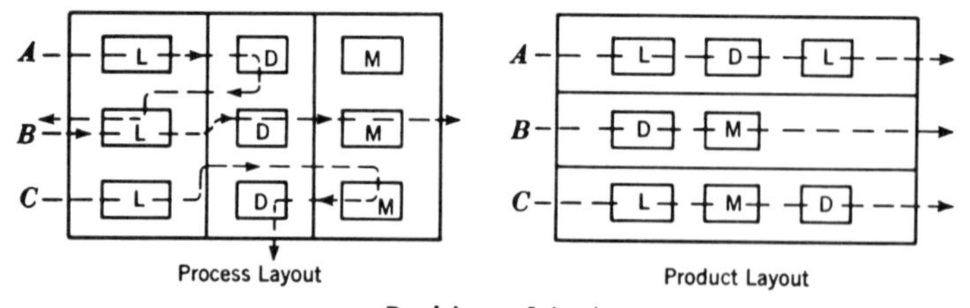

Problem 16–4.

16–5. A certain type and size container can be manufactured either on a semiautomatic "hand" line or on a fully automatic line. The cost of setting up the hand line for an order is $17; for the automatic line it is $135. Labor costs for the hand line are $16.30 per hour; for the automatic line $9.40 per hour. Those labor extras and indirect manufacturing expenses that are variable with direct labor are estimated to be $.60 for every dollar of direct labor cost. The hand line produces at the rate of 2100 cans per hour; the automatic line produces 15,000 per hour. What order size represents the break-even point between the two lines?

Solution: (a) Semiautomatic "hand" line:

Set-up cost/order = \$17, fixed cost	
Direct labor	= \$16.30
Indirect costs = 0.60 per \$1 of direct labor = 16.30×0.60	= 9.78 per hour
	\$26.08 for 2100 cans
Total variable cost per hour	= \$12.40 for 1000 cans

(b) Fully automatic line:

Set-up cost per order = \$135, fixed cost	
Direct labor	\$ 9.40 per hour
Indirect costs 0.60 (9.40)	= 5.64 per hour
Total variable cost per hour	= \$15.04 for 15,000 cans
	= \$ 1.00 for 1000 cans

Let X = number of 1000-can orders; then

$$\text{total costs (a)} = \text{total costs (b)}$$
$$17 + 12.40X = 135 + 1.00X$$
$$\text{and } X = 10.35 \text{ orders of 1000 cans}$$

Below 10,350 use "hand" line; above 10,350 use fully automatic line.

16–6. (a) A safety device to shut off the motive power in the event of an interruption in gas supply is being considered for installation on a number of continuous-type ovens used in painting and varnishing sheet iron for car bodies. The installed cost for each oven is \$800; the estimated life for the device is 12 years. In the event of interrupted gas supply, damage to product in each oven will amount to approximately \$175 if the automatic cutoff is not installed; if it is installed, the damage will amount to \$30. The interruptions of gas supply occur, on the average, about twice in every 3 years. Maintenance costs for each device are estimated at \$5 per year. Consider 10 per cent to be the minimum attractive return. (1) Should the safety device be installed? (2) What are the cost figures for or against installation of the device? (3) What price could be paid for the device to be relieved of the hazard forever? (Assume a device that would last forever.)

(b) There is one chance in five that a flood will close down your factory in any year. The flood will cost the company \$27,000. With a present return on your capital investment of 5½ per cent, what present expenditure is justified to eliminate this risk for 20 years?

Solution: (a) Data: P = \$800, n = 12 years, i = 10 per cent, maintenance = \$5 per year per device.

Calculation of Annual Damage

Without device	\$175 per interruption
With device	30
Saving	\$145 per interruption
Interruptions per year	$= \frac{2}{3}$
Saving per year	$= 145 \times \frac{2}{3} = 290/3 = \$97$
Annual savings	$= \$97$
Annual cost of device	$= P$ (capital recovery factor) $+ \$5$
	$= \$800\,(0.14676) + \$5 = \$122.40$

For (1) and (2): Do not install the device; net annual savings are \$97 compared with annual cost of \$122.

(3) Let P=price to pay for device of infinite life, n=infinity, i=10 per cent. Then

$$\text{Annual cost of device} = \text{annual net saving}$$
$$P\ (\text{capital recovery factor}) + 5 = 97$$
$$P\ (0.1000) = 92$$
$$P = \frac{92}{0.1} = \$920$$

(b) Flood damage=\$27,000 when flood occurs. With one chance in 5, occurrence would be every 5 years. Average annual damage would be \$27,000/5=\$5400. Data: Given R=5400, i=5½ per cent, n=20; find P.

$$P = \$5400\ (\text{pwf})$$
$$= \$5400\ (11.950) = \$64,530$$

16–7. A former method of assembling partitions in boxes produced 200 finished assemblies per hour. A suggested revision of method was timed, resulting in the following data: observed time, 0.20 min; operator rating, 72 points (60=avg); allowances for delay and fatigue, 10 per cent; allowance for personal needs, 24 min/8-hr day. Calculate the per cent increase in production and per cent saving in time.

16–8. The ABC Electrical Company uses several gages of varnished insulated copper wire for small motor and coil windings. The bare copper wire is supplied in 1200-ft spools. The operator of the varnish insulating machine has filed a grievance concerning the established standard for the varnish insulating operation and has requested a restudy of the job. Analysis of the operation yields these data:

Activity Elements	Elapsed Minutes
Stop machine	0.47
Remove take-up reel (insulated wire)	1.16
Roll reel of insulated wire to stock room	3.58
Record production of insulated wire into inventory	0.11
Check out reel of bare wire into production	0.13
Roll reel of bare wire to machine	3.60
Remove empty reel from supply spindle of machine and place on floor	1.11
Place reel of bare wire on supply spindle	2.23
Thread bare wire through machine	2.46
Move empty reel to take-up spindle (other side of machine)	2.72
Place empty reel on take-up spindle	2.61
Fasten threaded end of wire to take-up reel	2.67
Start machine	0.68
Machine time to varnish one reel, 1200 ft of wire (independent of wire gage)	8.45

NOTE: The operator is idle while the machine is running. The machine requires no attention while running. There are start and stop buttons on both supply and take-up sides of the machine. The given times include allowances for delays, personal time, etc.

(a) Chart the activity of the operator and the machine (Man and Machine Chart) showing their interrelationship. (b) How many reels of wire should be insulated per hour when the operator follows the present procedure? (c) What changes would you recommend to improve the present work procedure of the operator? (Do not change the layout of the plant, materials, or the machines.) (d) Chart the activity of the operator and the insulating machine, showing their interrelationship following your recommended procedures. (e) How many reels of wire should be insulated per hour following your recommended procedure? (f) What is the expected increase in production? (g) What is the saving in the time required to insulate each reel of wire?

16–9. Utilizing the following elemental time values, construct a formula which will give the allowed time for cutting and trimming rectangular lawns, of various dimensions, which surround a rectangular flower bed.

Element Description	Time (min)
Unload equipment from truck	8.6 per occurrence
Lubricate equipment (once per lawn)	4.50 per occurrence
Cut grass	0.80 per 100 linear feet
Turn mower around for return cut	0.35 per turn
Trim grass	0.85 per 100 linear feet
Return equipment to truck and load	9.2 per occurrence

Notes: 1) The lawn mower will cut an effective 16-in. swath and will cut to within 3 in. of the lawn borders. 2) One turn-around for each swath cut by mower. 3) The trimmer will cut a 6-in. effective swath to the flower bed edge or lawn edge.

Question: A 40 ft × 25 ft flower bed is centered with the long dimension of the flower bed parallel to the short dimension of a 100 ft × 200 ft lot. Is it more economical to cut this lawn with the swath path in the long dimension of the lawn or in the short dimension? Support your answer with the time difference between the two methods.

16–10. Three successive operations using different machines require the following standard times, in minutes, for each part of the operation. (a) Determine the ratio of machines of each type

Element	Operation A	Operation B	Operation C
Load machine	0.125	0.170	0.204
Automatic-machine time	0.410	0.118	0.660
Unload and move to next operation	0.095	0.132	0.186
Total	0.630	0.420	1.050

required to accomplish balanced production through the three operations. (b) Compute the cost of 1000 pieces if one operator is available for each machine and operators are paid $1.20 per hour. Assume one machine for each operation and the burden rate on all machines at $1.80 per hour. (c) Compute the cost of 1000 pieces if one man operates all three pieces of equipment, using the same unit costs as in (b). (d) Determine the number of operators required to bring about the most economical operating efficiency for balanced production.

16–11. It is desired to determine total allowances necessary in a foundry for molding work. Work sampling studies were taken for a period of 10 days. The following data which resulted from the studies have been summarized daily. It is thought, from past experience, that total allowances for allowable delays amount to about 10 per cent. The employee representation agrees to this 10 per cent figure and accepts an accuracy of ±10 per cent of it as being acceptable provided it can be shown that the allowable delay will fall within this range 95 per cent of the time. You, as an industrial engineer, are requested to work up the data on the delay study for analyses of conformance with the employees' request.

Number of Occurrences

Workday	Personal Delays	Avoidable Delays	Unavoidable Delays	Productive Work
1	5	15	10	98
2	8	2	5	100
3	10	4	3	95
4	8	4	5	110
5	9	7	2	116
6	12	6	2	96
7	8	5	4	109
8	4	9	6	106
9	5	8	5	105
10	6	5	8	110
Total	75	65	50	1045

(a) What is the per cent of total allowable delay occurrences (unavoidable and personal) as shown by the 10-day study? (b) What is the accuracy for all delays for the 95 per cent probability condition for the data taken during the 10-day study? (c) Does this deviation meet the acceptable accuracy from the 10 per cent figure that the employees agree to? (d) If not, how many observations should be taken of the molding work in order to statistically insure the conditions that have been agreed upon by the employees and management?

16–12. We are manufacturing a relay arm which has a small clip spot-welded to it. Standards established by our customer specify that the relay arms shall not have a shear strength of the weld less than 17 lb. We do not feel that it is practicable to obtain this assurance by a method involving sampling by attributes. A 100 per cent inspection does not seem practicable either, for testing damages the clips, and is very costly in proportion to the value of the product. We feel that we have all of the process variables affecting the weld strength under control at the present time. Destructive tests of representative parts yielded the data given in the table. (a) What is the probability of producing a weld which

Shear Strength X (lb.)	Number of Occurrences f	fX	X^2	fX^2
25.5	1	25.5	650.25	650.25
25.0	2	50.0	625.00	1,250.00
24.5	6	147.0	600.25	3,601.50
24.0	9	216.0	576.00	5,184.00
23.5	14	329.0	552.25	7,731.50
23.0	14	322.0	529.00	7,406.00
22.5	31	697.5	506.25	15,693.75
22.0	34	748.0	484.00	16,456.00
21.5	33	709.5	462.25	15,254.25
21.0	41	861.0	441.00	18,081.00
20.5	26	533.0	420.25	10,926.50
20.0	24	480.0	400.00	9,600.00
19.5	12	234.0	380.25	4,562.00
19.0	7	133.0	361.00	2,527.00
18.5	2	37.0	342.25	684.50
18.0	0	0.0	324.00	0.00
17.5	2	35.0	306.25	612.50
17.0	0	0.0	289.00	0.00
16.5	1	16.5	272.25	272.25
16.0	0	0.0	256.00	0.00
15.5	1	15.5	240.25	240.25
Totals	260	5,589.5	.....	120,733.25

will not meet our customer's specifications (assuming all process variables are still under control)? Should this be acceptable to our customer? (b) If you adopted an in-process control chart procedure using destructive tests on 4 welds from each 300 relay arms produced, what limits would you establish for weld strength to indicate that the process variables were no longer under control? Compute these limits. (c) What would you do if you obtained a sample with a weld strength less than the established lower control limit? Explain. (d) Sketch a control chart adapted to this situation.

16–13. The following table gives the data on inspection of rubber belts. Compute trial control limits and plot an *np* chart.

Lot Number	Number Inspected	Number of Defectives	Lot Number	Number Inspected	Number of Defectives
1	2300	230	12	2300	394
2	2300	435	13	2300	285
3	2300	221	14	2300	331
4	2300	346	15	2300	198
5	2300	230	16	2300	414
6	2300	327	17	2300	131
7	2300	285	18	2300	269
8	2300	311	19	2300	221
9	2300	342	20	2300	407
10	2300	308			
11	2300	456	Total	46,000	6141

16–14. An auto filling station is to incorporate the following items: four gasoline pumps, two greasing pits, free air, office, toilets, repair shed for two cars, and parking space for twelve cars. (a) List five kinds of services which will be rendered in order of their importance. (b) Make a layout of the station to approximate scale, assuming a corner lot. Place equipment according to the importance of the service rendered.

16–15. The Wells Company has an average of 1200 employees who work 40 hr/week. During the last 6-month period for which figures are available, the plant had 14 disabling injuries, involving 624 days lost from work. Compute accident frequency and severity rates for this plant. How do these compare with the averages for all industry in the United States?

16–16. It will cost $12,000 to build a special machine whose salvage value at the end of an estimated service life of 8000 hours will be $1000. The cost of housing the machine is estimated at $360 per year. Maintenance of the machine is estimated at $0.15 per hour, and its power consumption is estimated at $0.32 per hour of operation. Labor costs per hour of operation are to be taken at $1.56 and interest is 6 per cent. It will require 1 hr to process a unit of the product to be made on the machine. (a) Calculate the cost of processing a unit of product if 8000 units are produced per year. (b) Calculate the cost of processing a unit of product if 4000 units are produced per year.

16–17. A utility using fuel oil at a rate of 1,500,000 barrels per year wishes to determine if it would be economical to establish bulk storage near a fuel oil supply terminal and deliver fuel oil to its plant by pipeline rather than by barge. The delivery by pipeline would eliminate 15 cents/barrel barging costs. Land and easements would cost $75,000, and tank, pipelines, etc., would cost $500,000. The money for these facilities would come from the following sources: 50 per cent from mortgage bonds drawing 4½ per cent per annum, 35 per cent from common stock drawing 5 per cent per annum, 15 per cent from preferred stock drawing 6 per cent per annum. Other fixed charges are city and state taxes, 1 per cent; insurance, ½ per cent; and depreciation period, 25 years. Annual operating expenses, including maintenance, would be $18,500. Federal taxes on net profit would be 45 per cent. Find the net profit after all taxes, stock dividends, charges, etc., have been paid.

16–18. In order to keep its productive capacity more fully engaged, Electrothermal Castings has expanded from its original line of business, which was producing fine iron and steel castings to customer order, to the manufacture of a few assembled products whose major components are castings. This has required that the company establish a machine shop in addition to its original foundry so that it can machine components for assembly. This departure was made 8 years ago. The original foundry is almost 50 years old. At present the company employs about 300 men in its foundry and 100 in the machine shop. It has in addition about 50 general maintenance employees and nearly 50 office personnel.

An item which Electrothermal Castings purchases for use in one of its assemblies is a brass globe valve for 1½-in. pipe. Usage of these valves is 200 per month at present and promises to continue at the same rate. They are stored in an area in which the floor space value is determined as $0.96 per square foot per year. The valves are kept in bins that hold four per cubic feet. The bins are stacked in racks that permit a height of 12 ft to be used for storage. The floor loading permitted by the building's construction, however, is 200 lb/sq ft. A valve weighs 6 lb.

Last year the purchasing department processed 2947 purchase orders. The cost of operating the department was $17,260. Upon getting quotations for these valves, purchasing found the delivered cost to be as follows, with a lead time of 15 days, counting procurement time:

Lot size...........	100–199	200–499	500–999
Price per valve....	$1.94	$1.75	$1.45

It has been found at Electrothermal that inventory carrying charges to cover the risk of obsolescence, interest, taxes, and insurance on investment should be charged at 25 per cent per year.

Determine (a) the economic purchase quantity for globe valves if it is management's policy to keep a 2 weeks' supply on hand in inventory as a reserve stock, (b) order point quantity (in units), (c) normal maximum in units, and (d) normal minimum.

16–19. (a) Give a definition of production control, what functions or duties it comprises, and the desired results that are brought about by proper control of its functions. (b) What is a Gantt chart? Give three different items of production control information that can be obtained by an analysis of a Gantt chart. (c) State three ways by which an overloading of a group of machines can be corrected. (d) Give the information and services that are furnished by the various departments listed to provide the production control department with adequate data to effectively route an order through the plant: (1) sales department, (2) engineering department, (3) production standards department, (4) materials stores, (5) purchasing department.

16–20. A mine hoist system consists of two balanced cages operated by a motor direct-connected to the drum. The drum diameter is 8 ft; the depth of the mine is 350 ft. The running speed of the system is 1100 fpm; the system is accelerated from rest to full speed in 4 sec and brought to rest from full speed in 6 sec. (a) How long will it take one cage to make the trip from bottom to top? (b) Compute horsepower requirements if (to lift the coal only) 800 tons of coal are to be hoisted from the mine in 7 hr. The weight of coal per trip is 2 tons. The acceleration and retardation are as given in the statement of the problem. The cage going down is empty.

16–21. (a) A manufacturing company became involved in a grievance with the union about the standard time for a specific operation and about the general level of effort required for all operations. The specific operation standard time of 0.5 min per piece had been established 5 years previously, and the company had some important changes in equipment, layout, etc., since that time. Therefore, the company wanted to change the standard time, which contract provisions said they could (the company had made the changes in method). After thorough time studies (the company had a good time-study department and the union had respected the results previously), the standard time was established as 0.33 min. The union objected but did not offer a counter proposal for the standard time. Prior to arbitration, both parties agreed to have an outside consultant study the operation and establish a standard time. His time turned out to be 0.25 min. The company then insisted on using 0.25 min for the standard time. (1) Discuss the relationship of this case to rating. (2) What can be done to solve this problem (other than arbitration)?

(b) Time study consists of a number of steps used to find the standard or allowed time. The most controversial phase of time study is the rating, or leveling procedure. What is rating, or leveling, and why do we rate? (Describe fully in general terms; do not refer to a special rating system.) What is its relationship to the other steps of time study?

(c) The incentive earnings for an operator for production on 20 lots of the same part were, in per cent, 30, 22, 27, 25, 36, 18, 28, 39, 25, 25, 26, 30, 23, 33, 33, 15, 40, 31, 27, and 22. If the operator produced 50 per cent the next time, what could you conclude? 18 per cent? 2 per cent? 39 per cent?

16–22. Name, and give briefly, the main contributions of three pioneers in industrial engineering.

16–23. Discuss recent trends in industrial engineering in relation to the American Institute of Industrial Engineers' definition of it.

16–24. Assume that you are hired to make a survey of a company to determine the extent to which it applies modern industrial engineering methods and practices in an integrated way. Prepare a check list or list of questions which you could use to analyze present practices. (Make answer as complete as time permits.)

16–25. In a survey made by the Methods Engineering Council, 20 to 35 per cent of all the industrial operations studied were found to be unnecessary. The following eight reasons were given as the cause of permanent unnecessary operations: 1) snap judgment, 2) traditional methods, 3) misunderstandings, 4) misuse of supplier, 5) no change since development stage, 6) faulty inspection requirements, 7) temporary operations, and 8) unauthorized personnel work.

In your experiences in industrial engineering, describe five (5) unnecessary operations which you have personally observed. Explain the reason which you believe was the major cause for the existence of each set of conditions.

16–26. A research project is to be scheduled using the PERT technique. The project is comprised of various activities, represented by letters, which are interrelated according to the information provided in the list (not in sequential order). 1) Activities B and C both start when activity A has been completed. 2) The start of activities D and E is dependent upon the completion of activity B. 3) Activity F can start as soon as activity C has been completed. 4) Job M is dependent upon completion of activities Q and F. 5) Activity H follows activity D. 6) Activities N and P both start upon completion of activity L. 7) Job L depends upon the completion of Job F. 8) Activity R cannot start until M, N, P, and Q are finished. 9) J follows G. 10) Activity G is dependent upon the completion of activities C and E. 11) Jobs K and Q start upon the completion of H and J.

(a) Draw the logic network for the research project. (b) Determine the earliest start, latest completion, and slack time for each activity. (c) Indicate the location and length of the critical path. (d) Find the probability of completing this project in 35 weeks. Time estimates are given in the table.

Activity	A	B	C	D	E	F	G	H	J	K	L	M	N	P	R	Q
Optimistic time	2	1	2	1	7	5	3	1	3	1	2	2	1	7	1	2
Most likely time	4	3	5	4	8	11	3	3	7	5	6	6	3	8	2	2
Pessimistic time	6	8	9	12	10	19	3	6	10	9	18	14	7	12	5	2

16–27. Draw an operating characteristics curve assuming that the lot fraction defective is a continuous parameter. Label this curve completely indicating the producer's risk, the consumer's risk, the acceptable quality level, and the rejectable quality level.

16–28. Find the reliability of the system illustrated for a mission of 100 hr when three of four units number 7 through number 10 are needed for system success. Assume components follow an exponential failure rate pattern. Failure rates in failures per million hours are $\lambda_1 = 100$, $\lambda_2 = 500$, $\lambda_3 = 250$, $\lambda_4 = 50$, $\lambda_5 = 100$.

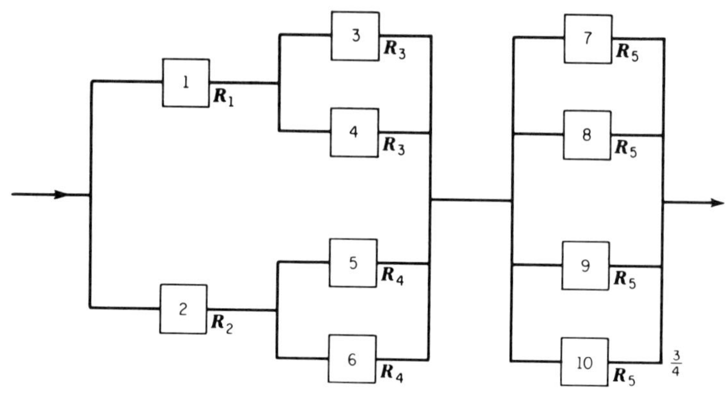

Problem 16–28.

16–29. A producer of 3 types of feed additives maintains 2 production facilities at the same location from which he manufactures his entire output. Plant No. 1 is designed to produce the biggest demand items, A and B, most economically. Plant No. 1, however, is less economical than plant No. 2 for additive 3. Using the information provided, determine how the production should be allocated to the 2 plants for the 3 additives in order to maximize profits.

Additive	Hrs/100 Lb		Sales Revenue/100 Lb	Maximum Demand/Week
	No. 1	No. 2		
A	0.25	0.20	$100	31,000
B	0.40	0.25	$120	30,000
C	0.35	0.40	$150	12,500

Plant No. 1 has a maximum of 100 hr available for production per week with an associated variable cost per hour of $250 which includes all labor, supplies and power, but not raw materials. Plant No. 2 also has a maximum of 100 hr available, however the variable costs per hour associated with plant No. 2 are $300.

16–30. In scheduling the production of a single lot of a given item, the production manager desires to allow for rejects so that the expected costs are a minimum. Currently the process is producing at a level of 5 per cent defective and is in a state of statistical control. The schedule calls for 200 good pieces. If 200 are not obtained, enough defective parts can be repaired at a cost of

$10 each to make up the schedule. Excess parts have no value. The variable cost of production is $20 per unit. What is the optimal number of pieces to produce if the criterion is minimum expected cost of production and repair, subject to the constraint that the schedule of 200 good pieces must be met?

16–31. Two factories can each make 4 products A, B, C, and D. Their total capacity for all 4 products is 70,000 and 90,000 lb per week, respectively. If overtime is worked, the capacities can be increased by up to 14,000 and 18,000 lb per week respectively. The table given shows costs and sales demands. Which factory should make which products on normal and overtime production? (Note that a factory may make several products.)

COST PER POUND

	Factory I		Factory II		
Product	Normal	Overtime	Normal	Overtime	Weekly Demand
A	$1.30	$1.40	$1.30	$1.50	30,000 lb
B	1.40	1.50	1.40	1.50	40,000
C	1.40	1.50	1.50	1.70	50,000
D	1.20	1.40	1.40	1.70	60,000

16–32. Three components, A, B, and C have to be produced on 4 machines, M_1, M_2, M_3, and M_4. Sequence of operations and times are given in the following table:

Product	A				B			C			
Operation	1	2	3	4	1	2	3	1	2	3	4
Machine	M_1	M_3	M_2	M_4	M_1	M_2	M_3	M_2	M_3	M_4	M_3
Time (Days)	2	4	3	6	4	3	4	4	5	3	4

Assume all machines are now available for assignment. Determine a schedule by which the production of all 3 products can be completed in the shortest possible time. No overlap is permitted.

16–33. The Greenough Corporation manufactures chains of all types, and in so doing, has to move 2110 tons of material in process each day. It has been decided by the traffic manager of the plant to use tractors drawing trailers to accomplish this movement. The Greenough plant is well supplied with load-bearing trailers which it can employ to transport the material in process. Each trailer weighs 2500 lb and can carry a load of 2.5 tons. The number of tractors needed to meet present demands must be determined. A local dealer quotes $1146.75 for machines with a tractive effort sufficient to pull 15.6 tons over the steepest grade in the Greenough plant. Another dealer quotes a price of $860 each for tractors which can draw 13.4 tons over the steepest grade in the plant. The two tractors have approximately the same operating costs. Distance to be traveled in the plant is 3750 ft each trip, average speed is 150 ft/min, and 15 min are allowed each trip for loading and unloading the trailers. The plant runs on a 12-hr day (two 6-hr shifts). How many tractors will be needed? Which tractor should be purchased? Why?

16–34. A midwestern company in a city of 350,000 people manufactures parts for aircraft and automobile engines. From a small start in 1943, it now employs over 650 in its 10 factory departments. Prospects for continued expansion make it imperative that the company install job evaluation. Accordingly, a consultant has been engaged, the assistant personnel director has been designated the key man to carry through the program, and the stage set to begin job analysis.

Assuming you are the consultant, design the forms necessary, and outline the method of analyzing factory jobs. Include selection, training, and supervision of job analysts, information to executives and employees, scope and uses of job information, editing and approving job analyses, scheduling of the work, and any other points that should be part of the plan.

16–35. A repairman is to be hired to fix machines which break down at an average rate of 3 per hr. Breakdowns are distributed in time in a manner regarded as Poisson. Non-productive time on any one machine is considered to cost the company $5 per hr. The company has narrowed the choice to 2 repairmen, one slow but cheap, the other fast but expensive. The slow repairman asks $3 per hr and will service broken-down machines exponentially at an average rate of 4 per hr. The fast repairman demands $5 per hr but will fix machines exponentially at an average rate of 6 per hr. Which repairman should be hired?

Mining and Metallurgy

17

17–1. Consider the following plain carbon steels: 0.40 per cent carbon, 0.80 per cent carbon, and 1.40 per cent carbon. For each one determine (a) the temperature at which the solid solution (austenite) begins to decompose and the name of the new phase appearing, (b) the temperature at which the decomposition of austenite is completed, and (c) the amount (in per cent) of proeutectoid phase and pearlite in the 0.40 per cent C steel at room temperature. (d) Sketch the structure of each at room temperature.

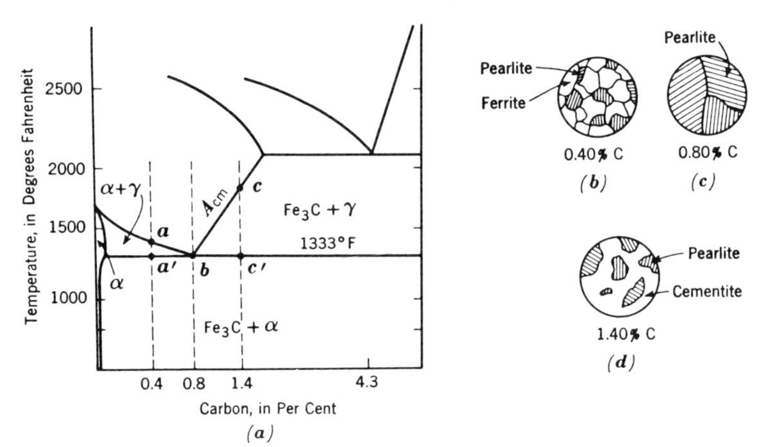

Problem 17–1. (*a*) Fe: Fe_3C equilibrium diagram. (*b*), (*c*), and (*d*) Structures of plain carbon steels.

Solution: (a), (b) The equilibrium diagram shown in view (*a*) is a plot of the composition of phases as a function of temperature in the iron–iron carbide system. Assuming a starting temperature of 2000°F, the three alloys are composed of a single phase, austenite. Upon cooling, transformation of austenite will start at the critical temperatures or critical points *a*, *b*, and *c*. Proeutectoid ferrite begins to form in the 0.4 per cent carbon steel at the critical point *a* (1505°F) and continues until the alloy cools down to the next critical point *a′* (1333°F), where all of the remaining austenite will be transformed to the eutectoid phase called pearlite, as shown in view (*b*).

The 0.80 per cent carbon steel corresponds to the eutectoid composition and will therefore remain as austenite until the eutectoid temperature (*b*,

1333°F) is reached where all the austenite will be transformed into pearlite. This transformation is isothermal, so only one critical point exists. The upper critical temperature for the 1.4 per cent C alloy lies on the A_{cm} line at point c (1820°F). From view (a), the new phase is seen to be cementite, Fe_3C. This proeutectoid phase continues to form down to the eutectoid temperature, where the remaining austenite is transformed to pearlite.

(c) The amount of any two phases coexisting at any temperature can be obtained by applying the lever rule as follows:

0.40 per cent C alloy

$$\text{Amount } \alpha = \frac{ab}{xb}(100) = \frac{0.80-0.40(100)}{0.80-0.025} = 49 \text{ per cent}$$

$$\text{Amount pearlite} = \frac{ax}{xb}(100) = \frac{0.40-0.025}{0.80-0.025}(100) = 51 \text{ per cent}$$

(d) See views (b), (c), and (d).

17–2. A natural-gas transmission line operated for only several months before a series of breaks occurred. Most of the breaks originated in the failure of blisters which formed in the 0.25 per cent carbon steel. The gas in the line contained 15 mole per cent carbon dioxide and 1 mole per cent hydrogen sulfide. Gas from a blister was analyzed and found to contain 94 per cent hydrogen, 2 per cent methane, and traces of both carbon dioxide and carbon monoxide. The hydrogen content of the gas in the line never exceeded 0.2 mole per cent prior to the failures. What was the source of the hydrogen causing the blisters and how does the hydrogen enter the steel? What remedies would you recommend to prevent similar failures?

Solution: H_2S and CO_2 gases dissolved in water (from condensation) within the pipeline to form dilute acid solutions which attacked iron according to the following equation:

$$\begin{array}{ccccccc} 2Fe & + & 2HA_c & \leftrightharpoons & 2FeA_c & + & H_2 \\ \text{iron} & + & \text{weak acid} & \leftrightharpoons & \text{iron salts} & + & \text{molecular hydrogen} \end{array}$$

In this reaction, iron is the anode and undergoes the following oxidation reaction:

$$Fe^0 \leftrightharpoons Fe^{++} + 2e$$

Hydrogen ions are in turn reduced as follows:

$$2H^+ + 2e \leftrightharpoons 2H^0$$

$$2H^0 \leftrightharpoons H_2$$

The presence of H_2S prevented atomic hydrogen to form molecular hydrogen and also made the steel surface more susceptible to absorption of the atomic hydrogen. This atomic hydrogen can move freely through interstices of the iron's atomic structure. When a sufficient number of them come to some internal discontinuity, they will combine to form molecular hydrogen. Extremely high localized pressures are created and blisters result. This type of attack can be prevented by adding an organic inhibitor to the line or by altering the interior surface of the steel. Linings of chromium or molybdenum alloys, or austenitic stainless steels, will prevent attack at all temperatures and pressures. Polysulfide injections into the line have also been used.

17–3. Discuss the effect of grain size on the physical properties of brasses.

Solution: There is a marked relationship between grain size and many of the properties of these alloys. Normally, hardness, yield strength and tensile strength decrease with increasing grain size; ductility and therefore both the capacity and ease of working brasses increase. The surface of brasses which have been subjected to forming operations becomes rougher as grain size increases, making it more difficult to polish and grind the surface.

The ability of brasses to withstand elevated temperatures without excessive creep is closely connected to grain size. At temperatures well above the recrystallization temperature, coarse grained materials have superior creep resistance. Below the recrystallization temperature, fine-grained alloys have higher creep strengths. Fatigue strength has been shown to increase as grain size decreases. Stress-corrosion cracking occurs often in brasses with high zinc content exposed to corrosive atmospheres in service. Finer grained materials are more resistant to this type of failure. No definite correlation has been found between electrical conductivity and grain size.

17–4. (a) Outline the method of precipitation (dispersion) hardening for nonferrous alloys. (b) Sketch microstructures to show how metals are strengthened by this method.

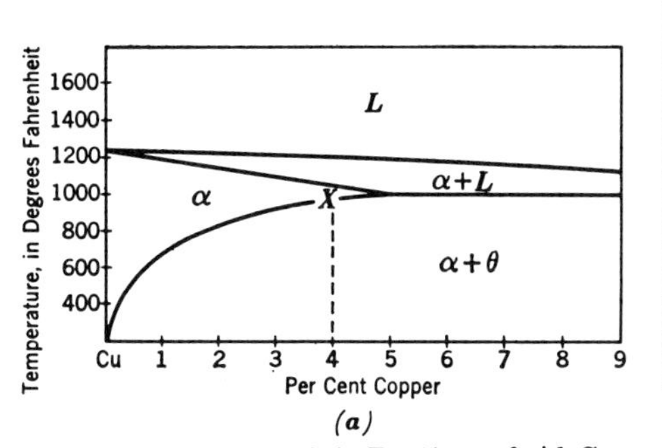

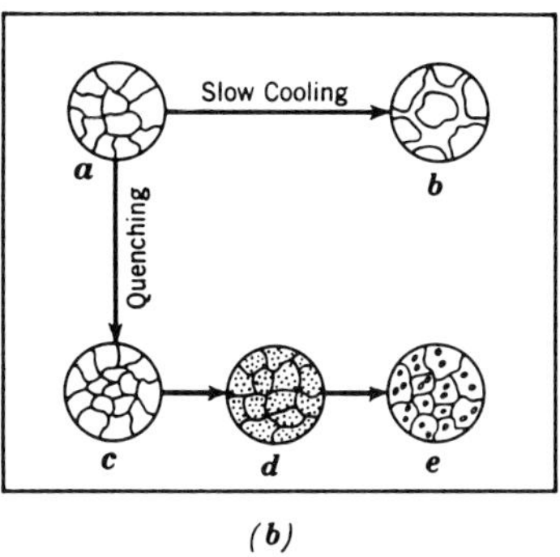

Problem 17–4. (*a*) Portion of Al-Cu equilibrium diagram. (*b*) Structures obtainable with precipitation-hardenable alloys.

Solution: (a) Assume an AlCu alloy containing 4 per cent Cu. At room temperature this alloy consists of both α and θ solid solutions. The θ solid solution is sometimes characterized structurally as $CuAl_2$. The steps in heat treatment follow: 1) Solution heat-treat at 1000°F to obtain a homogeneous structure composed of only α. 2) Quench in cold water. Metastable supersaturated solid solution is the only phase present in the alloy. 3) Artificially age at 300°F. This allows submicroscopic θ particles to precipitate throughout the structure. The high elastic stresses under which the θ solid solution exists are believed to lead to balancing localized elastic stresses and deformation in the matrix phase, thus strengthening and hardening it. The equilibrium diagram in view (*a*) shows this composition of phases.

(b) In view (*b*): a. Homogeneous α after solution treatment. b. Structure resulting from slow cooling. Physical properties are low. c. Metastable supersaturated α after quench. d. Artificially aged (hardened) structure (θ particles are submicroscopic). e. Overaged alloy. Soft, with low physicals.

17–5. A steel containing 0.55 per cent carbon, 3.6 per cent nickel, and 2.25 per cent chromium was tempered and cooled in the following two ways. Explain the large difference in the Charpy impact strength for the two cooling rates and give a means of eliminating the loss of ductility upon slow cooling.

Cooling Rate	Charpy Impact Strength
Air-cooled from 680°C	15
Water-quenched from 680°C	70

17–6. Briefly describe four of the following surface-treatment processes; what metals are they used on principally and what advantages are derived from their use? (a) Ihrigizing. (b) Coronizing. (c) Calorizing. (d) Nitriding. (e) Carburizing. (f) Sherardizing. (g) Chromizing.

17–7. List the precautions to take in conjunction with annealing stainless steels. (b) What composition would you suggest for a pickling solution to remove light scale formed during annealing? Give optimum temperature for use. (c) What type of annealing furnace atmosphere must be used to obtain completely scale-free parts?

17–8. (a) List five types of tests performed in the process of qualifying welders. (b) What information is obtained from each of the above tests?

17–9. Give one use for each of the following forms of cast iron and show how each is obtained: (a) white cast iron, (b) meehanite, (c) malleable iron.

17–10. What metallurgical difficulties encountered in the production of titanium from its ores contribute to its high cost?

17–11. (a) Which of the steels listed could be substituted for AISI 4340 H steel used for a 3-in.-diameter shaft? The minimum as quenched hardness at the center of the shaft must be Rockwell C 55. AISI 9260 H; AISI 5150 H; AISI 4640 H; AISI 4150 H; AISI 4140 H. (b) What heat treatment would you recommend if the shaft was to have a yield strength of 125,000 psi throughout?

17–12. On a TTT diagram point out the controlling factor for hardenability and draw cooling curve for martempering (delayed quenching).

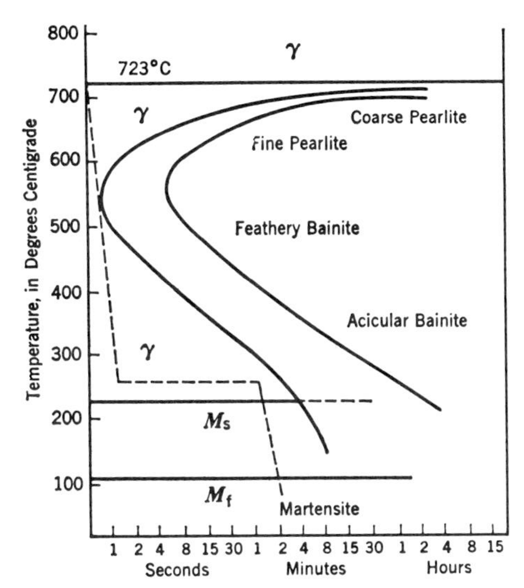

Problem 17–12. A TTT diagram for 0.80 per cent carbon steel.

Solution: See illustration.

17–13. Select a bearing metal for each of the following parts: (a) an automobile crankshaft, (b) a locomotive turntable, (c) the shaft of a motor very difficult to reach for servicing.

17–14. (a) If a liquid solution containing 60 per cent A and

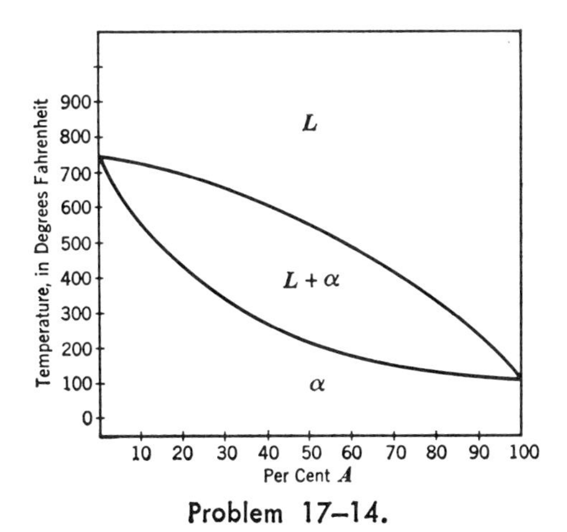

Problem 17–14.

40 per cent B is cooled slowly from 800°F, (1) what is the composition of the first solid formed in terms of A and B, (2) what is the amount of liquid found at 550°F, and (3) what is the composition of the last liquid just at the temperature of solidification? (b) A liquid solution containing 80 per cent A and 20 per cent B is cooled slowly to 300°F. (1) What is the per cent liquid present? (2) What is the composition of the solid phase at this temperature?

17–15. In blending raw lead sulfide ores and concentrates for sintering prior to smelting in the lead blast furnace, what factors must be controlled so as to produce a sintered material which will permit more efficient smelting?

17–16. (a) What is the most common composition of tungsten high-speed tool steel? (b) What mechanical and heat treatments must be given the cast alloy to make it a useful tool steel?

17–17. You are employed by an exploration group to look over a section of land on public domain that is suspected of having lode or fissure type deposits of certain minerals and metals. Your examination reveals that some of these values are present as suspected. An outcrop is located and you have placed markers along the outcrop for a considerable distance as guides for future work. (a) What are the procedures to follow in claiming this land for several years? (b) How many claims can your company have on the vein? (c) What are withdrawn lands?

17–18. *Sunshot Reference* 1959 Ephemeris (K&E) Given: Lat. N38°10.1′ (from map); Temp. 70°F; Elev. 1200 ft; Date April 4, 1959; Transit at A, backsight on B; Averaged and corrected angle right from backsight B to sun and vertical angle are respectively 156°24.2′ and 31°43.4′; Time of observation 2:47 P.M. (central time). Find bearing from A to B.

17–19. If 3000 cfm of air at 100 psi are needed in a mine, what size compressor is required? The elevation of the mine is 4000 ft. State any assumptions that you make.

17–20. What weight locomotive should be used to haul a 15-ton trailing load on level track? Assume that there is no accelerating force and that the locomotive has steel wheels. Consider that the resistance of the trailing load is 1.5 per cent of the total weight of the trailing load.

17–21. A mining company borrows $200,000 to buy a new hoist. It is estimated that there will be a direct saving of $27,000 each year in operating costs. Assume that the hoist has a life of 18 years and a new hoist will cost $225,000. The owner wishes to use the entire $27,000 each year, first to repay the borrowed capital, and second, to set up a sinking fund to meet the entire cost of the new hoist. He wants the two accounts to terminate at the same time. How shall the money be split and how long must the present equipment last? Assume that the interest rate on each account is 5 per cent.

17–22. A circular tunnel 20 ft in diameter is to be sunk through medium-hard limestone, and you are employed as a consultant on the project. What recommendations would you make on the following: (a) safety, (b) possible influx of water, (c) type of round to use?

17–23. (a) Calculate the gross value of your ore (in place) given the following data:

Analysis of Ore	Quoted Prices on Metals
Au....0.12 oz/ton	Au....$35.00 per ounce
Ag....6.0 oz/ton	Ag.... 0.88 per ounce
Pb....5.0 per cent	Pb.... 0.13 per pound
Cu....1.5 per cent	Cu.... 0.30 per pound
Zn....6.0 per cent	Zn.... 0.11 per pound
Fe....9.0 per cent	

(b) Given the following percentages of recoverable metallics, calculate the net value of the ore in place: Au, 88 per cent; Ag, 85 per cent; Pb, 87 per cent; Cu, 58 per cent; Zn, 64 per cent. (c) Determine the net cost per ton and the indicated profit from the following data: mining cost, $6.37 per ton; milling cost, $3.02 per ton; smelting cost, $2.04 per ton; overhead, $1.42 per ton. (d) Knowing the net indicated profit per ton of ore in place, what allowable development cost per ton of ore would you recommend to management?

17–24. Sketch a flow sheet to show how you would treat a complex sulfide ore containing sulfides of lead, copper, and zinc. Include the following: (a) necessary grinding stages, (b) reagents, and (c) sampling necessary.

17–25. A mining property is sold for $100,000 in payments of $15,000 cash and $5000 per year for 17 years. With interest at 5 per cent per annum what is the total cash value, now, of the property?

Mechanical Engineering 18

Representative problems are included from the following areas: steam power equipment; refrigeration and air conditioning; gas turbines, compressors, fans, and pumps; heat transfer and fluid flow; combustion processes; internal combustion engines; and general mechanical design.

Some examination problems specify solution by ASME code and, in some instances, specify a solution by state code. A review of Chapter 10, Engineering Economy, and Chapter 12, Aeronautical Engineering, may be helpful as similar problems also appear in the Mechanical Engineering examinations.

The solution of some problems requires assumptions to be made where certain information is missing; those necessary are included with the answers. Some examinations include problems requiring practical experience for the preliminary design of various systems or processes. Such problems are omitted because they will not normally be attempted by men not having experience in that particular area.

18–1. The design of a small power plant is to be based upon the following conditions:

Power output at generator terminals	5000 kw
Building heating steam, extraction pressure	30 psia
Building heating steam, quantity	60,000 lb/hr
Turbine inlet pressure	175 psia
Turbine inlet temperature	500°F
Exhaust pressure	2 psia
Generator efficiency	98 per cent

The brake turbine efficiency is 75 per cent for each part (before and after extraction opening). If the extracted steam is returned to the boiler as liquid at 200°F and if the exhaust steam is returned to the boiler as liquid at 120°F, determine (a) how much steam must be supplied to the turbine per hour and (b) how much heat must be supplied to the boiler per hour.

Solution: From Mollier diagram, $h_1 = 1273$ Btu/lb and $h_2 = 1124$ Btu/lb. For brake turbine efficiency of 75 per cent,

$$h_2' = h_1 - \eta_t(h_1 - h_2) = 1273 - 0.75(1273 - 1124) = 1161.3 \text{ Btu/lb}$$

At constant entropy on the Mollier diagram, $h_3 = 985$ Btu/lb.

$$h_3' = h_2' - 0.75(h_2' - h_3) = 1161.3 - 0.75(1161.3 - 985)$$
$$= 1029.1 \text{ Btu/lb}$$

$$\text{Turbine output} = \frac{(5000 \text{ kw})(3412 \text{ Btu/kwhr})}{0.98} = 1.74 \times 10^7 \text{ Btu/hr}$$

For throttle flow W lb/hr and 60,000 lb/hr extraction,

(a) $W(h_1 - h_2') + (W - 60{,}000)(h_2' - h_3') = 1.74 \times 10^7$ Btu/hr

$W(1273 - 1161.3) + (W - 60{,}000)(1161.3 - 1029.1) = 1.74 \times 10^7$

$W = 104{,}000$ lb/hr

Condensate to boiler = 60,000 lb/hr at 168 Btu/lb

104,000 − 60,000 = 44,000 lb/hr at 88 Btu/lb

Boiler output = 60,000(1273 − 168) + 44,000(1273 − 88)

$= 1.184 \times 10^8$ Btu/hr

(b) Heat supplied to boiler, assuming 75 per cent efficiency:

$$\frac{1.184 \times 10^8}{0.75} = 1.58 \times 10^8 \text{ Btu/hr}$$

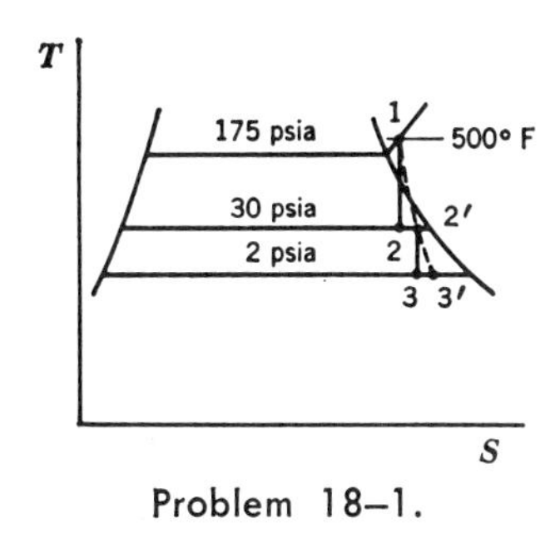

Problem 18–1.

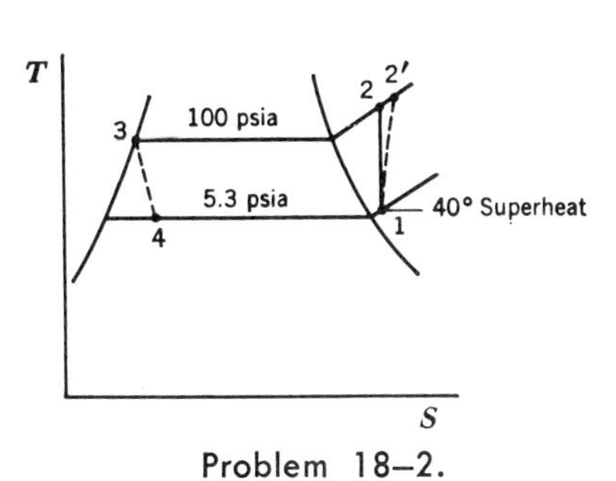

Problem 18–2.

18–2. A Freon-12 vapor compression refrigeration system has a compressor of 80 per cent adiabatic efficiency. At inlet to the compressor, the refrigerant is at a pressure of 5.3 psia and has 40° superheat; at discharge from the compressor, the pressure is 100 psia. Saturated liquid Freon at 100 psia leaves the condenser and passes through an expansion valve into the evaporator coils. The condenser is supplied with cooling water which enters at 60°F and which leaves at 70°F. For a plant capacity of 5 tons, find (a) the horsepower required to drive the compressor if it has a mechanical efficiency of 92 per cent and (b) the required capacity, in gallons per minute, of the cooling-water pump.

Solution: From tables of Freon-12 properties, $h_1 = 76.34$ Btu/lb, $h_2 = 101.2$ Btu/lb, and $h_3 = h_4 = 26.5$ Btu/lb.

From adiabatic compression efficiency,

$$0.80 = \frac{h_2 - h_1}{h_2' - h_1}$$

$$h_2' = \frac{h_2 - h_1}{0.80} + h_1 = \frac{101.2 - 76.34}{0.80} + 76.34 = 107.44 \text{ Btu/lb}$$

$$\text{Refrigerant circulated, } W = \frac{(5 \text{ tons})(200 \text{ Btu/(min)(ton)})}{h_1 - h_4}$$

$$= \frac{5(200)}{76.34 - 26.5} = 20.1 \text{ lb/min}$$

(a)

$$\text{Compressor horsepower} = \frac{w(h_2' - h_1)}{\eta_m (42.4 \text{ Btu/(min)(hp)})}$$

$$= \frac{20.1(107.44 - 76.34)}{0.92(42.4)} = 16 \text{ hp}$$

(b) Weight of cooling water, for a 10-degree temperature rise:

$$\frac{W(h_2' - h_3)}{10} = \frac{20.1(107.44 - 26.5)}{10} = 162.5 \text{ lb/min}$$

$$\text{Cooling-pump capacity} = \frac{162.5 \text{ lb/hr}}{8.33 \text{ lb/gal}} = 19.5 \text{ gpm}$$

18–3. Given the following data and performance of a fan in an installed fan system when handling air at a density of 0.075 lb/cu ft (barometer 29.92): static pressure, 1 in. water gage; capacity, 1910 cfm, fan outlet dimensions, 12⅛ in. × 15⅛ in.; fan speed, 736 rpm; shaft horsepower, 0.55 hp.

(a) Calculate the air velocity at the fan outlet. (b) Calculate the velocity pressure at the fan outlet, in inches of water gage. (c) If the fan speed is increased to 1104 rpm, determine the following: cubic feet per minute, velocity, static pressure, velocity pressure, shaft horsepower.

Solution:

$$\text{Fan outlet area} = \frac{12\tfrac{1}{8} \text{ in.} \times 15\tfrac{1}{8} \text{ in.}}{144 \text{ sq in./sq ft}} = 1.275 \text{ sq ft}$$

(a)

$$\text{Outlet velocity} = \frac{Q \text{ cfm}}{A \text{ sq ft}} = \frac{1910 \text{ cfm}}{1.275 \text{ sq ft}} = 1500 \text{ fpm}$$

(b)

$$\text{Velocity pressure } h_v = \frac{V^2}{2g} = \frac{(1500 \text{ fpm})^2}{(64.4 \text{ ft/sec}^2)(60 \text{ sec/min})^2}$$

$$= 9.71 \text{ ft air}$$

$$h_v = \frac{(9.71 \text{ ft air})(12 \text{ in./ft})(0.075 \text{ lb/cu ft air})}{62.4 \text{ lb/cu ft } H_2O}$$

$$= 0.14 \text{ in. } H_2O$$

(c) At 1104 rpm

$$Q = 1910 \text{ cfm} \frac{(1104 \text{ rpm})}{(736 \text{ rpm})} = 2870 \text{ cfm}$$

$$V = \frac{2870 \text{ cfm}}{1.275 \text{ sq ft}} = 2245 \text{ fpm}$$

$$\text{Static pressure } h_s = (1 \text{ in.}) \frac{(1104)^2}{(736)^2} = 2.25 \text{ in. } H_2O$$

$$h_v = 0.14 \text{ in. } \frac{(1104)^2}{(736)^2} = 0.315 \text{ in. } H_2O$$

$$\text{hp} = \frac{(0.55 \text{ hp})(1104)^3}{(736)^3} = 1.86 \text{ hp}$$

18–4. A twin-cylinder, double-acting, four-stroke-cycle, blast-furnace-gas engine is to develop 4000 bhp at 170 rpm. If the ratio of the length of stroke to the diameter of the bore is 1.45, probable brake mean effective pressure is 60 psi, and estimated mechanical efficiency is 86 per cent, determine the cylinder dimensions. Estimate the fuel consumption, in cubic feet per brake horsepower per hour, if the compression ratio is 7, probable brake engine efficiency is 66 per cent, K for the gas is 1.33, and the fuel will average 86.6 Btu/cu ft.

Solution: From horsepower equation, hp $= PLAN/33{,}000$, with $L/D = 1.45$ and

$$N = (2 \text{ cyl}) \left[\frac{1 \text{ power stroke}}{(\text{rev})(\text{cyl})} \right] (170 \text{ rpm}) = 340$$

$$\text{hp} = \frac{(60 \text{ lb/sq in.})(1.45D \text{ in.})(\pi/4)(D \text{ in.})^2(340)}{(12 \text{ in./ft})(33{,}000)} = 4000 \text{ hp}$$

Solving for D, $D = 41$ in., $L = 1.45(41) = 59.5$ in.

Ideal thermal efficiency

$$e = 1 - \frac{1}{r_K^{K-1}} = 1 - \frac{1}{7^{1.33-1}} = 47.4 \text{ per cent}$$

where r_K is the compression ratio. Brake engine efficiency

$$\eta_b = \frac{e_b}{e} = 0.66 \qquad e_b = 0.66(0.474) = 0.312$$

where e_b is the brake thermal efficiency. e_b is also (brake work)/(heat supplied), where the heat supplied is the quantity of fuel W_f cubic feet per hour multiplied by its heating value q Btu per cubic foot.

$$e_b = \frac{(4000 \text{ hp})[2544 \text{ Btu/(hp)(hr)}]}{(W_f \text{ cu ft/hr})(86.6 \text{ Btu/cu ft})} = 0.312 \qquad W_f = 376{,}000 \text{ cu ft/hr}$$

$$\text{Fuel consumption} = \frac{376{,}000 \text{ cu ft/hr}}{4000 \text{ Bhp}} = 94 \text{ cu ft/(Bhp)(hr)}$$

18–5. The 4 in. long crank of a slider-crank mechanism rotates at a constant angular velocity of 1800 rpm clockwise. The equivalent slider weight, including an appropriate portion of the 15 in.

long connecting rod, is 6 lb. Compute the slider inertia force acting when the angle between crank and motion-of-slider direction is 30°.

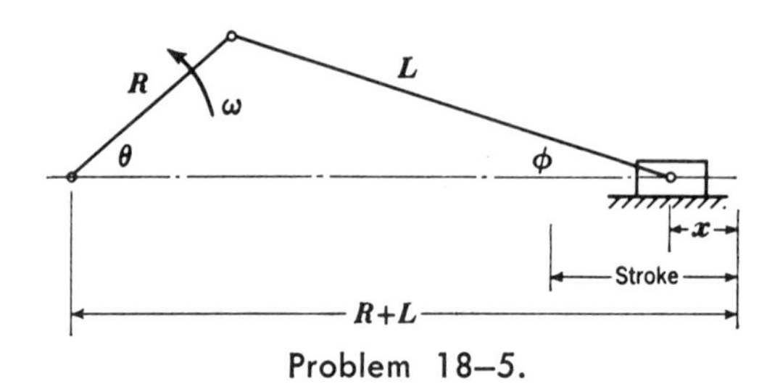

Problem 18–5.

Solution:

$$x = R + L - R\cos\theta - L\cos\phi = R(1-\cos\theta) + L(1-\cos\phi)$$

$$\cos\phi = \sqrt{1-\sin\phi} = \sqrt{1-\frac{R^2}{L^2}\sin^2\theta} \cong 1 - \frac{1}{2}\left(\frac{R}{L}\sin\theta\right)^2 \quad \text{since } \frac{R}{L} = \frac{4}{15}$$

$$x = R(1-\cos\theta) + L\left(1-1+\frac{1}{2}\frac{R^2}{L^2}\sin^2\theta\right) \qquad \dot{x} = R\omega\left(\sin\theta + \frac{1}{2}\frac{R}{L}\sin 2\theta\right)$$

$$\ddot{x} = R\omega^2\left(\cos\theta + \frac{R}{L}\cos 2\theta\right) = \frac{1}{3}(18.8)^2\left(\cos 30° + \frac{4}{15}\cos 60°\right) \text{ and}$$

$$\omega = \frac{1800\pi}{30} = 18.8 \text{ radians/sec}$$

$$x = 117.8 \text{ fps}$$

$$F = Ma\ddot{x} = \frac{6}{32.2}\ddot{x} = \frac{6}{32.2}(117.8) = 21.9 \text{ lb}$$

18–6. A cast-iron flywheel is constructed with the following dimensions: radius to center of rim, 32 in.; width of rim, 10 in.; depth of rim, 3½ in. Spoke cross-sectional area = 10 sq in. The iron is plain cast iron. There are six spokes, and the flywheel is well balanced dynamically. Assuming residual stresses are negligible and the flywheel is very slowly accelerated to 900 rpm, what safety factor (based on ultimate tensile strength of 20,000 psi) exists in the flywheel when it is rotating at 900 rpm?

Solution:

$$H = \frac{2/3}{0.0203r^2/h^2 + 0.957 + (A/A_1)} = \frac{2/3}{0.0203\ (32/3.5)^2 + 0.957 + 3.5} = 0.108$$

Force in spokes is determined from

$$F_1 = \frac{\omega r^2 n^2}{35{,}200}H = \frac{8.95\ (32)^2(900)^2}{35{,}200}(0.108) = 23{,}000 \text{ lb}$$

$$S = \frac{F_1}{A_1} = \frac{23{,}000}{10} = 2300 \text{ psi}$$

Force in rim due to centrifugal force:

$$F=\frac{\omega r^2 n^2}{35{,}200}(1-0.866\,H)=\frac{8.95\,(32)^2(900)^2}{35{,}200}[1-0.866\,(0.108)]=191{,}500 \text{ lb}$$

$$S_{CF}=\frac{191{,}500}{10\,(3.5)}=5480 \text{ psi}$$

Bending stress in rim:

$$S_B=\frac{6M}{bh^2}=\frac{6(0.0889F_1r)}{bh^2}=\frac{6(0.0889)(23{,}000)(32)}{10(3.5)^2}=3200 \text{ psi}$$

Resulting stress in rim:

$$\sigma=S_{CF}+S_B=5480+3200=8680 \text{ psi}$$

$$\text{Safety factor}=\frac{20{,}000}{8680}=11.5$$

18–7. A conical friction clutch with cast-iron contact surfaces transmits 100 hp at 1500 rpm. The cone slope is 20° and the coefficient of friction is 0.2. If the mean diameter of the bearing surface is 15 in. and the limiting value of the normal pressure is 35 psi, determine the width of the conical bearing surface and the axial load required to hold the clutch.

Solution:

$$T_f=\frac{63{,}000(\text{hp})}{n}=\frac{63{,}000(100)}{1500}=4200 \text{ lb-in.}$$

$$T_f=\frac{\pi f p_{\max} ri(r_o^2-r_i^2)}{\sin 20°} \qquad 4200=\frac{\pi(0.2)(0.35)(15-r_o)[r_o^2-(r_o-15)^2]}{\sin 20°}$$

$$r_o=7.9 \text{ in.} \qquad r_i=15-r_o=7.1 \text{ in.}$$

$$W=\frac{7.9-7.1}{\sin 20°}=2.34 \text{ in.}$$

$$R=2\pi P_{\max} ri(r_o-r_i)=6.28(35)(7.1)(0.8)=1250 \text{ lb}$$

for steady operation after load has been put in motion.

18–8. A steel valve spring for an automotive engine is loaded to 75 lb when the valve is closed and 120 lb when the valve is open. The valve lift is 0.32 in. The outside diameter of the spring must be not less than 1½ in. nor more than 1¾ in., and the permissible stress is 60,000 psi. Determine the wire diameter, outside diameter, and number of effective turns.

Solution: Assume closely coiled helical spring. For curvature effect and direct shear, let $C=D_m/D_W\geq 3$ and assume $C=7$. Stress factor is then

$$K_a=\frac{4C-1}{4C-4}+\frac{0.615}{C}=\frac{28-1}{28-4}+\frac{0.615}{7}=1.21$$

$$T=\frac{K_a 8FD_m}{\pi D_W^3} \qquad \frac{D_m}{D_W}=7$$

$$D_W = \sqrt{\frac{1.21(8)(120)(7)}{\pi(60{,}000)}} = 0.207 \text{ in.}$$

$$D_m = 7(0.207) = 1.449 \text{ in.}$$

$$D_o = D_m + D_W = 1.449 + 0.207 = 1.656 \text{ in.}$$

To determine the number of effective coils

$$\delta = \frac{8FC^3N_c}{GD_W} \quad \text{or} \quad \Delta\delta = \frac{8\Delta FC^3N_c}{GD_W} \text{ for linear spring}$$

$$N_c = \frac{\Delta\delta(G)(D_W)}{8(\Delta F)C^3} = \frac{0.32(1.15\times10^7)(0.207)}{8(120-75)(7)^3} = 6.15 \text{ effective turns}$$

$D_W = 0.207$ in., or Washburn and Moen Gage #5

$D_o = 1.66$ in.

$N_c = 6.15$ turns

18–9. A boiler has an over-all efficiency of 70 per cent when burning coal at the rate of 500 lb/hr. Coal contains 6 per cent moisture and has 12,000 Btu/lb as fired. Boiler pressure is 150 psi and steam temperature is 460°F. Determine the following: (a) pounds of steam discharged per hour, (b) boiler horsepower developed, (c) equivalent evaporation per pound of dry coal, (d) fuel cost of evaporating 1000 lb of steam from and at 212°F if coal costs $7.00 per ton.

18–10. A steam turbine operates with 75,000 lb/hr of throttle steam at 1200 psia and 1000°F and with exhaust to the condenser at 2 psia and an enthalpy of 1110 Btu/lb. Steam is extracted from the turbine at 100 psia and saturated, and it is used to heat feed water in a single closed heater to a temperature of 315°F; condensate resulting from the extracted steam passes to the condenser where it mixes with the condensed turbine exhaust. Mechanical efficiency of the turbine is 98 per cent and the generator efficiency is also 98 per cent. Neglecting losses not specifically referred to, (a) estimate flow rate in extraction steam line, in pounds per hour, (b) estimate internal turbine work, (c) estimate gross generator output, in kilowatts, and (d) estimate plant thermal efficiency.

18–11. Calculate a boiler heat balance from these data: Coal analysis: C, 60.74; H_2, 4.00; S, 1.32; O_2, 8.24; N_2, 1.15; H_2O, 12.85; ash, 11.70; Q_h=11,300 Btu/lb. Flue gas analysis: CO_2, 12; CO, 1; O_2, 7; N_2, 80. Atmospheric temperature, 70°F; flue gas temperature, 500°F. Heat transferred to steam per pound coal, 8400 Btu. Refuse in pit per ton coal burned 94 lb, free of combustible. Fly ash sampling showed 25 per cent combustible in it. The generating unit has capacity of 65,000 lb/hr, was tested at a load of 50,000 lb/hr. Two of the furnace side walls are water-cooled.

18–12. An ideal regenerative cycle with two heaters generates steam at 700 psia and 900°F and condenses at 1 in. Hg abs. The heaters operate at 20 and 160 psia. (a) Compute the efficiency of a Rankine cycle. Compute the efficiency of the regenerative cycle (b) if both heaters are open, (c) if both heaters are closed and condensate from the second heater is returned to the first, (d) if the second heater is closed and condensate is returned to the first, which is open. Neglect pump work.

18–13. A 20,000-kw steam turbine operates with 1200 psia and 1000°F inlet conditions. Condenser pressure is 2 in. Hg abs. The equivalent length of the pipe connecting to boiler is 150 ft. The maximum velocity should be 1500 fps per inch of pipe diameter. Find the correct pipe size and the pressure drop between boiler and turbine.

18–14. A reheat regenerative steam cycle operates with a condenser pressure of 2 in. Hg abs. Steam at 2000 psia and 1000°F leaves the superheater outlet header. At entrance to the turbine, the pressure is 1900 psia and the temperature is 1000°F. Expansion takes place in the turbine to a pressure of 500 psia and a temperature of 660°F. At this condition, the steam is removed and reheated without pressure drop to a temperature of 900°F. The reheated steam continues its expansion through the turbine until, at 100 psia and 500°F, a portion of the steam is extracted to an open feedwater heater. The balance of the steam continues its expansion through the turbine to a final condition of 2 in. Hg abs and a quality of 88 per cent. Neglecting the effect of pump work and losses not specifically referred to above, estimate the cycle heat rate, in Btu per kilowatthour.

18–15. A test of an ammonia vapor compression refrigeration system gave the following results: condenser pressure, 170 psia; evaporator pressure, 25 psia; temperature of vapor leaving evaporator coils, 10°F; temperature entering compressor, 20°F; temperature entering condenser, 210°F; temperature of liquid leaving condenser and entering expansion valve, 70°F; compression, isentropic. (a) Find heat lost or gained by ammonia per pound (1) between evaporator coils and compressor, (2) between compressor and condenser, and, (3) to condenser water. (b) Find (1) temperature in the evaporator coils in saturated state and (2) quality of the vapor in the evaporator coils following expansion through valve. (c) Find (1) the refrigeration effect per pound, (2) the net work per pound, and (3) the c.p.

18–16. The temperature in the evaporator of a vacuum refrigeration system is 42°F. Water at 60°F is supplied to the evaporator, which has a capacity of 100,000 Btu/hour of cooling effect. The evaporator is exhausted by a steam ejector using 40 lb of steam per ton of refrigeration. The ejector discharges to a condenser with a 92°F temperature in the steam space. Water for cooling enters the condenser at 77°F and leaves at 88°F. (a) Compute the cubic feet per minute of steam removed from the evaporator. (b) Compute the condenser water flow, in pound per hour.

18–17. In a vapor-compression refrigeration system using NH_3, saturated vapor at 10°F is received by the compressor. The compression is isentropic to 180 psia. The ammonia enters the expansion valve at 70°F. Neglecting all radiation losses, find (on the basis of 1 lb), (a) the refrigeration effect, (b) the heat rejected to condenser, (c) net work, (d) the c.p., (e) pounds of ammonia per minute per ton of refrigeration.

18–18. A certain space is to be air-conditioned with supply air entering at 65 dbt. Sensible and latent heat loads are 600,000 and 250,000 Btu/hr, respectively. Air leaving the conditioned space is to be at 80 dbt and 50 per cent relative humidity. The room air is to be recirculated through a cooling coil, except that enough room air is to bypass the cooling coil to satisfy the specific humidity requirements at the supply state. With zero requirements for ventilating air, and assuming that the air which leaves the cooling coil is saturated at the coil surface temperature (apparatus dew point), determine: (a) mass flow rate of supply air, in pounds of dry air per hour, (b) specific humidity of supply air, in grains per pound of dry air, and (c) mass flow rate of air through the cooling coil, in pounds of dry air per hour.

18–19. If 5000 cfm of air at 75°F and 50 per cent RH is mixed with 8000 cfm air at 95°F and 60 per cent RH and then dehumidified to 50°F at 90 per cent RH, determine: (a) the dry-bulb temperature and wet-bulb temperature of the mixture entering cooler, (b) the grains of moisture per pound of dry air removed in the cooler, and (c) the Btu per hour removed in the cooler.

18–20. A mechanical-draft cooling tower receives 250,000 cfm of atmospheric air at 29.60 in. Hg abs, 84° dry-bulb, 45 per cent relative humidity, and discharges the air saturated at 98°F. If the tower receives 3500 gpm of water at 104°F, what will be the exit temperature of the cooled water?

18–21. An auditorium seating 1800 people is to be maintained at 78°F dry-bulb and 67°F wet-bulb temperature when the outdoor air is at 90°F dry-bulb and 75°F wet-bulb. Solar heat load is 120,000 Btu/hr. Determine (a) cubic feet per minute of outdoor air required for ventilation, (b) volume, in cubic feet per minute, of conditioned air at 65°F dry-bulb that must be circulated to carry the total sensible heat load, (c) wet-bulb temperature of the conditioned air to absorb the moisture load.

18–22. A gas turbine is to be designed for an upper temperature limit of 1100°F with intake air at 80°F and 14.7 psia. (a) What should be temperature at the end of compression for maximum work? (b) What would be the corresponding compression ratio and thermal efficiency? (c) If 8000 lb/hr of fuel are burned, approximately what horsepower will be developed ideally by the cycle?

18–23. One stage of intercooling, one stage of reheating, and regeneration are incorporated in a gas-turbine plant. Air enters the low-pressure compressor at 14.7 psi and 60°F and leaves at 34 psi, passes through an intercooler where it is cooled to 75°F, enters the high-pressure compressor at a temperature of 60°F, and leaves it at 140 psi. The gas enters the high-pressure turbine at 1500°F and leaves at a pressure of 98 psi, passes through a reheater where its temperature is increased to 1500°F, and expands in the low-pressure turbine to 14.7 psi. A regenerator with an effectiveness of 70 per cent exchanges heat from the gases leaving the low-pressure turbine with the air leaving the high-pressure compressor. Compute, on the basis of an air-standard analysis, (a) the compression work in each compression stage, (b) the expansion work in each expansion stage, (c) the ratio of the total expansion work to the total compression work, (d) the net work done in the cycle, (e) the heat added in the cycle, (f) the thermal efficiency, and (g) the heat rejected in the cycle. (h) If cooling water is available for the intercooler at 70°F and is discharged at 85°F, compute the number of pounds mass of water required per pound mass of air flowing through the intercooler.

18–24. A single-stage, double-acting, reciprocating air compressor is guaranteed to deliver 500 cfm of free air with clearance of 3 per cent and suction conditions of 14.7 psi abs and temperature 70°F and discharge pressure of 105 psi abs. When tested under these conditions, it satisfied the manufacturer's guarantee, and test results show that compression and reexpansion curves follow $pv^n =$

constant with $n=1.34$. (a) What is the piston displacement of the unit, in cubic feet per minute? (b) If compression ratio is held constant and the unit is operated at an altitude of 6000 ft where barometric pressure and temperature are 23.8 in. Hg and 70°F, respectively, what will be its capacity and discharge pressure? (c) Assuming that bore, stroke, and clearance remain unchanged, what would you suggest doing to the compressor under (b) to make it deliver the same weight of air per minute at the same discharge pressure as under guaranteed sea level test conditions?

18–25. A turbo–air compressor is used to compress 10,000 cfm of air from a pressure of 14 psia to a final pressure of 80 psia. The initial and final air temperatures are 70°F and 150°F, respectively. The inlet and outlet pipes are 2 sq ft and 0.3 sq ft, respectively. The water enters the water jacket at a temperature of 65°F and discharges at 115°F. If the weight of water circulated per minute is 700 lb and the inlet and outlet pipes are at the same level, compute the theoretical horsepower required, using the steady-flow energy equation.

18–26. A ventilation system includes a fan of 20,000-cfm capacity discharging through a 4 ft × 3 ft duct with a static pressure of 1.15 in. of water. The temperature of the air is 85°F, the barometric pressure is 28.75 in. of Hg, and the fluid density is 62.1 lb/cu ft. What input horsepower will be required to give a fan mechanical efficiency of 44.3 per cent? What will be the static efficiency?

18–27. A condensate pump is to deliver 300,000 lb/hr of water from a condenser maintained at 1.0 psia to a deaerating heater maintained at 90 psia. Preliminary design data are as follows:

Static head on suction, referred to pump center line	15 ft
Friction drop in suction pipe	2 ft
Size of suction piping	12 in., sched. 40
Size of discharge piping	8 in., sched. 40
Static head on discharge, referred to pump center line....	60 ft
Friction drop in discharge line, including all valves	70 ft

Supply the following information: (a) dynamic head at entrance to pump, (b) dynamic head at pump discharge, (c) total dynamic head across the pump, (d) net positive suction head, and (e) the electrical power load at this design condition if over-all efficiency of pump and motor is 60 per cent.

18–28. A pump is to deliver oil with specific gravity 60/60 of 0.74 to a tank in which the elevation of the oil surface is 20 ft above the surface of the suction bin. Pressure in the discharge tank is 20 psig. Oil velocity in the 3-in. standard steel pipeline is 16.04 fps, and kinematic viscosity is 0.000008 sq ft/sec. There are 100 ft of straight pipe, two elbows, flush entrance, and submerged discharge. Calculate the brake horsepower of the driving motor for a pump efficiency of 60 per cent.

18–29. What horsepower motor would be required to supply 250 gpm of water under the following conditions: efficiency of pump, 60 per cent; intake, 10 ft below pump; discharge line, 2½ in. diameter; pressure gage reading on the discharge line at the pump, 41 psi?

18–30. A two-pass surface condenser is to be designed using an over-all heat-transfer coefficient of 480 Btu/(hr)(sq ft)(°F) with reference to the square feet of outside tube surface. The tubes are to be 1 in. OD with 1/16-in. walls. Entering circulating water velocity is to be 6 fps. Steam enters the condensers at a rate of 1,000,000 lb/hr at a pressure of 1 psia and an enthalpy of 1090 Btu/lb. Condensate leaves as saturated liquid at 1 psia. Circulating water enters the condenser at 85°F and leaves at 95°F. Calculate the required number and length of condenser tubes.

18–31. A 1000-kw turbogenerator uses 12 lb/kwhr of steam when operating with steam at 200 psia and 450°F, and exhaust pressure is 3 in. Hg abs. Determine the area of 1-in. tube surface in a surface condenser: inlet water, 70°F; outlet water, 90°F; condensate temperature, 5°F below saturation temperature; water velocity, 6 fps; mechanical efficiency of turbine unit, 94 per cent; and tube thickness, 0.049 in. If the tube length is limited to 20 ft, find number and length of tubes.

18–32. A condenser serving a 60,000-kw turbogenerator is to have 7/8-in. tubes. Water velocity in the tubes is assumed to be 7 fps. Inlet cooling-water temperature is 70°F, and a 5°F terminal difference is allowable. Vacuum is 1.5 in. of mercury, and the exhaust steam contains 950 Btu/lb. The turbine steam rate is 6.5 lb/kwhr. Calculate the square feet of tube surface required.

18–33. Steam, initially saturated at 300 psia, passes through a 4-in. standard steel pipe for a total distance of 500 ft. The steam line is insulated with a 2-in. thickness of 85 per cent magnesia. For an ambient temperature of 20°F, estimate the quality of the steam which arrives at its destination if the mass flow rate is 1000 lb/hr of steam.

18–34. Calculate the heat loss per hour from a 20 ft × 12 ft room 10 ft high, with one 20-ft side and outer wall of 4-in. brick, ½-in. air space, 4-in. brick, and lath and plaster on the inside. Outside temperature zero with severe winds. Inside temperature 70°F, with surrounding rooms and room below at same temperature. Floored attic above at 32°F. Outer wall has two 3 ft × 7 ft windows.

18–35. A duct 45 in. in diameter and 120 ft long is carrying 15,000 cfm of air at 70°F and 50 per cent relative humidity. Air pressure is 14.7 psi abs. What is the friction loss in the duct?

18–36. An 8-in. cast-iron water main (good condition) 1600 ft long is delivering 450 gpm under a head of 8 ft. It is desired to increase the delivery by paralleling this line with another 8-in. line for part of its length. What must be the length of the addition in order to get 675 gpm without increasing the head?

18–37. A 3-in. × 1½-in. venturi tube, with $\eta_d = 0.98$, is used to measure the flow of air in a 3-in.-ID pipe. The barometer is 30.05 in. of Hg, and the room temperature is 96°F. The impact temperature of the air is 114°F, and the static pressure ahead of the venturi is 3.9 in. H_2O. The pressure drop in the venturi is 11.4 in. H_2O. Account for the initial velocity. How much free (room) air is flowing, in cubic feet per minute?

18–38. Calculate the capacity, in cubic feet per minute, of an induced-draft fan for a boiler plant based on the following operating conditions:

Coal consumption	2000 lb/hr
Flue-gas temperature	400°F

Coal Analysis (per cent)				Orsat Analysis of Flue Gas (per cent)	
C	62.5	N	1.1	CO_2	13.0
H	5.1	O	15.2	O_2	5.4
S	3.4	Ash	12.6	CO	0.5

18–39. A flue gas shows the following by Orsat analysis: $CO_2 = 13$ per cent, $CO = 1$ per cent, $O_2 = 6$ per cent, and $N_2 = 80$ per cent. The fuel burned was coal which analyzed $C = 78$ per cent, $H_2 = 4$ per cent, $O_2 = 3$ per cent. Find (a) theoretical weight of air, in pounds per pound of coal, (b) actual weight of air, in pounds per pound of coal, (c) pounds of dry flue gas per pound of coal.

18–40. The exhaust gases from an automotive engine operating on octane, C_8H_{18}, showed the following analysis, in per cent by volume: $CO_2=11.3$, $O_2=4.02$, $CO=0.35$, $N_2=84.33$. Find (a) the weight of air used per pound of fuel, (b) the percentage of excess air, and (c) the weight, in pounds per pound of fuel, of each of the products of combustion.

18–41. A fuel gas is composed of $CH_4=52$ per cent, $C_2H_6=11$ per cent, $H_2=21$ per cent, $CO_2=12$ per cent, and $N_2=4$ per cent by volume. Calculate the amount of air required, in cubic feet of air per cubic foot of gas, if it is to be burned with 10 per cent excess air.

18–42. A six-cylinder, four-stroke-cycle, single-acting automotive engine is required to develop 80 bhp at 3600 rpm. The probable friction horsepower, including fluid losses, is 36, and the probable brake mean effective pressure is 86 psi. (a) For $L/D=1.4$, what are the bore and stroke? (b) What are the probable brake torque, mechanical efficiency, and indicated mean effective pressure?

18–43. A 2000-kw diesel generator unit uses 1261 lb/hr of fuel at full load. The higher heating value of the fuel is 18,650 Btu/lb. The eight-cylinder, two-stroke-cycle engine turns at 360 rpm and has a displacement of 7000 cfm. The generator efficiency is 92 per cent; the mechanical efficiency of the engine is 80 per cent. The temperature and pressure of air entering the engine are 90°F and 14 psia. The compression ratio is 13.5. (a) Determine the brake, indicated, and combined thermal efficiencies. (b) Estimate the weight of such an engine. (c) Estimate the volume of exhaust gases, in cubic feet per minute.

18–44. Given the following performance data for an eight-cylinder $3\frac{1}{4} \times 3\frac{3}{4}$ automotive engine:

Actual speed	3210 rpm
Brake torque	125 lb-ft
Fuel rate	55.9 lb/hr
Higher heating value of fuel	20,300 Btu/lb
Air-to-fuel ratio	12:1
Atmospheric pressure	28.36 in. Hg abs
Carburetor air temperature	84°F
Friction horsepower at 3210 rpm	34.9 hp

Determine the (a) brake thermal efficiency, (b) mechanical efficiency, (c) volumetric efficiency.

18–45. During 60° rotation of a disk cam revolving at 120 rpm the follower moves radially ½ in. from rest at constant acceleration. The follower is then brought to rest at constant deceleration during the next 90° rotation of cam. Compute the total radial travel of the follower during this 150° rotation of the cam.

18–46. A 3000-lb automobile, moving on level ground at 60 mph, is to be stopped in a distance of 160 ft. The diameter of the tires is 30 in. (a) What total average braking torque must be applied? Neglect all frictional effects except that of the brakes. (b) What must be the coefficient of friction between the tires and the road in order for the wheels not to skid? Assume that the weight is equally distributed among the four wheels. (c) If the entire energy absorbed is momentarily stored in the brake drums (which weigh 50 lb and have a specific heat of 0.13), what is the temperature rise of the drums?

18–47. (a) A pair of helical gears connect shafts 90° apart. Speed ratio=2:1. One gear has a pitch diameter of 8 in. and a helix angle of 30°. Find the helix angle and pitch diameter of the second gear. (b) A triple-threaded worm drives a gear wheel with 72 teeth. The linear pitch is 1½ in. The pitch diameter of the worm is 4 in. Determine the lead angle, the velocity ratio, pitch diameter of the gear wheel, and the distance between centers. (c) Design an epicyclic gear train with as small a number of gears as possible to give a reduction ratio of 10:1.

18–48. Suppose that 40 hp at 1500 rpm is delivered to shaft *1*. Gear *A* has 18 teeth; gear *B*, 45 teeth; gear *C*, 12 teeth; and gear *D*, 24 teeth. The loss of power between shafts *1* and *2* is assumed to be 5 per cent and between shafts *2* and *3* also 5 per cent. What are the torques, in pound-inches exerted by shafts *1, 2,* and *3?*

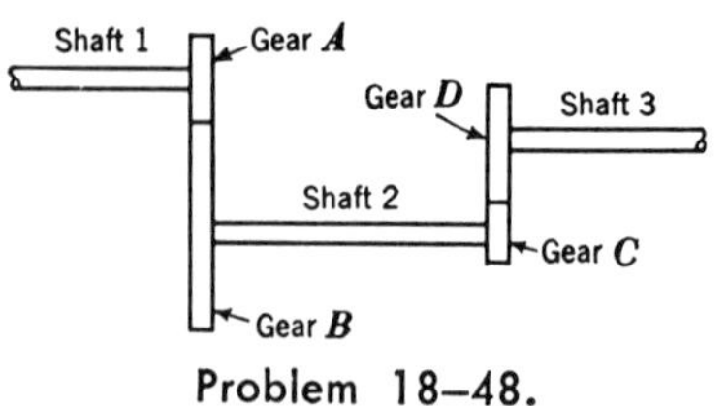

Problem 18–48.

18–49. The sketch represents the gearing of a chain hoist in which *A* is the fixed gear having 49 teeth meshing with the spur gear *B* with 12 teeth, and gear *C* is fast to the same shaft as *B* which revolves in bearings in the arm E. Gear C, with 31 teeth, meshes with gear D, having 13 teeth, which is rigidly attached to the shaft of the pull-chain sprocket G. Sprocket F has a pitch diameter of $3\frac{1}{8}$ in., and the pull-chain sprocket has a diameter of $9\frac{3}{4}$ in. If the pull chain moves at 50 fpm, how fast will the load rise?

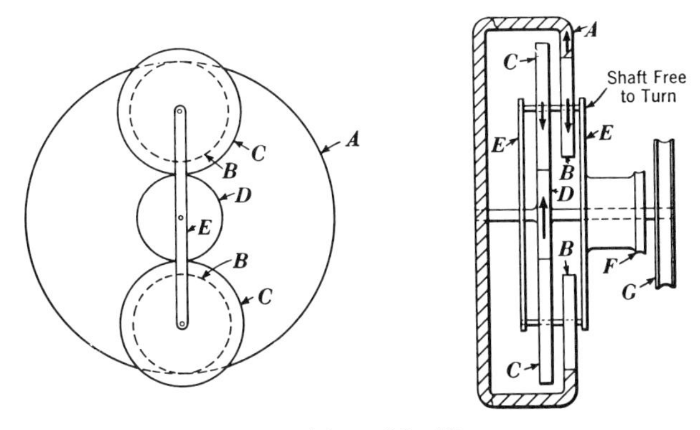

Problem 18–49.

18–50. In a pin-connected joint the pin is $1\frac{1}{4}$ in. in diameter, its effective length is 2 in., and it is supported on both ends. The pin material has an ultimate strength of 60,000 psi, a yield strength of 30,000 psi, a shear strength of one-half the tensile, and allowable bearing pressure of 4000 psi of projected area. Use design factor of 5 based on ultimate. (a) Determine by calculation loads for all possible ways of pin failure. (b) Show by calculation the maximum safe load for the pin.

18–51. The yoke of a turnbuckle is fastened to a plate inserted in the fork by means of a pin. All parts are made of SAE-1015 steel at a factor of safety of 3. If the yoke rod is $\frac{1}{2}$ in. in diameter, compute the minimum size pin required. Pin is also of SAE-1015.

18–52. A machine element consists of a cast-iron beam 5 ft long. Its axis is horizontal, and it is subjected to a vertical load lying in its plane of symmetry 2 ft from one end. The section under the maximum bending moment consists of two flanges, 2 in. and 5 in. wide, respectively, connected by a vertical web 5 in. high. The thickness is uniformly 1.0 in. The permissible tensile stress is 5000 psi. Considering the section to be used most advantageously, calculate the permissible load. Stress due to dead weight may be disregarded.

18–53. A cylindrical pedestal, 8 in. long and made of gray cast iron, is to support a load of 26,000 lb. The pedestal must not shorten more than 0.016 in. due to the load. Compute the diameter required.

18–54. Determine the maximum value of the repeated tensile stress for mild steel if the stress alternates from zero stress up to this maximum value. Give brief explanation as to how this value was obtained.

18–55. A bracket is needed to transfer a load F varying cyclically between 1000 and 10,000 lb from pin A to pin B over the obstruction C (see sketch). The pins 1 in. in diameter are made of cold-drawn SAE-1045 carbon steel, surface-hardened for good wear. The bracket is to be made of SAE-2330 steel. Completely design a bracket suitable and safe for this application. Draw a working sketch of your design.

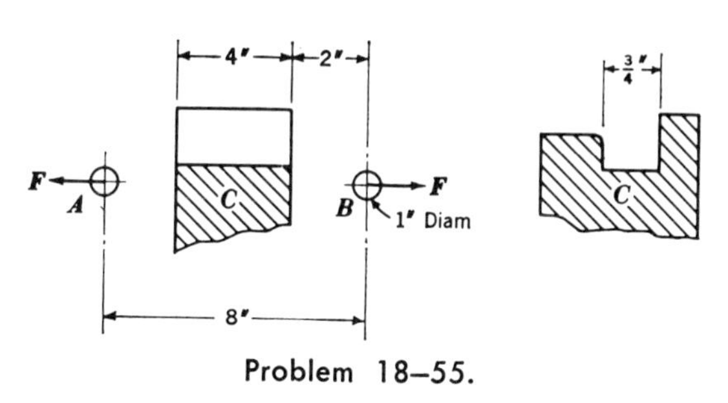

Problem 18–55.

18–56. Find the lowest natural frequency for a valve spring #4 steel wire of 10 active coils and mean diameter of helix of 2 in.

18–57. An automobile engine operating at 3800 rpm and full load delivers 90 hp at the crankshaft. Of this power, 10 per cent is used to overcome friction between the crankshaft and the rear axle at low gear and 5 per cent at high gear. The differential ratio is 4.7:1, and the transmission reduction in low gear is 2.8:1; the axle diameter is 1⅜ in. Write a power equation, in which all quantities are represented by algebraic symbols, in which the left side of the equation represents the mechanical power delivered by the engine, in terms of speed and torque of the crankshaft, and the right side of the equation represents the power delivered to the rear axle plus the losses between the engine and the rear axle. Check the dimensional correctness of the equation and then use the equation to find the maximum shearing stress due to torsion in the rear axle at full load conditions (a) in low gear, (b) in high gear. Calculate what the above stress would be if there were no keyways, splines, or stress concentrations.

18–58. A motor rotor is mounted between bearings 5 ft apart. The center of gravity of the rotor and shaft is 2 ft from one of the bearings and 0.1 in. away from the axis of rotation. If the weight of rotor and shaft is 600 lb, find the maximum bearing loads when rotating at 500 rpm.

18–59. A diesel engine developing 1850 hp at 105 rpm is used to drive a ship's propeller. The propeller shaft is made of 3½ per cent nickel steel, heat-treated to an ultimate strength of 130,000 psi, and ultimate in shear about 70 per cent of the ultimate in tension. Angular twist is limited to 1° in a length equal to 20 diameters. Apparent factor safety is 6. Find the diameter of a hollow shaft if the outside diameter is taken as twice the inside diameter.

18–60. The engine of an automobile is capable of developing a maximum brake horsepower of 80 at an engine speed of 3300 rpm, 90 per cent of which is delivered to the rear axle. The velocity ratio between the engine and the rear axle is 13.2 when the transmission is set in low gear. Assuming that the full power is developed in low gear, determine the shearing stresses in the axle if it has a keyway and a diameter of 2 in.

18–61. A shaft in torsion only is to transmit with medium shock 3000 hp at 200 rpm. The material of the shaft is to be SAE-1045. (a) What should be the diameter of a solid shaft for these conditions? (b) If the shaft is made hollow, the outer diameter being twice the inner, what size shaft will be required? (c) What is the weight per foot of length of each of the shafts found? Which is the lighter? What is the per cent saving in weight? (d) Which shaft is the more rigid? Compute the torsional deflection of each for a length of 10 ft.

18–62. A manufacturer of ball bearings rates his bearings on the basis of 500 rpm and a life of 1000 hr. If a bearing is desired to be operated at 1750 rpm and for 16 hr/day, 5 days per week, for a period of 1 year, what load rating would be used to select the bearing from the catalog if the bearing is to carry a radial load of 500 lb and an axial load of 200 lb? The bearing is to be of the self-aligning type with outer race stationary.

18–63. The main bearings of a steam engine are 7 in. in diameter; the load coming upon each bearing is 15,000 lb; and the engine speed is 135 rpm. Determine (a) the length of the bearing, (b) the necessary running clearance, using SAE 60 oil, and (c) the horsepower lost in friction at each bearing.

18–64. A 20-tooth manganese-bronze pinion meshes with a cast-iron gear. The velocity ratio is 5; the diametral pitch is 5; the face is 2 in.; and the gear turns 200 rpm. The teeth are $14\frac{1}{2}°$ standard height and commercially cut. (a) Which is stronger, the tooth on the pinion or the tooth on the gear? Show the reasons for your answer. (b) What horsepower will the combination safely transmit in continuous service?

18–65. A 5000-lb load is being raised at the rate of 450 fpm by a drum hoist having a drum diameter of 12 in. Between the drum and the hoist engine is a speed-reducing unit which consists of the following gear train: On the drum shaft is a 52-tooth gear which meshes with a 24-tooth pinion on an idler shaft; compounded with this pinion is a 60-tooth gear which meshes with a 15-tooth pinion on a second idler shaft; compounded with this pinion is a 42-tooth gear which meshes with a 16-tooth pinion on the engine shaft. All gears are of 3 pitch. (a) Sketch the rig from drum to engine shaft. (b) Using 7500 psi allowable stress in shear, compute the required standard shaft size for the drum and engine shaft, neglecting bending stresses. (c) Assuming 88 per cent efficiency in the rig, compute the horsepower delivered by the engine and its revolutions per minute. (d) Using reasonable allowable tooth stresses, determine the face widths of the 52-tooth and the 24-tooth cast-steel spur gears.

18–66. A pair of spur gears with 20° stub teeth must transmit 25 hp at a speed of 5000 rpm of the pinion. The velocity ratio is 10, and the diameter of the pinion is 3 in. The material of the pinion is SAE 1045, tempered at 1000°F. The gear is made of cast iron. Determine the pitch and face for continuous service if the margin of safety is 0.25.

18–67. A cone clutch has a face angle of 15° with a maximum diameter of 24 in. and a face width of 3 in. The coefficient of friction is 0.20 and the permissible pressure on the cone surface is 12 psi. (a) What torque may be transmitted? (b) What axial force must be exerted to obtain this torque?

18–68. A drive shaft rotating at 1500 rpm is connected to the source of power by means of a cone clutch. The mean diameter of the clutch is 16 in., and the cone angle is 10°. What horsepower can be transmitted if the axial force pressing the two halves together is 200 lb and the coefficient of friction is 0.35?

18–69. A hollow steel shaft with an outside diameter of 5.998 in. and a 1-in. inside diameter is to be pressed into a steel disk whose outside diameter is 27 in. Determine the maximum stresses in the disk and the shaft and also the pressure between the disk and shaft, using standard class 8 fit and the proper tolerance for the hole in the disk.

18–70. A closed steel shell 18 in. in diameter and 60 in. long is completely filled with water at 68°F and 30 psig. How high can the temperature of the surrounding air get before there is serious danger of rupture of the shell? The shell and heads are made of ¼ in. thick steel plate, SAE 1015. The heads are ellipsoidal with the minor axis equal to one-half the radius of the shell.

18–71. A circular plate is used as a diaphragm as shown and is edge-fixed. Steam at a pressure of 150 psig is applied to one side and atmospheric pressure on the other side. Calculate the thickness of the plate required, the maximum stress in the plate, and the maximum deflection. Use $S_s = 60{,}000$ psi and an apparent factor of safety of 6.

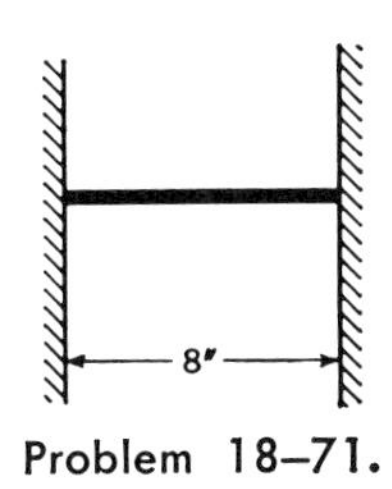

Problem 18–71.

18–72. A T-joint welded on both sides with an E-6010 electrode is to transmit a load of 24,000 lb. If the fillet size is ⁵⁄₁₆ in., how long must each weld be?

18–73. A 3-ft-diameter welded cylindrical closed tank made of ⅜-in. steel plate having a tensile strength of 55,000 psi contains air at a pressure of 200 psig. What is the longitudinal stress in the plate? What is the transverse stress (hoop tension) in the plate? (Assume the welds have the same tensile strength as the plate and neglect the difference between inside and outside diameters in calculation of internal pressure.)

18–74. A cold shear is to cut 1-in. square bars at 15 strokes per minute. Shearing stress=48,000 psi; friction=20 per cent; flywheel rpm=120; speed reduction=5 per cent; flywheel mean rim diameter=5 ft; rim depth=1.25 times rim width; weight of cast iron=0.26 lb/cu in. Calculate rim weight and cross section.

18–75. A steel crank web having an outside diameter of 16 in. is to be shrunk on a hollow shaft. The diameter of the contact surface is 9 in. and that of the hole in the shaft is 4 in. What original difference exists between the inside diameter of the hole in the web and the outside diameter of the shaft if a radial pressure of 5000 psi is to be secured?

18–76. A constant-force snubber is proposed for stopping side-tracked railroad cars. Determine the magnitude of force to be provided if a car is to be stopped in a distance of 2 ft, given the following data:

(a) Weight of the car, excluding wheels = 20,000 lb
(b) Weight of each of 8 wheels = 250 lb
(c) Wheel diameter (assume disk with uniform thickness) = 2 ft
(d) Car velocity at initial impact (assume track friction provides a constant retarding force equal to 200 lb) = 2 mph

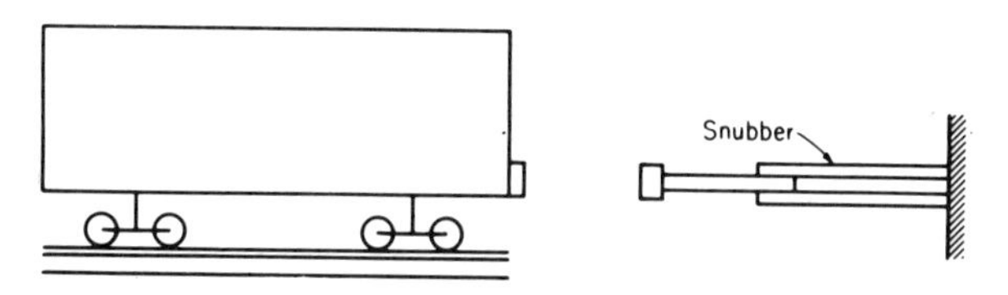

Problem 18–76.

18–77. The load cycle for a shaft is as shown. The shaft is driven by a belt and can be assumed to receive a constant driving torque. For a coefficient of fluctuation of one-tenth and a speed of 150 rpm, what should the outside diameter of the flywheel be if it is solid and cut from 2½-in. steel plate?

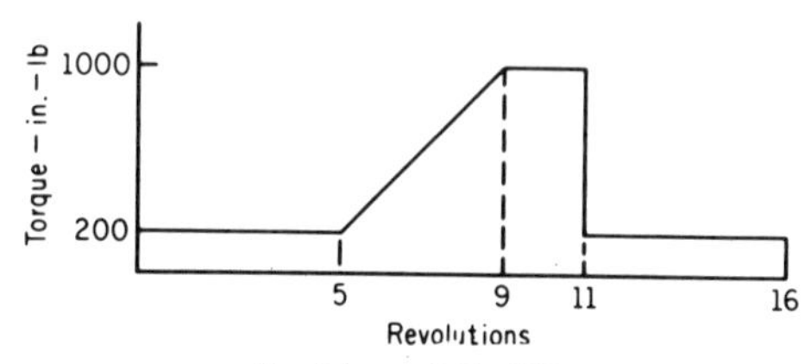

Problem 18–77.

18–78. A load cell in the form of a bent aluminum strip is shown in the diagram. The strip is ¼ in. wide and $\frac{1}{10}$ in. thick. Determine the strain gage reading for a 5 lb load.

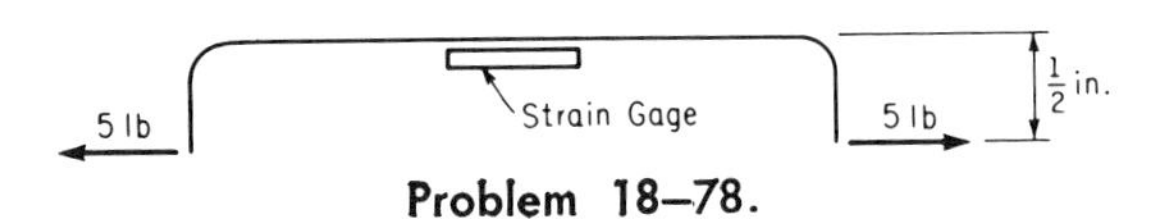

Problem 18–78.

18–79. In order to prevent the transmission of vibrations to surrounding machines, 16 helical springs are to be used to support a percussion machine for testing rock bits. The total static load on all springs is 50,000 lb, under which each spring is to deflect 0.4 in. The maximum possible deflection is to be at least 1 in. Use a wire diameter of $1\frac{3}{16}$ in., and an outside coil diameter of $5\frac{7}{16}$ in. Find (a) the spring constant of the springs; (b) the number of free coils in each spring; (c) the stress caused by the static load; (d) the solid height if the ends are closed and ground; and (e) the free length and "solid stress."

18–80. A 2-in. diameter steel rod supports a 2000-lb load and, in addition, is subjected to a torsional moment of 1000 in.-lb as shown in the accompanying figure. Determine the maximum tensile and the maximum shear stress.

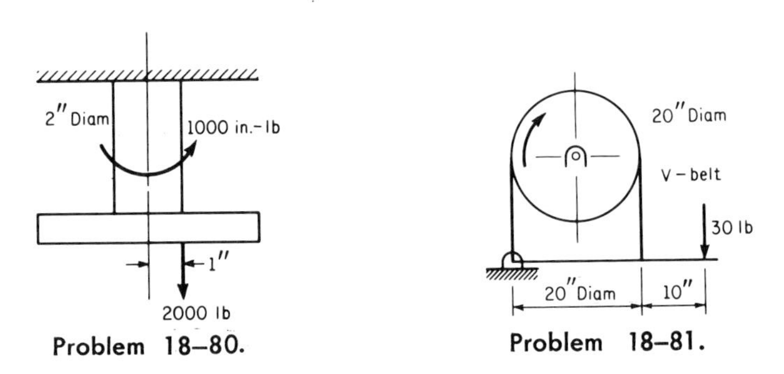

Problem 18–80. Problem 18–81.

18–81. A band brake uses a V-belt. The pitch diameter of the V-grooved sheave is 20 in. The groove angle is 45° and the coefficient of friction is 0.25. For the dimensions shown in the accompanying figure, determine the maximum horsepower rating for 300 rpm.

18–82. Illustrated is a rotation system which is to be balanced by removing mass from the two correction planes which are designated as L and R. Calculate the magnitude in ounce-inches and the angular location of the two corrections.

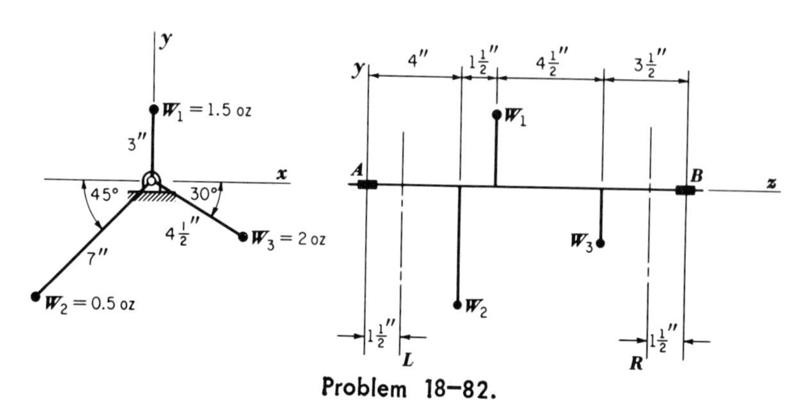

Problem 18–82.

18–83. A vehicle using the differential shown in the figure turns to the right at a speed of 30 mph on a curve of 80-ft radius. The tooth numbers are $N_2 = 11$, $N_3 = 54$, $N_4 = 11$, and $N_5 = N_6 = 16$. The tires are 15 in. in diameter. Use 60 in. as the center-to-center distance between treads. (a) Calculate the speed of each rear wheel. (b) What is the speed of the ring gear?

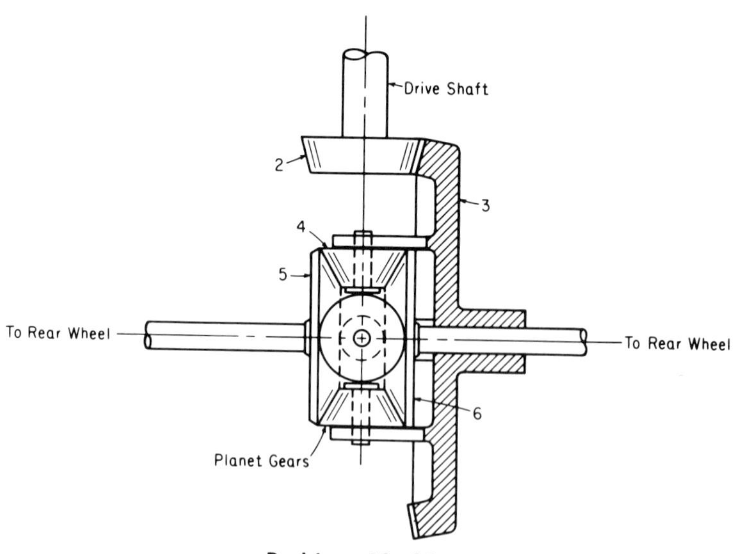

Problem 18–83

18–84. The diagram shows a rigid body suspended as a compound pendulum. When supported by a knife edge as shown, following an initial small angular displacement the time interval required for ten complete oscillations is 9.09 sec. By a balancing operation, the mass center of the connecting rod is found to be 5.75 in. below the knife edge support. Compute the square of the radius of gyration of the body about an axis which passes through the mass center and is parallel to the knife edge, in sq in.

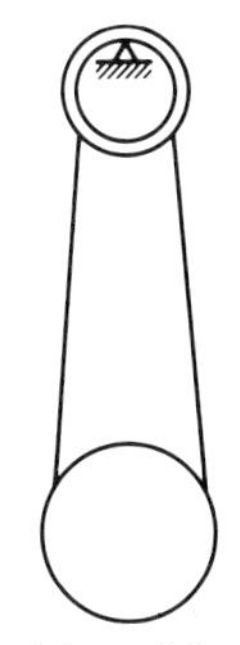

Problem 18–84.

18–85. A multiple-disk clutch having four pairs of mating friction surfaces operates at a speed of 945 rpm. The maximum permissible magnitude of the axial actuating force is 800 lb. Coefficient of friction equals 0.15. The inside and outside radii of contact of the friction surfaces are 1 in. and 2 in., respectively. If conditions are such that uniform wear prevails, determine the (a) torque capacity per pair of friction surfaces; (b) total horsepower capacity; (c) maximum pressure; (d) minimum pressure.

18–86. A horizontal hollow shaft weighing 320 lb/ft is supported by two bearings 25 ft apart. The inside and outside diameters of the shaft are 9 in. and 15 in., respectively. Maximum power of 4400 hp is transmitted to the input-end of the shaft (right-bearing end) at a speed of 126 rpm. At the output-end of the shaft (left-bearing end) there is a thrust load of 300,000 lb (in addition to the torque load). Assume that the load is applied gradually. Determine maximum shearing stress developed in the shaft.

18–87. The schematic diagram shows a quick-return mechanism used in a machine tool. Crank OB is driven counter-clockwise at a constant speed of 10 radians/sec and drives slotted arm AD through crankpin B. The resultant oscillation of arm AD drives the arm R through pin C. Friction and gravity effects are to be neglected. For the instantaneous position shown, the angular acceleration of arm AD is 26 radians/sec^2 counter-clockwise and the contact force at pin C is 150 lb in a direction opposing the motion. What is the instantaneous force on crankpin B for this same position?

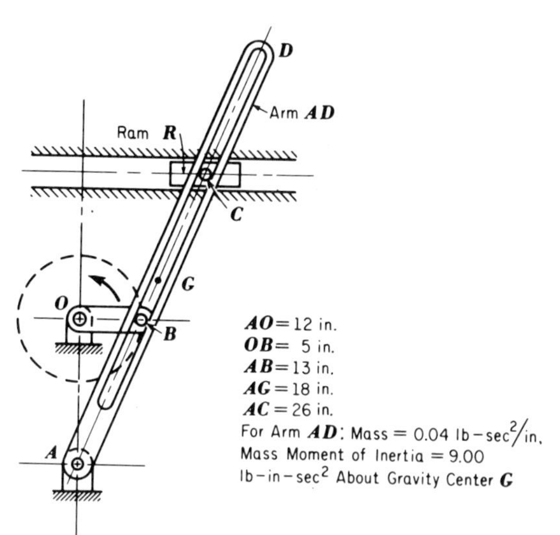

Problem 18–87.

18–88. A cantilever beam, with a tip mass weighing 1 lb, is mounted on a flywheel as shown in the diagram. Strain gages generate a signal proportional to bending moment, and are to be used as a means of indicating flywheel speed. What should the mounting angle θ be for maximum sensitivity? (That is, maximum bending moment for a given speed.)

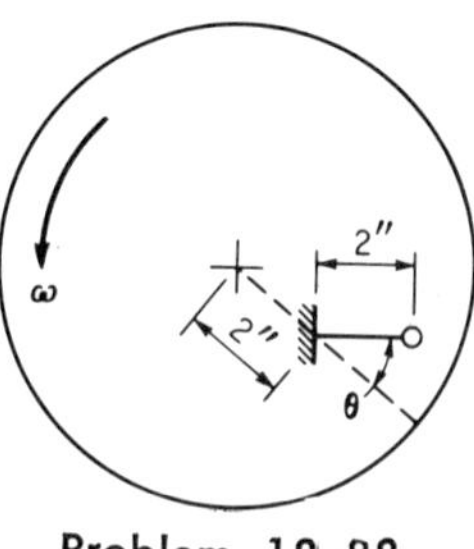

Problem 18–88.

18–89. A pair of helical spur gears is mounted as shown. The maximum peak torque is 6000 in-lb. The gears are cut with 20° involute teeth having a 15° helix angle. The diametral pitch is

5 and the driving gear has 60 teeth. What are the loads on the bearing on the input shaft? For solution assume a single direction of rotation and either a right- or left-hand helix.

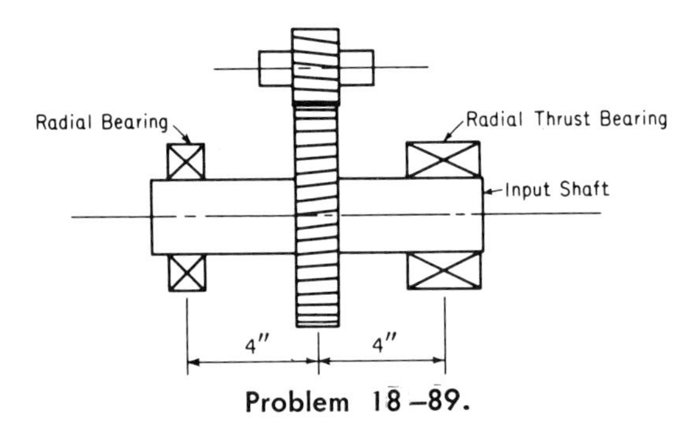

Problem 18–89.

18–90. An 8 WF 31 simply supported beam is reinforced by a 10 WF 49 cantilever as shown. The strut between them was installed while both beams were unloaded.

Compute for the cantilever beam: The load, the deflection, and the bending stress. Neglect the weights of both beams.

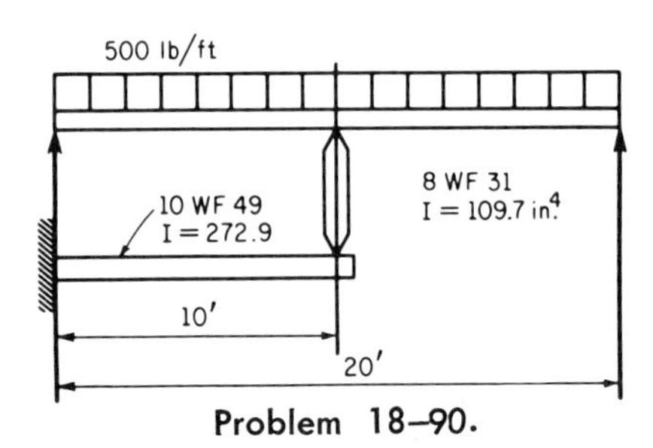

Problem 18–90.

18–91. Steam with a 5-psi gage pressure passes through a vertical 2-in. nominal pipe located in a room maintained at 75°F. Determine the minimum insulation thickness that should be used to prevent the surface from exceeding 125°F. The insulation is available in ¼-in. increments of thickness, and has thermal conductivity of 0.07 Btu/hr-sq ft-deg. The outside surface is to be enameled, providing a convection film coefficient of 1.0 Btu/hr-sq ft-deg and a radiation emissivity of 0.95.

18–92. Determine the heat transfer rate (Btu/hr) from the exposed top surface of a cube-shaped metal tank that is otherwise insulated. The tank is 2 ft on each edge and the heat transfer is assumed to be by natural convection to still room air at 90°F. A thermocouple fixed to the top of the tank indicates a steady temperature of 380°F.

18–93. The thermal conductivity of a material is to be determined by fabricating the material into the shape of a hollow sphere, placing an electric heater at the center, and measuring the surface temperature with thermocouples when steady-state has been reached.

Experimental Data: $r_1 = 1.12''$, $r_2 = 3.06''$. For an electrical energy input at the rate of 11.1 watts to the heater, $t_1 = 203$°F and $t_2 = 184$°F.

Determine (a) the experimental value of the thermal conductivity and (b) the temperature at a point half way through the sphere wall.

18–94. A centrifugal pump having four stages in parallel delivers 2400 gal/min of liquid against a head of 81 ft, the diameter of the impellers being 9 in. and speed 1700 rpm. Another pump is to be built with a number of identical stages in series, hydrodynamically similar to those in the first pump, to run at 1250 rpm, and to deliver 3200 gal/min against a head of 820 ft. Find the diameter of the impellers and the number of stages required.

18–95. Two hundred gallons of oil are pumped through a pipe 2000 ft long and 4 in. in diameter. The oil has an absolute viscosity of 0.00011 slug/ft sec and a specific weight of 58 lb/ft^3. Find the head lost in friction if the friction coefficient f of the Fanning equation is given by $f = 0.064 \text{ Re}^{-0.23}$ where Re is the Reynolds number. The discharge end of the pipe line is 60 ft higher in elevation than the inlet. Both inlet and discharge are at atmospheric pressure. Determine the power required to drive the pump, assuming pump efficiency of 65 per cent.

18–96. A perfect gas flows from a reservoir having a pressure of 42 psia and a temperature of 60°F. It passes through a converging-diverging nozzle having a throat area of 20 sq in. A static pressure survey along the nozzle indicates a normal shock wave downstream of the throat at a section of the nozzle where the cross-sectional area is 60 sq in. What would you expect the pressure, velocity, temperature, and density of the gas flow to be at a section downstream of the shock wave where the cross-sectional area is 100 sq in.? Assume that the ratio of specific heats, k, is 1.40.

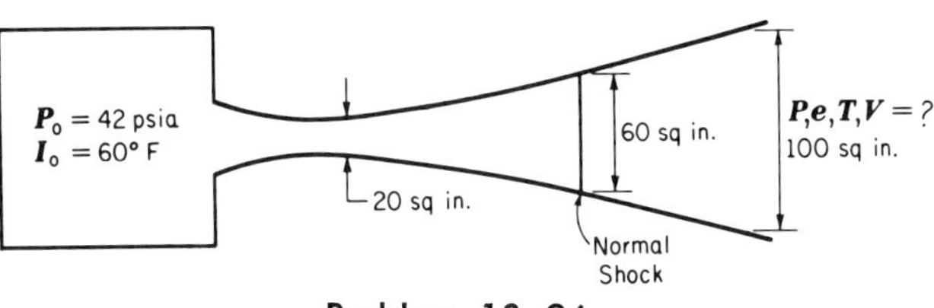

Problem 18–96.

18–97. The resistance of a certain boat to motion through fresh water is expressed by $F = 0.4V^2$ where V is the velocity of the boat through the water. A pump which is capable of pumping 5 cfs is installed in the boat so as to take water in through the bottom and discharge it to the rear through a pipe having an exit 0.1 sq ft in area. (a) How fast can the pump drive the boat? (b) What is the velocity of the jet of water leaving the boat relative to the water in the lake?

18–98. A drying room is to be maintained at a dry-bulb temperature of 95°F and 30 per cent relative humidity. The room has a sensible heat gain of 72,000 Btu/hr. The total weight of moisture to be evaporated from the objects being dried amounts to 40 lb/hr. Chilled air is introduced to the room at a dry bulb temperature of 65°F to absorb the moisture and sensible heat gain to the space. Find (a) the required wet bulb temperature of the 65°F air furnished to maintain the desired room condition; and (b) the volume of chilled air to be furnished in cubic feet per minute.

18–99. A residence having 12,000 cu ft of occupied space is to be maintained at 71.50° dry bulb temperature and 35 per cent relative humidity. The house has one air change per hour when the outside air temperature is 0°F with a relative humidity of 100 per cent. Find the number of gallons of water per 24-hr period of humidification. Assume standard atmospheric pressure.

18–100. Recirculated water enters a cooling tower at 100°F and leaves at 80°F. Air enters at 100°F dry-bulb, 73°F wet-bulb, and leaves at 85°F and 95 per cent relative humidity. Make-up water temperature is 60°F. Tower basin solids concentration shall not increase by more than a factor of five. (a) Determine volume of air to be moved per minute by the induced draft fan to give 1000 kw of cooling to the water. (b) Determine gallons of water per minute make-up required with 100,000 cfm of air passing through the induced draft fan. (c) Determine the amount of water in gallons that can be cooled in a minute by 50,000 cfm of free air.

Surveying

19

Surveying problems are sometimes included in the Fundamentals section (Part I) and in the Civil Engineering Section (Part II), besides the Land Surveying examination. Typical fundamental problems cover taping, leveling, and computation of bearings, latitudes, departures, and areas. The Civil Engineering examination may include these as well as simple curves, vertical curves, earthwork computations, and property descriptions. Land Surveying examinations vary widely, depending upon the state and its location. Legal questions and property descriptions, in both metes and bounds and public lands systems, are frequently emphasized. Short questions on diverse subjects, true or false statements, and multiple choice arrangements are becoming more common for parts of the registration examination. So are problems involving electronic measuring instruments, computer programs, and photogrammetric theory and equipment. A comprehensive compilation of surveying problems is given in a book devoted exclusively to this subject.[1]

19–1. (a) A line was measured horizontally with a 100-ft steel tape and the distance recorded as 1235.75 ft on the assumption that the tape was 100.00 ft in length. The temperature of the tape during the measurement was 100°F. Upon checking the tape it was found to be 100.00 ft in length at 68°F. What is the true length of the line? (b) What would be the recorded measurement of the line in (a) if the temperature was 30°F? Make calculations to the nearest 0.01 ft. Coefficient of linear expansion of the tape is 0.0000065 per deg F.

Solution: (a) $\text{Correction} = (100° - 68°)0.0000065(1235.75) = 0.26$ ft

$\text{True length} = 1235.75 + 0.26 = 1236.01$ ft

(b) $\text{Correction} = 38°(0.0000065)1236.01 = 0.31$ ft

$\text{Recorded length} = 1236.01 + 0.31 = 1236.32$ ft

19–2. On a certain survey, the field notes show that a level reading of 3.55 ft was taken on *B* at a distance of 2115 ft from the instrument at *A*. The height of instrument was recorded as

[1] R. C. Brinker, *3701 Review Questions for Surveyors* (published and sold by author, Box 893, University Park, N. M. 88070).

4.34 ft above A. Correction in feet for the earth's curvature is $0.66K^2$, and for the earth's atmospheric refraction $0.09K^2$, where K is in miles. What is the difference in elevation between A and B?

Solution: Total correction $= (0.66 - 0.09)(2115/5280)^2 = 0.09$ ft

B is $+4.34 - (3.55 - 0.09) = 0.88$ ft higher

19–3. A surveyor must find the difference in elevation between point A located in a canyon and point B on the canyon wall. Point B is inaccessible but visible from points A and C. Point C is 100.00 ft from A toward B on a direct line between A and B, but is 15.82 ft higher than A. The surveyor's notes show that when set up on A, he read an angle of 30°00′ from the horizontal to B, and when set up on C he read an angle of 40°00′ from the horizontal to B. The H.I. in each case was 4.51 ft. (a) Draw a diagram showing the known distances and angles. (b) Find the line-of-sight distance between B and the center of the transit telescope at A. (c) Find the difference in elevation between A and B.

19–4. To measure the width of a river, two points A and B are set 150.0 ft apart on one bank. A tree on the other side of the river is very close to the bank and designated point C. Angle CAB is adjusted to be 90°, after which CBA is found to be 36°00′. (a) What is the width of the river at this point, in feet? (b) If the angle at point A between the horizontal and the top of the tree is 30°, what is the height of the tree, in feet?

19–5. The elevation and distance to station A is to be determined by stadia. A backsight taken on a bench mark, elevation 1366.4 ft, gives a stadia interval of 7.25 and a vertical angle of +4°20′ with the center cross hair at 5.2 ft on the rod. The H.I. at station A is 4.3 ft. Determine the elevation of point A and the horizontal distance from the bench mark.

19–6. Determine the length and bearing of line DA for the notes shown.

Course	Horizontal Distance (ft)	True Bearing
A to B	600.0	N30°E
B to C	400.0	S45°E
C to D	200.0	S60°W

19–7. Balance the traverse data listed, using the compass rule, and compute the double-meridian distance for each side.

Side	Latitude	Departure	Corrections	Corrected	
				Latitude	Departure
AB	N 364.24	E 293.62			
BC	N 796.12	E 86.78			
CD	S 1684.61	E 212.65			
DE	S 120.42	W586.27			
EA	N 644.20	W 6.58			

19–8. A proposed 2°00′ highway curve has an inaccessible P.I. Measurement of the closing traverse line *AB* gives a distance of 244.6 ft. The station at *A* is 132+64.6. Degree of curve is to be defined as the angle at the center subtended by a chord of 100 ft. Find the (a) radius of the curve, (b) central angle △, (c) tangent distance *T*, (d) external distance *E*, and (e) station of P.C. and P.T.

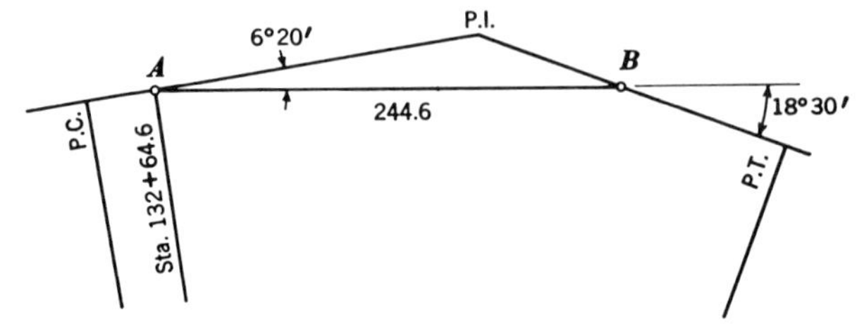

Problem 19–8.

19–9. Calculate the elevations at 50-ft stations for a vertical curve 400 ft long between tangent grades of +5 per cent and −7 per cent meeting at station 11+00 and elevation 110.00 ft.

19–10. Given the slope stake notes shown in which C represents cut and F fill. The width of roadway is 40 ft. Find the end areas, and the volume of earthwork between the two stations in cubic yards.

85+00	$\frac{F\ 5.4}{28.1}$	F 7.2	$\frac{F\ 6.8}{30.2}$
84+00	$\frac{F\ 4.8}{27.2}$	F 3.0	$\frac{F\ 5.2}{27.8}$

19–11. Write a legal description for a tract of six sides, two of which are on the legal border of a ¼-mile-wide river. Draw a sketch showing all data assumed for the tract.

19–12. Explain the difference, if any, between the "north half" of a lot, and the "north half, measured along the east and west lines" of a lot.

19–13. A steel tape has a cross-sectional area of 0.010 sq in. and is exactly 500.000 ft long at 70°F when subjected to a horizontal tension of 12 lb and supported throughout its entire length. Its weight is 18 lb, its modulus of elasticity 30,000,000 psi, and its coefficient of expansion 0.0000065 per deg F. In order to establish an elevation in a mine shaft, this tape with a 25-lb weight on its end is hung vertically in the shaft and simultaneously observed by two levels. The level at the surface, H.I.=760.327, reads 437.000 on the tape. The other level, near the foot of the shaft, reads 0.709 ft on the tape. If the temperature of the tape is 50°F, calculate the H.I. of the lower level to the nearest 0.001 ft.

19–14. A point on the ceiling of a corridor in a building has an elevation of 140.00 ft. A backsight taken on B.M. 1, elevation 130.00, is 3.47 ft. What should be the reading on a vertical rod held upside down from the point in the ceiling?

19–15. Lot *ABCD* between two parallel street lines is 100 ft deep; it has an 80-ft frontage (*AB*) on one street and a 120-ft frontage (*CD*) on the other. The interior angles at *A* and *B* are equal, as are those at *C* and *D*. What distances *AE* and *BF* should be laid off by a surveyor in order to divide the lot into two equal areas by means of a line *EF* parallel to *AB*?

19–16. In making a two-peg test, two points *A* and *B* were set about 300 ft apart. With the level adjacent to point *A* the rod reading on *A* is 5.368 and the reading on *B* is 7.135 ft. With the level at *B* the rod reading on *A* is 3.453 and the reading on *B* is 5.180 ft. Determine the true difference in elevation between points *A* and *B*. What is the error of the level in 300 ft? In which direction must the line of sight be adjusted?

19–17. The magnetic bearing of a property line was recorded in 1858 as N56°12′W, at which time the magnetic declination was 4°16′E. What is the magnetic bearing of the line in 1960 if the declination for this area is 2°27′W?

19–18. A minus grade g_1 intersects a plus grade g_2 at station *S*. If the length of a vertical curve joining these two grades is *L*, at what point on the curve (in terms given) should an engineer place an embankment-protecting spillway?

19–19. If the convergence of meridians at latitude 37° is 1 ft/mile, what is the theoretical length of the northern boundary of a township at this latitude?

19–20. Find the length of AB in the figure shown.

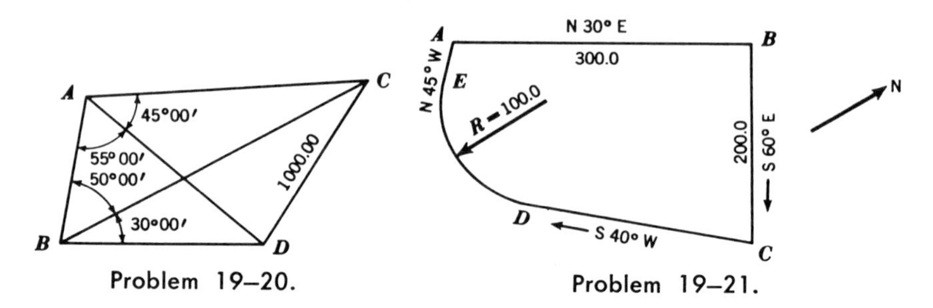

Problem 19–20.

Problem 19–21.

19–21. Compute the distance AE in the figure shown. Lines CD and AE are tangent to the curve.

19–22. Does the plumb bob at rest always hang toward the center of the earth? Explain.

19–23. How many acres are contained in the NW¼ of the NE¼ of the SW¼ of section 16?

19–24. What is a surveyor's legal position in the settlement of a boundary dispute?

19–25. A surveyor is hired by a client to make a survey of a tract of land and to stake out a large building. Discuss the liability of the surveyor.

19–26. Examine each of the following statements and mark whether true or false. (a) In setting bench marks on bridge foundations, new bridge foundations are preferable to old ones. (b) A surveying party has the legal right to cross private property without obtaining permission. (c) In a properly balanced closed survey, the sum of the latitudes should equal the sum of the departures. (d) In land surveying, neither the area nor the description by course and distance are allowed to hold against the proved location of the original monuments.

19–27. Draw an appropriate map symbol for each of the following: (a) Bridge over a waterway, (b) ford across a waterway, (c) triangulation station, (d) power line, (e) depressed area, and (f) bench mark showing elevation.

19–28. A land surveyor must be concerned with errors of many types. Give a definition of each of the following types of errors: (a) accidental, (b) systematic, (c) discrepancies, (d) compensating, (e) mistake, and (f) natural.

19–29. When a ruling grade is reduced to allow for resistance due to curvature, it is said to be ______.

19–30. Electronic computers are designated by one of two different categories. What are the two categories? (a) ______, (b) ______.

19–31. When an alluvial deposit is attached to the land of a riparian owner, the owner acquires title to such land. The term applied to this land growth is ______.

19–32. The Transit Rule and the Compass Rule are frequently used in land survey work. State in words the essence of each, describe what they are used for, why they are necessary, which of the two rules you prefer to use, and why.

19–33. In a regular township, what is the number of the section that may have fractional lots along both the north and west sides?

19–34. Standard time zones in the United States are established on longitude intervals of (a) 5° (b) 7½° (c) 10° (d) 15° (e) 25°.

19–35. The sun and stars are located by the celestial coordinates: (a) declination and right ascension, (b) right ascension and sidereal hour angle, (c) prime vertical and hour circle, (d) hour angle and equation of time, (e) latitude and longitude.

part three

TYPICAL EXAMINATIONS

Typical Actual Examinations 20

The typical actual examinations reproduced in this chapter have been selected from tests given in 40 states over a 10-year span. They provide a full-scale "final examination" under the conditions stipulated for time and references as contrasted with problems in previous chapters which were grouped in specific categories. Answers are given for nearly all problems except the All-Engineering Branches examination which is useful for assignments in formal review courses.

Study of hundreds of EIT examinations shows there is no truly typical one for the entire United States. Examinations E and F are examples of different approaches. At least 30 states, however, now use the National EIT examination represented by tests A, B, and C which were given during the past six months to two years. The Southern Zone examination continues to be used by some states and differs very little from the National one.

Professional engineering registration examinations vary considerably in type and subject material, even in the same state in successive years. For Civil Engineers, emphasis may be placed on structures, or sanitary engineering and fluids, with different weights on engineering economy, highways, and surveying. Problems in Chemical, Electrical, Industrial, and Mechanical Engineering are broad and changing as noted in Chapters 13, 15, 16, and 18 respectively. The All-Engineering Branches examination permits a versatile applicant to spread his choices over a broad field.

TYPICAL EXAMINATION A

Fundamentals

PART I

Time limit 4 hours. Work any 6 problems from any 4 of the groups. Use of references permitted.

Mathematics

20–1A. The cross section of a tank 10 ft long is an equilateral triangle, as in the diagram. Water runs into the tank at the rate of 2 cu ft/min. At what rate is the depth of the water increasing when the depth is 6 in.?

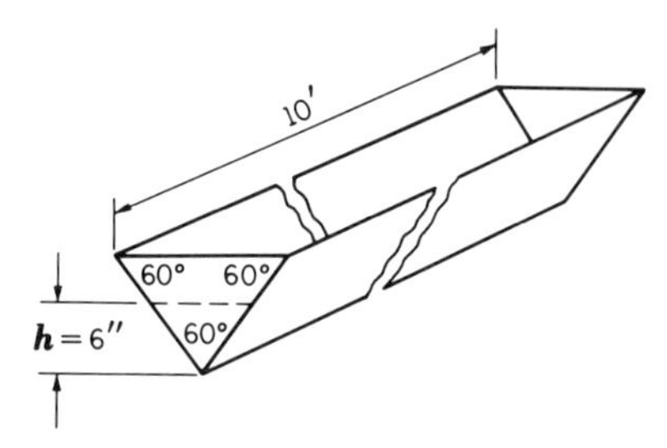

Problem 20–1A.

20–2A. A porous material dries in the open air at a rate proportional to its moisture content. If a slab hung in the wind loses half its free moisture in one hour, how long will it take to lose 99 per cent, weather conditions remaining the same? Let a = original amount of moisture in the slab and x = amount of moisture removed in time, t.

20–3A. At what distance along the x-axis is the centroid of the shaded area located which is bounded by the two curves whose equations are: $y = x$ and $y = 3x - x^2$?

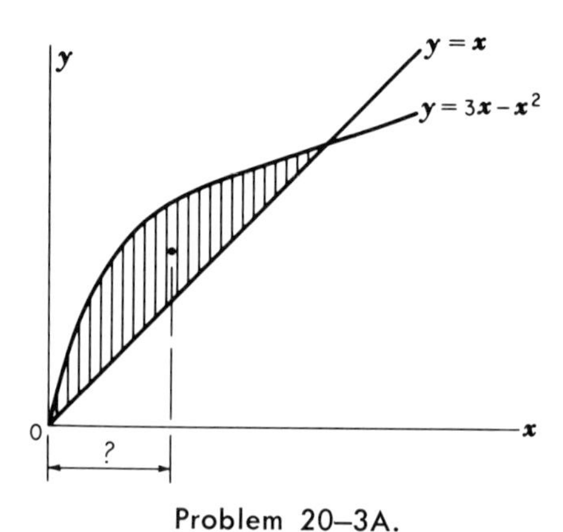

Problem 20–3A.

Chemistry

20–4A. How many cubic feet of dry air at 70°F and 28.01 in. of mercury will be required to burn a cubic foot of gas whose analysis by volume is CH_4 = 46 per cent; CO = 38 per cent; O_2 = 5 per cent; and N_2 = 11 per cent? The gas is also at 70°F and its pressure is 28.01 in. of mercury.

20–5A. The waste water from an industrial plant was 10,000 gpd. While essentially water, it contained 0.02 weight per cent of hydrochloric acid, HCl. Before discharge to the city sewer, this acid was neutralized with soda ash (sodium carbonate, Na_2CO_3). How many pounds of soda ash were needed per day? (At. wts are: H=1, Cl=35.5, Na=23.0, C=12.0, and O=16.0.)

20–6A. A transportation company ships gaseous materials. (a) If they had standard size tanks of 10, 20, and 30 liters, and they received an order for 100 liters of gas at S.T.P., which size container would be used if the gas were to be shipped at a temperature of 80°F and a pressure of 8 atm? (b) A tank tested to withstand a pressure of 15 atm is filled with gas at 20°F and 12 atm pressure. If the temperature increases to 65°F, what percentage of the margin of safety has been lost?

Fluid Mechanics

20-7A. A CI pipeline, 12-in. ID, and 10,000 ft long leading from a reservoir, terminates in a nozzle of 2-in. diameter, discharging into the atmosphere. The center of this nozzle is 100 ft below the free surface of the water in the reservoir supplying the pipeline. Find the flow rate, cfs, and the power in the jet if the coefficient of friction in the pipe line is 0.02. Neglect minor losses.

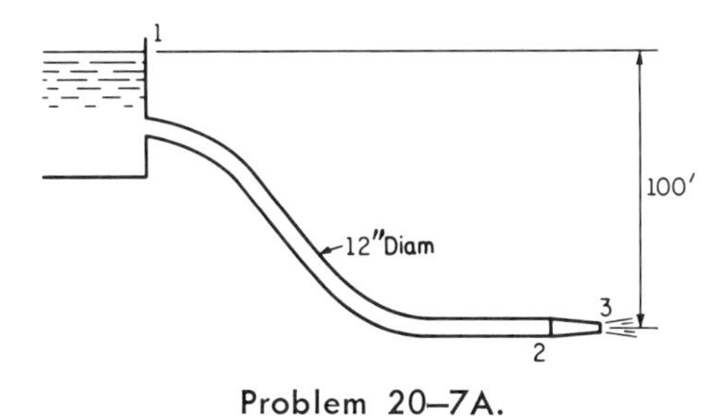

Problem 20–7A.

20–8A. Pressure gages at the top and bottom of the triangular conduit shown read 10 and 16 psi respectively. Calculate the magnitude and line of action of the resultant fluid force on the triangular end of the conduit.

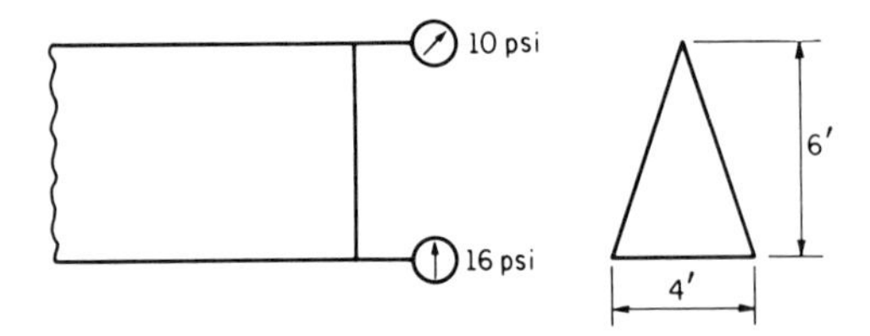

Problem 20–8A.

20–9A. A smooth cement-lined canal, Manning $n = 0.010$, is of semicircular cross-section. The radius of the canal is 4 ft and the canal is laid on a slope of 0.0028. What uniform flow rate exists when the water flows to a depth of 3 ft?

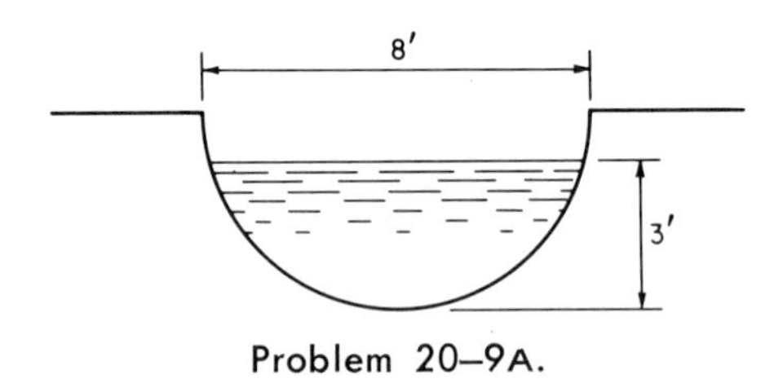

Problem 20–9A.

Thermodynamics

20–10A. If 200 cfm of air at 50°F and a relative humidity of 60 per cent are to be modified to 85°F and 95 per cent relative humidity and a total pressure of 14.7 psi absolute, determine the heat and water requirements.

20–11A. A vessel with volume of 50 cu ft is being filled with air, which is to be considered as a perfect gas. At a particular instant of time the instruments recorded a temperature of 240°F and a pressure of 200 psia. At this instant the pressure is increasing at a rate of 20 psia per second and the temperature is increasing at the rate of 50°F per second. Calculate the rate of air flow into the tank at this instant of time in pound mass per second. Do not calculate for any specific time interval.

20–12A. A steam turbine produces 1000 kw on test and consumes 16,000 lb of steam per hour. Steam enters the turbine at 200 psia and 540°F and leaves at 3 in. of Hg absolute. There is no subcooling in the condenser. Using the Mollier diagram calculate: (a) the ideal steam rate, (b) the actual steam rate, (c) the actual thermal efficiency.

Statics

20–13A. The pin-connected frame sketched in the diagram is loaded as shown. Determine the total stresses in members a, b, and c.

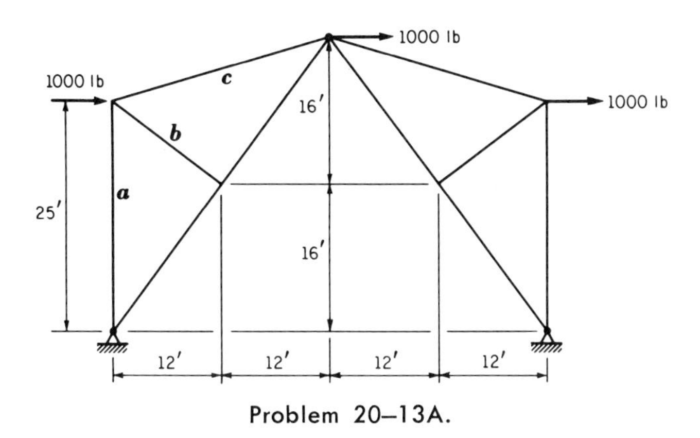

Problem 20–13A.

20–14A. What value of the force P in the sketch will just prevent downward movement of the 3000 lb weight? The rope makes two complete turns around the post, and the pulley turns on a frictionless bearing. $\mu = 0.25$.

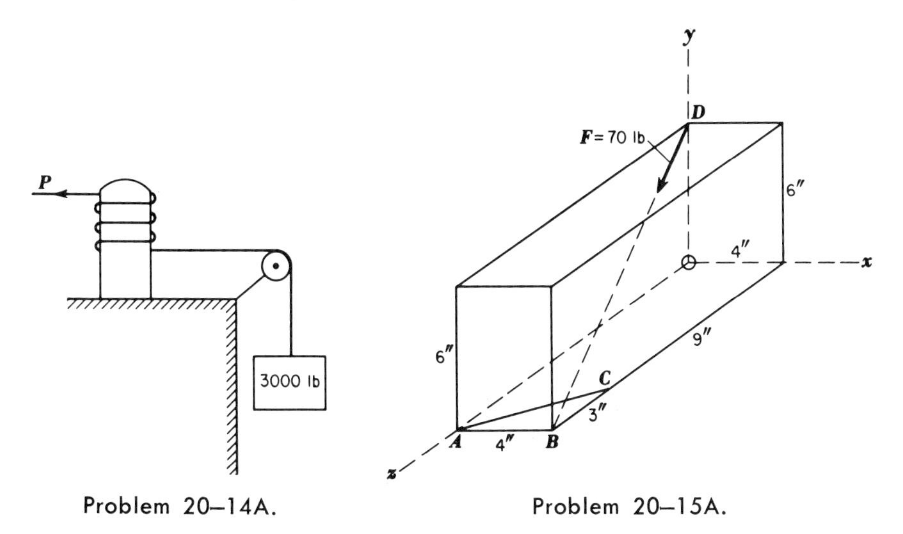

Problem 20–14A. Problem 20–15A.

20–15A. (a) Determine the moment of force $F = 70$ lb, acting along line DB, about the line AC. (b) Determine the shortest distance from line DB to the point A.

PART II

Work any 6 problems from 4 different groups. Time Limit: 4 hours. Use of references permitted.

Dynamics

20–16A. A wheel, consisting of two solid, homogeneous cylinders joined together with a common axis as shown, rolls on the rail without slipping under the action of the horizontal force P of 40 lb. Determine the acceleration of the center of the wheel, and the frictional force between the rail and the smaller cylinder.

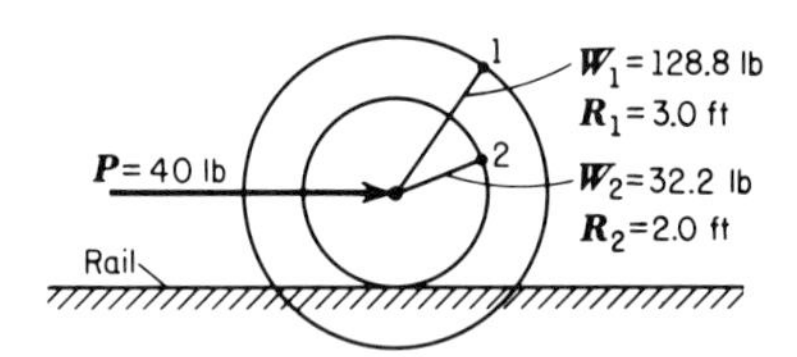

Problem 20–16A.

20–17A. In the position shown, the spring A is stretched 0.5 ft and the system is being held at rest by an upward force F, on B. If the force F is removed, find the velocity of C after B moves down 2 ft. All pulleys are frictionless and negligible weight. $k = 100$ lb/ft, $B = 322$ lb, $C = 64.4$ lb. Assume only vertical movement occurs.

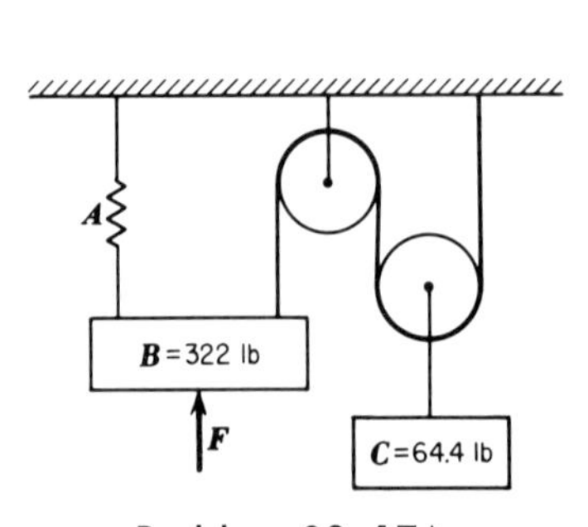

Problem 20–17A.

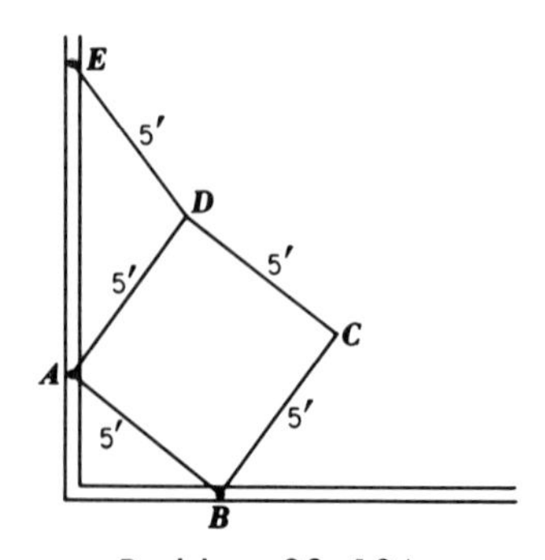

Problem 20–18A.

20–18A. The rigid square in the diagram measures 5 ft on each side. Rod DE is also 5 ft long. Points A and E move in the vertical slot, and B moves horizontally. In the position shown, A has a constant velocity upward of 12 fps. Determine (a) the velocity of points B, D, and E, (b) the acceleration of points B and D.

Mechanics of Materials

20–19A. A shaft loaded as indicated rotates at 1890 rpm. If $G = 12 \times 10^6$ psi, find the maximum shear stress and the angle of twist of gear A relative to gear C.

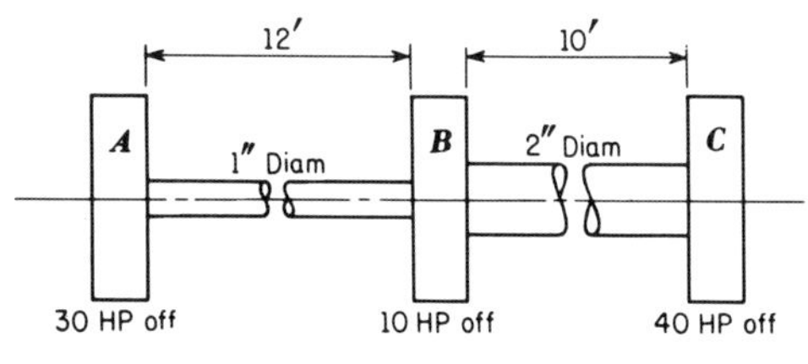

Problem 20–19A.

20–20A. A steel cylinder and copper tube as shown in the diagram are compressed between parallel plates. Determine the stresses in the steel and copper, and total in kips for each material. $E_s = 30 \times 10^6$ psi, $E_c = 16 \times 10^6$ psi.

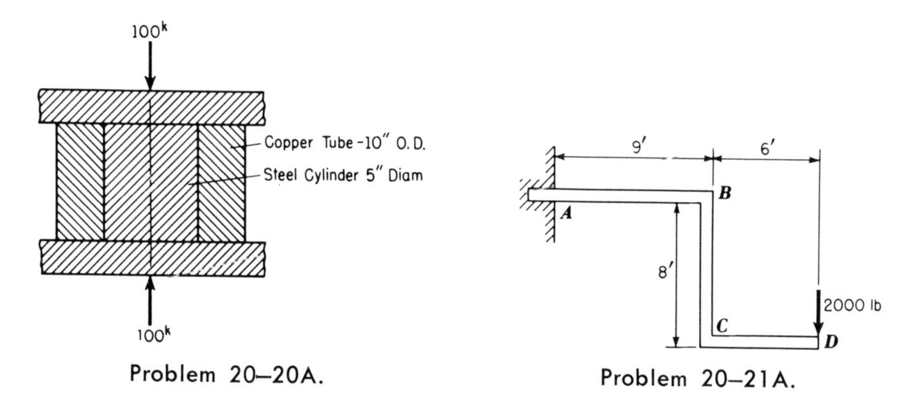

Problem 20–20A.

Problem 20–21A.

20–21A. The offset cantilever beam is shown. It is fabricated from structural steel. Its properties are $E = 30 \times 10^6$ psi and $I = 60$ in.^{4}. Neglect the weight of the beam. Determine the horizontal and vertical deflection at D with respect to A in inches.

Physics

20–22A. A vessel at rest explodes, breaking into three pieces, A, B, and C. Piece A weighs 1 lb and flies off in a vertical direction with a velocity of 30 fps. Piece B weighs 1 lb and flies off horizontally to the right with a velocity of 40 fps. Determine the direction and magnitude of the velocity of piece C which weighs 2 lb immediately after the explosion.

20–23A. A 300-watt heater is attached to a water faucet. If the water runs at a rate that permits it to be heated from 60°F to 120°F, how long will it take to obtain a gallon and what will be the cost at three cents a kilowatt-hour? Assume that 95 per cent of the electrical energy will be utilized in heating the water.

20–24A. You have an illuminated lantern slide in which the slide is 10 ft from a projection screen. You wish to form an image of this slide on the screen which is 4 times as large as the slide and therefore the information on the slide will also be magnified 4 times. If you wish to do this with a single simple lens, state whether this can be accomplished by either a diverging or a converging lens and determine the focal length of the lens which will accomplish your objective.

Electrical Theory

20–25A. The following information is given in connection with tests performed on a 25-kva 2400/240-volt, single phase, 60-cycle transformer. Open circuit test: 240 volts, 250 watts; short circuit test: 72 volts, 380 watts, 10.4 amp (rated current). Calculate the per cent efficiency at 1.3 times rated kva at a power factor of 0.85.

20–26A. The equivalent circuit of a two-stage triode amplifier is shown along with a tabulation of the circuit and tube parameters.

e_1 = input voltage to amplifier
R_{in} = input resistance of amplifier
μ_1 = multiplication factor of tube 1
r_{p1} = plate resistance of tube 1
R_{L1} = load resistance on tube 1
e_2 = output voltage of stage 1
μ_2 = multiplication factor of tube 2
r_{p2} = plate resistance of tube 2
R_{L2} = load resistance on tube 2
e_{out} = output voltage of stage 2

i_1 = plate current in tube 1
i_2 = plate current in tube 2
$R_{in} = 2\times10^6$ ohms
$\mu_1 = 15$
r_{p1} = 50,000 ohms
R_{L1} = 100,000 ohms
$\mu_2 = 20$
r_{p2} = 30,000 ohms
R_{L2} = 90,000 ohms

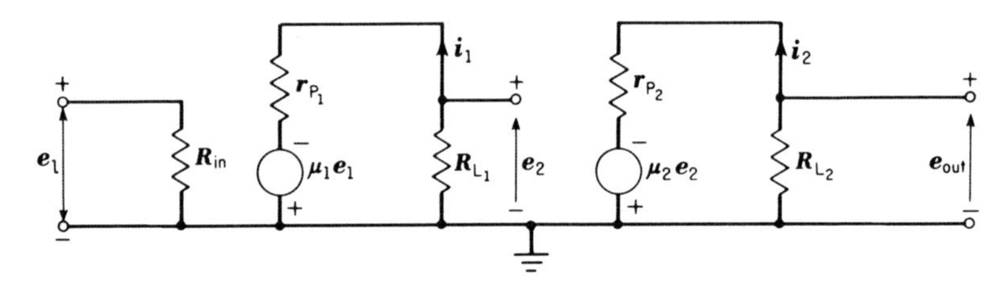

Problem 20–26A.

Find the voltage amplification for each stage and the over-all voltage amplification for the amplifier.

20–27A. A three-phase, three-wire, 208-volt, 60-cycle system draws 10 kw at 80 per cent power factor, lagging. It is desired to connect three capacitors in delta across this line to raise the power factor to 90 per cent lagging. What should be the rating of each capacitor in kva, and what is the capacitance of each capacitor?

Economic Analysis

20–28A. A man bought an electric typewriter for $50 down and $30 a month for two years. He could have bought the same typewriter for $675 cash. What true effective annual rate of return, before taxes, did the time payment indicate?

20–29A. To finance a sewage plant a sanitary district issues $50,000.00 worth of bonds bearing interest at 5 per cent annually, that will mature in 30 years. Equal annual amounts will be invested by the sanitary district in a sinking fund to earn 4 per cent interest. What will be the total annual cost of the bond issue, to the nearest $100?

20–30A. A 30,000 kw hydroelectric development will cost $7,500,000. A steam plant of equal capacity will cost $3,000,000. Corresponding cost data for the two installations are estimated as follows:

	Hydroelectric	Steam
Interest on investment	5 per cent	5 per cent
Taxes	4 per cent	4 per cent
Annual operating cost (other than fuel)	$ 50,000	$ 90,000
Annual maintenance	40,000	80,000
Annual depreciation	125,000	100,000

Cost of coal is $5 a ton and one pound will be required per kwhr generated. If each plant is to operate on an annual use factor of 50 per cent, which will produce the cheaper energy?

EXAMINATION B

Fundamentals

PART I

Time allowed—4 hours. Work 6 problems including at least one problem from 4 groups. Use of references permitted.

Mathematics

20–1B. A closed circular cylindrical can is to have a volume, V. If the cost of the material per square inch in the top and bottom is twice that used in the curved sides, find the ratio of the height to diameter for minimum cost.

20–2B. A parabolic arch has a span of 120 ft and a height of 25 ft. Derive the equation of the parabola; compute the heights of the arch at points 10 ft, 20 ft, and 40 ft from the center. See figure for standard position.

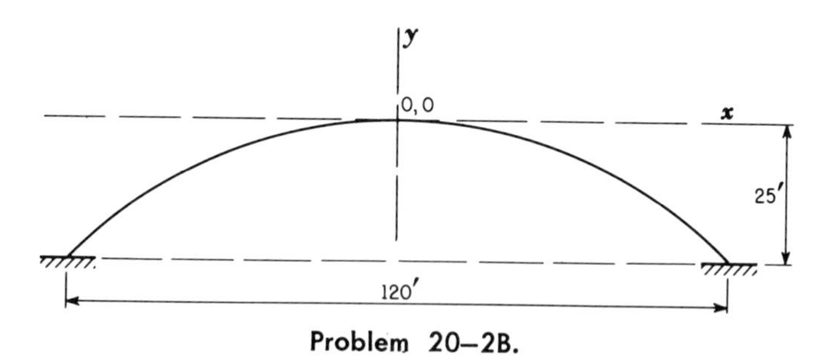

Problem 20–2B.

20–3B. An airplane headed N30°E, climbing on a 20° incline at a speed of 240 mph passes 1 mile directly over a car headed south on a flat road at a rate of 60 mph. At what rate of speed are they separating after 10 min?

Chemistry

20–4B. If 0.3150 grams of a gas occupies 250 ml at 20°C and 740 mm of Hg pressure, calculate the molecular weight of the gas.

20–5B. A 250 ml sample of a 0.264 *M* gold chloride solution ($AuCl_3$) was used to gold plate several objects. A constant current of 3.50 amperes was used for a total of 9 min. (a) What weight of gold metal was plated out on the objects? (b) What was the molarity of the solution of gold chloride at the conclusion of the process? (Au is 197, Cl is 35.5.)

20–6B. Balance the following equations:

(a) ___ CO_2 + ___ H_2O → ___ $C_6H_{12}O_6$ + ___ O_2
(b) ___ $CaCO_3$ + ___ HCl → ___ $CaCl_2$ + ___ H_2O + ___ CO_2
(c) ___ BaO_2 + ___ HCl → ___ $BaCl_2$ + ___ H_2O_2
(d) ___ $(NH_4)_2SO_4$ + ___ $NaOH$ → ___ Na_2SO_4 + ___ H_2O + ___ NH_3
(e) ___ $NaCH$ + ___ H_2SO_4 → ___ $NaHSO_4$ + HCN ↗

Fluid Mechanics

20–7B. When water is pumped at the rate of 2 cfs from a reservoir located 20 ft above the pump to a point located 90 ft above the pump where free discharge takes place, the pressure on the intake side of the pump is 5 psi and the pressure on the discharge side is 50 psi. If all pipes are 6 in. in diameter, determine the head supplied by the pump, the head loss in friction between the reservoir and the pump, and the head loss in friction between the pump and the point of free discharge.

20–8B. Air at a static pressure of 20 psia, 40°F, flows through a smooth 10-in. diameter duct. A pitot-static tube is located at the center of the duct and the manometer connected to it indicates a differential pressure of 2.0 in. of water. Calculate the flow rate in pounds per second. Assume $f = 0.0126$.

20–9B. Water is pumped from tank A to tank B, through the system shown in the figure, which includes a square-edged entry, three elbows, and free discharge. The system contains 100 ft of 3-in. pipe for which f is taken as 0.030. Assume loss entry to be $0.5v^2/2g$ and loss due to each elbow to be $0.8v^2/2g$. Calculate the required horsepower input to the pump if Q is 0.56 cfs and the pump efficiency is 70 per cent.

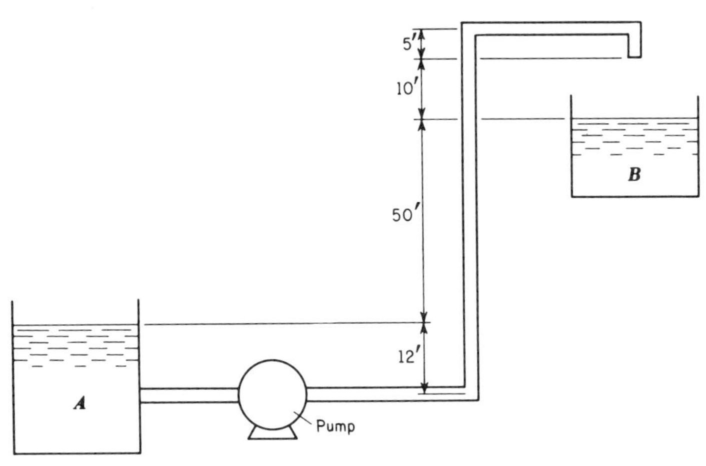

Problem 20–9B.

Thermodynamics

20–10B. A small steam turbine is supplied with steam at 1000 psia and 100 per cent quality, and exhausts at 14.7 psia. The turbine uses 40 lb of steam for each horsepower delivered at the turbine shaft. Heat losses from the turbine to its surroundings are negligible. What is the entropy per pound of the exhaust steam?

20–11B. In a Freon vapor-compression refrigeration cycle, the saturated liquid refrigerant expands isentropically from 100°F to 30°F through a turbine which is used to replace the expansion valve. The vapor leaving the evaporator is saturated. Calculate the work output of the turbine and the refrigeration effect in Btu per pound of refrigerant. For a system of 100 tons capacity, what is the power output of the reversible turbine? Would you recommend replacing the expansion valve with the turbine? Give reasons for your answer.

THERMODYNAMIC PROPERTIES OF FREON

TEMP (°F)	ABS PR (*psi*)	SATURATED FREON					
		Enthalpy (Btu/lb m)			Entropy (Btu/lb m °R)		
		Sat Liq (h_{f_g})	Evap (h_{f_g})	Sat Vapor (h_g)	Sat Liq (s_f)	Evap (s_{f_g})	Sat Vapor (s_g)
0	23.849	8.5207	68.750	77.271	0.01932	0.14956	0.16888
30	43.148	15.0580	65.361	80.419	0.03301	0.13347	0.16648
70	84.888	24.0500	60.309	84.359	0.05048	0.11386	0.16434
80	98.870	26.3650	58.917	85.282	0.05475	0.10917	0.16392
100	131.860	31.1000	55.929	87.029	0.06323	0.09992	0.16315

20–12B. One hundred linear feet of schedule 40, 1-in. steel pipe, carries saturated steam at a pressure of 150 psig. The pipe is lagged with 2 in. of magnesia covering [K_{av} = 0.04 Btu/hr (sq ft) (°F) (ft)]. The temperature directly under the canvas is 90°F. Neglect inside film coefficient and resistance of the pipe. Calculate (a) the over-all coefficient of heat transfer based on the outside area and (b) the hourly heat loss in Btu.

Statics

20–13B. Determine the reactions on the beams at *A*, *B*, and *C*. Neglect the weights of the members.

20–14B. In the truss shown, find the stresses in members *a*, *b*, and *c*.

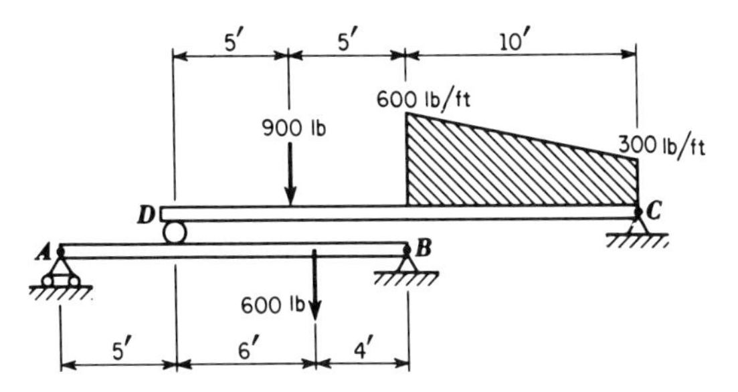

Problem 20–13B.

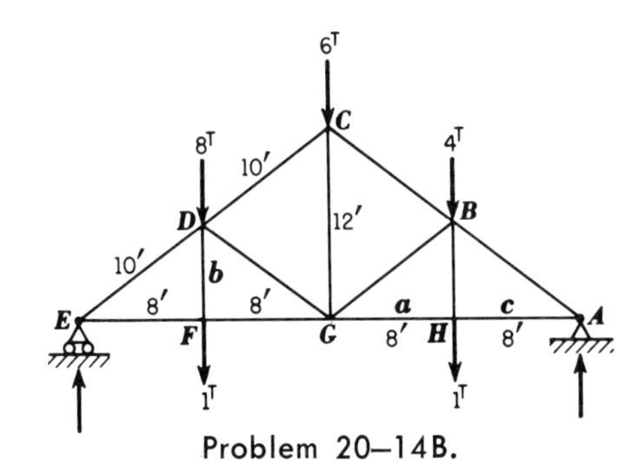

Problem 20–14B.

20–15B. The weight of 500 lb is to be raised by means of a lever supported at one end with a force G, and with a force F at the other end. The lever weighs 5 lb/ft and weight is applied at a point 2 ft from the support. Find the length of the lever in order that the force required is a minimum.

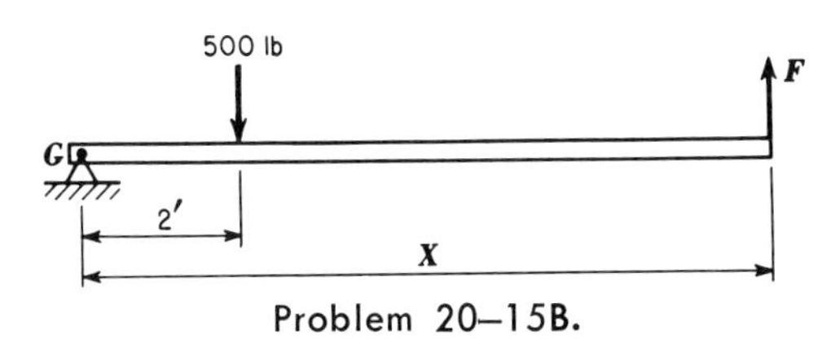

Problem 20–15B.

PART II

Time allowed—4 hours. Work any 6 problems including at least one problem from each of 4 groups. References allowed.

Dynamics

20–16B. A body A weighing 8 lb which rests on a smooth horizontal plane is attached to a second body B, weighing 16 lb, by a string passing over a smooth peg C. Find the acceleration of body B and the tension in the string.

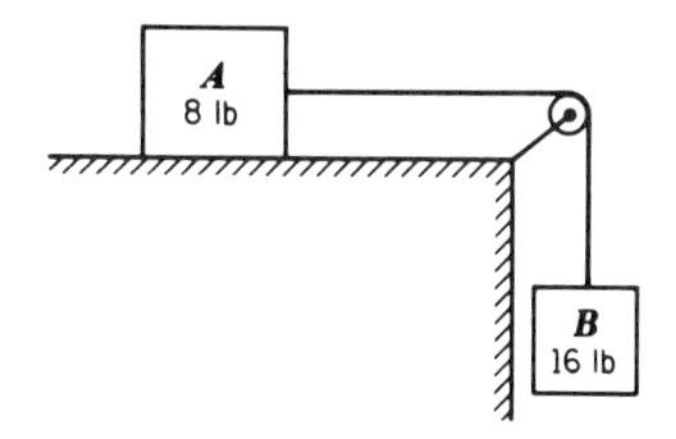

Problem 20–16B.

20–17B. A particle moves in a straight line with an acceleration of $3t$-4. Find the distance of the particle from its starting point at any time, t, if $s = 0$ and $v = 4$ when $t = 0$.

20–18B. In the figure, wheel A and block B each weigh 32.2 lb, $d_1 = 16$ in., $d_2 = 4$ in., angle $a = 30°$, and $h = 2$ ft. Disregard the weight of the pulley and friction at G. Block A rolls along the plane without slipping. The radius of gyration of mass A with respect to a horizontal axis through $G = 4.0$ in. In the position shown, B has a velocity of 5 fps downward. When it is stopped by the plane at D after falling h feet, determine the distance G will move up the plane after B stops.

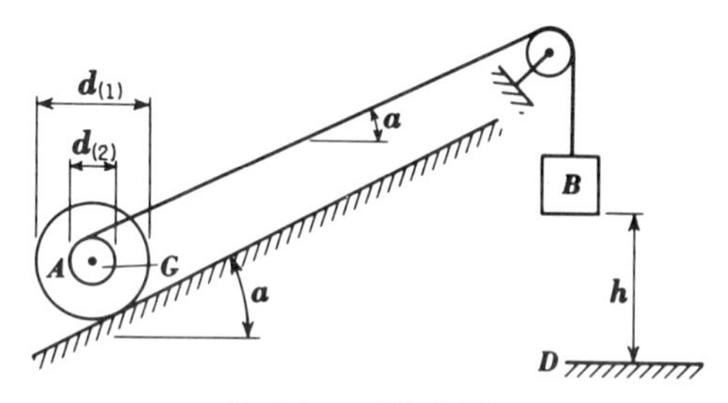

Problem 20–18B.

Mechanics of Materials

20–19B. A cast-iron cantilever beam 5 ft long has a T-shaped cross section. Both the flange and the stem have dimensions of 1 in. × 6 in. The beam is placed with the flange of the T at the top. The allowable compressive stress is 16,000 psi. Neglecting the weight of the beam, what is the maximum safe concentrated load that can be placed at the free end of the beam?

20–20B. A 12-in. 35-lb I beam, 30 ft long is supported at 5 ft from each end and carries a uniformly distributed load of 1600 lb/ft including the beam weight. Determine the maximum flexural stress.

20–21B. All bars in the figure have the same area and are of the same material. Assuming no stress in the bars before the load is applied, find the load carried by each bar following application of the load F.

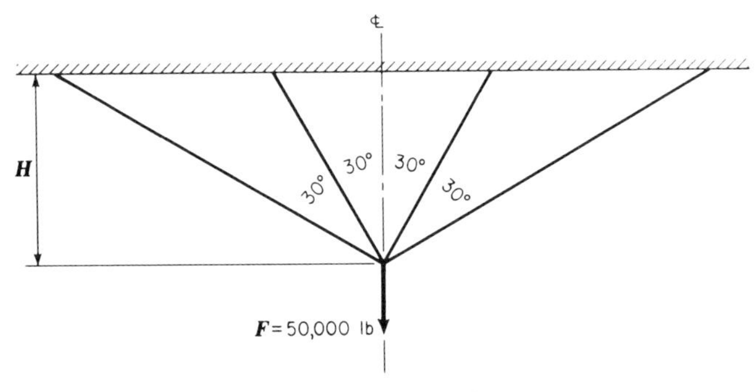

Problem 20–21B.

Physics

20–22B. A pitcher throws a ball with a speed of 120 fps, the ball leaving his hand horizontally at a height of 5 ft. If the distance from the pitcher is 60 ft, at what height will the ball pass the batter?

20–23B. (a) A spherical concave shaving mirror has a radius of curvature of 1 ft. What is the magnification when the face is 4 in. from the vertex of the mirror? (b) An object is 6 in. from the center of a silvered spherical glass (Christmas tree ornament) 3 in. in diameter. What is the position and magnification of its image?

20–24B. The silver rod of circular cross section has one end immersed in a steam bath and the other end immersed in a mixture of ice and water. The distance between the two ends is 6 cm, and the diameter of the rod is 0.3 cm. Calculate the amount of heat that is conducted through the rod in 2 min.

Electrical Theory

20–25B. An industrial plant is supplied from a 3-phase/480-

volt, 60-cps system. The load is primarily induction motors. A check shows that the plant draws 1000 amp at 0.80 lagging power factor when motors are loaded, and 625 amp at 0.707 lagging power factor when the motors are not loaded. How much capacitance is required across the load to insure that the power factor is never below 0.90 lagging?

20–26B. Find I_A in the circuit shown.

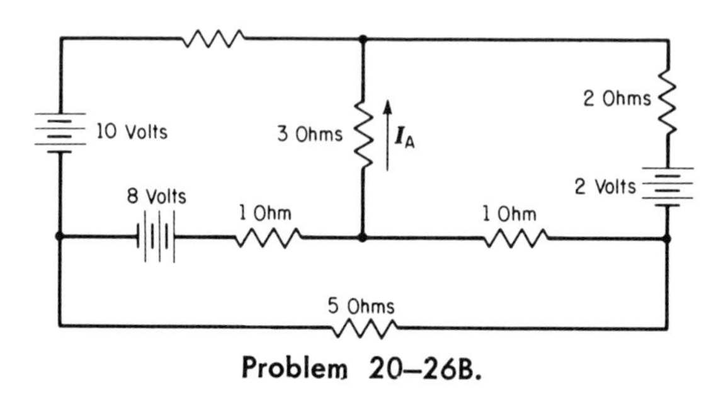

Problem 20–26B.

20–27B. A cathode follower is composed of a triode tube, a 3000-ohm cathode resistor, and a 200-volt plate power supply. The tube parameters are: Amplification factor = 30, plate resistance = 10,000. Determine the voltage amplification.

Economic Analysis

20–28B. A company purchased a fleet of trucks for $78,000. Terms included a down payment of $5000 and 12 end-of-month payments of $7000. Another dealer offered the same purchase at an interest rate of 1 per cent per month on the unpaid balance. Which offer should the company have accepted? Show all computations.

20–29B. An inventor sold his patent to a corporation and was given his choice of three offers: (a) $100,000 in cash; (b) an annual royalty of 7 per cent on sales estimated at $150,000 per year during the remaining 10 years of the patent life; or (c) a 20 year annuity of $7500, payments to be made at the end of each year. If money is worth 6 per cent to the inventor, which offer should he accept? (Neglect tax differences.)

20–30B. An electronic digital computer can be purchased by a professional engineer for $23,000. He estimates a useful life of 8 years for the computer with a salvage value of $3000. A maintenance contract is available for the computer at a rate of \$1200 per year, and an operator will cost \$5.00 per hr when the machine is in use. A computer service is available to the engineer to do all of his electronic digital computing at a rate of \$12 per hr. Assuming interest at 4 per cent, compounded annually, with taxes and insurance at 3 per cent of the purchase price: (a) Tabulate all of the annual costs involved with owning and operating the computer, except the daily cost of the operator, evaluating each numerically, and (b) write a simple equation and compute the number of hours the computer must be required to operate each year to justify its purchase.

EXAMINATION C

Fundamentals

PART I

Work 6 problems including at least one problem from at least 4 different groups. Use of references permitted. Time limit 4 hours.

Mathematics

20–1C. A farmer decides to build a rectangular feed lot with a semi-circular pen at one end. If he has 500 ft of fencing, find the radius of the pen which would give a maximum area for the feed lot.

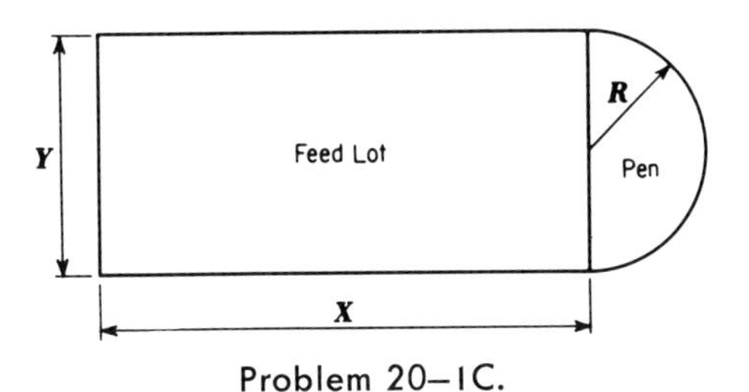

Problem 20–1C.

20–2C. A rectangle lies in the first quadrant, has two of its sides on the x and y axis, one vertex at the origin, and the opposite vertex on the curve $x^2 + 2y^2 = 9$. Find either coordinate of the latter vertex so that the area of the rectangle is a maximum.

20–3C. Brine, containing 1 lb of salt per gallon, runs into a 200-gal tank, initially full of brine containing 3 lb of salt per gallon, at the rate of 4 gpm. If the mixture runs out at the rate of 5 gpm, when will the concentration of salt in the tank reach 1.01 lb/gal? Let x = amount of salt in the tank at time t. Let c = concentration of salt at time t.

Chemistry

20–4C. Calculate the weight of water in pounds required to produce by electrolysis 500 cu ft of hydrogen measured at 32°F and 14.7 psia. Assume the process is 100 per cent efficient.

20–5C. Calculate the weight in tons of NaCl to produce 100 tons of chlorine when the process is 95 per cent efficient.

20–6C. Balance the following equations:

(a) ___ Na + ___ $H_2O \rightarrow$ ___ $NaOH$ + ___ H_2
(b) ___ $AlCl_3$ + ___ $H_2SO_4 \rightarrow$ ___ $Al_2(SO_4)_3$ + ___ HCl
(c) ___ MnO_2 + ___ $NaCl$ + ___ $H_2SO_4 \rightarrow$
___ Na_2SO_4 + ___ $MnSO_4$ + ___ H_2O + ___ Cl_2
(d) ___ Zn + ___ $HNO_3 \rightarrow$ ___ $Zn(No_3)_2$ + ___ $NO \nearrow$ +
___ H_2O
(e) ___ $AlCl_3$ + ___ $NH_4OH \rightarrow$ ___ NH_4Cl + ___ $Al(OH)_3$

Fluid Mechanics

20–7C. A horizontal venturi meter for measuring oil flow has a main diameter of ¾ in. (area = 0.00307 sq ft) and a throat diameter of ¼ in. (area = 0.00034 sq ft). The pressure difference between the throat and the main is 10.4 psi. The specific gravity of oil is 0.84. Determine the quantity of oil in cubic feet per second. Assume that there is no loss.

20–8C. Air at 20 psia, 40°F, flows through a 12-in. diameter duct. A pitot-static tube is located at the center of the duct and the manometer connected to it indicates a differential pressure of 2.0 in. of water. Calculate the flow rate in pounds per second. Assume $f = 0.0120$.

20–9C. A 30-in. water pipe carries 20 cfs. At point B the pressure is 25.5 psi and the elevation is 120 ft. At point C, which is 5000 ft down stream from B, the pressure is 30.5 psi and the elevation is 100 ft. Find: (a) the head loss between B and C, (b) the horsepower lost between B and C and (c) the friction factor f.

Thermodynamics

20–10C. Steam enters the turbine of an industrial plant at 200 psia, 600°F. The turbine has an internal efficiency of 70 per cent and is to deliver 1000 kw of power. Exhaust takes place to heating mains which are maintained at 25 psia. Determine the exhaust flow rate in pounds per hour.

20–11C. The following data are known with respect to a one-ton simple vapor-compression refrigeration cycle, using Freon-12 refrigerant.

Pressure of evaporating refrigerant .... 20 psia
Pressure in condenser .... 90 psia
Temperature of refrigerant entering expansion valve ..... 70°F
Temperature of refrigerant leaving evaporator .... 20°F

Assuming reversible adiabatic compression, determine: (a) weight of refrigerant circulated per minute, (b) horsepower required, (c) heat removed by the condenser, Btu per minute.

Data from Freon-12 Tables

Temp (°F)	PSIA	Saturated Freon					
		Enthalpy (Btu/lb)			Entropy		
		h_f	h_{fg}	h_g	s_f	s_{fg}	s_g
70	84.89	24.05	60.31	84.36	0.05048	0.11386	0.16434
80	98.87	26.37	58.92	85.28	0.05475	0.10917	0.16392

Superheated Freon

Temperature at 20 psia			Temperature at 90 psia		
°F	h	s	°F	h	s
20	80.403	0.17829	100	89.175	0.17234
40	83.289	0.18419	120	92.536	0.17824
			140	95.879	0.18391

20–12C. A steam turbine exhausts 10,000 lb of steam per hour to a surface condenser at 1 psia and 90 per cent quality. Cooling water enters the condenser at 70°F and leaves at the steam temperature. How many pounds of cooling water are required per hour?

Statics

20–13C. The weights of the members of the smooth pin-connected frame may be neglected. Determine the components of the pin reactions at B, C, and E.

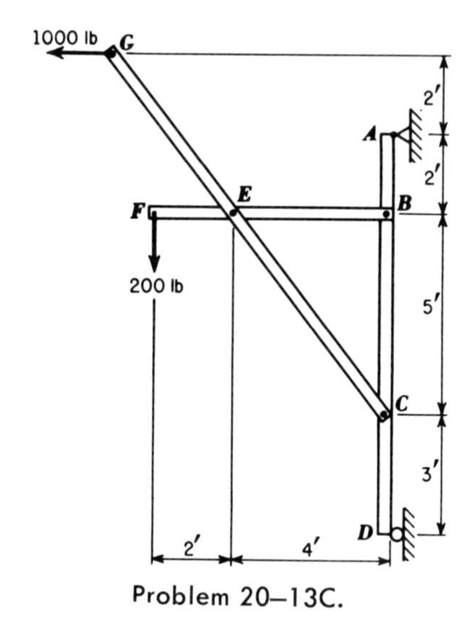

Problem 20–13C.

20–14C. Solve for the magnitude and kind of force in the members a, b, and c of this pin-connected truss.

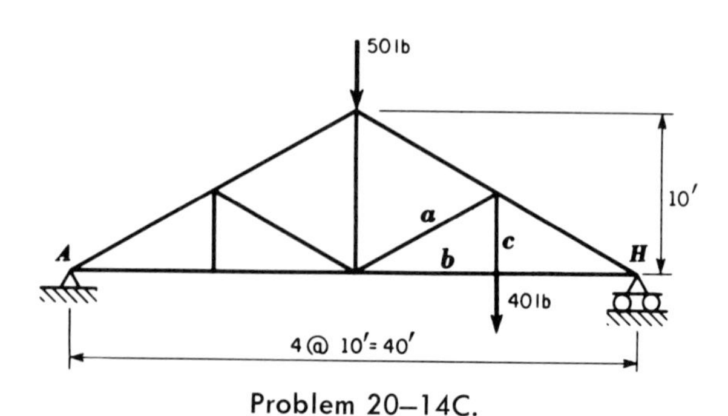

Problem 20–14C.

20–15C. The 10-ft long non-homogeneous bar AB in the diagram weighs 100 lb and moves with its ends in contact with smooth horizontal floor and vertical wall surfaces. The spring constant is 10 lb/ft, and it is unstretched when the lower end B of the bar is in contact with the vertical wall. Determine the angle θ in degrees for equilibrium position of the bar other than when $\theta = 0$, (HINT: can be solved using method of virtual work.)

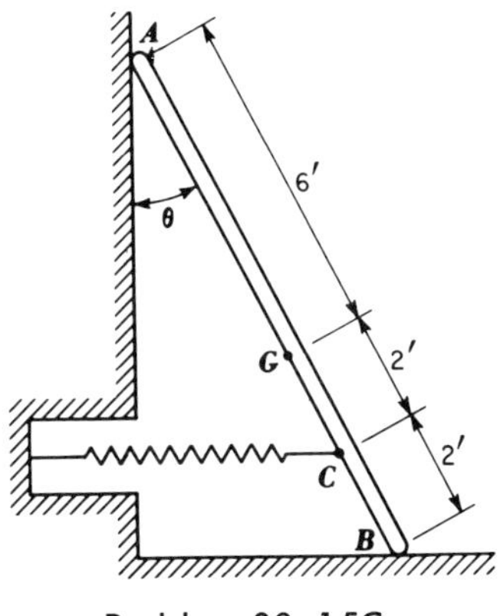

Problem 20–15C.

PART II

Time Limit 4 hours. Use of references permitted. Work at least 6 problems from any 4 of the groups.

Dynamics

20–16C. Two bodies, A and B, weighing 10 lb and 30 lb respectively, rest upon rough inclined planes. They are connected by a string passing over a smooth peg C. Find the acceleration of either body if the coefficient of friction is 0.3. Also find the distance the body moves from rest in 4 sec.

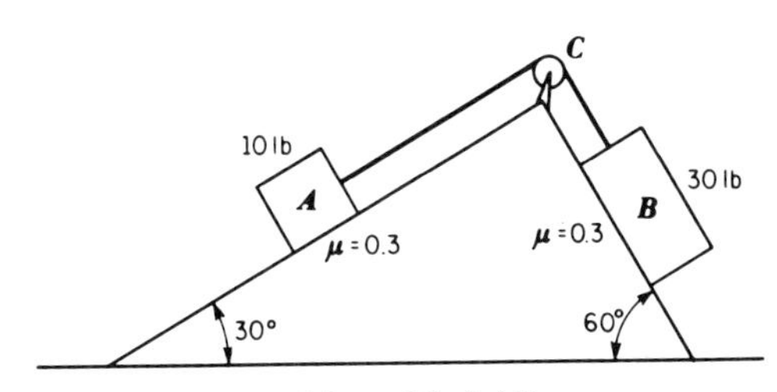

Problem 20–16C.

20–17C. A point moves along a curve whose equation is $16y^2 = x^3$, in which x and y are expressed in feet. The motion is such that $v_x = 4$ fps and is constant. It is also known that $t = 0$ at the instant when the moving point is at the origin. Calculate the magnitude of the velocity at the instant when $t = 9$ sec.

20–18C. A particle has simple harmonic motion. When it is displaced 12 in. from the center of its path, the magnitude of its velocity and acceleration are 40 ips and 250 ips^2, respectively. Determine: (a) the period of the motion, (b) the amplitude of the motion.

Mechanics of Materials

20–19C. A continuous beam is shown with a uniform moment of inertia – 1200 in.^{4}. Assume the beam to be made of steel. Determine: (a) reaction at B, (b) moment curve with ordinates, and (c) direction and slope of the beam at C in radians.

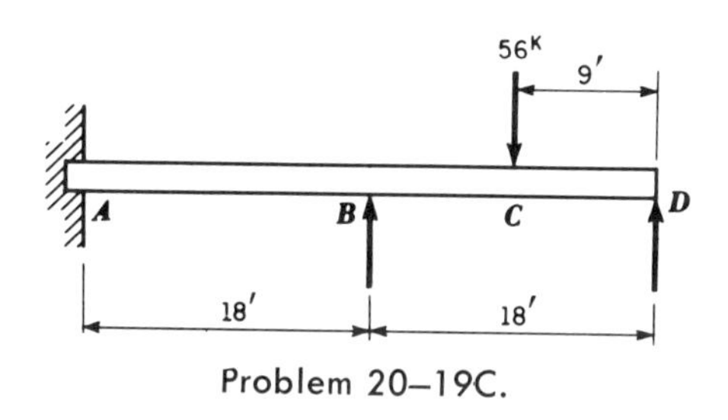

Problem 20–19C.

20–20C. A horizontal solid shaft of steel, 4-in. in diameter and 8 ft long, is rigidly attached to a supporting member at each end. A torque of 12,000 lb-ft is applied to a pulley keyed to the shaft 2 ft from the left end. Calculate the maximum torsional stress in the shaft.

20–21C. Find the deflection of point A in the figure shown. Assume the modulus of elasticity to be 30×10^6 psi.

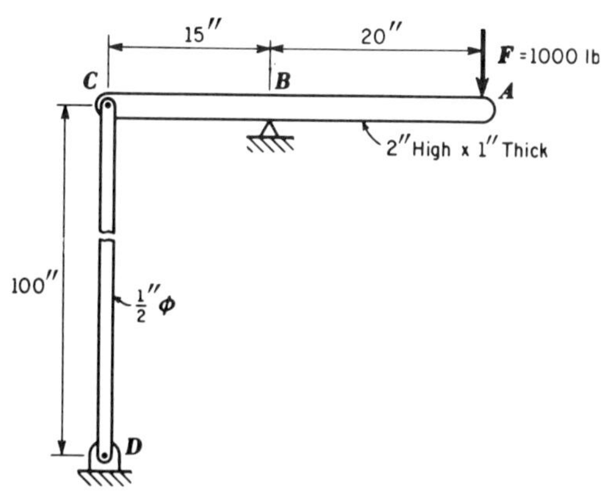

Problem 20–21C.

Physics

20–22C. An electron is accelerated from rest along a straight line to a final velocity of 10^8 cm/sec in a distance of 1 cm. (a) What is the acceleration of this electron? (b) How long did it take to reach this velocity? (c) If the electron then went in a circle with a constant speed of 10^8 cm/sec, what must be the radius of the circle in order to produce the same magnitude of acceleration that it had along the straight line?

20–23C. A thin converging lens has a focal length of 10 in. An object is placed 15 in. from the lens. (a) How far from the lens does the image appear? (b) What is the ratio of image size to object size?

20–24C. The heating required for a structure is determined to be 100,000 Btu/hr. The structure is to be maintained at a temperature of 98°F while the outside temperature is 40°F. Find the minimum horsepower input to a heat pump meeting this requirement.

Electrical Theory

20–25C. A 20-hp, 1750-rpm, 3-phase, 440-volt (line to line), 60-cps induction motor is operating at full load output. Assume the motor efficiency is 90 per cent and the power factor is 80 per cent. Determine: (a) line current, (b) kilovolt amperes of capacitors needed to increase power factor to 90 per cent, (c) approximate no-load speed.

20–26C. A battery of 40 volts emf, has an internal resistance of 2 ohms. It supplies current to the circuit shown. Determine the current supplied by the battery.

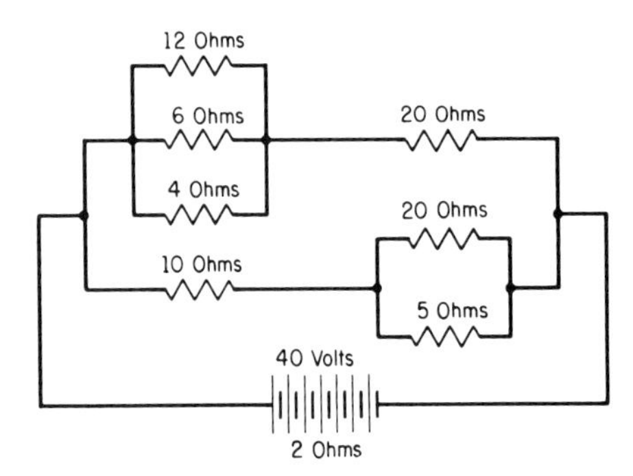

Problem 20–26C.

20–27C. The current waveform shown in the figure may be considered a good approximation of a current impulse. If this impulse is applied to a capacitor as shown in the figure (*b*), how much energy is transferred to the capacitor?

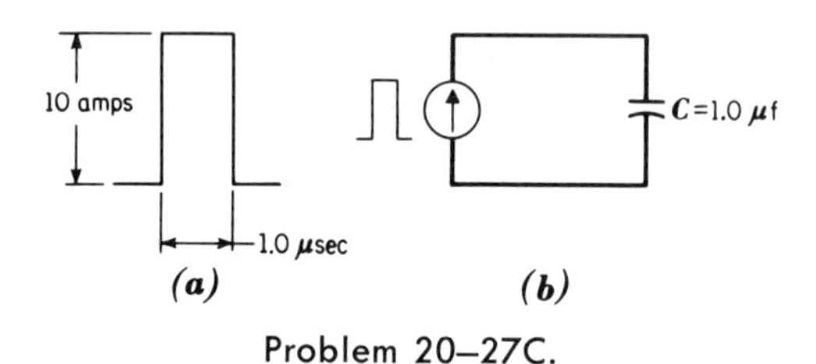

Problem 20–27C.

Economic Analysis

20–28C. An L-shaped structure can be built for the service contemplated at a cost of $18,000,000, but 15 years hence an addition to this building will be necessary for storage at a cost of $10,000,000. A T-shaped structure can be built at the present time which will furnish adequate space for the entire period of planning at a cost of $25,000,000. Both types of structures are of permanent construction, so that depreciation can be neglected in a comparison of costs. With interest at 6 per cent, which is the more economical plan for construction?

20–29C. A company is planning purchasing a 10-hp electric motor which it estimates will run an average of 6 hr/day for 250 days per year. Past experience indicates that: (a) its annual cost of taxes and insurance averages 2.5 per cent of first cost, (b) it must make 10 per cent on invested capital before income tax consideration, and (c) it must recover capital invested in machinery within five years. Two motors are offered to the company. Motor A costs $340 and has a guaranteed efficiency of 85 per cent at the indicated operating load. Motor B has a guaranteed efficiency of 80 per cent at the same operating load and costs $290. Electric energy costs 2.3 cents per kwhr. Calculate the annual cost of each motor and indicate which motor should be purchased. (1 hp = 746 watts.)

20–30C. One year ago a machine was purchased at a cost of $2,000.00, to be useful for 5 years. However, the machine failed to perform properly and has cost $200 per month for repairs, adjustments, and shutdowns. A new machine designed to perform the functions desired is quoted at $3500.00. Cost of repairs and adjustments are estimated to be $50 per month, for its useful life of 5 years. Except for repairs and adjustments, the operating costs for the two machines are substantially equal. With interest at 8 per cent, show whether it is economical to purchase the new machine.

EXAMINATION D

Fundamentals

PART I

Indicate the one answer of your choice for each of the problems 1 through 20 by showing the letter, a, b, c, d, or e in the space provided on the answer sheet. You may use any available space for computations. Only the answer shown on your letter sheet will be graded. Problems 1 through 20 have a grading weight of one point each.

20–1D. Brass is basically an alloy of copper and (a) zinc, (b) tin, (c) aluminum, (d) lead, (e) nickel.

20–2D. Telstar is the name given to (a) a long-span steel joist, (b) a concrete retarder, (c) an expansion-joint filler, (d) a compound to fill cracks in concrete, (e) a communication satellite.

20–3D. Split rings are commonly used in construction of (a) bearing piles, (b) concrete pipes, (c) steel joists, (d) timber trusses, (e) earth-fill dams.

20–4D. Which of the following is not a physical property of hydrogen gas? (a) About one-half as soluble in water as is oxygen, (b) colorless, odorless, and tasteless, (c) lowest specific heat of all gases, (d) best heat conductor of all gases, (e) lightest known substance.

20–5D. An alidade is used primarily in (a) determining the BOD of sewage, (b) a chemical laboratory, (c) mass-diagram plotting, (d) high-order triangulation, (e) plane-table survey.

20–6D. The $\log_{10}$ of 2 is 0.30103. The log of ½ is (a) 9.30103-10, (b) 0.30103/2, (c) 1-0.20103, (d) 9.69897-10, (e) 1/0.30103.

20–7D. The chemical formula for the compound commonly called caustic soda is (a) $NaHSO_4$, (b) $Ca(OH)_2$, (c) Na_2SO_4, (d) $NaOH$, (e) Na_2CO_3.

20–8D. Capillarity results from (a) excess pore water pressure, (b) surface tension, (c) seismic forces, (d) inadequate compaction, (e) second degree indetermining.

20–9D. The Ross-Forel, modified Mercalli, and the Richter are scales used to measure (a) propeller pitch, (b) concrete densities, (c) ductility of steel, (d) earthquake intensity, (e) turbine pressure.

20–10D. Pressure applied everywhere on a confined liquid is transmitted undiminished in every direction. The force thus exerted by the confined fluid acts at right angles to every portion of the surface of the container and is equal upon equal areas. This principle was formulated by (a) Archimedes, (b) Pascal, (c) Hooke, (d) Bernoulli, (e) Charles.

20–11D. The maximum unit fiber stress at any vertical section in a beam is obtained by dividing the moment at that section by (a) the section modulus, (b) the cross-sectional area, (c) one-half the distance to the point where the shear is zero, (d) the radius of gyration, (e) the moment of inertia.

20–12D. To increase the power factor in a series a-c circuit with a lagging power factor, you would increase the (a) current, (b) voltage, (c) inductance, (d) capacitance, (e) frequency.

20–13D. Pan joists are generally used in construction of (a) railroad bridges, (b) timber wharves, (c) roof trusses, (d) concrete flooring, (e) wood frame ceilings.

20–14D. The maximum shear stress in a solid round shaft subject only to torsion occurs (a) on principal planes, (b) on planes containing the axis of the shaft, (c) on the surface of the shaft, (d) on planes perpendicular to the axis of the shaft, (e) at the neutral axis.

20–15D. Entropy (a) remains constant during an irreversible process, (b) is independent of temperature, (c) is a maximum at absolute zero, (d) is a measure of unavailable energy, (e) is the reciprocal of enthalpy.

20–16D. Which measurement listed below is the most precise? (a) A mile measured to the nearest foot, (b) a degree measured to the nearest second, (c) a kilogram measured to the nearest gram, (d) 1.004 in. measured to the nearest thousandth of an inch, (e) a second measured to the nearest millisecond.

20–17D. The rpm of an a-c electric motor (a) varies directly as the number of poles, (b) varies inversely as the number of poles, (c) is independent of the number of poles, (d) is independent of the frequency, (e) is directly proportional to the square of the frequency.

20–18D. Which of the following is incorrect? (a) $\cos^2 A = \tan A \cot A$, (b) $\sin A = \cos A \tan A$, (c) $\cos 2A = \cos^2 A - \sin^2 A$, (d) $2 \sin^2 A = 1 - \cos 2A$, (e) $\sin (A + B) = \sin A \cos B + \cos A \sin B$.

20–19D. On exposure to air a deliquescent substance (a) oxidizes, (b) crystallizes, (c) loses water of hydration, (d) becomes moist, (e) disappears.

20–20D. The transition between laminar and turbulent flow usually occurs at a Reynolds number of approximately (a) 350, (b) 900, (c) 1800, (d) 2100, (e) 3850.

In solving the following problems, be sure to show all of the steps of the solution in sequence. The method of solving the problems is considered in the scoring. Problems 21 through 30 have a weight of 3 points each.

20–21D. What is the tangent of an angle whose cosine is X?

20–22D. What is the value of the determinant D when:

$$D = \begin{vmatrix} 1 & 1 & 1 \\ 2 & -1 & 1 \\ 1 & 2 & -1 \end{vmatrix}$$

20–23D. Water is flowing through a pipe. The following data are known: $D = 2$ in. ID, $P = 70$ psig, $N = 0.015$, $h_f = 20$ ft, $N_R = 1590$, $V = 25$ fps. What is the rate of flow in gallons per minute?

20–24D. A helical spring has a natural length of 6 in. It requires a force of 20 lb to hold it extended to a length of 12 in. How much work in in.-lb does it take to stretch the spring from a total length of 9 in. to 11 in. long? Assume that the spring does not exceed its elastic limit.

20–25D. Find the area formed by the boundaries $y = 1$, $x = 1$, and $y = e^{-x}$.

20–26D. Find the acceleration of the masses and the tension in the rope for the arrangement shown. Assume no friction and weightless pulleys.

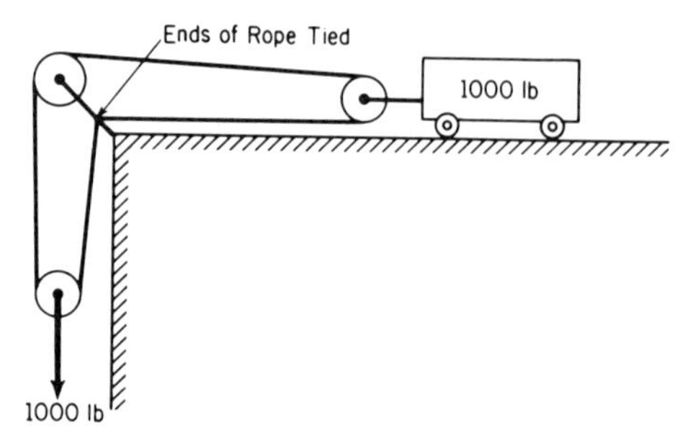

Problem 20–26D.

20–27D. What is the hp required to propel a 3-ton vehicle up a 6 per cent grade at 60 mph, assuming only 75 per cent of the engine power is available to pull the vehicle? (25 per cent of the power is used in driving engine accessories, overcoming friction, drag, etc.)

20–28D. A 150-lb man stands at the rear of a 250-lb boat. The distance from the man to the pier is 30 ft and the length of the boat is 16 ft. What is the distance of the man from the pier after he walks to the front of the boat at a velocity of 3 mph? Assume no friction between boat and water.

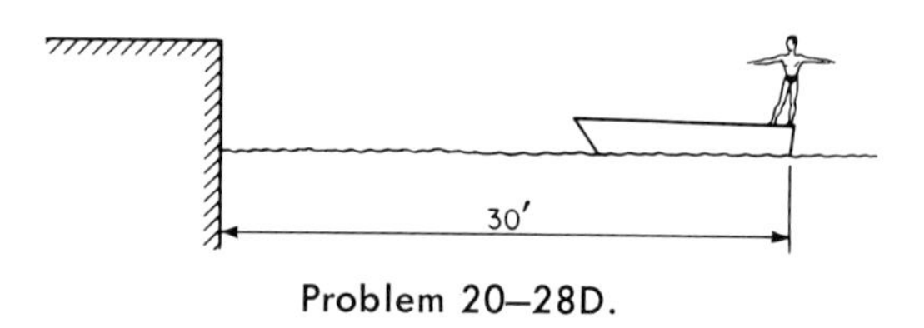

Problem 20–28D.

20–29D. What is the total equivalent resistance of the circuit between A and B?

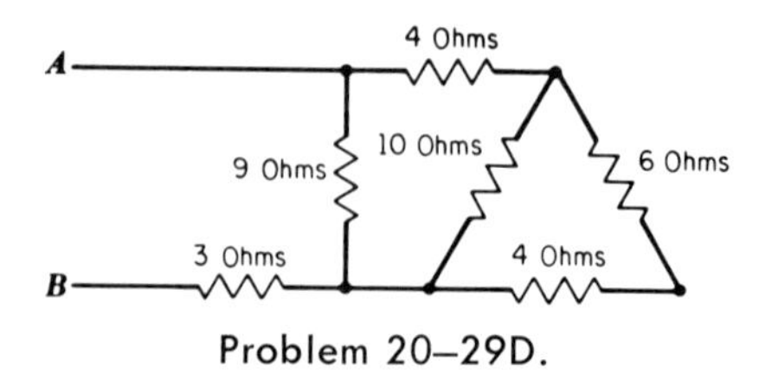

Problem 20–29D.

20–30D. Prove mathematically that the average value of the amplitude of a half sine-wave is $2/\pi$ times the maximum value.

PART II

20–31D. How much force does a 160-lb man exert on an airplane seat when it is at the top of a vertical loop of radius 1000 ft if the plane's speed is 180 mph?

20–32D. Theoretically, how many pounds of air are required for complete combustion of 10 lb of ethane gas (C_2H_6), and how many pounds of water vapor are produced by the products of combustion? Assume that the air contains 23 per cent oxygen by weight.

20–33D. A batted baseball leaves the bat at an angle of 30° above the horizontal, and is caught by a fielder 400 ft from home plate. What is the initial velocity of the ball? Assume the ball's height when hit is the same as when caught and that air resistance is negligible.

20–34D. Two 3-lb weights are connected by a massless string hanging over a smooth frictionless peg. If a third weight of 3 lb is added to one of the weights and the system is released, by how much is the force on the peg increased?

20–35D. A body experiences acceleration as given by the equation $a = At - Bt^2$, where A and B are constants and t is time. If, at the time $t = 0$, the body has a zero displacement and velocity, at what next value of time does the body again have zero displacement?

20–36D. A uniform solid rod 24 in. long is supported at one end by a string 6 in. from the water. If the specific gravity of the rod is 5/9, find the length of the rod that is immersed in water. Assume the cross-section of the rod is small.

20–37D. A steel bar having a 1 in. square cross-section is 150 in. long when lying horizontally. What is its length if suspended vertically from one end? Steel weighs 0.283 lb/cu in.

20–38D. Define the following terms: (a) friction head, (b) present worth, (c) standard deviation, (d) *p*H, (e) anti-logarithm, (f) nomograph, (g) bourdon tube, (h) circular mil, (i) dyne, (j) kinetic energy.

20–39D. Given: Universe = (1,2,3,4,5,6,7); A = (1,3,6), B = (1,2,6,7). Find: (a) $\overline{A}$, (b) $\overline{B}$, (c) $A \cap B$, (d) $A \cap \overline{B}$, (e) $\overline{A} \cup B$.

20-40D. An athletic field 450 ft on each side is illuminated by 6 towers supporting banks of 1000-watt incandescent lamps rated at 20 lumens per watt. If the desired illuminance has been set at 20 lumens per sq ft, how many lamps are required in each bank if there is a 50 per cent loss of luminous flux from the towers to the field?

20–41D. A vertical cylindrical water softener is to operate under the following conditions: (1) water flow of 307 gpm, (2) maximum flow rate of 8.0/gpm/sq ft of area, (3) supply water with a hardness of 12.0 grains/gal., (4) softener contains 95.0 cu ft of exchange resin, (5) exchange value of resin is 24,000 grains/cu ft. Determine: (a) diameter of softener to nearest foot, (b) number of gallons of water softened between regenerations, (c) length of time softener will operate before requiring regeneration.

20–42D. A rectangular wooden beam is loaded as shown. Beam weight is neglected. (a) Is the beam overloaded in bending if the maximum allowable bending stress is 2000 psi? (b) Is the beam overloaded in horizontal shear if the maximum allowable shearing stress is 100 psi? Show proof of answers.

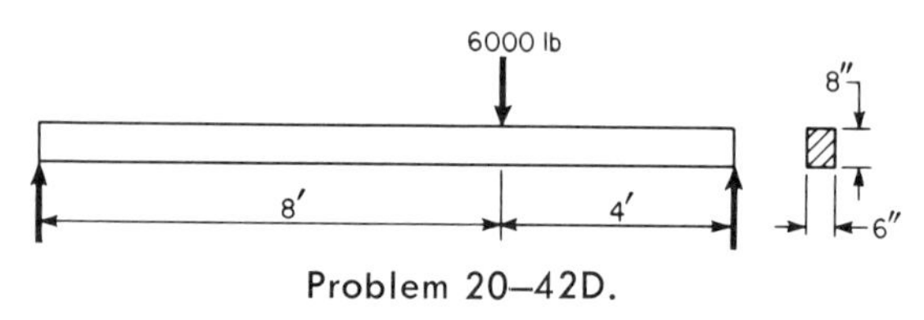

Problem 20–42D.

20–43D. In the figure, the pipe is of uniform diameter. The gage pressure at A is 20 psi, and at B is 30 psi. In which direction is the flow, and what is the head loss if the liquid has a specific weight of 30 pcf?

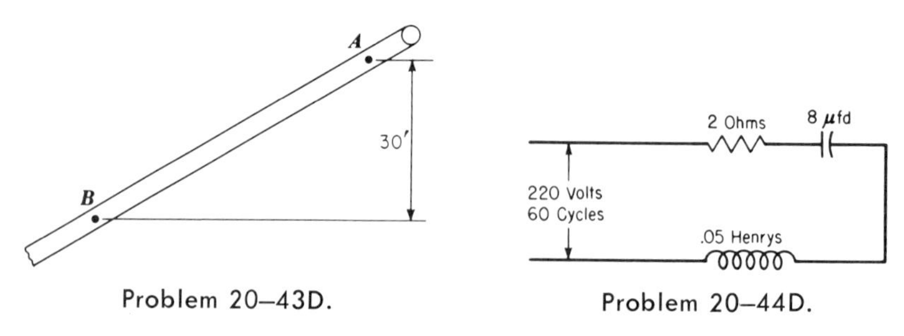

Problem 20–43D. Problem 20–44D.

20–44D. In the circuit shown, find: (a) the impedance, (b) the line current, (c) the power factor.

20–45D. A counterflow heat exchanger is operating with the hot liquid entering at 400°F and leaving at 327°F. The cool liquid enters at 100°F and leaves at 284°F. What is the log mean temperature difference between the hot and cold liquids?

20–46D. In the circuit shown, compute the voltage drop across the 7-ohm resistor. Assume the inductance has negligible resistance.

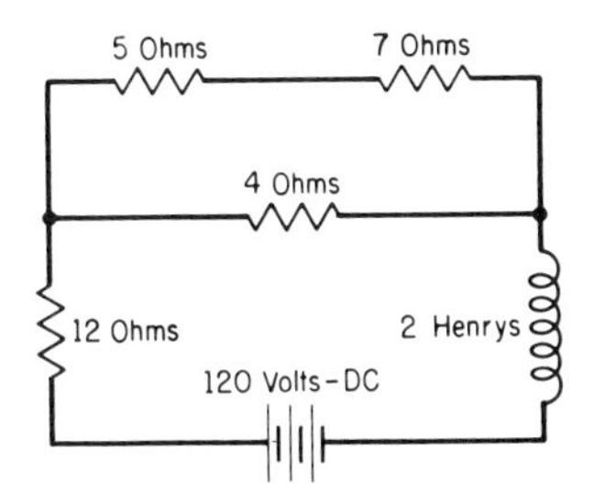

Problem 20–46D.

20–47D. (a) Write the equation for the formation of aluminum oxide. (b) Define and give an example of an exothermic reaction. (c) Define and give an example of an endothermic reaction.

20–48D. Water flows through two orifices in the side of a large water tank. The water surface in the tank is held constant. The upper orifice is 16 ft above the ground surface, and this stream strikes the ground 8 ft from the base of the tank. The stream from the lower orifice strikes the ground 10 ft away from the base of the tank. (Assume $g = 32$ fps^2.) (a) Find the height of the water surface above the ground. (b) Find the height of the lower orifice above the ground.

20–49D. A distance from A to B was measured to be 5368.25 ft with a tape. The temperature during this time was 22°F. The steel tape used was standardized at 100.00 ft at a temperature of 68°F. If the coefficient of expansion of steel is 0.0000065, what is the true distance from A to B?

20–50D. What is the probability that of 5 persons in a room, at least two will have birthdays that fall on the same day of the year? Use one year = 365 days.

EXAMINATION E

Engineer-in-Training Examination

FUNDAMENTALS (Morning)

Instructions: The use of textbooks, interest tables, logarithm tables and slide rules for calculation is permitted. Time allowed, 4 hours. Answer 5 questions, using at least 4 subjects.

Mathematics

20–1E. (a) Find M if $\log_5 M = \log_{25} 4$. (b) Find the equation of the parabola in the form $y = f(x)$ which passes through the points (1,2), (3,20), and (4,35).

20–2E. Determine the error in the calculated volume of a sphere 10 in. in diameter if the possible error in the diameter measurement is 0.10 per cent.

Physics

20–3E. A glass rod of refractive index=1.50 has hemispherical surfaces of 5 cm radius at each end. An object 25 cm from one end, and outside the rod, creates a final image 30 cm from the opposite end but within the rod. What is the *length of the rod?*

20–4E. A tuning fork of 512 frequency makes 2 beats/sec with a vibrating string. Tightening the string eliminates the beats so that the fork and the string vibrate in unison. Find in what proportion tension in the string was increased.

Chemistry

20–5E. The complete combustion of propane gas is represented by the following skeleton equation: $C_3H_8 + O_2 = CO_2 + H_2O$. (a) Balance the equation. (b) How many cubic feet of air (air is 21 per cent O_2 by volume and 79 per cent N_2 by volume) measured at 25°C and a pressure of 760 mm of Hg would be required to burn 10,500 cu ft of propane gas measured at the same conditions of temperature and pressure?

20–6E. The specific gravity of a 10 per cent calcium chloride solution ($CaCl_2$ dissolved in water) is 1.0835. Water weighs 62.43 lb/cu ft at 39°F and there are 7.48 gal in a cubic foot. Calculate the number of pounds of calcium chloride required to make 55 gal of a 10 per cent solution of this salt at 39°F.

Economics

20–7E. An asset has a first cost of $13,000, an estimated life of 15 years, and a salvage value of $1000. For depreciation use the sinking-fund method with interest at 5 per cent compounded annually and find: (a) the annual sinking-fund annuity or depreciation charge, and (b) the balance in the sinking fund, i.e., the amount accumulated toward depreciation of the asset at the end of 9 years. (c) If the asset were to be sold for $4000 at the end of 9 years, what would be the *net book value gain* or *loss*?

20–8E. A certain product is selling for $8.20. The production cost is $7.38. (a) What per cent of the selling price represents profit? (b) What per cent of reduction in production costs will increase the margin of profit 60 per cent?

Electrical

20–9E. An electrical milliameter, having an internal resistance of 500 ohms, reads full scale when 1 ma (0.001 amp) of current is flowing. (a) If the meter is to be used as an ammeter reading 0.1 amp full scale, what size (ohms) resistor should be used in parallel with it? (b) If used as a voltmeter reading 100 volts full scale, what size (ohms) resistor should be used in series with the milliameter?

20–10E. (a) Battery A has a no-load terminal voltage of 9 volts and an internal resistance of 2 ohms. Battery B has a no-load terminal voltage of 6.5 volts with an internal resistance of 1 ohm. When the positive terminals of the two batteries are connected together, the negative terminals are connected together, and a 3-ohm resistor is connected between positive and negative terminals, what current will flow through each battery?

(b) A 1-h inductor and a 100-ohm resistor are paralleled and the combination is placed in series with a 50-ohm resistor. This series-parallel circuit is placed across a 60-cycle source, and the voltage across the inductor is 100 volts. What is the source voltage?

FUNDAMENTALS (Afternoon)

Instructions: The use of textbooks, interest tables, logarithm tables, and slide rules for calculations is permitted. Time allowed, 4 hours. Answer 5 questions, using at least 4 subjects.

Statics

20–11E. The weights A and B are supported by a continuous rope which is attached at points C and D and passes around frictionless pulleys as shown. Neglect the weight of the rope and pulleys. Find the position of pulley P relative to the point O for equilibrium.

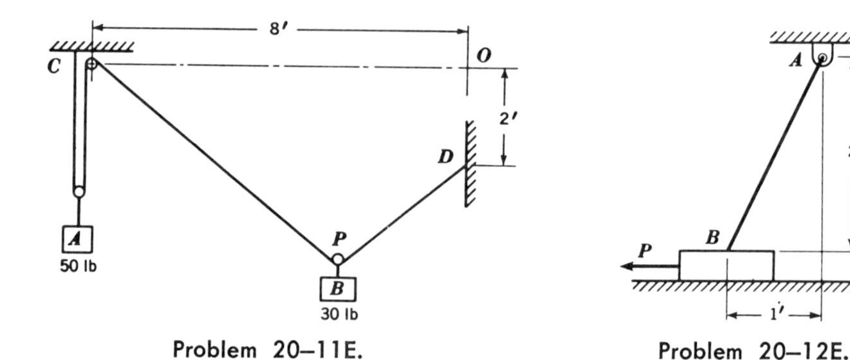

Problem 20–11E. Problem 20–12E.

20–12E. A homogeneous rod weighing 50 lb is hinged at A and rests on a block at B as shown. The block weighing 3 lb rests on a horizontal floor. If the coefficient of friction for all surfaces is $\frac{1}{3}$, find the horizontal force P necessary to cause the block to slide to the left. Consider the hinge at A to be frictionless.

Kinetics

20–13E. A drop hammer of 1-ton dead-weight capacity is propelled downward by a 12-in. diameter air cylinder. At 100 psi air pressure, what is the impact velocity if the stroke is 28 in.? What is the impact energy?

20–14E. A 10-hp 1750-rpm motor is connected directly to a 30-lb/ft torque brake. The rotating system has a total inertia (WR^2) of 10 lb ft^2. How long will it take the system to stop if the brake is set at the instant the motor is shut off? How much energy must be dissipated?

Strength of Materials

20–15E. A new column is to be used to aid an existing column to carry a load. The allowable stress in the new column is 10 ksi and the length is 10 ft. The modulus of elasticity is 30,000 ksi, and the coefficient of thermal expansion of the material is 6.7×10^{-6}. The final temperature of both columns is assumed to be 80°F. Find the temperature to which the new column will have to be cooled in order to have $\frac{1}{32}$ in. clearance for insertion and to take up its load when raised to 80°F.

20–16E. Where does the maximum bending moment occur in a beam with a 30-ft span with the following loads and what is that moment: A uniformly distributed load of 1000 lb/ft is carried, along with an additional load of 2000 lb/ft starting 6 ft from the left support and extending over 8 ft of the beam to the right?

Thermo-Heat-Power

20–17E. (a) One pound of saturated steam at 400°F expands isothermally to 60 psia. Determine (1) change of entropy, (2) heat transferred, (3) change of enthalpy, (4) change of internal energy, and (5) work. (b) One pound of steam at 400 psia and 600°F expands isentropically to a final temperature of 200°F. Determine (1) initial a) enthalpy, b) entropy, c) volume, d) internal energy; (2) final a) pressure, b) quality, c) volume, d) enthalpy, e) internal energy; (3) heat transferred; (4) change of internal energy; (5) work done during the process; (6) sketch on temperature-entropy plane showing saturated liquid and vapor lines.

20–18E. (a) Tests of a six-cylinder 4-in. bore and 3⅛-in. stroke aircraft engine at full throttle show a brake horsepower of 79.5 at 3400 rpm. The compression ratio is 8:1, the specific fuel consumption is 0.56 lb/brake hp-hr. The higher heating value of the fuel is 19,800 Btu/lb. Determine (1) the brake mean effective pressure; (2) the brake torque; (3) the brake thermal efficiency; (4) the brake engine efficiency based on cold air standard if the ideal efficiency e is:

$$e = 1 - \frac{1}{r_k^{k-1}}$$

where r_k=compression ratio.

(b) An exhaust gas has the following volumetric analysis, in per cent: CO_2=12, CO=2, O_2=4, and N_2=82. Find the corresponding gravimetric (by weight) analysis.

Fluid Mechanics

20–19E. Water flows through 3000 ft of 36-in. diameter pipe which branches into 2000 ft of 18-in. diameter pipe and 2400 ft of 24-in. diameter pipe. These rejoin, and the water continues through 1500 ft of 30-in. diameter pipe. All pipes are horizontal, and the friction factors are 0.016 for the 36-in. pipe, 0.017 for the 24-in. and 30-in. pipe, and 0.019 for the 18-in. pipe. Find the pressure drop, in pounds per square inch, between the beginning and the end of the system if the steady flow is 60 cfs in the 36-in. pipe. Neglect minor losses.

20–20E. A horizontal bend in a pipeline reduces the pipe from a 30-in. diameter to an 18-in. diameter while bending through an angle of 135° from its original direction. The flow rate is 10,000 gpm, and the direction of flow is from the 30-in. to the 18-in. pipe. If the pressure at the entrance is 60 psig, what must be the magnitude of the resultant force necessary to keep the bend in place? Consider the bend to be adequately supported in a vertical direction.

EXAMINATION F

Fundamentals

PART I ONLY

Time allowed, 4 hours. Answer enough problems to add up to 50 points. No text or reference material may be used.

20–1F. (Wt. 1) tan (arcsin 0.5) is equal to (a) $\frac{1}{4}$, (b) $\frac{1}{2}$, (c) $1/\sqrt{3}$, (d) 1, (e) $\sqrt{3}$.

20–2F. (Wt. 1) $\log_{10} (100)^2 - \ln_e 2.718$ is equal to (a) 2, (b) 3, (c) 4, (d) 5, (e) 6.

20–3F. (Wt. 1). For the position-time function $x=3t^2+2t$ the velocity in the x direction at $t=1$ is (a) 4, (b) 5, (c) 6, (d) 7, (e) 8.

20–4F. (Wt. 1) The wavelength of blue light is longer than the wavelength of (a) green light, (b) orange light, (c) red light, (d) violet light, (e) yellow light.

20–5F. (Wt. 1) A kilowatthour is a unit of (a) momentum, (b) power, (c) acceleration, (d) energy, and (e) impulse.

20–6F. (Wt. 1) Which one of the following statements is false? (a) The atomic weight of oxygen is exactly 16. (b) Alcohol has a freezing point of —40°F. (c) 788 ft-lb equals 1 Btu. (d) Absolute zero on the temperature scale is approximately —460°F. (e) A coulomb of electricity can be defined as that quantity which will deposit a stated fraction of a gram of silver from a stated normal solution of silver nitrate under certain conditions.

20–7F. (Wt. 1) Which one of the following statements is false? (a) A Btu is $\frac{1}{100}$ of the quantity of heat required to raise 1 lb of water from 32°F to 212°F at a pressure of 1 atm. (b) Concrete weighs approximately 150 lb/cu ft. (c) Structural steel has an ultimate strength in tension of over 60,000 psi. (d) The area of an ellipse is πab, where a and b are respectively one-half the major and minor axes. (e) A #14 Awg copper conductor, such as commonly used in household circuits, has a current-carrying capacity of at least 15 amp.

20–8F. (Wt. 1) Kinetic energy is a function of (a) mass and position, (b) moment of inertia, momentum, and speed, (c) mass and velocity, (d) moment of inertia and acceleration, (e) mass and acceleration.

20–9F. (Wt. 1) The sum of the interior angles of a polygon with seven sides is (a) 540°, (b) 630°, (c) 720°, (d) 810°, (e) 900°.

20–10F. (Wt. 1) For a d-c shunt motor, operating from a constant potential supply, (a) increasing the shunt field resistance will cause the motor speed to increase, (b) increasing the shunt field resistance will cause the motor speed to decrease, (c) increasing the shunt field resistance will cause the shunt field current to increase, (d) decreasing the shunt field resistance will cause the shunt field current to decrease, (e) increasing the shunt field resistance will cause the armature current to decrease.

20–11F. (Wt. 1) A four-pole synchronous motor operating from a 50-cps supply will have a synchronous speed of (a) 3600 rpm, (b) 3000 rpm, (c) 1800 rpm, (d) 1500 rpm, (e) 1200 rpm.

20–12F. (Wt. 1) The volume of 1 mole of oxygen at 0°C and 1 atm of pressure is approximately (a) 1.0 liter, (b) 16.0 liters, (c) 22.4 liters, (d) 1.0 cu ft, (e) 62.4 cu ft.

20–13F. (Wt. 1) The numbers of liters of oxygen necessary to burn 10 liters of H_2S gas according to the reaction $2H_2S+3O_2 \rightarrow 2H_2O+2SO_2$ is (a) 3, (b) 6, (c) 10, (d) 15, (e) 30.

20–14F. (Wt. 1) The concentration of a solution of H_2SO_4 is given in terms of moles per liter as 0.2 M H_2SO_4. The normal concentration of this solution would be designated as (a) 0.05 N H_2SO_4, (b) 0.1 N H_2SO_4, (c) 0.2 N H_2SO_4, (d) 0.4 N H_2SO_4, (e) 0.5 N H_2SO_4.

20–15F. (Wt. 2) Which one of the following chemical equations is correct? The valences of the various elements or radicals are listed as follows: H^+, Na^+, Ag^+, Ca^{++}, Zn^{++}, C^{++++}, $(OH)^-$, Cl^-, NO_3^-, O^{--}, CO_3^{--}, SO_4^{--}. (a) $H_2+O_2 \rightarrow H_2O$, (b) $NaCl+2AgNO_3 \rightarrow NaNO_3 + AgCl$, (c) $CaO+H_2O \rightarrow Ca(OH)_3$, (d) $CaSO_4+Na_2CO_3 \rightarrow CaCO_3 + Na_2SO_4$, (e) $ZnCO_3 \rightarrow ZnO+2CO_2$.

20–16F. (Wt. 2) A sum of money invested at 4 per cent interest, compounded semiannually, will double in amount in approximately (a) 15½ years, (b) 17½ years, (c) 19½ years, (d) 21½ years, (e) 23½ years.

20–17F. (Wt. 2) In the equation $y=(-x^3+3x+2)/(x^2+2x+1)$, the limit of y as x approaches a value of -1 (minus one) is (a) zero, (b) 1, (c) 2, (d) 3, (e) infinity.

20–18F. (Wt. 3) List three ways in which a current or voltage may be developed.

20–19F. (Wt. 3) Define the following chemical terms: (a) catalyst, (b) oxidation, (c) reduction.

20–20F. (Wt. 3) Derive the equation of the largest circle that is tangent to both coordinate axes and has its center on the line $2x+y-6=0$.

20–21F. (Wt. 3) The melting rate of snow will normally be accelerated when warm rains fall. Using the following data, determine the percentage of a 50-in. snow pack that will be melted by the rain water. Snow: depth, 50 in.; water content, 40 per cent; temperature, 32°F (melting point), heat of fusion, 144.0 Btu/lb. Rain: Amount, 2 in.; temperature, 68°F. Assume weight of melted snow and rain water as 62.4 lb/cu ft.

20–22F. (Wt. 3) Determine the theoretical mechanical advantage (ratio of applied force F to load W) of the system shown in sketch.

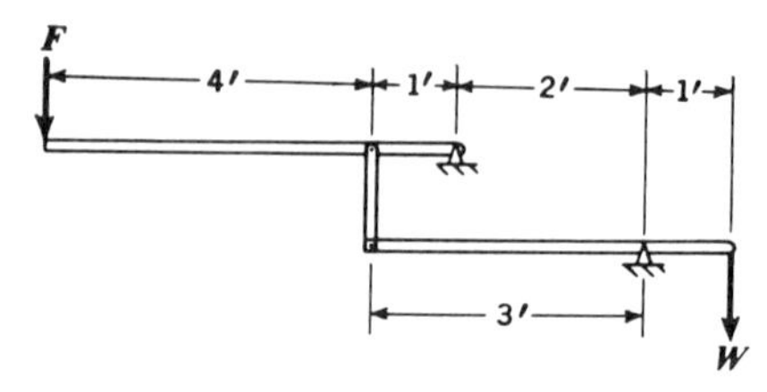

Problem 20–22F.

20–23F. (Wt. 4) Circular cylindrical cans of volume V_0 are to be manufactured with both ends closed. Determine the ratio between the diameter and height that will require the minimum amount of metal to make each can.

20–24F. (Wt. 6) Boat A is chasing boat B and wishes to fire its gun such that a hit may be scored. Boat A and boat B are traveling in the same direction at constant velocities V_A and V_B, respectively. The gun on boat A has a muzzle velocity of V_1 and is inclined an angle θ to the horizontal. What must be the separation of the boats L in order for the hit to be scored? Obtain the distance L in terms of the variables V_A, V_B, V_1, and θ. Neglect air friction, and assume that the shell leaves the gun at the same elevation as the point of impact on boat B.

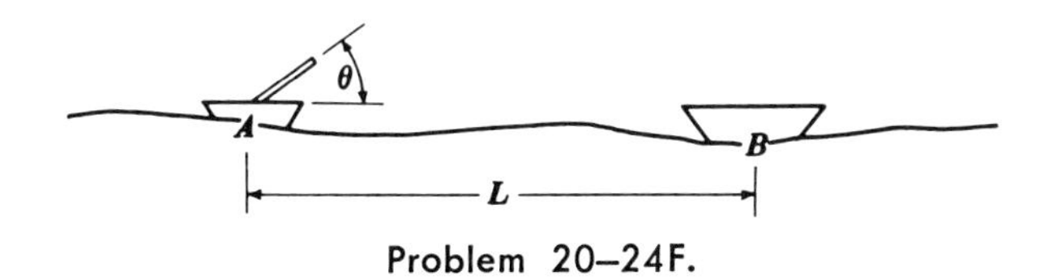

Problem 20–24F.

20–25F. (Wt. 4) A bullet of mass m, traveling at velocity V_1, makes an inelastic impact with a simple pendulum composed of a mass M on the end of a flexible cord. If the impact occurs a distance L below the pendulum's suspension point, through what angle θ will the pendulum move? (Assume the impact occurs at right angles to the vertical.)

20–26F. (Wt. 5) The stiffness of a rectangular timber beam is proportional to the width and the cube of the depth. Find the dimensions of the cross section of the stiffest beam that can be made out of a circular log whose diameter is 20 in.

20–27F. (Wt. 6) Given a rigid bar hanging from three wires of length L, modulus of elasticity E, cross-sectional area A, spaced a distance a apart as shown in the figure. Calculate the force in each wire caused by load P. Neglect weight of bar.

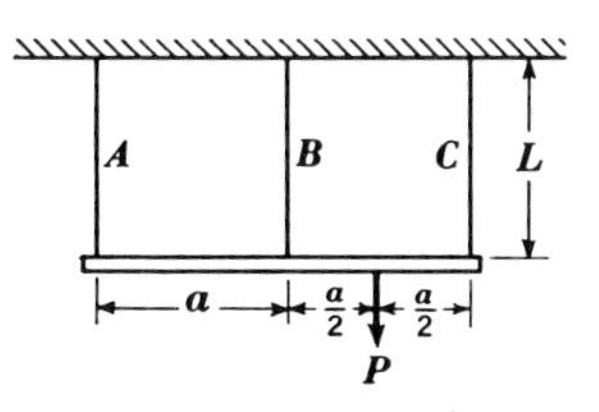

Problem 20–27F.

20–28F. (Wt. 3) The circuit shown is composed of resistors which have equal resistance of R. What is the resistance between points A and B?

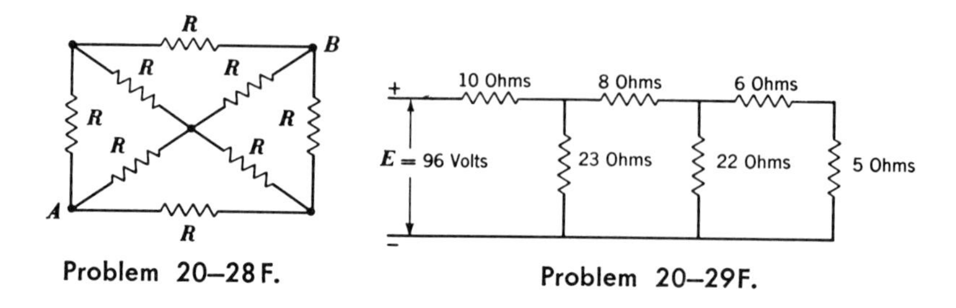

Problem 20–28 F.

Problem 20–29F.

20–29F. (Wt. 4) Find the current input to the circuit shown.

20–30F. (Wt. 4) What are the power, in watts, the reactive power, in vars, the total volt-amperes input, and the power factor of the circuit shown?

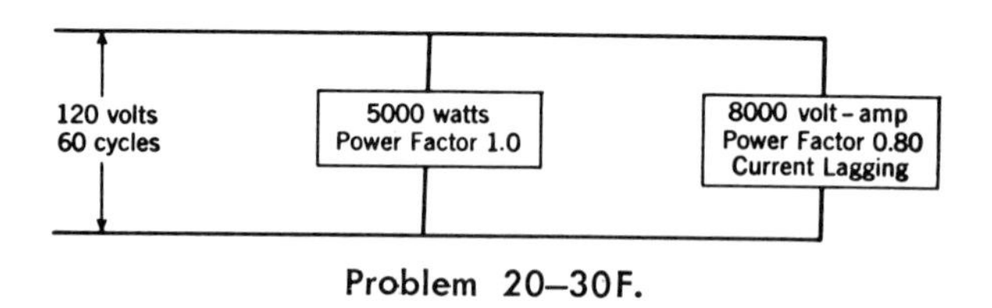

Problem 20–30F.

20–31F. (Wt. 5) Two control cables for an aircraft are partially shown in the full-scale plan and elevation views as *AB* and *CD*. Determine, graphically, the minimum clearance between the two control cables and indicate the minimum clearance as a line on the plan and elevation views.

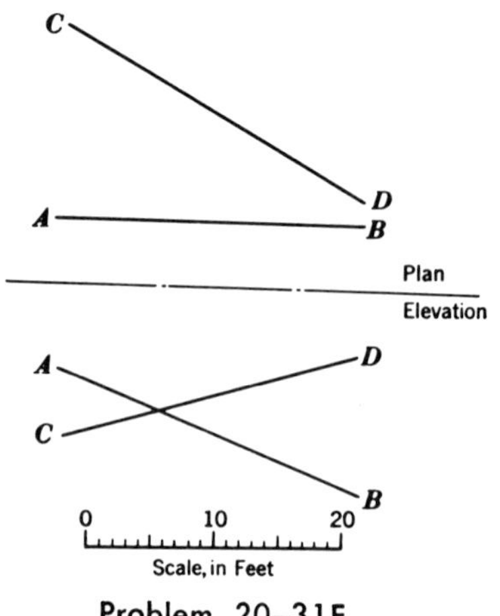

Problem 20–31F.

EXAMINATION G

Aeronautical Engineering

PART I

Time allowed, 4 hours. No references permitted. Work any 5 of the 7 problems.

20–1G. A ½-hp motor operating at 1000 rpm rotates a ¾–0.035 aluminum alloy torque tube 30 in. long which drives the gear mechanism for operating a wing flap. Determine the maximum torsional stress in the torque shaft under full power and revolutions per minute. Find the angular deflection of shaft in the 30-in. length. Polar moment of inertia of tube is 0.01 in.^{4}. Modulus of rigidity $G=3.8\times10^6$ psi.

20–2G. The lateral dynamic stability quartic for an airplane may be written as $A\lambda^4+B\lambda^3+C\lambda^2+D\lambda+E=0$. The first two roots were found to be $\lambda_1=0.2$ and $\lambda_2=-10.1$ and the remaining second-order differential equation is

$$\frac{d^2\beta}{dt^2}+3\frac{d\beta}{dt}+40\beta=0$$

(a) If A, B, C, and D are positive and E is negative, the airplane will be (stable, unstable) in the ____________ mode. The root describing this mode is ____________. (b) If $E=0$ in the lateral stability quartic, the condition is called the ____________ boundary. (c) What does λ_2 above reveal? (d) Write the solution of the second-order equation using the numbers given. Assume the solution in the form $\beta=\beta_1 e^{\lambda t}$. (e) Find the time to damp to one-half amplitude or to double amplitude in (d), if the motion is oscillatory. (f) Find the period of the oscillation in (d) if the motion is oscillatory.

20–3G. (a) If an airplane has a rolling moment due to rolling velocity of $C_{l_p}=-0.1$, what must the length of the span be in order that the airplane have a rolling velocity of 45.85° per second, at a forward velocity of 300 fps? Assume that the opposing rolling moment coefficient developed at this speed is -0.008. (b) The yawing moment due to the rolling velocity for a given airplane is $C_n=\pm0.016$, and the adverse yaw due to the rolling control is $C_n=0.004$. If the directional stability of the airplane is $C_{n\psi}=-0.001$, how many degrees of sideslip would this airplane develop during abrupt rolling maneuvers? (c) How much rudder power

$C_{n_{\delta r}}$ must the airplane in (b) have for 30° of rudder throw to overcome the adverse yaw? (d) If the airplane in (b) has $a_{vT}=0.02$, $S_t/S_w=0.1$, $l_v/b=1.0$, and $\eta_v=0.8$, will it have sufficient rudder power for 30° of rudder as described in (c)? (e) If an airplane has a rudder throw power $C_{n_{\delta r}}=-0.002$ and the directional stability is $C_{n\psi}=-0.001$, 10° of rudder will produce how many degrees of yaw?

20–4G. (a) If a representative variation of $u=f(y)$ for air flow parallel to a plane surface is $u=30{,}000\ (y-50y^2)$, where u is measured in feet per second and y in feet, find (1) The height of the boundary layer. (2) The viscous shear stress at the plane surface, in pounds per square foot. (3) The viscous shear stress at $y=0.1$ in. and 0.12 in. (b) An airfoil of the laminar type is placed in a wind tunnel which has 6 per cent turbulence. The rectangular wing has a 6-ft chord and 18-ft span. If the average velocity in the working section is 100 fps under standard conditions, what is the viscous drag of the airfoil, considering the surfaces flat? Zero angle of attack. (c) Find the drag of the wing in (b) assuming the flow to be purely laminar over the entire wing.

20–5G. A Karman vortex street is formed behind a bluff body with a distance of 5.62 ft between the rows, and the vortices are spaced 20 ft apart. The free-stream velocity ahead of the body is 5 fps. Timed photographs showed that every 20 sec a large vortex was shed at one edge of the body, i.e., the alternate shedding of the vortices from the two edges (two-dimensional flow only) was such that a vortex was produced in the wake every 10 sec. Assuming the fluid to be standard air, find the drag, in pounds.

20–6G. An airplane with an elliptical wing flies at 10,000 ft. If the span of the wing is 80 ft and the air speed is 250 mph, find the lateral center of pressure, in feet, measured from the center line.

20–7G. A two-dimensional symmetrical diamond airfoil with 2° semi-angle (4° opening angle) is at 3° angle of attack. Find, by linearized supersonic theory, for a free-stream Mach number of 3: (a) the pressure distribution (show a plot), (b) the lift, in pounds per foot of span, if the chord is 10 ft and the free stream is standard conditions, (c) the slope of the lift curve, and (d) the drag, in pounds per foot of span, if chord is 10 ft (standard conditions).

PART II

Time allowed, 4 hours. No references permitted. Work any 5 of the 7 problems.

20–8G. There are six commonly used designs of solid-propellant grain configurations. By proper geometrical design of the propellant grain, practically any desired thrust-vs.-time curve can be achieved. Name and sketch three typical solid-propellant grain configurations such that one exhibits neutral (cigarette) burning, one exhibits regressive burning, and one exhibits progressive burning.

20–9G. There are three distinct conditions under which a ram-jet engine diffuser can operate, depending on the heat release in the combustion chamber. (a) First, make a sketch of these three conditions and identify each (be sure to show the position of the normal shock). (b) Discuss the conditions under which these can exist and state which is the *design* condition.

20–10G. (a) In two-dimensional supersonic flow a detached bow wave exists for some bodies, while others have attached straight shock waves. Explain why this occurs. (b) In so-called linearized supersonic theory, the Mach angle is assumed to be the angle of inclination of the shock wave. In the actual case, what is the situation regarding the shock and Mach angles? (c) Define transonic flow. (d) Define pure supersonic flow. (e) Explain what is meant by the so-called exact supersonic or shock-expansion theory. (f) A two-dimensional wedge with 46° semi-angle is flying at a very high supersonic Mach number. Discuss briefly.

20–11G. (a) Given a three-dimensional cone and a two-dimensional wedge with the same opening angle. Discuss briefly the shock attachment Mach number. (b) Define wave drag and pressure drag. (c) Explain briefly the difficulties encountered in testing at Mach number 1 in a wind tunnel with a solid-wall working section. (d) How may a solid-wall working section be altered so that one may test models at Mach number 1? (e) In subsonic flow a real fluid cannot negotiate a sharp corner. Discuss briefly this type of flow in the supersonic case. (f) In a fixed-wall subsonic wind tunnel the Mach number can be varied by increasing the power. Explain the analogous situation in a fixed-wall supersonic tunnel.

20–12G. (a) The heat-transfer rate at the stagnation point of an axially symmetric body is given by the expression

$$q_{w\ \text{stag}} = \frac{0.763}{Pr^{0.6}} \sqrt{\beta \rho_\infty \mu_\infty c_p} (T_w - T_{aw})$$

where β is the stagnation velocity gradient dU/dx. If the Mach number and altitude are given, what single factor does the designer have that will give him some control over the heat-transfer rate? What parameter is involved? (Assume that he has no artificial means of cooling such as magnetogasdynamic techniques, refrigeration, ablation, etc.)

(b) It is known that the *incompressible* (Blasius) solution for local skin friction coefficient c_f for a flat plate can be written as $c_f=0.664/\sqrt{\text{Re}}$, where $\text{Re}=\rho_\infty V_\infty x/\mu_\infty$ is the "freestream" Reynolds number. Assume that the Mach number over a flat plate is 5, the recovery factor unity, the y-momentum equation is $\partial p/\partial y=0$, the equation of state is $p=\rho RT$, and the viscosity-temperature relation is $\mu_1/\mu_2=(T_1/T_2)^n$. Show how you can alter Blasius incompressible solution to find the local skin friction coefficient for the hypersonic Mach number 5. Be explicit.

(c) State the exact formula for Reynolds analogy (between the skin friction and heat transfer) for laminar flow and explain physically what it means. Next, state the modified Reynolds analogy for turbulent flow and conclude from the results why one would prefer laminar flow at extreme speeds.

(d) If, for the flow over a flat plate, one uses the expression

$$\frac{T_w}{T_\infty}=1+\frac{\gamma-1}{2}M_\infty{}^2$$

to calculate wall temperature T_w, what assumption is automatically made? Criticize the use of the above expression for calculating the "wall" temperature at the stagnation point for a hypersonic Mach number of 15.

(e) Of what value is the Mangler transformation?

20–13G. (a) Suppose a rectangular wing has full-span differential ailerons and is flying at 100 fps. If the total aileron deflection is 20° and the wing span is 30 ft, find the steady-state rolling velocity, in degrees per second, by using the strip integration method. Assume that the aileron effectiveness factor is 0.5. (b) What type of wing section is required on a flying-wing aircraft? (c) In what way does the elevator trim tab affect the longitudinal stability index? (d) What considerations should be given to the rudder design (for directional stability purposes) for a re-entry missile at a design Mach number of 15? Ignore aerodynamic heating.

20–14G. Outline the steps required to design a two-dimensional minimum-length supersonic nozzle. Assume design Mach number given.

EXAMINATION H

Chemical Engineering

Time allowed, 5 hours. Reference books, textbooks, and slide-rule may be used. Answer 5 of the 9 problems, including at least one in each group.

GROUP I

20–1H. You are asked to prepare the process flow sheet and obtain preliminary design data for sizing of equipment for the manufacture of KNO_3 from Chilean nitrate and commercial KCl. Indicate the kind of data you require, the places where you will find it in the literature, and how you would employ it.

20–2H. A bare pipe carrying steam at 150 psi loses 1000 Btu/ hr per foot of length and is 1200 ft long. The line is fed 101.2 million Btu/hr and delivers 100 million Btu/hr at the exit end. If insulated at a cost of $1.00 per foot of length, the line will lose 166 Btu/hr per foot of length. Fuel cost is $0.10 per million Btu. Fixed charges on the boiler plant, auxiliaries, and line are $25.00 per hr. Calculate the hours of service of the insulated line when the thermal savings will equal the cost of insulation.

20–3H. For the production of sulfuric acid by the contact process, iron pyrites, FeS_2, is burned with air in 100 per cent excess of that required to oxidize all iron to Fe_2O_3 and all sulfur to SO_2. It may be assumed that the combustion of the pyrites is complete to form these products and that no SO_3 is formed in the burner. The gases from the burner are cleaned and passed into a catalytic converter in which 80 per cent of the SO_2 is oxidized to SO_3 by combination with the oxygen present in the gases. The gases enter the converter at a temperature of 400°C.

Assuming that the converter is thermally insulated so that heat loss is negligible, calculate the temperature of the gases leaving the converter.

$$4FeS_2 + 11O_2 \rightarrow 2Fe_2O_3 + 8SO_2$$

$$SO_2 + \tfrac{1}{2}O_2 \rightarrow SO_3$$

GROUP II

20–4H. Methanol at 70°F flows from a tank in which the pressure is 10 psig through a 300-ft length of 2½-in. schedule 40 steel pipe into another tank where the pressure is atmospheric. The liquid level in the second tank is at the same height as the liquid level in the first tank. There are two standard-radius 90° elbows and one open globe valve in the line. (a) Calculate the rate of flow, in gallons per minute. (b) A sharp-edged orifice 1.75 in. in diameter equipped with throat taps is placed in the line, and the pressure in the first tank is increased so as to maintain the same rate of flow as before. What is the reading on a mercury manometer connected to the taps, if the leads are filled with methanol? (c) What is the required pressure in the first tank?

20–5H. A vapor condenser condensing saturated vapor at 190°F has 20 copper tubes, ¾ in. OD, #16 bwg, each 12 ft in length. Water at 60°F enters the tubes in parallel at the rate of 20,000 lb/hr. The vapor film coefficient is known to be 1400 Btu/(hr)(sq ft)(°F), and the thermal resistance of the tube wall may be neglected. Find (a) the temperature of the water leaving the condenser and (b) the pounds per hour of vapor condensed if the latent heat of vaporization is 900 Btu/lb.

20–6H. A single-stage single-acting compressor has an 8-in. bore and a 10-in. stroke and turns at 200 rpm. The compressor takes in dry saturated ammonia vapor at 0°F and compresses the ammonia adiabatically but irreversibly to 140 psia. The actual shaft work of the compressor is 20 per cent more than if the compression was reversible. The volumetric efficiency of the compressor is 88 per cent. The ammonia leaving the compressor enters a condenser where it is cooled and condensed, leaving the condenser as a liquid at 70°F. Potential and kinetic energy changes are negligible. Calculate, with the aid of ammonia tables or an ammonia chart, (a) the horsepower input to the compressor if the mechanical efficiency is 85 per cent, (b) the pounds per minute of ammonia handled by the compressor, (c) the Btu per minute of heat removed in the condenser, (d) the quality of the resulting vapor-liquid mixture if the ammonia leaving the condenser is throttled to a pressure of 30.42 psia.

GROUP III

20–7H. A quantity of 1000 lb of a solution containing 50 per cent by weight of component *A* and 50 per cent by weight of component *C* is to be reduced to a concentration of 10 per cent of component *C* by extracting with a solvent *B* which is immiscible with *A* and partially miscible with *C* (data in table). The extraction is to be carried out isothermally by using 200 lb of solvent *B* in each stage of a multiple contact cocurrent extraction system. Determine the number of stages required.

Point . . .	1	2	3	4	5	6	7	8	9
Material	Concentration per cent								
A	85	65	46	35	20	8	3	2	1
B	2	5	8	10	20	35	47	55	79
C	13	30	46	55	60	57	50	43	20

TIE LINE DATA

	Weight (per cent)		
	A	*B*	*C*
Raffinate	59	6	35
Extract	5	40	55

20–8H. A mixture of *A* and *B* which contains 50 mole per cent *A* is to be rectified in a bubble-cap column with a top product 95 per cent *A* and a bottoms of 5 per cent *A*. The equilibrium data are as follows:

Mole per cent *A* in liquid	0	5.75	16.25	28.85	42.6	56.1	64.25	78.20	94.5
Mole per cent *A* in vapor	0	12.7	31.1	49.11	64.3	75.5	81.2	89.9	97.4

The boiling point of the bottoms is 105°C and that of the top fraction is 76°C. The feed may be considered to be at its boiling point. The latent heat of vaporization of component *A* is 12,800 Btu/lb mole at 76°C and 11,700 Btu/lb mole at 105°C. The latent heat of vaporization of component *B* is 15,300 Btu/lb mole at 76°C and 14,500 Btu/lb mole at 105°C. How many moles per hour of the feed mixture can be processed in an existing still that has the following operating characteristics: 1) actual plates, 18; 2) diameter, 2 ft; 3) plate efficiency (over-all), 50 per cent for superficial velocity of 1.97 fps; 4) reboiler, 70 sq ft of effective heating surface with an over-all coefficient of heat transfer of 300 Btu/(hr) (sq ft) (°F); 5) available steam, 20 psig; 6) condenser, 45 sq ft effective area with an over-all heat-transfer coefficient of 180 Btu/(hr) (sq ft) (°F); 7) available cooling water at 70°F with a permissible temperature rise of 50°F? Assume condensate to be returned as a saturated liquid.

20–9H. (a) Determine the pressure that must be maintained on a condenser in order to liquefy completely at 90°F a mixture of 25 per cent ethane, 35 per cent propane, 25 per cent butane, 10 per cent isobutane, 5 per cent isopentane. (b) One pound of water at 80°F and 250 psia is heated at constant pressure to the boiling point and then is completely vaporized at this pressure. Assuming the enthalpy of liquid water is independent of pressure, determine what portion of the heat added is unavailable for work in a heat engine if the lowest temperature at which heat can be rejected by the system is 60°F. (c) Calculate the velocities of water that will be necessary to sort a mixture of spherical particles ($\rho_s = 2.65$ gm/cu cm) into the following gradations: (1) 0.5 to 0.2 mm, (2) 0.2 to 0.1 mm, (3) 0.1 to 0.01 mm. The particles 0.5 mm to 0.01 mm were originally present in a mixture.

EXAMINATION I

Civil Engineering

PART I

Time allowed, 4 hours. Texts or reference books may be consulted. Answer any 5 of the 7 questions. Answers must be accompanied by a proper solution.

20–1I. A saturated sample of soil has a volume of 1.00 cu ft and a weight of 130 lb. The specific gravity of the particles is 2.76. Determine the water content and the void ratio.

20–2I. A polar planimeter is used to measure the area of a farm drawn to a scale of 1 in. = 300 ft. The roller of the planimeter turns 3.475 revolutions as the tracing point is moved once around the boundary. To calibrate the planimeter, it is repeatedly used to measure a circle whose diameter is 4.00 in. The average reading was 1.302 revolutions of the roller. How many acres does the farm contain?

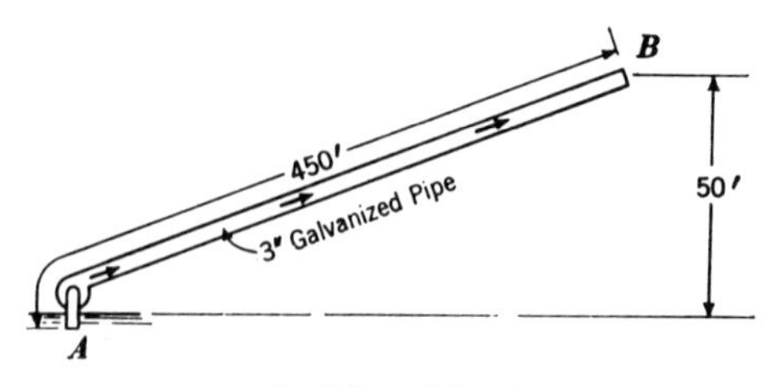

Problem 20–3I.

20–3I. Oil which weighs 58.0 lb/cu ft and has a kinematic viscosity of 0.000093 sq ft/sec is pumped at an average velocity of 4 fps from A to B (see illustration). If the pump has an efficiency of 72 per cent, find the horsepower required to drive it.

20–4I. (a) What is the flattest satisfactory slope on which a 12-in.-diameter concrete *storm drain* should be constructed? (b) What is the flattest satisfactory slope on which a 12-in. concrete *sanitary sewer* should be constructed? (c) List the advantages and disadvantages of catch basins on a storm sewer system. (d) A 12-in. vitrified-clay sewer on a slope of 3 ft/1000 ft carries sewage at a depth of 4 in. in uniform flow. Estimate the average velocity. (e) Find the discharge (gallons per minute) in part (d).

20–5I. A watershed containing 4.59 sq miles has been receiving rainfall at 2.75 in./hr long enough that all of the area is contributing runoff. If the runoff is found to be 3600 cfs, what is the runoff coefficient?

20–6I. Trusses are spaced 20 ft apart to support the roof of a building. A wind load of 20 psf is applied as shown. (a) For an interior truss, calculate the top chord panel load due to wind. (b) Find the reactions at the ends of the truss.

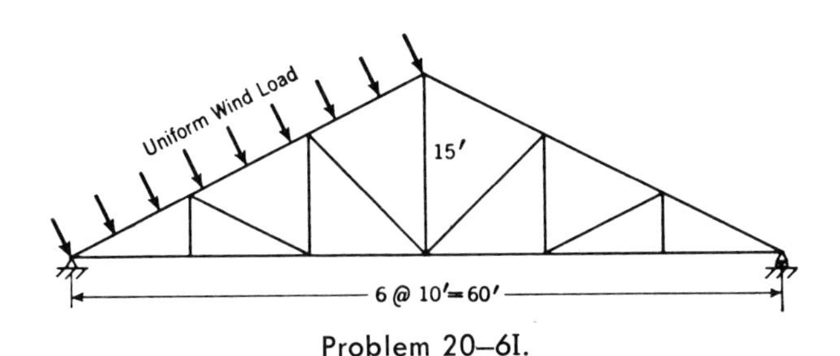

Problem 20–6I.

20–7I. A rapid sand filter cost $25,000 to build and equip. It is expected to be usable for 30 years, after which it will have a scrap value of $1000. Operation and maintenance together cost $1500 per year. Assume that construction costs are constant, that depreciation is calculated on a sinking-fund basis, and that the interest rate is constant at 5 per cent compounded annually. (a) Find the capitalized cost of the filter. (b) What will be its book value after 10 years of service?

PART II

Time allowed, 4 hours. Answer any 5 of the 6 questions. Other information same as for Part I.

20–8I. A rising 4.32 per cent grade tangent to station 78+50 (where the elevation is 974.00) is followed by a descending 3.72 per cent grade tangent. The grades are connected by a 400-ft parabolic vertical curve. Compute the grade elevation for each 50-ft station on the curve.

20–9I. A concrete dam has a vertical upstream face. Its cross section is a trapezoid 9 ft wide at the top, 30 ft wide at the bottom, and 51 ft high. Water stands h feet deep on the upstream face, and hydrostatic uplift is negligible. The resultant foundation pressure force passes through the center of the base. If concrete weighs 150 lb/cu ft, (a) find the foundation pressure (pounds per square foot) at both edges of the base and (b) find h.

20–10I. A steel gas pipe has an internal diameter of 24 in. and a wall thickness of $\frac{5}{16}$ in. At a stream crossing it is weighted with concrete (150 lb/cu ft) cylinders which are 3 ft long, 25 in. ID, and 40 in. OD. To have a safety factor of 1.25 against floatation, how far apart (center to center) should the cylinders be placed on the pipe?

20–11I. The bottom of a television antenna rests on a single spherical bearing. The antenna is 450 ft high and is guyed in a vertical position by four cables which lie in east-west and north-south planes. The cables are attached to the tower 250 ft above its base. At the point of attachment they slope at 45° from the vertical. During a storm, wind blows from 30° north of east and exerts a horizontal force of 75 lb on each linear foot of tower. Due to the wind force stated (a) find the tension (pounds in each cable and (b) find the magnitude and direction of the force on the spherical bearing.

20–12I. A beam 20 ft long is simply supported by two reactions 16 ft apart. The left end of the beam is at the left support and the right end of the beam extends 4 ft beyond the right support. The beam is to support a pair of movable loads which are always 6 ft apart. The loads are 5 tons and 10 tons. Calculate the maximum live-load bending moment which the beam must resist.

20–13I. A rectangular open channel is 6 ft wide and horizontal. Water enters it at a depth of 1.5 ft and a velocity of 21.5 fps.

(a) Is a hydraulic jump possible from this depth? (b) If so, what will be the depth of water just downstream from the jump? (c) Referring all elevations to the horizontal bottom of the channel, what horsepower is dissipated in the jump?

EXAMINATION J

Electrical Engineering

PART I (Morning)

Time allowed, 4 hours. Answer question 1 and any 4 others. References may be used.

20–1J. Write a short essay on the nature of the engineering work involved in your present position.

20–2J. Calculate the general circuit constants *A, B, C,* and *D* for the pi network shown.

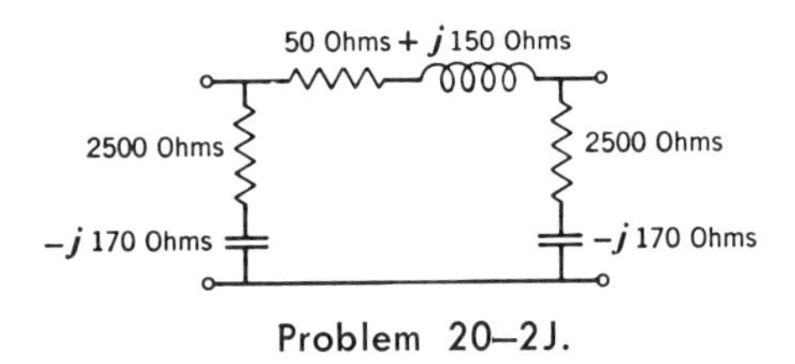

Problem 20–2J.

20–3J. A power transmission line has three 500,000–circular mil ACSR conductors with 30 strands of aluminum and 7 strands of steel in each. The three conductors are arranged on the towers in a horizontal plane and have a spacing of 10 ft between the center conductor and each outside conductor. Find the 60-cycle positive-sequence inductive reactance of one conductor of the above line, in ohms per conductor per mile. The line is transposed.

20–4J. A schematic diagram of a voltage-regulated power supply is shown in the figure. (a) Explain how the voltage regulator circuit stabilizes the output voltages against fluctuations in input voltage or against changes in the load resistance. (b) Assume $\mu_1=4$, $r_{p1}=1$ kilohm (for 2A3), $\mu_2=1000$, $r_{p2}=$ 700 kilohms (for 6SJ7), and the d-c output voltage is 250 volts. What is the ripple factor if 1 volt rms is applied to the voltage regulator circuit, the ripple voltage being the second harmonic of the driving voltage?

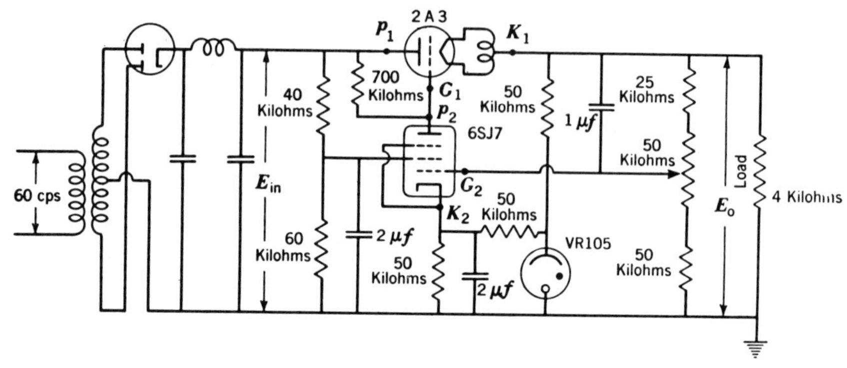

Problem 20–4J.

20–5J. In a test on a 15-kva, 2300/230-volt transformer it is found that 65 volts are required to produce a rated current in the high side while the low voltage coil is short-circuited. The power input during this test is 350 watts. The core loss is 220 watts at rated voltage. Calculate the per-unit voltage regulation at full load and 80 per cent lagging power factor. Calculate the loads, in per cent of rated, that will produce the maximum efficiency.

20–6J. A load consisting of 208-volt three-phase motors is supplied by a bank of three single-phase 2200/208-volt 30-kva transformers from a 2200-volt line. Additional motors are to be installed and will increase the total load from 90 to 150 kva. The transformers of the original bank are fully loaded, and no more of the same voltage are available. However, three single-phase 2200/120-volt 25-kva transformers are available. Show, by means of vector diagrams, how the second bank of transformers can be used and point out any precautions that must be taken.

20–7J. Neglect the reactances in the figure of all blocking con-

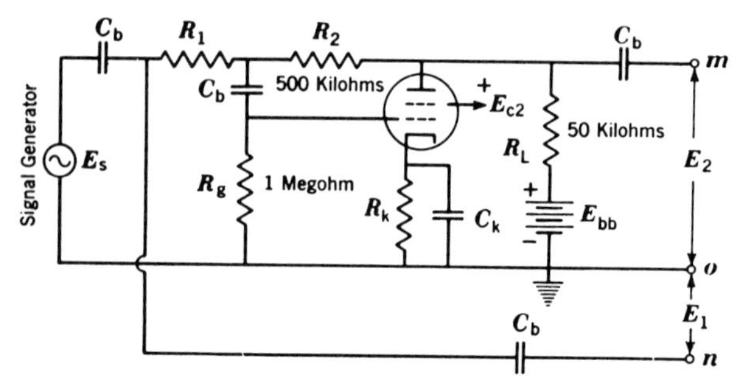

Problem 20–7J.

densers C_b and bypassing condenser C_k, stray capacitances, and the r_p of the pentode. Assume G_m of the tube is 3500 μmhos. Find (a) R_1 for balanced voltage output $E_1=-E_2$, (b) the input impedance seen by E_s, and (c) the output impedance between output terminals m and ground with the signal generator removed.

20–8J. A group of 50 lamps, each rated at 120 volts and 100 watts, is to be controlled by an inductively reactive dimmer of negligible resistance. For the purposes of this problem, it may be assumed that the luminous flux emitted by the lamps varies as the 3.5 power of the impressed voltage, and the power drawn by the lamps varies as the 1.5 power of the impressed voltage. Calculate from these data the maximum inductance of the dimmer required to reduce the luminous flux to 50 per cent of the rated value for the lamps. Electric power is supplied at 120 volts and 60 cycles. Neglect the losses of the dimmer.

20–9J. A small industrial plant operates with an average load of 400 kw consisting of small induction motors with some electric heating. The average power factor is 70 per cent lagging. A 200-hp synchronous motor driving a compressor is added to the plant. Neglecting the effect of motor losses, calculate the power factor at which this motor must be operated in order to raise the power factor of the plant to 80 per cent.

PART II (Afternoon)

Time allowed, 4 hours. Answer question 10 and any 4 others. References may be used.

20–10J. Prepare a question that may be used on this part of the examination in the future. Submit the solution with the question.

20–11J. Measurements made at the three terminals of a source show the following voltage values between terminals: $V_{ab}=200$ volts, $V_{bc}=173.2$ volts, $V_{ca}=100$ volts. A resistance of 100 ohms and an inductive reactance of 100 ohms are connected in series and between terminals A and B with the resistor connected to A. The voltage between terminal C and the point between the resistor and inductor is found to be smaller than any of the voltages between terminals given above. (a) Determine the phase sequence of the described source. Draw a vector diagram and explain how you obtained the sequence. (b) Find the positive, negative, and zero sequence components of the above voltage set.

20–12J. (a) A 150-hp 2300-volt Y-connected, three-phase synchronous motor has values of resistance and synchronous reactance of 1.0 ohm and 12 ohms per phase, respectively. Determine the value of generated voltage per phase when the motor is operating at full load on the rated line voltage with a line current of 38 amp at 0.8 leading power factor. (b) Determine the values of line current and power factor when the load is removed while the line voltage and excitation are maintained constant. (c) Determine the maximum possible power output with this line voltage and excitation.

20–13J. It will be assumed that $\omega = \omega_0 = 1/\sqrt{LC}$, that r_p can be considered infinite, and that $G_m = 2000$ μmhos. Compare the input impedance of part (a) of the figure with that of part (b). Neglect interelectrode capacitances.

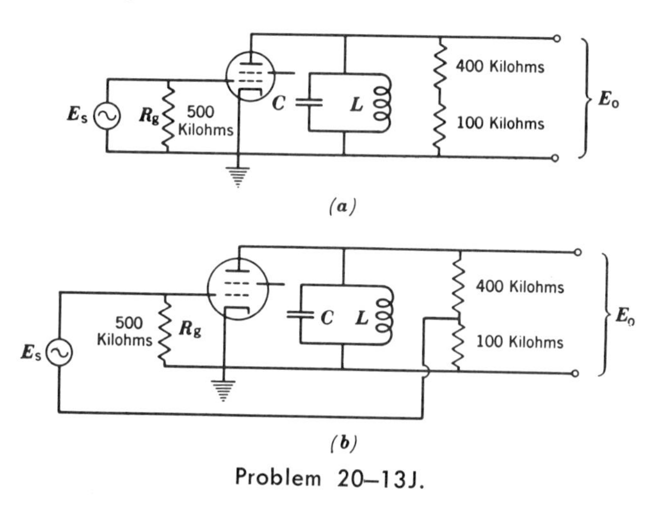

Problem 20–13J.

20–14J. A 220-volt d-c motor has an armature resistance of 0.4 ohm, a shunt field of 175 ohms, and a series field of 0.4 ohm. This machine is connected as a short-shunt compound machine to 220-volt mains. Calculate the line current and the total or gross mechanical horsepower generated in the armature when the armature current is 30 amp. Neglect the brush loss. If the speed under this load condition is 1460 rpm, what is the torque developed?

20–15J. In the process of connecting a delta-delta bank of three identical single-phase transformers, one of the secondaries was connected in reverse of what it should have been. Rated line voltage was applied to the primary. The line on the secondary was not connected to the bank. The per-unit impedance of each transformer is 0.1. Determine the currents in the secondary and in the primary lines.

20–16J. The circuit shown in the sketch is a simplified version of a relaxation oscillator which produces a time-varying voltage E_o across its output terminals. The characteristics of the gas triode shown are such that, with the given bias, the tube fires at anode voltage=200 volts and extinguishes when the capacitor voltage drops to 30 volts. During discharge of C, the effects of the circuit to the left of C are negligible, as is the tube drop. (a) For what length of time is the capacitor charging? Discharging? What is the period of E_o? Its frequency? (b) To what value should R_1 be changed if the frequency of E_o is to be 2000 cps? (c) Sketch at least one complete cycle of E_o, showing the scale on both axes. Only the general shape of E_o with respect to time is expected in this sketch.

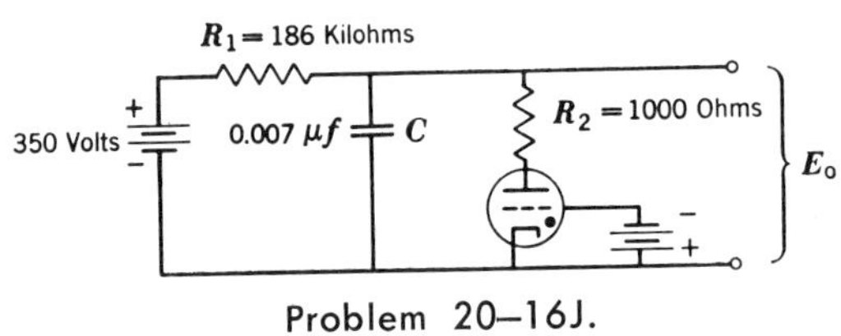

Problem 20–16J.

20–17J. A load having an admittance of $0.015-j0.020$ mho is to be matched to a transmission line by means of an open-circuit stub located as near as possible to the load. Both the line and the stub have a characteristic impedance of 100 ohms, and operation is at 500 megacycles. Calculate the length and location of the stub, in centimeters.

20–18J. Explain the principles of operation of induction heating and dielectric heating apparatus. List some typical applications of each. What are the relative advantages of these methods of heating with respect to other methods?

EXAMINATION K

Industrial Engineering

PART I

Time allowed, 4 hours. References permitted. Answer 5 of the 6 questions.

20–1K. A company is faced with the following three alternatives with regard to the installation of a machine: Assume annual

Item	Machine A	Machine B	Machine C
Original price	$12,000	$16,000	$20,000
Useful life	10 years	15 years	20 years
Salvage value	$2000	$1000	0
Yearly maintenance	$1000	$750	$600

interest of 6 per cent on the unpaid balance. Which machine will be the economical choice?

20–2K. The Georgia Company standards department has recorded the following observed times for three elements of performing a task (in hundredths of minutes): Element 1: 21, 22, 19, 17, 20, 22. Element 2: 29, 30, 31, 30, 32, 31. Element 3: 20, 23, 21, 18, 22, 23. Select elemental time by averaging. The operator is rated as 75 per cent efficient. The job allowances are: fatigue, 4 per cent; miscellaneous and personal allowance, 12 per cent. Determine the standard time for the task.

20–3K. A local shop which specializes in the production of plastic bags operates 8 hr/day, 300 days/year, and produces at the rate of 100,000 bags/day. The shop is operating now at 75 per cent of its theoretical capacity. The estimated yearly operating costs are as listed in the table. The owners of the shop expect to earn a $12,000 return on their investment each year. Sales quotations have been based on a selling price of $6.00 per 1000 bags. (a) Draw a break-even chart based upon the above data. (b) What is the break-even point for no profit–no loss? (c) What is the break-even

Item	Fixed	Variable	Item	Fixed	Variable
Labor	$6,750	$28,250	Equipment maintenance	....	$ 870
Material	....	45,600	Tool and die maintenance	....	2,400
Tools and dies ..	....	5,200	Building maintenance .	$ 960	....
Power and light .	700	4,900	Insurance	2,200	....
Heat	450	....	Depreciation	23,200	....
Water	70	....	Administration	15,000	....
Taxes	1,530	....	Selling	10,000	....
Supplies	200	700			

point for expected profit of $12,000? (d) What is the required selling price per 1000 bags to earn the expected return when operating at 40 per cent capacity? (e) If market conditions are such that bags can be sold for only $4.00 per 1000 bags, would you recommend that the plant shut down rather than accept orders at this price? (Assume that the low sales price is a reflection of temporary economic conditions.) Explain your answer.

20–4K. (a) Prepare a process flow chart for the process as shown. (b) Prepare a revised layout for the process using the equipment noted in the sketch.

The chickens are taken individually from the crates, stuck inside the throat with a thin sticking knife, and then hung by the chicken sticker in a vat of scalding water. The chicken sticker watches these chickens so as to keep a supply ahead of the pickers and prevent any bird from being kept an undue length of time in the vat. He tries to keep four or five chickens scalding at once.

When necessary, the pickers walk to the vat, get a bird, take it to their workplace, hang it by one or both legs from a hook, and pick it clean. When it is completely defeathered, they walk with it to the singeing table and place it on the pile on the "in" side. They then walk back to the vat and repeat the process.

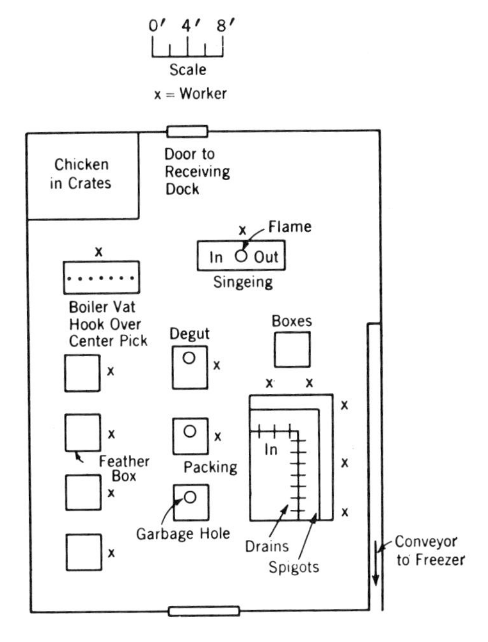

Problem 20–4K.

The singer singes each chicken and looks at it for pinfeathers. About one chicken out of five has pinfeathers to be pulled. The singer removes the pinfeathers as necessary and piles the singed and de-pinfeathered chickens on the right side of his table.

The degutters walk to the singeing table as necessary, get a bird at a time, take it to their workplace, and while it lies on their table they draw it (remove the innards), replace the giblets, and then carry the bird and place it on the pile on the packing table. They then walk to the singeing table for another bird.

As necessary, each packer walks around the table to get a bird, takes it to his work area with a box, which he takes from the pile, cuts the chicken into frying sections, and places the box on the conveyor that carries the box into a quick freezer.

20–5K. Make a left- and right-hand chart of the motions required to fill a fountain pen with a lever-type plunger. The ink is in a bottle with the cap screwed on tightly. Assume that the purpose of the chart is to break the operation down for methods analysis.

20–6K. The following data were collected on the weight of a critical material fed into a mixer. Each sample consists of four measurements of the weight, in ounces, on four consecutive mixes. (a) Draw an $\overline{X}$ and R chart for the data. (b) Explain the difference between $\overline{X}$ and R charts. What does each show? (c) Why

Mix . . .	1	2	3	4
Sample No.		Weight (oz)		
1	4.015	4.016	4.014	4.015
2	4.012	4.011	4.015	4.014
3	4.011	4.013	4.016	4.012
4	4.020	4.010	4.009	4.021
5	4.021	4.014	4.014	4.017
6	4.008	4.012	4.011	4.009
7	4.012	4.017	4.019	4.016
8	4.010	4.013	4.014	4.012
9	4.018	4.016	4.012	4.014
10	4.015	4.011	4.017	4.014

are averages of samples taken instead of individual readings in quality control work? (d) Should specification tolerance limits be shown on an $\overline{X}$ chart? Explain.

PART II

Time allowed, 4 hours. References permitted. Answer 7 out of 10.

20–7K. Determine graphically the approximate economic lot size for the following conditions: 1) annual sales, 10,000 units; 2) factory cost, $3.00 per unit; 3) inventory carrying charges, interest at 4 per cent, insurance at 2 per cent, taxes 2 per cent; 4) set-up and preparation cost per lot, $10.00. It is recommended that the various costs be tabulated prior to constructing the graph.

20–8K. Estimates show that a building which can be constructed for $200,000 requires $10,000 per year for operating expenses and will return a gross annual income of $20,000. Estimates also show that an additional investment of $50,000 in the building will increase the annual income by $10,000, but will also increase the annual operating expenses by $1000. Based on a life of 50 years, which is the better investment, and what rate of return would be realized on the additional investment of $50,000?

20–9K. Define in your own words and give an example of practical use of each of the following: (a) work sampling, (b) MTM, (c) operations research, (d) Monte Carlo method, (e) Poisson distribution, (f) factor comparison method, (g) automation, (h) feedback, (i) MAPI, (j) linear programming.

20–10K. A plant wants to expand and needs more space for processing equipment. A contractor is asked to submit costs on two different types of buildings, one a cinder block structure and the other a metal frame sheet-steel building. The contractor estimates the cinder block will cost $100,000 to build and the sheet-steel $35,000. Additional costs to consider are as shown in the table. Compare the two structures on the basis of annual cost.

Cost Factor	Cinder-Block Building	Sheet-Steel Building
Life	50 years	20 years
Annual maintenance	$500	$750
Insurance	$2 per $1000	$4 per $1000
Taxes	$1 per $100 per year on 50 per cent evaluation	
Depreciation	Straight-line on life of structure	
Interest	5 per cent	
Salvage	20 per cent of initial cost of building	

20–11K. The Greenough Corporation manufactures chains of all types and in so doing has to move 2110 tons of material in process a day. It has been decided by the traffic manager of the plant to use tractors drawing trailers to accomplish this movement. The Greenough plant is well supplied with load-bearing trailers which it can use to move the material in process. Each of these trailers weighs 2500 lb and can bear a load of $2\frac{1}{2}$ tons. The immediate problem is to determine the number of tractors that will be needed in order to meet the present needs of the plant. A local dealer has quoted a price of $1146.75 for tractors with a tractive effort sufficient to pull 15.6 tons over the steepest grade in the Greenough plant. A dealer in a nearby city has quoted a price of $860 for a tractor which can draw 13.4 tons over the steepest grade in the plant. The two tractors have approximately the same costs of operation. The distance to be traveled in the plant is 3750 ft each trip. The tractors can progress at an average of 150 fpm. Fifteen minutes are allowed each trip for loading and unloading the trailers. The plant runs on a 12-hr day (two 6-hr shifts). How many tractors will be needed? Which tractor should be purchased? Why?

20–12K. (a) Give a definition for job evaluation. (b) Give the three major steps involved in the mechanics of installing a job evaluation program, and a brief description of each step. (c) State at least five benefits to be derived from a job evaluation plan. (d) What is the correlation between job evaluation, merit rating, and wage incentives? What phase of manufacturing does each concern itself with?

20–13K. At one step in a manufacturing process, a standard crew of one man performs a completely manual operation made up of five elements. From time studies the following data were obtained:

Element 1....0.20 min rated at 110%
Element 2....0.08 min rated at 95%
Element 3....0.14 min rated at 100%
Element 4....0.07 min rated at 125%
Element 5....0.16 min rated at 105%

Personal, fatigue, and delay allowances of 12 per cent will be applied to the normal time on an elemental basis. (a) Develop the standard time for this operation and express it to two decimal places as man-hours per 100 units. (b) The incentive plan used in this plant has a guaranteed base rate and pays 1 per cent incentive earnings for each 1 per cent increase in production above standard.

(Plan is 1 for 1 with guaranteed base rate participation beginning at 100 per cent efficiency.) Use the standard developed in (a) and this information: base rate, $1.50 per hr; hours of work, 8; hours on unmeasured work, 2; production, 600 units. Determine (1) per cent performance (or efficiency) on measured work, (2) earnings for the day, (3) number of units produced if on measured work 8 hr, (4) earnings if on measured work 8 hr at same performance level.

20–14K. (a) To abide by the provisions of the Taft-Hartley Labor Law, (1) what conditions must a union fulfill before it can call a legal strike and (2) under what conditions can a company-union agreement contain a) closed shop, b) union shop, c) maintenance of membership clause?

(b) Under the Taft-Hartley Labor Law, what are the factors in the organizing of the following employees into a bargaining unit? (1) Skilled craftsmen. (2) Supervisors and foremen. (3) Plant guards. (4) Professional employees.

(c) Under the Taft-Hartley Labor Law, it is possible for a company to sue a union for various acts committed by the union. What constitute some of these acts?

20–15K. On June 30, 1948, the business of Sam White had assets of $40,000 and liabilities of $15,000. Six months later it had assets of $35,000 and liabilities of $9000. During the six months White withdrew $5000 and loaned it to Jim Brown to purchase a business. In the same period he placed in his business a note receivable for $2000, a year-old loan repaid by Gary Moore. The note had not matured by December 30, 1948. (a) Would the note be included in the $35,000 total of business assets on December 30, 1948? (b) Would the total of the business assets be the same if the note had matured and been paid by the maker? Explain. (c) What is the net increase or decrease in proprietorship for the 6-month period? (d) Determine the amount of the net profit or loss for the period. (e) What would have been the net worth of the business on December 30, 1948, if Brown had not made an added investment and a withdrawal of assets?

20–16K. (a) State steps preliminary to drawing the first quality-control chart in your plant. (b) Under what conditions and in what type of manufacturing would you use the following? (1) A 100 per cent sampling plan of inspection. (2) A statistical quality-control plan of inspection. (c) What are the advantages of using statistical methods in quality control?

EXAMINATION L

Mechanical Engineering

Time allowed, 5 hours. Solve problems 1 and 2 and any other 3 questions. Reference books, textbooks, and slide rule may be used.

20–1L. Assume you are called upon to make preliminary estimates for a new district heating plant to supply an estimated 80,000 lb/hr of steam at about 175 psia and 50° superheat. The plant will be a peak load station, supplementing other steam generating facilities of the company, and will operate only a few hours a day during the heating season. A plot about 100 ft × 130 ft is under consideration in a neighborhood occupied largely by hotels and apartments. No above-ground space is available for fuel storage. City water of hardness 6 to 8 grains/gal will be used, and condensate will not be returned. (a) What major equipment or facilities *must* be provided? (b) What other major equipment or facilities *may* be found desirable after further study? (c) What type of feed-water treatment is indicated, if any? (d) Estimate the volume of flue gas produced, in cubic feet per minute, when plant is operated at rating.

20–2L. A steel plate 15 ft × 2 ft × ¼ in. lying flat on the ground is to be lifted by means of slings attached to clamps at the midpoints of the long sides. (a) How high must the crane hook be raised before the plate clears the ground? (b) What maximum stress is developed in the plate? (c) Will the plate be permanently deformed? Why?

20–3L. There are bypassed around an air-conditioning unit 100 cfm of air at 80°F and 70 per cent relative humidity. Passing through the conditioner are 150 cfm of air which leave the conditioner in a saturated condition at 50°F. Mixture pressure is 29.92 in. Hg. (a) Estimate the capacity of the refrigeration unit, in standard commercial tons. (b) After the two streams have merged beyond the conditioner, determine (1) temperature, (2) humidity ratio, in pounds of water vapor per pound of dry air, and (3) relative humidity.

20–4L. A horizontal shaft 60 in. long is supported in bearings at each end. A pure torque of 10,000 in.-lb is applied 15 in. from the left-hand support, and the shaft is prevented from turning by a single cylindrical pin inserted transversely in each bearing in such a way as to pass completely through bearing and shaft, i.e., similar to a cotter pin. Find the size of pins required if pins and shaft are made of SAE 1045 steel.

20–5L. A d-c motor-driven pump running at 100 rpm delivers 500 gpm of water against a total pumping head of 90 ft with a pump efficiency of 60 per cent. (a) What motor horsepower is required? (b) What speed and capacity would result if the pump rpm was increased to produce a pumping head of 120 ft, assuming no change in efficiency? (c) Can a 25-hp motor be used under conditions indicated in (b)?

20–6L. An unfired pressure vessel 50 in. in diameter and 10 ft long is made of 1-in. steel plate butt-welded longitudinally. The ends are made of ½-in. plates of the same material. The ends are riveted, using a single riveted lap joint. The rivets are 1 in. in diameter, and rivet pitch is 2½ in. Allowable stresses are tension, 11,000 psi; bearing, 20,000 psi; and shear, 8800 psi. Determine the maximum safe operating pressure.

20–7L. A steam-electric generating station has three 20,000-kw turbine-generators. Steam is supplied at 200 psia and 600°F. Exhaust is at 1 psia. Daily load factor is 60 per cent. Assuming average steam rates and efficiencies, estimate (a) tons of coal required per day, (b) average condenser cooling-water requirement, in gallons per minute, (c) air requirement, in cubic feet per minute.

20–8L. An oak-tanned leather belt $\frac{5}{16}$ in. × 8 in. is mounted on 36-in.-diameter cast-iron pulleys set on 12 ft centers. The belting weighs 0.035 lb/cu in., and the pulleys turn at 360 rpm. If the center-to-center distance is increased 3 in. beyond the point of no slack and zero stress, what horsepower may be transmitted?

EXAMINATION M

All Engineering Branches

Most handbooks acceptable, except Chemical Engineering handbooks. Slide rule may be used. Answer any ten (10) of the 90 questions.

20–1M. A tunnel survey is established between the two portals by means of an open deflection-angle traverse. For the deflection angles and distances given, find the bearing and length of the tunnel.

Line	Bearing	Deflection angle	Length
x-1	N16°21′E	....	726.91
1-2	....	37°21′ L	331.66
2-3	....	22°40′ L	879.61
3-4	....	118°46′ R	416.83
4-5	....	10°15′ R	921.76
5-Y	....	69°30′ L	1348.61

20–2M. Calculate in field-note form the complete notes necessary for establishing in the field a simple circular curve. Indicate how this curve would be located and checked in the field. The data are P.I.=18+61.8, $\triangle=46°22'$, and $D=5°20'$.

20–3M. Describe fully how you would construct a topographic map for a proposed plant site of 80 acres. The plant will consist of buildings, parking, and roads and will utilize the entire site. The terrain is steep and sparsely wooded. What scale and contour interval should be recommended? What equipment and type of party would you recommend?

20–4M. Determine the diameter of the largest inscribed circle within the four boundary lines. What is the length of each boundary line?

Line	Bearing	Length (ft)
AB	N58°30′E	
BC	S46°00′E	
CD	S45°15′W	400.0
DA	N32°40′W	

20–5M. A continuous beam, 50 ft long, is supported at the ends and at 30 ft from one end. It is to be designed to carry a uniformly distributed load of 3000 lb/ft over its entire length. It is laterally unsupported except at the reactions. Select the lightest WF section for this beam that would be permitted by the latest revision of the AISC Code.

20–6M. The columns of an industrial-building bent support the walls, roof truss, and a crane runway girder on a bracket. The unsupported length for the major axis is 27 ft, and for the minor axis it is 18 ft. Analysis of the bent shows that the following two loading conditions should be considered in the design of the columns: 1) With wind, an axial load of 93.0^k and a moment of $117.5'^k$ about the major axis. 2) Without wind, an axial load of 112.0^k and a moment of $72.0'^k$ about the major axis. Select the lightest 12WF section suitable for these columns using the latest revision of the AISC Code.

20–7M. A single-plate bracket is to be attached perpendicularly to the flange face of a 12WF65 column, the plate lying in the plane of the column web. It carries a vertically downward load of 30^k acting 12 in. from the face of the column. Assume that the bracket plate is ½ in. thick. Design the riveted connection of the bracket to the column flange.

20–8M. A 50-ft simply supported welded plate girder is to span an opening in a building. It is to be designed for a total uniform load of 3 klf over its entire length and a concentrated load of 140^k at mid-span. Lateral support shall be assumed over the entire length. The web is to be a single plate limited in depth to 48 in., and each flange is to be a single plate limited in width to 14 in. Determine the required thickness of the web plate and the maximum required thickness of the flange plates.

20–9M. Design a reinforced-concrete beam for a 15-ft simple span. Applied loads are 2 klf uniformly distributed and two 10^k concentrated loads at the third points of the span. Assume b equal to approximately $\frac{2}{3}d$. Use 3000-psi concrete and intermediate-grade steel, 1963 ACI Code. Show results with a clear sketch.

20–10M. Design a spiral column, 20 ft long, to carry a concentric load of 800^k. Assume 3000-psi concrete and 50,000-psi yield point steel. Use 1963 ACI Code.

20–11M. Design a square spread footing to support a column 30 in. square carrying a load of 1000^k. Soil pressure is limited to 7 ksf. Assume 3000-psi concrete and intermediate-grade steel, 1963 ACI Code. Show results with a clear sketch.

20–12M. Given a one-way slab, 12 ft simple span, with an effective depth of 7 in., reinforced with #6 deformed bars on 6-in. centers. Compare the safe superimposed uniform load allowable by conventional design to the load allowed by ultimate strength design of the 1963 ACI Code. Neglect wind and earthquake loading. Assume 3000-psi concrete and 50,000-psi yield point steel, intermediate grade.

20–13M. Design a butt splice for a tension member carrying a normal load of 33,000 lb. Main member is a 4 × 10 S4S Douglas fir, Coast region; side plates are 2 × 10 S4S of the same material. Use ¾-in. bolts and find the number required in the joint. Sketch a detail of the joint.

20–14M. Design a simple beam on a 15-ft span to carry a concentrated moving load of 6500 lb. This load may be any place on the beam. Deflection is limited to 1/240 of span. Neglect weight of beam. Data are $f=1800$ psi, $H=120$ psi, $E=1{,}760{,}000$ psi.

20–15M. Design a compression member of a truss that may carry any proper combination of the following loads: dead load $=-10{,}000$ lb, snow load $=-20{,}000$ lb, wind load $=-16{,}000$ lb. Unsupported length $=9$ ft, $c=1400$ psi, $E=1{,}760{,}000$ psi.

20–16M. Design a column 14 ft long to carry a concentric normal load of 60,000 lb and a moment due to wind of 11,500 ft-lb. Data are $f=1900$ psi, $c=1450$ psi, $E=1{,}760{,}000$ psi.

20–17M. A fire department pumping truck delivers 250 gpm through 200 ft of 2½-in. diameter smooth rubber-lined cotton hose terminating in a 1¼-in. diameter nozzle. The pump is 70 per cent efficient, and pressure in the hydrant is 30 psi. Find the horsepower required.

20–18M. A gravity wall has a height of 10 ft, top width of 2 ft, and base width of 8 ft, with one face vertical. It is constructed of masonry weighing 150 lb/cu ft and has water to a depth of 9 ft on the vertical face only. The foundation material has an allowable bearing pressure of 1 ton/sq ft and coefficient of friction on masonry of 0.40. Investigate the stability of the structure.

20–19M. A clay sewer pipe is 4 ft in diameter and is laid on a grade of 5 ft/1000 ft. It discharges into a river whose level stands 1 ft above the top of the pipe. During a certain storm the water level in a manhole 1500 ft from the river rises 5 ft above the top of the pipe. What is the discharge of the sewer?

20–20M. A power plant at elevation 2350 is supplied from a reservoir of surface elevation 3100 by a welded-steel penstock of uniform diameter and 4000 ft long. Plant is to operate continuously with a discharge of 60 cfs. List the additional data required and outline the procedure for determining the most economical pipe diameter. Neglect water hammer.

20–21M. In a certain town the pressure at the pumping plant at

1st St. and Broadway is 90 psi. A 5-in. diameter main leaves the plant and runs south on Broadway 12 blocks to 13th St. A second main 6 in. in diameter runs from the plant east 6 blocks on 1st St., then south to 13th, then west to rejoin the 5-in. main. If all pipes are cast iron, what pressure may be expected at 13th and Broadway when the demand at that point is 750 gpm, neglecting other demands on the system? All blocks are 330 ft in length.

20–22M. A standard ogee spillway has a crest elevation 15 ft above the stream bed and is designed for a head of 3 ft over the crest. Approximately what tail-water depth is required downstream to produce a hydraulic jump on an apron at stream-bed level? What should be done if the tail-water depth is somewhat less than required?

20–23M. An irrigation canal has a bottom width of 5 ft and 1:1 side slopes. It carries 100 cfs at a depth of 3 ft. A bulkhead is placed in the canal to divert the entire flow into a lateral at 90° to the main canal. Find the force on the bulkhead.

20–24M. The space between two retaining walls with smooth backs is filled with sand weighing 113 lb/cu ft. The foundations of the walls are interconnected by a reinforced-concrete floor, and the crests of the walls by heavy steel tie rods. The walls are 15 ft high and 50 ft apart. The surface of the sand is used for storing pig iron weighing 300 lb/sq ft. If the coefficient of the earth pressure at rest is $K_0=0.50$, what is the total pressure against the walls before and after the application of the surcharge?

20–25M. A footing with a trapezoidal base is 12 ft long, 3 ft wide at one end, and 6 ft wide at the other. It supports two columns along its center line, one at a distance of 2 ft from the narrow end and the other 3 ft from the wide end. The load on the first column is 18 tons, and on the second, 36 tons. Assuming the footing is rigid, what is the subgrade reaction at each end? Sketch the probable pressure distribution considering that nc footing is actually rigid.

20–26M. Given a capped group of nine piles in a square pattern 2 ft on centers. The average diameter of each pile is 12 in. and length is 36 ft. Borings indicate a fairly uniform clay to a depth of 72 ft with an average unconfined compressive strength of 1.2 tons/sq ft. The sensitivity of the clay is low, and the water content is considerably below the liquid limit. Using a factor of safety of 3, what is the allowable load on the group?

20–27M. Three resistors, each of 1 ohm, are connected in delta. Inside the delta, a 1-ohm resistor is connected from each corner to a common point, thus forming a wye inside the delta. Six batteries, each of a different unknown emf and negligible internal resistance, are inserted into the network, one in each of the six branches. The current in one of the delta resistors is found to be 5 amp. Now an additional resistance of 2 ohms is inserted in the branch which was carrying 5 amp, making a total of 3 ohms in this branch under the new condition. What is the new current in this branch?

20–28M. Three circuit elements are in parallel: a resistance R of 20 ohms, a capacitance C of 100 μf, an inductance L of 0.125 h. The voltage impressed on this circuit is of triangular shape, the voltage changing linearly from -100 volts to $+100$ volts in 0.01 sec and then changing linearly from $+100$ volts to -100 volts in the next 0.01 sec, the cycle then repeating. The current through the inductance has a zero value when the voltage has its maximum value. For one complete cycle sketch the current through each element and the total current. Indicate the maximum value of each current.

20–29M. An RC-coupled triode stage has circuit constants of such values that its mid-frequency gain is 11 and its high and low half-power frequencies are 50 cps and 25 kc, respectively. Two of these identical stages are now cascaded, and voltage feedback is employed around the system, such that the gain for the two-stage system is now 11 in the mid-frequency region. (a) Draw a block diagram of the system, showing the feedback loop. (b) What is the required mid-frequency feedback factor of this system? (c) Assuming that β is constant throughout the frequency range of the system, calculate the complex gain of this system at 50 cps, without feedback and with feedback. (d) The percentage amplitude distortion of either stage under maximum output conditions and without feedback is measured to be 8 per cent in the mid-frequency region. What percentage distortion does the two-stage system have in the mid-frequency region if the feedback given above is employed, and under maximum voltage output conditions?

20–30M. Each phase of a wye load had $(10/\sqrt{3})\ \underline{/30^\circ}$ ohms. A delta load has 10 ohms of pure resistance as one side, 10 ohms of pure capacitive reactance as a second side, and 10 ohms of pure inductive reactance as the third side. The wye and delta loads are connected in parallel. Calculate the magnitudes of the line currents, the total power consumed, and the power factor of the combination.

20–31M. An a-c source, $V \sin \omega t$, is switched in series with an inductor L and a resistor R. (a) What is the differential equation in current i governing conditions after the switch is closed? (b) What is the general solution for current in this circuit after the switch is closed? (c) What initial condition on current must be used to evaluate the constant of integration appearing in the general solution? Why? Assume the switch is closed at $t=t_1$. (d) Show at what instant of time t_1 that the switch may be closed in order that no transient current will flow in the mesh.

20–32M. The characteristic impedance per mile, $\bar{Z}_0=\sqrt{\bar{Z}/\bar{Y}}$, of a transmission line is $1.72\underline{/-5.6^\circ}$. The propagation constant per mile, $\gamma=\sqrt{\bar{Z}\,\bar{Y}}$, is $0.00208\underline{/84.5^\circ}$. Line length=225 miles; $\bar{A}=\cosh \gamma l=0.894\underline{/1.2^\circ}$, and $\bar{B}=\bar{Z}_0 \sinh \gamma l=176\underline{/80.3^\circ}$. Verify the values of $\bar{A}$ and $\bar{B}$.

20–33M. Tests on a certain 20-kva 400/100-volt transformer give the following results: During the short-circuit test, the instruments are in the high side, and during the open-circuit test they are in

		I	P
Short-circuit test	24.4	50	220
Open-circuit test	100	5	140

the low side. Calculate voltage regulation and efficiency for a load of 20 kva and 0.8 power factor lag.

20–34M. A sinusoidal voltage source with an internal impedance of pure resistance R_g feeds a load of pure resistance R_L. Show that an L-type network which is purely reactive can be placed between source and load so that the circuit is image-matched, i.e., the source sees a load resistance equal to R_g and the load sees a resistance equal to R_L. Assume that the network consists essentially of an impedance Z_a which is in series with R_L and an impedance Z_b which is parallel with the series combination of Z_a and R_L. Assume also that R_g is greater than R_L. Determine the expressions for Z_a and Z_b.

20–35M. A cast-iron ring magnet has a cross-sectional area of 2 sq in. and a mean length of 10 in. The air gap is 0.1 in., and 80,000 lines are desired in the gap. Neglect fringing. (a) Calculate the ampere-turns needed for the gap. (b) Give the procedure for determining the total number of ampere-turns needed.

20–36M. (a) Sketch on the same set of axes the applied sinusoidal voltage and primary current of a single-phase, half-wave rectifier with resistance load. Assume an ideal rectifier and transformer. (b) If the utilization factor is defined as the ratio of the d-c output of a rectifier to the volt-ampere input for the transformer primary, determine the utilization factor of the primary for a single-phase, full-wave rectifier with resistance load. Assume an ideal transformer and rectifier tubes.

20–37M. An amplifier has a gain equal to A. The output is then coupled to the input so that there is 100 per cent negative feedback. What is the gain of the modified amplifier?

20–38M. A resistance-coupled audio-amplifier stage uses a tube having a μ of 30 and an r_p of 25,000. The plate-circuit load resistor is 100,000 ohms and the grid-leak resistor of the next following tube is 250,000 ohms. The bias is obtained by means of a cathode resistor of 8000 ohms, but the bypass condenser is defective (a lead has come loose inside the unit) and it acts as an open circuit. Draw the a-c equivalent circuit and compute the voltage gain of the stage.

20–39M. Diagram a class C tuned power amplifier, showing a suitable neutralizing circuit; use capacitive coupling from the preceding stage and both grid-leak and cathode bias. Carefully sketch, all on the same time axis, waveforms of grid voltage, plate current, and plate voltage for this amplifier when operating under typical conditions.

20–40M. It is desired to design the stator winding for a 200-kva 60-cycle 2200-volt Y-connected three-phase a-c generator to operate at 900 rpm. The stator will have 72 slots with two coil sides per slot. The lowest-order harmonic which can be tolerated in the output voltage is the seventh. If the total sinusoidally distributed flux per pole is 936,000 lines, calculate the number of turns per coil.

20–41M. The flux density produced by the fundamental component or armature current in phase a of a round-rotor synchronous machine may be given by the expression $B_a = B_\mu \cos \gamma \cos \omega t$, where γ is the space angle from a reference 0 and ωt is the time angle from reference 0. (a) Determine the speed and direction of the flux density wave produced by a fifth space harmonic assuming sinusoidal armature current and a pitch 4/5. (b) Determine the speed and direction of the flux density wave produced by a fifth time harmonic of the armature current.

20–42M. Determine the friction loss, in inches of water, in a 100-ft-long, 6-in. ID commercial steel pipe carrying 100 lb/min of carbon dioxide initially at 70°F and 50 psia.

20–43M. Determine the number of passes and the number of tubes per pass in a steam condenser condensing at standard atmospheric pressure if 10,000 lb/hour of circulating water is heated from 70°F to 110°F. Tubes are admiralty metal 1 in. OD and 0.9 in. ID. Space limitations restrict tube lengths to 6 ft. Assume a water velocity of 4 fps. No promoter is to be used.

20–44M. A steam-turbine-driven centrifugal blower operates at 3300 rpm. The turbine is a two-row impulse type with a pitch diameter of 20 in., nozzle angle of 20°, and nozzle throat area of 0.220 sq in. It operates initially on steam at 550 psig and 600°F, with a back pressure on the exhaust of 60 psig. (a) If steam-chest pressure under a certain load is 300 psig, estimate steam requirements of the turbine, in pounds per hour. (b) If a 7-in. diameter flow nozzle placed in the blower intake indicates a pressure drop of 1.8 in. of Hg at 75°F and the blower is compressing the air to a static pressure of 24 in. of water, what would you estimate as the horsepower requirements of the blower?

20–45M. A package delivery service operates a fleet of trucks capable of 60,000 lb-miles service per day and is presently operating at 50 per cent capacity and serving many small businesses. Present daily expenses are as follows: drivers, $36.00; overhead, $12.00; operation, $0.0002 per lb-mile; repairs and maintenance, $2.00 plus $0.0001 per lb-mile. The present income is $0.002 per lb-mile. What minimum bid could be made, per pound-mile, to a new large business for an additional 15,000 lb-miles service per day which would permit the delivery service to realize a gross profit of $11.50 per day?

20–46M. Air enters a pipe of 2 sq ft area at 14.7 psia and at velocity of 800 fps and temperature 59°F. One-twelfth pound of fuel per pound of air is injected between entrance and exit and is ignited, providing 16,000 Btu/lb of fuel. The exit area is 1 sq ft. Exit pressure 14.7 psia. Neglect friction losses. Take $C_p = 0.24$ for air. Assume complete combustion of fuel and assume that the process continues in one direction (as in ramjet). Using the steady-flow energy equation, find (a) exit temperature and (b) exit velocity. Using the momentum equation, find (c) the net thrust, considering both intake and exhaust.

20–47M. A single-pass steam surface condenser is to be designed using an over-all heat-transfer coefficient of 388 Btu/hr/°F/sq ft based on the outside tube surface. The tubes are to be ⅞ in. OD with a wall thickness of 0.049 in. Water velocity through the tubes is to be 4 fps. Steam enters the condenser at a rate of 450,000 lb/hr at a pressure of 2 in. Hg abs and an enthalpy of 1019.1 Btu/lb and leaves as saturated liquid at 2 in. Hg abs. Circulating water enters at 80° and leaves with a terminal temperature difference of 11.6°F. Find the required number of tubes and effective length of tubes (between tube sheets) and the circulating water required, in gallons per minute.

20–48M. An austenitic stainless steel (18–8) container is to operate in a corrosive environment at temperature in the vicinity of 1200°F. Specify the type which should be used and explain why.

20–49M. Specify, from the materials available the table given, the most economical material for a component 10 in. long, 8 uniform cross sections to operate under a static tensile load of 10,000 lb with a total elongation not to exceed 0.01 in. Assume density of all materials to be 0.28 lb cu in.

Material	Elastic Limit (psi)	Tensile strength (psi)	Modulus of Elasticity (psi)	Cost per pound (dollars)
0.3% C steel, hot-rolled ..	35,000	65,000	30×10^6	0.21
Structural Ni steel, hot-rolled	60,000	110,000	30×10^6	0.30
Ni-Cr steel, heat-treated ..	110,000	130,000	30×10^6	0.60
Alloy cast iron	None	45,000	20×10^6	0.16

20–50M. What would be the per cent saving in actual horsepower required, if there is a saving, by using a two-stage compressor as compared to a single-stage compressor in compressing 2000 cfm of free air from a barometric pressure of 24.43 in. Hg and a temperature of 60°F to a receiver pressure of 118 psig? The isentropic compression efficiency of each machine is 85 per cent, and the mechanical efficiency of each machine is 85 per cent. The value of n in $PV^n=C$ is 1.3.

20–51M. Calculate the dry flue-gas analysis as would be obtained with an Orsat apparatus, per cent by volume, in burning the following gaseous fuel with 30 per cent excess air.

Gas	CH_4	C_2H_6	CO_2	N_2	O_2
Per cent by volume	52	18	10	10	10

20–52M. Oil of specific gravity 0.90 flows in a length AB of $D_o=9$-in. diameter pipe of length $L_o=2000$ ft and friction factor

$f_o=0.015$ (assumed). At B there is a junction where the pipe divides into two parallel pipes of different diameters, different lengths, and different friction factors. These pipes join again to form a single pipe at point C. Assume points A and C are at the same elevation and that the difference of pressure $(p_A-p_C)=25$ psi. Branch *1* has diameter $D_1=3$ in., length $L_1=3000$ ft, friction factor $f_1=0.02$ (assumed). Branch *2* has $D_2=8$ in., $L_2=4500$ ft, $f_2=0.03$ (assumed). (a) Use the D'Arcy equation for head loss, $h=f(l/D)(V^2/2g)$, and any other considerations to find the rate of flow in each of the three sections of pipe, in cubic feet per second. (b) Compute the pump horsepower necessary to maintain these flow rates. (NOTE: The assumed values of friction factor are supposed to allow for roughness and Reynolds number, to a first approximation.)

20–53M. A spark-ignition engine is directly connected to an electrical generator. An output of 150 kw is to be maintained. The generator efficiency is 90 per cent; 115 lb/hr of 18,000-Btu fuel is used. Assume that a spark-ignition engine of this capacity will operate on an efficiency which is 50 per cent of that of the ideal Otto cycle of the same compression ratio. Determine what will be the horsepower output of the spark-ignition engine and what compression ratio it must have. Use a value of $k=1.40$ for the ideal cycle.

20–54M. A dry-plate friction clutch on a hoist drive has seven driving disks and six driven disks with outside diameters of 4½ in. and inside diameters of 2 in. Assuming coefficient of friction as 0.20, and maximum allowable pressure between disks of 40 psi, find horsepower that can be transmitted at 600 rpm.

20–55M. A pharmaceutical manufacturer packages insulin in ½-oz glass bottles with rubber stoppers. The bottling is carried out under sterile conditions in a 6-ft-square cubicle in which a positive pressure of sterilized air is maintained. Three women rotate every hour between filling and capping and remain seated at a bench in the cubicle for a 3-hr period. All equipment and materials are set up in the cubicle prior to commencing the filling. Sterilized bottles are brought in in covered copper boxes from the autoclaves. During the operation the bottles are removed individually by the filling-machine operator, filled, handed to one of two cappers alternately, capped, and placed individually in cardboard boxes holding 1 gross. Boxes are restacked as filled. At the end of the filling shift all boxes are removed, the cardboard boxes containing the insulin being taken on hand carts to the refrigerator for the noon hour. After lunch these boxes are brought out to an inspection room adjoining the filling cubicle where the three women inspect the morning's filling, holding two control and one new bottle at one time in one hand before a fluorescent lamp. No filling is done after lunch because of the required inspection, which cannot be done in the cubicle. Time study reveals the following cycle times in minutes. What method changes will improve the efficiency of the over-all operation, and to what extent may efficiency be expected to improve.

One Bottle One Operation	Unadjusted Actual Time	Operator Rating as Per Cent of Normal	Adjusted Normal Time
Filling	0.070	120	0.084
Capping	0.120	80	0.096
Inspecting	0.083	100	0.083

20–56M. As plant industrial engineer, you believe that a present materials handling operation employing hand trucks could be made more efficient by the use of an electric lift truck. The present crew consists of one unloader, one loader, four hand-truck operators each earning \$1.10 per hour on an 8-hr shift. It is estimated that a revised crew would consist of three loaders at \$1.10 per hour and one lift operator at \$1.50 per hour. The operation is continuous throughout the working day, and the plant works 250 days/year. The burden rate on direct labor is 10 per cent. The operation is employed in warehousing and would have no direct effect on production. The fork lift has an estimated life of 4 years and an annual power cost of \$400.00. Allowing 5 per cent of maintenance, 6 per cent for insurance, and 6 per cent for interest on investment, what price lift truck is justified?

20–57M. As an engineer, would you encourage, in so far as practicable, standard cost systems in your company? If so, why? If not, why not?

20–58M. The density of 78 per cent (by weight) sulfuric acid solution is 1.70 g/cc. What volume, in gallons, of this acid is needed to make 100 gal of 1.5 molar (gram moles per liter) acid? Atomic weights: S=32, O=16, H=1. One gallon=3.78 liters.

20–59M. Calculate the heat necessary to raise the temperature of 10 lb of water from 80°F to 400°F at 1 atm pressure, using the following data: C_p of H_2O, liquid=1 Btu/(lb) (°F), heat of vaporization of water=970 Btu/lb at 212°F, C_p of steam=approximately 8.0 Btu/lb mole/°F. Also, calculate the change in enthalpy and entropy.

20–60M. A pump which is 80 per cent efficient has 4 hp applied to its shaft. It delivers 25 gpm of water from a tank at atmospheric pressure to another tank situated 10 ft lower and under a pressure of 100 psig. How much power is lost due to friction in the pipe if the pipe is ½ in. ID? (1 hp=33,000 ft-lb/min)

20–61M. Define or explain briefly the following terms as they apply to the petroleum industry: (a) hypersorption, (b) reforming, (c) polymerization, (d) partial oxidation, (e) isomerization, and (f) alkylation.

20–62M. Outline or sketch one method for separating a mixture containing about equal amounts of the following four chemicals: aniline, benzene, benzoic acid, and ethyl alcohol.

20–63M. List what you consider to be the chief chemical raw materials necessary for the synthesis of the following chemicals: (a) chlorine, (b) glycerine, (c) nitric acid, (d) styrene, (e) sulfuric acid, and (f) methanol.

20–64M. (a) Differentiate between a partial and a total condenser for a distillation operation. (b) Define or explain adiabatic and isentropic.

20–65M. Draw schematic phase diagrams for the following systems, labeling all areas of the diagram: (a) A three-component system, at constant pressure and temperature, in which two of the components are gases and the other is a liquid. (b) A two-component system, at constant pressure, which forms a minimum boiling point homogeneous azeotrope, with the two components completely miscible in the liquid region. (c) The same as (b), but with the two components only partially miscible in the liquid region.

20–66M. Indicate schematically, by use of a y-x diagram, the procedure for determining the number of theoretical trays in an absorber calculation.

20–67M. Assuming that ice has a molal volume of 19.6 cc/mole, water has a density of 1 g/cc, and the heat of fusion of water is 80 cal/g, what is the melting point of ice 1500 ft beneath the surface of the ocean? The density of water may be taken as 62.4 lb/cu ft. Note also that 1 liter-atm = 24.21 cal.

20–68M. In a certain plant, 7000 lb/hr of a salt solution are being heated from 60°F to 190°F by passing through a 150-ft copper tube 1.2 in. ID. Outside the tube, water entering at 210°F and leaving at 110°F is circulated (countercurrent to the flow of salt solution) at a rate of 7200 lb/hr. The resistance of the copper tube to heat transfer is very small and may be neglected. Calculate (a) the over-all coefficient of heat transfer, in Btu per hour per square foot per degree Fahrenheit based on the inside area of the copper tube, and (b) the length of exchanger required to double the capacity. (The rates of flow of both liquids are to be doubled, and thus the terminal temperatures are the same as before.)

20–69M. A technician determines a bubble point of 21°F at 1 atm on a mixture known to contain propane, *n*-butane, and *n*-pentane. In analyzing for the individual components, the gas partitioner fails after obtaining only the amount of *n*-butane in the original sample. This was found to be 67.3 mole per cent. What are the compositions of the propane and *n*-pentane in the original sample? The vapor pressure data for propane, *n*-butane, and *n*-pentane at 21°F are 2950, 620, and 135 mm Hg, respectively.

20–70M. What are some of the factors affecting the selection of a stoping method?

20–71M. List four types of underground track haulage and give advantages and disadvantages of each.

20–72M. Describe in detail the procedure used in the location of a lode claim in your state on government land.

20–73M. Describe the advantages and disadvantages of a burn cut and an angle cut which are used in drill rounds.

20–74M. In what way does a mine differ from most other types of industry?

20–75M. In selecting equipment for any given job, more than just the first cost must be considered. The cheapest to buy may, in the long run, be most expensive. For example, in pumping water through a long pipe, the larger the pipe diameter the more expensive will be the initial cost and the installation, but the smaller the pipe the greater will be the power required to pump a given quantity of water through it. Given: *A* thousand gallons of water per minute to be pumped vertically out of a mine; *B* feet, the vertical distance it is to be pumped, and also the length of the pipe itself; $0.015 per kilowatthour, the cost of power for pumping; $0.30 per pound, the cost of installing the pipe, including cost of the pipe; 10 years, the estimated life of the project. Show by outline the sequence of steps by which the most economical diameter of pipe can be determined.

20–76M. Discuss the methods of transporting material from an open pit.

20–77M. Discuss four different classes of resistance to air flow in ventilating an underground mine.

20–78M. Name at least nine minerals that are used in construction of buildings, of any type. (That is, minerals that may be "processed" but not changed chemically. For example, gypsum is changed chemically and as a result is used as plaster of paris; hence gypsum would not qualify in this question. Therefore, confine your listing to minerals that are used either raw or only after mechanical but not chemical processing.)

20–79M. Draw an idealized cross section of an acidic batholith that has digested sediments of limestone, sandstone, and argillaceous shale but has not reached the "ground water" level. (a) Indicate where mineralization would most likely occur. (b) Name a few probable species of minerals that would be found at each such point. (c) Name at least four or more "mineralizer" elements or compounds that an acidic batholith would contain.

20–80M. This question will require three sheets of paper. (a) Draw a simple topographic map (at least six contour lines). (b) Draw a structural contour map of the same area, of violently different contour directions and elevations. (c) Superimpose, on the third sheet, *both* sets of contours. (d) Draw a "drillers' map" that will show the estimated drilling depth from the surface to the horizon of (b) above.

20–81M. In a petroleum exploration program, there are known to be three "marker beds." One is largely gypsum; one is purely calcite; one is anhydrite. All three beds are crystalline. Assume that you are equipped only with a binocular microscope, and without chemical reagents, far from other consultants or supplies. How would you distinguish these marker beds as your cuttings samples went through them, with ONLY a binocular microscope for equipment?

20–82M. Under each of the following conditions, name the type of geophysical exploration methods (gravity, magnetic, seismic, etc.) you would recommend to a client: (a) A disturbed section about 10,000 ft thick of sediments; low topographic relief; no evidence of "structure." (b) Evidence of violent structure of both ancient and recent sediments overlying ancient metamorphics. (c) A large area of Miocene sand dunes, say, 500 ft thick, lying on Paleocene sediments.

20–83M. The owners of a rather large oil-producing area will lease certain geologic time units of sediments, to wit: Miocene, Ordovician, Dakota, and Proterozoic. Organize these terms in their proper sequence into a geologic time table. Place the oldest intervals at the bottom of the list and fill in the missing intervals, in terms of ages, periods, and epochs.

20–84M. Give two "rules of thumb" by which the depth of a body of ore, oil, etc. might be roughly estimated, by a magnetic anomaly.

20–85M. Show, by sketches, how you would determine the upthrow side of a fault that cuts off a vein of ore in underground workings. Assume that the country rock of the area includes granite-like minerals (quartz and feldspar) and that the fault plane is filled with gouge (clay). Assume further that there is only one level of the mine and that there is only one 6 ft × 8 ft tunnel.

20–86M. Uranium is a highly important element in our atomic age economy. Its "daughter products" are closely tied in with what is known as "equilibrium." Describe briefly, or by a series of sketches, what is meant by this statement: "The deposit is badly out of equilibrium, and radiometric assays are not conclusive."

20–87M. What is meant by "structural control" to a geologist-engineer? Give at least three examples in which the structural features of an area would control the direction and possible distance of looking for *more* ore, of whatever kind. (Specific locations need not be named. Possible conditions of local or regional structure are important.)

20–88M. Read this question before you start to answer it! Tabulate at least ten important features of an "exhausted oil field" that you would explore and critically examine BEFORE you would recommend ANY program for secondary recovery. (Assume that equipment is on hand and in good working order, during the productive period of the field; assume that markets and prices, wages, and taxes are of the same order; also power costs, drilling costs, logging, cementing, and casing and tubing costs are all within small brackets of capital outlay.) NOW: Give ten important features besides the known factors just mentioned. Some of these features have particular physical units of measurement and others do not. In your tabulation, give the physical units of measurement.

20–89M. Give a *brief* outline of your concept of a "petroleum reservoir engineer." What are his functions? When do they start? What educational background in subject matter do they imply as necessary? Do YOU have that background? If so, where did you acquire it? If you were head of your own corporation, could you act as your own "reservoir engineer"? Or could you select, by interview, competent reservoir engineers from your knowledge of the subject?

20–90M. Give at least eight valid reasons as to *why* you are taking this examination. Limit yourself to 50 words or less for each reason. Do not overlap motives. (This is a test question for brief and succinct expression of your thinking.)

appendix

Answers

A

CHAPTER 1

1–13. 1.732 **1–14.** 0.875 ft/min **1–15.** 20, 10 **1–16.** 15 miles
1–17. 3 **1–18.** Problem has no solution **1–19.** $y + x/3 = 11/3$
1–20. 1.40, 1.00 **1–21.** $\phi = 35.5°, x = 3.68; \phi = 215.5°, x = -3.68$
1–22. $y = \frac{3}{2}x - 7$ **1–23.** 0.42 **1–24.** 0.912, 0.908, 0.904
1–25. $x = 36/49, y = 18/49, z = 12/49$
1–26. 3.85 sta. (impractical) **1–27.** 0.8609
1–28. 6.04; 6.63; 2, 1; 0, π, 2π, 3π . . . **1–29.** 5, 1 **1–30.** 0.0251
1–31. 3.7 **1–32.** 120°
1–33. $c^2 = 1 + b^2 - 2b \cos C, b^2 = 1 + c^2 - 2c \cos B, A = \sqrt{s\ (s\text{-}a)\ (s\text{-}b)\ (s\text{-}c)}$
1–34. $t_{ca} - t_{ba} = 1.24/V_s$ (V_s in miles/sec); 640 acres **1–35.** 71.5 ft
1–36. 0.18 mile; 0.105 mile **1–37.** $DG = 579$ ft, $CB = 819$ ft
1–38. 3.76 miles **1–39.** No answer **1–40.** 16,420 ft **1–41.** 30°, 150°
1–42. $b = h = 20.5$ ft **1–43.** $3x^2 - 8x + 4$, 22 **1–44.** 16 ft lb/sec
1–45. v at 2 sec = 236 ft/sec², at 15 sec = −180 ft/sec², $a = -32$ ft/sec²
1–46. $y = \frac{x^3}{6} - 1800\,x + 72{,}001$ **1–47.** 0.66, $(e + 1)/2$, $\frac{2}{3}L_n\ (1 + x\sqrt{x}) + C$
1–48. $\tan^{-1} (\sin 2) = 0.74$ **1–49.** 45 units² **1–50.** $\frac{512}{9}\pi$ units³, $\frac{64}{3}\pi$ units³
1–51. $\pi^2 - 4$ **1–52.** $y_t = -3x/4 + 25/4, y_n = 4x/3 - 25/3$
1–53. Base = 10 ft, $h = 12.50$ ft, \$150 **1–54.** 1.21 in. **1–55.** 110 yd
1–56. 35 **1–57.** $x = 0.85D, y = 0.53D$ **1–58.** 12 ft
1–59. $r = 5.1$ ft, $h = 13.2$ ft; \$192.40 **1–60.** $r = h = 1/\sqrt[3]{\pi}$ **1–61.** 1186, 50%
1–62. $\tan^{-1}\sqrt{2}$ **1–63.** 14.82 ft **1–64.** $\sqrt{52}$ ft **1–65.** 24.6° **1–66.** 19.1 sec
1–67. $35\,\pi$ ft³ (Simpson's rule) **1–68.** 3600 lb **1–69.** 1 sec, 84 ft
1–70. 106.6 ft, 6.99 sec **1–71.** $780 \sin\left(\frac{\pi t}{12} - \frac{\pi}{2}\right) + 820$
1–72. 30 radians/hr **1–73.** $a \sinh\left(\frac{x}{a}1\right)$ **1–74.** $1/18\pi$ft/min
1–75. 0.6 ft/min; 0.333 ft/min
1–76. Base = 10 ft, height = 5 ft **1–77.** $x = 0, y = 4r/3\pi$
1–78. Area = 130.5 units², $x = 4.15$ units **1–79.** −1/3 **1–80.** −11.8 ft/sec

CHAPTER 2

2–17. 20 liters **2–18.** 37%
2–19. $CO_2 = 18.2\%$; $CO = 0.5\%$; $O_2 = 6.8\%$; $N_2 = 74.5\%$

2–20. 49.7 lb **2–21.** 1.5 cu ft, 75.3 lb

2–22. 25 moles of O_2, 16 moles of CO_2, 18 moles of H_2O **2–23.** 21.4 kg

2–24. 8.0 g (Cu), 2.26 g (H_2O)

2–25. 3.5 lb of O_2, 3.1 lb of CO_2, 1.4 lb of H_2O

2–26. 28.2 lb of SO_2, 7.9 lb of H_2O, 21.2 lb of O_2

2–27. **(a)** 0.2 lb **(b)** 0.19 g **2–28.** 2430 g

2–29. **(a)** 0.64 g **(b)** 1.87% **2–30.** 95.2 lb **2–31.** 2994 lb **2–32.** 28.1%

2–33. 4.2 g **2–34.** 20 cu ft **2–35.** 952 cu ft **2–36.** 476,200 cu ft

2–37. 2.47 lb **2–38.** **(a)** 109 g **(b)** 24.9 liters

2–39. **(a)** 73.4 lb **(b)** 169.5 liters

2–40. **(a)** one **(b)** 0.142 lb **(c)** 0.84 cu ft

2–41. **(a)** 5150 lb **(b)** 862 lb **(c)** 7010 cu ft

2–42. **(a)** 1147 **(b)** 24,500 **2–43.** 483 cu ft

2–44. **(a)** 522 lb **(b)** 2851 cu ft

2–45. 161.5 g of residue; 49,700 cc of HF **2–46.** 232,200 g **2–47.** 164 g

2–48. 68.6 g/liter **2–49.** 4.06 g **2–50.** 1.25 qt **2–51.** 7.34 liters

2–52. 0.030 liter of HCl; 12.2 g of Zn **2–53.** 74.5%

2–54. **(a)** Emphasize ionic character of reactants and/or products, shows only the substances actually undergoing chemical change, more realistic
(b) Equation for oxidation (loss of electrons) or reduction (gain of electrons) step in redox reactions $3e^- + 4H^+ + NO_3^- \rightarrow NO + 2H_2O$, $Cu \rightarrow Cu^{++} + 2e^-$
(c) (2,2,1,1,1) (2,2,2,1)

2–57. (4,1,8,2,4,4) silver, oxygen, sodium, carbon, nitrogen, hydrogen, cyanide, hydroxide

2–58. Concentration of reactants, temperature, catalysts, nature of reactants, pressure (in case of gases)

2–59. **(1)** Increase temperature shifts equilibrium left, decrease shifts right
(2) Increase pressure shifts right, decrease shifts left

2–60. $pH = \log \frac{1}{(H^+)} = -\log (H^+)$

2–63. **(a)** Bond formed by transfer of electrons between atoms; bond force is electrostatic attraction between positive and negative ions.
(b) Bond formed by sharing of electrons between atoms; bond force is electromagnetic attraction between electrons of opposite spin.

2–64. Alkali metal and alkaline earth metal silicates plus excess SiO_2

2–65. Some silica replaced by boron (III) oxide, possess low coefficient of expansion, high softening point, resistance to chemicals, shock resistance

2–67. Na, Ca, Al, K, Li, Be **2–68.** Sn, Cr **2–69.** Hematite, Fe_2O_3

2–70. Iron ore, coke, limestone, air **2–71.** Mg **2–72.** Zn

2–73. Cu, Zn, Hg

2–74. Molten pig iron mixed with excess of scrap iron, along with a little limestone. Subject to air blast, skim off slag, cool

2–75. Faster, more economical

2–76. Higher quality steel due to closer control possible

2–77. (a) and (e) **2–78.** (b)

2–79. Low carbon steel. Only the surface is desired to be tough (high carbon), not the interior

2–81. **(a)** 651 mm **(b)** 46.1%

2–82. **(a)** $CO_2 = 15.5\%$; $CO = 1.3\%$; $O_2 = 8.7\%$; $N_2 = 74.5\%$. **(b)** 4.8 lb

2–83. $4C_3H_5(NO_3)_3 \rightarrow 12CO_2 + 10H_2O + 6N_2 + O_2$

2–84. **(a)** 21% CO_2; 79% N_2 **(b)** 13.1% CO_2; 13.1% CO; 73.8% N_2

2–85. 14,350 cu ft **2–86.** 18.6 lb **2–87.** 38.8 g

2–88. 235g Na_2CO_3, 487g HCl

2–89. **(a)** $C_3H_8 + 5O_2 \rightarrow 3CO_2 + 4H_2O$; **(b)** 53.3 lb/hr; **(c)** 10,870 cu ft/hr

2–90. 64.6%

2–91. **(a)** 31.61 g of $KMnO_4$/liter of solution; **(b)** 126.76 g of $FeCl_2$/liter of solution

2–92. **(a)** 525 ml of 2N; 175 ml of 6N **2–93.** 180

2–94. CH_3S — simplest; $C_3H_9S_3$ — molecular **2–95.** 20 moles **2–96.** 0.72 M

2–97. 1.0×10^{-7} N **2–98.** Acid 1-7; base 7-14; 2.45 grains **2–99.** 237

2–100. **(a)** Yes; **(b)** no; **(c)** 1390 liter **2–101.** 12,700 g **2–102.** 91.1 lb

2–103. **(a)** six; **(b)** H; **(c)** ionic; **(d)** E; **(e)** six; **(f)** 2; **(g)** 6, 4, 2, 0, −1, −2; **(h)** c; **(i)** Y_2C_3; **(j)** $1s^2$; $2s^2$, $2p^6$, $3s^2$, $3p^5$

CHAPTER 3

3–11. 1330 lb, 77.8° W of S **3–12.** **(a)** 1720 lb, **(b)** 41.2° W of S

3–13. **(a)** 10 lb at 7 ft left of center of board, **(b)** 20 lb down at 4 ft right of center of board, **(c)** 22.4 lb, 26.6° from horizontal, 0.892 ft from center of board

3–14. 30 lb down, 16.7 ft from left end

3–15. **(a)** $\Sigma M_A = 0 = rw - 0.707rN_c$, $\Sigma F_x = 0 = N_A - 0.707N_c$, $\Sigma F_y = 0 = W - 0.707N_c$ **(b)** $N_A = 100$ lb, $N_c = 141.3$ lb

3–16. $A = 3160$ lb, $B = 2033$ lb, $C = 2123$ lb, $D = 2890$ lb

3–17. $F = 972$ lb compression **3–18.** $F = 1346$ lb **3–19.** $F = 588$ lb

3–20. **(a)** 2000 lb, **(b)** 2000 lb, **(c)** 2830 lb

3–21. **(a)** 10,000 lb, **(b)** 4840 lb

3–22. 5.83 lb at 31° from horizontal and 5.23 ft left and above c.g.

3–23. Yes **3–24.** $AB = 1492$ lb compression, $AC = 105.8$ lb tension

3–25. P is 4 ft below point O and 2.67 ft to left of point O

3–26. Tension $= 6360$ lb, $P = 990$ lb

3–27. 4.13 ft left of right support, 5.5 ft below it

3–28. 3720 lb tension, $R = 3870$ lb

3–29. 450 lb tension, thrust $= 780$ lb **3–30.** 114 lb

3–31. $A = B = C = 50$ lb

3–32. $A = 278$ lb, $B = 388$ lb, $C = 333.3$ lb (all up)

3–33. **(a)** 5 lb up, **(b)** 5.23 lb along each leg

3–34. $R_1 = 3120$ lb, $R_2 = 1930$ lb, $Q = 64{,}800$ in.-lb

3–35. $B = +900$, $C = 0$ lb, $D = -900$ lb

3–36. $\bar{y} = 4.38$ in. up, $\bar{x} = 8.99$ in. left, $I_{xx} = 698.28$ in.^{4}

3–37. $\bar{y} = 16$ in. up, $I_{xx} = 187{,}620$ in.^{4} **3–38.** $I_{xx} = 346.6$ in.^{4}

3–39. $\dfrac{h^2}{2h + r}$ above base **3–40.** $\bar{x} = 9.2$ in. from end of rod

3–41. **(a)** $\theta = 42.6°$, $X = 3.4$ tons, **(b)** $\theta = 58.4°$, $X = 4.76$ tons

3–42. 3.36 ft from wall **3–43.** $P = 43.1$ lb **3–44.** $W_2 = 46.8$ lb

3–45. $A_v = 195$ lb up, $A_h = 43.1$ lb to right, $B_h = 43.1$ lb to left

3–46. $W = 101.5$ lb **3–47.** $P = 89$ lb **3–48.** $P = 11$ lb to left

3–49. $\theta = 50°$ **3–50.** 0.375 **3–51.** Will not tip **3–52.** 35°

3–53. **(a)** Yes, **(b)** 4 lb **3–54.** **(a)** 67.2 lb, **(b)** 0 lb **3–55.** 2.33 times

3–56. 4.14 ft

3–57. $R_h = 560$ lb to left, $R_v = 830$ lb up, $S_h = 1120$ lb to right, $S_v = 820$ lb up

3–58. $A_h = 14.25^k$ to left, $A_v = 42.8^k$ up, $B_h = 85.6^k$ to left, $B_v = 57.2^k$ up

3–59. $A = 20{,}000$ lb tension, $B = 30{,}000$ lb compression

3–60. $A = 11.25$ kip tension, $B = 6.25$ kip tension, $C = 15$ kip compression

3–61. **(a)** 1413 lb, **(b)** 2828 lb **3–62.** $A_h = 67.7$ lb to left, $A_v = 33.3$ lb up

3–63. B_x 120 lb

3–64. $BE = 12.5$ kip tension, $DF = 10$ kip compression, $DE = 0$

3–65. 177.9 ft, −690 lb **3–66.** $a = -6$ kip, $b = 0$, $c = +6.69$ kip

3–67. $I_y = 2a^3b/7$ 3–68. $\bar{x} = 3.28$ in., $\bar{y} = 0.71$ in.

3–69. **(a)** 544 lb at 28.4° **(b)** 3.27 ft **(c)** 3.72 ft below point 0

3–70. $A_v = 46.7$ lb, $A_h = 86.6$ lb, $C_v = 64.4$ lb, $C_h = 55.7$ lb

3–71. 1150 lb each **3–72.** **(a)** 350 lb, **(b)** 200 lb at 30°

3–73. $BE = 1390$ lb; $BD = 1210$ lb; $A_x = 2450$ lb; $A_y = -472$ lb; $A_z = -137$ lb

3–74. 2020 lb **3–75.** 16.15 ft **3–76.** 4.7 ft

3–77. $a = -3.5P$; $b = +0.87P$ **3–78.** (c) **3–79.** 8 ft **3–80.** 11.3°

CHAPTER 4

4–13. 4 ft/sec^2 **4–14.** 4 ft/sec **4–15.** 458 sec

4–16. **(b)** 38,274 ft, **(c)** 0.406 ft/sec^2, **(d)** −0.284 ft/sec^2

4–17. 138.98 ft **4–18.** 10 ft/sec^2 **4–19.** 168.9 lb **4–20.** 4.03 ft/sec^2

4–21. 900 ft

4–22. **(a)** 33.4 ft/sec, **(b)** 221 sec, **(c)** 16,820,000 ft-lb, **(d)** 160.5 hp, 971 hp, **(e)** 685 hp

4–23. **(a)** 19,200 lb, **(b)** 2560 hp **4–24.** **(a)** 554.6 ft, **(b)** 8.35 sec

4–25. 0.033 radian/sec

4–26. **(a)** 2895 ft/sec, **(b)** 2895 ft/sec, **(c)** 776 ft/sec, **(d)** 139,600 ft, **(e)** 9350 ft, **(f)** 48.2 sec

4–27. **(a)** 23,430 ft, 20.2 sec, **(b)** 1500 ft, 9.65 sec **4–28.** 15.3 ft/sec

4–29. 18.5°, no **4–30.** **(a)** 150.5 ft/sec, **(b)** 40.3 ft/sec

4–31. **(a)** 1.00 radian/sec, **(b)** 24,900 ft-lb

4–32. **(a)** 25.8 radians/sec^2, **(b)** 48.6 rpm

4–33. Front = 1754 lb, rear = 1446 lb **4–34.** 7.41 ft/sec^2
4–35. **(a)** 15 ft/sec^2, **(b)** R_A = 3760 lb, R_B = 2680 lb **(c)** 1790 lb
4–36. **(a)** 6.44 ft/sec^2, **(b)** 10.72 ft/sec^2
4–37. 9.55 ft/sec **4–38.** **(a)** down, **(b)** 253.3 lb, **(c)** 0.43 ft/sec^2
4–39. 7.5 lb **4–40.** 0.347 **4–41.** 3125 in.-lb **4–42.** **(a)** 2.77 ft, **(b)** 189 ft
4–43. 31.6 ft/sec, 31,060 ft-lb **4–44.** 88.2 hp **4–45.** 7.55 hp
4–46. **(a)** 2.25 to 1, **(b)** 143 hp **4–47.** **(a)** 14,600,000 ft-lb, **(b)** 17.7 sec
4–48. 125 hp **4–49.** 3.52 ft/sec **4–50.** 5.68 ft/sec
4–51. **(a)** Yes, **(b)** 3 to 2, **(c)** no **4–52.** 40.4 ft/sec ∠21.8° N of E
4–53. **(a)** 87.6 ft/sec ∠33.8° N of E, **(b)** 611 ft-lb **4–54.** 248 in./sec
4–55. T_1 = 75.64 lb, T_2 = 78.54 lb **4–56.** 125 sec **4–57.** 9270 ft-lb
4–58. **(a)** 2.74 lb, **(b)** 150 lb, **(c)** 5170 ft-lb, **(d)** 49.3 revolutions
4–59. 61 sec, 167,500 ft-lb **4–60.** 4.89 revolutions
4–61. **(a)** 131 lb, **(b)** 199 lb at ↘41.2°, **(c)** 247,000 ft-lb, **(d)** 2360 revolutions
4–62. **(a)** 1600 ft-lb, **(b)** roll **4–63.** 46.5 ft/sec **4–64.** 0.315 ft-lb
4–65. **(a)** 66.65 ft, **(b)** 13.34 ft/sec
4–66. **(a)** 2 in. from midpoint of BC on line perpendicular to BC
(b) 4 radians/sec, **(c)** 11.32 fps ↖45°
4–67. **(a)** 19.5 ft/sec ←, **(b)** 4.88 radians/sec(CW)
4–68. 11.45 radians/sec^2 (CW)
4–69. 32.9 ft/sec^2 →, 118 lb **4–70.** 115.4 lb **4–71.** 31.9 deg
4–72. 16.1 ft **4–73.** 136.5 lb, 68.3 lb, 170 ft-lb **4–74.** 22.0 hp **4–75.** 58.3 lb
4–76. 165 ft **4–77.** 9.47 fps **4–78.** 890 ft., 890 ft. **4–79.** 3.94 lb/ft
4–80. V_B' = 3.81 fps →, V_A' = 6.93 fps ↗88.4°
4–81. 33.5 in. **4–82.** 342 lb **4–83.** 30.6 ft **4–84.** 18.6 in.
4–85. 183.5 lb ↓ **4–86.** 0.675 sec **4–87.** 6500 rpm (CW), 9.44 radians/sec^2
4–88. **(a)** 12.6 radians/sec (CCW) **(b)** 5.25 lb ↗45°, 48.0 lb ↖45
4–89. **(a)** 10.65 ft/sec^2 **(b)** 0.25 lb **(c)** No **4–90.** 29.3 radians/sec^2 (CCW)

CHAPTER 5

5–17. 12 lb, direction of 20-lb force **5–18.** 7 in. 5 in.
5–19. 2.5 ft/sec^2, 5 lb **5–20.** 160 ft-lb, 5 ft/sec^2
5–21. 6.4 ft/sec^2, 2000 ft-lb **5–22.** 1.81 × 10^7 ft-lb, 32.8 sec **5–23.** Zero
5–24. 185 ft **5–25.** 3.75 lb **5–26.** 0.25 **5–27.** 2.3 lb, 14.9 lb
5–28. 2π radians/sec, 20π ft/sec, $40\pi^2$ ft/sec^2, $80\pi^2$ lb
5–29. 87.2° **5–30.** 1.13 × 10^7 kwhr **5–31.** 856 ft/sec
5–32. 1.26 × 10^5 lb/sq ft **5–33.** 224 lb **5–34.** 1 cu ft, 200 lb/cu ft, 3.2
5–35. 1872 lb **5–36.** 4.75, 0.71, 44.3 lb/cu ft **5–37.** 675π **5–38.** 12,000 lb
5–39. 66 ft **5–40.** 27°C, −40°C **5–41.** 13,170 Btu, 20.3 Btu, 0.24 Btu/°F
5–42. 2260°F **5–43.** 209 cu in. **5–44.** 176 ft-lb **5–45.** 2.19 × 10^6 Btu
5–46. 76.2 Btu, 397°F **5–47.** 4.6 in., $128\pi k$ (k in Btu/in. sec°F), $3.0/k$ sec
5–48. 0.044 lb/cu ft **5–49.** 76 Btu **5–50.** 1440 ft/sec **5–51.** 0.244 in.
5–52. 153,600 Btu **5–53.** 16.6% **5–54.** $T_2 = 1.01\ T_1$ **5–55.** 238 ft
5–56. 68 ft **5–57.** 209 ft/sec **5–58.** 1.65 × 10^4 ft/sec **5–59.** 2.29 × 10^4 ft

5–60. 0.67 ft to right of lens and inverter, 1/3
5–61. 5 diopters, —20 cm (object side of lens), 1, virtual **5–62.** 58.2 cm
5–63. —5 in., 2 in. **5–64.** 1.42 in. **5–65.** 22 cp, 15.7 cp **5–66.** 30 ft
5–67. 4 amp **5–68.** No numerical answer **5–69.** $0.018
5–70. 22.9 amp, 17.1 amp, 137 volts **5–71.** 22,800 cycles/sec
5–72. 0.105 henrys **5–73.** 280 ohms **5–74.** 141 ohms, 45°
5–75. 0.436μf **5–76.** 98.5 ft **5–77.** 1.55 ev **5–78.** 16 amps
5–79. 5.58 miles **5–80.** 13,100 watts/sq m

CHAPTER 6

6–21. (c)
6–23. **(a)** $P = 7850$ lb; **(b)** diam. required = 2.14 in.; **(c)** 850 psi, 61.2 tons/sq ft
6–24. 16,100,000 psi **6–25.** 125,000 lb
6–26. Aluminum = 8.68 in.; brass = 1.32 in. **6–27.** 1300 psf, 8500 psf
6–28. **(a)** 122 lb; **(b)** 41.2 lb, **(c)** aluminum = 24,000—28,000 psi, steel =50,000—65,000 psi
6–29. 12.2 in.× 17.3 in.
6–30. **(a)** 231 lb; **(b)** 0.0604 in. vertical and 0.0098 in. horizontal
6–31. $Pa = 4000$ lb; $Pb = 16,000$ lb **6–32.** 10,540 lb in shear
6–33. **(a)** Six; **(b)** four **6–34.** 6750 lb at the center
6–35. 12,800 psi; 758 psi **6–36.** 19,980 psi **6–37.** **(a)** 4.85 in.; **(b)** 1.85°
6–38. **(a)** **(b)** $hp_a = 1.395\ hp_b$; **(c)** B
6–39. **(a)** 1108π in.-lb; **(b)** 0.000732 radian
6–40. **(a)** 1070 psi, **(b)** yes, **(c)** varies as the radius
6–41. **(a)** 2.68 hp; **(b)** 6820 Btu/hr
6–42. **(a)** 14 ft-lb; **(b)** driver = 720 in.-lb, driven = 1080 in.-lb; **(c)** 17.1 hp
6–43. **(a)** 26,300 psi, **(b)** 22%
6–44. **(a)** 2650 lb, using Eulers Eq.; **(b)** 1760 using AISC
6–45. Column is OK, $0.852 < 1$ **6–46.** Aluminum = 5570 lb; steel = 9430 lb
6–47. $P = 11,550$ lb with standard 1½ in. pipe **6–48.** 31°F **6–49.** 8.05 in.
6–50. 7′6″ square, with 13-#6 bars each way, (ACI)
6–51. **(a)** 14,000 psi at 45°; **(b)** 13,000 psi and 12,100 psi.
6–52. $L_1L_2 = 145$, $L_2L_4 = -145$, $U_1U_3 = -1445$, $L_0U_1 = -1156$, $U_1L_2 = 866$, $L_2U_3 = 1446$, $U_3L_4 = -1446$
6–54. 14,950 lb **6–55.** $AB = 10.45$ kip, CB = DB = 1.75 kip (partial answers)
6–56. $BC = -707$ lb, $CD = -707$ lb, BD = AE = 0, $AB = -500$ lb, $AD = 625$ lb, $DE = -875$ lb
6–57. Top chord in compression, bottom chord in tension, interior diagonals in tension, zero stress in alternate verticals.
6–58. $AB = BD = 1080$ lb, $CE = -3510$ lb
6–59. $R_b = 20$, $A_v = 10$, $A_h = 0$, $AC = 10$, $BC = EF = FG = ED = 0$ $CE = -7.5$, $BD = -20$, $DF = HF = -10$, $HI = 7.5$
6–60. Top chord, l to r, = —6.3, —4.6, —3.33, —3.75; bottom chord, l to r, = 1.0, 1.0, 2.0, 2.0 interior members, l to r, = 0, —1.67, 2.7, —2.92, 0

6–61. $R_1 = 10.86$ kip, $R_2 = 12.3$ kip

6–62. $L_0L_1 = L_1L_2 = 6$, $L_0U_1 = -8.48$, $U_1L_2 = 4.24$, $U_1U_2 = -9.0$, right side is symmetrical, all verticals = 0

6–63. $R_a = 22.13$, $R_b = 27.67$, $V_c = 8.2$ kip

6–64. At left end, $V = 6200$ lb, $M = 44{,}900$ ft-lb

6–65. Inflection points are 5.8 ft from left end and 3.25 ft from right end, $M_{max} =$ 6950 ft-lb under concentrated load.

6–66. (c)

6–67. $M_{max} = -16$ ft-kip under left reaction, $M_{max} = 38.8$ ft-kip, 11.4 ft from left end. Points of inflection are 5.16 ft from left end and 2.3 ft from right end.

6–68. Reactions are 10.2 kip each.

6–69. $M_{max} = 18$ ft-kip, 6 ft from left end and -12 ft-kip at right reaction.

6–70. $M_{max} = 10{,}800$ ft-lb, 5.6 ft to left of concentrated load, and $M_{max} = -2500$ ft-lb at right reaction.

6–71. M_{max} is negative at right reaction and is equal to 1600 ft-lb. I/c required $= 0.96$ in.^{3}

6–72. $R_1 = 870$ lb, $R_2 = 10{,}530$ lb, $M_{max} = 4360$ ft-lb under concentrated load and $-19{,}200$ ft-lb over right reaction, I/c required $= 11.5$ in.^{3}

6–73. M_{max} is 16,000 ft-lb at right reaction.

6–74. $R_L = 47.5$ kip, $R_R = 23.5$ kip, $M_{max} = -85$ ft-kip at left reaction, and 80.75 ft-kip, 9 ft to left of right reaction.

6–75. $V = 9.87$ kip, $M_{5000} = 11.1$ ft-kip

6–76. **(a)** $R_2 = 11.5$, $R_1 = 4.5$; **(b)** 1366 psi, 4 ft to left of R_1, and 2130 psi at R_2; **(c)** 141.8 psi just to left of R_2.

6–77. 42.2 ft

6–78. 1.13 in. × 2.26 in., theoretical size, not including deflection.

6–79. 2 in. × 8 in. beam.

6–80. 2″×8″ flanges and 4″×8″ web, or 2″×8″ flange and 2″×16″ web if permissible.

6–81. 5.04 in., with deflection of L/360 included, or 9½ in. without deflection.

6–82. (b) Deflects less

6–83. 2″×10″

6–84. **(a)** Section B, **(b)** section A

6–85. **(a)** I/c required: $A = 36$, $B = 20.2$, $C = 21.6$, $D = 40.6$ in^3 **(b)** A = 14WF30, $B =$ 10WF21, $C =$ 10WF25, $D =$ 14WF30 **(c)** 952 psi

6–86. 0.296 in. **6–87.** $E\Delta_C = 937.5$ **6–88.** $R = 2640$ lb

6–89. **(a)** 20,600 psi, **(b)** -8350 psi, **(c)** 616 psi

6–90. 1062 psi, 44 psi **6–91.** 185 lb/ft, shear governing

6–93. $L_v = 3980$ lb, $L_h = 600$ lb, $R_h = 0$, $R_v = 3980$ lb

6–96. 26,800 psi, 9050 psi. **6–97.** (1) b, (2) a, (3) e, (4) a

6–98. **(a)** T, **(b)** F, **(c)** F, **(d)** T, **(e)** F

6–99. **(a)** Compression, **(b)** moment of inertia or deflection, **(c)** spark test, **(d)** hardness, **(e)** tensile

CHAPTER 7

7–7. 10 cm **7–8.** $P_{O2} = 2.94$ psia, $P_{N2} = 11.76$ psia

7–9. 2 atmos., 15.8 Btu **7–10.** 2.5 cu ft **7–11.** 176 Btu/lb

7–12. $v = 6.17$ cu ft, $u = 6.87$ Btu/lb, $h = 9.6$ Btu/lb; $v = 2.30$ cu ft, $t = 283°F$, $W = 41.7$ Btu/lb

7–13. $W = 43.7$ Btu/lb, $Q = 43.7$ Btu/lb **7–14.** 79.34 lb, 1003 cu ft

7–15. 55 cu ft, 9660°F, −411.4°F

7–16. 0.30 lb, 0.324 Btu/lb °F, 20.4 Btu, 5.83 Btu

7–17. 480°F, 28.9 cu ft, 720 Btu

7–18. $\Delta t = -243°F$, $\Delta u = -167$ Btu, $\Delta H = -234$ Btu, $W = 167$ Btu, $Q = 0$

7–19. 32 hp **7–20.** 7.08 cu ft, 40.5 Btu, −40.5 Btu **7–21.** 18 psig

7–22. $P_{N_2} = 14.0$ psia, $P_{CO_2} = 4.0$ psia, $P_{CO} = 2.0$ psia; $N_2 = 62.8\%$, $CO_2 = 28.2\%$, $CO = 9.0\%$

7–23. 68°F, 0.0803 cu ft; 168°F, 0.0822 cu ft; 227.2°F, 84 cu ft; 318.8°F, 114.5 cu ft

7–24. 4.1×10^7 Btu/hr **7–25.** 38 lb/min, 40.4 lb/min

7–26. $0.54/1000 lb **7–27.** 328.6 Btu/lb **7–28.** 68.4%

7–29. **(a)** $\Delta S = 0.1865$ Btu/lb °R, $Q = 160.3$ Btu/lb, $\Delta h = 32.8$ Btu/lb, $\Delta u = 25.3$ Btu/lb, $W = 160.3$ Btu/lb; **(b)** **(1)** $h = 1307$ Btu/lb, $s = 1.5897$ Btu/lb °R, $v = 1.478$ cu ft/lb, $u = 1198$ Btu/lb; **(2)** $P = 11.53$ psia, $x = 87.3\%$, $v = 29.36$ cu ft/lb, $h = 1020$ Btu/lb, $u = 958$ Btu/lb; **(3)** $Q = 0$; **(4)** $\Delta u = -240$ Btu/lb; **(5)** $W = 287$ Btu/lb

7–30. 10,600 kw **7–31.** 3140 ft/sec

7–32. 446 Btu/lb, 35.2%, 7.65 lb/kwhr; $e_k = 24.1\%$, $\eta_k = 68.5\%$

7–33. 101.7 Btu/min **7–34.** 212 Btu/lb, 36.9%

7–35. **(b)** 40.4% **7–36.** 69%

7–37. $Q_A = 6220$ Btu/min, $Q_R = 1980$ Btu/min, $e = 68.1\%$

7–38. **(a)** 78.7 psi, 1473 lb-in., $e_b = 23\%$, $\eta_b = 40.7\%$; **(b)** $CO_2 = 17.55\%$, $CO = 1.86\%$, $O_2 = 4.26\%$, $N_2 = 76.33\%$

7–39. 82.2 Btu/lb **7–40.** 42.4%, 407°F

7–41. 54.4%; $W_k = 14.28$ lb/kwhr, $e_k = 47.3\%$; 38.4%; 8040 gpm; Regenerative Cycle; 6400 lb/hr

7–42. $W_M = 14{,}500$ lb/hr, $W_S = 5500$ lb/hr

7–43. 4.15 lb/min, 415 Btu/min, 201 lb/min, 15.4%, 4.82

7–44. 843 Btu/lb, 674 Btu/lb, 2390 hp, 283 hp, 20.5%

7–45. **(b)** Adiabatic: $Q = 0$, $W = -27.4$ Btu, $\Delta u = 27.4$ Btu; constant pressure: $Q = 158$ Btu, $W = 45.2$ Btu, $\Delta u = 112.8$ Btu; constant volume: $Q = -140.5$ Btu, $W = 0$, $\Delta u = -140.5$ Btu

7–46. 1210 cfm **7–47.** 38 tons, 5.97

7–48. $P_{MH} = 26.9$ psi, $P_{MC} = 28.4$ psi, $W_F = 5.35$ hp

7–49. $W_B = 20$ hp, $W_T = 22.5$ hp, $e = 27.3\%$

7–50. 2190 hp, 1970 hp, 53.5 mph, 1725 tons

7–51. 33.6%, 57.4 Btu/min **7–52.** 9.14 Btu/hr sq ft, 9°F

7–53. 1.13×10^7 kwhr **7–54.** 160°F

7–55. 59 grains/lb dry air, 31.6%, 51.6°F, 29.6 Btu/lb dry air

7–56. **(a)** 2360 fps; **(b)** 80,500 ft-lb_f/lb_m; **(c)** 30.3 kw

7–57. **(a)** 620°F; **(b)** 47.2%; **(c)** 133.3 psia; **(d)** 1.59 Btu

7–58. 256 Btu/lb_m decrease **7–59.** 250 Btu by the gas **7–60.** 350 psia

7–61. 35.3 Btu/lb_m; –38.2 Btu/lb_m **7–62.** 18,100 Btu **7–63.** 107.6 psia

7–64. **(a)** 51°F; **(b)** 4.27 cu ft/lb_m; **(c)** 965 fps; **(d)** 0.00708 ft^2; **(e)** 86°F; **(f)** either

7–65. 12,850 cu ft/hr **7–66.** **(a)** 446°F; **(b)** 98 cu ft; **(c)** 895 Btu

7–67. 3.78; 1.68 **7–68.** **(a)** 69.2°F; **(b)** 1665 Btu, 1822 Btu **7–69.** 0.195 lb_m

7–70. **(a)** 17,500 Btu/hr; **(b)** 37.2°F **7–71.** 0.43 Btu/R net

7–72. ΔS net = 0 is basis for solution **7–73.** 9000 hp transmitted

7–74. 576 Btu **7–75.** **(a)** 0; **(b)** 1.9 Btu out; **(c)** 1.9 Btu on

CHAPTER 8

8–7. 12,000 lb **8–8.** 4000 lb, 2.33 ft below top of gate

8–9. 4.10 ft × 4.10 ft × 4.10 ft **8–10.** 15,170 lb, 1.56 ft from top of gate

8–11. **(a)** 55 min, **(b)** 169,000 lb (S.G. = 0.92), **(c)** 32,200 lb (S.G. = 0.92)

8–12. **(a)** 1,005,000 lb, **(b)** 0.0305 ft below center

8–13. Top, 0.00; bottom, 123.2 lb/in. of width of hoop **8–14.** 14.0 psia

8–14. 0.398 ft **8–15.** 8.26 ft **8–16.** 14.0 psia

8–17. 1.5 in. **8–18.** 98.5 psi **8–19.** 0.908 in.

8–20. With ideal, steady continuous flow of an incompressible fluid, the total mechanical energy per unit of weight (heads) is the same at any point in the closed channel $\frac{P_1}{w} + \frac{V_1^2}{2g} + z_1 = \frac{P_2}{w} + \frac{V_2^2}{2g} + z_2$; venturi meter

8–21. **(a)** From B to A; **(b)** 10.1 ft of water; **(c)** 7.65 fps, 2.75 fps

8–22. 40.7 fps **8–23.** 2.03 cfs **8–24.** 2.70 gps **8–25.** 0.925 cfs

8–26. 43.3 psi, 0.437 cfs **8–27.** 47.6 fps **8–28.** 14.5 ft, 3.88 cfs

8–29. 166 cfm **8–30.** 0.0143 in. **8–31.** 0.554 cfs

8–32. 8.25 cfs **8–33.** 12.7 ft/sec **8–34.** 31.6 psi

8–35. 1360 psi **8–36.** 497 hp **8–37.** **(a)** 148 ft, **(b)** 129 ft, **(c)** 19.0 ft

8–38. 1050 kw (f = 0.018) **8–39.** Q_{24} = 53.3 cfs, Q_{12} = 6.70 cfs

8–40. 17 psi **8–41.** 4.32 cfs (c = 120)

8–42. **(a)** 5000 ft (c = 120); **(b)** 2000 gpm, 458 ft

8–43. 4.60 ft (c = 130)

8–44. 3.78 cfs **8–45.** 72.6 ft, 4,120 hp **8–46.** 2.21 cfs

8–47. **(a)** 7.75 cfs, **(b)** 1510 hp **8–48.** 58%

8–49. 102 ft salt water **8–50.** 1450 hp **8–51.** **(a)** 0.121 hp, **(b)** 0.200 hp

8–52. **(a)** 10.0 hp, **(b)** 9.2 kw, **(c)** $57.10 **8–53.** 94.6 hp

8–54. **(a)** 708 hp, **(b)** 1380 hp **8–55.** 2.26 cfs (n = 0.013)

8–56. 229 ft/1000 ft (n = 0.013) **8–57.** 76.5 cfs

8–58. Area of cross section of stream, wetted perimeter of channel, roughness coefficient of channel, slope of channel

8–59. **(a)** circle **8–60.** 3 ft high × 6 ft wide

8–61. 0.02, 570 cfs **8–62.** **(a)** 80.2 fps, **(b)** 272 lb **8–63.** 353 lb

8–64. $F_H = \underleftarrow{2430 \text{ lb}}$, $F_v = 0.00$ **8–65.** $\underrightarrow{245 \text{ lb}}$

8–66. 2560 lb →, 4450 lb↓ **8–67.** **(a)** 834 lb ←, **(b)** 834 lb → @ Pa = 14.7 psi

8–68. 21.6 lb **8–69.** 52.0 lb $\angle 10°$ ↘ **8–70.** 2570 lb

CHAPTER 9

9–15. ⅚ R **9–16.** 136 volts **9–17.** **(a)** 900 ohms, **(b)** 75 volts

9–18. **(a)** Assuming a nominal 8-hr rate of discharge, 78.8 volts, **(b)** 2.75 ohms

9–19. 6-ohm : 1.35 kw; 8-ohm : 1.02 kw **9–20.** 0.2 ohm, 12.5 volts

9–21. 0.5 ohm **9–22.** **(a)** 52.5 volts, **(b)** 63.5 volts, **(c)** 21.9%

9–23. 44.7 watts **9–24.** 4.40 kw, $0.22 **9–25.** 10.0 divisions

9–26. 540 kilohms **9–27.** 1.08 megohms **9–28.** 16.7 ohms

9–29. 0.0894 ohms **9–30.** **(a)** 8.68 ohms, **(b)** 2.50 ohms

9–31. **(a)** 300 MCM, **(b)** $0.67 per year

9–32. **(a)** 15.9 volts, **(b)** 47% increase

9–33. **(a)** Insert additional resistance in the armature circuit, **(b)** in the range of 0.2 ohm, **(c)** in series with the armature to partially replace the drop normally produced by the back emf of the armature, **(d)** to prevent damage to armature windings, brushes, and commutator bars, **(e)** usually within 150% to 300% of rated value

9–34. (c) **9–35.** 77.4% **9–36.** 382 amp **9–37.** 25.8 amp

9–38. **(a)** 0.384 volts/turn, **(b)** $E_{average} = 0.6\,E_{max}$; $E_{rms} = 0.775\,E_{max}$

9–39. **(a)** Add windings in parallel, fields aiding, **(b)** add windings in series, fields aiding, **(c)** add windings in parallel, fields aiding, **(d)** add windings in series, fields aiding

9–40. **(a)** 25.4 kilolines/sq-in., **(b)** 29 amp-turns, **(c)** 2380 amp-turns

9–41. **(a)** $0.16 + j0.12$ ohm, **(b)** 0.16 ohm

9–42. $R = 1500$ ohms, $L = 1.59$ henrys, $C = 0.0156\ \mu$f

9–43. $6.15 + j1.86$ ohms, 6.42 ohms

9–44. **(a)** **(1)** 10 ohms, **(2)** 20 ohms, **(3)** 17.32 ohms, **(4)** 0.046 henry; **(c)** 4.11 amp

9–45. 17.32 amp, lagging line voltages by 30° **9–46.** 5.77 amp, rms

9–47. **(a)** 7.78 $\angle 45°$ amp, **(b)** 11.0 $\angle -36.9°$ amp, **(c)** 156 $\angle -45°$ volts, **(d)** 14.4 $\angle -4.4°$ amp, **(e)** 126 $\angle 6.0°$ volts, **(f)** 0.984, inductive, **(g)** 0.0159 henry

9–48. 389 kva **9–49** **(a)** 887 watts, **(b)** 0.944, capacitive

9–50. **(a)** 5.12 hp, **(b)** 232 volts, **(c)** 98.0%

9–51. **(a)** A three-phase power system achieves the conversion and/or transfer of three trains of a-c energy, each of which has a definite time relation with respect to the other two.

(b) The Edison three-wire distribution system is one in which the voltage between two of the conductors is twice the voltage between either of these conductors and a third conductor.
(c) (1) For a fixed amount of power transferred a fixed distance at a fixed line voltage and a fixed power factor, the three-phase system will accomplish the same efficiency as the single-phase system with only 75% of the copper required of the single-phase system; (2) in three-phase power systems the third harmonic can be controlled by the correct connections (eliminated from the line terminals of three-wire, Y-connected and delta-connected generators; conserved and beneficial in the windings of a delta-connected transformer).
(d) A power transformer is one of relatively high efficiency designed to transform normally large rates of energy.
(e) By connecting capacitors at various points in a power system the power factor can be kept at a higher value by partially offsetting the lagging power factor of most a-c machinery; thus, the same power can be transferred with a lower line current.

9–52. 19.5 hp

9–53. **(a)** 245 amp, **(b)** 461 kvars

9–54. **(a)** 40.6 amp; **(b)** 30.4 amp; **(c)** 120 volts, 55.6 amp; **(d)** 1.0

9–55. **(a)** 37.5 lb-ft, **(b)** 100 amp

9–56. **(a)** Interchange any two line terminals, **(b)** reverse either the starting or the running winding, **(c)** reverse either the shunt-field winding or the armature terminals, **(d)** reverse either the series-field winding or the armature terminals.

9–57. Connect the 2280 volts to the innermost taps; connect the secondary windings in parallel.

9–58. **(a)** 9.90-db gain; **(b)** 46.9 volts, rms; **(c)** 0.44 watt

9–59. **(a)** 21 volts, rms; **(b)** the output would become distorted; **(c)** 30 kilohms

9–60. (d)

9–61. **(a)** $r_p = 7.36 \times 10^3$ ohm, $\mu = 16$; **(b)** 381 volts; **(c)** 11.7;

(d) $\sqrt{\dfrac{A_2^2 + B_2^2}{A_1^2 + B_1^2}}$ (100) where $A_n = \dfrac{\omega a}{\pi} \displaystyle\int_0^{\frac{2\pi}{\omega}} [1 + b \sin \omega t]^{1.5} \sin n\omega t dt$

$a = 7.63$

$b = 0.889$

$B_n = \dfrac{\omega a}{\pi} \displaystyle\int_0^{\frac{2\pi}{\omega}} [1 + b \sin \omega t]^{1.5} \cos n\omega t dt$

9–62. **(a)** $A_v = 62.6$, $V_o = 0.626$ volts, **(b)** 920 ohm, **(c)** 2.71×10^5 ohm, **(d)** 25, **(e)** 1600, **(f)** 170 ohm

9–63. 4860

9–64. **(a)** 50 amp, **(b)** 5 volts, **(c)** 250 watts, **(d)** 25 amp

9–65. **(a)** The two 100-watt lamps paralleled, in series with the 200-watt lamp, **(b)** 200-watt : 1.67 amp; 100-watt : 0.833 amp, **(c)** 1.67 amp

9–66. $R_{3\min} = 9.23$ ohm, $R_{3\max} = 216$ ohm

9–67. **(a)** $I_1 = 0.73$ amp, $I_2 = 0.98$ amp; **(b)** 131.2 watts; **(c)** 5.85 watts

9–68. $I_1 = 0.725$ amp, $I_2 = 0.545$ amp, $I_3 = 1.545$ amp

9–69. Answer is in form of circuit diagrams

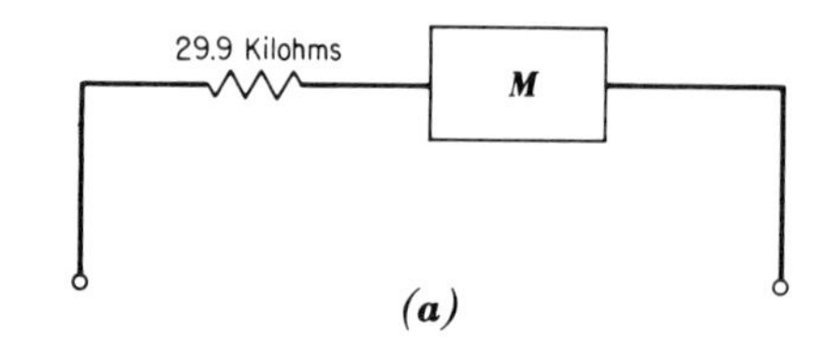

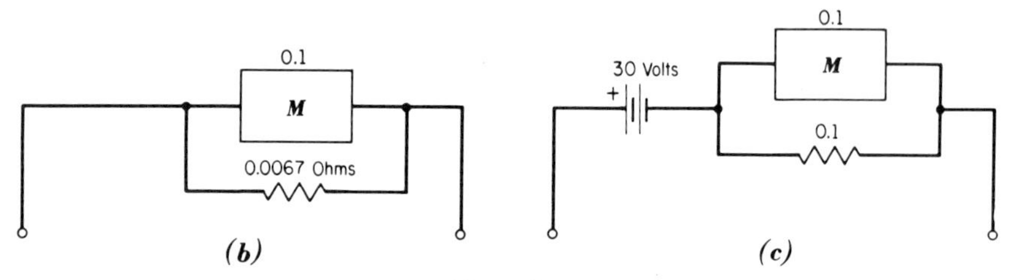

Problem 9–69.

9–70. **(a)** 262.5 volts, **(b)** 15,748 watts, **(c)** 235 volts **9–71.** 1970 rpm

9–72. **(a)** $3.66 \angle -60.8°$ amp, **(b)** 428 watts, **(c)** 57.33 ohm, **(d)** 0.29 μf

9–73. **(a)** $7.54 \angle -16.6°$ ohms, **(b)** $I_1 = 26.8 \angle 63.43°$ amp, $I_2 = 17 \angle -80.55°$ amp

9–74. **(a)** 1592 cps, **(b)** 1 volt **9–75.** 1.63 watts **9–76.** 2.86×10^{-6} mhos

9–77. Source: $I = 100$ amp, $v = 2000$ volts, pf = 50%, kw = 100, kvar = 173.2, kva = 200
Line: $I = 100$ amp, $kw_{loss} = 29.3$, $kvar_{loss} = 102.5$, Reg. = 50%, Eff. = 70.7%
Load: $I = 100$ amp, $V = 1000$ volts, pf = 70.7%, kw =70.7, kvar = 70.7, kva = 100

9–78. $122.00 **9–79.** **(b)** $E_s = 240$ volts, $I_s = 60$ amp, $I_p = 2$ amps

9–80. 67.1 mph

CHAPTER 10

10–10. **(a)** The net income of a business; financial or monetary gain obtained from the use of capital in a transaction or series of transactions.
(b) The present worth of the cost of perpetual service.
(c) Money paid for the use of money.
(d) The certain point in the increase of capital or labor beyond which there is a proportionately smaller increase in productivity.

10–11. **(a)** Serial bonds—interest and principal paid off each year. Sinking fund—deposits made accumulate with interest to pay off all bonds at one time.
(b) Factor for converting costs from one period and area to another. An example is the Engineering News-Record index.

10–12. 19 years; last payment = $61,732 **10–13.** I—$114,360, II—$109,860

10–14. A—$44,642, B—$53,265

10–15. A—$16,500, $183,430; B—$19,240, $213,945

10–16. $411, buy new machine **10–17.** $5484, $4793

10–18. A—$19,880, B—$13,890

10–19. Old—$14,228; hydro—$11,783; new—$15,311

10–20. New plant, $20,860 **10–21.** New machine, $3874

10–22. Metal, $2265; wood, $3108; 11.1% (average interest used)

10–23. **(a)** $24.32, **(b)** $21,290

10–24. Tossup. Old = $48,412 versus new = $50,050

10–25. **(a)** $62,310, **(b)** $3083, **(c)** $69,828, **(d)** $36,532

10–26. **(a)** $44,866, **(b)** land may be gone, price inflated, possibility of sooner use, etc.

10–27. Prestressed concrete; urgency of need, possibility of floods, safety, etc.

10–28. $698,130, 72.26% **10–29.** $16,470 **10–30.** $3963 **10–31.** $341.60

10–32. $9950 **10–33.** A—$2,304,790, B—$2,203,680

10–34. **(a)** $14,180, **(b)** $6083 **10–35.** $35,508 **10–36.** Timber, $49,440

10–37. **(a)** $1920; **(b)** $1772.45, $1843.35, etc.; **(c)** $4740, $2493, etc.

10–38. **(a)** 12 in., $7333; **(b)** 3700 hr **10–39.** 5770 units **10–40.** 1714 hr

10–41. $42,810 **10–42.** 59.7%

10–43. 5488 miles (using straight-line depreciation and average interest)

10–44. 34 **10–45.** $2.07 **10–46.** 10% **10–47.** Work overtime; 50%

10–48. Build plant, $131,830

10–49. Rent (if own $10,000 used and interest lost) **10–50.** $35,750

10–51. $8000 cash **10–52.** $2806 **10–53.** 1 in. better, $218

10–54. B—annual cost = $835,100

10–55. Savings—highway, $25,360; railroad, $40,000. Highway offer is low, railroad about right.

10–56. $1745 **10–57.** $34,341

10–58. Build four-lane, now cost = $315,140

10–59. Land and construction costs, labor costs and supply, shipping and storage facilities, funds available, interest rate, etc.

10–61. $31,439 **10–62.** $1,831,875 **10–63.** Approximately 6.5%

10–64. $16,395 **10–65.** **(a)** $A = \$128, B = \$137$; **(b)** $A = \$124, B = \$135$

10–66. Every 4 years **10–67.** $2,902

10–68. **(a)** $\sqrt{K_1/K_D}$, **(b)** $2\sqrt{K_1K_D} + C_3$

10–69. 21.6% **10–70.** **(a)** 42% per year, **(b)** 51.5% per year

10–71. 18.5 years **10–72.** $3,429 **10–73.** 7.1% to 12.6%

10–74. No. Interest counted 3 times in (1), (2), and (4). Capital repayment counted 3 times in (2), (3), and (4). Annual cost found by (1) + (3) + (5) if salvage value is zero or by (4) + (5) if debt ratio is 100% and salvage value is zero

10–75. Plan A, $4,938 **10–76.** 16.2 or 17 days **10–77.** D, $2,128 per year

10–78. $897 **10–79.** $5,800,000 **10–80.** Lease, $272,760

CHAPTER 11

NOTE: Other useful references for the questions in this chapter include: (a) The Manual of Professional Practice in particular states, i.e., for example, The Manual of the Texas Society of Professional Engineers, entitled "The

Manual of Professional Practice, General Engineering Services." (b) Technical Society Manuals, for example, American Society of Civil Engineers Manual No. 38, "Private Practice of Civil Engineering—For Use of Engineers and Clients."

11–1. Yes. Ethical and legal integrity constitute honesty, courtesy, etc.

11–2. **(a)** State Registration Board, **(b)** pertinent technical society

11–3. Probably not

11–4. Complete; clear and definite; specify results desired, not method; give tolerances permitted; make plans part of specifications; divide into General Conditions and Technical Specifications; define authority of engineer; define responsibility of contractor; state provisions for changes, extra work; specify beginning and completion times; etc.

11–5. The question apparently means "specify one particular material or product." On this assumption, answers are: if one item is best for the job, or if no other suitable material or product is available.

11–6. Colleague (Cannons Sec. 13)

11–7. Lump sum, per cent of cost, cost plus a fixed fee, daily fee as suggested by professional societies

11–8. **(a)** Possibly, but not without permission of the client, **(b)** not without permission of the client

11–9. Yes

11–10. The requirement of one state: "Every holder of a license shall display it in a conspicuous place in his principal office, place of business or employment"

11–11. Should be reported to the professional society, or if serious, to the state board. (Answer assumes the question meant "What should you do about it?")

11–12. Not ethical, even though he may assume less work will be required because of confidence in fabricator (Cannons Sec. 17)

11–13. Refuse to compete on basis of fee (Cannons Sec. 26) and inform client of the requirements of ethical practice

11–14. **(a)** Unethical (Cannons Sec. 25). **(b)** The question itself presumes unethical practice is in operation. After engineers have submitted brochures and offered their services, "negotiations" for scope of the work and fee are carried on with *only one* engineer selected on the basis of his qualifications. Aside from this point, if the other engineers had offered their services without special invitation, and the "negotiation" process has not yet been reached, Engineer A could offer his services also.

11–15. "—present clearly the consequences to be expected from deviations—" (Cannons Sec. 12)

11–16. **(a)** Should not be taken on contingency basis, **(b)** not ethical—all engineers should protest

11–17. **(a)** For a contractor, reasonable if the certain product is just as good and the owner who has approved the original design is informed and agreeable. For a design engineer, since the owner does not profit, the engineer must presumably. This leads to a conclusion of unethical practice on the engineer's part, and probably the supplier also. **(b)** Not unreasonable on the basis of greater responsibility

11–18. **(a)** Unethical, **(b)** same, unless D is informed of the situation or has been completely discharged

11–19. Refuse, unless you honestly believe the equipment best fits the job, and inform your client of the arrangement (Cannons Sec. 15, 16)

11–20. **(a)** Not required to be registered as a professional engineer in many states but may need a contractor's license to collect. Use of term "engineer" was misleading and may bar recovery. **(b)** Can check the work and cost to determine whether they are satisfactory

11–21. **(a)** Unethical; **(b)** may be permissible if his judgment is not swayed by gratuity and he determines they best meet the requirements; **(c)** may be done if he tells client and can justify the use to competent unbiased engineers (Cannons Sec. 10)

11–22. **(a)** That he has satisfied legal requirements set up for the protection of the public as to his qualifications to do engineering work; **(b)** no, unless the original engineer has been fully discharged from the job

11–23. **(a)** Written contract should govern. He can, however, require first engineer to do entire job and since the work was not finished, the contract is breached. **(b)** First engineer is obligated to finish the job he started, unless the owner approves a change. The owner contracted with him

11–24. **(a)** Tell both companies of the situation and prorate expenses; **(b)** no; **(c)** return expense money to first company

11–25. Inform consulting engineers and employer and ask for a review and changes

11–26. **(a)** Unfair to contractor; **(b)** "All work must be done in accordance with the best local practice as demonstrated on specified projects X, Y, etc., to fulfill the requirements of the owner"

11–27. **(a)** "Legally right" means within the law, "legally wrong" is contrary to the law. The spirit of the law may be violated, yet no legal liability result; **(b)** an act may be ethically wrong, yet within the law. Examples: stealing is wrong, legally and ethically. Specifying a brand item on a non-Government contract may be legally all right but ethically wrong.

11–28. Competent parties, legal subject matter, sufficient consideration, mutual agreement between the parties; (b) a voidable contract permits one of the parties to reject or affirm the agreement. A contract is void (actually not a contract) if one of the essentials is missing.

11–29. Must be filed to protect pubiic, client, and engineer

11–30. **(a)** A true "mechanics lien" is attached by common law only to personal property. As customarily applied, however, it is the priority right of one person in the property of another, which has been given him by law because of his contribution in services or materials to the property. It is imposed by law, rather than by an agreement between the parties. **(b)** Part of the work done, such as supervising construction, and "labor", may be considered as "work" performed on the structure, within the mechanics lien statute. Drawing plans and specifications, and work not performed on the premises, are excluded.

11–31. He has the right as a professional employee to a separate vote apart from production and other employees, to determine the wishes of the professional personnel with regard to representation for collective bargaining.

11–32. Partnerships acceptable in most or all states but requirements vary as to whether only one or all partners must be registered. Practice by corporations permitted in some states if top officers are registered (some on basis of grandfather clause), denied in others

11–33. **(a)** A promise to pay if a certain thing is not done; a "surety" bond is designed to protect the owner against liability and loss caused by acts or failures of the contractor; **(b)** bond (or certified check) to protect owner in case successful bidder refuses to sign contract; **(c)** the compensation to an employee for injury or occupational disease suffered in connection with his employment, paid under a government supervised insurance system contributed to by employers; **(d)** insurance carried by contractor to protect contractor, subcontractors, and owner from claims for personal injury, death, and property damage arising from operations under the contract; **(e)** a provision for increasing the price of services, materials, etc., if costs rise. For example, wages may be increased if the cost-of-living index rises, resulting in higher contract unit prices.

11–36. See Engineers Council for Professional Development Canons of Ethics

11–37. Yes, if he does not use municipal equipment or facilities (without agreement and reasonable rental) and does not use his salaried position to compete unfairly in any way with other professional engineers.

11–38. Survey records are public records so his knowledge does not prevent a municipal engineer from making property surveys if he does not undercut prices or receive special favors in recording.

11–39. Engineering educators and their students do benefit by a *reasonable* amount of private consulting work if university facilities, and time for class preparation and student conferences, are not abused.

11–40. Yes, if in so doing normal consulting or engineering services are not affected. This is part of the duties of citizenship.

11–41. See ECPD Canons Section 2

11–42. Individual liability is difficult to fix in the event of an infraction of the law or engineering canons of ethics. Also, there is a major question as to which officers (or all) must be registered professional engineers.

11–43. **(a)** No, **(b)** yes, **(c)** yes—zero. Only ordinary courtesies such as a cigar, cigarette, etc. should be offered or accepted.

11–44. Any violation of the licensing law provisions

11–45. If the person is duly registered in another state a reciprocity agreement can be arranged for a limited period of time, say 30-60 days. In case the work extends over a longer period the engineer should obtain a license in the state where the work is being done.

11–46. The non-engineer violates the law if his work is offered for practical use and paid for, thus, the registered engineer who certifies such work compounds the violation. If a registered engineer carefully checks each step of the work, is suitably paid, and accepts liability for the design and specifications, he is only following normal practice in a large office.

11–47. **(a)** No—this is contrary to the ECPD Canon of Ethics; **(b)** no—all work is supposed to be correct and the engineer is legally responsible for his work; **(c)** no—but the contractor might hire the inspector for his own organization.

11–48. **(a)** Specifications. Lawyers like words. **(b)** No, **(c)** yes (usually in contracts a legal address for notices is given)

11–49. **(a)** Yes—plans are the property of the owner unless paid for or covered by a statement in the contract. **(b)** Yes, except for the usual exclusion of an Act of God, and perhaps a strike

11–50. **(a)** **(b)** A municipal franchise usually requires poles inside the R-W limits to be moved by the utility without cost to the municipality. If one ft outside the R-W and the municipality acquires additional R-W, negotiation is used. **(c)** For new state highway R-W, estimate of cost to move utilities is requested, checked, approved, and a purchase order issued to the utility for the work. **(d)** Contractors get authority from the highway department and are not involved unless they go beyond the job requirements.

CHAPTER 12

12–6. **(a)** $\varepsilon^\circ = 2.03^\circ$, $C_{D_1} = 0.0284$, $D_i = 87.2$ lb

12–7. $\alpha = 8.3^\circ$. $C_D = 0.109$ 12–8. **(a)** $D_i = 73$ lb, **(b)** hp $= 16.6$

12–9. The elliptical planform wing, based on downwash theory

12–10. **(a)** Integrating the second equation gives:

$$u = \frac{1}{r_2^2 - r_1^2}\left[r(\omega_2 r_2^2 - \omega_1 r_1^2) - \frac{r_1^2 r_2^2}{r}(\omega_2 - \omega_1)\right]$$

(b) Using the Newton friction law gives:

$$M_2 = 4\pi\mu h\left(\frac{r_1^2 r_2^2}{r_2^2 - r_1^2}\omega_2\right)$$

12–11. Using the boundary condition $w = 0$ at $R = y$ (where R is the maximum radius of the pipe), two integrations of the Navier-Stokes equation yields:

$$u = -\frac{1}{4\mu}\frac{dp}{dx}\left(R^2 - y^2\right)$$

12–12. Reynolds number $= \dfrac{\rho u(\partial u/\partial x)}{\mu(\partial u/\partial y)^2} = \dfrac{\rho V d}{\mu}$

12–13. This is the analogy between skin friction and heat transfer. It states that of the whole work of friction 50% goes into heating.

12–14. Heating is proportional to the square root of the stagnation velocity gradient. By making the shape of the nose flat, one can reduce heating.

12–15. For two-dimensional flow, $1>n>\frac{2}{3}$; for axially symmetric flow, $1>n>\frac{1}{2}$

12–16. $C_L = \frac{2}{3}$

12–17. $\gamma = 1.2, \frac{\rho_2}{\rho_1} = 10; \gamma = 1, \frac{\rho_2}{\rho_1} = 100$

$$M = \infty \; (\gamma = 1.2) \; \frac{\rho_2}{\rho_1} = 1; \; (\gamma = 1) \; \frac{\rho_2}{\rho_1} = \infty$$

12–18. $\theta = 60°, C_D = \frac{3}{4}$

12–19. 1.98 lb, 0.497 lb/in.

12–20. (1) Chemical reaction rate (should be rapid), (2) heat of combustion (should be large), (3) density of propellant (large), (4) vapor pressure (should be small), (5) chemical stability (stable), (6) rapid ignition, (7) low freezing point, (8) low viscosity, (9) high specific heat, and (10) low corrosion

12–21. $A = 5.9$ sq in., 1.35, 4760 fps

12–22. **(a)** 93,200 lb, **(b)** 5360 fps

12–23. $\delta = \frac{Pb^2}{EIL^2}\int_0^a x^2 dx + \frac{Pa^2}{EIL^2}\int_0^b x_1^2 dx \quad$ or $\quad \delta = \frac{Pa^2b^2}{3EIL}$

12–24. Roots are $-$ 1.48 $\pm$ 6.01 $\quad \tau = 2.0$
Period is 2.1 sec. Damping is good since oscillation is damped to half-amplitude in 0.45 cycles.

12–25. (1) I. Newton—laws of motion, (2) O. Reynolds—Reynolds number, (3) T. von Karman—theories in supersonic flow, transonic flow, subsonic flow, (4) L. Prandtl—concept of boundary layer, (5) Helmholtz—vortex flows, and (6) G. G. Stokes—viscous flow theory

CHAPTER 13

13–10. 0.128 vol %

13–11. **(a)** 500°F, $H_c = -121{,}538$ Btu/lb-mole
(b) 1000°F, $H_c = -121{,}434$ Btu/lb-mole
(c) 2000°F, $H_c = -120{,}425$ Btu/lb-mole

13–12.

	(cycle) Btu	(a) Btu	(b) Btu	(c) Btu	(d) Btu
Q	+750	+1850	−980	+1000	−1120
W	+750	+1348	−278	0	−320
ΔE	0	+502	−702	+1000	−800
ΔH	0	+804	−980	+1396	−1120

13–13. Assume 25°C as standard temperature for H^0 and S^0, $K = 32.4 \times 10^9$

13–14. Answers are based on the following assumptions: 8-hr pumping time; design liquid velocity, 6 fps; pumping head equals lost work. **(a)** 2 in., **(b)** 21.7 psi

13–15. Hydrogen = 11.3 wt%, carbon = 83.5 wt%, sulfur = 5.2 wt%

13–16. **(a)** 21.2 fps, **(b)** 5.3 fps, **(c)** 207.5 gpm

13–17.

Composition	Moles	Mole %
CO_2	35.50	16.47
O_2	6.55	3.04
N_2	173.50	80.49
Total	215.55	100.00

13–18. **(a)** 16.50 in., **(b)** 2.25 in.

13–19. **(a)** 1895 Btu/hr sq ft before insulation, 394 Btu/hr sq ft after insulation, **(b)** junction firebrick and red brick = 1277°F, junction red brick and magnesia = 1203°F

13–20. 10.65 hr based on the following assumptions: no boiling point elevation, no liquid head, feed enters at 70°F, specific heat of feed is 1.0 Btu/lb °F

13–21. 84 wt%

13–22.

Purchased Concentration	Final Concentration (10%)	Cost, Dollars/Lb (54%)
50%	0.0054	——
73%	0.00592	0.01909
100%	0.00306	0.0235

13–23. **(a)** 60 lb, **(b)** 25%

13–24. 53.7 moles

13–25. **(a)** Air entering = 0.0305 lb H_2O/lb bone-dry air, air leaving = 0.0483 lb H_2O/lb bone-dry air, **(b)** 76.3 lb H_2O/day, **(c)** 9.08 tons/day

13–26. 19.25 hr based on the following assumptions: falling rate portion of curve is linear, and no change in volume of cake during drying

13–27. N_{tog} (both cases) $= \dfrac{\ln\left(\dfrac{0.8\,mG}{L} + 0.2\right)}{1 - \dfrac{mG}{L}}$ G = gas rate, L = liquid rate, $m = y^*/x$, Z = tower height

HTU (both cases) $= \dfrac{Z}{N_{tog}}$

13–28. **(a)** 0.376 moles/mole, **(b)** 0.624 moles/mole, **(c)** 4.0 trays, **(d)** 0.242 moles/mole

13–29. **(a)** $K_c = T_1/4R_1T_2$ for $\zeta = 1$ critically damped, **(b)** $1/K_c$

13–30. **(a)** 352 ft^2, **(b)** 222 ft^2, **(c)** 230 ft^2, **(d)** 242 ft^2

13–31. 31.1 hr **13–32.** **(a)** $\tau = 50.0$ sec

13–33. (a) Product = 570 mols/day, bottoms = 680 mols/day; **(b)** $(L/D)_{min}$ = 1.86, (c, 1) 8.5, (c, 2) 6th plate from top of column, (c-3) 7th plate from top of column

13–34. **(a)** 0.4 ft^3, **(b)** 2.0 ft^3, **(c)** 2.4 ft^3 **13–35.** Tubular reactor

13–36. 73.32 Btu/lb water **13–37.** 9.9(10^5) lb/hr

13–38. **(a)** ID = 3.54 in. **13–39.** **(a)** 1,894 gal, **(b)** 4.3

13–40. 358°K, 358°K (dew point = bubble point within slide rule accuracy only by coincidence of the composition).

CHAPTER 14

14–7. **(a)** 6.41 sacks/yd, **(b)** 5.12 gal/sack, **(c)** 3.98% **14–8.** 35.2 cu ft

14–9. Cement 15.1, sand 33.2, stone 49.8, water 11.6 cu ft

14–10. 1.52 lb, 151 pcf

14–11. **(a)** 2.205, **(b)** 2.320, **(c)** 4.96%, **(d)** yes, **(e)** 149.5 lb

14–12. **(a)** 2.46, **(b)** 5.70%, **(c)** 96.5%

14–13. **(a)** 9,888 gal @ 60 F, **(b)** flash point, viscosity, distillation, penetration, ductility, solubility of residue, per cent residue from distillation

14–14. **(a)** 2.41, 3.7%; **(b)** 2.32

14–15. **(a)** 73.2%, **(b)** 43%, **(c)** no—aggregate voids too high and per cent of voids filled too low (mix most likely unstable)

14–16. For 20 years service, 1 in. asphalt concrete surfacing, 5 in. asphalt base (or other combinations)

14–17. **(a)** B = 20.2% and A = 79.8% to B = 62.5% and A = 37.5%, **(b)** B = 47.4% and A = 52.6%

14–18. 212 lb sand, 386 lb gravel, 41.9 lb water

14–19. Heating water and/or aggregates, placing as stiff a mix as soon as possible, protection to retain heat, avoiding early removal of forms

14–20. Acts as a filler, combining with asphalt to coat and bind larger aggregate

14–21. **(a)** A dispersing agent, **(b)** initial tension applied to flexural steel which, upon release, places all or nearly all of cross section in compression, **(c)** powdered material added to improve workability

14–22. Increased resistance to freezing and thawing; reduction of strength at high air contents

14–23. **(a)** Shows gradation of aggregate, **(b)** test for organic matter, **(c)** measures consistency, **(d)** measures compressive strength

14–24. **(a)** Membrane curing, ponding, tarp, paper or sand covering and kept damp; **(b)** no, possible re-starting resistance; **(c)** consolidates concrete better, lower w/c rates possible, but overvibration must be avoided; **(d)** sheepsfoot roller, rubber tired roller, vibration from crawler-tractor; **(e)** 14 days, 2-3 days, 14-21 days, 14-21 days

14–25. **(a)** True, **(b)** questionable, **(c)** partially true, **(d)** false, **(e)** partially true

14–26. **(a)** Steel bars across longitudinal joints; **(b)** #4 or #5, 30 in. maximum spacing; **(c)** volume is too inaccurate

14–27. **(a)** Use of a tremie with valve, richer mix, 6-7 in. slump, continuous pour; **(b)** high air pressure to balance water pressures, equipped with air lock for entrance and exit of men and materials; **(c)** driving head or cap, wood or rope cushion, strike head squarely; **(d)** drop hammer—simple and very slow; double-acting steam hammer—fast, light hammer; single-acting steam hammer—simple, low velocity heavy blow

14–28. **(a)** Chipping and flaking of surface; **(b)** failure or loss of subgrade support usually due to water; **(c)** irregular surface cracking

14–29. **(a)** Successive layers of smaller angular stones, consolidated and keyed by rolling, then sprayed with a bituminous binder. Final application of chips rolled to lock them in place. **(b)** Clean and tough aggregate with strong interlock between particles plus a firm, well-drained base, and proper binder. **(c)** Freezing and thawing, failure of base or subgrade, abrasion by traffic

14–31. 257.5 lb sand, 307.5 lb gravel, 50.8 lb water

14–32. **(a)** T, **(b)** F, **(c)** T, **(d)** T, **(e)** F **14–33.** 350

14–34. **(a)** \$64,700; **(b)** 564 lb cement, 907 lb F.A., 2070 lb C.A., 325 lb water, 1.08 cu ft air

14–35. 4.31 cu ft; 590 lb cement, 1255 lb F.A., 1950 lb C.A., 267 lb water

14–36. 481 lb cement, 1790 lb F.A., 1535 lb C.A., 255 lb water

14–37. 20.8 lb cement, 47.7 lb F.A., 65.4 lb C.A., 11.1 lb water

14–38. PCA method, dry aggregate: absolute volume in cu ft, cement 0.477, F.A. 1.09, C.A. 2.40, water 0.70, 6% air 0.28

14–39. **(a)** 31% A, 69% B; **(b)** material C

14–40. **(a)** Allow for expansion (30 to over 1000 ft) and contraction (12 to 30 ft), prevent relative vertical movement of slabs; **(b)** keep adjacent edges at same elevation; **(c)** 9-in. slab; **(d)** prevent widening of cracks, A = 0.0338 sq in./ft; **(e)** not necessary for concrete pavement.

14–45. 0.00 **14–46.** 0.95 cu ft **14–47.** 2.57 ft, 544 tons

14–48. **(a)** Fx = 13,000 lb at 6.96 ft above base; Fy = 16,100 lb at 7.63 ft left of toe; F.S. = 1.36; **(b)** F.S. = 0.556 (unsafe).

14–49. 5730 lb **14–50.** **(a)** 9900 lb, **(b)** 24,000 lb **14–51.** 0.0212

14–52. 238 hp, c = 120 **14–53.** 3.5 ft/hr

14–54. 19.2 sec **14–55.** Yes

14–56. **(a)** $Q = 0.281\ Cd^{2.63}s^{0.54}$; **(b)** 334 ft, 490 gpm, 53 hp

14–57. −3.56 psi (f = 0.019)

14–58. *A*, 1.24 cfs clockwise; *B*, 4.24 cfs clockwise; *C*, 1.77 cfs counterclockwise; *D*, 2.77 cfs counterclockwise

14–59. #1, 11.4%; #2, 23.8%; #3, 64.8%

14–60. 5370 cfs (n = 0.0225)

14–61. **(a)** 0.9 ft depth × 1.8 ft width, **(b)** 0.64 ft **14–62.** 21 in.

14–63. 96.6 ft/mile (n = 0.0225), 7.98 ft depth × 3.68 ft width

14–64. 79.5 cfs, 60 in. **14–65.** 5.32 ft

14–66. 3.88 ft, 1.78 $\frac{\text{ft - lb}}{\text{lb}}$

14–67. 14,250 gpm **14–68.** \$5.00 **14–69.** 34.6 hp **14–70.** 540 gpm

14–71. 74.6 cfs

14–72. **(a)** 2.91 ft; **(b)** 221 cfs; **(c)** 123.2; **(d)** 0.0135; **(e)** 2.46 ft/sec; **(f)** 2.80 ft/sec, 220 cfs; **(g)** 1.80 cfs

14–73. 3.51 hp **14–74.** 8.86 ft **14–75.** 700 kw

14–76. **(a)** 50 hp, **(b)** 64,000 gpm, **(c)** 48,000 gpm

14–77. **(a)** 564 gpm, 77.9 ft, 13.1 hp; **(b)** 622 gpm, 94.9 ft, 17.6; **(c)** 2220 rpm

14–78. 226 lb **14–79.** 8.60 ft

14–80. **(a)** 1.3 ft, **(b)** 1.8 ft **14–85.** 35.8 cfs

14–86. 12.3 mgd **14–87.** Mean 3.1, Standard deviation 5.3

14–88. 9300 cfs (Fanning); 15,000 cfs (Myers, p= 15); A 24-hr flood of 10,400 cfs will occur, on the average, 50 times in each 100-year period.

14–89. 2000 cfs

14–90. **(a)** **(b)** Wells are developed to remove fine sand from the vicinity of the screen and to determine the hydraulic characteristics of the aquifer and well so that the proper permanent pumping equipment may be selected. A temporary turbine pump without a foot valve may be installed along with facilities to measure rate of pumping and drawdown. The pump is then started and stopped until the fine sand is removed and then is operated continuously for a specified period of time. Rate of pumping and drawdown are recorded and specific capacity of well and proper pumping equipment are determined.

14–91. **(a)** 3830 sq ft, **(b)** 9 filters, **(c)** 5.73, **(d)** 67.6 lb/24 hr

14–92. 125,000 gal **14–93.** $1,138,000

14–94. 30 ppm; 7-6000 lb/day, 4-2000 lb/day, 2-400 lb/day

14–95. 1.45 lb/mg

14–96. $Al_2(SO_4)_3 \cdot 18\ H_2O + 3\ Ca(HCO_3)_2 \rightarrow 2\ Al(OH)_3 + 3\ CaSO_4 + 18\ H_2O + 6\ CO_2$, 270 parts of alkalinity as $CaCO_3$

14–97. 532 lb/day, 9.62 ppm, 158 lb/day

14–98. 1.8 hr: 7.75×10^{-3} fps, 250 lb/day

14–99. **(a)** 0.1635 in.; **(b)** 0.306 in.: **(c)** yes, stresses are opposite

14–100. New line, $82,830; pump station, $47,160

14–101. **(a)** 53.3 ft; **(b)** 896 gal/sq ft/day; **(c)** 11,950 gal/lineal ft/day; for (b)—no, (c)—no; no, Water Supply and Sewerage—Steel; for (b)—no, (c)—yes, Water Supply and Sewerage—Steel

14–102. Essentially an Imhoff tank combines sedimentation and sludge digestion with each taking place in a separate compartment. The tank is arranged so that gases formed during digestion do not interfere with sedimentation. Imhoff tanks are generally recommended for primary treatment of sewage from small towns employing the trickling filter process, but are not generally recommended for primary treatment preceding the activated sludge process.

14–103. 1,265,000 Btu/hr

14–104. 176 ft in diameter; two filters, 100 ft in diameter by 9.33 ft deep

14–105. **(a)** 2 filters, **(b)** 1 filter

14–106. Line

1 Openings between bars in the bar screens shall be 1
2 in. or greater and the total clear space between the bars shall be designed to
3 not less than 8 *to* not greater than 3
5 2 cu ft *to* 4 cu ft
6 in solid form *to* in solution
7 no mixing shall be permitted *to* Flocculation shall be provided
8 after the rapid mixing of
9 2 to 3 hr *to* 10 to 30 min
11 no opening such as entries or *to* provisions for complete draining of tanks

12 *to* Emergency power sources for
13 control *to* operation
14 *to* Where trickling filters are used
16 2 *to* 3 and No *to* The
17 *to* is 10 ft. Sizes between 2½ to 3½ in. should
18 Adequate protection *to* Facilities
19 against *to* for
20 *to* Primary treatment shall not be bypassed and
21 filter *to* chemical
24 6 *to* 18
25 *to* sand with an effective size between 0.20 and 0.50 mm. All
26 *to* underdrains shall be surrounded by crushed stone or gravel and laid with joints about ⅜ in. apart
27 *to* The underdrains shall be laid on a grade of 0.5% or greater
28 *to* and the maximum distance between lines shall be 30 ft
29 *to* Detention periods in the flow-through chamber of Imhoff tanks shall be not less
30 1 *to* 2

14–107. 63.7 cu ft, 62.8 lb/cu ft, 15.2 cu ft

14–108. 4.0 acre-ft, 1.00 acre, 4.0 ft

14–109. 100,000 to 130,000 cu ft, 115,000 cu ft used, 2 circular digestors—60 ft in diameter and 20 ft deep

14–110. Based on 80 gpcd, 0.0 BOD, and 100% oxygen saturation of stream before entrance of sewage, plain sedimentation is sufficient treatment. DO_c —6.5 ppm, t_c —1.24 days, $f = 2.88$

14–111. 27 in. sewer for 5-year storm

14–112. **(a)** 83 cfs; **(b)** 130 cfs; **(c)** 5.28 ft/sec

14–113. **(a)** At center, **(b)** 0.92 full depth, **(c)** 0.82 full depth, **(d)** 0.82 full depth, **(e)** minimum grade is that slope which will give a velocity of flow of 2 fps when flowing full. This is the velocity which should prevent the sedimentation of solids in the sewer.

14–114. **(a)** R.C. pipe, 200% concrete cradle; **(b)** 9450 lb

14–115.

Station	0+00	0+50	1+00	1+50	2+00
Cut	5.2 ft	5.5 ft	4.8 ft	4.5 ft	5.5 ft

14–116. Install, in parallel, a new 36-in. line on slope of 0.0035 from manhole *2* to stream

14–117. **A** bathing, **B** ferric chloride, **C** sewer line being cleaned of stoppage, **D** root troubles in sewer, **E** testing for presence of oxygen after it is known that no explosive gas is present

14–118. 32,400 persons

14–119. **(a)** Superchlorination followed by coagulation and sedimentation. Sufficient reduction in BOD so that BOD of mixed waste entering plant does not exceed 400 ppm. **(b)** Biological filtration of waste. Sufficient reduction in BOD so that BOD of mixed waste entering plant does not exceed 400 ppm. **(c)** No copper bearing wastes shall be discharged to sewer.

14–120. **(a)** Public Health Engineering is the application of the principles of engineering to the field of public health. **(b)** Bovine tuberculosis—tests and slaughter of positive cows. Brucellosis—eradication plans recommended by Bureau of Animal Industry. **(c)** Vector mosquitoes reduced by drainage and efficient larvicides, medical agents to reduce the parasites in human population, educational campaigns, keep infected vector population, and parasitic infections in humans so low that there will be an interruption in transmission. **(d)** Controlled by preventive measures against the rat and flea. Means of rodent control include trapping, poisoning, fumigation, ratproofing, and elimination of harborages. Ectoparasite control by application of DDT dust to runways and burrows is practical. **(e)** Flea, while feeding, takes blood from host animal and the plague organism within the flea mixes with this blood. Flea then regurgitates the mixture back into host animal. **(f)** Diatoma—taste and odors. Crenothrix—red water. Synura—tastes and odors. **(g)** Bacilli, Cocci, Spirilla. **(h)** Obtain case history of each typhoid case, preparation of spot map showing where cases occurred and time of occurrence. If no points of contact are found, check water plant and plant records. **(i)** Incineration—high construction and operation costs. Sanitary landfill—cheap and simple, may deteriorate into a dump unless properly operated. Sufficient land at a reasonable cost must be available. **(j)** The grams of H^+ ions per liter of solution. **(k)** **(1)** 2.891 cases per 1000 population, **(2)** 0.652 deaths per 1000 population, **(3)** 45%.

14–127. **(a)** Flow curve, **(b)** shrinkage ratio, **(c)** void ratio, **(d)** moisture content, **(e)** shear strength, **(f)** coefficient of volumetric compressibility, **(g)** neutral stress or pore pressure, **(h)** coefficient of compressibility.

14–128. **(a)** Shattering or breaking, **(b)** transfers loads into a soil or to a soil of adequate bearing capacity (partial answers)

14–129. **(a)** Shear strength, PI, limits, cohesion, grain size analysis; **(b)** changes in moisture content or by stabilization; **(c)** loss of support or failure of base material often near slab corners leading to pavement failure.

14–130. 780 psf, $\theta = 25°$

14–131. With five flow paths and 13 spaces, $Q_t = 965$ cu ft/hr

14–132. 65.2%, 2.24, 78.7%

14–133. 106 pcf, 13.8% and 120.5 pcf, 130.5 pcf, 1.15%

14–134. 162.4 lb/lineal ft of bulkhead **14–136.** $P = 3980$ lb/ft of wall

14–137. $P = 4095$ lb/ft of wall **14–139.** No

14–144. Replace frost susceptible soil, lower water table, or prevent rise of capillary water in soil subgrade by other means.

14–145. 10.1% and 1.81 g/cc, 0.622 and 43%

14–146. (1) CL, (2) SM, (3) SC, (4) CH, (5) SC-ML or SC-OL **14–147.** 11.4 ft

14–148. 0.5 ft **14–149.** 128-129 pcf at 13%

14–150. 14 in. to top of pavement

14–151. **(a)** 86,000 by ENR, **(b)** 3.7 by Stren **14–152.** 25 sq ft, 100 sq ft

14–153. 16%, 0.614. **14–154.** No, maximum load is 14.5 tons

14–156. **(a)** $P_{30} = 944$ psf

14–157. Depth = least dimension of building, uniformity of strata, density, water table, shear strength, consolidation.

14–177. **(a)** 7 in. and 13 in., **(b)** six ⅞-in. rivets (partial answer)

14–178. $14\frac{3}{4}$-in. along back of outstanding leg, 8 in. end weld, 30 in. total length required

14–179. Using $1\frac{1}{2}$-in. plates, fourteen $1\frac{1}{8}$-in. rivets required on each side

14–180. Using ACI creep method, $P = 470^k$

14–181. Two 15-in. 33.9 lb channels (partial answer) **14–182.** 329^k

14–183. 12WF106, possibly 12WF99 **14–184.** Column OK

14–185. $\#7 = -18^k$, $\#8 = +18^k$, $\#9 = +18^k$, $\#10 = -42^k$

14–186. $CD = 240^k$, $DE = 1440^k$, $cD = 1560^k$, all tension

14–187. $b\text{-}1 = -12{,}350$ lb, $2\text{-}3 = +7700$ lb, $4\text{-}5 = 0$

14–188. $C_h = 22.86^k$, $M_b = 685'^k$

14–189. $AB = +42{,}500$ lb, $BD = -40{,}000$ lb, $DC = -50{,}000$ lb, $BC = +36{,}000$ lb

14–190. Horizontal = 3.84 in., vertical = 15.15 in.

14–191. Max. mom. = $115.2'^k$, max. shear = 2660 psi, max. axial = 645 psi

14–192. Typical footing: 9′ 8″ sq, $d = 17$ in., $A_s = 24\text{-}\#6$ each way

14–193. $A_s = 17\text{-}\#11$ each way, $v = 67$ psi (partial answer)

14–194. 20^k wheel located 1.33 ft to right of beam center, **(a)** $M = 169'^k$, **(b)** $V = 6.58^k$, **(c)** $V_{max} = 28.56^k$ at reaction with 20^k load located there

14–195. $M_P = 160$

14–196. Typical section 12WF144 with 12-in., 30.9 lb channel

14–197. 1 in. × 12 in. cover plates

14–198. $a = -60$ kip, $b = 38.8$ kip, $c = 80$ kip

14–199. $A_h = 29.8$, $A_v = 15.1$, $C_h = 50.2$, $C_v = 34.9$ kip

14–200. **(a)** 31,000 psi, **(b)** 21.3^k

14–201. 40 ft-kip, 18 kip, 23.33 kip, —1.33 kip

14–202. **(a)** 2000 lb/ft LL, **(b)** 21.6 ft from ends

14–203. $\frac{12}{3} M_a + \frac{6}{3} M_b = 0$, $\frac{6}{3} M_a + \frac{22}{3} M_b + \frac{5}{3} M_c = 1500$, $\frac{5}{3} M_b + \frac{10}{3} M_c = 1500$

14–204. 64,500 in.-lb, governed by steel

14–205. **(a)** 102,500 ft-lb, **(b)** $v = 76$ psi

14–206. 5.08 in. **14–207.** 2370 lb/ft **14–208.** $d = 25$ in., $As = 2.31$ sq in.

14–209. 127 kip **14–210.** 8980 lb, concrete governs

14–211. 42.5 psf **14–212.** Wood = 1540 psi at the top, steel = 19,080 psi

14–213. $\theta_C = wL^3/48EI$, $\Delta_B = wL^4/128EI$, $\Delta_C = 7wL^4/384EI$

14–214. I/C uncut section = 541 cu in., I/C cut section using flange only (no web) = 697 cu in.

14–215. $\Delta A = 0.52$ in. (partial answer)

14–216. $\Delta_C = 0.36$ in., $\Delta_D = 0.06$ in.

14–217. I/C original beam = 100 cu in., I/C new beam = 604 cu in.

14–218. $d = 4.9$ in., 3.32 in. c-c (theoretical dimensions)

14–219. $b = 13$ in., $d = 19$ in., $A_s = 3\text{-}\#10$ bars

14–220. **(a)** 3.92 in. × 7.84 in., **(b)** $v = 80.6$ psi over reaction

14–221. 27WF94

14–222. v_{max} = 952 psi, v_{max} allowable with web reinforce = 360 psi (ACI)

14–223. **(a)** k = 0.327, j = 0.892, M = 1060'^{k} due to steel, **(b)** bond = 214 psi

14–224. M_{max} = 154 ft-kip under load, V_{max} = 26 kip at left reaction

14–225. M_{max} = 137.5 ft-kip under load, −25 ft-kip over right reaction

14–226. M = −1600 ft-kip at C, +700 ft-kip *between* E and F.

14–230. M = 1490 ft-kip under wheel #3, 84%.

CHAPTER 15

15–5. 49.5 units **15–6.** **(a)** Leave, **(b)** 0.747 amp **15–7.** $5.76

15–9. **(a)** 4.08 amp, **(b)** 2.50 amp

15–10. **(a)** 1000 ohms, 0.01 h, 100 $\mu\mu$f; **(b)** 0.173 ω_r

15–11. **(a)** 1.12 megacycles, **(b)** 140 volts, **(c)** 1.38 watts

15–12. **(a)** 4610 ohms, **(b)** unity

15–13. **(a)** A series combination of resistance and capacitance, R_3 and C_3, respectively; **(b)** $R_x = \dfrac{R_1R_2}{R_3}$, $L_x = R_1R_2C_3$

15–14. 351 volts **15–15.** 16.6 amp, 2340 watt, 0.81

15–16. 1022 kva, less line current means better efficiency and smaller equipment

15–17. 45.0 amp **15–18.** 10.6 kw, 39.4 kw

15–19. P_a = 1840 watts, P_b = 6290 watts **15–20** **(a)** 20 amp, **(b)** 10 amp

15–21. **(a)** 200 volts, a negative with respect to b; **(b)** there will be a very high voltage developed between a and b, a negative with respect to b

15–22. 16.8 ohms in each series arm, 98.8 ohms in the shunt arm

15–23. **(a)** 0.5 h in each series arm, 4 μf in the shunt arm; **(b)** 22.9 db

15–24. **(a)** 796 cps, **(b)** 995 cps, **(c)** 14.9 db

15–25. 0.0866 h, 0.137 μf **15–30.** 12.5 volts, rms; 270 volts

15–26. $I(t) = 1.65 \times 10^4 \sin \omega t - 1.31 \times 10^{-2} \cos \omega t + e^{-12.2t}$ $(7.25 \times 10^3 \cos \omega t + 6.46 \sin 3\,\omega t)$

15–27. $L_1 = 1h$, $L_2 = 3h$, $C_2 = 1/12\,f$

15–28. $E_3(s) = \dfrac{s^2 + 1.43}{s(0.11s^5 + 0.522s^4 + 0.821s^3 + 1.65s^2 + 1.93s - 1.36)}$

15–29. **(a)** 13.1, **(b)** 17.86, **(c)** −0.855

15–30. (a) $R(t_1, t_2) = e^{-2\lambda\,|t_1 - t_2|}$ volts²/sec

(b) See diagram

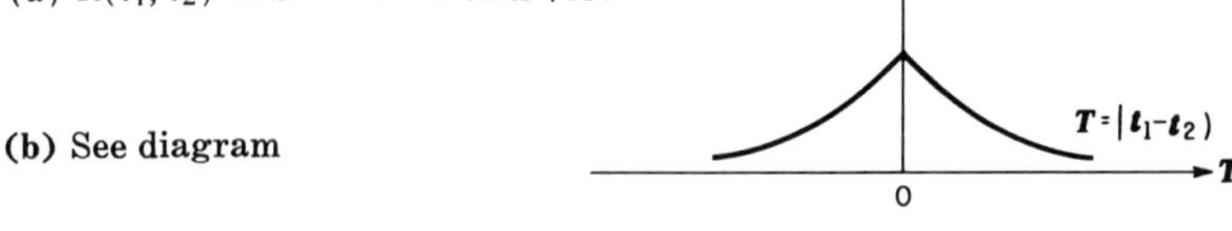

Problem 15–30.

(c) $S(\omega) = \dfrac{4\lambda}{4\lambda^2 + \omega^2}$ volts² cycle

15–36. 12.5 volts, rms; 270 volts **15–37.** **(a)** 16.2 db, **(b)** 5440 megahertz

15–38. **(a)** 50.1 db; **(b)** 47.0 db; **(c)** 41.8 db, the output impedance will be reduced

15–39. **(a)** 1.15 ma, rms; **(b)** 7.68 watts; **(c)** 1.49 watts, a-c; 4.42 watts, total; **(d)** 12.1 db

15–41. 30.9 db **15–42.** **(a)** 8.33%, **(b)** 2

15–43. $E_{oa} = E_{ob} = 32.9$ volts, rms; $E_{ba} = 65.8$ volts, rms **15–44.** 89.4 volts

15–45. **(a)** 6.26 watts; **(b)** 1000-ohm resistor, 2.5 watts; 500-ohm resistor, 1.88 watts; **(c)** 3.10 watts

15–46. $0.578I$ amp, rms **15–47.** **(b)** 99.1 volts

15–48. **(a)** See: Samuel Seely. *Electronic Engineering.* New York: McGraw-Hill Book Company, Inc., 1956, pp. 374-376. **(b)** The grid voltage will always lead the plate voltage, and the tube will fire every time the plate goes positive; there will be no control over the plate current, and the plate current will be the total half-wave rectified current.

15–49. 32.5 hertz

15–50. 85%; 351 Khertz; 451 Khertz; 185 volts, peak; 42.5 volts, peak

15–51. See any standard electronics text on Lissajous patterns

15–52. $h_{11} = 30$ ohm, $h_{12} = 5\times10^{-4}$, $h_{21} = -0.98$, $h_{22} = 10^{-6}$ mhos

15–53. $A_v = \dfrac{-R_L\ (r_m - r_e)}{r_b + r_e + R_i\ [r_e + r_c\ (1-a) + R_L] + r_e\ (r_m - r_e)}$

15–54. **(a)** 1400 ohm (zero), 13.4×10^6 ohm (infinite); **(b)** 31.3 ohm (zero), 3×10^5 ohm (infinite); **(c)** 41.6

15–55. First stage: 24.1 db; second stage: 32.4 db; total: 56.5 db
Interstage losses: 26.7% if available power of first stage. Pre-first stage losses: 77.4% of input power

15–56. $A_v = \dfrac{\alpha\ R_2 R_3 R_4 r_c}{[(2R_1 + R_2)\ r_b + R_1R_2]\ [r_c(R_3 + R_4) + R_3R_4]}$

15–57. -40; 2.25×10^{-4} mhos

15–58. **(a)** 150 ohm; **(b)** 16,230 hertz; **(c)** (1) 516 ohm, (2) no oscillation possible, (3) 227 ohm.

15–59. **(a)** 6.66 amp, **(b)** 4.28 kv, **(c)** 10.4 kv

15–60. **(a)** 6.19 μvolts, **(b)** 14.5 μvolts **15–61.** 200 volts

15–62. **(a)** 1:8.5; **(b)** $I_{\text{peak}} = 0.246$ amp, $I_{\text{ave}} = 0.154$ amp; **(c)** $\gamma = 48\%$

15–63. **(a)**

$J_0 = 30$	$J_4 = 15.7$	$J_8 = 12.8$
$J_1 = 1$	$J_5 = 34.7$	$J_9 = 5.9$
$J_2 = 30$	$J_6 = 33.9$	$J_{10} = 2.3$
$J_3 = 16.7$	$J_7 = 23.4$	

(b) 140 kc

(c) See diagram

(d) $7\sin 62800t + c$

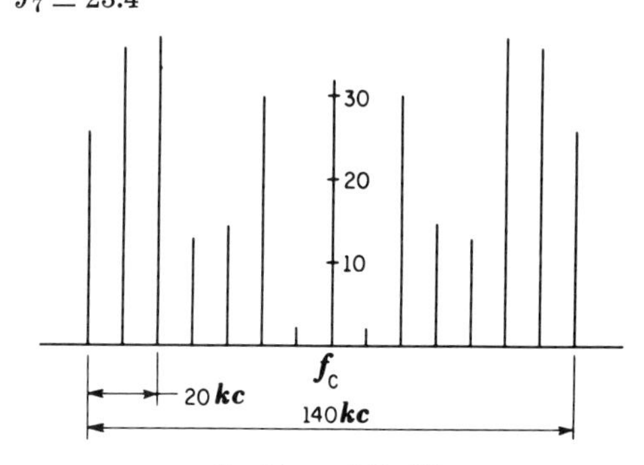

Problem 15–63.

15–64. **(a)** See diagram

(b) $K = 7$

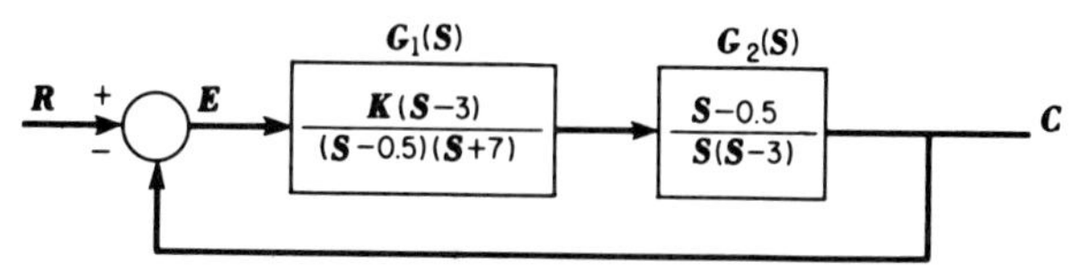

Problem 15–64.

15–65. **(a)** $C/R = \dfrac{k_1(1 + 0.33s)}{s(1 + 0.2s)\ (1 + 0.125s) + k_1(1 + 0.33s)}$

(b) type 1

(c) k_1

(d) 0

(e) See diagram

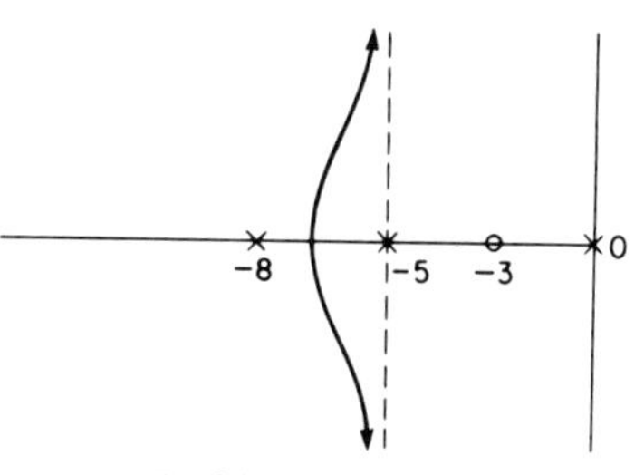

Problem 15–65.

15–67. 3.20 ft-candles **15–68.** 31.6 ft-candles

15–69. 62.1% of design value **15–70.** 13.3 ft-candles

15–71. $N = 1015$ **15–72.** $L = 433.45$ lumens

15–73. **(a)** $N = 78$, **(b)** $L = 8.73 \times 10^5$ lumens

15–80. **(a)** 125 volts, 2000 amp, 250 kw; **(b)** no changes necessary if separately excited; if self-excited, reconnect the shunt field as two parallel circuits of three poles each

15–81. **(a)** 15.1 h; **(b)** 0.160 sec, 1.05 sec; **(c)** 188 volts; **(d)** 1180 joules

15–82. **(b)** (1) Insert resistance in the field circuit; an increase in resistance will result in an increase in speed. (2) Insert resistance in the armature circuit; an increase in resistance will result in a decrease in speed. (3) Insert resistance in series with the line; in a series motor, an increase in resistance will result in a decrease in speed; in a shunt motor, an increase in resistance will produce a relatively small decrease in speed. The first method is the least expensive and yields the best efficiency and speed regulation. **(c)** 1180 rpm

15–83. 1260 rpm **15–84.** 945 lb-ft

15–85. **(a)** $R = 1.82$ ohms, $X = 6.38$ ohms; **(b)** 98.4%

15–86. **(a)** 916 volts; **(b)** $P_e = 34.3$ watts, $P_h = 165.7$ watts

15–87. Unity and 0.500 lagging

15–88. **(a)** 400 ohms, **(b)** 100 ohms, **(c)** 0

15–89. $jX_x = -j28{,}800$ ohms

15–90. **(a)** 8170 volts, rms; **(b)** 23.8%

15–91. **(a)** 5000-kva alternator, 3810 kw; 2500-kva alternator, 1190 kw; **(b)** 6720 kw

15–92. **(a)** 95.8%, **(b)** 94.5%

15–93. 838 amp; 6010 volts, line-to-neutral

15–94. **(a)** 881 hp, **(b)** 2280 volts

15–95. 364 kva

15–96. **(a)** Decreased, **(b)** increased, **(c)** increased, **(d)** increased, **(e)** unchanged, **(f)** decreased

15–97. **(a)** 11.5 hp, **(b)** 82.0%, **(c)** 0.866

15–98. **(a)** 2.00 hp, 1140 rpm; **(b)** 1860 watts, 6.46 amp

15–99. **(a)** pf = 0.782 lag, **(b)** 30.54 kw

15–100. 1.56 newtons

15–101. **(a)** 184.5 watts, **(b)** 82.8°, **(c)** 3%, **(d)** 1.3%, **(e)** −1.09%, **(f)** 98.4%, **(g)** 98.6% at unity p.f.

15–104. **(a)** 97.0%, **(b)** 11,600 volts, **(c)** 0.499

15–105. 7890 volts **15–106.** 37.6 amp

15–107. **(a)** 13,700 volts, **(b)** 1690 watts

15–108. **(a)** 730-j163 ohms, **(b)** 2.06

15–109. 77.5 ohms, 2450 volts

15–110. **(a)** A line of appreciable length in comparison to a quarter wavelength of the voltage or current wave on the line; **(b)** the impedance to the voltage traveling in one direction on the line; **(c)** there are many ways, one of which is to take the geometric mean of the open-circuit impedance (input impedance of the line when terminated in an open circuit) and the short-circuit impedance (input impedance of the line when terminated in a short circuit); **(d)** the ratio of the maximum line voltage to the minimum line voltage on the standing wave pattern; **(e)** part of the incident power to the receiving end is reflected back toward the sending end; for a certain amount of power to be transferred, a higher standing wave ratio means a higher peak line voltage and a greater possibility of flashover; the input impedance will vary as a function of frequency; **(f)** (1) capacitance, (2) open circuit, (3) open circuit; **(g)** one way would be to insert two quarter wavelengths between the lines—the one closer to the 500-ohm line with a characteristic impedance of 308 ohms, and the other of 117 ohms

15–111. See any standard text on transmission lines for the correct standing wave patterns. **(a)** the maximum line voltage is 5 times the minimum line voltage; the voltage maxima and the current minima occur at a quarter wavelength from the receiving end and every half wavelength thereafter up the line; **(b)** the minima are 0; voltage maxima and the current minima occur at 0.188 wavelength from the receiving end and every half wavelength thereafter up the line

15–112. Location: 0.098λ length: 0.348λ

15–113. 29-j19 ohms

15–114. **(a)** $f_{min} = 7.5 \times 10^9$ hertz, **(b)** $f_{max} = 1.5 \times 10^{10}$ hertz

15–115. **(a)** 50 ft (nearest); 111 ft (farthest) **(b)** 114 db, **(c)** 68 ft, **(d)** —12 dbm

CHAPTER 16

16–7. 7.95% increase in production, 7.37% saving in time.

16–8. **(a)** Man and machine chart, **(b)** 1.88 reels/hr, **(c)** have stockroom activity overlap machine time, **(d)** revised man and machine chart, **(e)** 2.44/hr. **(f)** 30.5% increase, **(g)** 7.42 min saved each reel

16–9. Cut in long dimension; long dimension takes 179 min, short dimension takes 194 min

16–10. **(a)** 3, operation A; 2, operation B, 5, operation C; **(b)** $105; **(c)** $115.50; **(d)** one man on operation A, two on B, two on C

16–11. **(a)** 10%; **(b)** 17%; **(c)** no, this is ±17% not ±10%; **(d)** 3600 observations (using formula in Barnes, *Work Sampling*, 2d ed., Chapter 5)

16–12. **(a)** Probability is 0.00118, or approximately 1 in 1000; **(b)** x chart UCL = 23.72, LCL = 19.28, R chart, UCL = 6.92, LCL = 0

16–13. Upper control limit = 307 + 49 = 356, lower control limit = 307 − 49 = 258

16–14. **(a)** (1) Gasoline sales and air, (2) customer rest rooms, (3) greasing service, (4) repair facilities, (5) parking; **(b)** layout

16–15.

	Wells Company	U.S. All-industry Rate, 1958
Frequency rate	11.22	6.17
Severity rate	500.0	744.0

16–16. **(a)** $3.54 per unit; **(b)** $3.63 per unit, using straight-line depreciation and average interest

16–17. $75,685 net profit, using straight-line depreciation

16–18. **(a)** 10 lots of 240 each, **(b)** 191, **(c)** 332, **(d)** 92

16–19. Production Control: **(a)** production control covers routing, scheduling, dispatching and follow-up; **(b)** a Gantt chart uses time and output as its abscissa. It can show schedule, actual performance in relation to schedule, and status of work on each piece of equipment at any given time; **(c)** overloading can be corrected by: (1) more machines, (2) more work hours, (3) improved methods; **(d)** (1) sales furnishes requirements, (2) specifications, (3) production rates, (4) inventory records, (5) delivery dates

16–20. **(a)** 24.1 sec for trip; **(b)** 306 hp to accelerate the load, 133 hp at top speed

16–21. **(a)** Although standardization of rating of workers is improving, there is still difference between companies as to concepts of what is normal pace for similar tasks. Consistency within a company is important. Bringing in a consultant brings in another concept of pace. His time of 0.25 min showed that the company's time of 0.33 min was not too tight. For consistency within the plant the 0.33 standard should be retained. The consultant's result should convince the union that the company's value is not too tight, and arbitration therefore should be unnecessary. **(b)** Rating or leveling is the evaluation of the speed or performance level of an observed operator compared to a "normal" or expected rate of performance. This rating is used to adjust the observed time to conform to the normal or expected time for the job, which is the time required for a qualified operator to do the work when working steadily at a pace which he can maintain all day without undue fatigue. **(c)** Inspection of the incentive earnings for 20 lots shows a range from 15 to 40 with an average around 26. If the operator produced 50% the next time, investigation should be made as to how this was accomplished. Either abnormal effort or perfect working conditions could explain it; if not, question is raised regarding the accuracy of the standard. Values of 18, 26, or 39% are all possible within the pattern of previous earnings.

16–22. **(a)** Frederick W. Taylor, Principles of Management Science, Exponent of time standards, Development of planned supervision, Production control and planning, Selection of proper employee. **(b)** Frank L. Gilbreth, Therbligs-Analytical methods improvement, *The One Best Way,* Micro motion analysis, process charts, adjustable scaffold, etc. **(c)** Henry L. Gantt-Wage incentive plans, Gantt Control charts for scheduling. (See standard texts for other pioneers.)

16–23. The AIIE definition of Industrial Engineering emphasizes the systems approach. Instead of designing individual work-places or jobs, combining these into production lines and layouts, the objectives of the system as a whole are defined, outputs, inputs and feedbacks are identified, with the components, such as production lines and work places, handled as the last step in design.

16–24. *Example*—Quality control: (1) Does company use statistical quality control? (2) Are specification limits considered in relation to statistical limits? (3) Is quality related to quantity standards? (4) Are statistical methods used in determining number of cycles and otherwise analyzing time study data? (5) Is control chart program effective to the point of permitting reduced sampling inspection of final product? Etc.

16–26. **(a)** Logic network shown.

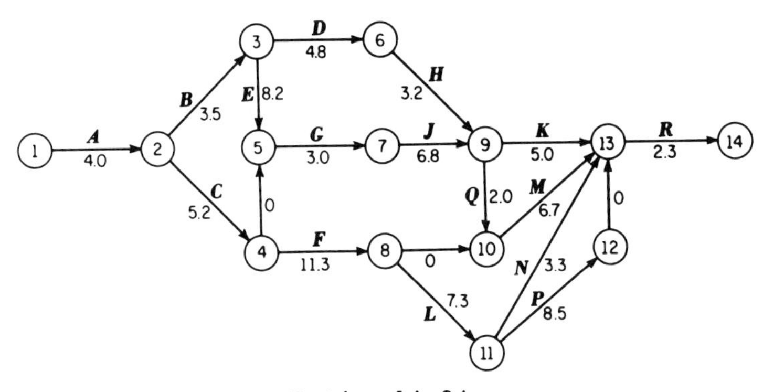

Problem 16–26.

(b)

Activities		Earliest Start T_E	Latest Completion T_L	Activity Slack $T_L - T_E$
Successor Event j	Predecessor Event i			
14	13	38.6	38.6	0.0
13	12	36.3	36.3	0.0
	11	31.1	36.3	5.2
	10	34.2	36.3	2.1
	9	30.5	36.3	5.8
12	11	36.3	36.3	0.0
11	8	27.8	27.8	0.0
10	9	27.5	29.6	2.1
	8	20.5	29.6	9.1
9	7	25.5	27.6	2.1
	6	15.5	27.6	12.1
8	4	20.5	20.5	0.0
7	5	18.7	20.8	2.1
6	3	12.3	24.4	12.1
5	4	9.2	17.8	8.6
	3	15.7	17.8	2.1
4	2	9.2	9.2	0.0
3	2	7.5	9.6	12.1
2	1	4.0	4.0	0.0

(c) Critical Path: A-C-F-L-P-R; **(d)** P (completing task in 35 weeks) = 18.14%.

16–27.

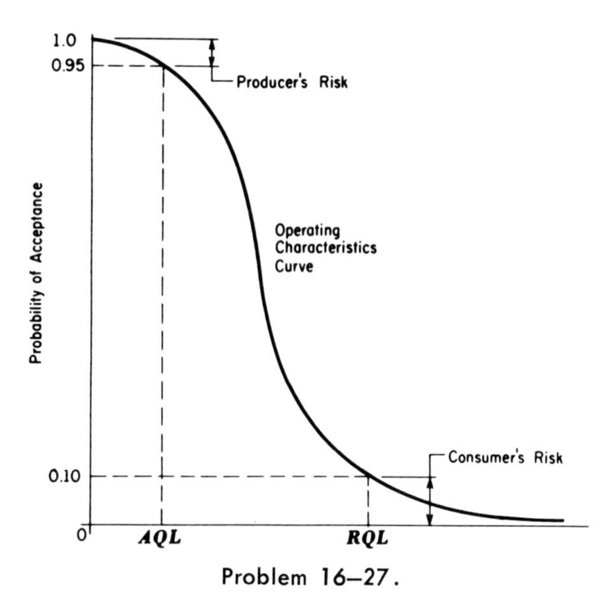

Problem 16–27.

16–28. $R_s = 0.998{,}899$

16–29. Maximum marginal income = $33,260 from production schedule of Item A: Plant 1, 18,500 lb, Plant 2 = 12,500 lb; Item B: Plant 2, 30,000 lb; Item C: Plant 1, 12,500 lb.

16–30. 200 pieces

16–31.

Factory	Product	Products Scheduled	
		Normal Time	Overtime
I	C D	10,000 60,000	14,000
II	A B C	30,000 34,000 26,000	6,000

16–32.

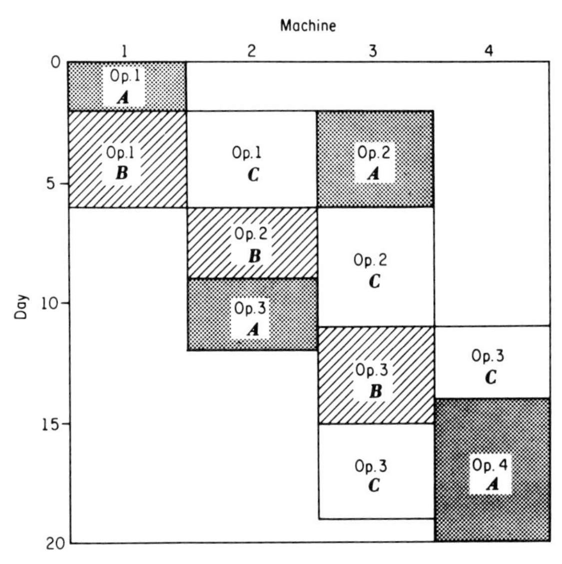

Problem 16–32.

16–33. Tractors required: 12 of type A, 75% less operating cost for same capital outlay.

16–34. Include such items as Job Description and Job Specification

16–35. Fast man

CHAPTER 17

17–5. **(a)** The presence of chromium makes the steel temper-brittle when slowly cooled from tempering temperatures above 1000°F. **(b)** Temper brittleness may be prevented by adding molybdenum in amounts ranging from 0.20 to 1.0%.

17–6. **(a)** Ihrigizing—The impregnation of an iron-base material with silicon. This treatment makes material more resistant to corrosion, high-temperature exposure, and wear. **(b)** Calorizing—The impregnation of plain carbon steel or alloy steels with aluminum. Calorized parts are highly resistant to oxidation and corrosion by flue gases and sulfurous fumes at temperatures up to 1500°F. **(c)** Sherardizing—The impregnation of iron-base materials with zinc. The resulting coating is anodic to the iron base and thus protects it from atmospheric corrosion. **(d)** Chromizing —The impregnation of low-carbon steel with chromium. These coatings raise the steel's resistance to wear, have a low coefficient of friction, good resistance to high temperatures, and can resist 10% nitric acid for long periods of time.

17–7. **(a)** Use an oxidizing atmosphere in the annealing furnace since reducing atmospheres lead to the formation of scale which is difficult to remove and to embrittlement of the stainless steel. Before annealing, all traces of grease, oil, and zinc must be removed from the steel to prevent carbon pickup and embrittlement. **(b)** 12 to 15% nitric acid with 1% hydrofluoric acid in aqueous solution will remove light scale. Use a temperature of 150°F. **(c)** Dry, cracked ammonia or dry hydrogen atmospheres will give scale-free parts.

17–8. **(a)** Qualifying tests may be classified as (1) transverse tension tests, (2) all-weld-metal tension test, (3) guided face bend test, (4) guided root bend test, and (5) free face bend. **(b)** The transverse and all-weld-metal tests are used to check the strength of the weld metal. The free bent test measures ductility and the results from this test can be compared with the data from the all-weld-metal tension test. All three bend tests indicate soundness and proper fusion.

17–9. **(a)** White cast iron is not used for structural parts because it is excessively brittle. Used mostly to resist wear by abrasion. Rapid cooling prevents graphitization and results in the typical white cast iron structure. Used for pump liners. **(b)** Meehanite is produced by adding calcium silicide to a melt having the composition of a gray iron. This produces a fine distribution of graphite which imparts excellent physical properties to the alloy. May be used for cylinders and pistons for internal combustion engines. **(c)** Malleable iron is produced by annealing white cast iron at 900°C for 48 hr and then slowly cooling until the alloy reaches a temperature of 725°C. This treatment decomposes the iron-carbide phase into small particles of graphite called "temper carbon." May be used for pipe fittings.

17–10. Some of the metallurgical difficulties encountered in the production of titanium from its ores are (1) extreme affinity for oxygen, which makes it extremely difficult to reduce the ore; (2) high melting point; (3) high affinity for carbon, nitrogen, and oxygen, which makes it necessary to melt under a protective atmosphere; (4) high reactivity in the molten state.

17–11. **(a)** AISI 4150 H. **(b)** A yield strength of 125,000 psi is obtained from any alloy steel which has been tempered to a hardness of RC 33. The tempering curves given for AISI 4150 H show that tempering at 950°F will give a hardness of RC 33. Complete heat treatment would then include the following steps: (1) normalize at 1650°F, (2) hold for ½ hr at 1550°F, (3) quench in oil, (4) temper at 950°F, (5) cool as desired.

17–12. The figure shows that the critical cooling rate must be exceeded or equalled to avoid transformation until the steel cools to a sufficiently low temperature where martensite can form.

17–13. **(a)** Bearing would be subjected to a high operating speed and fairly heavy pressure. Use an arsenical-lead babbitt alloy. **(b)** Bearing would operate at very heavy load level and low speed. Use a high-tin phosphor bronze alloy. **(c)** A powder metal bearing of copper or brass of the graphitic type or the "oilless" type would be most suitable.

17–14. **(a)** **(1)** 6% A, 94% B, **(2)** 75%, **(3)** 88% A, 12% B; **(b)** **(1)** 56%, **(2)** 42% A, 58% B

17–15. (1) Keep total metal content below 30%. Charges with higher metal content become difficult to smelt. (2) Maintain 8:10 ratio between lime and silica. (3) Keep zinc content of blended material below 15%. Higher zinc contents make blast furnace slag mushy. (4) Adjust moisture content and the ratio of fine to coarse material so as to obtain optimum burning rate.

17–16. **(a)** 18% tungsten, 4% chromium, 1% vanadium, and 0.7% carbon; **(b)** hot-forge the cast billets at 1200°C to break up the massive carbide network formed during solidification. This working will also produce homogenization and reduce the billet to a size suitable for tool stock. After forming is completed, austenitize the steel at 1200°C, quench in oil, and temper at 600°C.

17–17. **(a)** The process of locating a claim on a vein varies somewhat in the different states. In general, most states require the following procedure to be followed: (1) Post notice of location at the point of discovery; (2) define the boundaries of the claim by placing posts or stone monuments at the corners of the claim; (3) record a copy of the location notice with the county recorder; (4) sink a discovery shaft within a specified time after the date of location; (5) $100 worth of labor or improvements must be made yearly on each claim to maintain legal rights. **(b)** Any number of claims may be located along the vein as long as each claim does not exceed 1500 ft in length along the vein and a width of 300 ft on each side of the vein. **(c)** Withdrawn lands are any public lands of the United States which the President orders temporarily withdrawn from settlement, location, sale, or entry. These lands may be reserved for some public purpose, such as water-power sites.

17–18. S86°10.5′E **17–19.** 575 hp **17–20.** 0.90 ton

17–21. Present equipment must last 17.29 years. Yearly payment toward retirement of borrowed capital will be $17,544. Sinking fund annual payment will be $9446.

17–22. **(a)** Safety measures should include (1) hiring only competent, careful, experienced men; (2) provide a bulkhead covering the entire shaft; (3) have sufficient ventilation and adequate pumps available; (4) use electric firing only. **(b)** Have grouting equipment on hand if preliminary borings indicate a possible influx of water. **(c)** A pyramid cut consisting of 8 holes, together with 8 first relievers, 16 second relievers, and 28 trim holes should be the most efficient round.

17–23. **(a)** $44.68, **(b)** $33.16, **(c)** $20.31, **(d)** $2.00 **17–25.** $71, 370

CHAPTER 18

18–9. **(a)** 3550 lb/hr, **(b)** 125 hp, **(c)** 9.20 lb/lb dry coal, **(d)** 40.5/M lb

18–10. **(a)** 16,100 lb/hr, **(b)** 8200 kw, **(c)** 7870 kw, **(d)** 29.4%

18–11. Heat absorbed by boiler, 8400 Btu/lb coal; losses due to: dry flue gas,

1190 Btu/lb coal; moisture in fuel, 165; moisture from H_2, 463; incomplete combustion, 460; combustible in flue gas, 256; radiation and unaccounted for, 366 Btu/lb coal

18–12. **(a)** 40.2%, **(b)** 43.7%, **(c)** 42.6%, **(d)** 43.5%

18–13. 5 in., 52 psi, based on 15,000 fpm velocity **18–14.** 7780 Btu/kwhr

18–15. **(a)** **(1)** 5.6 Btu/lb, **(2)** −46.2 Btu/lb, **(3)** −593 Btu/lb; **(b)** **(1)** −7.96°F, **(2)** 15%; **(c)** **(1)** 499 Btu/lb, **(2)** 131 Btu/lb, **(3)** 3.82

18–16. **(a)** 3610 cfm, **(b)** 42,800 lb/hr

18–17. **(a)** 494 Btu/lb, **(b)** 591 Btu/lb, **(c)** 97 Btu/lb, **(d)** 5.09, **(e)** 0.405

18–18. **(a)** 167,000 lb/hr, **(b)** 66.4 gr/lb dry air, **(c)** 93,500 lb/hr

18–19. **(a)** 87°F dry bulb, 75.9°F wet bulb; **(b)** 69 gr/lb dry air; **(c)** 1.092 $\times$ 10^6 Btu/hr

18–20. 83°F **18–21.** **(a)** 13,500 cfm, **(b)** 39,400 cfm, **(c)** 60°F wet bulb

18–22. **(a)** 558°F; **(b)** 3.76, 41.2%; **(c)** 30,000 hp (23,000 Btu/lb fuel)

18–23. **(a)** 33.8, 62.4 Btu/lb; **(b)** 45.6, 197 Btu/lb; **(c)** 2.52; **(d)** 146.4 Btu/lb; **(e)** 270.6 Btu/lb; **(f)** 54%; **(g)** 118.5 Btu/lb; **(h)** 2.02

18–24. **(a)** 566 cfm; **(b)** 500 cfm, 83.5 psia; **(c)** increase rpm 26%

18–25. 1150 hp **18–26.** 9.33 hp, 38.8%

18–27. **(a)** 18.85 ft, **(b)** 304.95 ft, **(c)** 323.8 ft, **(d)** 13.0 ft, **(e)** 61 kw

18–28. 14.6 hp **18–29.** 11.5 hp **18–30.** 36,400 tubes, 20.2 ft

18–31. 94 tubes, 20 ft (*U* for new tubes, 615 Btu/hr sq ft °F)

18–32. 48,700 sq ft (*U* for new tubes, 670 Btu/hr sq ft °F)

18–33. 94% **18–34.** 12,800 Btu/hr (no infiltration) **18–35.** 0.055 in. H_2O

18–36. 1450 ft **18–37.** 170 cfm **18–38.** 10,300 cfm

18–39. **(a)** 7.31 lb/lb coal, **(b)** 13.6 lb/lb coal, **(c)** 14.05 lb dry product/lb

18–40. **(a)** 18.5 lb/lb fuel; **(b)** 21.8%; **(c)** CO_2, 3.00; O_2, 0.77; CO, 0.06; H_2O, 1.42; N_2, 14.22

18–41. 8 cu ft/cu ft fuel

18–42. **(a)** 3⁹⁄₆₄ in. $\times$ 4¹³⁄₃₂ in.; **(b)** 117 lb-ft, 69%, 125 psi

18–43. **(a)** e_b = 31.4%, e_i = 39.3%, e_k = 29%; **(b)** 300,000 lb; **(c)** 8100 cfm at 15 psia, 600°F, assumed volumetric efficiency of 60%

18–44. **(a)** 17.2%, **(b)** 68.6%, **(c)** 71.3% **18–45.** 1.25 in.

18–46. **(a)** 2810 lb-ft, **(b)** 0.75, **(c)** 71°

18–47. **(a)** 60°, 27.7 in.; **(b)** 19.7°, 24, 34.4 in., 19.2 in.; **(c)** one answer is $N_C = 10$, $N_D = 40$, $N_E = 90$

18–48. Shaft 1, 1680 lb-in.; shaft 2, 4000 lb-in.; shaft 3, 7600 lb-in.

18–49. 1.83 fpm

18–50. **(a)** Shear = 73,600 lb, bearing = 10,000 lb, bending = 11,500 lb; **(b)** shear = 14,750 lb, bearing = 10,000 lb, bending = 2300 lb

18–51. 0.456 in. (use ²⁹⁄₆₄-in. diam.) **18–52.** 8475 lb **18–53.** 1.18 in.

18–54. 31,000 psi

18–55. 10 in. $\times$ 3½ in. $\times$ ¾ in. over-all, 2 in. $\times$ 1½ in. projects, all corner radii = 0.20 in.

18–56. 78.4 cps **18–57.** **(a)** 34,700 psi, **(b)** 13,050 psi **18–58.** 615 lb, 410 lb

18–59. 10.75 in., 5.375 in., std. size shaft

18-60. 22,900 psi, shock and fatigue factor of 1.5

18-61. **(a)** 6.5 in.–7.5 in.; **(b)** 6.75 in.–7.50 in., 3.38 in.–3.75 in.; **(c)** 19.2%–25%; **(d)** 0.056–0.032 radian (solid), 0.051–0.034 radian (hollow)

18-62. 1715 lb for uniform steady load

18-63. **(a)** 7 in., **(b)** 0.005 in. running clearance, **(c)** 0.26/bearing

18-64. **(a)** Pinion 1925 lb, gear 1765 lb; **(b)** 13.5

18-65. **(b)** 2 15/16 in. diam. for drum shaft, 1 7/16 in. diam. for engine shaft; **(c)** 71.5 hp, 1430 rpm; **(d)** 1.04 in.

18-66. $P_d = 5$, $b = 2.0$ in. **18-67.** **(a)** 5100 lb-in., **(b)** 660 lb **18-68.** 76.8

18-69. 13,900 psi radial, 15,835 psi max. circum. in disk, 32,500 psi max. circum. in shaft

18-70. 665°F **18-71.** $t = 0.425$ in., max. defl. = 0.0086 in.

18-72. 3.87 in. shielded, 4.72 in. non-shielded

18-73. 4800 psi longitudinal, 9600 psi hoop

18-74. $b = 7$ in., $t = 4.66$ in., weight of rim = 1150 lb **18-75.** 0.00504 in.

18-76. 1342 lb **18-77.** 21.5 in. **18-78.** 680 μ in./in.

18-79. **(a)** 7810 lb/in.; **(b)** 5; **(c)** 29,400 psi; **(d)** 8.3 in.; **(e)** 9.3 in., 73,800 psi

18-80. 3300 psi, 1710 psi **18-81.** 14.4 hp

18-82. $R = 6.2 \underline{/-23^\circ}$ oz-in., $L = 0.405 \underline{/-171.5^\circ}$ oz-in.

18-83. **(a)** $\omega_R = 652$ rpm, $\omega_L = 695$ rpm; **(b)** 674 rpm **18-84.** 13.4 sq in.

18-85. **(a)** 180 in.-lb; **(b)** 10.8 hp; **(c)** 127 psi; **(d)** 63.7 psi

18-86. 4660 psi **18-87.** 337 $\underline{/-22.6^\circ}$ lb **18-88.** 90°

18-89. $F_R = 268I - 383J + 500K$ lb, $F_L = 19J + 500K$ lb

18-90. 3460 lb, 0.244 in., 7600 psi **18-91.** 2 in. **18-92.** 2300 Btu/hr

18-93. **(a)** 1.075 Btu/hr-ft-°F; **(b)** 189°F **18-94.** 17.4 in., five stages

18-95. 14.8 ft, 5.4 hp **18-96.** 17.2 psia, 304 fps, 52°F, 0.0905 lb_m/cu-ft

18-97. **(a)** 24.7 fps; **(b)** −25.3 fps **18-98.** **(a)** 53.5°, **(b)** 1980 cfm

18-99. 12.6 gal **18-100.** **(a)** 78,600 cfm; **(b)** 14.4 gal/min; **(c)** 217 gpm

CHAPTER 19

19-3. **(b)** BA = 300.3 ft, **(c)** elevation difference = 154.6 ft

19-4. **(a)** 109.0 ft, **(b)** 62.9 ft

19-5. Elevation of A = 1312.7 ft, horizontal distance = 721 ft

19-6. DA length = 431.8 ft, bearing = S 71°32′W

19-7. DE latitude = S120.35, departure = W586.30, double-meridian distance = 599.52, etc.

19-8. $R = 2864.93$, $\Delta = 24°50'$, $T = 630.8$ ft, $E = 68.6$ ft, P.C. = 128 + 18.6 and P.T. = 140 + 60.3

19-9. At 10 + 50, elevation = 104.12, etc. **19-10.** 953 cu yd

19-12. North half is ½ total area; area north of line connecting north half of side lines

19-13. 324.060 ft **19-14.** 6.53 ft **19-15.** AE = 56.1 ft, EF = 102.0 ft

19-16. 0.020 ft, adjust line of sight down when setup at B

19-17. N 49°29′W **19-18.** $g_1L/(g_1 - g_2)$

19–19. Length = 6 miles minus 36 ft

19–20. Angle x = 30°56′20″, angle y = 74°03′40″, AB = 887.60 ft

19–21. AE = 36.3 ft **19–22.** No. Deflected by any adjacent mountain mass

19–23. 10 acres

19–24. None, except to offer expert testimony to assist court in decision

19–25. Liable to his client as a professional man to exercise the degree of care that a skilled surveyor of ordinary prudence would exercise under similar circumstances

19–26. **(a)** F, **(b)** F, **(c)** F, **(d)** T **19–27.** See any topo symbols book

19–28. See ELEMENTARY SURVEYING by Brinker & Taylor, pp. 14-16

19–29. Compensated **19–30.** Digital, analog **19–31.** Accretion

19–32. See ELEMENTARY SURVEYING by Brinker & Taylor, pp. 213-214

19–33. 6 **19–34.** d **19–35.** a

CHAPTER 20

Examination A

20–1A. 0.347 fpm **20–2A.** 6.57 hr **20–3A.** $\bar{x} = 1$ **20–4A.** 5.05 cu ft

20–5A. 24.2 lb/day **20–6A.** **(a)** 20 liter, **(b)** 36.7%

20–7A. 1.91 cfs, 25.8 hp

20–8A. 24,400 lb perp. to triangle, 0.0139 ft below centroid of triangle

20–9A. 190 cfs **20–10A.** 462 Btu/min; 0.317 lb/min **20–11A.** 1.10 lb_m/sec

20–12A. **(a)** 9.9 lb/kwhr; **(b)** 16 lb/kwhr; **(c)** 17.7%

20–13A. **(a)** −310 lb; **(b)** −1050 lb **20–14A.** 131.5 lb

20–15A. 360 in.-lb, 3.6 in.

20–16A. 4.00fps² →, 20 lb ← **20–17A.** 5.04 fps ↑

20–18A. $v_B = 12$ fps ←, $v_D = 6$ fps ←, $v_E = 12$ fps ↑, $a_B = 30$ fps² ←, $a_D = 20$ fps² ↖ 30°

20–19A. 0.0205 rad **20–20A.** 1962 psi, 1042 psi

20–21A. $\Delta_H = 1.4$ in.; $\Delta_V = 1.2$ in. **20–22A.** 216.8° ∠; 25 fps

20–23A. 31 sec/gal; 0.00462 cents/gal

20–24A. Converging lens; 3.2 ft **20–25A.** 97.4%

20–26A. $A_1 = 10, A_2 = 15, A_T = 150$ **20–27A.** **(a)** 0.883 kva, **(b)** 54.4 μf

20–28A. 51.11%/yr **20–29A.** $33,900 **20–30A.** Steam, $868,500

Examination B

20–1B. H = 2D **20–2B.** 24.3 ft, 22.2 ft, 13.9 ft

20–3B. 256 mph N—S, 82 mph vert., 113 mph E—W **20–4B.** 31.1 **20–5B.** 1.32 g

20–6B. **(a)** $6CO_2 + 6H_2O \rightarrow C_6H_{12}O_6, + 6O_2$, **(b)** $CaCO_3 + 2HCl \rightarrow CaCl_2 + H_2O + CO_2$, **(c)** $BaO_2 + 2HCl \rightarrow BaCl_2 + H_2O_2$, **(d)** $(NH_4)_2SO_4 + 2NaOH \rightarrow Na_2SO_4 + 2H_2O + 2NH_3$, **(e)** $NaCN + H_2SO_4 \rightarrow NaHSO_4 + HCN$

20–7B. $E_p = 104$ ft, $(h_f)_i = 6.84$ ft, $(h_f)_o = 25.5$ ft

20–8B. 4.10 lb/sec **20–9B.** 8.38 hp **20–10B.** 1.72 Btu/lb_m —°F

20–11B. 1.3 Btu-lb; 50.6 Btu/lb; 12.2 hp; No

20–12B. **(a)** 0.14 Btu/hr-ft² —°F; **(b)** 6350 Btu/hr

20–13B. $Ra = 1450$ lb, $Rb = 975$ lb, $Rc = 3475$ lb

20–14B. $a = +12$ ton, $b = +1$ ton, $c = +12$ ton **20–15B.** $x = 20$ ft
20–16B. 21.5 fps^2, 5.3 lb **20–17B.** $s = 0.5t^3 - 2t^2 + 4t$
20–18B. 3.42 ft
20–19B. 1230 lb **20–20B.** 19,000 psi **20–21B.** 8060 lb, 24,200 lb
20–22B. 0.975 ft **20–23B.** **(a)** 3, **(b)** 1/7 **20–24B.** 1.42 K cal
20–25B. C = .0164 farad **20–26B.** $I_a = 0.298$ amp
20–27B. $A_v = 0.874$ **20–28B.** 1%/month **20–29B.** Plan A
20–30B. **(a)** $4,981, **(b)** 712 hr/yr

Examination C

20–1C. $500/(4 + \pi)$ **20–2C.** $x = +2.45$; $y = +1.22$
20–3C. 32 min **20–4C.** 25.1 lb **20–5C.** 173 lb
20–6C. **(a)** $2Na + 2H_2O \rightarrow 2NaOH + H_2$
(b) $2AlCl_3 + 3H_2SO_4 \rightarrow Al_2(SO_4)_3 + 6HCl$
(c) $MnO_2 + 2NaCl + 2H_2SO_4 \rightarrow Na_2SO_4 + MnSO_4 + 2H_2O + Cl_2$
(d) $3Zn + 8HNO_3 \rightarrow 3Zn(NO_3)_2 + 2NO + 4H_2O$
(e) $AlCl_3 + 3NH_4OH \rightarrow 3NH_4Cl + Al(OH)_3$
20–7C. 0.0147 cfs **20–8C.** 5.91 lb/sec
20–9C. **(a)** 8.40 ft, **(b)** 19.1, **(c)** 0.0369
20–10C. 26,000 lb$_m$/hr **20–11C.** 3.55 lb$_m$/min; 1.02 hp; 242 Btu/min
20–12C. 293,000 lb$_m$/hr
20–13C. $B_h = 2040$ lb, $B_v = 100$ lb, $C_h = 1040$ lb, $C_v = 300$ lb,
$E_h = 2040$ lb, $E_v = 300$ lb
20–14C. $a = -44.7$ lb; $b = +110$ lb; $c = +40$ lb
20–15C. 11.3° **20–16C.** 11.2 fps^2, 89.6 ft **20–17C.** 9.83 fps
20–18C. **(a)** 1.38 sec, **(b)** 9.15 in.
20–19C. $R_b = 36.9$ kip; $M_a = 54$ ft-kip; $M_b = 108$ ft-kip; $M_d = 0$;
$\theta_c = .0066$ rad
20–20C. 8590 psi **20–21C.** $\Delta_A = 0.0303$ in. (neglect bending in AC)
20–22C. **(a)** 5×10^{15} cm/sec^2; **(b)** 2×10^{-8} sec; **(c)** 2 cm
20–23C. **(a)** 30 in.; **(b)** 2 **20–24C.** 4.1 hp
20–25C. **(a)** 27 amp, **(b)** 4.0 kva, **(c)** 1800 rpm
20–26C. 3.79 amp **20–27C.** 50×10^{-6} joules **20–28C.** L-shaped, $416,651
20–29C. A, $400.98
20–30C. New machine (present value of old machine should have been given)

Examination D

20–1D. (a) **20–2D.** (e) **20–3D.** (d) **20–4D.** (c) **20–5D.** (e)
20–6D. (d) **20–7D.** (d) **20–8D.** (b) **20–9D.** (d) **20–10D.** (b)
20–11D. (a) **20–12D.** (d) **20–13D.** (d) **20–14D.** (c)
20–15D. (d) **20–16D.** (a) **20–17D.** (b) **20–18D.** (a)
20–19D. (d) **20–20D.** (d) **20–21D.** $\sqrt{1 - x^2}/x$ **20–22D.** 7
20–23D. 245 gpm **20–24D.** 26.7 in.-lb **20–25D.** $(1-1/e)$
20–26D. 16.1 fps^2, 250 lb **20–27D.** 76.7 hp **20–28D.** 20.0 ft

20–29D. 7.5 ohm **20–30D.** $E_{ave} = (2/\pi)E_{max}$ **20–31D.** 185.0 lb

20–32D. 162 lb air, 18 lb water **20–33D.** 121.5 fps **20–34D.** 2.00 lb

20–35D. $t = 2A/B$ **20–36D.** 8.00 in. **20–37D.** $e = 0.0106$ in.

20–38D. **(a)** Loss of energy in flowing system expressed in terms of feet of water, **(b)** Current worth of a future sum considering compound interest n years from now, **(c)** positive square root of the variance, **(d)** common log of reciprocal of hydrogen ion concentration, **(e)** the number corresponding to a logarithm, **(f)** a graph alignment chart, on which using a straight edge, the values of a dependent variable may be read, **(g)** part of mechanism of bourdon spring-type gage for measuring pressure, **(h)** 360° = 6400 mils, **(i)** unit of force in CGS system, **(j)** energy owing to motion

20–39D. $\overline{A} = 2,4,5,7$; $\overline{B} = 3,4,5$; $A \cap B = 1.6$; $A \cap \overline{B} = 3$, $\overline{A} \cap B = 2.7$

20–40D. 68 **20–41D.** **(a)** 7 ft, **(b)** 190,000 gal, **(c)** 61.7 min

20–42D. **(a)** 3000 psi, **(b)** 125 psi **20–43D.** B to A, 18.0 ft

20–44D. **(a)** $14.45 \underline{|-82.05°}$, **(b)** $15.2 \underline{|82.05°}$, **(c)** pf = 0.138 lead

20–45D. 145°F **20–46D.** 14 volts

20–47D. **(a)** $4Al + 3O_2 \rightarrow 2Al_2O_3$
(b) Evolves heat energy, $2H_2 + O_2 \rightarrow 2H_2O$
(c) Absorbs heat energy, $6CO_2 + 6H_2O \rightarrow C_6H_{12}O_6 + 6O_2$

20–48D. **(a)** 20 ft, **(b)** 10 ft

20–49D. 5366.64 ft **20–50D.** 0.0271

Examination E

20–1E. **(a)** $M = 2$, **(b)** $y = 2x^2 + x - 1$

20–2E. $\frac{\pi}{2} \times 10^{-1}$ cu in. **20–3E.** 36.25 in. **20–4E.** 1.01

20–5E. 250,000 cu ft **20–6E.** 49.8 lb

20–7E. **(a)** \$556, **(b)** \$6132, **(c)** loss = \$2868 **20–8E.** **(a)** 10%, **(b)** 6.6%

20–9E. **(a)** 5.05, **(b)** 99,500 **20–10E.** **(a)** 1.5 amp, 0.5 amp; **(b)** 151 volts

20–11E. 4 ft below and 2.67 ft to left of point O **20–12E.** 11 lb to left

20–13E. 31.6 fps, 31,060 ft-lb **20–14E.** 61 sec, 167,200 ft-lb

20–15E. −8.5°F **20–16E.** 12.55 ft from left end

20–17E. **(a)** **(1)** 0.187 Btu lb °F, **(2)** 161 Btu lb, **(3)** 33 Btu lb, **(4)** 25.8 Btu lb, **(5)** 135.2 Btu lb; **(b)** **(1)** **a)** 1307 Btu lb, **b)** 1.589 Btu lb °F, **c)** 1.48 cu ft/lb, **d)** 1197.5 Btu lb; **(2)** **a)** 11.52 psia, **b)** 87.3%, **c)** 29.4 cu ft/lb, **d)** 1022 Btu lb, **e)** 959.3 Btu lb; **(3)** 0; **(4)** −238.2 Btu lb; **(5)** 238.2 Btu lb

20–18E. **(a)** **(1)** 78.6 psi, **(2)** 1470 in.-lb, **(3)** 23%, **(4)** 40.7%; **(b)** CO_2 = 17.6%, CO = 1.9%, O_2 = 4.3%, N_2 = 76.2%

20–19E. 40 psi **20–20E.** For $h_B = h_C = 0$, 54,700 lb

Examination F

20–1F. (c) **20–2F.** (b) **20–3F.** (d) **20–4F.** (d) **20–5F.** (d)
20–6F. (b) **20–7F.** (a) **20–8F.** (c) **20–9F.** (e) **20–10F.** (a)
20–11F. (d) **20–12F.** (c) **20–13F.** (d) **20–14F.** (d) **20–15F.** (d)
20–16F. (e) **20–17F.** (d)

20–18F. Chemical to electrical conversion, flux cutting conductor, varying flux within an electrical loop

20–19F. **(a)** Substance which alters rate of reaction, without being consumed by reaction; **(b)** loss of electrons by a substance in a chemical reaction; **(c)** gain of electrons by a substance in a chemical reaction

20–20F. $x^2 + y^2 - 4(x + y) + 4 = 0$ **20–21F.** 2.5%

20–22F. $F = W/15$ **20–23F.** $d/h = 1$

20–24F. $L = [V_1 \cos\theta + (V_A - V_B)]\left[\dfrac{-V_1 \sin\theta \pm \sqrt{(V_1 \sin\theta)^2}}{32.2}\right]$

20–25F. $\cos\theta = \dfrac{L - (V'/2g)^2}{L}$ **20–26F.** 11.55 in., 16.33 in.

20–27F. $F_A = \dfrac{P}{12}, F_B = \dfrac{P}{3}, F_C = \dfrac{7P}{12}$

20–28F. $\dfrac{2R}{3}$ **20–29F.** 5.0 amp

20–30F. 11.4 kw, 4800 vars, 12.4 kva, 0.92 **20–31F.** 8.4 ft

Examination G

20–1G. $T = 31.5$ in.-lb, $0 = 0.299$

20–2G. **(a)** Unstable, spiral, λ_1; **(b)** spiral; **(c)** heavy convergence;

(d) $\dfrac{-3}{2} \pm i\sqrt{\dfrac{151}{4}}$; **(e)** 0.462 sec to damp to one-half amplitude;

(f) $\dfrac{4\pi}{\sqrt{151}}$

20–3G. **(a)** 60.0, **(b)** $-20°$, **(c)** 0.000667 C_n/degree, **(d)** yes, **(e)** 20°

20–4G. **(a)** **(1)** 0.01, **(2)** 0.01116 psf, **(3)** 0 psf at 0.12 in.; **(b)** 9 lb; **(c)** 1.75 lb

20–5G. -0.514 lb/ft of span **20–6G.** $\bar{y} = 17$ ft

20–7G. **(a)** $\pm \dfrac{2\theta}{\sqrt{M_\infty^2 - 1}}$ where θ is the local angle of surface with respect to free-stream direction; **(b)** 2116 psf; **(c)** $\dfrac{4}{\sqrt{M_\infty^2 - 1}}$; **(d)** $L\alpha$

20–8G. End-burning charge exhibits neutral burning; internal burning star, regressive burning; tubular configurations, progressive burning.

20–9G. **(a)** Critical, supercritical, and subcritical operation. Shock is located at inlet under critical conditions. In supercritical operation, shock is near exit; in subcritical operation, shock is a detached one. **(b)** Critical is the design condition when heat released in chamber is of such magnitude that back pressure at exit of subsonic diffuser causes normal shock to be located at inlet.

20–10G. **(a)** A straight shock exists if, and only if, the resultant velocity downstream is essentially sonic or greater. By continuity, momentum, and energy considerations, if resultant subsonic flow exists downstream, a straight shock cannot exist and the wave becomes curved. If a local surface exceeds 45°, in two-dimensional flow, the shock must be curved regardless of the value of the free-stream Mach number. **(b)** The shock angle is greater than the Mach angle since a shock wave moves faster normal to itself than a sound wave. **(c)** Transonic flow occurs when the local Mach number anywhere reaches the value unity; the governing equations no longer can be treated as linear ones. **(d)** Pure supersonic flow is one in which at all points the flow is such that the Mach number is greater than unity. **(e)** The Shock-Expansion theory is the application of the oblique shock and the Prandtl-Meyer equations to airfoil problems in two-dimensional supersonic flow; a step-by-step solution. **(f)** The shock will always be detached.

20–11G. **(a)** Shock attachment Mach number is less for cone than for wedge. **(b)** The drag due to formation of a shock wave; they are the same. **(c)** One cannot test under such conditions, due to the interference between wall and body which chokes the flow. **(d)** Slots or perforations. **(e)** In supersonic case, the flow can negotiate a sharp corner (Prandtl-Meyer flow). **(f)** In a fixed-wall supersonic tunnel, increasing the power has no effect; the Mach number stays the same, except for viscous effects.

20–12G. **(a)** Only parameter over which the designer has any control is the stagnation velocity gradient. This parameter is a function of the shape of the nose. The flatter the nose, the less the heat transfer at the nose. **(b)** It is only necessary to base the Reynolds number on the wall conditions, i.e., the viscosity and density must be based on wall conditions. **(c)** For laminar flow, $c_h = 0.5\ c_f$, which says that one-half of the work due to friction is converted to heating the body. For turbulent flow the relation is $c_h = 0.6\ c_f$, which shows that the heat transfer is greater for the turbulent case. **(d)** It is assumed that the Prandtl number is unity, or that the recovery factor is unity. The recovery factor is not unity anywhere and, in particular, the wall temperature at the stagnation point must take into account the shape of the nose. **(e)** The Mangler transformation allows, in some cases, the use of two-dimensional boundary layer results in the axiallary symmetric case.

20–13G. (a) 0.873°/sec. **(b)** One that has a reflex trailing edge such that the pitching moment coefficient is a small positive quantity. **(c)** No effect. **(d)** Rudder should be located at bottom of fuselage only, since at hypersonic speeds in reentry the upper surface of rudder is in the "shadow" of the fuselage and would hence be ineffective.

20–14G. Assume symmetric nozzle and no viscous effects. For the given Mach number, determine by the Prandtl-Meyer expansion the angle ν required to give design Mach number. Plot $\nu/2$ at the end of throat with the Mach angle corresponding to the average value between Mach number unity and that corresponding to $\nu/2$. Plot this Mach wave until it strikes centerline; let it bounce on centerline at an angle ν_1 with the centerline direction (which is average Mach angle for region 2–3). When wave reaches outer wall, cancel it by turning wall $\nu/2$ degrees.

Examination H

20–1H. The information which follows should be used only as a guide in answering this type of question. Briefly:

Data on	Data Required	Location of Data
Process	Flowsheet, equipment, material and auxiliary requirements	An encyclopedia of inorganic processes
Chilean nitrate	Analysis, supply quantities, physical properties	Supplier or process reference
Process chemicals	Analysis, supply quantities, physical properties	*Chemical Materials Catalog*, Chemistry & Physics Handbook
Process equipment	Materials of construction, standard capacities, etc.	*Chemical Equipment Catalog*

20–2H. 10,900 hr **20–3H.** 543°C

20–4H. **(a)** 100 gpm, **(b)** 4.0 in. Hg, **(c)** 11.06 psig

20–5H. **(a)** 81°F, **(b)** 467 lb/hr

20–6H. **(a)** 17.6 hp, **(b)** 5.68 lb/min, **(c)** 3280 Btu/min, **(d)** 14.5%

20–7H. Assuming the system is ideal and Henry's law applies, the theoretical number of stages is 3.6.

20–8H. Based on condenser limitations, 27 lb-moles/hr

20–9H. **(a)** 233 psia; **(b)** 65%; **(c)** **(1)** 22.2 cm/sec, **(2)** 3.5 cm/sec, **(3)** 0.89 cm/sec

Examination I

20–1I. 11.75% water, 0.325 **20–2I.** 69.3 **20–3I.** 1.36 hp

20–4I. **(a)** 0.003; **(b)** 0.002; **(c)** Advantages: prevent (1) silting of drainage system having flat grades, (2) stoppage of drainage system by debris. Disadvantages: (1) require frequent cleaning, (2) can provide mosquito breeding areas and foul odors if not properly maintained; **(d)** 1.95 fps; **(e)** 194 gpm

20–5I. 0.445

20–6I. **(a)** 8 panels at 1675 lb each; **(b)** at left, $V = 8260$ lb up, $H = 6000$ lb to left; at right, $V = 3740$ lb up

20–7I. **(a)** \$62,224, **(b)** \$20,457 **20–8I.** At 79 + 00, 969.88

20–9I. **(a)** Toe 4986 psf, heel 4966 psf; **(b)** 39.6 ft **20–10I.** 8.67 ft

20–11I. **(a)** East cable = 21,500 lb, north = 37,200 lb, south = west = 0; **(b)** east 1675 lb, north 2900 lb, up 41,500 lb

20–12I. $91.8'^k$ with 20^k load 1 ft to right of center

20–13I. **(a)** Yes, **(b)** 2.35 ft, **(c)** 75 hp

Examination J

20–2J. $A = D = 1.02 \angle 3.4°$; $B = 158 \angle 71.6°$; $C = (8.04 \times 10^{-4}) \angle 5.6°$

20–3J. 0.729 ohm per conductor per mile

20–4J. **(a)** See: Samuel Seely. *Electronic Engineering.* New York: McGraw-Hill Book Company, Inc., 1956, pp. 401–406; **(b)** 5.98×10^{-6}

20–5J. 0.03 voltage regulation; 79.4% rated load

20–6J. The primaries of the 25-kva transformers should be connected in delta to the 2200-volt line. A 208-volt line voltage can be obtained by connecting the secondaries in wye such that the line-to-neutral voltages are 120° apart. The additional 60 kva of load should be supplied separately by the 25-kva transformers, because if the secondaries of the two banks are connected in parallel, there will be a high circulating current caused by the 30° phase difference in the secondary line voltages of the two banks.

20–7J. **(a)** 492 kilohms, **(b)** 495 kilohms, **(c)** 429 ohms

20–8J. 4.81 m **20–9J.** Unity

20–11J. **(a)** *AB–BC–CA*; **(b)** positive sequence components = 153 volts, one of which lags V_{ab} by 10.9°; negative sequence components = 57.7 volts, one of which leads V_{ab} by 30.0°; zero sequence components = 0

20–12J. **(a)** 1620 volts; **(b)** 24 amp, 0.08 leading power factor; **(c)** 636 hp

20–13J. 1:201 **20–14J.** 31.2 amp, 8.17 hp, 3.60 ft-lb

20–15J. 20 per unit, 34.6 per unit

20–16J. **(a)** Charging time = 1.28×10^{-3} sec, discharge time = 1.14×10^{-6} sec, period = 1.28×10^{-3} sec, 783 cps; **(b)** 72.8 kilohms

20–17J. Length = 9.86 cm, location = 1.03 cm

20–18J. See: E. May. *Industrial High Frequency Electric Power.* New York: John Wiley & Sons Inc., 1950, Chapters 6 & 7

Examination K

20–1K. Choose C. Annual costs: A = \$2479, B = \$2354, C = \$2344

20–2K. 0.624 min with allowances based on normal time, or 0.640 with allowances based on standard time

20–3K. **(b)** 19.9 million bags per year; **(c)** 23.8 million bags per year; **(d)** \$7.50; **(e)** no, loss of \$28,980 is less than fixed cost of \$61,060. Old-time customers and workers might be lost permanently

20–4K. **(a)**

Symbol	Description	Symbol	Description
▽	in storage crates	⑤ (in square)	inspect and de-pinfeather
⇨	to scalding vat	D	await degut
①	stick in throat with knife	⇨	to degut table
②	hang in scalding vat	⑥	degut
⇨	to picker rack	⇨	to packing
③	defeather	D	await packing
⇨	to singe table	⑦	pack and box
D	await singe	⇨	to freezer
④	singe		

(b) No fixed answer. Solution must (1) place singe table between pickers and degut, (2) move box storage close to pack table, and (3) reduce over-all distances between pickers, singe, degut, pack. Solution should also (1) recommend chutes or conveyors and (2) eliminate walking by operators

20–6K. **(a)** $\overline{X}$ chart: UCL = 4.018 oz, LCL = 4.010 oz. *R* chart: UCL =

0.013 oz, LCL = 0. **(b)** X charts indicate changes and trends in process averages. R charts indicate changes in spread. **(c)** Individual readings are less secure. Averages of samples tend to follow a normal distribution even though individuals may not. Fewer readings are required. **(d)** No, specifications are set for individual readings which are not plotted on the X chart.

20–7K. Eleven lots per year of 909 units per lot

20–8K. The additional investment is justified since 16% (18% return if exact compound-interest method is used) will be earned on the additional $50,000

20–10K. Use sheet steel. Cost will be $3550 vs. $5840 for cinder block (using straight-line depreciation and average interest)

20–11K. Eight local tractors cost $9174; 9 outside-dealer tractors cost $7740, so buy these

20–12K. **(a)** A definition should include the following (1) work requirements expressed in common factors, (2) common factors used to appraise relative work requirements, (3) relative requirements set forth in points, levels or money, (4) relative ratings become basis for base pay for every job. **(b)** (1) Job analysis (descriptions and specifications, (2) selection of factors and weightings and application to each job to determine relative requirements, (3) assignment of classifications (groupings) and wages in money for each class of job. **(c)** Benefits: Better industrial relations by eliminating many evils of other systems of wage and salary payments: (1) high wages to persons whose jobs do not require great amounts of skill, effort, and responsibility, (2) paying beginners less than they are entitled to, (3) giving raises to those who do not deserve them, (4) deciding pay on basis of seniority rather than ability, (5) payment of various rates for the same or equal jobs, (6) unequal wages paid because of race, sex, religion, etc. **(d)** Job evaluation classifies the job according to its importance and its requirements. Merit rating evaluates the *man's* performance at his job. Wage incentives are a means of paying the worker for the degree of performance he displays.

20–13K. **(a)** 1.29 man-hours per 100 pieces, **(b)** (1) 129%, (2) $14.61, (3) 800, (4) $15.48.

20–14K. **(a)** **(1)** A legal strike may be called *at any time* with the following exceptions: a) Government employees may not strike, b) a jurisdictional strike is not allowed, c) a sympathetic strike is not allowed, d) a strike that violates the Taft-Hartley Act is not allowed, e) a strike to obtain an unlawful end is not allowed. **(2)** The following conditions are necessary: a) A closed shop is illegal, b) a union shop is legal in any state which does not restrict its use. It is legal under Federal law, c) same as b). **(b)** **(1)** Skilled craftsmen *may* petition to be placed in a bargaining unit of their own craft—otherwise, they will be included in the regular production bargaining, **(2)** the Taft-Hartley Act has no provisions for supervisors or foremen, **(3)** plant guards must bargain in a unit distinct from the production and maintenance employees, **(4)** same as **(3)**. **(c)** The company may sue to remedy breach of contract and to enforce contract agreements

20–15K. **(a)** Yes; **(b)** no, slight difference between accrued interest and total interest; **(c)** increase $4000; **(d)** $29,000

20–16K. **(a)** Sell management, orient foremen, orient inspectors, observe selected operations, collect data; **(b)** **(1)** small number of identical units, precision work required, **(2)** ordinary mass production and assembly jobs; **(c)** reduced inspection costs, more uniform quality, better identification of production trouble, provides better basis for engineering tolerances

Examination L

20–1L. Solution of this type of problem depends on the area or state in which it is given. Factors such as type and cost of fuel and water available, common practice in the climate of particular area, legal and economic aspects of area, must be considered. A complete solution is not offered but a brief indication of possible answers follows: **(a)** Choose a self-contained gas-fired boiler unit. Due to the neighborhood location and considering the climate, provide a suitable building. A low pressure, deaerating feed-water heater with level control, steam reducing valve from boiler main, and small storage to serve feed pump suction should be provided. Consideration might be given to operation for short periods without feed-water treatment, in which case provisions must be made for internal treatment such as phosphate addition. For such operation, blowdown would be about 20% and equipment to eliminate noise and steam emission required. **(b)** Further study might indicate use of heat recovery equipment, such as air preheater, blowdown flash tank, etc. **(c)** Since the condensate is probably returned to other parts of the system, and anticipating increasing use of the facilities, external feed-water treatment should be provided. Hot-process softening to reduce hardness and bicarbonate alkalinity would materially reduce boiler scale and system corrosion problems. The softener would also provide heating and deaeration. **(d)** Approximately 30,000 cfm of products at 350°.

20–2L. Assuming for analysis that sling force acts vertically, and transverse deflection is negligible, **(a)** from time slack is taken from cable, 15.75 in., **(b)** 29,200 psi, **(c)** no, yield strength not exceeded.

20–3L. **(a)** 0.85 ton, **(b)** 62°F, **(c)** 0.0107, **(d)** 90%

20–4L. $d = 0.65$ in., 0.375 in.

20–5L. **(a)** 20 hp; **(b)** 116 rpm, 580 gpm; **(c)** no (29.5 hp)

20–6L. 228 psi

20–7L. **(a)** 476, **(b)** 49,500 gpm (15°F rise), **(c)** 87,500 at 14.7 psia and 80°F

20–8L. 15 hp

appendix

Symbols and Abbreviations B

SYMBOLS

Symbol	Meaning
A, a	area
C_c	coefficient of velocity
C_D	drag coefficient
C_{D0}	profile drag coefficient
C_L	lift coefficient
C_v	coefficient of velocity
D	drag
E	voltage; modulus of elasticity
e	elongation
e_L	distance along plane of surface; center of gravity to center of pressure
F_c	column force
f	natural frequency; stress
f_c	concrete stress
f_s	steel stress
g	acceleration of gravity
h_f	friction head
I	current; static moment of inertia
I_G	moment of inertia
I/C	section modulus
K	thermal conductivity; spring modulus
L	lift; length of beam
l/r	slenderness ratio
M	moment
m	moment (unit load)
N	number of revolutions
N_R	Reynolds number
n	ratio; modulus of steel to modulus of concrete
P	pressure; allowable load; concentrated load
p	static pressure
R	resistance; radius
r	body radius; damping constant
r_1	inner radius
r_2	outer radius
S	section modulus
T	temperature; torque
T_s	temperature
t	thickness
t_s	throat temperature
u	circumferential velocity
V, v	volume
V_t	throat velocity
W	weight
w	uniform load per unit length
x	axial distance
Z	impedance
$\cup$	union
$\cap$	intersection
$^\circ$	degree (angle)
$'$	minute (angle)
[	channel section
$\angle$	angle section
α	angle of attack
γ	ratio of specific heats
Δ	angle of intersection of curve; deflection
δ	deflection; body thickness ratio; logarithmic decrement
ε	strain
θ	angle change; slope
λ	latent heat of vaporization; dimensionless time
μ	coefficient of viscosity; airplane density factor; micro (prefix)
π	pi
ρ	mass density
L/ρ	slenderness ratio
Σ	sum
σ	stress, direct
τ	stress, shear; root of characteristic equation
ω	angular velocity
ω_1	inner angular velocity
ω_2	outer radius

ABBREVIATIONS

abs	absolute
a-c	alternating current
acre-ft	acre-foot
amp	ampere
amp-hr	ampere-hour
amp-turn	ampere-turn
atm	atmosphere
Awg	American wire gage
bhp	brake horsepower
B.M.	bench mark
BOD	biochemical oxygen demand
Btu	British thermal unit
Bwg	Birmingham wire gage
°C	degrees centigrade
cal	calorie
cc	cubic centimeter
cfm	cubic feet per minute
cfs	cubic feet per second
c.g.	center of gravity
cm	centimeter
c.p.	coefficient of performance
cu ft	cubic foot
cu yd	cubic yard
db	decibel
dbt	dry-bulb temperature
d-c	direct current
deg	degree
DL	dead load
emf	electromotive force
EW	equivalent weight
°F	degrees Fahrenheit
f	farad
fpm	feet per minute
fps	feet per second
ft	foot
ft-lb	foot-pound
g	gram
gal	gallon
gpcd	gallons per capita per day
gpd	gallons per day
gpm	gallons per minute
h	henry
H.I.	height of instrument
hp	horsepower
hp-hr	horsepower-hour
hr	hour
I	I-beam
ID	inside diameter
ips	inches per second
ips^2	inches per $second^2$
°K	degrees Kelvin
k	kilopound (kip); 1000 pounds
′k	foot-kilopound
″k	inch-kilopounds
kc	kilocycle
KE	kinetic energy
kg	kilogram
klf	kilopounds per linear foot
ksf	kilopounds per square foot
ksi	kilopounds per square inch
kv	kilovolt
kva	kilovolt-ampere
kw	kilowatt
kwhr	kilowatt-hour
lb	pound
LL	live load
ln	natural logarithm
m	meter
meq	milliequivalent
ma	milliampere
mgd	million gallons per day
mh	millihenry
mi	mile
min	minute
ml	milliliter
mm	millimeter
mph	miles per hour
mv	millivolt
MW	molecular weight
μf	microfarad
μμf	micromicrofarad
μh	microhenry
μmho	micromho
N.A.	neutral axis
OD	outer diameter
oz	ounce
pcf	pounds per cubic foot
PE	potential energy
pf	power factor
plf	pounds per linear foot
ppm	parts per million
psi	pounds per square inch

psia	pounds per square inch absolute
psig	pounds per square inch gage
pw	present worth
qt	quart
°R	degrees Rankine
r-f	radio-frequency
RH	relative humidity
rms	root-mean-square
rpm	revolutions per minute
rps	revolutions per second
SC	Smith chart
sec	second
sp gr	specific gravity
sq ft	square foot
sq in	square inch
sq m	square meter
SSD	saturated surface dry
Sta.	station
tds	total dynamic head
VC	vitrified clay
WF	wide-flange section
whp	water horsepower
yd	yard

appendix

C

Addresses of State Registration Boards

Alabama State Board of Registration for Professional Engineers and Land Surveyors, 64 North Union St., Room 606, Montgomery, Alabama 36104.

Alaska State Board of Engineers and Architects Examiners, Box 1416, Juneau, Alaska 99801

Arizona State Board of Technical Registration for Architects, Assayers, Engineers, Geologists and Land Surveyors, Guarantee Bank Building, 3550 North Central Ave., Phoenix, Arizona 85012

Arkansas State Board of Registration for Professional Engineers, P.O. Box 4067, Park Hill Station, North Little Rock, Arkansas 72116

California State Board of Registration for Civil and Professional Engineers, Room A-102, 1021 "O" Street, Sacramento, California 95814

Canal Zone Board of Registration for Architects and Professional Engineers, P.O. Box 223, Balboa Heights, Canal Zone

Colorado State Board of Registration for Professional Engineers and Land Surveyors, Room 102, State Services Building, 1525 Sherman St., Denver, Colorado 80203

Connecticut State Board of Registration for Professional Engineers and Land Surveyors, Room 543, State Office Bldg., Hartford, Connecticut 06115

Delaware State Board of Registration for Professional Engineers and Land Surveyors, 1000 Washington St., Wilmington, Delaware 19801

District of Columbia Board of Registration for Professional Engineers, 1145 19th St., N.W., Washington, D.C. 20036

Florida State Board of Engineer Examiners, 808 John F. Seagel Building, Gainesville, Florida 32601

Georgia State Board of Registration for Professional Engineers and Land Surveyors, 224 State Capitol, Atlanta, Georgia 30334

Hawaii State Board of Registration for Professional Engineers, Architects and Land Surveyors, 424 South Beretania Street, P.O. Box 3469, Honolulu, Hawaii 96801

Idaho State Board of Engineering Examiners, 1205 Capitol Blvd., Boise, Idaho 83706

Illinois Department of Registration and Education, 112 Capitol Bldg., Springfield, Illinois 62706

Indiana State Board of Registration for Professional Engineers and Land Surveyors, 1007 State Office Bldg., 100 N. Senate Ave., Indianapolis, Indiana 46204

Ohio State Board of Registration for Professional Engineers and Surveyors, 21 West Broad Street, Columbus, Ohio 43215

Iowa State Board of Engineering Examiners, State House, Des Moines, Iowa 50319

Kansas State Board of Engineering Examiners, 1159 W. State Office Building, Topeka, Kansas 66612

Kentucky State Board of Registration for Professional Engineers, 223 Mineral Industries Building, 120 Graham Ave., Lexington, Kentucky 40506

Louisiana State Board of Registration for Professional Engineers and Land Surveyors, 4747 Earhart Blvd., Suite 207, New Orleans, Louisiana 70125

Maine State Board of Registration for Professional Engineers, State Office Bldg., Augusta, Maine 04330

Maryland State Board of Registration for Professional Engineers and Land Surveyors, 301 West Preston St., State Office Building, Baltimore, Maryland 21201

Massachusetts State Board of Registration of Professional Engineers and Land Surveyors, Room 34, State House, Boston, Massachusetts 02133

Michigan State Board of Registration for Architects, Professional Engineers and Land Surveyors, 1604 Cadillac Square Building, Detroit, Michigan 48226

Minnesota State Board of Registration for Architects, Engineers and Land Surveyors, 1512 Pioneer Bldg., St. Paul, Minnesota 55101

Mississippi State Board of Registration for Professional Engineers and Land Surveyors, P.O. Box 3, Jackson, Mississippi 39205

Missouri State Board of Registration for Architects and Professional Engineers, Box 184, Jefferson City, Missouri 65101

Montana State Board of Registration for Professional Engineers and Land Surveyors, P.O. Box 1706, Capitol Post Office, Helena, Montana 59601

Nebraska State Board of Examiners for Professional Engineers and Architects, 512 Terminal Bldg., 941 "O" Street, Lincoln, Nebraska 68508

Nevada State Board of Registered Professional Engineers, P.O. Box 5208, Reno, Nevada 89503

New Hampshire State Board of Registration for Professional Engineers, c/o Secretary of State, State House, Concord, New Hampshire 03301

New Jersey State Board of Professional Engineers and Land Surveyors, 1100 Raymond Blvd., Newark, New Jersey 07102

New Mexico State Board of Registration for Professional Engineers and Land Surveyors, P.O. Box 4847, 1300 Louisa St., Santa Fe, New Mexico 87502

New York State Board of Examiners of Professional Engineers and Land Surveyors, c/o New York State Education Dept., Albany, New York 12224

North Carolina State Board of Registration for Professional Engineers and Land Surveyors, 1307 Glenwood Avenue, Suite 152, Raleigh, North Carolina 27605

North Dakota State Board of Registration for Professional Engineers, P.O. Box 1264, Minot, North Dakota 58702

Oklahoma State Board of Registration for Professional Engineers, 516 Sequogah Office Bldg., Oklahoma City, Oklahoma 73105

Oregon State Board of Engineering Examiners, 158 12th St., N.E., Salem, Oregon 97310

Pennsylvania State Registration Board for Professional Engineers, Room 404, 279 Boas St., P.O. Box 2649, Harrisburg, Pennsylvania 17105

Puerto Rico Board of Examiners of Engineers, Architects and Surveyors, P.O. Box 3271, San Juan, Puerto Rico 00904

Rhode Island State Board of Professional Engineers and Land Surveyors, 246 State Office Building, Providence, R.I. 02903

South Carolina State Board of Engineering Examiners, 710 Palmetto State Life Building, Columbia, S.C. 29202

South Dakota State Board of Engineering and Architectural Examiners, Engineering Hall, South Dakota State University, Brookings, South Dakota 57006

Tennessee State Board of Architectural and Engineering Examiners, P.O. Box 1810, Station "B", Nashville, Tennessee 37203

Texas State Board of Registration for Professional Engineers, State Office Building, Room 200, 1400 Congress Avenue, Austin, Texas 78701

Utah Department of Registration Representative Committee for Engineers and Land Surveyors, 330 East 4th South Street, Salt Lake City, Utah 84111

Vermont State Board of Registration for Professional Engineers, Norwich University, Northfield, Vermont 05663

Virginia State Board for the Examination and Certification of Architects, Professional Engineers and Land Surveyors, 605 East Main Street, Richmond, Virginia 23202

Washington State Board of Registration for Professional Engineers and Land Surveyors, Division of Professional Licensing, P.O. Box 649, Olympia, Washington 98502

West Virginia State Registration Board for Professional Engineers, 301 Morrison Building, Charleston, West Virginia 25301

Wisconsin State Registration Board of Architects and Professional Engineers, Room 1100 State Office Building, 1 West Wilson Street, Madison, Wisconsin 53702

Wyoming State Board of Examining Engineers, 201 Capitol Building, Cheyenne, Wyoming 82001

NOTE: For certification by The National Bureau of Engineering Registration which assists registered engineers who require registration or licensing in several states, write to Mr. James H. Sams, Executive Secretary, National Council of State Boards of Engineering Examiners, Box 752, Clemson, South Carolina, 29631. If any state board cannot be reached at the address listed (changes are rather frequent), contact the NCSBEE office in Clemson, S.C.

appendix

Recommended Reference Books

Any recent standard college textbook and handbook familiar to its user is suggested for review of each of the subjects, Mathematics, Chemistry, Physics, Statics, etc. The large number of satisfactory books available in all of the areas makes it unnecessary to tablulate representative examples herein. A brief list of helpful reference books covering specific items included in the EIT and Professional Engineering Registration examinations is given below in the same sequence as the chapter to which they most nearly pertain.

BURINGTON, RICHARD S. *Handbook of Mathematical Tables and Formulas.* Sandusky, Ohio: Handbook Publishers, Inc., 1945.

MCNEESE, DONALD C., and HOAG, ALBERT L. *Engineering and Technical Handbook.* New York: Prentice Hall, Inc., 1957.

HODGMAN, CHARLES D. *Handbook of Chemistry and Physics.* Cleveland: Chemical Rubber Publishing Company, latest edition.

LARGE, NORBERT A. *Handbook of Chemistry.* Sandusky: Handbook Publishers, Inc., 1956. *Steel Construction.* New York: American Institute of Steel Construction, latest edition.

KING, H. W., and BRATER, E. F. *Handbook of Hydraulics,* 5th ed. New York: McGraw-Hill Book Company, Inc., 1963.

GLENDINNING, WILLIAM. *Electrical Engineering Problems.* Published by the author, Bayside, N. Y., latest edition.

GLENDINNING, WILLIAM, and STEINBERG, MAX J. *Engineering Economics and Practice.* Published by the authors, Bayside, N. Y., latest edition.

GRANT, EUGENE L., and IRESON, W. GRANT. *Principles of Engineering Economy.* New York: Ronald Press Company, 1964.

CONSTANCE, JOHN D. *How to Become a Professional Engineer,* 2d ed. New York: McGraw-Hill Book Company, Inc., 1966.

LALONDE, WILLIAM S. *Professional Engineers' Examination Questions and Answers,* 2d ed. New York: McGraw-Hill Book Company, Inc., 1966.

PERRY, JOHN H., CHILTON, and KIRKPATRICK. *Chemical Engineers Handbook,* 4th ed. New York: McGraw-Hill Book Company, Inc., 1963.

GLENDINNING, WILLIAM. *Civil Engineering Problems.* Published by the author, Bayside, N. Y., latest edition.

U. S. NATIONAL BUREAU OF STANDARDS. *National Electrical Safety Code.*

AMERICAN CONCRETE INSTITUTE. *Reinforced Concrete Design Handbook,* 3d ed. Detroit, Michigan, 1965.

AMERICAN INSTITUTE OF STEEL CONSTRUCTION. *Manual of Steel Construction.* 6th ed. New York, N.Y., 1966.

SEELYE, ELWYN E. *Data Book for Civil Engineers,* Vol. 1, 3d ed. New York: John Wiley & Sons, Inc., 1960.

ESHBACH, O. W. *Handbook of Engineering Fundamentals,* 2d ed. New York: John Wiley & Sons, Inc., 1952.

MAYNARD, HAROLD B. *Industrial Engineering Handbook,* 2d ed. New York: McGraw-Hill Book Company, Inc., 1963.

AMERICAN SOCIETY FOR METALS. *Metals Handbook.* 1948 (with supplements).

PEELE, ROBERT. *Mining Engineers' Handbook.* New York: John Wiley & Sons, Inc., 1941.

ELLENWOOD, FRANK O., and MACKAY, CHARLES O. *Thermodynamics Charts.* New York: John Wiley & Sons, Inc., 1944.

GLENDINNING, WILLIAM. *Mechanical Engineering Problems.* Published by the author, Bayside, N. Y., latest edition.

KEENAN, JOSEPH H. *Steam Tables and Mollier Diagram.* New York: American Society of Mechanical Engineers, 1930.

KEENAN, JOSEPH H., and KEYES, F. G. *Mollier Diagram.* New York: John Wiley & Sons, Inc., 1946.

KENT, WILLIAM. *Mechanical Engineers Handbook,* 12th ed. New York: John Wiley & Sons, Inc., 1950.

MARKS, LIONEL S. *Mechanical Engineering Handbook,* 6th ed. Mc-Graw-Hill Book Company, Inc., 1958.

BRINKER, RUSSELL C. *3701 Review Questions for Surveyors.* Published by the author, Box 893, University Park, N.M. 88070, 1965.

BROWN, CURTIS M., and ELDRIDGE, WINFIELD H. *Evidence and Procedures for Boundary Location.* New York: John Wiley & Sons, Inc., 1962.

U. S. BUREAU OF LAND MANAGEMENT. *Manual of Instructions for the Survey of the Public Lands of the United States.* Washington, D. C.: Government Printing Office, 1947.